THE BOOK OF
COSTUME

VOLUME I

XVc. 1467. Italian (see Ill. 743.)

Fra Carnevale: Birth of the Virgin.

Courtesy of the Metropolitan Museum of Art

XVIIc. 1603. English (see Ill. 1471). Unknown Artist: Henry Frederick, Prince of Wales, and Sir John Harington (detail).

Courtesy of the Metropolitan Museum of Art

THE
BOOK
OF
COSTUME

BY
MILLIA DAVENPORT

VOLUME I

New York
CROWN PUBLISHERS

First Printing

PRINTED IN THE UNITED STATES OF AMERICA

To Hark—my greatest help and hindrance

CONTENTS

VOLUME I

LIST OF COLOR PLATES

Introduction

YEARS OF WORK, research and study in the field of costume have led me to three conclusions about books on costume which I do not think are valid for me alone.

1. Books illustrated by the author are usually to be deplored, and many of them are terrible.

2. The best book is the one with the most pictures, all of them contemporary documents; the best text is based on the words of contemporaries—friends, enemies, or travelers.

3. The physical location or source of every picture, and the number of every manuscript should be given, if possible, as a help in finding colored reproductions, further information, or more illustrations from a series.

The ideal book of costume, to my way of thinking, would provide so many pictures (all documents, arranged chronologically, and in color) that the story would tell itself without words.

This book was originally planned, when commissioned more than seven years ago, as a "Dictionary of Costume" in one volume, with compressed chart-outlines of the development of dress, by civilization or century. Because of difficulties in obtaining pictures, the book lay in abeyance through the war. During these years, I found time to read more source books than research for the theater had previously permitted. I had long known that plays have a stubborn will of their own. Now I discovered that this is true also of books. The proposed dictionary had become, after the first Christian centuries, a documented survey of European and American dress and ways, calling for a very large number of illustrations.

The Book of Costume is now chronological survey of dress through the ages. Each segment-civilization or century has been given an historical summary and an outline of changes in its dress. These are followed by a picture section, which is subdivided by centuries and by countries, as regional differentiations become well established. When a great culture is segregated by time, it has been massed under one heading, for example: Egypt, under which will be found neighboring peoples and aliens as seen by the Egyptians. The order in which countries are presented changes with the fluctuations of their influence on dress. Basic comments will be found under the leading country, and differentiations defined under the dress of others. By XIXc., when all fashion is basically French, illustrations are again massed by chronology alone.

It became clear that bibliographical and documentary material and acknowledgments might clutter and disturb the text. An Appendix was established to hold such material, which will be found there, either under general chapter headings, or under the number of relevant illustrations. The Appendix also gives primary sources; manuscripts, with indications about their availability in reprint or facsimile; early engraved books and series of plates on costume; present-day authorities, and more recently published books to which we are indebted for facts and pictures (since they are apt to be well illustrated, comprehensive, and to lead to collateral material). When space allowed, the words of original authorities are quoted in the text. Limitations of space have occasionally made it necessary to withdraw them to the Appendix, under the illustration number. For reasons which are explained in the Appendix, no bibliography of books on costume has been attempted, but a few books with documentary illustrations or special usefulness have been indicated there.

In the Index, three sorts of material will be found: names and the location of biographies of artists; of named subjects shown in illustrations; and material immediately relative to costume. A complete index would obviously be more unwieldy than useful. Our costume index has selected outstanding examples in illustration and important references in text, from the many thousands of possibilities in our two volumes.

It is almost impossible to redraw (even with the most laudable intention of clarification) without falsifying another age in terms of one's own. Illustrations redrawn at several removes from Racinet (where they were not very good to begin with, although largely taken from Willemin, an excellent book of its kind) seem to me inexcusable in the age of photo-engraving. The amount of collateral information you absorb, as you get facts from documentary illustrations, more than repays the extra effort which may be required in research. Where we have used redrawings, it is usually because the original has disappeared, has deteriorated since the record was made, or is difficult or impossible to photograph. Since there can never be enough pictures, they must be threaded together on a text, and texts are even more suspect than redrawings. All clues to the original authority for a statement are apt to have been sieved out, many books back.

The best and often the only really good information about dress comes from books which are not concerned primarily—or at all—with costume: old histories, books of travel, diaries, memoirs and account books, even novels; works on archaeology; histories of civilizations and their arts; catalogs and volumes sponsored by museums, libraries, universities, learned societies, and organizations like the Roxburghe Club, Walpole Society and Society of Antiquaries; compilations of photographs and prints and art books, sponsored by such publishers as Georg Hirth, Belvedere, Hyperion, Pantheon, Phaidon, and éd. Tel and Belles-lettres; volumes like those of D'Allemagne and Max von Boehn, dealing with textiles, accessories, toys and games, etc.; and periodicals devoted to the arts and antiquities.

Many disparate dates, spellings and attributions appear, as one collects data from even the most scrupulous museum sources. Each eminent authority has his own pet chronology, opinions and preferred way of spelling. These things are constantly being altered in the light of further research. Art objects change hands, not to mention the dislocations of war. I have not made desperate attempts to reconcile these inconsistencies, and have chosen many middle roads. Because a Pharaoh was familiar in my childhood as Sesostris is no reason why we should insist on using the Greek form of his name when many modern Egyptologists prefer Sen-Wosret. On the other hand, I have used the familiar Nefretity in place of more meticulous modern spellings.

I hope I have given enough quotations from sources to show in how many ways it was possible not so long ago for one man to spell the same word, even his own name, in the space of one paragraph. Changes in orthography, sometimes within less than a century, are so interesting that I have attempted, here and there, to preserve them within the limitations of type-faces available in the U.S.A., and by circumventing the diligence of proof-readers.

Many alternative and equally correct spellings for certain words in costume use will be found, even in the abridged Oxford Dictionary. The most anglicized of half a dozen or more forms is apt to be a long way from the original, which was probably French. Words change their spelling, and even their meaning, with time, country and use. I try to hold to a spelling which retains some of the significance of its origin without being archaic; but I make deliberate use of others (to which you will constantly be exposed in other books), if only to draw them to your attention.

People, events and new usages are taken up, along the way, as they present themselves in relation to illustrations. Once in a while, we have lingered over a family like the Pastons, whose rise from Saxon bondsmen is part of England's story; a family of bourgeois bankers, like the Medici, turned merchant princes, patrons of arts and letters; a court like Louis XIV's, which formed manners and taste; a sainted ecclesiastic in contrast to a hideously worldly one, at a time when French society was rent by its opinions of the Church, and divided *paniers* were called *jansénistes;* or a Cavalier like Buckingham, in contrast to the Protestant general who became his father-in-law. These things were not premeditated; but there are all sorts of disproportions which are not necessarily accidental. There is apt, for instance, to be more biographical material about obscure painters than about familiar ones. There may be more about helmets than about the rest of the equipment, just because I am a theatrical designer who has learned how much the right helmet helps, when you have to concoct extra soldiers from nearly nothing.

The end of the American Civil War, when clothing began to be mass-produced, and international exhibitions multiplied, seemed like a logical stopping place. The following eighty-odd years would require at least another volume, and a great deal of time and travel. I think it is very much needed, and I should like to do it, if ever I get my garden in shape, and my courage back; and we are still alive, and interested in such matters.

Acknowledgments

IT IS NOT possible to collect thousands of pictures and information about them without receiving more kindness and help than one can ever acknowledge.

I have worked so long at the Metropolitan Museum that I must be under obligation to almost everybody on its payroll. Mr. Horace H. F. Jayne, its Vice-Director, made available the Museum's collection of negatives just when the low point of discouragement about photographs from Europe had been reached, and the book had kept me from going to Hollywood to do *Macbeth* for Orson Welles. In the order in which the Museum lists its departments in the Bulletin, I must thank Mr. Ambrose Lansing, Curator of Egyptology; Miss Gisela Richter and her Associate in Greek and Roman Art, Miss Christine Alexander; Mr. William H. Forsyth and Miss Margaret B. Freeman, in Mediaeval Art; Mrs. A. Ten Eyck Gardner, Miss Margaretta M. Salinger, and Miss Margaret Scherer, in the Department of Paintings. Mr. William J. Ivins, Jr., Curator Emeritus, and Mr. A. Hyatt Mayor, present Curator of the Print Department, and the staff have shown so much interest, made so many suggestions, and answered so many cries for help from the country that I must thank them all, Miss Alice Newlin, Miss Olivia H. Paine, and Miss Janet S. Byrne in particular. My greatest regret is that the physical mass of my material, which was filed in the country, made it impossible for me to avail myself of the extraordinarily kind offer of Mr. Stephen V. Grancsay, Curator of the Arms and Armor Department, to go over all of that material in the illustrations. The Executive Director of the Costume Institute, Miss Polaire Weissman, was very helpful, as was Miss Marian P. Bolles of the Textile Collection. For a year, the Photograph Collection, whose Curator, Miss Alice Franklin, had gone to Barnard with me, was practically my office, while I selected material and consulted about its suitability for reproduction with Mr. Alexander, the ablest photostat man I ever met, now unfortunately lost to the Museum. Nobody could have been friendlier than Miss Franklin's entire staff have been for many years. I spent pleasant months in the Lending and the Lantern Slide Collections, both under Mrs. Ruth J. Terrill, and then put Mr. Edward J. Milla, who is responsible for the Museum's fine photographs, and his assistants to a great deal of trouble. Literally thousands of orders were filled by Miss Evelyn B. Grier's Information and Sales service. Mr. Walter Hauser's staff in the Library showed much helpful interest.

I am greatly indebted to Dr. Guido Schoenberger of the Institute of Fine Arts of New York University for being given access to the Institute's collection of lantern slide negatives, and to the help of Mr. Russell and other members of the staff. As we met at the files, Dr. Karl Lehmann-Hartleben of N.Y.U. was good enough to indicate material which I should otherwise have missed, and give me information about the content of other photographs.

The wonderful resources of the Frick Art Reference Library were made available by Miss Ethelwny Manning and her assistant, Miss Hanna Johnson; and research by Miss M. Steinbach and Miss V. Seery was a godsend when I had to stay for long periods in the country.

The principal source of manuscript material and XVIIc. costume plates was, of course, the Pierpont Morgan Library, under Miss Belle de Acosta Green, and endless courtesies were extended by Miss Meta Harssen.

Near-by Cooper Union was always a great help. I am particularly obliged to Mr. Calvin Hathaway, the Director of the Museum for the Arts of Decoration, the late Miss Elizabeth Haines, and Miss Edna Donnell. Mr. Richard E. Morse and Mrs. E. Volkov, in the Museum's delightful little library, were tireless in looking up details for us, as were the staff of the main library, and the library of the Art School, many of whom I met only by telephone.

At the New York Public Library, Mr. Paul Kup and Mr. Lamar Trotter in the Print Collection; Mr. Percy Clapp in the Rare Book Room; Miss Eleanor Mitchell and her successor, Miss Muriel Baldwin, in Arts and Architecture; Mr. George Freedley and his successor, Mrs. E. P. Barrett, in the Theater Section; the staff of the Genealogy Room, who clarified so many relationships by telephone; Mr. Robert Kingery, the Readers' Adviser; Miss Romana Javitz of the Picture Collection; and perhaps most of all, the many services of the Reference Department under Mr. Paul North Rice, must be thanked for their assistance.

At the Hispanic Society, Miss Ruth M. Anderson was generous with time and information.

We are under great obligation to Mr. John D. Cooney, Curator of Egyptology at the Brooklyn Museum, and to his assistant, my old friend Mrs. Elizabeth Riefstahl, for the loan of illustrations from the precious out-of-print catalogue of the exhibition of "Pagan and Christian Egypt" in 1941. The Museum is also the source of many photographs of actual costumes.

Very special thanks indeed are given to Miss Gertrude Townsend of the Boston Museum of Fine Arts, and to another old friend, her assistant in charge of Costume, Mrs. Jean Reed. They put off vacations in order to show me a glimpse of the wonders of the Elizabeth Day McCormick Collection of Costume, which was still being accessioned. In beginning the photography of the collection (which will take a lifetime to complete), they were good enough to select objects in which I had shown special interest, and accompanied each with detailed descriptions, in case there were lacunae in the notes I took during two and a half frantic days at the Museum, in the midst of a collection which cannot possibly be seen in so short a time as a month. I am also obliged to the Director, Mr. G. H. Edgell, and to Mr. Henry P. Rossiter, the Curator of Prints.

Mrs. Fern Rusk Shapley and her assistant, Miss Caroline L. Huddle, at the National Gallery of Art in Washington, D.C., have answered many questions, as have Miss Louisa Dresser of the Worcester Art Museum; Mr. James W. Foster, Director of the Maryland Historical Society; Mr. James L. Cogar, Curator of Colonial Williamsburg; Mr. Heinrich Schwarz, of the Museum of the Rhode Island School of Design; Mr. David Wilder, Librarian of Hamilton College; the Secretary of the Elizabethan Club, and Miss Anna S. Pratt, Reference Librarian, at Yale University; Mrs. Alexander Quarrier Smith; and Sir Osbert Sitwell.

Special questions have been answered by Mr. Benjamin Parry, head of the United States Weather Bureau in New York, and Mr. Merrill Barnard of the Washington headquarters; by the Very Rev. Msgr. Thomas J. McMahon, S.T.D.; by Prof. Edgar Wind of Smith College; by Henri Marceau, Curator of the John G. Johnson Collection in Philadelphia; by Mr. Francis Thompson, Librarian and Keeper of the Collections of the Duke of Devonshire; by the Directors of the Victoria and Albert, and of the South Kensington Museums; and by Monsieur J. Porcher, Curator of the Manuscript Collection of the Bibliothèque nationale.

Not nearly enough residents of New York State have ever heard about the wonders of their State Library. No matter how far back in the woods you may find yourself, practically any book you may require will be sent down within three days after application to your nearest branch library. I am obliged to Mr. Charles F. Gosnell, the State Librarian, and to Miss Powell and Miss Halstead of the excellent library at Nyack, for many weeks' use of books which no city library would ever circulate, such as the five volumes of the superb Clark edition of Anthony Wood.

I cannot begin to thank another old and dear friend, M. Jacques E. J. Manuel, for his help in gathering material in Paris. While directing a motion picture, he was still able to slash red tape and shortages which made it difficult to get permission to photograph material in French government collections. My aunt, Miss Millia Crotty, also procured pictures in Paris, and Mrs. Don Blatchley was helpful in London.

During the years when my old friend and brother in Local 829, Hermann Rosse, was detained with the rest of his family in Occupied Holland, his daughter and son-in-law, Jannelisa and Paul Galdone, enabled me to avoid visitors and telephones by letting me work in the chauffeur's quarters in the garage-stable which has since become their own home.

I am much obliged for the loan of books or photographs, to Henry Varnum Poor, Marion Hargrove, Aline Bernstein, and to Lee Simonson, whose enthusiasm has been very heartening.

Mr. William D. Allen, formerly of Cooper Union Museum, has given invaluable last-minute help in editorial and historical checking.

I believe that permission to use illustrations was refused in two cases only, and that another unanswered series of letters can be laid to the dislocations of war. I am grateful to all the private owners and institutions, authors and publishers, who have been gracious in granting permissions for use.

THE BOOK OF
COSTUME

The Ancient Orient

THE BABYLONIANS were merchants, traders by land and sea, and farmers; a population of mixed races, with relatively little caste system, under a king who was also a priest. Education was general; common also to women, who occupied a position of respect. The cultural level was high, providing libraries, astronomical observatories, dated legal documents and contracts on clay tablets. There was little stone available between the Tigris and the Euphrates, so clay brick was used for building; glazed tiles, colored fresco. Cylindrical seals of precious and semi-precious stones were minutely engraved with the aid of crystal lenses ground on a wheel.

During the *Early Sumerian Dynasties* c. 3000-2500 B.C., the chief cities were Nippur, Tello, Susa, Lagash, Kish. The influence of Babylonian art was felt as far as Syria and Egypt.

BABYLONIAN COSTUME

Male clothing consisted of a *cape,* a rectangle around the body, over shoulders, and a *kaunakes,* a long shaggy skirt, probably closed in front. It was made of hanks of wool fastened in horizontal lines like coarse fringe, on cloth; or perhaps twisted locks of wool, still fastened to the hide. Sometimes it covered the left shoulder. The women wore a form of *kaunakes,* but more enveloping, and the female cape was worn over the shoulder or caught at the center front.

Gods, and priests, or noblemen as priests, shaved their hair. Other men wore their hair long, looped and braided into the *catogan.* Women also used the *catogan,* but more elaborately arranged, with bands and knobbed pins. Male and female feet were bare, but on arms and legs they wore beads of lapis, carnelian, onyx, agate. In addition, they wore gold and bronze bracelets, earrings, and ornaments. Pins and hairpins were used.

Men wore hats.

During the *Agade Dynasty,* there was the rise to power of the Semitic servant class (*Akkad*).

Sargon (a Semite) subdued Babylonia, Elam, Syria, Palestine. Art was marked by the finest cylinder seals. Culture flourished to the greatest extent, reaching the Mediterranean during the Arabian-Semitic *Ur Dynasty* c. 2700 B.C. Its chief cities were Ur, Lagash, Kish, Nina (later Nineveh).

The *kaunakes* led to a garment often fringed, worn over the left shoulder, under the right arm, which eventually became a short-sleeved shirt. Kings and nobles wore high turbans; others wore round hats with cylindrical brims.

During the *Babylonian Dynasty,* Babylonia was invaded and eventually divided, North Babylonia going to the South Arabians, South Babylonia to the Elamites. About 2250 B.C., Hammurabi shook off the Elamites, consolidated the monarchy to the Mediterranean; Syria and Canaan became dependencies. An excellent code of laws was formulated. The new city of Babylon became the capital; Susa, Larsa and Nineveh flourished.

The *Kassite Dynasty* c. 1786 B.C., contemporaneous with the Hyksos (Egypt), was marked by the loss of West Asia and the independence of Palestine and Syria.

About 1700 B.C., the horse appeared from the East in Babylonia, Greece, Egypt.

The Assyrians, living since Sargon's time in the Tigris valley, and coming of the same stock, increased their power as that of Babylonia weakened. The kingship of Assyria was assumed by the high priests of Assur. There was correspondence, and relationships, with Egypt (Amenophis IV to Deltaic Dynasty when Egypt became Assyria's vassal). The kings became generals; the population completely militarized, ruthlessly aggressive and cruel. The great culture of Babylonia was entirely and uncritically taken over. The personal portraits of Egyptians never appear in the stylized bas-reliefs of the Assyrians (in which one king might be any other). But details, such as those of the costumes of aliens, are much more accurately observed in Assyrian than in Egyptian art. The Assyrian code of laws differed from the Babylonian, and their women were veiled.

ASSYRIAN COSTUME DETAILS

Costume was dyed madder red, indigo blue, saffron yellow (combined in a dull green), snail purple; priests wore bleached linen.

The basic garment was the shirt, worn by everybody. The female shirt was long, with or without rolled belt, accompanied by a mantle worn over the head. The male shirt was short, with a belt often rolled. Common soldiers wore the short shirt with a wide protective belt. Kings and personages wore a long shirt—embroidered, brocaded, tasseled, fringed in a manner commensurate with rank.

Other garments of important personages were like the shirt in respect to material and decoration. The king's cloak, originally like that of *Aamu-Ribu* (see Egyptian, Semitic Nomads), followed the same mutations of cut and eventually became a tabard.

Scarves were worn by all important persons and the wearer's position was indicated by the number, disposition, and width of fringe of the scarves. Scarves were worn by kings to the Second Assyrian Empire only.

Priests' costumes were of two sorts: *spiral*, of which another variety was worn by kings, and *cloaked* or *aproned*, of bleached linen. The *spiral* was a triangular fringed garment, rolled spirally around the body over the shirt, with the point brought over the right shoulder to the belt. The king's *spiral* was a fringed rectangle, wound around the body in an ascending spiral and ending in a pointed piece brought over the right shoulder while a rectangular piece was brought around the left arm.

The High Priest's apron was worn around the back of the body, fastened with hanging tasseled cords, and was ankle-length, exposing the hem of the short shirt in front. He also wore a cloak.

The king's headdress was a truncated conical *tiara* of white felt, with a spiked top; and purple *infulae*, two narrow tabs hanging almost to the waist in back. It was duplicated in gold for use in war. Bullocks' horns were added around this headdress for the priest or for the king as priest.

Women and common men went barefoot, as did soldiers in early days. Soldiers later were superbly shod. Kings and personages wore sandals enclosing the heel, beautifully made yet relatively plain in comparison with the costume.

Jewelry consisted of arm bands, bracelets, necklaces, and weapons of gold.

The conical helmet of peaked Assyrian form eventually assumed the Graeco-Carian crest. It was made of copper, then bronze, and finally of iron. The king's helmet was a gold replica of his tiara.

The shield was oblong or round, and convexly pointed, made of bronze.

The archer's shirt was short so that the body, left relatively unprotected, had freedom in the use of the bow. The archer also wore a wrist-band with a protective, often decorative, boss.

The officer's shirt was a cuirasse of bronze plates fastened on a short leather shirt. The leaders had long shirts of plates of mail, very like Egyptian (Tomb of Ken-Amun). The belt was wide and protective. There were crossed straps on the breast, with a protective metal plate at the intersection.

Kings and officers wore fringed scarves, indicative of rank, and fringed and tasseled aprons. The end of the scarf was drawn through the belt.

Soldiers originally went barefoot; then they were given excellent high leggings and boots, which often were worn over long, apparently quilted stockings. No spurs were used.

Their arms were a bow with case, arrows in quiver, spears, glaives, and daggers in sheath.

THE ASSYRIAN EMPIRE

Four great emperors from Shalmaneser I in 1310 B.C. to Shalmaneser II 856-881 B.C. helped to build the *First Assyrian Empire*. Under the first Shalmaneser the Assyrians took the place formerly held by their nominal masters, though Babylon itself was conquered by a later king. Tiglath-pileser I, 1129 B.C., conquered Armenia and Cappadocia. Assur-nasir-pal II, 883-858 B.C., and Shalmaneser II also extended the Empire. Both kings built palaces at Nimrud. This was a period of coalitions, revolts, plagues, ruthless militarized life, and strong, simple sculpture.

The *Second Assyrian Empire* began under a series of professional soldiers but the usurper Tiglath-pileser III, 745 B.C., consolidated and co-ordinated the Empire, perfected the army. Art was at a low ebb. Sculpture was definitely inferior, though in reliefs at Balawat there is some useful military detail. But later, under Sargon, sculpture shows meticulous realism (Khorsabad). In fact, the following two-thirds of the century is the great period of Assyrian sculpture.

During the reign of Sargon's son, Sennacherib, 705-681 B.C., Babylon was destroyed as the result of a revolt, and a palace was built at Nineveh. Under Sennacherib's grandson, Assur-bani-pal, 668-626 B.C., the Empire began to fall apart. Egypt was lost, there were struggles with Elam and Babylonia, and Assyria was left exhausted, prey to the invading Scythians and Medes, whose court costume was affected by Assyrian fashions.

With the Aryan Scythians and Persians appears an entirely new costume: the fitted sleeved coat, opening down the front, long trousers, and boots —the basis of our own costume today. The dress (and diet based on fermented milk) of the present-day Siberians is almost identical with that of the Scythians.

The garments of the Greeks and Egyptians, as well as those we have just been considering, were made from, or evolved out of the use of, draped rectangles of woven materials.

The tailoring of our own clothes was influenced by the invading Indo-Germanic peoples of the cold Eastern plateau, cattle-raising nomads in search of pasture, mounted warriors who brought with them the horse, "the ass of the East," and who dressed in the skins and hides of their beasts. The comparatively intricate cut of their garments was determined first by the resemblance, and then by the disparities, between the patterns of the skins of different animals, and of man.

Thus came about pattern, cut, piecing, and tailoring. With these people went their tailored garments which will be found on Celt and German, as on Persian and Parthian; Scythian and Sarmathian of the steppes; Dacians, Lydians, and Phrygians; spreading amongst the gentry of Cyprus and Cappadocia and Asia Minor; and given by the Greeks to the mythical Amazons.

PERSIAN (ACHAEMENIAN) EMPIRE

Cyrus, 558-528 B.C., Aryan king of Semitic Elam, conquered his Median sovereign and capital, Ecbatana; became king of Persia; united Medes and Persians into the greatest empire yet seen; defeated the coalition of Sparta, Lydia, Babylon, and Egypt.

The Median national costume, very different from the Persian, was adopted for court wear. Silk and cotton cloth, instead of leather and fur, became known to the Persians. There were six great Persian families in addition to that of the king; but Medians and other peoples, subjugated by relatively humane warfare, were allowed to retain power and serve in important Empire posts as officers of court, in the colonies as satraps, and in the army. The court served as training school and proving ground for all of noble birth.

The superb army, under a number of great warrior-kings, included every able-bodied citizen. Its tactics were based on a massive offensive hail of arrows. The bow, native weapon of the Iranians, was drawn from behind light standing shields, by kneeling men, unhampered by defensive armor except metal helmets; meanwhile their cavalry darted into, broke up, and pursued the enemy. Only the leaders were strongly armed. The short lances and daggers which Persian soldiers carried in addition to the bow were of little use in hand-to-hand battle, when, as finally at Marathon, the Persian ranks were penetrated by the heavily armed *hoplite*.

The peasantry were strong and manly, brought up in a healthy climate, and habituated to all hardships, Herodotus tells us, adding that "of all mankind" they "were the readiest to adopt foreign customs, good or bad." The art forms of Babylonia and Assyria were taken over by the Persians, and produced for them by craftsmen of many races.

During the Luristan period, the Medes wore a *kilt,* wrapped around the hips, lapped on the right side; and a *shirt* which went halfway down the thigh, or, in the case of kings and attendants, down to the ankles. It had a diagonal closing across the breast, quarter sleeves, and it was belted, with bands of braid or thin gold strips (Scythic) at the borders, and in suspender lines.

Later, the Medes used the *kandys,* a long, flowing cloth gown, looped up to a belt at the sides; with or without voluminous sleeves, widening from shoulder to cuff, much as the garment itself widened from shoulder to hem.

Headcoverings included Median caps or *kyrbasia* (the modern *bashlik*), like the Phrygian bonnet. There was a soft, high crown which fell forward; and usually there were flaps at the neck and at either side which could be fastened under the chin. One form, without these flaps, had a hanging cord. Another headcovering was the *padom,* a hood worn by the royal entourage, surrounding the face and often concealing the chin, falling in flaps which covered the back and chest. Courtiers and satraps were allowed to wear round spreading caps. Blue and white cord designated the royal family (Cyrus).

The king wore the *kidaris,* a ribbed tiara, or embroidered hat. His kandys was purple, crimson, or saffron, with a white stripe down the center front. The king also carried a staff.

The garments of the priests, regarded as "magicians" (of whom the king was chief), varied in cut with rank and duties. They were white or purple.

The High Priest wore a purple girdled kandys, a shaped cape which also was purple, a spreading cylindrical hat, and a staff with a gold knob head.

Lesser priests wore a plain white shirt with a belt (*kosti*) which was the only ornament allowed.

The cape was a folded rectangle with tasseled corners and a triangular collar.

PERSIAN COSTUME

Persian costume was originally of leather, and later of cloth. The nobility used polychrome fabrics brocaded and embroidered in lines, stars, animal and floral motifs, edged with gold. They affected the costume of the nobility of Phrygia, Lydia, Cappadocia, Lycia, and Cyprus.

The male wore a coat that was open down the front, had a fitted waist, and long tight sleeves sewn into the armholes. At first it was knee-length, later calf-length. Trousers were wide but close at the ankle. High boots and leggings were worn over the trousers. The nobility had shoes with edged tops and three straps over the instep; or colored slippers.

The *overcoat* was a sleeved kandys, often fur-collared. It was slung over the shoulder by cord, the sleeves hanging unused except on great occasions.

For *headcovering,* the king wore a modified Assyrian tiara which had assumed the flaps of the Median cap. It was conical, spiralled in two colors; or a truncated cone, swathed with a turban. Hair and beard were worn in Assyrian cut. Nobles wore the *kulah,* a high cylindrical felt hat; or the *kyrbasia* (bashlik) either with flaps or as a round felt hat with cord but no flaps.

Women wore the same garments as the men, with the adition of a long veil. The female coat was longer than the male's. It had a closed front, with a slit for the head, and wide sleeves for court wear or narrow sleeves for ordinary dress.

Soldiers wore Persian national costume, but the use of Median court dress was granted by Darius to his bodyguard, the 10,000 Immortals. Persian arms are listed in the *Zend Avesta.* Ring-mail originated in Persia between the ninth and eighth centuries B.C.

During the Achaemenian period, helmets were leather or metal, some with movable sections very like mediaeval helmets. The *padom,* with chin protectors and flaps covering the back and chest, was worn by the royal entourage. The *"Phrygian" bonnet,* a segmented conical casque, was worn particularly by heavily armed Parthian and Sarmathian cavalry. Sarmathians shown on the Trajan Column wear short, pointed conical caps with cheek plates and splints covering the neck.

Armor consisted of a cuirasse made of metal scales, or rings of bronze, iron, or gold, on leather; arm and leg plates; a shield, rectangular, round, or rondache (violin-shaped), made of wicker or leather.

Arms consisted of a sword, fifteen to sixteen inches long; javelin; knife; club; bow; quiver with thirty brass-headed arrows; and a sling with thirty stones.

During the reign of Darius I, 521-485 B.C., there was considerable infiltration of Greek culture at court. The art was imperial rather than national, and craftsmen generally were foreigners. Darius adopted the crenellated tiara, long used in Assyria and Asia Minor.

The turning point of the Persian Empire came during the rule of Xerxes I, 485-465 B.C. There was a war with Greece in which the Persian archers were defeated by the Greek phalanx. Macedonia started its ascendancy.

THE SELEUCID EMPIRE

Alexander the Great, 331-323 B.C., adopted the Persian dress and ceremonial in newly-united Persia and Macedonia. The brilliant Greek court, and the city colonies in conquered lands, spread Greek culture throughout Asia. The reaction against Hellenic culture began during the Parthian period, when Mithridates (124-88 B.C.) was king and nomadic Scythians gradually were establishing themselves as great proprietors and serf owners in Parthia.

There were notable changes in style during the Seleucid and Parthian periods. *Trousers* were wide at the top and very tight at the ankle; they were strapped under the foot, and also under the crotch for riding. The *coat* was knee-length and had narrow sleeves. The king's *mantle* was knee-length, and an *apron* came into general use. The king's *mitre* was a cylindrical Assyrian battle-mented crown from which longer and wider infulae fluttered. His *hood* was a lighter, smaller, and shorter kyrbasia, with the point of its crown more vertical and the flaps hanging loose. Scarves of ribbons in fluttering bows on the chest, sash, infulae, and shoes were worn through the Sassanian period. Sovereigns also took to wearing knots of hair on the top of their heads.

Under Ardashir I, 226 A.D., and Shapur I, the Iranians were welded into one nation (the Sassanian Neo-Persian Empire) in the old Achaemenian tradition. There was a return to old Persian styles, and Median fashions disappeared except for the Median bandeau. High tiaras and jewelry —necklaces, beads, and earrings—were popular. Hair was worn bushy. Revers and rounded aprons were worn on coats, and trousers were wide and fluttering. The kulah (either round or conical, sometimes with flaps) carried a bandeau. The kyrbasia disappeared. Women wore a smaller veil and bandeau with a knot at the back of the head.

During the Sassanian period, heavy cavalry and horse were armed remarkably like the mediaeval knight and steed. The helm was conical with a ribbon floating from the crest; visor and mail-coif extended to the shoulders. The cuirasse was made of ring- and scale-mail combined; ring-mail encased the legs and feet. The head, chest, and shoulders of the horse also were mailed.

The struggle between Rome and Persia gradually weakened both until Persia fell victim in 641 A.D. to the Arab (Islamic) conquest.

1. **Sumerian, Agade Dyn. Relief Tablet. c. III mill. B.C. Tello. (Louvre.)**

King Or-Nina and Family. Kaunakes worn by seated and standing figures, one shown with a basket on his head.

2. **Sumerian 2800 B.C. Votive Mace Head. Lagash (Tello) (British Museum.)**

Enannatum 1, patesi of Lagash. Wearing the

sheep's wool kaunakes of the early Sumerian.

3. **Sumerian e. III mill. B.C. (Berlin Museum.)**

Goddess of Vegetation. In horned headdress, and cape garment.

4. **Sumerian c. 2800 B.C. Marble statue. (British Mus.)**

Priestess. Hair elaborately clubbed up in a catogan with a band; fringed cape.

Courtesy of British Museum (2), (4); the Louvre (1)

5-7. Elamite 2000 B.C. Ivory statue. Susa. (Louvre.)

Elamite lady. Cape garment, under right arm, caught on left shoulder; fringed scarf over bare shoulder; collar, bracelets.

8, 9. Sumerian mid-III mill. B.C. Statue. Summer Palace, Tello. (Louvre.)

Goudea. Patesi (high priest) of Lagash: showing arrangement of cape. The headdress is also shown on a number of other statues of Goudea, which exist together with elaborate accounts of his greatness as a builder, and plans and specifications for his palace.

10. Babylonian II mill. B.C. Koudourrou of King. Susa. (Louvre.)

King Hammurabi as judge. Spiral garments; tiara.

11. Babylonian e. XIIc. B.C. Koudourrou of King. Susa. (Louvre.)

Goddess Nanaï on throne, King Melishpak II, and his daughter. With symbols of sun, moon, and planet Venus (Goddess Ishtar).

12. Babylonian e. I mill. B.C. Relief. Susa. (Louvre.)

Lady of rank spinning, fanned by servant. Elaborate catogan of type worn since archaic times. Simple garments, heavy belts, borders, bracelets; bare feet. (See Ill. 273.)

Courtesy of The Louvre (8, 10)

About a hundred years ago, the excavations of the Englishman, Layard, (*Discoveries at Nineveh*), and of the Frenchman, Botta (*Monuments at Nineveh*), brought to light the first great Assyrian remains and laid the foundations for the great collections of the British Museum and the Louvre, respectively, the third important collection being that at Constantinople.

The engraved illustrations in their books give information on artifacts which in some cases no longer remains in clear form for recording by photography.

As the titles of the books indicate, each thought that what he was excavating was Nineveh, whereas Layard's was actually Nimrud, and that of Botta (who had turned away from Quyunjig, the actual Nineveh) was Sargon's Khorsabad.

13-16. 1st Assyrian Emp. 885-856 B.C. Reliefs, Nimrud (Calah). (British Museum.)

Assur-nasir-pal; young male attendants; priest dressed as a winged god. The priest, carrying a pail and pine-cone, is about to anoint the king with the "juice of the Enurta," in a fertility rite. He wears the priest's headdress with bullock horns; the priest's apron, fastened by knotted cords; and fringed scarf of rank, over short fringed shirt.

The young male attendants with fly whisks may or may not be eunuchs, as was formerly believed. One is offering the king a libation; the other carries dagger, bow and quiver.

The king wears a spiked tiara with infulae; and royal cloak over long shirt. These personages wear fine but simple sandals (which the Greeks criticized as being disparately plain). They have richly embroidered and fringed garments and jewelry—earrings, necklaces, arm-bands and bracelets with medallions.

17. 1st Assyrian Emp. 885-856 B.C. Alabastrine limestone statue Nimrud (Calah). (Louvre.)

Assur-nasir-pal. In spiral garments of a priest of the Temple of the War-God Enurta, without headdress, carrying crook-shaped sceptre, long dagger. This is the only perfect example of Assyrian sculpture in the round, not relief.

From Layard: Discoveries at Nineveh.

18

19

18. 2nd Assyrian Empire 705-680 B.C. Relief. Kuyunjik (Nineveh) s.w. palace, passage LI. (British Museum.)

Sennacherib's horses: being led by men with carefully arranged hair and beards. Simple shirts, with fringed scarves, indicative of rank, are tucked into wide belts which have handsome webbed fastenings. Sandals enclose heel.

19. 1st Assyrian Empire 824-810 B.C. Limestone relief, Nabu Temple, Nimrud. (British Museum.)

Shamshi-Adad V, husband of Semiramis, brother of Sardanapalus: king with divine emblems. Above to king's right:—sun, moon, planet Venus (goddess Ishtar). He wears the king's tiara with infulae, set on typically curled Assyrian hair; beard. Simple shirt, with heavily fringed hem, indicative of rank; mystic cross on breast.

Courtesy of British Museum

20. 2nd Assyrian Emp. 705-680 B.C. Reliefs, Kuyunjik.

Flight of the inhabitants of Lachish from Senna-cherib's soldiers. Soldier: in Graeco-Carian helmet, long spear, round shield, dagger; short shirt with wide protective belt and crossed straps with plate at intersection; high quilted or knitted stockings, gartered, under strapped boots. Officer: cuirasse of metal plates, fringed scarf of rank, and wide baldric; mace and dagger. Canaanite peasant women, with mantles like veils over their heads, carrying their belongings, and followed by their captive men, in short shirts with thick belts, and high laced buskins; their hair cropped shorter than that of Assyrians.

21. Assyrian Empire. Relief, Nimrud.

King before the walls of a besieged city. King as an archer, with little defense; tiara, probably in metal (as helmet) distinguishes monarch; wide protective belt and baldric, overlong shirt and tasseled apron. Shield-bearer, in shirt of mail, carrying rectangular wicker shield, which could be set up for archer's protection; conical helmet; heavy wide belt. Attendants (eunuchs) carrying quiver, baton, umbrella. Soldier with mace, dagger, bow and arrows pursuing child and three women in long patterned shirts, and thick rolled belts. Other soldiers in loin cloths or shirts, and helmets; daggers, spears, bows.

From Layard: Discoveries at Nineveh.

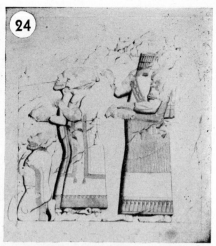

22. 2nd Assyrian Emp. 722-705 B.C. Reliefs, Khorsabad.

Sargon II and his Vizier. Traces of color, red, ochre and black, still remain.

Sargon, in spiked tiara with infulae; magnificent hair and beard; cruciform earrings; fringed mantle brocaded in rosettes; over brocaded shirt; sword with lion's heads; arm bands, bracelets; baton of rank; laced sandals covering heel; ring on big toe.

Vizier: bareheaded; rich bandeau with infulae; earrings, necklace, bracelets, arm-band; scarf with very wide fringe, indicating his importance.

23, 24. Same provenance as 22.

Hebrew tribute bearers (23) *and prisoners* (24): with small "prayer curls" in front of ear.

The costume of Semitic noblemen assumed many Assyrian characteristics, during the Assyrian domination, while retaining specific Semitic characteristics. All these figures wear a long fringed linen shirt, the belt of which, when worn, is quite different from that of an Assyrian. They also wear a characteristic shorter woolen garment: either the caftan, a sleeved coat, open down the front, the edges of which are caught together in front by elaborate clasps and cord; or a tabard-like garment, open at the sides. These

From Botta and Flandin: Monuments de Nineveh (22-24).

garments carried purple tassels at the corners to commemorate the 4 statutes of Jehovah. Some wear tasselled "stocking" caps; the others a wound headcloth, over hair which differs from the Assyrians in length and arrangement.

25. Hittite VIIIc. B.C. (Berlin Museum.)

Grave stela of a queen in the time of King Barrekub: the fibula which she wears pinned to her gown above the left breast will have a long life in Semitic use, as will the distaff (see Ill. 273).

26. 2nd Assyrian Emp. 655 B.C. Relief, Kuyunjik. (British Museum.)

Assur-bani-pal and his queen celebrating the death of Te-Umman. The only Assyrian sculpture showing a female. Similar furniture, fillets and jewelry, patterned and fringed garments with weighted corners, and fine shoes, can be found in Etruria and N. Italy in VI-V c. use.

27. Achaemenian Persian Vc. (British Museum.)

Silver figurine of a man in dress previously seen on reliefs.

28-32. Achaemenian, Artaxerxes II. 404-359 B.C. Persepolis, Apadena Stair.

28. Men in alternating Persian and Median dress. The Median robe has a dagger of Scythic type, with characteristic wide guard, thrust into belt; bow cases not of Scythic type. Shoes with three lacings. Fluted, flat-topped headdresses. The Persian garments are of the nomad type, with short swords ingeniously slung and held in place by a strap under the crotch. Round-topped felt bonnets (*bashlik*), without lappets, some with a forward rake. Some overcoats with collars and ribbon ties slung over the shoulders without using sleeves (like XVc. Magyar *huszars,* see XIXc. huzzar costume). Shoes tie around ankles. Hair in Assyrian curls, but bushier shape; beards more natural. Necklaces of the twisted torque variety brought by the nomad people (see Frankish guard, Ill. 283). *Engraving by Flandin.* 29. Photograph of the relief, detail near the one shown in 28. 30. Anatolians bringing tribute; cups of Scythic round-bottomed type, bowls of kumyss, and Scythic bracelets. Conical segmented felt hats, brought by Central Asiatic nomads, but gowns and tassels of Semitic type. 31. Bactrian with camel: wider breeches, from Sacian conquerors; Assyrian bandeau instead of *kyrbasia* (*bashlik*). 32. Others, in nomad costume: conical hats with flaps; short swords, slung out of the way for riding; shoes tied at ankle; carry Scythic bracelets.

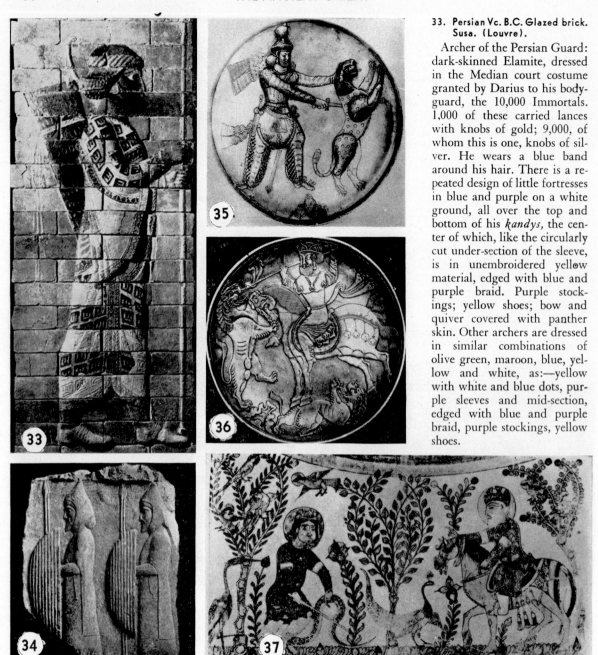

33. Persian Vc. B.C. Glazed brick. Susa. (Louvre).

Archer of the Persian Guard: dark-skinned Elamite, dressed in the Median court costume granted by Darius to his body-guard, the 10,000 Immortals. 1,000 of these carried lances with knobs of gold; 9,000, of whom this is one, knobs of sil-ver. He wears a blue band around his hair. There is a re-peated design of little fortresses in blue and purple on a white ground, all over the top and bottom of his *kandys,* the cen-ter of which, like the circularly cut under-section of the sleeve, is in unembroidered yellow material, edged with blue and purple braid. Purple stock-ings; yellow shoes; bow and quiver covered with panther skin. Other archers are dressed in similar combinations of olive green, maroon, blue, yel-low and white, as:—yellow with white and blue dots, pur-ple sleeves and mid-section, edged with blue and purple braid, purple stockings, yellow shoes.

34. Darius 521-485 B.C. (Berlin Museum.)
Anatolian guards.

35. Persian 383-388 A.D. Silver Plate, repousse, en-graved, partly gilded. (Hermitage Museum, Lenin-grad.)

Shapur III dispatching a lion: fluttering ribboned effects show on *infulae* sash; wide trousers, caught up at the crotch, bows on shoes. Crown set on bushy hair with puffed knot on top (since Ardashir I); each ruler now makes additions and modifications in head-dress.

36. Persian IXc. A.D. Post-Sassanian. Silver Plate, re-pousse, engraved, partly gilded. (Hermitage Mu-seum, Lenigrad.)

Bahram Gur hunting lions: grandson of Shapur III, and a Vc. king of legendary beauty, called the "Wild Ass" for his strength and valor; combatted Christianity, warred with Rome, but he was actually just the weak aristocrat he appears here, wearing the headdress with eagle wings, adopted by him.

37. Persian XIIIc. A.D. Galen Manuscript, Seljuk School. (Staatsbibliothek, Vienna.)

Andromachus and the boy bitten by the snake: manuscript leaf filled with the new ideas to which Europe was exposed by the Crusades: the turban; band about the upper arm; ideas of design and manu-script illumination, using leaves, flowers, and birds, which profoundly affected European manuscript style. Venice was a "boom town" during the Cru-sades; East and West met there in trade; and it was by way of Venice that "pantaloons" entered Euro-pean dress.

The Nile

EGYPTIAN COSTUME

EGYPTIAN costume was based on two elements: the wrapped loin cloth of men, and the sewed *kalasiris* (a sheath which developed into a shirt) of women; by the New Kingdom, it became incorporated into male costume as well. Increasingly finer materials were used, and were worn, from the Middle Kingdom, in increasingly numerous combinations and superimpositions of garments of different lengths, and different weights: such as a long pleated skirt of gauzy linen over a short plain one of heavy material.

From the earliest times a mantle was occasionally worn; it became an important part of both male and female costume by the New Kingdom, arranged around the body or tied about the buttocks, ends arranged at center front.

Female entertainers and slaves frequently wore nothing but jewelry.

The strong lay position in Egyptian religion lost out to the professional priesthood, which had become extremely powerful by the Eighteenth Dynasty. As lay costume became more elaborate and colorful, the priesthood retained the simple white loin cloth (linen, never wool) and leopard skin of earlier days; the priestly functions of the king increased, and the spotted animal skin became, late, a granted honorific.

A notably cleanly people, the Egyptians of both sexes clipped or shaved their heads, and the men their beards, which for ceremonious occasions they replaced with wigs of wool or hair, and artificial beards. Common people wore their own hair.

Materials: Egyptians dressed almost entirely in white linen. Linen more than half again as fine as today's handkerchief has been found in First Dynasty tombs, c. 3000 B.C. Fringed ends are knotted into tassels on loin cloths of the Fifth Dynasty. Linen was stiffened and pleated with exquisite art in horizontal and vertical patterns; herring-bone pleating is used by the Fifth Dynasty. Some line patterns may have been produced by weaving cords into the fabric. Cords are used to give elaborate bands, lines, and zigzags by the Eleventh Dynasty (c. 2000 B.C.). Long furry loops are woven into cloth by the Eighteenth Dynasty.

The few sheep native to Egypt had dark, goat-like hair; fleecy sheep began to appear from the East during the New Kingdom. Herodotus says Egyptians had wool mantles in his time (Vc. B.C), but wool was considered unclean, and not to be worn in temples by priests and worshippers. There was little silk and cotton until the late dynasties.

The Egyptians, expert leather-workers, used the spotted patterns of hides, and imitated them in paint; they cut leather into netted patterns. Leopard skins were worn by kings and priests.

Defensive mail armor was imported during the Eighteeth Dynasty; until that time, defensive garments were quilted, or covered with feathers, symbolic of divine guardianship."*

Color: Egyptian garments were largely white, because of the difficulties in dyeing linen permanently without mordants, with which Pliny says the Egyptians had become familiar by Ic. A.D.

Cloths were dipped in safflower for yellows and orange reds; native woad for blue; combinations of these for dull green; madder for a fugitive red; kermes (cochineal) for a more permanent red.

Color was most used in the earliest, and in the latest periods, and in the dress of royalty, gods, and the dead; entertainers' costumes were often yellow. Dark blue was the color of mourning.

Color was applied in many ways; netted or zigzag patterns of bead strings were sewed and caught into the fabric as it was woven. Feathers or their imitations were applied. Cut-leather nettings appear to have been used, together with patterned hides, and their painted imitations, which became stylized into rosettes. Woven patterns and embroidery were introduced from the East during the Eighteenth Dynasty, together with wool, which could be dyed satisfactorily.

Jewelry: A great deal of the color of Egyptian costume was furnished by its wonderful jewelry which included collars, necklaces, arm and leg bands, bracelets, earrings, fillets, diadems, and rings. Colored pebbles were replaced by beautiful glazed beads during the Old Kingdom. Semiprecious stones (turquoise, lapis-lazuli, carnelian), glass, and faience were used in beads, inlay, and pendants. Gold was worked in granular and filigree techniques on scarabs and seals.

Flowers were dearly loved. They were worn in necklaces and headdresses or carried in the hand. Eventually they were stylized in jewelry.

Fans of papyrus and feathers were used.

Cosmetics: Eyebrows were blackened, blue eyeshadow came into use, nails were hennaed, and lips were colored.

Symbols of Pharaoh were a *crook* (originally

---

* I am much indebted to Elizabeth Riefstahl: *Patterned Textiles in Pharaonic Egypt;* Brooklyn Museum, 1944; 56 pages, 8" x 11", and 56 excellent photographs. Since no one interested in the subject will fail to get it, I use Riefstahl page references for statements which are verified in eight pages of scholarly notes. Mrs. Riefstahl is in charge of the Wilbour Library of Egyptology at Brooklyn Museum, an institution which is rich in Coptic textiles.

the boomerang), a *flail* with three lashes, and a tall, animal-headed *staff*. Two staffs or scepters, the straight *was* and the wavy *tsam,* were carried by dignitaries to signify support of heaven. Crowns signified the district ruled. The red crown of Lower Egypt, and the white tiara or *atef* of Upper Egypt were worn together by kings of both regions. Crowns were often decorated with the *uraeus* (a rearing viper), a common symbol of royalty, and with the *Ankh cross* as a sign of life.

Gods (as priests) were depicted with the *as,* a lock of hair hanging on one side as worn by the young prince-god Horus, and with a tail which hung from the girdle or the headdress.

The costume of royalty of one dynasty would become that of nobility, and in turn the "best" clothes of lower classes in later dynasties. The short, pleated, gold-trimmed loin cloth of kings became an assumed or granted honorific, as did the lock of hair, animal tail, and spotted animal skin. This skin, taken from gentlemen by priests, was later reassumed by gentlemen.

EGYPTIAN COSTUME DETAILS

The geographical situation of Egypt brought her into contact with African, Aegean, and Asiatic civilizations. Representations of the costumes of these aliens—nomads, allies, subject peoples, mercenaries, and slaves—appear plentifully in Egyptian wall paintings, almost synchronously with the peoples themselves in Egypt.

A large number of these illustrations is included here for two reasons. Enmeshed though it is in Egyptian life, alien dress is seldom shown in works on Egyptian costume. It is from Asia that most of our ideas of textile design, our long tight sleeves, and trousers have evolved.

THE OLD KINGDOM

The First through the Eighth Dynasties center around Memphis. First Dynasty sculpture was noble, serene, and naturalistic. Jewelry: characterized by fine goldsmith's work and by blue and green glazed beads. The Second and Third Dynasties saw the beginning of conventionalization in sculpture, and in architecture the use of glazed tiles and brick mastaba tombs (Sakkara).

The Fourth to Sixth Dynasties, 2830-2530 B.C.* was the period of Cheops and the Pyramid Kings. The pyramids—Gizeh, Abusir, and Sakkara—illustrate its grand conventionalized style in architecture, and it is the best period in sculpture.

Men wore the loin cloth or kilt, ends tucked in belt and hanging down in front. The dress of nobles and of common men differed little, except in fineness of materials. Linen and other woven fabrics, including rushes, were used, with leather for reinforcement at the seat. Sailors wore cord looped in front into a bow as loin cloth. The

* Meyer's chronology.

king's loin cloth, which was finely pleated and rounded off, showed gold trimming on the right side and was worn with a lion's tail hanging from the belt. Noblemen wore capes made either of cloth rectangles or leopard skins, drawn under the left arm and knotted on the right shoulder. Nobility were distinguished also by a strip of white stuff, worn hanging over the shoulder. The governor and the chief justice wore a long skirt, suspended at breast height from shoulder bands.

By the Fifth Dynasty, a triangular erection rose at the front of the starched or pleated loin cloth. Nobility copied the king's short, old-style, gold-trimmed loin cloth, without lion tail but with a beautiful catch on the belt; Fifth and Sixth Dynasties: loin cloth was longer, wider, gathered in front. Leopard skin was frequently stylized in fabric with simulated head and claws.

Women's dress, to the Eighteenth Dynasty, consisted of the *kalasiris,* a form-fitting sheath extending from the breast to the ankles, made of thick, flexible materials (possibly knitted), attached either by single or double shoulder straps or else by a wide collar of beads. This garment, worn by all classes of women, was generally yellow or red or occasionally white, with multicolored decoration in bead netting or feathers. Working women wore a shorter skirt, and often were nude above the waist.

From the Fifth to the Eighteenth Dynasty men and women both wore their hair clipped rather than shaved. Wigs replaced natural hair; short and woolly, in little curls all over the head, or simple and straight to the breast, separated or shortened over the shoulders. The size of all wigs gradually increased, but women's were always larger than men's except in the Thirteenth Dynasty.

THE MIDDLE KINGDOM

From the Ninth to the Seventeenth Dynasty, Memphis gradually declined. Thebes rose as the civilization's center.

In the Twelfth Dynasty (Heraclite Kings), 2130 B.C., the workmanship of sculpture was vigorous and fine, particularly in the characteristic low reliefs of the period. This was also the finest period in architecture; tombs with wall paintings (Beni-Hassan). Jewelry of inlay, cloisonné and gold filigree.

The male loin cloth lengthened into a skirt, which was frequently multiplied, i.e., a short thick underskirt combined with a longer, stiffened, transparent overskirt. There was usually a border around the hem, which dipped in front. These skirts, often overlapping, were worn high under the armpits as late as the Eighteenth Dynasty. Men's attire was almost universally white, with gold reserved for king and nobility. A cloak or shoulder cape gathered at the center-front was common. Sandals, which the master might need, were carried by a servant who followed him.

Women's clothes were green, white, or multi-colored, but beyond this there was little change in female attire down to the Eighteenth Dynasty.

Toward the end of the Twelfth Dynasty, Asiatic nomads began to appear in patterned, woven and painted wool and leather clothes. The ensuing long period of Asiatic invasions was artistically sterile; little change in dress to Eighteenth Dynasty.

THE NEW EMPIRE

The periord from the Eighteenth to Twentieth Dynasty was one of great expansion and conquest, plunder and tribute. Egypt ruled the East. The Hyksos Shepherd Kings were over thrown and a succession of great kings—AmenophisI, Thutmosis I, Thutmosis III (greatest of the Pharaohs), and others to Tutankhamun in 1350 B.C.—extended Egypt's power and dominion.

Woven and embroidered patterns in color, found in Egyptian tombs of the Eighteenth Dynasty, were the work of captive Syrian weavers.*

Coats of mail were brought in tribute from Syria, and fleecy sheep were imported from Asia.

It was in 1320 B.C. during the Nineteenth Dynasty, founded by Rameses I, that the great hall of Karnak and a magnificent painted tomb in the Valley of the Kings were completed by Seti I, Rameses' son. During the later years of this dynasty and well into the Twentieth Dynasty—1180 B.C.—revolts, unrest, strikes, tomb-robbing, and starvation plagued the people. Rameses III finally effected peace and some revival of the old glory.

NEW EMPIRE CHARACTERISTICS

Magnificent architecture characterized the extensive tomb and temple building, although this activity began to degenerate during the Nineteenth Dynasty. Wall painting was natural, lively, and charming in its careful detail. Beads used as jewelry were not simply glazed but rather were made of glass, and gold was used extravagantly.

During the New Empire and after, simplicity in costume was gone. Wealth and luxury made for increasingly greater use of color and pattern so that, by the Nineteenth Dynasty, embroidery was common. Garments were full, with vertical pleats. The *kalasiris,* now worn by men as well as women, in varying lengths and widths, was either sleeveless, supported by a shoulder strap; or with a short sleeve on the left arm only, sometimes with a hole cut for the head. Often the *kalasiris* in this period was worn in bolero-jacket length.

There was considerable variety in skirts. The thin, pleated outer skirt gradually became less important than the underskirt. By the end of the Eighteenth Dynasty, this outer skirt characteristically was tucked back and up, often covering only the rear of the body and revealing a long

fringed undershirt which was also tucked up and puffed. During the Nineteenth Dynasty this underskirt was fully pleated and longer, but less puffed, and until the Twentieth Dynasty there were apron arrangements in front. By the end of the Twentieth Dynasty the outer skirt had disappeared. At this time an apron was added to the front of the old-style nobleman's short skirt.

The mantle, made of wool or pleated linen, was either an oblong or a wide oval with a hole for the head, thus forming a covering for the shoulders. It was often gathered up at the center of the chest, giving the appearance of pleated sleeves.

In women's dress, kalasiris was worn covering left shoulder with little deviation until time of Twentieth Dynasty, when left sleeves were added. Often two kalasiris were worn, the lower one being heavier and plainer. The mantle had an embroidered edge, and was gathered and caught at center front thus giving the appearance of sleeves.

Men's and women's wigs were commonly wide and short, although occasionally they were long, perhaps covering the whole upper body and ending in a fringe of curls. By the end of the Eighteenth Dynasty ladies sometimes dispensed with wigs and set their headdresses directly on the shaved head, which in many cases had been deliberately deformed from childhood.

THE XXI-XXV DELTAIC DYNASTIES

During the period from 1100 B.C. to 668 B.C., Libyan mercenaries gradually rose in power as the Egyptians became less warlike. Egyptian influence abroad weakened. Syria was repeatedly lost and then regained. Assyria captured Memphis in 668 B.C. and made the Pharaohs their vassals.

Trade, extended by the Phoenicians (Carthage) to the western shore of the Mediterranean, had brought new ideas to the rich delta of Egypt. Religion had gained in power over the masses. Egypt became less warlike and more interested in culture and the sciences.

After fighting off the Scythians, Egypt succumbed to the Assyrians in 664 B.C.

By the Twenty-fifth Dynasty, the taste for archaic simplicity began to revive. Fifth Dynasty round wigs and loin cloths in plain colors reappeared.

LATER HISTORY

Then followed the Persian period, the conquest by Alexander the Great, and the spread of Greek culture in the Ptolemaic period, circa 323 B.C., after thousands of years of Egyptian antipathy to the Greeks. It was at this time that Alexandria was founded. Although Greek influence became strong in the Delta region, it did not affect Upper Egypt. Egyptian decline persisted through the Roman Period (beginning 30 B.C.), and the Coptic Period, to the Moslem conquest in 640 A.D.

---

* *Riefstahl,* p. 31.

The Egyptian Army; Adversaries and Mercenaries

The Egyptians were faced by a series of enemies, many of whom appeared later in the Egyptian army as slave or mercenary troops, often fighting against their own kind. (For the Nubian and Ethiopian types, see Ills. 60, 62, 77.)

Libya, to Egypt's west, was her most dreaded neighbor from the Eleventh through the Twentieth Dynasties. The nomad Ribu, Tehennu, etc., were probably indigenous Berbers.

The *Libyans* wore their hair divided, sometimes partly shaved above the ear, with a long braided lock falling in front of the ear at one side and curling up at the end. Two feathers were worn in hair typically, but in illustrations of battles on Tombs of Seti I, Merneptah, and Rameses III the feathers are often shown on captive leaders only. The third distinguishing Libyan characteristic is tattooing of arms, wrists, thighs, shanks, and instep in dotted and crosshatched patterns.

Loin cloths took two forms: either the straight or wrapped kilt, or the belt with an ornamented, tasseled pendant strip in front.

A wrap of fabric or painted ox-hide with large patterns was worn, carried around the body under one arm and caught up or tied to cover the other shoulder. Selvage edges were left open, and like the hem, were richly bordered

Warriors, led by a standard bearer, carried boomerangs, lassos, spears, javelins, double-headed axes, maces, bows and arrows, and shields which might be oblong, ovoid, or pear-shaped

The "Sea People," "Island People," "Barbarians," "whom the miserable Libyans had led thither" (reigns of Seti I and Merneptah) were legion.

The *Shardana* (Sardinians?), *Shakarusha,* and *Turusha* (Tyrrhennians), of the first wave, were Mediterranean coast peoples who wore armor of the Mycenaean type. Armor of the Mycenaean type was also worn by the Lycian members of the Hittite confederacy against Rameses II, and the other "Sea People" who, with the *Purasati,* came from the north to trouble Rameses III.

The *Shardana* had lighter skin and hair than the Egyptians. Notable is the helmet they wore, which is different from any other. The helmet was "white" (tinned bronze?) and had horns and a knob, usually on a projection. This helmet was often fastened under the chin, and while it sometimes had hinged ear flaps, it never had feathers like the helmets of the other "Sea People." The *Shardana* were sometimes bearded; hair trimmed so short that it never showed under the helmet.

The *Shardana* wore a cuirasse of overlapping plates of mail which were usually arranged in an inverted "V" pattern, and a kilt like that of the Keftiu, dipping to a "V" in front. There were several lines of decoration parallel to the hem, and another line down the center front, where, as also at the sides and hips, three small tassels often hung. They carried a good-sized round shield without a boss, long spears, and pointed swords.

By the time of Rameses III, the Shardana enemies of Seti I fought with the Egyptian forces.

The *Shakarusha* and the *Purasati* (Philistines), who were always beardless, wore a feather headdress of the Mycenaean-Lycian type. This headdress consisted of a wide, decorated band about the forehead, and a spreading crown of feathers from the center of which, at later periods, rose a Carian crest. The feathers were mounted on a close-fitting, apparently quilted, cap which covered the whole head and usually tied under the chin. These peoples wore the same type of kilt and carried the same weapons as the Shardana.

The *Turusha* (Tyrrhennians), shown with Rameses III hunting lions between campaigns, wore a feather headdress entirely different in shape from that of the Shakarusha. The Turusha headdress, instead of being set on the brow in a spreading tiara, raked back from the forehead in a diminishing rather than spreading form. The Turusha wore their beards narrow and trimmed square at the end. They wore the same kilt and carried the same arms as the Shakarusha and the Shardana. The Turusha wore a circular medallion hanging around the neck.

The *Hittites* were shown with distinctively beaked noses and receding foreheads. They wore headdresses of a baggy, hanging, conical cap variety, or else they wore simple helmets which frequently were furnished with one horn set with a backward rake. Their shields were either oblong or of the Amazonian violin shape, and were made of basket-work. Their garments ranged from a wrapped one like that of the nomad Semite, to a long, sleeved gown, like the Cappadocian, which was elaborately colored in vertical red and blue stripes and was often worn over a yellow undergarment. The *Kheta* (Syrians) also carried an oblong shield. They wore the long gown, caped and girdled, of the Retennu, frequently in a quilted, defensive form. The *Canaanite* soldiers had simple low helmets, horizontally laminated mail, battle axes, spears, and javelins.

The Egyptians wore defensive armor: helmet, shirt and shield; never greaves. The helmet was a metal or quilted cap, often tasseled at the crown but never crested. The shirt, quilted or made of metal plates, had either one or two sleeves shorter than elbow-length. The shield, oblong with rounded top or flat-iron shaped, made of wood covered with patterned ox-hide (see Ill. 47), was carried by the heavily armed infantry.

Egyptian offensive arms were bows and arrows, the quiver being slung horizontally across the back and reached from under the arm; spears and javelins up to six feet long; swords from two and one-half to three feet long and daggers, all double edged for cut and thrust; falchions and axes of many varieties; clubs; maces; slings; boomerangs.

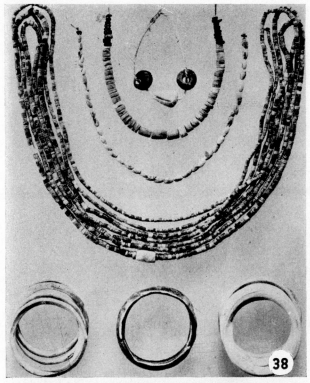

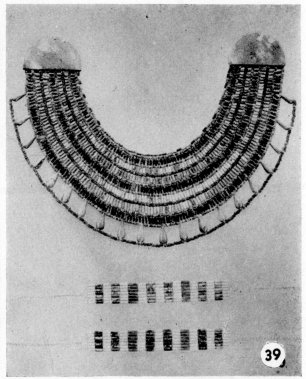

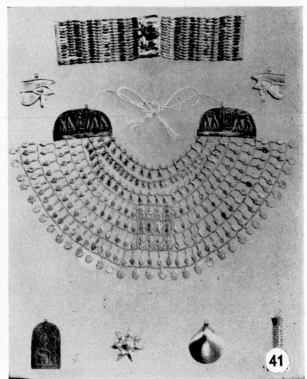

38. Egypt. Badarian per.; before 4000 B.C.
Strings of shell and stone beads.
38a. Pre-Dynastic per.; c. 3500 B.C.
Shell bracelets.
38b. II Dyn.; c. 2800 B.C.
Hollow gold bracelet of Kha'-sekhemwy.
39. XII Dyn. 2000-1788 B.C.
Funerary jewelry: broad collar of faience; neutralized greens, variegated beiges, colors of utmost distinction and elegance. Anklets of carnelian and faience. Similar jewelry worn during Old Kingdom.

40, 41. Early XVIII Dyn. 1501-1447 B.C. Thutmosis III.
Headdress of a court lady at a period of great wealth and luxury: gold inlaid with carnelian and glass. The flowers the Egyptians loved are used here in a stylized form, covering the wig.

Jewelry of a court lady: lavish use of gold in jewelry, with inlay of semi-precious stones and glass. The eye has an amuletic significance, connected with the god Horus.

Courtesy of Metropolitan Museum

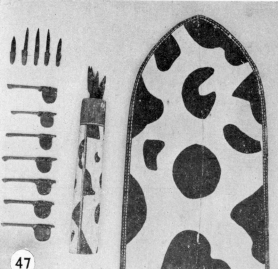

42. XII Dyn. from Lisht, Tomb of Inhotep. Cedarwood statue.

Sen-Wosret I.

43. XII Dyn. from Lisht, North Pyramid. Limestone statue.

A Priest: horizontal pleating as decoration of a dignitary.

44. XII Dyn. reign of Sen-Wosret I. c. 1950 B.C. Limestone statue.

The Steward Au: artificial beard, fine pleating.

45. XII-XIII Dyn. from Thebes. Wood statue.

The Vizir Yuy: long, skirt-like loin cloth, dipping in front, worn high; probably pleated horizontally to give a design often seen on important personages.

46. XII Dyn. 2000-1788 B.C. Basalt statuette.

Khnuma-hotpe (inscribed with a prayer that the god Ptah-Sokar pray for his soul); wrap covering shoulder.

47. XII Dyn. 2000-1788 B.C. from Assiut.

Models of arms and armor (see Ill. 63), painted imitation of patterned hide.

Courtesy of the Metropolitan Museum

48. V Dyn. c. 2500 B.C. Wood statue from Mitry tomb -at Sakkara.

The Official Mitry: fine pleating at one end of kilt; fine catch of belt.

49, 50. XI Dyn. Thebes, Tomb of Mehenkwetre. Funerary model, painted wood.

Peasant girl bearing offerings of meats and a live duck; wig and hem blue; feather decoration and jewelry blue, green, beige, and henna; similar garments were covered with zig-zag patterns in beads (example in Louvre).

51. XII Dyn., from Meir. Wooden statue.

Senba, Superintendent of the Palace: kilt stiffened into a trapezoid.

52. VI-XII Dyn. Painted Limestone. Stela.

Stiffened triangular point of kilt.

53. VI Dyn. Giza, Tomb of Kaemonkh. Wall Painting.

Cattle boats; there are fascinating representations of slaves, busy at every possible occupation, throughout Egyptian art, but their costume remains a comfortable loin-cloth. The hides of these spotted oxen give pattern to Egyptian shields and quivers.

54. XI-XII Dyn., from Assiut. Wooden statues, inscribed.

Four men.

Courtesy of Metropolitan Museum

Other peoples as seen by the Egyptians

55-57. XII Dyn. Beni-Hasan, Tomb of Khnumi-hotpe. Wall painting.

55. Two nomads: red and blue. Garment wider at top, probably made of painted skins.

56. Semite with donkey: rosy red and deep pink pattern.

57. Group of Semite women: patterned in blue, henna, green and red. Shoes with contrasting tops. Men also wore similar garments of same length.

SEMITIC NOMADS IN EGYPT

In contrast to the simple, short, mainly white garments of the Egyptians, those of the Semitic nomads, the *Aamu,* who began to appear in Egypt in the Twelfth Dynasty, were long, brightly patterned in elaborations of vertical stripes or spots, and decorated with fringe and tassels. The shape of the garments shows that they had been developed out of hides; the Libyans continued to dress in leather until Roman times.*

Men: loin cloth, longer than worn by Egyptians of the period.

Men and Women: wrap, worn long by women, in varying lengths by men. Rectangular, widening at the top; when not of leather, which naturally has that form, small triangles could be sewn on the selvage at the top. Wrap went around body under right arm and fastened on left shoulder, the selvage edges on the left side remaining open.

The *Ribu,* an Aamu tribe, wore a garment developed out of this, with a further refinement of a slit for the right arm, and a hole left for the head. The decorative selvage edges on the left side were caught together at the waist. The *Tehennu,* a maritime Aamu tribe, wore a similar garment with a sleeve on the right arm; it tied on the left shoulder in long ears, and was belted. The *Cheli,* a tribe of the interior, wore a garment of the same type, which tied under the left arm, and had a turned-over collar which covered the right shoulder. (See Ills. 78, 79-86).

NORTHERN SEMITES

Cappadocians (*Retennu-Tehennu*): The garments of the peoples of the colder Upper Euphrates covered the body more completely than those of the South Syrians.

The costume was based on a fitted shirt (see Ill. 58), shown on armed soldiers; and longer, on persons of rank, with or without spiral scarf about the skirt, but in the latter case, worn with a cape.

Shirt: long; from halfway down calf to ankle length. A fitted garment with long tight sleeves, perhaps in the case of soldiers made of leather, it was of plain material; but all seams were covered with patterned colored braids, which were used to form a design, frequently cruciform at the neck which closed by a tasseled cord. Tassels also hung at hem from ends of seams. Upper and lower sections of sleeve, frequently divided by a line of braid around the arm, were often made of different materials, by the time of Remeses II.

* Riefstahl, p. 11

Spiral: like that of Assyrian priest, worn by men of rank. An elongated triangle, examples of which, 3'x30' long, have been found in Egyptian tombs. On the garments of the Retennu princes it is made of plain material, edged with colored braid, and wound from waist to hips over the long seamed shirt. When it is omitted, a braid-edged cape, of another color, might be worn.

Asiatics to the East: *Retennu;* Assyrian origins. (See Ills. 58, 59, 61).

Spiral: as a complete garment; a square, just large enough to go around the body, to which was seamed an enormously long, narrow triangle, which was wound about the body, leaving the right arm and shoulder bare. These were usually embroidered in bright madder reds, indigo blues, and Tyrian purples; worn with matching *shoulder cape:* fitted, pushed up on one shoulder to permit use of arm.

58, 59. XVIII Dyn. 1470-1445 B.C., Thutmosis III. Egyptian wall painting. Thebes, Tomb of Rekh-mi-re.

58. Syrian tribute bearers: fair-haired "white Syrians" (Hittites); one with a clipped beard and shock of hair; garments natural color, trimmed with red and blue braid, blue tassels. 59. Keftiu tribute bearers: The Keftiu were the non-Semitic people who lived at "the Back of Beyond" in "the Land of the Very Green Sea,"—"the land of the Ring" (i.e., of islands of the Mediterranean, and to the N.W. of Egypt, Rhodes, Crete, Cyprus and S.W. Asia Minor). They were never Phoenicians, though their commerce with Egypt passed through Phoenician ports. After the Eighteenth Dynasty the generic word "Keftiu" disappears, and the tribes are referred to specifically, as Lycian, etc.

The prototype of all these Aegean costumes was that of Crete, in which the belt was tighter, the hair more elaborately looped, knotted and horned, though the hair of the Keftiu is sometimes represented in the Egyptian fashion. All wore elaborately colored and patterned sandals, leggings, boots, and loin cloths fringed and tasseled. Animal skins were often tucked into the belt, as here shown. The tribute carried has a definitely Mycenaean character, like the metal beer-warmer held by its handle, and the bulls' heads borne by other figures, not reproduced here. The boots and loin cloths are embroidered in blue, red, yellow, browns and grays. Conical Cretan caps.

60. XVIII Dyn. 1420-1411 B.C. Thebes, Tomb of Tjanuy, No. 74. Wall painting.

Nubian soldiers with standard-bearer: black and white costume, and tails (description, see Ill. 77); nets, probably cut leather.

61. XVIII Dyn. 1420-1411 B.C. Thutmosis IV. Thebes, Tomb of Sebkhopte, No. 63. Wall painting.

62. XVIII Dyn. 1411-1375 B.C. Amenophis III. Thebes, Tomb of unknown nobleman, No. 226. Wall painting.

Syrian tribute bearers: Kheta, whose white costumes the Egyptians rather admired, as they did not the red and blue costumes of other Syrian peoples. Spiral edged with one braid, shirt with another, red and blue, alone or in combination.

Foreigners beneath the royal throne: Nubians (Cushites): in white loin cloths, and red sashes edged with white. Syrians: man with fillet on hair; white garment edged in red and green. Asiatic: man with shaved head; white garment, red and green edge; cape, green above, with a red and white edge; henna below, with an edge of henna, green and white.

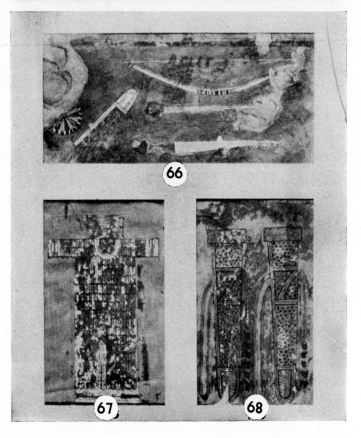

63. XVIII Dyn. c. 1430 B.C. Thebes, from Tomb of Ken-Amun, Chief Steward and Overseer of Cattle. Wall painting.

Attendants of Ken-Amun: carrying his stool, with an animal skin to sit on; sandals, staff and bag of clothing, boomerang, bow and case (made of leopard or painted like it); and a quiver with fur tail, which was carried horizontally across the back, and reached from under the arm. The shield (see Ill. 75): oblong with rounded top and boss, hide-covered over a wood or wicker frame. Egyptian armor also included quilted caps of helmet or wig shape, quilted cuirasses, spears and javelins, short-straight swords, slings, battle-axes, and maces. Greaves were not worn.

64. XVIII Dyn. c. 1415 B.C. Thebes, Tomb of Zeser-ka-Ra-sonbe, Scribe and Counter of Gold. Wall painting.

Musicians: the first and last in saffron yellow (conventional for entertainers). Two female slaves, naked except belt below waist, and jewelry.

65-68. XVIII Dyn. c. 1430. Thebes, Tomb of Ken-Amun, Chief Steward and Over-seer of Cattle. Wall Painting.

65. Dancing girls in funeral procession.

66. New Year's Gifts: bow; whip; dagger, quivers. 67. gold and bronze scales on a heavy cloth backing, blue bordered with red bands. 68. covered or painted like hide, and with fur tails: coat of mail.

Courtesy of Metropolitan Museum

69, 70. XVIII Dyn. c. 1415 B.C. Thebes, Tomb of Menena, Scribe of the Fields of the Lord of Two Lands. Wall painting.

69. Harvest: Overseers and scribes in long and short kalasiris, and one or two loin cloths. Male slaves in loin cloth, one carrying master's "Was" staff with stylized animal head; female slaves in kalasiris held by one shoulder strap. All barefoot, some shaven heads without wigs. 70. Fishing and fowling in the marshes: Gentlemen in long sheer kalasiris,

and heavier loin cloth; shoulder-length bobbed wig. Ladies, kalasiris with left arm covered, heavy wig with long horizontal bottom line. Male slaves, triangular loin cloth. Female slave, naked except for belt below waist.

71. XIX Dyn. after 1350 B.C. Thebes, Tomb of Apuy the Sculptor. Wall painting.

Apuy and his wife receiving an offering: Wife with lotus flower and cone of perfumed fat on her

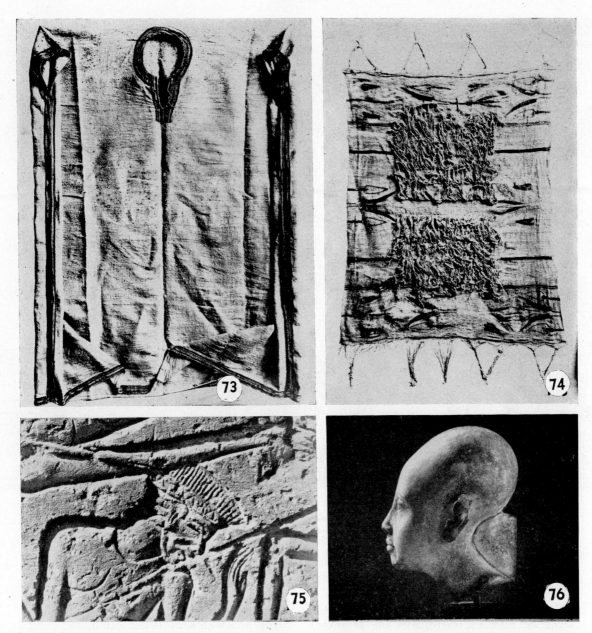

long enveloping wig ending in a fringe of tiny ring-lets; pleated cape, equivalent to sleeves; fringed robe. Apuy, like the priest, wears sandals (see Ill. 78) and wears on his cape an eye amulet (see jewelry Ill. 41). The priest wears the simple loin cloth of earlier times, though lengthened and elaborated, and the animal skin.

72. End XVIII Dyn. Amenophis III. 1411-1375 B.C. Thebes, Tomb of Ra-mose No. 55. Wall painting.

Mourners: in gray costumes, although dark blue had been traditional for mourning since the earliest dynasties.

73, 74. XVIII Dyn. Amenophis III-IV. 1405-1352 B.C. Thebes, Tomb of Cha, the Architect. (Turin Museum.)

73. Tunic: edged with colored braid. 74. Fringed cloth, with tapestry-woven lotus pattern, looped on the reverse to give a furry warmth or solidity to the fabric. It is possible that some such technique was

responsible for the shaggy garments worn by the Sumerians. Ten pieces of patterned cloth, antedating Tutenkhamun, have been discovered. Of these, two are similar fringed cloths, and a third is one of the seventeen linen tunics found in the tomb of the Architect Cha; no color notes are available.*

75. Egyptian, XIX-XX Dyn. Rameses III. Medinet Habu.

North wall relief: Naval battle with Northerners: head of a dead Philistine.

76. Egyptian, XVIII Dyn. El Amarna. (Neues Museum, Berlin.)

Head of a princess: skull deformed deliberately from birth, and shaved. Many well-known heads of the lovely Nefret-ity show her similarly deformed skull, shaved and without headdress, or with the headdress set directly on the head, without a wig.

* Riefstahl, 21-5.

Courtesy of Metropolitan Museum

77. Egyptian, XVIII Dyn. c. 1350 B.C. Tutankhamun.
Tomb of Hoy, viceregent of Nubia. Wall painting.
(Neues Museum, Berlin.)

Drawings taken from the papers of Lepesius.
Made when the state of preservation of the paintings
was more complete than at present.

Nubian tribute (west wall, south side): above Hoy:
shields and furniture, covered with hide or painted,
often to resemble hide; stools, fixed and folding;
chairs; beds with head rests; loaded wheelbarrow.

Top row, r. to l.: Chiefs of Wawat (Lower Nubia),
Nubian princes and princess in Egyptian dress, collars and sandals, differenced by leopard skins over
shoulders; bands over shoulders and sashes with
apron ends, of embroidered red; hoop, and other earrings; cat's tails at sleeves; feathers or ostrich plumes
in hair; feather insignia in hands of chiefs. Gifts of
rings of gold, animal skins. Ox-drawn chariot with
parasol. Followers of princess in patterned ox-hide
loin cloths, over sashes, with animal tails fastened

on rear (see Ill. 60), and narrow scarves knotted at
neck. Women in many-colored patterned skirts. Children naked, with tufted hair.

Rows 2 & 3: Princes of Cush (Upper Nubia), over
whom there had been an Egyptian viceroy since
Thutmosis I, 1540 B.C. More Negroid, barefoot, bearing giraffe tails, rings of gold, patterned skins, a
giraffe, oxen with horns tipped with hands.

Row 3: The tall men of Trk and the men of Irmi,
in loin cloths, sandals, and many bracelets, carrying
fans of feathers and gold on long jewelled and gold
trimmed staves.

Large figures: Hoy being greeted by his household
on his return: wearing kalasiris, tucked up, under
overskirt, reduced to a swathing of the back of the
figure. Feather fan, insignia of his viceroyalty (originally an actual feather, now probably stylized). Collar, bracelets of massive gold; cone of perfumed fat
on head as for a banquet.

78. Egyptian, c. 1350 B.C., Tutankhamun. Tomb of Hoy, viceregent of Nubia. Wall painting. (Neues Museum, Berlin.) From Lepesius' papers.

Tribute of the Princes of Asia, the Retennu and Syria.

Large figures: Tutankhamun: with ankh (crux ansata) in r. hand; flail with 3 lashes, and crook (symbols of sovereignty) in l. hand. War helmet, with uraeus (rearing viper, symbol of royalty) and colored triangular apron of Pharaoh. Collar, bracelets and arm bands. Pleated collar-sleeves, long pleated skirt. Hoy: with crook and feather (symbol of vice-royalty), collar, sandals with a beak point, the cords held from toe and heel by a metal plaque.

Next smaller figures: Hoy, carrying a bowl of lapis lazuli and a necklace with exaggeratedly enlarged pectoral, "tribute offered by Retennu (Syria) the vile," as well as carnelian, vases in nets and on standards, animal skins, offered by the chieftains of Upper Retennu and ambassadors and "chieftains of distant lands" (smaller figures) wearing wound costumes of 2 superimposed spirals of different materials, and followed by slaves in tasseled loin cloths.

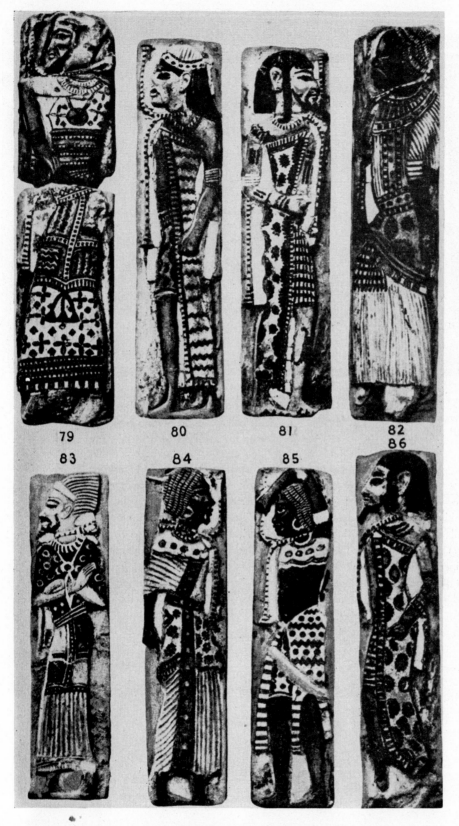

79-86. XX Dyn. c. 1180 B.C. from Medinet Habu. Glazed tiles. (Cairo Museum.)

races. In the case of important Negro personages, where the decorative elements of native costume are superimposed on an Egyptian base, this is very clear. With the Phoenician traders, Semitic patterns and cut, tassels and fringe, travelled west by water to combine with Aegean and Mediterranean native costume. The advance and alteration of an element in costume can be followed like the mutations of an insect, except that among insects fewer fantastic marriages prove fertile than in costume. The descent of many of these patterned, perhaps painted, garments from a pattern of an animal hide, is unmistakable.

79. Philistines: simple helmet fastened under chin; medallion on chest; horizontally laminated cuirasse; Keftiu-type loin cloth, tasseled; over long, patterned, short-sleeved tunic.

80. Differs from Libyan in hair form, fillet, beardlessness, absence of side-lock (which might be on other side). Similar costume, and apparently some tattooing.

81. Libyan: lock of hair in front of ear; tattooed designs on arms, and on lower leg the shuttle of the goddess Neït; straight loin cloth; patterned and bordered upper garment of hide; typical feathers in hair lacking, but unmistakably a Libyan.

82, 84, 85. Negroes: (See Ill. 77.)

83. Shakalousha.

86. Hittite or Syrian, Asiatic in beard trimmed like the Tourcha; horizontal stripes of loin cloth; curved lower edge of wrap; lock in front of ear, like prayer-curl rather than Libyan side-lock.

Identification of the costumes of alien peoples is complicated by the mistaken attributions made by the Egyptians themselves, as well as by the mingling, sometimes mistaken, frequently actual, of the costumes of different

87. XVIII Dyn. after 1350 B.C. Thebes, Tomb of Tutan-khamun. (Cairo Museum.)

Painted ivory carving from a ceremonial baton: Syrian in typical narrow-sleeved yellow undergarment, and red and blue overgarment; almost the identical costume in which the Lords of Lebanon are shown cutting cedar for tribute to Seti I.

88. Late XVIII Dyn. 1375-50 B.C. Thebes, Valley of the Kings.

Ostracon (artist's sketch): painted on limestone. King in the act of spearing a lion; short-sleeved shirt, slit horizontally across the breast, lower part tied around the midriff; skirt draped in horizontal pleating, shows the triangular, decorated apron of a king; red crown of Lower Egypt.

89. XVIII Dyn. Painted Limestone.

Priest presenting an official and his son.

90. XIX Dyn., from Assiut. Limestone.

Ini and Rennut, his wife. Garments more cut and fitted; wigs, especially of women, enclose whole upper body, and are elaborately dressed. Men now wear kalasiris with a neck opening, pleated into sleeves; apron effect of skirt front is probably the mantle tied around the hips. Kalasiris of women covers left shoulder.

91. XVIII Dyn. Basalt statue.

General Harmhab, last king of Eighteenth Dynasty. Sleeved kalasiris, short slit at center of throat, puffed apron arrangement of skirt.

Courtesy of Metropolitan Museum (88-91)

92

93

94

92. XIX Dyn., Rameses II. Thebes, Tomb of Nekht-Amun. Wall painting.

Funeral procession: shaved heads, sign of mourning. Priest with shaved head, in loin cloth and skin.

93. Egyptian, 1292-1225 B.C. Rameses II. Thebes, Tomb of Nefret-ity, Valley of the Queens. Wall painting.

Isis leading Nefret-ity: color is beginning to assume a place in the hitherto white Egyptian dress; strong primary colors and sharp greens, very unlike the grayed and yellowed greens of the earlier dynasties. The worship of Isis increased greatly toward the end of the New Kingdom, and she is shown in the tight garment of earlier days which has persisted as the costume of goddesses; red, with a zig-zag pattern in green and other colored beads. Many symbols related to her headdress of blue cow-horns (sacred to her), set on her blue wig; red disk (universe, phases of the moon), uraeus (rearing viper, of royalty), green staff with stylized jackal's head. Over her shoulder she carries a *menyet,* a necklace composed of a hank of green beads balanced by a gold plaque of equal weight at the other end, which could equally

well be carried and waved, during religious ceremonies.

Nefret-ity: in full white kalasiris, its pleats spreading into a cape; red girdle, gold collar and winged headdress, surmounted by stylized feathers of a queen, worn over blue wig, edged with gold. Uraeus of queen used as earring.

94. XX Dyn., Rameses III, 1198-1167 B.C. Thebes, Tomb of Prince Amenkhopshef. Wall painting.

Isis greets Rameses III and his son: increasing use of color.

Isis: barefoot, in traditional dress; yellow, red, and blue with red and blue sash, blue wig, green collar.

Rameses III: gold headdress; green collar and crossed bands; abbreviated short-sleeved shirt, now a jacket, over heavier white shirt; royal apron, over skirt of red, blue and green feather pattern; sash with one red and one blue end; sandals.

Amenkhopshef: in white, red sash, embroidered, with one red and one blue end, and red, blue and white tassels; gold collar; headdress, blue and gold, with black and white feathers; sandals.

Courtesy of Metropolitan Museum

95, 96. Egyptian. Late New Kingdom. 1360 B.C. Wood statuette. (Cairo Museum.)

Official: front and back views.

97, 98. XIX Dyn. c. 1250 B.C. Wood statuette. (Cairo Museum.)

Female: front and back views.

99. c. 210 B.C. Limestone statuette. (Metropolitan Museum.)

Arsinae.

100. Roman - Persian - Egyptian XXVII Dyn. Painted Headpiece. (Metropolitan Museum.)

Pharaoh: with atef crown, carrying ankh and jackal-headed staff, feather and other patterns. (See Ill. 78.)

Isis and her son, or adopted son, Horus, wearing the crowns of both Upper and Lower Egypt at the same time. Style mixed and impure: old netted bead pattern. (See Ill. 93.)

Courtesy of
Metropolitan Museum (99, 100);
Cairo Museum (95-98)

101. Egyptian XII Dyn. c. 1900 B.C.

Pectoral of Sit-Hat-Hor Yunet, daughter of Sen-Wosret II: "Tiny pieces of turquoise, carnelian, lapis lazuli, and garnet have been inlaid in cloisons to make a design consisting of two falcons, symbols of the god Horus, which face each other across a cartouche of the king, supported on a figure representing eternity. Not content with decorating only one side, the jeweller engraved details on the solid gold of the reverse side. The pectoral was suspended on a string of drop-shaped beads which repeat the color of the pendant."*

102, 103. Byzantine, Early Christian, prob. VIc. A.D. or earlier.

102. Bracelet of gold, pearls, sapphires, and emerald plasma. 103. Necklace and earrings of gold, pearls and sapphires.

104. Near East and Cyprus. VII-IIIc. B.C.

Necklace, earrings and bracelet.

105. Byzantine (prob. Russian) XI-XIIc. A.D.

Earrings and parts of a necklace in gold, with X-XIIc. cloisonné enameling, a technique of Eastern origin. One earring is still bordered with pearls.

106. Frankish Merovingian VI-VIIIc. A.D.

Costume ornaments from Merovingian graves; brooches, buckle,

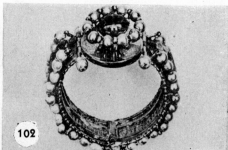

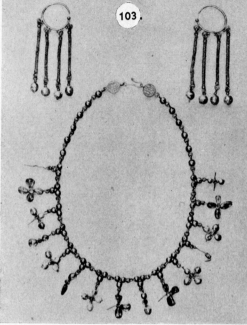

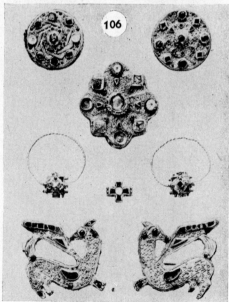

and earrings of gold and bronze-gilt, inlaid with glass and precious stones.

---

* Notes by Ambrose Lansing.

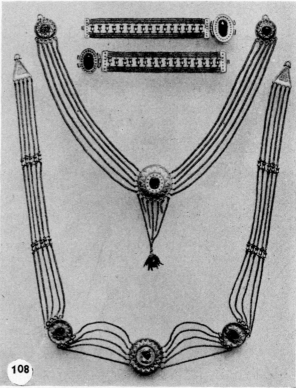

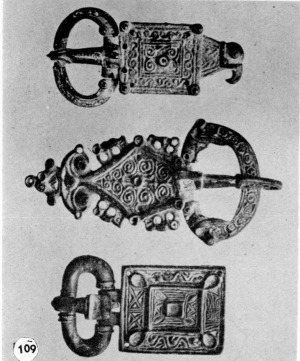

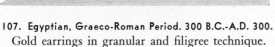

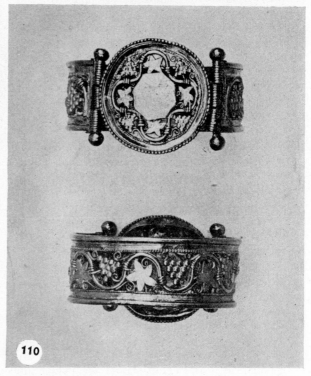

107. **Egyptian, Graeco-Roman Period. 300 B.C.-A.D. 300.**
Gold earrings in granular and filigree technique.

108. **Egyptian, Ptolemy III. 247-222 B.C.**
Bracelets, necklace and girdle of gold and precious stones in the Greek style. Braided gold chains connect the medallions, the central one of which is a coin of Ptolemy III.

109. **Barbarian. V-VIc. A.D.**
Bronze buckles; upper two, Ostrogothic; lower, Visigothic.

110. **Barbarian. VII-IXc. A.D.**
Gold belt ornaments found in Albania, presumably the work of migrants from Central Asia. Massive; high-lights and deep shadows.

Courtesy of Metropolitan Museum

COPTIC COSTUME

The cultural chaos of Egypt began to coalesce under the influence of Christianity.

The unification brought about by the Coptic church has caused the whole Early Christian period in Egypt, whether Christian or not, to be called "Coptic." It was actually a synthesis of Ancient Egyptian, Roman, Greek, and Near Eastern influences.

The cultural contributions of the early Church were limited to hymns and sermons. The only available vocabulary of art was formed out of old symbols and designs from pagan and classical life. These motifs and mythological figures had become meaningless and purely decorative; they were used freely on Christian dress in Egypt, which was substantially that of the whole Roman empire. In this way, a combination of Near Eastern and Mediterranean patterns passed into the dress of Early Mediaeval Europe.

Christianity made great strides among the lower classes during the desperately poor years of the IIIc. It rose to power in IVc.; Christians were the government workers, scribes and accountants, the surveyors and architects. With the Moslem persecutions, quantities of Christian material were destroyed, future development was inhibited, and "degrading dress" began to be imposed on Christians in IXc. In Xc., they were forced to assume heavy crosses and the black turbans native to one of Islam's most despised enemies; while Jews wore yellow, and Mohammedans, white or red turbans. In 1301, a dark-blue turban, the color of mourning since Ancient Egyptian times, was imposed, and many Christians turned to Islam, rather than wear it.

Coptic burial places furnish actual garments and jewelry of people of every class and sect; mummies are accompanied by portraits painted on wood or linen; there are funerary stelae, and frescos.

For our purposes, the actual garments, and the techniques and colors of their decoration, which formed European dress, are most significant.

There are reserve printed all-over patterns, usually blue. Linen tunics (usually undyed) and wool tunics (sometimes yellow), are both encrusted or inlaid with tapestry-woven borders, square patches, and roundels in colored wools. There is a great variety of purples, orange-yellow, red, blue, green, brown and black. Patterns are geometrical; leaves (grape, laurel, ivy, palm) and fruits, often combined with urns; animals (deer, lions, hare, fish); birds (peacock, eagle, dove and duck); figures and motifs from classical and pagan mythology (Europa and the bull, chariots, hunting and pastoral scenes, Persian figures); and portrait medallions.

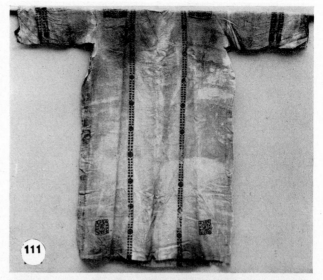

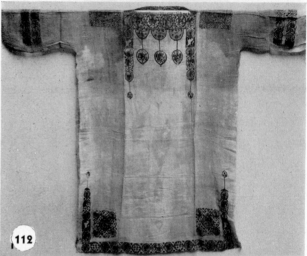

111. **Coptic. IVc. A.D., from Akhmen. (Metropolitan Museum.)**

Tunic: undyed linen; tapestry-woven decoration in purple wool and undyed linen. Cloth woven in loop technique.

112. **Coptic. IVc. A.D., from Akhmen. (Metropolitan Museum.)**

Tunic: same colors as above sample.

113. **Coptic. VI-VIIc. A.D., from Tuna. (Metropolitan Museum.)**

Tunic: tapestry-woven in undyed wool, with *clavi* and *orbiculi* in colors on a red ground. Applied woven bands at hem and cuffs, red on brown.

Courtesy of Metropolitan Museum

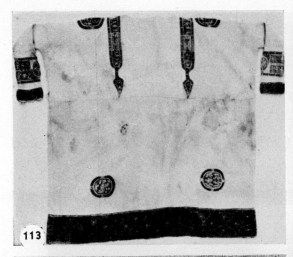

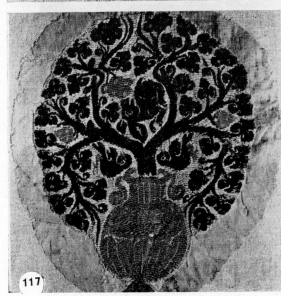

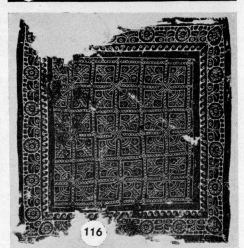

the Eastern legend of Alexander the Great's journey to Heaven, which was carried over into the Mohammedan period, and passed into mediaeval European use.

115. Coptic. IV-Vc. (Brooklyn Museum.)

Swimming amorino with dolphin: tapestry-woven square in deep purple and undyed linen.

116. Coptic. III-IVc. (Collection of N.Y. Hist. Soc., in Brooklyn Museum.)

Square with geometrical design: tapestry woven purple wool with fine design in undyed linen thread, used on hangings or the cloak, *pallium*.

117. Coptic. IV-Vc. (Brooklyn Museum.)

Vine growing from urn: tapestry weave in wool and linen; deep blue vine with hare and bird in the branches; gadrooned urn and clusters of fruit are red; pale greenish - blue high-light on urn.

118. Coptic. IV-Vc. (Cooper Union Museum.)

Female head in jewelled frame: naturalistic colors with black hair, on red ground; border imitating gold frame set with jewels. Splendid example of late classical portrait heads.

114. Coptic. VII-VIIIc. A.D., (Brooklyn Museum.)

Tunic: yellow wool rep, with tapestry-woven bands in dark blue with touches of pale purple, showing figures in niches. The figure at the neck, between griffons, is probably an illustration from

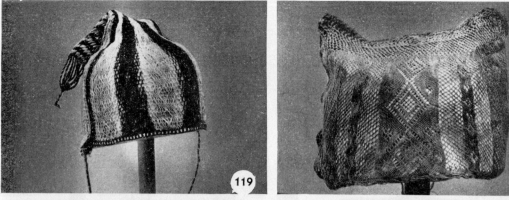

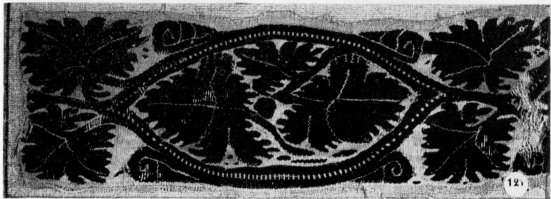

119. Coptic. V-VIc., from Sakkara. (Metropolitan Museum.)
Cap of red wool and undyed linen network.

120. Coptic. V-VIc., from Akhmen. (Metropolitan Museum.)
Cap of brownish linen network.

121. Coptic. V-VIc. (Brooklyn Museum.)
Border with grapevine motif, in purple wool and linen, forming oval cartouches with semi-naturalistic vine leaves and tendrils.

122. Coptic. Vc., said to be from Akhmen. (Brooklyn Museum.)
Looped linen fabric (see Ill. 74). with tapestry-woven bands of roundels, of vine stems and buds, containing floral and animal motifs.

123. Coptic. VII-VIIIc. (Brooklyn Museum.)

Front of green woolen tunic with tapestry-woven bands.

124. Coptic. V-VIc. (Brooklyn Museum.)

Border; very fine wool tapestry weave. Pale purplish-red ground, with design in red with tan shading outlined in undyed linen thread, combining late Classic and Sassanid motifs, lion, and portrait medallion. Border of undulated vines with pomegranates. A roundel with portrait heads probably from the same garment, is in the Textile Museum of the District of Columbia.

125. Coptic. VIc. (Brooklyn Museum.)

Front of tunic: yellow wool with tapestry-woven bands showing nymphs and sea-monsters, yellow on brown. At neck, in colors, jewelled chain with cross, and, in V formed by chain, a crude, nude female figure in dancing posture, with elaborate headdress and upraised hands holding heart-shaped red objects. Strzygowski speculates as to whether this combination of cross and dancing figures may not be a Gnostic symbol.

126. Greek VIc. 550-530 B.C.
    Athenian black-figured amphora, *The Judgment of Paris*. Hermes escorting the Three Goddesses.

127. Greek IV-IIIc. B.C.
    Tanagra type figurine of painted terra cotta.

128. Coptic IVc. A.D.
    Tapestry-woven decoration in wool on linen.

129. Coptic V-VIc. A.D.
    Tapestry-woven wool: detail of shoulder-band.

The Greek Sphere

CRETE

CRETE, situated between Egypt, Greece and the mainland of Europe, having very early established an art of immense and unmistakable character, greatly affected Cyprus and the coast of Palestine (where settlements were made by Cretans), Asia Minor, the Greek Islands, Italy, Sardinia and the western Mediterranean as far as Spain.

The Aegean culture falls into three periods, Early, Middle and Late Minoan:

Early Minoan I-III (3400-2100 B.C.): Crete a fertile island without defenses or enemies. Pottery as fine as any then being produced anywhere; spiral patterns, red, black, white. Early Minoan II contemporaneous with Twelfth Dynasty in Egypt.

Middle Minoan I (2100-1900 B.C.): Palace at Cnossos planned.

Middle Minoan II (1900-1700 B.C.): Palace built; frescos, mosaics, high reliefs (to L.M.Ia); gold, silver and bronze work; engraved gems; decorated pottery at its best, red, yellow, white on black. At end of M.M. II, there was a catastrophe, probably connected with Hyksos Dynasty in Egypt, with which country Crete had had age-old relations.

Middle Minoan III (1700-1580 B.C.): The period of Crete's greatest influence and trade. Palaces built in colonies at Mycenae, Tiryns, Troy.*

Middle Minoan IIIa: Palace of Cnossos rebuilt and decorated; baths, magnificent water and drainage system; luxury, gladiatorial sports, bullfighting by both men and women.

Middle Minoan IIIb: Catastrophe: fire? earthquake? Palace plundered.

Late Minoan I (1580-1450 B.C.): Cnossos rebuilt; cupbearer frescos. Egypt copies Aegean art.

Late Minoan I & II (1450-1375 B.C.): Eighteenth Dynasty in Egypt.

Late Minoan IIb: Cnossos burned, sacked, never recovered.

Late Minoan III (1375-1100 B.C.): Late Mycenaean (Aegean) period. Keftiu tributaries shown on wall paintings in Egypt. (Tombs of Rekhmi-ré and Senmut.) Cnossos partly reoccupied. Introduction of the pottery wheel brought about uniformity; the beginning of the end; horizontal line decoration in white on black. Lifelessness of Crete and whole Aegean.

About 1000 B.C., Cnossos was finally destroyed, probably by invading Dorians. Iron Age of Northern barbarians supplants the Bronze Age.

Cretan religion centered around a mother-goddess with her consort-son. Objects with religious significance were snakes, doves, lions, pillars, bulls, Double-Axe.

Cretan costume: the most elaborately cut, fitted, in many cases patterned, in all antiquity.

COSTUME DETAILS (FEMALE)

Up to M.M. period, in the case of common women even later, upper body was bare. Thereafter, they wore a short, tight bodice, possibly made of leather, sleeved, exposing breasts, laced close beneath them. Belt was very tight, wide with rolled edges, or a snake-like roll.

Skirt was bell-shaped, in superimposed tiers, or flounced; sometimes finely pleated. Slanting lines of decoration are seen, from Petsofá examples onward; by M.M. III., flounces follow a convex, dipping hemline; this is universal by L.M., and is paralleled by hemline of men's loin cloths.

Aprons: snake godesses. Curved front and back sections, over tiered skirts.

Loin cloths, like men's, were worn by women bullfighters. Capes had the high "Medici" collar (Petsofá). Headdress might be horned (Petsofá), a turban, or a high truncated cone (Cnossos).

Hair was worn long; up to L.M., it was covered, then knotted in back, high on the crown, with bound and flowing tail; falling loose at the sides; also clubbed in *catogan*.

Jewelry included diadems, hairpins, buttons and brooches, necklaces, bracelets—of gold, silver, bronze, semi-precious stones, glass beads.

Priestesses and goddesses are depicted with aprons, with snake-like hair and with snakes in their headdresses.

---

* See writings of Evans and Schliemann.

COSTUME DETAILS (MALE)

Cretan men are depicted with the tight "wasp waist" girdled by a belt, possibly of metal riveted on in youth. The loin cloth was worn under a kilt or apron. The kilt, a later development, was decorated characteristically, following a concave hemline, dipping in front, often fringed. Late examples are finished with a triangular beaded netting.

They wore boots of decorated light-colored leather. There were probably sandals and legbands, of white leather, as still worn in Crete.

Male hair was worn longer than that of women; looped, knotted, tied at top or back of head, in top-knot flowing from a metal spiral, or horns, or a *catogan* club at back. Headcoverings were the hood and the wide-brimmed *petasus*. Short hair was worn for mourning.

The cloak was shaped, often fringed.

Priests, like goddesses, wore the apron, which was long up to M.M. III, thereafter reduced to a flap behind. Gods were depicted with the feathered tiara, like the later Lycian headdress.

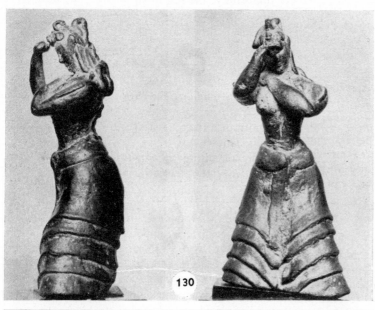

130

131

132

130. Aegean M.M. III. (Berlin Museum.)

Bronze statuette: worshipping woman. Snake-like loops of hair. Bodice cut away to expose breasts, and tightly laced below. Semi-circular wrapped-around skirt, apparently composed of 5 skirts, superimposed and shortening, all dipping at center front (see Ills. 59, 130, 133).

131. Aegean M.M. I., from Petsofa.

Terra cotta statuette: horned *Petsofá* headdress (covering the hair), and standing collar, on a bodice which is probably no more than a piece of leather wrapped around the torso. Snake-like roll of belt, bell-shaped skirt; decoration set at an angle (see Ill. 59).

132. Aegean M.M. III, from the Harbor Town of Cnossos. (Fitzwilliam Museum, Cambridge.)

Three views of a stone statuette of the Mother Goddess which omits the snakes of her underworld aspect. Tiered, truncated conical headdress. Cut-away, fitted, boned and laced bodice. Tight Cretan belt, concave with rolled edges. Patterned apron. Tiered, pleated skirt.

133. Aegean M.M. III, c. 1800-1500 B.C. Cnossos. (Metropolitan Museum.)

Faience figures of a snake goddess, attendant, and part of another. There are no more explicit representations of Cretan goddesses than these. The attendant wears the truncated conical hat. Skirts are now perfectly made, bell-shaped, and tiered with patterned pleating, rather than wrapped around. The Snake Goddess (r.) is costumed in blue-black, purplish-brown, with white and a variety of yellows, the darkest of which is used on the bodice. Her black and white turban is surmounted by a yellow lion (ritual significance). Figure (1); brown tiara; green and brown snakes; beige bodice scrolled in brown; gray apron; milky white skirt lined in purplish brown.

134. Aegean M. Minoan III. XVIc. B.C. (Boston Museum of Fine Arts.)

Cretan Snake Goddess. It is pure sacrilege to have a restoration of a wall painting appear on the same page with the Museum of Fine Arts' tiny snake goddess; it is undoubtedly one of the most enchanting

Courtesy of Metropolitan Museum of Art (133)

134

135

136

works of art in existence. It is sad that no photo-graphs can give any idea of the ritual exaltation of this little figure, carved from ivory, and banded in gold, with gold snakes and jutting gold nipples.

135. Aegean L. Minoan III. XIV-XIIIc. B.C., found at Ras-Shamra, Syria. (Louvre.)

Ivory cover from a pyxis. A goddess of fertility and fecundity (ears of wheat, rearing animals); originally received from the Orient, and now taken back by Mycenaean traders. Hair drawn to crown, bound, falling snake-like lock (as in Tiryns fresco). Head-dress, modelling of face, and skirts are Mycenaean; she sits on the altar which stands near the Gate of the Lions, Mycenae, where similar fragments have been found. (See Appendix.)

136. Aegean, Late Minoan from Cnossos. (Candia Museum.)

Stucco Relief: Priest-King of Cnossos. Crown, with Lycian plumes, and collar combine the *was* lily, (papyrus) of the Nile Delta, with the iris of Crete, in blue and henna red, which in these frescos are equivalent to silver and gold. Blue roll above red and white belt. Blue Mycenaean loin cloth of modesty, worn with a white apron, lined in red, which has been reduced to a flap behind, by the Late Minoan period. Ridged lines on the right thigh indicate a tiered white sash, related to the tiered skirts of snake-goddesses. Like the silver anklets shown on Oriental figures of antiquity, bracelets and necklaces indicate rank.

The Cupbearer, and other processional figures* in Late Minoan frescos show jutting rumps, like that of the woman in the Tiryns fresco, in kilts similar to those Aegeans in Egyptian wall paintings (See Egypt 1470-45, Rekhmi-Re), falling in a weighted point, from which hangs a triangle of blue-beaded network, finished with lilies and papyrus flowers.

137. Aegean Mainland. Late Minoan III, from Tiryns.

Restoration of a wall painting: The frescos are too badly damaged to give an informative photograph. This redrawing shows clearly the bustled aspect, which is seen in the Berlin Museum's worshipper, and in the VIIIc. dipylons. Hair remains snake-like through all the favorite Cretan methods of dressing it, shown here in combination: clubbed into a *catogan* at the nape; knotted and then flowing from the top of the head; bound in a snake; or falling in wriggling locks. Pattern follows the line of 4 concavities in the hemline, which gives this later skirt a curiously trouser-like look.

137

138. Aegean, M.M. II, from Hagada-Triada. (Candia Museum.)

Steatite Vase: Young Prince and officer of his guard outside the gate to his house.* Forelock and frontal curls; dirk with knobbed hilt at girdle (tra-

---

* Evans: Pal. of Minos, sup. pl. XXVII.

ditional); collar and bracelets, like officer's torque, indicate rank.

139. Aegean, MM.II., from Hagada-Triada. (Candia Museum.)
   The Harvester Vase.

140. Aegean, M.M.III., from Mycenae.
   Ivory relief: Warrior.

141. Aegean, Late Minoan III, 1350-1100 B.C. Mycenaean. (Metropolitan Museum.) Vases: Warriors.
   Vase: Warriors.

Hagada-Triada was destroyed before Cnossos. The illustrations on this page show the Aegean helmet with boar's tusks and crest; the exposed ear; hair clubbed at the nape in *catogans,* or knotted high with a falling lock. Shields and spears carried only by officers. Belted wasp-waists, even of naked harvesters. Characteristic dipping hemline of Aegean loin cloth; pattern following this line (on women's skirts, as well); scale decoration; fringe. Capes. High, elaborately patterned shoes and leggings. Compare with women's illustrations, Egyptian wall paintings of Cretans, and XVIIIc. Dipylons.

———
* Evans

GREECE, HER COLONIES AND NEIGHBORS

PRE-HELLENIC

3400-1375 B.C. *Minoan Period* (Crete).
1375-1100 B.C. *Mycenaean Period* (Aegean).

HELLENIC

Homeric Age: monarchy; position of women free and more dignified than in IVc. Athens. Archaic architecture: Greek Islands, S. Italy, Syracuse, 1000 B.C. Temple of Olympia. Achaean iron work.

VIIIc. Oligarchy.

VIIc. Tyrants; Temple of Selinus, Sicily and Temple of Assus, Asia Minor (archaic sculpture).

VIc. Return to oligarchy: establishment of Hellenic art, by Alexander's city-colonies; spread through Asia as far as India, and Asia Minor, Syria and Egypt. Greek architecture and vase painting at highest point. Sculpture: rigid. Great age of colonization to Aegean, Asia Minor, Italy, Sicily: contacts in Asia Minor with oriental art and costume. Increase in Persian arrogance and Greek apprehension. Greece divided into:

    Dorians: inheritors of Mycenaean civilization (Crete and Rhodes); also colonized Lesbos, Halicarnassus and Cos.

    Ionians: greatest of the colonizers and traders; most orientalized in art and costume; colonized Samos, Chios, and rich Miletus.

    Aeolians: sided with Ionians in Peloponnesian Wars.

    Spartans: last monarchy of the old style; preeminent infantry army.

Vc. Internal strife in Greece; Persian invasions; Persians defeated by Greeks.

Persian wars 499-480 B.C. under Spartan leadership; unity, power, increase in trade. Aegina: Temple of Aphaea; sculptures of Trojan War.

Great Age 480-338 B.C. Rise of Athens: political science; painting; poetry; mathematics; astronomy; philosophy. Architecture: Parthenon, Propylaea, Erectheum, Hall of Eleusinian Mysteries.

Peloponnesian War 431-404 B.C. Athens vs. Dorians and Sparta; decline of Athens, politically and artistically; prose.

Spartan Empire 405-371 B.C.: narrow, selfish oligarchy.

Rise of Macedonia to Roman conquest 146 B.C. Artistic development in Italy (painted Etruscan tombs), Sicily (Messina); Greek cities of Asia Minor, Temples of Diana at Ephesus, and Apollo at Miletus, Mausoleum at Halicarnassus, tombs in Lycia.

GREEK COSTUME DETAILS

Greek clothing was formed out of rectangles of material, and consisted of a garment and a wrap. There were two main varieties of the garment, the *Dorian peplos* and the *Ionian chiton.* The wrap, known as the *himation,* or the *chlamys,* was often the sole apparel worn by men, especially in the rude Dorian days and in the revival of earlier styles after the Persian Wars. The Minoan male was much more elaborately dressed than the Dorian invader of Crete.

The Dorian *peplos* was the simpler form, worn by all Greek women to VIc. (but only by women) and revived again after the Persian Wars. It was of wool, dyed indigo, madder or saffron, frequently patterned, especially at the turn of the Vc.; used also as a blanket.

Its upper edge was folded over to hang down on the breast; it was folded around the body, caught together on each shoulder by pins, leaving the arms uncovered, and though open down the right side, was held in place by the girdle over which it bloused. In Corinth and Attica it was sewed together down the side below the waistline.

With time, the garment grew wider, and the overfold deepened so that it was included in the girding, or hung over and concealed the girdle. When not girded, the overfold could be raised over the head in back as a shawl. Spartan girls and women wore the woolen Dorian peplos; married women the himation as well.

The *chiton* (Ionian) was of Phoenician origin; the word has the same root as the Hebrew "ketho-neth," our "cotton," and the Roman "tunica." It was worn first by men, later by women also. It was made of thin stuffs; probably crepe-like, similar to materials still woven in Greece; linen; or the gauzy materials from Cos in Asia Minor, patterned in murex purple. It was, therefore, more ample, made of two pieces sewed together, frequently pleated, and long, sometimes trailing.

It was sewed or caught together all the way down the arm, into the equivalent of sleeves, and sewed up the right side. It was worn in many ways: without a girdle, by musicians; and when long, by men; girdled at the waist, by women only, with the girdle worn lowest c. 450 B.C., and raised high under the breasts c. 200-150 B.C.; girded across the breast in various ways by both sexes, and by charioteers.

The chiton was often worn with a short wrap (*chlamydon*), pleated over a band which ran from the right shoulder under the left arm.

There was a short form of this chiton, worn by men at work or sport, which came to Greece from Asia Minor, perhaps originally from Babylon. The chiton was discarded as unmanly, during the return to the old, simple styles, after the Persian wars.

These two garments greatly affected and modified each other. They are found in all sorts of combinations from the Vc. Their colors were: yellow, worn only by women; various greens, purples, red, black, blue-gray, golden brown, as well as white.

There was also an intermediate form of *sleeveless chiton,* worn by Doric men, young girls, country folk; and, caught sometimes on one shoulder only (*exomis*) by athletes; and by workmen, often of sheepskin or leather. Sleeved garments were used, particularly in Asia Minor and Troy, where the Scythian and Persian styles spread, whence they were carried to Ionia. In Greek dress, a long-sleeved garment worn by a woman, in company of other people, indicates a servant or foreigner.

Animal skins were worn (as *aegis*), slit for passage of the wearer's head, with the head of the animal, usually a goat, on the breast. On the aegis of Athene, the hair at the edges developed into a fringe of snakes. The aegis was worn in Crete and early Athens, by women as well as men. Xerxes' Lycian archers wore goat, fox, fawn skins; Arcadians, the bear, wolf, sheep and goat.

The *himation* was a square of wool with weighted corners, slung over the left shoulder, leaving the right arm free; or worn, by married women, with the corner over the head like a shawl. Dorian men wore it as their only garment, as did the Athenians in their return to earlier simplicity; shortened, III-II B.C. A man wearing the himation alone was always adequately dressed, while the chiton, worn alone, was informal. It served also as a blanket. The colors were: gamut of natural wool colors: white, natural, browns, and black; or dyed scarlet, crimson or purple; woven patterns; selvages; embroidery.

The *pharos* was the linen equivalent of himation, worn only by noblemen upon occasions. The *chlamys* was a smaller woolen rectangle, of Macedonian or Italian origin; sometimes bordered, pinned at right shoulder or front: worn with short chiton or alone, by younger, more active men. The *chloene,* like the chlamys, was of coarse wool, worn hooked on one shoulder, running below the other breast; often folded over before fastening; originated in Macedonia or Thessaly. The equivalent female wrap was the *diplax.* The *chlamydon,* a long, narrow chlamys for women, was worn pleated over a band running beneath left breast from right shoulder. The *tribon* was worn by Spartan males over 12; a small, oblong cloak, of Balkan origin, as the only garment.

Footwear was not worn in the house by either sex; women, until late period, barefoot at all times, except goddesses, or for travelling. Sandals were red, black, white. Boots were high laced for hunting, travelling. Buskins, *cothurnus*: to mid-leg; with platform sole, for tragic actors. Common men had feet or legs swathed in skin or cloth. Slippers were Persian influenced, patterned.

Headcoverings consisted of hats worn only when their protection was actually needed for travelling, or by peasants. The *petasus* was a wide brimmed travelling hat, worn also by peasants, shepherds, etc. *Pilos* were caps worn by workmen, shepherds, sailors. The *causia* was a Thessalonian travelling hat for men or women, worn also by actors to indicate an arduous journey. The Tanagra figurines show the Boeotian headcovering and the "Phrygian bonnet" shows the Scythian-Persian influence.

Female headwear included the *ampyx* (diadem); *kekryphalos*: handkerchief, possibly hood or cap; the *kredemnon*: a veil worn over the head, if not covered by himation. It was probably of white linen; dark for mourning; worn to swathe and conceal the face.

Jewelry was of metal rather than jewels; much more worn by women than men. It included pins: stiletto-like, at shoulders of peplos; *fibulae* and brooches; hairpins of ivory, bone, gold; diadems (*ampyx*), and fillets; *sphendome* (sling); and *sakkos,* a completely enveloping form of hair binding; necklaces, earrings, rings.

Male hair was worn very long in the Achaean period, long in Homeric times, and shorter in the days of the Persian wars. Slaves wore short hair which was indicative of servitude. An athlete bound his hair in a *tellex* (cricket), in reference to segmented windings around the hair, which is clubbed at the neck. During the Classical Revival in Europe in late XVIII-early XIXc., both men's and women's hair was clubbed into Etruscan *catogans.* Spartans wore their hair long, carefully dressed.

MYCENAEAN AND GREEK WARRIORS

During the Mycenaean period, warriors fought naked, or with short linen tunic, without cuirasse or breastplates. They did wear a leather belt, protecting the abdomen; a conical helmet, leather edged with boar's tusks, crested in a tuft.

The shield was carried only by leaders. It was large, protecting the whole body: *ancillar,* 8-shaped; or *scutum,* oblong, sometimes notched at the corners, often bent semi-cylindrically to surround the body. Probably of leather, the form of shield related to the shape of an animal hide with legs trimmed off.

Likewise, the sword was carried only by leaders. It was bronze, three feet long, two-edged, was used for thrusting only and therefore at a disadvantage against the Homeric iron cutting blade.

The spear was bronze. The sling with balls, and

the bow and arrows with obsidian or bronze heads were used by common soldiers only.

Archers were not well regarded by the Greeks, but the Mycenaeans were excellent bowmen, down to the time of Xerxes' Lycian mercenaries. Archers are here, as everywhere, at all periods, relatively unprotected by armor which hampers mobility.

In the Homeric period the iron-armed Achaean proved superior to the bronze-armed Mycenaean in single combat. But there was little uniformity in arming.

The breastplate was the *thorex,* a corslet of metal plates fastened on cloth; worn tight over the tunic. It fitted Odysseus "like an onion skin." The helmet was a leather or bronze cap with leather chin-strap; crested, but not yet furnished with side pieces protecting ears and cheeks. The shield was round, iron, with a boss at the center, decorated with designs in concentric circles, slung by baldric. The sword was iron, good for cutting as well as thrusting. The spear had an iron head.

Greek warriors of the Homeric period wore a cloak (*chloene*) of rough wool, caught by pins of animal form, often elaborate; the *aegis,* animal hide over the shoulders, or thrown protectively over the arm; *cnemides,* greaves of shaped hide or bronze, sprung, not strapped around the shank; the *mitre,* a metal belt protecting the abdomen; it was wide in front, tapering toward the back.

The most important division of the Greek army during the Historical period was the *Hoplites,* the heavily armed infantry (of which the best was Spartan). There were also the Archers; the Slingers; the Light Armed Cavalry which used the javelin and the *peltast,* a leather-covered wicker frame shield; and the *Cataphract,* discussed below.

The *Hoplites* used:

Breastplate: front and back plates of metal or leather, with leather shoulder-straps and protective lappets below the waistline; it was not worn by common soldiers (who were given leather cuirasse, metal belt, greaves and helmet) or by archers.

Aegis: skin of goat, sheep, bear, wolf, fox, fawn, worn over head and down back, or over sword-arm. Worn by early Athenian townspeople, Arcadians and Thracians, and eventually by mercenary Lycian archers of Xerxes' army.

Helmet: Corinthian: surrounding face, protecting nose, cheeks, jaw-bone, neck, eye-slits; frequently painted; often crested, horsehair. *Athenian:* not surrounding face; frequently with hinged side-plates; crests, often multiple, adopted from Carians. *Spartan:* cap-shaped, without cheek-plates or crest.

Shield: smaller, round; or rondache with circular cut-outs at sides (like a violin). Handles in-side shield instead of strap adopted from Carians, as well as the use of a badge or device on the shield, (which led to the dropping of projecting center boss which interfered with the design).

Greaves: cnemides, bronze; not worn by archers.

Mantle: chlamys, often wound around arm to ward off blows.

Swords: become shorter, 2 foot, double-edged; Spartan's sword had curved blade.

Pike: 8 feet long.

The *Cataphract* was the heavily armed cavalry that developed with the improvement and increasing strength of horses. It had the advantage of armed mobility at a time when the short range of offensive weapons kept fighting at close range. But in this period, this cavalry still lacked the weight and momentum to penetrate the ranks of *Hoplites.* It used a small shield or none.

DETAILS OF COSTUMES OF PELASGIAN, MYCENAEAN AND OTHER SETTLEMENTS

Arcadia, Thrace, Asia Minor, Troy, Phrygia, Lydia, Cappadocia, Lycia, Cyprus, Etruria

Arcadians were small, dark Pelasgians of Mycenaean culture, who lived as shepherds and hunters, landlocked on a high plateau since the Stone Age. They were the most conservative and least Hellenized of Greeks. They fought without greaves or breastplate, protected by large oblong shields, spears and javelins. They wore the aegis of the skin of many animals: bear, wolf, as well as the sheep and goats of their flocks. Arcadia was the principal source of mercenary *peltasts* (lightly armed infantry) of the later Greek army.

Thracians were of two sorts: the Getae of the Danube were red-haired; used iron weapons, round shields with a central boss, and brooches. They were Celts of an entirely different culture from the Bessi of the mountains, who were dark Pelasgians like the Illyrians, and kin to the Trojans and Phrygians. Thracians and *Illyrians* of good family were tattooed to distinguish them from those of low birth. The Greeks considered them very dirty people of horrifyingly low morals. Descent was traced through the female line, and their young girls given complete license. Out of this arose the legends of the Satyrs, (from the Thracian tribe, Satrae) and the girl Bacchantae. Their climate was severe, and, like their Trojan kin and the Cretans, Lycians and early Athenians, they wore the aegis of goat skin; as mercenaries of Xerxes, of fox and fawn skin. They were literate; the greatest lovers of music in all Greece; fine metal workers in the Mycenaean manner; among the earliest coiners.

They wore their hair in a Cretan tuft on the top

of the head, enclosed in a spiral of metal, as did the *Trojans,* who likewise carried the *pelta* (round, Thracian shield) and the short sword. They wore a chiton and the national *zeirai* instead of the Macedonian chlamys.

Troy, fertile, wooded around Mount Ida, was settled by Mycenaean and later Aeolic peoples. Their chief cities were: Ilium (Troy: excavations at Hassarlik), Assus and Alexander Troas.

The *Phrygians* who had crossed from Thrace, colonized Armenia and Cappadocia, taking with them their high buskins and the small, round Thracian shield with boss, *pelta.* In return they received the conical nomad's cap with flaps, and the sleeved, fitted, embroidered garments worn in Asia Minor. They were shepherds and farmers, not sailors or warriors; loved music as did the Thracians, but were not quick-witted or literarily productive.

Lydians, living in a rich and fertile land (cities: Sardis, Magnesia, modern Smyrna, and Ephesus), were busy traders who invented coined money; lively people who first played the games of ball, dice and knuckle-bones; whose daughters earned their doweries by religious prostitution; and whose dances with shield and bow, before the shrine of Cybele (Artemis), played a part in the formation of the myths of the Amazons. They wore several superimposed Graeco-Persian garments, only one of which would be sleeved. Women wore long tight garments, long-sleeved, which might be belted high under the breasts, or not.

Lycians, like the *Philistine** "giants," were of strongly Mycenaean character, and the least Assyrianized of these peoples. Both wore a high tiara of feathers, and coats of plate mail or the goatskin aegis. The Lycians, bowmen like all Mycenaeans, fought as mercenaries with Xerxes. Other Lycians carried two swords, a long spear, and fought within a circle formed of their round shields. Lycian remains: rock tombs and sarcophagi. Philistine: painted tombs, excavations at Gaza.

Cappadocia, inhabited by the Hittite "White Syrians," was made up of salt desert, volcanic mountains and high, cold pasture-land for horses and sheep. There was a peasant population of slaves, of whom there were 6,000 at the Temple of Comana. These later became bond-servants.

Its capital, Pteria (now Boghaz Keui: rock sculptures), was enslaved by the Lydian king, Croesus, and Cappadocia later formed two of the Persian satrapies (illustrations under Egypt, foreigners).

The *Cypriots* were a stubborn, unimaginative people, slow to accept and to relinquish. But be-

cause of their rich copper deposits, there was, from the Bronze Age, a steady stream of Phoenician, Egyptian, Mycenaean and Assyrian trade and influence.

The *kefa,* the Cypriot loin cloth, was of Phoenician origin; as was the worship of Astarte (Gk. Aphrodite, R. Venus), goddess of moon (menstruation) and dew (fertilization); elements both male and female. As the androgynous Aphrodite of the Cypriots, her worship spread to Italy, Sicily and Greece (see Ill. 73).

Etruria: was a rich, well-wooded land, peopled by north Italian migrants and about 1000 B.C. by Lydian colonizers. The Etrurians were unaggressive farmers of fertile land, and middlemen who prospered through the passage of the German trade in metals and amber to Greek and Phoenician adventurers. They lived extremely well; beautiful furniture and table settings; ate to the music of flute and trumpet. They played games and had religious dances. Painted tombs giving minute details of their lives, and excellent granular gold filigree work give evidence of artistic development at a late period.

Etruscan costume, intermediate between Greek and Roman, shows strong Oriental influences. Rich patterned designs and borders are notable.

The *male tunic,* like a short tight Greek athlete's chiton, was often the only garment worn by the young and active. It was patterned in braid at neck, hem, edge of short sleeves, and down side closing. Older men wore a longer tunic with pleated chiton beneath.

The *tebenna,* a cape, was a typical Etruscan ceremonial garment, semi-circular like half of a Roman toga. It was the ancestor of the purple-bordered Roman *toga praetexta.* Another semi-circular cloak, worn by active young men, was buttoned or knotted at center-front or shoulder, not oblong and pinned by a brooch like the Greek chlamys. The Etruscans also used a shortened form of the chlamys, which was weighted and bordered; it became the Roman *paludamentum.*

The Etruscan hat besides the wide petasus was the *apex* or *galerius;* leather, conical, of Asiatic origin; its equivalent for women was the *tutulus.*

A *fillet* (*corona Etrusca*) was worn on important occasions.

Shoes had long pointed toes, of Oriental origin; displayed fine workmanship and decoration; were in demand in Greece and Rome, as *calcei repandi.*

The *Female tunic* was long, fitted, slit down in back from its bordered neck; its shoulder-seam was prominent. Early garments were often embroidered all over.

The *Cloak* was usually darker than the gown; patterned all over in sprawling designs; edges banded and weighted.

---

* See Ill. 75.

Hair was worn looped, bound with the Etruscan fillet. In the early period it was decorated with bells.

Necklaces and earrings were worn.

Women's *shoes*, like those of men, had pointed tips and showed fine workmanship.

Soldiers had body armor of bronze plates and leather, front and back, connected by shoulder straps. They wore belts, helmets (see Helmets, Etruria, Bronze Age), greaves, round shields, double-edged swords, and axes. The development of the Etruscan military costume was like that of the Roman.

HELMETS: ETRURIAN, BRONZE-IRON AGES, AND MIGRATIONS

The Bronze Age, which ran from c. 2000 B.C. in South Germany, to 100 B.C. in countries far removed from the necessary materials, was a culture of Oriental derivation, dependent on tin. Tin was found only in Saxony and Cornwall, where Phoenician traders had sought it, perhaps as early as 1400 B.C. Bronze Age culture reached Italy and France by way of the Danube and Elbe, as southern culture was taken to Denmark by the amber route.

Bronze Age culture and weapons were similar all over Europe. Helmets were conical; sword handles short and narrow; shields round; patterns of bosses, spirals, and concentric circles appeared on jewelry which was equally Eastern in origin: fibulae (like safety pins, at first), torque bracelets and necklets in spirals of wire were used.

The Iron Age, which brought Celtic supremacy, came from the Southeast of Europe and spread northward, from Greece and Etruria, reaching Gaul c. 800 B.C., and Denmark in Ic. A.D., and North Russia, c. 800 A.D.

Smelting of iron seems to have been understood in Etruria, which then included most of Northern Italy, as early as 1200 B.C. Etruria was the meeting place of Phoenician and Greek traders who wished to exchange gold and ivory from the East for tin, iron and amber from the northern countries, and the timber of North Italy. Etruria, at the height of its civilization when it first began to battle the Celts in Xc. was almost extinguished during the second great Celtic invasion of 400 B.C.

The Homeric Achaeans were Celts: tall, fair-haired, and blue-eyed. They brought iron weapons, the round shield with center boss, the habit of cremation, fibulae, and ornament of geometric pattern, instead of spirals and squirming animals. Their civilization slightly preceded the Hallstatt Iron period in Baden and Bavaria, VIII-Vc. B.C., and the Villanova culture in North Italy.

The La Tène period, c. IV-Ic. B.C. brought gold and enamel into Celtic use; its culture spread across the Danube and Balkans to South Russia, to Etruria and Rome, and through Greece to Asia Minor. Glass jewels appeared during the Roman period, Ic. A.D. The great Germanic migrations ran from IV-VIc. A.D.

SCYTHIA, SARMATIA, PARTHIA, ILLYRIA

Scythian and *Sarmatian* costume resembles that in which the Greeks represented the mythical Amazons, from whom Herotodus thought them descended (since the women fought, from horseback, and the men were easy-going and fat). It very much resembles Siberian peasant costume.

Nomadic cattlemen and horsemen, they dressed in leather, hides, furs and felt. They were rich in copper, silver and especially in gold. These metals were worked for them by Assyrian and Greek craftsmen into objects, many examples of which have been found in burial mounds on the steppes —weapons, cauldrons, cups, bridles, toilet articles, and quantities of metal plates and ornaments (which were sewn on their garments and animal-bridles) in all-over and line designs.

Trousers appear almost automatically in the costume of peoples who dress in fur and leather; the pattern of sleeve and trouser is inherent in the shape of the hide.

Men wore high pointed hoods or caps tied on by a cord. Their coats were fur-lined or -bordered, narrow sleeved, fitted, closed in front, often overlapping. The hemline often dipped low in front, and there were vents in the skirts of the coat.

Trousers were frequently stuffed into boots which were soft, high, or tied around the ankle.

Beards were worn and hair generally was longish.

Weapons used were the bow and arrows in a case, a round shield, spear, axe, dagger and sword. These latter were short and with a heart-shaped guard, peculiarly arranged to be slung out of the way in riding.

Articles of jewelry were gold, except for the poorer people who used bronze. There were bracelets, torques, fibulae and ornaments sewn on clothes. Sarmatian jewelry was pierced and interlaced, like the Finnish.

Women wore long gowns, long veils, high pointed hats. They painted their faces.

Parthians wore similar garments and armor, but with the sleeve typically prolonged to hang over the hand. Coats were wider, cut like the short kandys (width increasing from shoulder to hem, not fitted): sometimes several were worn superimposed.

Dacians and *Illyrians* wore the high, truncated conical hat, fez-shaped (see Roman, Traianic examples). Their trousers were narrower, tied at the ankle. Semi-circular, fringed capes were pinned at the right shoulder.

142. Greek. Attica VIIIc. B.C. (Metropolitan Museum.)

Geometric dipylon amphora: tasselled cloak (between handles).

143. Greek VIIIc. B.C. (Metropolitan Museum.)

Geometric dipylon amphorae: (larger) Procession of two-horse chariots, two-wheeled; line of women,

with long patterned and bustled skirts and flowing hair. (smaller) Round shield with Homeric center boss-crested helmet.

144. Greek VII-VIc. B.C. (Metropolitan Museum.)

Fragment of black-figured vase: beard and filleted

hair; long, ungirded chiton; patterned and tasselled himation.

145, 146. Greek Dorian School end VIIc. B.C. (Louvre.)

The Lady of Auxerre. No one knows how this yellowish-gray limestone statue arrived at Auxerre where it was found. It resembles Archaic sculpture from Crete, where it was probably made. The position of the hand indicated prayer (see Berlin Mus.

Aegean, M.M.). She retains the characteristic belt, bustle and hips; skirt fringed and geometrically patterned; snake-like hair represented as an Egyptian wig.

147. Greek VIIIc. B.C. (Metropolitan Museum.)

Geometric dipylon vase: Mycenean wasp-waist and shield with incurved sides; four wheeled chariot.

148. Italian mainland. c. 500 B.C. Italian Prehistoric Bronze Age. (Bologna Museum.)

The Situla of Certosa is "the great landmark of N. Italian Art."

Its information is reinforced by that of the Benvenuti situla (c. 500 B.C., also influenced by Etruscan art), and by the Arnaldi situla. The details of the Certosa situla are "Bolognese when not Etruscan"; the military equipment is "absolutely Etruscan, all well-known types."

The central band shows a religious procession, probably a cremation, which was the form of about one third of Etruscan burials. Women carrying bundles of faggots wear the familiar dark cloaks; the men, the familiar mantle, cross-hatched in blocks or diamonds (see Etruscan, and VIIIc. geometric dipylon amphorae), and the broad-brimmed petasus (*caere, chiusi*).

The lower band shows scenes of daily life. We see servants carrying a stag back from the hunt, slung on a pole, while hunters beat the brush for hare. Other sections show an ox, light plough, slaves dragging a pig, on which sits a bird. There is also an entertainment, in which there is a magnificent bronze divan with 6 ivory legs, and arms of lions eating a man and a rabbit; musicians with lyre and pipes, and a dignified onlooker in cloak and broad hat, dipping wine as he listens and watches the amusements.

149. Ancient Italy. Venetia. Este.

Bronze relief.

150. Prehistoric Italy VIc. B.C., from Abruzzi. (Rome M. delle Terme.)

Italian warrior from Capistrano.

I know relatively little about either of these wonderful costumes, which have turned up at the last minute; I give the reference for one and the location of the other, so that they may be looked up further.

The patterned garments and cuffed shoes of the relief show Etruscan influence, and the plumed headdress may be compared to the Priest-king of Cnossos. The Italiotic helmet of the Hallstatt Bronze period shows one form of combination of the age-old motifs of a standing ridge on the crown of a helmet, and projecting ridges specifically designed for the insertion of plumes; in their infinite permutations between Xc. B.C. and the casques of the Gallic legion, they can be studied in *Léon Coutil: Les Casques Proto-Etrusques, Etrusques et Gaulois, W. Sifter, Gand, 1914; and Franz Freiherr von Lipperheide: Antike helme,* and are utterly fascinating.

The Capistrano warrior's wasp-waist, apron, collar and bracelets, and dagger belted at the breast, can be seen on Ills. 136, 138, 155.

151. Etruscan VIc. B.C. (Louvre.)

Massive cast-bronze statue, found near Viterbo. Helmet protecting sides of face but shaped like the conical Etruscan hat of Phoenician origin. Body armor of metal-studded leather, with shoulder straps and lappeted hem (compare with identical forms in Roman armor usage). Metal greaves and shield; hole through fist originally held spear.

152, 153. Sicilian? VIc. B.C. (Louvre.)

Massive cast-bronze warrior, with inlaid silver eyes. Italiotic workmanship and face, found in Sicily. Short-sleeved leather jacket; cuirasse with circular protective plates, strapped over the shoulders, after the manner of the original breastplate in Rome. Helmet with flattened peaked ridge, and cheek-plates, greaves.

Belt with the Aegean edging.

154-156. Sardinian, Prehistoric, Bronze Age. (Caligari Museum.)

Three figures: warrior; head of tribe; archer in repose. Both warriors wear shallow, horned helmets, slightly peaked in front; narrow tunics, apparently of leather over longer tunics, both with horizontal hems separated by two hanging tabs at the front. Breastplates; greaves, bare feet. Shield with projecting point; bow; two-edged bronze swords. The head of the tribe wears a similar headdress, without horns; cape; same two tunics with paired tabs; staff; dagger on wide band across chest. The first protection added to the hawberk of a XIVc. knight will be a plate on chest, to which dagger and sword are chained.

157. Etruscan c. 500 B.C., from Viterbo. (Metropolitan Museum.)

Terra cotta votive statue: Etruscan warrior, showing strong Greek influence. Almost typical hoplite (heavily-armed infantryman). Bronze Corinthian casque protecting the whole face, carrying the Graeco-Carian horsehair crest; long hair. Moulded bronze cuirasse and greaves. Short athlete's chiton, "tight as an onion-skin," probably of leather, to protect body from chafing. The figure originally carried a shield and spear.

158, 159. Etruscan second half VIc. B.C. Bronze statue. (Metropolitan Museum.)

Woman, front and side views: Long, close-fitting tunic; shoulder-seams stressed in Etruria. Cloak, usually darker than gown (see Et. tomb paintings), patterned all-over, banded and weighted at the corners; laid in pleats. Looped hair exposing the ears: fillet with bells; bead necklace worn high; rosette earrings. Typically elongated point of beautifully made Etruscan shoes.

160. Etruscan Vc. B.C.

Bronze: Reclining youth: patterned chlamydon.

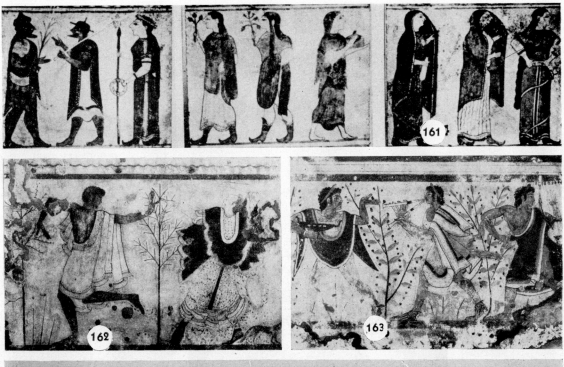

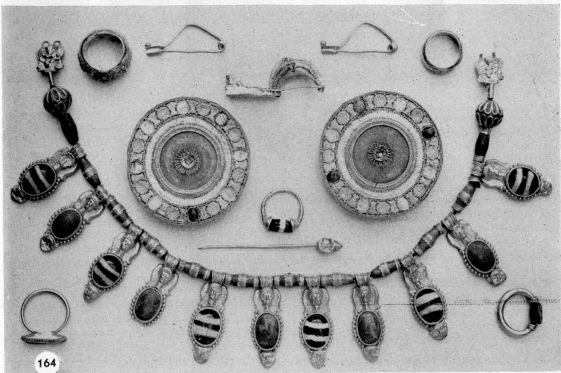

161. **Etruscan Vc. Cervetri. Tomba Banditaccia. (British Museum.)**

Tomb painting.

162. **Etruscan Vc. Corneto, Tarquinia. Grotto del Triclinio.**

Tomb painting: mourning dancers.

163. **Etruscan Vc. Corneto, Tarquinia. Tomba degli Leopardi.**

Tomb painting.

Etruscan tombs are rich in painted scenes of feasts, dances and ceremonies. They show, in color and movement, the fillets, patterned gowns, dark veils, wonderful shoes, the petasus, and fringed and bordered cloaks, about which Etruscan sculpture is so explicit.

164. **Etruscan VI-Vc. from Vulci. (Metropolitan Museum.)**

Necklace, two round brooches, fibulae, pin, and rings found in an Etruscan tomb. The exaggerated development of the vertical part of the catch (c. fibula), increases until the catch becomes all-important in the T-shaped fibulae of IIIc. A.D. onward. The circular forms of brooches became mediaeval European favorites.

The gold necklace had grayish-green glass beads, and alternating glass pendants of blue striped with white, and grayish flecked with reddish. The disk fibulae are garnet edged, with glass cabochon centers. Rings of brown and white-banded agate, or of carnelian.

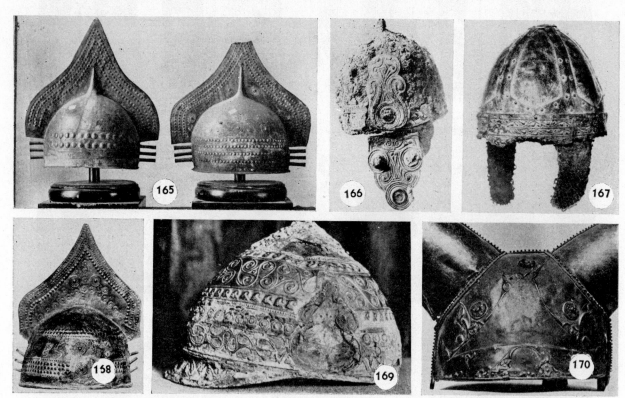

165. Italic end Bronze Age—beg. Hallstatt VII-VIc. B.C. (Tarquinia Municipal Mus.)

Two bronze helmets.

166. Italic La Tene Per. end VI-Vc., B.C., from Umbria. (Berlin Mus.)

Bronze helmet.

167. Celto-Iranian Migrations Frankish VIc. A.D., from Gammertingen (Sigmaringen Hohenzollernsches M.)

Spangelhelm; iron and bronze.

168. Italic XII-VIc. B.C. (Louvre.)

Bronze helmet.

169. Italic La Tene end VI-Vc. B.C., from Normandy. (Louvre.)

The Helmet of Amfreville-sur-Seine: gold and enamel.

170. Bronze Age Celtic. I B.C., found in the Thames. (British Museum.)

Repoussé bronze and enamel horned helmet.

Orientally inspired Etrurian bronze helmets, and imitative Gallic iron forms, found all over Europe, lead to the conical Norman iron helmet with nasal. They have been classified by Coutil* into twelve groups with many subdivisions between the original Xc. B.C. Etruscan form and the casques worn by Roman Legionaries. The original Etruscan form of Xc. B.C. was a more angular version of (165-168);

crest less elaborate, parallelled crown more narrowly and accurately; had three similar or analagous projections, fore and aft, presumably to hold feathers. Other forms are elaborately crested, with hinged flaps; or round-topped, with narrow crest, no points, but projecting triple bands at the bottom. The helmet (decorated with dots, concentric circles and bird-forms) shows up in Russia, Bavaria, Italy, the Rhine and Seine; and in bronze-studded terra-cotta, as lids for funerary urns at Corneto; they are the prototype of the Etruscan helmet. The crest, reduced to a ridge, with one spike, fore and aft, appears on globular casques with insistently projecting rims in Etruria, VII-IVc. B.C. These pass into Gallic legionary use, often with jugular flaps.

The Umbrian helmet (166), transitional in form between Attic-Ionian casques with uncovered ears and conical Mycenaean helmets, has been found at Paris, in Bavaria and N. Italy. Worn, if not made in Etruria, it appears on Etruscan wall-paintings, and often has an Etruscan inscription inside the brim. Its crown may be round, or of a very high conical form like the Gallic helmet of IIIc. A.D., decorated with

* Coutil: *Les Casques Proto-Etrusques, Etrusques, et Caulois*, W. Swifter, Gand, 1914.

170 B

170 A

The mastic-enamelled helmet (169) is the richest example of a type which has been found in Finisterre, Weisskirchen, Umbria and Ancona; either cut out around the ears, or with hinged jugular flaps, as this did; Celtic patterns of decoration.

The Celtic helmet (170) in the horned form worn by British chieftains, shows the style of decoration which is continued in VII-IXc. manuscripts (131-3). These remind us of the bright checked and striped garments of the N. W. Celts, which so impressed the Romans. They were worn with flowing hair, long moustaches; chieftain's torques and bracelets in returning spiral forms; animal skin cloaks in war; braccae or bound legs; feet wrapped or bound in hide.

170a. Bronze Age Celtic Ic. B.C., found in the Thames. (British Museum.)

170.b. Bronze Age Celtic Ic. B.C., found in the Thames. (British Museum.)

The *spangelhelm* (167), the conical Frankish helmet of VI-IXc. A.D. (of which ten examples exist*), has been found between Finland and Italy. One very similar to our photograph was found at Izere, where a battle was fought in 524 between Burgundians and the King of Orleans. We illustrate a typical example: the band is always elaborate; the outer frame is studded, and usually cross-hatched with geometric design; the inner panel is not always patterned, as it is in this case; and the helmet is always made of combinations of iron with bronze or copper, frequently gold-plated.

the palmetto leaves used here, but without jugular flaps. The knob may be elaborated into two horns, with a sort of 2-pronged fork between (which, in turn, may become a human figure with raised arms), from the horned Corinthian and Ionian casques with eyebrows and nasals, of VI-Vc.B.C.

---

* Sir Guy Francis Laking: *A Record of European Armour and Arms through Seven Centuries.*

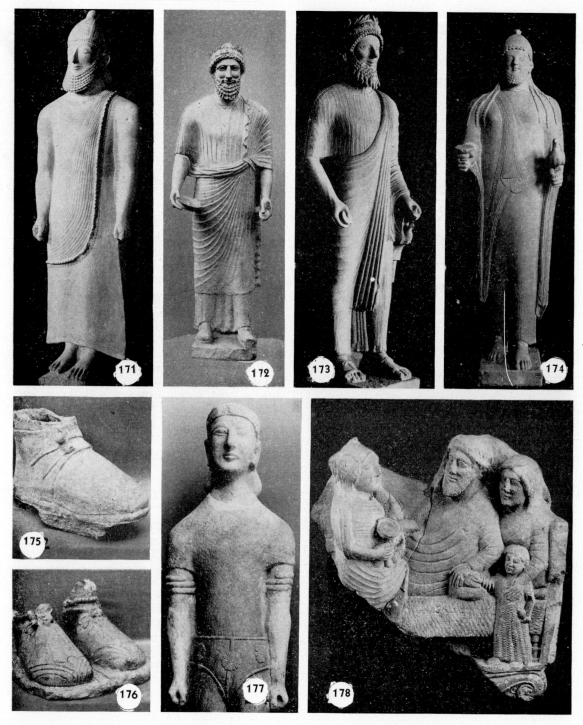

171, 172. Cypriot c. 700-650 B.C. Limestone statues.
Bearded votary; bearded priest or votary.

175, 176. Cypriot 700-600 B.C.
Fragments of statue: Feet, elaborate shoes.

Courtesy of Metropolitan Museum

173. Cypriot c. 500 B.C.
Bearded priest or votary, with bird and incense box. All three in pleated, ungirdled chiton (garment of Oriental derivation) and himation.

174. Cypriot c. 500 B.C.
Bearded Aphrodite: in Assyrian cap, of form still worn by priests in Cyprus. Narrow robe with embroidered hem; traces of red paint indicate embroidered stars around neck. Assyrian influence also shown in hair and beard.

177. Cypriot c. 650-500 B.C.
Limestone statuette: Beardless votary: hair clubbed in the *catogan* of nearby Crete (see Aegean); tight leather tunic; protective studded belt; coiled upper-arm bracelets, snake-like (see Aegean).

178. Cypriot Tomb.
Banquet: pleated garments of children (see Ill. 246).

179. Greek, Athenian, VIc. B.C. Black figured amphora.
Warrior bearing fallen comrade: crested Corinthian helmet; rondache shield with device of snakes. Fleeing male whose pointed cap with lappets, bow, quiver with hanging tail, all indicate Asiatic influences. Female in Athenian peplos.

180. Greek, VIc. B.C.
Lekythos (oil-jar): Battle scene: Persian archer whose conical hat with lappets, patterned garments with sleeves and trousers, form of bow and quiver, indicate origin. Kneeling, typical Greek hoplite.

181. Greek, VIc. 550-540 B.C. Amphora (Exekias).
Arming a warrior: for fighting in the archaic manner, naked except for greaves; spear; helmet with double crest; large shield with device of lion head. Badges on shields were a Carian fashion adopted by Greeks; the boss of the Homeric shield was dropped because of its interference with the design.

182. Greek, 550-540 B.C.
Detail of vase showing warriors.

183. Greek Marble, VIc. B.C.
Maiden, perhaps a Votary, bringing offerings to a Divinity: chiton with finely pleated top; skirt tucked into belt.

184. Greek, Vlc. B.C. Oil jug.

Chlamys pinned over short chiton of active young man. Shield, showing handles which Greeks took from Carian shield, slung over shoulders by cord; helmet painted with legendary beast. Other figure with short sword in scabbard, slung over shoulder on baldric, and chlamys wound, protectively, around arm.

185. Greek, Vlc. 550-500 B.C. Black figured cup

Warriors: crested Corinthian helmets; moulded breastplates with protective flange at bottom; over short pleated chiton; decorated shields; greaves, spears. Adversary in dress of Asia Minor: Phrygian bonnet and sleeved garment, without trousers.

Courtesy of Metropolitan Museum

186. Greek, Athenian, Vlc. 530 B.C. Black figured amphora.

Male: with patterned himation, held by baldric across shoulder sandals. Female with hair caught in high bunch of curls, and wearing patterned himation over Dorian peplos with border.

187. Greek, Athenian, Vlc. B.C. Black figured lekythos.

Women working wool: decorated Dorian peplos of the early narrow sort, sewed up the side in the Athenian way.

188. Greek, Athenian, Vlc. B.C. Black figured amphora.

Hermes, Dionysus and Athena, and an old man: Hermes in typical costume; petasus; sleeveless short chiton of Doric shepherd, bordered; patterned chlamys; winged boots. Athena holds a crested hel-met; she is dressed in a peplos with wide border and all-over diapered design. Dionysus: dotted short chiton, striped himation. He and the old man have long locks, and like Athena, he wears a wreath.

189. Greek, Athenian, Vlc. B.C. Black figured amphora.

Mercury: in hat, short chiton, chlamys with weighted corners, winged boots and carrying caduceus. Female in peplos, like a bolero, tightly belted; dotted himation with weights in corners; sandals; offering wreath. Man: with filleted long hair; long dotted chiton; decorated himation; spear.

190. Greek, Vlc. B.C. Vases.

Dionysus: in various guises: playing the pipes he wears the sleeved long gown of musician.

191. Greek, Attica, VIc. 500 B.C. Marriage vase.

Marriage bed: women in peplos, sewed up the right side, as was done in Attica. Riders, below, in boldly patterned chlamys.

192. Greek, c. 540 B.C.

Black-figured amphora, attributed to Exekias: Marriage Procession. Narrow, closed and patterned peplos; over-fold reaching almost to girdle.

193. Greek, VIc. B.C. Drinking cup

Warrior in crested helmet, shield and greaves. Woman rider wearing the peaked bonnet with lappets which, with the horse, came to Greece from the Eastern nomads.

194. Greek, c. 550 B.C.

Black-figured pottery aryballas (oil-jug): on lip, battle of pigmies and cranes. On handle: Perseus, Hermes and Satyrs: Hermes' winged boots.

195. Greek Vc. 459-431 B.C. Relief sculpture. Parthenon.

Detail of the procession of the people of Athens:
two young girls in wide peplos with deep ungirded overfold, and girded low on hips, characteristic of young girls. Man in himation.

196. Greek Vc. 435 B.C. Relief sculpture. Parthenon,
West Frieze.

Young man with horse: sleeveless chiton, girded
at waist and again below. Chlamys pinned at center front.

197. Greek Vc. 420 B.C. Sculpture, copy of last
original of the School of Phidias. (Nat. Mus.,
Naples.)

Orpheus, Eurydice and Hermes: Orpheus in
chiton girded twice at natural waistline, beneath
and above blousing; chiton knotted on right shoulder; petasus slung in back, sandals; Eurydice in
garment without overfold, but caught on shoulder
like peplos; deep blouse and low girdle; veil over
head; sandals. Hermes in cap and high boots, tops
dagged and turned down.

198. Greek, Vc. 480-470 B.C. Red figured pottery. (Metropolitan Museum.)

Youths and piper: in long ungirdled sleeved garment, Asiatic in origin, of Ionian musician. Young men in himation, probably their only garment. Sandals on musician and one youth.

199. Greek, Vc. 460-445 B.C. Red figured vase. (Metropolitan Museum.)

Young people conversing: Dorian male wearing only himation. Females with knotted and filletted hair, pleated white chitons, and bordered himations with weights at corners.

200. Greek, Vc. 490-480 B.C. Red figured pottery. (Metropolitan Museum.)

Man in himation. Woman in finely pleated transparent chiton, caught down the shoulder to form sleeves, and girdled at normal waistline.

201. Greek, Vc. B.C. (Metropolitan Museum.)

Red-figured kylix: Woman Dancing: the chiton has been folded in at the shoulder, and is belted low; its sides swing out in what looks like a sleeve, with the motion of the arm; petasus on the ground.

202. Greek, c. 480 B.C. (Metropolitan Museum.)

Red-figured amphora, attributed to "Providence Painter": Maenad pursued by a Satyr: peplos with border and clearly weighted ends.

203. Greek, Attica, first half Vc. B.C. (Louvre.)

Alabastrum with a white ground. Negro in a sleeved white blouse and trousers, patterned in black stripes and dots, which he certainly brought back from travels in Asia Minor.

204-206. Greek Classical Period.

From various vases:

204. Interior of an Athenian school; instruction in music and the use of arms.

205. Surgical clinic: doctor and patients; bandages, amputations and malformations.

206. Women in the linen room: wide chitons of the second period of decoration, entirely different from that of VIc.; girded low on the hips beneath an overfold like a peplos; one wears a chlamydon.

207. Greek (probably from W. Sicily) early Vc. B.C. Terra cotta statuette.

Maiden: chiton and chloene.

208. Roman copy of Vc. B.C. Greek work, found in Egypt. Bronze statuette.

Woman: in peplos with overfold concealing low, bloused girdling. Hair parted and rolled.

209, 210. Roman copy of Greek statue attributed to Polykleitos, 440-430 B.C. Marble statue.

Wounded Amazon: in sleeveless chiton of an athlete, caught on one shoulder only; girded above and below blousing. Hair parted, rolled back and up.

211. Greek, 450-400 B.C. Bronze mirror stand.

Woman: in peplos with long overfold concealing girdling: Laced shoes. Hair parted and rolled up.

212. Greek, Vc. B.C. Bronze mirror stand.

Woman: in peplos similar to 211, but arranged to form very short sleeves.

213. Greek, Attica, IVc. B.C., from Menidi. (Berlin Mus.)

Mourning girl: sleeves have actually been added to this chiton, but are girded into fitting under the arm.

214. Greek Vc. B.C.

Replica of a Phidias. *Athena with a collar.* The Athena Parthenos was a colossal statue of gold and ivory, made by Phidias c. 440 B.C. The original statue, which stood within the Parthenon, has been lost. This is one of many copies. The *aegis,* originally a skin tied around the neck by its legs, has become stylized; peplos with a girdle above the overfold. The lost right hand carried a winged victory; the left rested on a carved shield.

215, 216. Greek, IVc., from Gabi, Italy.

By Praxiteles. *Diana*: short chiton, girdled high under the breast, and again, low on the hips; pinning on a diplax or chloene; elaborate fenestrated sandals.

217. Greek, 450 B.C. Red figured vase.

L. to R.: 2nd. figure in bordered chloene, folded over in peplos effect, hooked over chiton. 3rd. in himation draped over chiton. 4th. in peplos, entirely open down right side; overfold included in girdling.

218. Greek, attributed to the Meletos painter, c. 455 B.C. Red figured bell krater, free style.

Nike and youth: the winged goddess of victory wears a chiton with a woven band a foot above the hem, girdled low on the hips. The chiton of the youth, like his chlamys, has woven decorative bands well up into the fabric and is gathered into a neck-band. Petasus hanging by cords with slide fastening.

219. Greek, Athenian, attributed to the Persephone painter, c. 440 B.C. Krater, red figured pottery, free style.

The Return of Persephone: led by Mercury, in

Courtesy of Metropolitan Museum (217-228)
Courtesy of The Louvre (214-216)

chiton. Females: in peplos girdled under the overfold; and in chiton and himation; hair with diadem, fillet, or knotted high.

220. Greek Vc. B.C. Red figured vase.

Girl: in bordered peplos, open down left side, girded beneath overfold; pursued by Poseidon with trident, laurel wreath, and himation.

221. Greek, Athenian, attributed to the Mannheim paint-

er, c. 450 B.C. Orinoche, red figured pottery, early free style.

Amazons starting for battle: showing combination of Eastern nomad and Greek costume: hood with lappets; cuirasse of strips of leather; battle axe; shield; arms and legs with flexible patterned covering; pleated Greek short chiton.

222. Greek, Athenian, attributed to an associate of Polygonates, c. 440 B.C. Calyx Krater, red figured pottery.

Kadmus slaying the dragon at the fountain of Ares: Athena with helmet and spear. Kadmus: brimmed hat slung over shoulder, chlamys pinned on right shoulder, short chiton, and high boots. Female figure with bound headdress. Ares: bearded, heavily armed as he is represented to Vc. (later as beardless youth). He wears the Athenian helmet with movable hinged flaps at the sides; body armor with shoulder straps and lappets below waist which developed out of the protective flange at the bottom of the breastplate.

223. Greek, Vc. B.C.

Orpheus among the Thracians: Orpheus in laurel wreath and himation, playing lyre to the music-loving Thracians. Man in nomad hood; outer garment the shape of which was derived from an animal skin, the quarters of which hung over the shoulders; high, laced boots with turned down, dagged tops. Woman, overfolded peplos in thin fabric of chitons.

224. Greek 460 B.C. Column Krater, red figured pottery.

Young warrior arming: Athenian helmet with hinged side flap turned up; body-armor of plate, scales and separate, comfortably flexible lappets protecting abdomen. Elders with staffs, wearing himation. Woman with shield and quiver: bound hair, chiton, himation.

225. Greek, Athenian. Column Krater, attributed to the Pan painter, c. 465 B.C.

Dionysus and a satyr: Dionysus wears a wreath of vine leaves; long pleated chiton, under bordered himation.

226. Greek, Athenian, attributed to the Pan painter, c. 465 B.C. Orinoche, red figured pottery. Early free style.

Ganymede: most beautiful of Greek boys, in bordered himation.

227. Greek, Relief Melian. c. 450 B.C.

Girl playing pipes and young man watching dancer: Girl, knotted hair, bound with fillet; chiton, himation, sandals. Man, himation, sandals.

228. Greek. Melian, first half Vc. Terra cotta relief, c. 450 B.C.

Return of Odysseus: in folded himation, chlamys, knotted animal skins, conical felt cap.

229, 230. Greek, 480 B.C. Temple of Aphaea, Aegina, (Munich, Glyptothek.)

Herakles: in the lion-headed helmet of Aegina; body armor of leather and bronze. One of a set of statues of the Trojan war. 230. Fallen Warrior: of Homeric period, fighting naked except for Athenian helmet, round shield, and greaves.

231. Greek, 480 B.C. (Berlin Altes Museum.)

Painted marble statue: Enthroned goddess: pleated chiton, under chlamydon fastened on a band running under breast from shoulder; long tresses.

232. Roman copy of Greek, c. 450-440 B.C. (Athens Nat. Museum.)

Pentelic marble relief: Demeter, Triptolemus and Persephone: peplos; naked boy with himation; chiton and himation; plain sandals, women; elaborate sandals, males.

233. Greek, Vc. (Delphi Museum.)

Bronze statue: Chariot Driver: chiton of the gir-dled form in which it was worn by charioteers, girt around the shoulders to form manageable sleeves.

234. Greek, c. 455-450 B.C. Island of Paros. (Metropolitan Museum.)

Marble grave relief: Girl feeding pigeons: peplos, sandals.

235. Roman copy of Greek work from Egypt, Vc. (Metropolitan Museum.)

Bronze statuette: Standing woman: back of peplos.

236. Greek, Athenian, Vc. B.C. (Metropolitan Mus.)

White lekythos: Hermes conducting a man to Charon's boat (detail): bearded man in workman's hat and animal skin.

237. Greek, V-IVc. B.C. (Metropolitan Museum.)

Arcadian? peasant, the pattern of whose cloak suggests that it is the upper part of a hide; the pin is not far removed from the classic shepherd's thorn; and he wears the hat of a man who is out in all weathers.

238. Late Greek, Tanagra type, IVc. B.C. Terra cotta
    statuette. (Metropolitan Museum.)
    Lady: with lotus leaf fan, hair dressed in high
krobyle above forehead. Gowns and scarves of figures
are in pale colors: rose, violet, lemon, blue, often with
deep border of different color on himation or robe.
239-241. Herculaneum, IV B.C. (Dresden, Albertinium.)
    Female statue: bare heads now draped, like future
Roman matron, mediaeval lady and madonna.
242. Greek, Tanagra type, IV-IIIc. B.C. Terra cotta
    statuette. (Metropolitan Museum.)
    Lady: with typical Tanagra headcovering and
swathing himation.
243. Terra cotta statuettes: a. Tanagra IVc., b. Asia
    Minor IIIc., c. Tanagra IVc. (Metropolitan Museum.)
244. IIIc. or later, (Metropolitan Museum.)
    Statuette: Nike flying.
245. Cyprus, IVc. (Metropolitan Museum.)
    Limestone statuette with traces of red paint: Tem-

ple Boy holding a Bird.
246. Hellenistic (?) (Metropolitan Museum.)
    Limestone: Seated Temple Boy, with a chain of
pendants, holding a hare.
247. Greek, Ic. B.C. (Istambul Museum.)
    Youth: tunic with short sleeves. The cloak of the
Middle Ages is emerging; high strapped boots.
248. Apulia, 350-300 B.C. (Metropolitan Museum.)
    Krater: Conversation Piece.
249. Etruscan, 3! B.C.-14 A.D. (Metropolitan Museum.)
    Relief: Paris and Helen.
    Outlying lands were subjected to the influence of
many neighbors before Greek culture began to spread
over the Mediterranean and Near East in Vc. It first
affected Phoenicia, Cyprus, and S. Russia through
the Black Sea; with Macedonian conquests, it spread
wide, and finally penetrated even Greek-hating Egypt.
    The temple boy from Cyprus (245) wears a Coptic

lappeted cap, trousers, and the long-sleeved garment, which he wears girdled in the Greek way. Apulia, on the Adriatic just above the Achilles tendon of the Italian boot, was peopled by indigenous Samnites, and dark pastoral Pelasgians from the Balkans, who brought Thracian Oriental influences.

250. Scythian, late. From Kul-Oba. (Leningrad, Hermitage.)

Gold plaque: male.

251. Scythian c. 400 B.C., from Kul-Oba. (Leningrad, Hermitage.)

The Kul-Oba Vase. Man stringing a bow.

252. Scythian c. 400 B.C. Nikopol, S. Russia. Chertomlyk Tomb. (Leningrad, Hermitage.)

The Chertomlyk or Nikopol Vase; parcel gilt. Scythic figures milking mares.

253. Nomadic.

Gold torque.

tunic with *clavi;* the shirt of the other (246) has been affected by Egypt's ancient methods of horizontal pleating, and he wears a necklace of amulets, which goes on into use on Roman children. Eastern trade influences have brought to Etruria the charioteer's

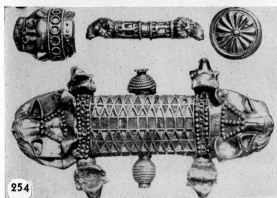

254. Scythian, VIc. B.C. Kelermes, Kuban. (Hermitage.)
Gold ornament inlaid with amber.

255. Scythian, Vc. B.C., said to be from Nikopol, S. Russia. (Metropolitan Museum.)

Gold plate for a sword-sheath: detail of top end. Contest between Greeks and Barbarians: l. to r., Greek, Barbarian, Greek and Persian.

256, 257. Scythian, VI-IIIc. B.C. Melitopol Tumulus of Solokha.

Gold comb: front and reverse. Bareheaded man on foot: typical Scythic garments; coat edged or lined with fur, hem dipping in front; trousers tied at ankle; gold bands and ornaments sewed on garments.

Heavily-armed cavalryman: scale armor (see Roman, Ill. 298); helmet of Greek type; very short Scythic spear; wicker shield of *pelta* form. Heavily-armed foot-soldier: low-peaked helmet, cap form, without flaps; armor of Greek type, edged with the peplum of plates which had evolved out of the spreading metal flange at the bottom of the cuirasse; wicker shield in a variation of the *rondache* form.

258. Sarmatian, Steppes, Siberia. (Hermitage.)
Gold (?) plaque: bird.

259. Scythian and Sarmatian, IIIc. B.C. Craiova. (Bucharest Musee des Antiquites.)

Silver appliqués: animal heads.

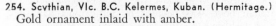

Romans and Barbarians

ROMAN COSTUME

MALE Roman costume consisted, basically, of a short-sleeved shirt, *tunica,* originally woolen, girded up to knee length; and of an elliptical woolen wrap, the *toga,* typically white, draped about the body from the left shoulder under the right arm. Purple bands, *clavi,* on the tunic indicated the wearer's rank. There were many additional wraps, restangular, semi-circular or fitted.

Women wore a sleeved, long, girded *tunica,* or *stola;* and an outdoor wrap, *palla,* which might be draped over the head, but did not obviate the necessity for wearing a veil or other head covering. Children were dressed like their elders, in *tunica* and *toga.*

Footwear in the house might be strapped slippers, *soleae;* light shoes, *soccae;* and on the street, leather shoes, *calcei,* strapped, cut-out, and laced sandals, varying in height from ankle to well up the calf. Those of senators were black; patricians and magistrates wore purple.

Jewelry consisted of *fibulae* and brooches, bracelets, earrings, necklaces and the Gallic *torque,* hairpins, fillets, and wreaths.

Popular colors were yellow (worn only by women, however), various greens, gray-blue, red, purple, natural wool colors, browns, blacks, and a great deal of white.

Toga: Outer garment, which was also the badge of the Roman citizen, rich or poor. A slave could not wear it; a freed man was granted permission to assume it; a banished citizen had to give up wearing it.

The *toga* was originally the rectangular Greek *pallium,* but became an ellipse, the draping of which developed infinite complications and subtleties. Folded lengthwise, with one end hanging to the ground in front, the *toga* was draped over the left shoulder, across the back, under the right arm and up across the body (in a mass of folds called the *sinus* which served as pockets), and over the left shoulder or arm, where it was held in place by its own texture, or by an added weight.

The *toga* was of wool, characteristically white, for the citizen. The *toga* of the Emperor was purple; those of artisans, the poor, and of people in mourning or at sacrifices (who wore the *toga*

draped over the head) were of the darker colors of natural wool. The *trabea* worn by the equites was a small scarlet-striped *toga.*

The *toga praetexta* had a purple hem. It was worn by senators, certain officials, priests, and by boys up to the age of sixteen, when they assumed the *toga virilis,* the plain white *toga* of the citizen. Senators could not appear in public without the *toga,* which was worn until the end of the IVc. A.D. To appear in the more convenient *paenula* was permitted only to the Prefect of Rome, who in his military capacity had always to be prepared to go anywhere without notice.

The late purple and gold embroidered *toga picta* or *palmata,* worn at triumphs, became the rigidly magnificent garb of those IV-Vc. consuls, whose most arduous duty was to celebrate the circus days. A wide strip of stiff embroidery, wound around the shoulders, simulated the folded bands of the *toga,* and a crescent-shaped apron to match, drawn across the thighs and up to the left arm was a formalization of the *sinus* (the drape of the *toga* under the right arm and across the body in front). (Compare with Diptych of Magnus and XIc Byz. Emperor Nich. Botaniate.)

Pallium: *Palla*: Roman outdoor garment, which could also be used as a bed covering. It was originally Greek, but in Rome it was draped like a Greek *himation,* or held by a *fibula;* not hooked, as in Greece.

It was a rectangle, as wide as from the wearer's shoulder to the floor, and about three times as long, and was worn by men, women and children, civil and military. Women wore the *palla* outdoors, often draped over the head, but always in conjunction with a veil or cap. As today in church, a head covering was customary among women in Rome.

The *pallium* was the characteristic garment of the scholar and philosopher (as the sole garment), the conventional mantle of Christ, and the name of the liturgical garment, though perhaps not the garment itself, derives from it.

Besides the *toga* and *pallium,* the Romans had many other mantles.

Paenula: This was a hooded, bell-shaped weatherproof garment of leather or wool, which was already in use by the Etruscans in IV B.C. It was worn by everybody, civil and military, particularly by centurions. By the time of Tacitus, it was worn by lawyers, and though much condemned and banned, it finally conquered the much less convenient toga even for senatorial use. It was lengthened, closed all the way, except for a slit at the chin, like a poncho, and its name changed to *casula,* from which (cf. Fr. *cagoulle*) we have the liturgical *chasuble.*

The *cucullus* was a Gallo-Roman IIc. hood with a small cape of its own to keep the neck snug, while used in conjunction with some other, more ample, often poncho-like, covering over it.

There were two purely military mantles, *paludamentum* and *saggum.* The paludamentum was the official military mantle of the general in command, or of the Emperor while in the field. It was used particularly in the earlier years, before I A.D. In cut it resembled the *chlamys* or *lacerna,* with two corners truncated to form an elongated primitive semi-circle.

The saggum was Gallic in origin: there it was a folded rectangle of striped cloth, held by a thorn, in place of a fibula. It became the military wrap of the Roman army; opened out it served as a blanket. Generals, as well, wore it in red or purple and L. M. Wilson* says that of 100 cloaked soldiers on Trajan's Column, two-thirds are wearing the saggum, and that of the remaining third, all, except Emperor, generals and 10 centurions, are wearing the paenula. "Putting on the saggum" was the equivalent of declaring war.

Chlamys: The chlamys was a semi-circular cape, hung over the left arm, and fastened by a fibula or clasp at the right shoulder. It can be seen, decorated with the *tablion,* on the Ravenna mosaics, and on the "Diptych of an Empress," and from the Byzantine court it will continue for many centuries as the outer garment of the upper classes of Western Europe.

Lacerna: This garment was the cloak similar to the chlamys, but light and short, which was worn by everybody in the last century of the Republic. Even senators wore it, in place of the toga, although doing so even then caused a scandal. The *abolla* and the red *byrrus* were other chlamys-like cloaks, often hooded.

Tunica - Stola: Wide shirt-like under-garment, the indoor dress of the Roman; worn outdoors, without the toga, only by working people. It was not, like the toga, distinctively Roman. Originally sleeveless and woolen, usually white, it acquired sleeves, and was later made of linen and cotton, as well. Until the late Empire, sleeves below the elbow were considered in poor taste, and were worn by priests only, or by actors and musicians.

The tunic was girded with meticulous care to the exact length which was considered correct for the sex and rank of the wearer: long, for women;

knee-length or a little below, for a man (longer was effeminate); shorter than knee-length and deeply bloused, for a centurion (who, under campaign conditions, might need the protection against cold furnished at night by its full, ungirdled length.) An ungirded tunic was considered slovenly. A workman's tunic might pass under the right arm and have only a right armhole; it could be made of leather or fur-hide.

The stola, the woman's tunica, was worn over the *tunica intima* (which was of similar cut, might or might not have sleeves, and which served as house-dress). The *stola* had sleeves like the men's, or pinned along the shoulder line and tight down the arms; or, after the IVc., very wide. It was girded once, under the breast (which was first held up in place by soft leather bands—equivalent of our brassiere) and was often girded again at the hips. It was frequently lengthened in appearance by the *instita,* an additional piece of stuff, fastened under the lower belt, forming a train in back on the gown of a matron.

The *tunica talaris,* which fell to the feet and had long loose sleeves, was the marriage dress for men, but was looked down upon by the citizens of Rome and did not compete with the short tunic until the IVc. A.D.

By the VIc., the long toga went out of civil use, and developed into the liturgical *alb,* or *surplice.*

As time went on, several tunics were worn, one over another, those beneath being narrower.

Dalmatica: (see Coptic text and plates). An outer garment, originally male, it was introduced c. 190 A.D. from Dalmatia; common in Rome by IIIc. A.D., it was cut like a tunic, but wider, and with wide short sleeves; went on over the head, was worn without girdle, and was characteristically decorated by the *clavus.*

The dalmatic was much worn by the early Christians: St. Cyprien went to his martyrdom dressed in dalmatic and cape; from it developed the liturgical *dalmatic* and *tunicle.*

Purple stripes (*clavi*) running up over each shoulder from hem to hem, on a customarily ungirded dalmatic, indicated the rank of the wearer: wide (*latisclavus*) *for senators;* narrow (*añgusticlavus*) for equites, knights.

With time, the clavus lost distinction, and by the Ic. it was worn by everyone. The *clavi* then became more elaborately decorative in character; broke into spots of decoration, and amalgamated with borders at the hem of the garment, which gradually moved below the knee-length at which it had stayed for 600 years. The dalmatic was, later, patterned all over, even in letters of the Greek alphabet used decoratively.

The original rectangularity of the dalmatic began to be lost by IVc. Diagonal cutting widened the hems of sleeves and shirts. By the Crusades it

---

* L. M. WILSON: *Clothing of Ancient Romans.*

became a gentleman's long, loose-sleeved gown of rich stuff.

From Vc., the dalmatic was more elaborately cut and fitted; also it was shortened. It became part of the coronation robes of the German Emperors, from XIc.; and in a form more nearly approaching the original, it is still part of the English, as it was of the French coronation regalia. It also distinguishes the vestments of a deacon of the modern Roman church.

BASIC EUROPEAN DRESS

During the first five centuries of the Christian era the basic dress of Western Europe was in process of evolution from its Latin, Barbarian and Hellenic sources. Dress varied little, during this period, between nations, or, except in length, between sexes. Its foundation was Roman, which remained for a thousand years a potent influence, the vestigial remains of which are still with us in liturgical vestments.

In the IIIc. Eastern influences added sleeves to the Roman tunic, which became the dalmatic. The Roman clavus had gradually lost distinction until, by the Imperial epoch, it was worn by the lowest servants. It was, proudly therefore, as "The servants of God," that the early Christians are shown in the paintings of the Catacombs, wearing the clavus on their wide, ungirdled, sleeved dalmatics.

The trouser, originally the badge of the Barbarian, had been taken up, for garrison wear, in rigorous climates, by the Roman army. During the Ic. Barbarian *bracae* began to filter back towards Rome; they were still an interesting novelty there in the IIIc. In the IV-Vc. they were repeatedly interdicted for wear in the city, but as Barbarians entered into and rose in the Roman service, through the III and IVc. to triumphant positions in the Vc., the Romans succumbed to what Toynbee calls the inverted snobbery of a mania for barbarism.

It was significant to find that among the IVc. illustrations, selected for intrinsic interest, we have, in the colossal statue of Barletta, the Emperor Valentinian I, a Pannonian, a barbarian partly Celtic in origin; in the guard on the Disk of Theodosius (whose daughter, incidentally, married the successor of Alaric), we see a long-haired Frank; and on the Diptych of Stilicho, a Vandal, married to Serena, niece of the Emperor Theodosius (whose son, Arcadius, had married Eudoxia, daughter of the barbarian, Banto). Another sort of trouser became familiar to Rome, from Persia.

Byzantine influences became of paramount importance as the Roman imperial system disintegrated and Constantinople became the capital of the Empire in the IVc.

The long-sleeved *tunica talaris* which the Romans had considered unmanly (actors' or musicians' garb) came into general use in the IVc., as did a linen undergarment.

The clavi changed from simple stripes to decorative ones. In the IVc. they began to shorten, running over the shoulders only, and perhaps up a little from the hem, ending in decorative motifs, *orbiculi*. Decorative roundels and squares were added at shoulder and knees; decorative bands to hems. A widening single band down the center front eventually joined with the shoulder decoration to form a patterned yoke, *superhumeral*, with an analogous border at the hem.

An embroidered square, the *tablion*, appears on the front and back edges of the semi-circular mantle, chlamys, which (covering the left arm and caught on the right shoulder by a fibula), had replaced the draped Roman toga. The folded bands of the late Roman toga persisted as the embroidered palla around the shoulders and hips of the ceremonial dress of the later Consuls, and in the costume of the XIc. Byzantine emperor Nicholas Botaniate; the palla was also the source of the pallium of episcopal vestments.

Roman footwear, slippers and calcei had developed, by IVc., into the Byzantine shoe.

By VIc the civil dress of Europe became that of the westerners and barbarians, breeched, short-cloaked; and the long hooded garments of earlier centuries were retained by the conservative church.

260. Rome Ic. A.D.

Claudius Family.

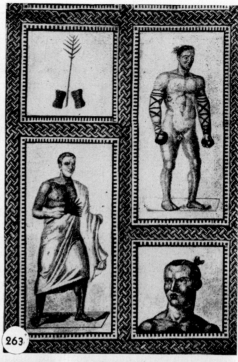

261. Roman. (Rome Conservatori.)

Magistrate: *calcei*: tunic (if two, the lower is longer and sleeved); toga draped in *sinus,* (used as pocket); its banded fold across the shoulder is commemorated in an embroidered band in the 518 A.D. Diptych of Magnus, together with the official handkerchief, *mappula,* which then serves to signal the start of contests in the games (Ludi Circensis).

262. Roman Mid-Ic. A.D. (Rome Mus. delle Terme.)

Augustus: toga draped over head.

263. Roman late. Baths of Caracalla. (Rome Lateran.)

Mosaic: athletes: boxer fighting naked; body oiled; hair bound up in a knot; hands, in *caestus* strapped around the arms, often held a block of metal. Victor's palms and *tesserae* of bone or ivory, (originally four-sided knuckle-bones), on the four sides of which are engraved the name of the athlete, of his patron, the fact that he has passed his trials, and the date.

264. Roman early Pompeii. (Naples National Museum.)

Mosaic: School of Plato: philosophers naked except for pallium and sandals.

265, 266. Roman. (Rome Lateran.)

Sophocles: toga only. Front and side views.

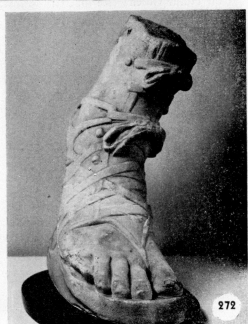

267. Roman adaptation (Greek work).

Marble statue restored as Ceres: *stola* equivalent to *chiton; palla* equivalent to *himation.*

268. Roman (Greek work). Ic. B.C.

Roman boy, of the Julio-Claudia family: bordered and patterned pallium with weighted corners; toga or pallium could be worn in public without tunic, but not tunic without toga.

269. Roman, Empire.

A Camillus: boy assisting at the altar (see also late Greek examples), in tunic and sandals.

270, 271. Roman Ic. B.C.—IIc. A.D.

Bronze: priest sacrificing: wreath, tunic, toga (mourners also wore toga over the head). Front and back views.

272. Roman.

Calcei.

Courtesy of the Metropolitan Museum

273. Syria. Palmyra Roman Epoch II A.D. (Louvre.)

Funerary portrait. "The wealthy Palmyrene merchants had gorgeously decorated sepulchres built for themselves. The bust of each deceased person was placed over the spot where he was laid and the last word of the epitaph inscribed thereon was 'habal'—alas! The deceased, who is veiled, holds a distaff. She is decked with many jewels—a frontlet, earrings, several rows of necklaces of pearl in particular, fibulas on her left shoulder, large bracelets and rings."*

Strong Persian influences in rosetted border of cloak; and, from a millennium earlier, in both the fibula caught on left breast of garment (independent of mantle) by female aristocrats since the Hittite Queen's (see Ill. 25); and in spinning, which has religious significance (see Ill. 12).

274. Roman. Traianic. e. IIc. A.D. (Louvre.)

Bust of Patrician Woman. Elaborate dressing of Roman Matron's hair.

275. Roman 69-96 A.D.

Funerary portrait: *Cominia Tyche.*

276. 114-116 A.D. Syria. (Dura-Europos, Temple of Zeus.)

Head of Baribonnaea.

Against a gray and buff ground, with dark gray and red lines, Baribonnaea is shown in a Palmyrene headdress and jewels. The stiff *tarboush* is pink, veiled in deep violet, the color of her dress. The tiara is banded above the brow in black, ornamented with a running chevron

in yellow (gold), set with pink and green leaves; white band above. The body of the headdress, dotted in yellow, carries a black center band and chevrons, dotted in yellow. The lining of the veil, seen above the ears, is yellow striped in green. Through a red loop on the central band, hangs a chain of braided silver, connected by silver disks and beads, and terminated by elaborate striated pendants.

The gown is almost concealed by five necklaces. From the top, the first, second and fourth strings are of round and cylindrical beads: white, red, black, yellow, and dark gray, the yellow probably representing gold and the white, pearls. The third is a silver braid, carrying a square pendant with a raised edge, and circles which might indicate enamel or stone settings. The fifth braided silver chain is hung with fusiform silver pendants.†

* From Enc. Phot. de l'Art, Louvre
† Information from Dura: Preliminary Report, 1933-5, Yale Univ.

Courtesy of Metropolitan Museum (275)

277. Syria. 245 A.D. from Dura-Europos (Damascus, New Museum.)

Synagogue frescos. The old pagan gods were losing power; the new proselytising religions of Judaism and Christianity were rising. Rome remained a stronghold of paganism. When Constantine was converted to Christianity and made it the official religion, he decided to move the seat of government to the East, and began to build Constantinople.

The victories of the Ptolemys had sent Jews to Syria, Mesopotamia and Palmyra; Babylonia had become tolerant of Judaism. Dura, lying on the Euphrates, midway between Baghdad and Aleppo, was a largely Semitic city, whose Greek inhabitants realized the unity between Zeus and Artemis, and the Semitic Solar-god and goddess of fertility. Judaism and Christianity were both established there early; the first Synagogue at the end II c. A.D.; the Christian meeting place in 232 A.D. The Synagogue was rebuilt in 245 A.D. by Samuel, the high priest, and other Jews. This unsuspected building came to light during Yale University's excavations at Dura. The frescos of the Synagogue were removed for their protection from moisture, and placed in an exact replica of the Synagogue in the New Museum at Damascus.

The Jewish prohibition of images began to be liberalized during I c. A.D. to allow illustrations of scenes from sacred books. The Dura Synagogue frescos show battles between Israelites and Philistines; episodes in the lives of Aaron as High Priest; Miriam, Saul and David, with horsemen in Iranian dress; Ahasuerus on Solomon's throne, with Esther and Mordecai; Elijah; and Moses. The exposure of Moses as a baby shows his rescue by Pharaoh's daughter.*

278. Syria. Palmyra. Roman Epoch IIc. A.D.?

Two young military men. Persian trousers tucked into high shoes.

* M. Rostovtzeff: Dura-Europos and its Art, Clarendon Press, Oxford, 1938, Yale University Expedition.

279. Byzantine c. 300 A.D. (Venice St. Marks.)

Two bearded Emperors giving the accolade to two beardless Tetrarchs. Tetrarchs in military costume, moulded cuirasses, elaborate sandals. These porphyry statues (sometimes classed VIIIc.) are dated by Peirce and Tyler, as symbolic representations of the Tetrarchal System, founded 285 A.D. by Diocletian, which was upset after his abdication in 305 A.D.*

280. Byzantine third-quarter IVc., from Barletta, Italy.

Colossal Bronze Statue. Probably the Emperor Valentinian I (364-374), a barbarian (Pannonian) of Celtic-Illyrian origin. The statue, brought from Constantinople in 1204, sank with the ship in the Adriatic; it was later raised, and the arms and legs badly restored in XVc. The diadem of pearls was originally set with stones.

Typical later Roman military costume: moulded lorica lengthened to protect abdomen, shows one of the shoulder straps which secured front and back plates. Costume of Augustus worn with long-sleeved tunic.

281, 282. Byzantine, c. 395 A.D. Monza, Italy (Cathedral Treasure.)

Diptych of Stilicon. Stilicon, the Vandal who defeated Alaric, may be taken as a type of the Barbarian, who by IVc. was rising to the highest military commands and civil honors of the Empire. Then, self-confident, the Barbarians went back to their native names, while the Roman emperors dressed in furs like Scythian warriors. Stilicon's wife, Serena, was the niece of the Emperor Theodosius, whose son Arcadius married Eudoxia, daughter of Banto, another Barbarian. With Stilicon and his wife is their son Eucherius in a Byzantine tunic. Chlamys, caught by a fibula—its *tablion* patterned with horizontal lines. Ser-

ena is a late-Roman matron: two tunics, palla, headdress, girdle and heavy Byzantine pearls and earrings. Stilicon's tunic and chlamys are richly embroidered all over in two patterns, but his fibula is an unjewelled one of metal, conforming strictly to the edict.

* From Hayforth Peirce and Royall Tyler: L'Art Byzantin, Librairie de France, Paris, 1932-4, 2 vols., to which I am almost completely indebted for information given under illustrations taken from them.

283. Byzantine 388-394 A.D. (Madrid Academy of History.)

Disk of Theodosius, detail: one of the Frankish Guards. The Disk of Theodosius was probably donated by the Viceroy of Spain, where it was found.

The hinged collar, *torque,* which he wears around his neck, was introduced from Gaul; it indicates rank. Torques were used to crown emperors, when a diadem was not available. Decorative patches on the tunic grow larger and more elaborate. Bossed barbarian shield.

284. Byzantine c. 500 A.D. (Florence Bargello.)

Ivory diptych of an Empress. Probably Ariane, daughter of Emperor Leon I. On the tablion of her chlamys is embroidered the portrait (as consul) of her son Leon II, who died emperor at seventeen in 474 A.D. She probably wears this in support of the imperial ambitions of her subsequent husband, in his position as son-in-law of one emperor and step-father of another. Her costume is the ultimate in Byzantine luxury, with feathered diadem, headdress, and collar and borders of fabulous pearls. Shoes such as she wears supplanted sandals in IVc.

285. Byzantine 518 A.D. (Paris Cabinet des Medailles.)

Diptych of Magnus: leaf. Typical costume of a consul celebrating circus day, at the time when the consulate had become a rich man's sinecure, before it was abolished in VIc. Over his tunic, which has bands of embroidery at neck and wrist, is the *toga picta* or *palmata.* The formalized remains of the folded bands of the toga show in the strip of embroidery around the shoulders and down the front. On Magnus' feet are gilded *calcei;* in one hand is the folded handkerchief, *mappa,* with which to signal the start of the games; in the other, the imperial eagle.

286. Byzantine 536-547 A.D. (Ravenna, St. Apollinare-in-Classe.)

Mosaic: *St. Michael*. Tunic with clavi, orbiculi, roundels on shoulder and cuffs: chlamys has patterned *tablion* and clasps at Byzantine shoulder-closing; beautiful embroidered shoes which continued in European use for centuries.

287. Byzantine before 553 A.D.

Pseudo Sassanian Textile. An attempt (probably Egyptian, but showing Greek influences), to approximate costly Eastern silk in local wool. The mounted archer was an Eastern military invention and the seated figure of the king also shows costume elements which had filtered westward.

288. Spanish-Hellenistic, second half VIc. A.D. (Seville, Ecija Santa Clara.)

Sarcophagus: *Isaac and the Good Shepherd Daniele*. Sarcophagus of local limestone, not imported marble, showing Greek influences working in Spain, where, after the Roman withdrawal, the Byzantine armies were confronted by the Visigoths* (whose contributions will in turn be seen—see Visigothic Spanish).

* A. Kingsley Porter: Spanish Romanesque Architecture.

289. Italian Vc. A.D. (Naples. San Gennaro, Catacomb 2.)

Grave of Theotecnus. Tombs hewn out of rock were a Jewish method of burial taken over by Christian communities in cities, like Rome and Venice, which were built on porous volcanic rock. Cemetery lots were bought, and excavated in layer on layer of galleries. Pilgrimages were made to these graves of the holy dead, many of them saints, and they were carefully catalogued under Pope Damasus (366-84); many of the catalogues and wall paintings still exist.

Theotecnus wears a tunic decorated on shoulder and cuff; a chlamys caught by a fibula. His wife, tunic, paenula, and scarf over her head. Their two-year-old son wears a long, rather fitted tunic, necklace, jewelled belt, earrings, and head-band.

290. Italian Vc. A.D. (Naples. San Gennaro, Catacomb 2.)

Grave of Cominia, with her daughter Nicatiola, and St. Januarius. All wear tunics with *clavi,* the woman's girdled. Cominia wears a *paenula,* and the embroidered scarf which had supplanted the *pallium,* with the advent of the sleeved dalmatic.

291, 292. Greek MS. 490 A.D.
(Vienna Library.)

These illustrations are from *The Genesis of Vienna* manuscript, the earliest existing Christian book, executed in silver letters and bright color on dark purple vellum.

(291) *Rebecca and Isaac at the court of Abimelech.* Short girdled tunic with short clavi and roundels. Ecclesiastic in chasuble. Beside Pharaoh's throne, soldiers and a man in chlamys with tablion. Women in girdled tunic and palla, under one of which the raised hand is concealed in a gesture which will persist for centuries.

(292) *Joseph interprets Pharaoh's* dream. Joseph in an ungirdled dalmatic short clavi; roundels at shoulder and knee. Both his tunic and Pharaoh's have wide sleeves closing in tightly from elbow toward wrist. Elaborate shoes and the long hose which came into use in VIc.

293. Greek MS. V-VIc. (Rome. Vatican Library codex. vat. Pal. Greco 431.)

Joshua Roll. Commander with soldiers and prisoners. Roman armor, trousers, *feminalia;* and high sandals, *calcei.*

294, 295. Byzantine VIc. 547 A.D. Ravenna. San Vitale Choir.

Mosaics: Justinian and followers, including:

294. *Archbishop Maximian and Deacons at the consecration of the church.*

295. *Theodora and her suite at the consecration.*

Justinian, nephew of an illiterate Slavonic peasant who rose, by way of the army, to emperor of the East, was designated by his uncle as his successor, with Theodora as empress—not merely consort. Her father had fed the bears in the ampitheatre; she had been a courtesan. Justinian was unable to marry her until the death of his aunt and the repeal of a law forbidding the marriage of emperors to actresses.

Theodora was small, exquisite, brilliantly intelligent, courageous and imperious; she ruled her very able husband who never remarried after her death from cancer.

Justinian was notable for his compact consolidation of centuries of Roman laws, and for his passionate interest in theology—which led him to built St. Sophia.

In these wonderfully rich mosaics we see Justinian in a white silk tunic embroidered in gold bands and roundels, a purple chlamys, with gold-embroidered *tablion* and the familiar Byzantine closing, from which radiate three lines of decoration.

The dalmatic is still being worn by laymen as well as clergy; from first half IVc. it is the outer garment of deacons, in both liturgical and everyday dress; a fresh garment, although of the same form, must be worn at the mass.

The *pallium,* which came to Rome from the Eastern church, is seen over the Archbishop's chasuble.

The *fibulae* fastening the chlamys of the noblemen; and the *torques* worn by the guards, indicative of rank, have already been seen (see Ill. 283).

The Empress and her suite stand against a basically yellowish-green background, enriched with gold, purple and colors; a scarlet, blue and white curtain is looped up on the right, and a white curtain, patterned in gold, blue-black and red, in the doorway.

The man on the extreme left wears a yellow chlamys with a tablion of the brownish purple which is used throughout. His tunic is white, with a red belt; all the male feet are white, with black tips. The man between him and the Empress is in white and purple.

Theodora's tunic is white, with a deep border in gold; her cloak purple, with human figures in gold embroidery; red appears in her gold and pearl diadem and in the Byzantine collar, dripping with pearls. Gold shoes.

Her attendants wear the palla, both embroidered and decorated, as well as plain; all-over patterned gowns with rich borders, roundels, squares and dalmatic-like vertical bands.

Running right from Empress, the first lady wears a gold-patterned white cloak; purple tunic with gold clavi, patterned in green and red. Next: white cloak, gold squares; white tunic with green and gold figures finished with a dark, pearl-trimmed multi-color band. Next, orange-red cloak with green dots; green gown dotted in red; she holds a fringed white *mappula.* To the extreme right: yellow cloak, green dots; white gown. All the ladies wear scarlet shoes.

THE ROMAN ARMY

The Roman army, which originally fought like the Greek phalanx, passed through three periods of development towards the most disciplined solidarity.

Servian. The army consisted of all citizens 17 to 60 years: there were two main arms, the *equites* (cavalry) and the bodies of heavily armed infantry called *hastati, princeps, triari.* The *equites* were the richest men. They were armed like the Greeks, with only a spear. The shield (*clipeus*) was large, round, oval; it was Argolic Greek, acquired through the Etruscans; in disuse by the time of the Republic. The *hastati, princeps,* and *triari* used a leather helmet and a shield, the oblong Mycenean *ancile.* It was brought by the Romans to the continent of Europe, where the existing circular shield of the Hallstatt Iron period had a projecting boss, *umbo.* The oblong shield assumed this boss and became the *scutum* of the heavily armed soldier, from 334 B.C.; of all Roman soldiers by Caesar's time; and of the Gauls by IVc.

The Republic (Legions). In this period the army saw long service and was paid. Besides the Roman citizens who made up the cavalry and the heavily armed infantry there were also light skirmishers, *velites,* made up of allies, *socii,* and recruits, *auxilia.* The *equites,* or cavalry, used breastplate or cuirasse of scale armor; the spear and the shield. Of the heavily armed infantry, *hastati* and *princeps* used *pilae,* two heavy-throwing spears, seven feet long, one-third iron. About one-third of the *hastati* were without *scutum,* with *hasta,* long spear, and *gaesa,* javelin. *Triari* used the *hasta.* All three bodies used a metal-crested helmet, a leather cuirasse or, in the case of poor men, a nine-inch metal plate worn on the breast. They bore also the *scutum* which was about four feet by two and a half feet, made of wood, hide, and canvas glued or bound with iron and with an iron boss; also the *gladius* which was a two-foot Spanish sword, double edged, worn on the right side on the *cingulum,* belt, or the *balteus,* baldric. The greave, leg armor, was worn on the right leg only. *The socii* (allies) and *velites* (light skirmishers), used the *hasta* and the *spathus,* long sword, toward the end of the Republic. Their tunic was leather with a scalloped bottom; their shield, *parma,* was three feet across, round, light, iron trimmed. Their helmet, *galea,* was leather.

The proportions of these three main bodies were about 300 *equites* to 3,000 heavily armed bodies to 1,200 light skirmishers. The recruits, *auxilia,* were Cretan bowmen, African horsemen, etc.

Empire (Cohorts). The army consisted of recruited Roman citizens and recruited subjects, who were free but not Roman citizens. These could gain citizenship for themselves and family by long service. In this period the *equites* and *velites* disappeared and we have the *legions,* with centurions, standard bearers, etc., infantry, cavalry, Praetorian guard, etc., costume detailed below. The *auxilia* continue with the *spathus,* the long, single-edged sword, and the *hasta.*

The Emperor and the officers like the soldiers were shaved and their hair was clipped. The officers carried no shields. The helmet was crested, or animal-headed. The breastplate, *lorica,* was made of metal scales or moulded in body-form, over a leather protective doublet, the bottom of which was slit into knee-length straps with metal studs which were both protective and decorative. There was the same effect at the armholes, covering shoulder and upper arm. The tunic was wool. Mantles included the scarlet or white *paludamentum,* often fringed and embroidered; *abolla;* red *byrrus;* and *saggum.* The sword was worn in a belt over the *lorica.* The footwear was high-laced sandals or boots, tops often turned down, with animal-head effects.

The *Standard Bearer* had an animal skin on his head instead of a helmet with the paws tied about the neck and the hide hanging down back.

The *Centurion* wore the crested helmet, but the crest varied, sometimes running across the head, ear to ear. He carried also the *vitis,* the official baton, a short plain stick. During the Empire he wore a greave, *ocrea,* on the right leg and the *paenula,* a mantle particularly favored by centurions.

The *Praetorian* used the *lorica squamata,* and *hamata,* and the typical helmet.

The Legionary's helmet was metal, Greek type, protecting the sides of the face, but no longer crested by the time of the Empire. He wore also a cuirasse, the *lorica segmentata,* a corselet of overlapping leather strips, from underarm to waist, usually closed in front, held up by three to six vertical strips over each shoulder, often finished with fringed skirt of leather strips, waist to mid-thigh. During the Empire, his cuirasse was the *lorica squamata* made of metal plates or the *lorica hamata* of chain mail, both on leather or canvas. The tunic was wool, above the knees. He wore also a *focale,* wool muffler; a belt, *cingulum,* with three vertical protective lappets hanging below; a mantle, *saggum,* brown-red wool. There was no leg-wear until the campaigns in Gaul. The *bracae* were the breeches of barbarians adopted for garrison wear; not used in Rome until III-IVc. They used leg-swathings called *fasciae.*

The footwear was called *caligae,* heavy, often hob-nailed boots; or sandals with straps and lacings going well up the leg. Auxiliaries wore native footwear. The sword was the *gladius,* about 20 to 24 inches long, two-edged, worn on the belt or baldric. During the Empire, there was the *spatha,*

the long single-edged sword worn on the left side. The dagger worn on the right side was called the *pugio.*

From 334 B.C. onwards, the shield became the *scutum,* which was oblong, oval, hexagonal, octagonal, about two and a half feet by four feet. It was curved about the body, made of wood, leather covered, with an iron band around the edge and the iron boss, *umbo,* in the center. After IIc. A.D., it was oval. The *clipeus,* the large round leather shield, was used before the Republic; and later, smaller, in iron, it was used by the commander's attendants. The *parma* was the round, light, iron-trimmed shield used by *velites* under the Republic, and by gladiators.

The Legionaries also used the *hasta,* long spear, and the *pila,* the heavy seven-foot, one-third iron spear.

296. Roman 20 B.C. Statue. (Metropolitan Museum.)

Augustus as Commander. Paludamentum; magnificent moulded *lorica* with typically shaped shoulder straps connecting its sections (see also No. 297); pleated leather doublet, its edges cut into fringe, worn between woolen tunic and cuirasse to give additional protection and to prevent chafing.

297. Roman, Traianic. II A.D. Relief Sculpture. (Louvre.)

Praetorians. The feathered Attic crest, often red and black, on the helmets of the Praetorian guards, was removable for wartime use; chin strap outline and studding protects the face. Moulded loricas of handsomely worked metal on ranking officers; doublets elaborately cut into fringes; belt with apron of three protective leather lappets, or a wide protective belt; tunics; boots; oblong shield, decorated, without center boss.

298. Roman II A.D. (Rome, Column of Trajan.)

Battle at walls. Trajan (whose father had risen from the ranks, fighting in Spain) was a soldier whom all soldiers, enemy as well as friends, admired. He was open, simple, solicitous of his men's comfort, and lived and ate as they did. His wonderfully disciplined and organized army fought to secure the northeastern frontier between the Rhine and the Danube. The Column of Trajan, built early in IIc. is a monument to his great Dacian campaign, and shows "Barbarians" of many sorts, both as adversaries, and as Roman auxiliaries.

All the archers, most of the cavalry and much of the infantry is now composed of "Barbarians"; the top leadership was Roman, but more immediately they were commanded by their own tribal leaders, and were allowed to keep their native dress and weapons. The equipment of Roman soldiers began to be standardized in I A.D., but in early II A.D. it is often difficult to distinguish the origins of soldiers shown on triumphal monuments. The dress of the

Roman legionaries became affected by barbarian ways, while the barbarians were being Romanized, gaining citizenship, and preparing to become the most powerful men of the Empire.

In the battle for the walled town, we see hairy and bearded barbarians in breeches and sleeved tunics.

Two Asiatic horsemen (perhaps Iranians from the steppes of Southern Russia) wear conical helmets of metal banded leather, and scale-mail which was made to cover the horse as completely as the rider.

299. Roman Traianic 98-114 A.D., from Forum of Trajan. (Rome, Conservatori.)

Captive Barbarian Chief. The prisoner-of-war is Dacian, an Indo-European tribe from what is now Roumania. Cloak is a rectangle, heavily fringed on three sides, folded double, pinned with a fibula on one shoulder and folded up over the other; long bordered tunic with long sleeves; full, horizontally-striped breeches caught with a decorative knot, into shoes which are folded around the foot like a moccasin and laced across an ovally cut-out instep.

300. Danish Early Iron Age 250 B.C.—45 A.D., from Thorsbjerg.

Trousers, stocking feet; cloak materials. In mid-XIXc., remarkable finds were made in Sleswig.* In peat-bogs, situated always between rivers near the sea, and in connection with barrows on adjacent high land, were discovered quantities of objects, in orderly heaps. All had been hastily and deliberately made useless (clay vessels were filled with stones to sink them, and there were traces of fire), whether in some religious ceremony, no one knows.

Iron objects had disintegrated, but the peat had preserved other metals, wood, leather and textiles; a huge boat; clothing; fibulae, buttons and buckles; shields, helmets; weapons and bridles; reed baskets, wood rakes, troughs and spoons; ring-money; lathe-turned awls, knives; nets and pottery.

The clothing at Thorsbjerg consisted of a handsome wool shirt in herring-bone weave, with sleeves of a different diaper-pattern, finished with cuffs of decorative braid; cloaks; and a pair of breeches, with a foot, in a diaper-weave. The breeches have loops to hold a belt, reinforced with a woven braid.

There were also several shirts of fine, linked, iron ring mail, in alternately riveted asd welded rows, bordered in bronze rings. These are of immense importance because it had been supposed that rings were sewed onto canvas until after the period of the Bayeux tapestries; now a considerable amount of linked chain-mail has been found antedating IIIc. A.D.

Dressed corpses have been recovered from other peat-bogs in Denmark, Northwest Germany, and Holland. Roughly summarized: they are dressed in fur, leather, wool in many weaves (some dyed and striped like ticking) trimmed with good-looking fancy braids; later, shirts of linen, over which wool tunics became belted. Conical caps, fitted hoods, and shaped or rectangular capes (the latter, often of striped wool, caught by a fibula) of fur, leather, or wool. Shirts, sleeveless, or with long sleeves which are often of a different weave and finished with a braid, were of hip-to-knee lengths. Trousers, knee-to-ankle length, the shorter ones finished with woven bands, and often worn with leg-wrappings. Extremely good leather shoes, folded about the foot, cut out and slit in handsome decorations (usually diagonal) trimmed in bronze and laced at the ankle.

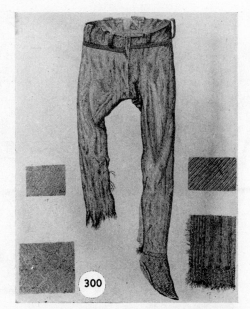

300

Women, in the grave found near Aarhus, Jutland, wore shorter, sleeved shirts with a slit neck-closing; skirts made of a long piece gathered together into a ruffled top, above a handsome braid girdle going several times around the waist, and ending in tassels of expertly made fringe. Hair was gathered up in back in net hammocks, elaborately patterned; the top tied around the forehead and the lower part over the crown, to hold the net in place.†

Besides fine shoes and decorative braids, the barbarians had wonderful jewelry of gold, silver, bronze and niello, often set with stones; fibulae and buckles, necklets, bracelets, and rings; golden combs.

Sidonius Apollinarius (430-485 A.D.) says that the Franks of the IV-V c. had red hair which they wore knotted high; shaved but carried moustaches; wore tight-fitting knee-length trousers; tunics with sleeves barely covering the shoulders (i.e. a sleeveless shirt, made of a strip of material sewed part-way up the sides, with a hole for the head), made of striped materials; a red *saggum* with a green edging; a wide, studded belt; and hung the sword from a baldric slung across the breast. The Teutonic *braie* (bracchae) were later worn by the Gauls with *pedules* (long socks drawn up to the knee and turned down), which became the national dress of the Franks.

* C. Engelhardt: *Denmark in the Early Iron Age*. Williams and Norgate, London, 1866. Illustrated with scrupulously accurate engravings, such as Ill. 300.

† Other Jutland finds have been made at Borum-Eshoi, Marx-Etzel, Bernuthsfeld, and Oben-Altendorf.

301. Roman Traianic IIc. A.D. (Rome. Column of Trajan.)

Barbarians who are Roman auxiliaries in uniform, and impossible to identify.* The auxiliaries are less well paid and equipped than the legionaries. They retain their bossed shields; *saggum* caught on shoulder with a *fibula;* breeches reaching to the calves; handsomely-cut shoes finished with patterned bands at the ankle. The figure on the right, next to top, shows the segmented form of *lorica.*

302. Roman Traianic IIc. A.D. (Rome. Column of Trajan.

Barbarians and Romans before a walled town. Various tribes of the Balkan Peninsula, and possibly southern Russia. Right to left; the three men facing the emperor are Germanic, possibly tribes of the Bastarnae. To the left, the man in a pointed cap is Dacian, or of a related Thracian tribe. Two, with gathered skirts, to the left, wear mittens; they are northern

tribesmen, perhaps nomads from the southern steppes of Russia. The two at extreme left are supposedly Sarmatians, of the tribe of the Jazygi; (who at the time occupied what is now Hungary).*

303. 304. Roman. Aurelian. IIc. A.D. (Rome, Arch of Constantine.)

Two Reliefs. (303) Legionaires in breeches; various leather cuirasses segmented or scale-covered; one crested Attic helmet. In back, standard-bearers with animal skins over their heads; praetorians.

(304) Persian soldier in conical helmet, extended in splints to protect the back of the neck; long, segmented cuirasse with segmented shoulder caps.

* Prof. Karl Lehmann-Hartleben of New York University has been good enough to identify some of the races represented in these Traianic sculptures, many of which were photographed by him. All identifications are conjectural.

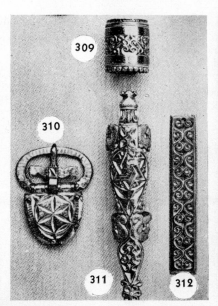

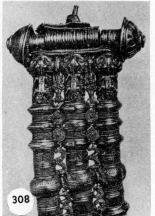

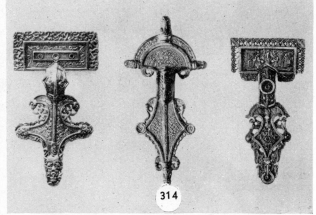

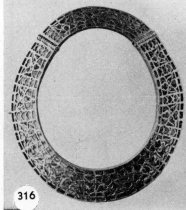

niello: apparently the insignia of office of a chief of Roman legionary troops; done in the perforated "Kerbschnitt" technique, found along the borders of the Roman Empire: Belgium, N. France, and the Rhineland; it utilized the Scandinavian and Sarmatian coiled animals (magical properties), which can barely be seen on piece 311.

313. Moorish, from excavations. N. Germany.
Silver ornaments and sword shields.

314. Scandinavian Iron Age. c. 500-700 A.D.
Fibulae in silver and bronze: T-shaped fibulae become frog-like in Scandinavia, and are found wherever the Vikings went. The most extremely cut out and interlaced patterns, which went south with the Sarmatians and north with the Finns (both of whom cast them in white-metal and tin), form the basis of the great Celtic manuscript style. Fibulae sometimes reached a length of 15 inches.

315, 316. Roumania V-VIc. A.D., from Petrossa.
315. Vc. Gold fibula: bird: cabochon carbuncles, glass paste.
316. VIc. Gorget: openwork set with garnets, vitreous paste, and lapis-lazuli.

317-326. Frankish VI-VIIIc., A.D., Marne and Rhineland.
Ten rosette-shaped fibulae. The Franks were Teutonic Eastern barbarians, who began their invasion of W. Germany and N. France in IV-V c. They settled in the Frankish kingdoms of Austrasia, Neustria,

Jewelry of III-VIIIc. Migrations.
305. Pontine S. Russia IIIc. A.D., from N. France.
Gold bracelet: 3 twists of heavy wire, bound in fine wire; finished in approximations of animal heads.
306. Germanic-Celtic-Iranian, La Tene Period, from Trichtingen.
Silver bracelet, ending in sheeps' heads.
307, 308. N. Germany Iron Age from Olleberg.
Gold collar: details.
309-312. Gallo-Roman. France IV-Vc. A.D., from tomb at Vermand.
Buckle and spear-mounts in silver, parcel-gilt and

and Acquitaine, and joined the Romans and Visigoths in fighting the Huns in the Vc. Under Clovis (465-511) they ruled Northern and Central France; in VIIc., they joined the culturally allied Burgundians to the south.

Frankish jewelry includes T-shaped parcel-gilt fibulae, and rosette-shaped fibulae, which are usually of bronze, the face silvered or gilded—and inlaid with glass and stones, cloisonné enamel, or filigreed.

Courtesy of Metropolitan Museum (305, 309-312); Stuttgart Museum (306); Flensburg State Museum (313); Oslo, Stockholm, and Copenhagen Museum (314); Bucharest Museum (315, 316).

317. Marne VIII c.
318. Frankish-Allemanian VII c.
319. Frankish VII c.
320. Marne VII c.
321. VII-VIII c. (rare type).
322. Niederbreisig VI-VII c.
323. VII-VIII c. (rare type).
324. Late VII-e.VIII c.
325. Niederbreisig e.VIII c.
326. Niederbreisig VII-e.VIII (extremely rare).

Courtesy Metropolitan Museum. Gift of J. Pierpont Morgan

Roman Catholic Church

DEVELOPMENT OF ECCLESIASTICAL VESTMENTS

DURING the first three Christian centuries the dress of a priest differed from that of a dignified, scholarly layman only in that the Mass had to be celebrated in fresh, clean garments—our "Sunday clothes."

Liturgical dress as we know it was evolved between the IV-IXc. out of elements: Roman, Byzantine, Western. Before the VIIIc. there was little attempt on Rome's part to impose direction on the development of the churches of Gaul and Spain, and from Rome those churches took only the pall, dalmatic, maniple and buskins. The distinctly Roman dalmatic and pall were sent as gifts to honor distinguished prelates of the Western church. But Roman usages were brought to the continent rather by the missionaries to Germany from the British Isles, where Christianity had long been established under Roman rule. By IXc. Roman usage was firmly established in the West and liturgical costume was further defined, to XIIIc. Change, between XIII-XVIc. was in the direction of closer fit and richer ornamentation. Since XVIc. it has become progressively less aesthetically satisfying.

The first vestments to appear were the *Pall* and *Stole,* well established by the IV and Vc. as distinguishing marks of bishop and deacon.

The *Paenula,* common to laity and clergy from III-IVc., was separated for liturgical use by the IVc. and, as the *Chasuble,* was retained in its long form by the conservative church, after shorter garments had become the rule in daily life. To XIc. it was worn by all priests, even by acolytes, and later became a Mass vestment.

By the VIc., when gentlemen were wearing the paenula (chasuble) and dalmatic, bishops wore besides these garments the pallium, but deacons wore the dalmatic only and sub-deacons the tunic only. The clergy were tonsured.

In the VIIIc. the *Cope* first appears as a processional garment, worn both by clergy and secular, particularly singers; by Xc. its use is widespread; by XIIc. fixed; by XIIIc. it has replaced the chasuble except at the celebration of the Mass.

The IXc. liturgical garments of a Pope or a Roman deacon, given in *Amalarius: De officis ecclesiastices,* consisted of *amice* (anagolaium), *alb* (tunica alba) girdled with *cingulum, maniple, stole* (orarium), *tunicle* (dalmatica minor), *dalmatic* (dalmatica major), *chasuble* (planeta), *pallium, sandals, pontifical stockings.*

XIc. ecclesiastical costume is still unembroidered, the *clavi* or the folds of handsome woven stuff the only decoration.

Pontifical *gloves* appear in the XIc.: the *mitre* in the Xc., *liturgical shoes* in the XIc.

The *surplice* (super-pellicia) is first mentioned in the XIc. Originally worn over fur garments, by the choir and lower clergy, it replaced the alb, which it resembled, by the XIIIc.

By the XIIc. the mitre and gloves are worn by all Bishops, who are gaining in temporal power and magnificence,* and are, especially in Germany, sometimes assuming a new ornament, the *rationale,* resembling the pallium. The XIIIc. is full of complaints by a scandalized laity, that priests dressed in a way more suitable to knights. The 4th Lateran Council (1215) forbade the clergy to wear green and red clothing, brooches, and copes with sleeves, and exhorted them to wear unextravagant dress, closed down the front.

The red apparel of cardinals had appeared before Innocent IV conferred the cardinals' hat in 1245.

Until the early Middle Ages, prelates of the Church might appear in full regalia, as for the Mass, at a banquet at the palace on a great feast day or in honor of a visiting sovereign.

By XIIc. liturgical color was established and may be roughly charted as follows:

* In 1042 the abbot of the Monastery of St. Gall was responsible for providing the Emperor with an army of 60,000 men and was seated at the Emperor's right. Until the XIIc. knighthood might be received from abbots and bishops.

	Priest	Bishop	Arch-Bishop	Cardinal	Pope	Deacon	Other and Lower Orders	Sub-Deacon
CASSOCK Non-liturgical but worn under liturgical.	Black	Black Red or Purple edged	Black Red or Purple edged	Red or Black-edged Red	White	Black	Monks in color of Order	Black
BIRETTA General use; limited liturgical use.	Black	Purple	Purple	Red	White	Black		Black
TIARA					Processional			
SURPLICE (Cotte, rochet) liturgical but not blessed.	Administering sacramental blessing	✓	✓	Proper to all clerics particularly to			Choir and Lower Clergy	✓
COPE Liturgical but not sacerdotal.	✓	Purple	Purple	Red or Purple	Red mantle Morse of precious stones		Early Church Festivals Lay and Choir	
ALMUCE Choir vestment of dignitaries to XVc.; by XIVc. largely superseded by **MOZETTA**		Purple	Purple	Red	Ermine-Edged Red Velvet		Choir Vestments of Canons. Since XIVc.	
LITURGICAL								
AMICE	✓	✓	✓	✓	✓	✓		✓
ALB	✓	✓	✓	✓	✓	✓		✓
CINCTURE	✓	Purple	Purple	Red	White	✓		✓
MANIPLE	✓	✓	✓	✓	✓	✓		particular to
STOLE	✓	✓	✓	✓	✓	✓		
TUNICLE		✓	✓	✓	✓			particular to
DALMATIC		✓	✓	✓	✓	particular to		
CHASUBLE	✓	✓	✓	✓	✓			
SANDALS		Color of Vestments of			Day			
STOCKINGS-BUSKINS		‖	‖	‖	‖			
GLOVES		‖	‖	‖	‖			
MITRE		White	White	White	liturgical			
PALLIUM		particular to White		✓	✓			
SUB-CINCTORIUM					✓			
FANION					✓			
PECTORALCROSS		✓	✓	✓	✓			
PONTIFICAL RING		✓	✓	✓	✓			
PASTORAL STAFF		✓	✓	✓				

CHART OF ECCLESIASTICAL VESTMENTS AND COLORS

White (or silver) was used for festivals, consecrations, coronations and such events; red, signifying blood, was used on occasions commemorating the sufferings of Christ, the Apostles, martyrs, etc.; green was used during specified periods (over half of the year) before Lent and after Trinity. Gold brocade could be used instead of any one of these three colors.

Violet and black signified mourning, violet for intercessional and penitential and black for funerals and Masses for the dead.

Hierarchal rank is also indicated by color: white for the Pope, red for cardinals, violet for bishops, black for priests.

ECCLESIASTICAL VESTMENT DETAILS

Alb: liturgical vestment of Catholic Church; derived, with *surplice and rochet,* from the long *tunica alba,* which passed out of Roman civil usage in VIc. It is of white linen, narrow-sleeved, slit for the head to pass through, and girdled to clear the ground. It is worn over the cassock and under the other liturgical garments and ornamented with embroidery or lace.

In the IXc. Rabanus Maurus gives the alb as an integral part of priests' attire; in Spain and Gaul is was often worn instead of the dalmatic, by deacons. In the Xc. it began to be ornamented with embroidered bands at hem, neck and wrists.

During the XIIc. at the day-long services of the Benedictine Monastery at Cluny, albs were worn both by the priests officiating at the altar and by the monks assisting in the stalls.

By the XIIIc. 4-6 brocade or embroidered patches (*apparels, parures* or *orphreys*) at center front and back of hem, wrists, and sometimes at breast and back, began to supplant bands. Spreading from N. France, this became general.

In the XIVc. the alb was reserved for celebration of mass; surplice used otherwise. During the Middle Ages the hem widened to 5 yards, and by XVIc. to more than 7 yards. In the XVI-XVIIc. lace replaced apparels.

The "colored" albs found in church inventories during the Middle Ages were probably carelessly listed dalmatics, or references are to the colors of the embroidery.

Since the XIIc. the alb has gradually been replaced by the *surplice,* originally the vestment proper to the lower orders; except for priests, bishops, deacons and sub-deacons.

Almuce (O. Fr., O. Eng. *Aumuce*): Fur-lined, hooded choir vestment worn from the XIIc. by church canons over the surplices, against cold; by the XVIc. hung over left arm as badge of office. Certain academic and monastic bodies were also granted its use, and by the XIIc. the laity also wore it. Originally open in front and tied at the neck, it became closed and was dropped over the head. As hats began to be worn, the almuce became progressively more cape-like; by the XIVc. it was often shortened at each shoulder for convenience, but hung down in front in two long points, which must not, however be confused with the *stole.* The almuce will sometimes be seen edged with fur tails.

Amice (*Anagolaium*): Liturgical vestment, the first in order to be assumed by a priest vesting himself for the Mass. Developed out of the Roman neckcloth, it is a strip of linen, laid, hood-like, over the head, dropped to the shoulders and tied in position around the upper body with tapes sewed to two corners, forming a collar. Its use is recorded in Rome in the VIIIc. and spread with other Roman usages in the IXc. By the XIIc. the amice, like the alb, was decorated with embroidered apparels, which stiffen it to form an apparent collar. Since the end of the XVIc. there is always a cross at the center of the apparel.

Biretta (*Biretum, Barret-Cap,* cf. *Beret*): Since XVIIc. a ridged cap peculiar to Catholic clergy; of limited liturgical function, worn also outside the Church, as at processionals. It developed out of a close skull-cap (*pileus*), which appeared in XIIIc. and was worn by dignitaries and officials, legal, academic, as well as ecclesiastic, when hoods were the only common head coverings. It had a center tuft, like a modern beret, and, like it, was susceptible of arrangement; out of this developed its present pinched shape. By the XVIc. it was worn by all people of standing, women and men.

In its mediaeval form it is the hat familiar in the portraits by Holbein, and survives in the academic mortarboard.

The ecclesiastical biretta derives from a cap identical in form with the modern beret: it became squarer as it became ampler, and now, completely stiffened, has the excess material at the top seamed into upright folds, forming a cross. Its color: black, purple, red, or white indicates its wearer's rank as priest, bishop, cardinal, pope.

Cassock (*Pellicium*): *Soutane.* Originally the daily wear of everybody, especially the dignified and elderly; and fur-lined, according to the wearer's means, for winter use. It was retained by the church, after the change in lay fashion. It is now the ordinary dress of Roman, and to a more limited extent, of Church of England clergy, upon which vestments, eucharistic and processional, and monastic habit, are super-imposed. Its color: black, purple, red, or black with red pipings, white indicate rank: priest, bishop, cardinal, pope. Monks' cassocks are of the color of the habit of their order.

Chasuble (*Planeta,* Late L. *Casula*: little house): Outermost, and a most important liturgical garment of the Catholic church. The shape varies by period and country. Essentially it is a cape of silk or metal cloth, never linen or cotton, with a hole for the head, shortened at the sides to the shoulder to leave the arms uncovered, and falling down the front and back. Derived from the Roman *paenula,* originally a barbarian garment, adopted by soldiers and low people.

In the IVc. it was considered permissible wear for senators, and its everyday and liturgical uses had been separated, although the cut remained identical. By the VIc. still common to clergy and laity. In his life of St. Germanus of Paris, Fortunatus of Poitiers says that the saint wore tunic and chasuble, but retained only one of each, giving any duplicates to the poor. The portrait of St. Gregory with his layman father shows both wearing dalmatic and chasuble, the saint distinguished by his tonsure and pall.

In 742 A.D. priests in Gaul were ordered to wear the casula instead of the short military saggum. At the end of the Xc. *apparels* common, as border, vertical stripe, or forked cross with arms lifted up.

It was worn by all churchmen, even acolytes, during the XIc. It had become distinctly a Mass vestment, with the establishment of the *cope* as a processional and choral vestment. The chasuble, being a cape sewed up into a pastry-tube shape, was inconvenient. By the VIIc the sides of the tent-like cape are cut away for more convenient celebration of the Mass.

Apparels became wider and more decorative during the mid-XIIIc. In this century the symbolic meaning of the cross began to be emphasized, and the cross with horizontal arms began to appear on the back of the chasuble only, with a vertical strip down the front. In the XIVc. a crucified Christ was added, and in the XVc. a horizontal cross; or vertical apparels, front and back, with short horizontal apparel at base of neck opening in front.

By the XVIc. it had its scapular-like modern form.

The chasuble typical of the Church of England carries the forked cross in front and in back.

Chimere (It. *zimarre*): Liturgical and ceremonial civil vestment of Anglican bishops; developed, together with certain academic robes, out of the *tabard* (*collobium*), the common outer garment of all mediaeval Europe. It is a long sleeveless gown of satin or silk, full across the shoulders in back, and is worn over the *rochet,* the lawn sleeves of which pass through the slits at the sides of the chimere, and were, at a late period, sometimes transferred to the chimere. After the advent of wigs, it was opened down the front to facilitate donning, as were the academic robes.

The various colors in which the chimere is listed during the Middle Ages may have designated academic rank. The chimere is now black or red.

The continental *zimarre* (*simmara*) is a *soutane* with a short cape and short, slit sleeves; and like the soutane is worn by clerics of all ranks, professors, and formerly by Roman senators.

Cope (*Cappa, Pluviale*): liturgical vestment of Catholic and choir vestment of some Anglican churches. Semi-circular cape brocaded or embroidered, fastened across chest by a broad ornamented band, sewed to one edge and hooked or pinned by a jewelled *morse* to the other, and with an embroidered flap, a vestigial hood, hanging down back.

Originally, a protective outer garment, of the same derivation as *chasuble,* open instead of seamed up, common to laity of both sexes and to churchmen.

In VIIIc. the black *Cappa Choralis* (non-liturgical) was worn in outdoor procession by singers, secular and regular clergy; it is the present Dominican winter garment. In 888 in Metz, the laity were forbidden to wear copes. In Xc. the influence of opulent Cluniac ceremonies spread the use of decorative vestment, particularly at high mass for choir-master and choir, who on lesser occasions would wear albs.

By the XIIIc. it was fixed in liturgical use, and substituted, outside the Mass, for the less convenient chasuble. The flap at this period was triangular. The shape and size of the hood evolved with the passage of time. In the XIV-XVc. it was shield-shaped, in the XVIIc. it was rounded at the bottom and by the XVIIIc. the hood was enormously enlarged.

Dalmatic (*Dalmatica Major*): (as a liturgical garment of the Catholic Church). In Rome the dalmatic is now a knee-length, wide-sleeved gown, slit up the sides; outside of Italy it is a poncho-like garment with square flaps hanging from upper arm over shoulder. It is decorated with two vertical stripes over the shoulder to the hem. In Rome these are narrow and are united by two narrow horizontal stripes at the bottom; outside Italy, broad, joined higher up by a broad stripe. The dalmatic of a Bishop is fringed on both sides and sleeves, and that of a Deacon is (properly) fringed on the left side and sleeve only.

Since the IVc. the dalmatic has been distinctly a vestment of the Pope and his Deacons, and always a festal garment, worn (under chasuble, never under cope) during Mass, benedictions, processions, never on penitential days.

In the VIIc. it was wool or linen, fringed at sleeves and side openings. Up to the VIIIc. long tunic, long wide sleeves. In the IXc. shorter and narrower outside Italy; tuft of red fringe began to be set in clavi, especially outside Italy (to the XIIIc).

In the Xc. color came into use, especially outside Italy. The Pope granted it to cardinal-priests and abbots in XIc. When granted to priests, may be worn on specified days only. Changes in the following century: in Italy, it was shorter and narrower; silk began to be used; also it was slit up sides for easier donning, gradually up to sleeves, unless widened by gores.

By the XIIIc. color was the rule (liturgical colors). Its length was 51"-55" outside Italy but to the XIVc. in Italy also. In the XVc. sleeves were opened for convenience, outside Italy.

The dalmatic gradually became shorter, 47" in the XVIc. and 39"-35" by the XVIIIIc. Sleeves were correspondingly narrower.

Maniple (Mappula) liturgical vestment of all orders of Catholic church above sub-deacon. It is a narrow strip of silk, three feet long, decorated with three crosses, now hung or fastened over left forearm. It is one of the four distinctly Roman contributions to liturgical costume, originally a linen handkerchief or cloth derived from the folded consular *mappula*, its use spread from Rome to Ravenna, and thence westward. Originally linen, it lost its useful character, and, like the stole, became silk .

In the IXc. it was already band-like, carried in the left hand, and in the IX-XIc. either carried in left hand or worn on left wrist. By the XIIc. it was worn over the left arm.

Mitre: liturgical headdress of Catholic church, specifically that of bishops, but occasionally worn by abbots and other church dignitaries, by grant of the Pope. Now a high hat composed of two identical stiffened pieces which fold flat against each other when not spread horn-like by being set on the head. From back half depend two narrow fringed strips.

Mitres are of three sorts: *simplex*: white linen or silk, undecorated, except that dependent strips terminate in red fringe; *aurifrigiata*: gold or silver embroidered orphreys on white silk; *pretiosa*: overlayed with gold plates, set with jewels.

The mitre seems to have developed out of the cone-shaped cap of the early Popes. It was established in Rome in the Xc.: conical shape with band around brow. In the XIc. it was frequently granted by the Pope to cardinals in Rome; first granted to an English abbot in 1063, and to some secular dignitaries, and the Roman emperor.

In the XIIc. all western bishops wore it, and it was granted to many abbots; rounder shape; added band running over crown from front to back forced a horned side effect which persisted to the XIIIc. when the mitre had already begun to be turned so that horns were at front and back; decorative embroidery spread from horizontal and vertical bands to triangular spaces outlined by them. Low triangular shape of mitre progressively rises from the XIVc., spreads and becomes arched, XV-XVIc.; the increasingly rich decoration based on horizontal and vertical bands is supplanted by symmetrical scrolled embroidery.

Mozetta: ceremonial and processional vestment worn by Catholic prelates, in colors designating rank. A short hooded cape, buttoned down front, worn over *rochet*. Also developed out of the cappa, like the cope, it is not a liturgical garment.

Pallium (Omorphion, Pall): vestment worn by Catholic archbishops. It is a woven band of white lambs' wool, "three fingers broad," worn over chasuble. Derived from Roman *pallium*, it was originally a longer strip draped over both shoulders and pinned to the left one; now a strip, decorated with four crosses, made into a circle which is dropped on the shoulders and fastened, front and back, with gold pins, at those points from which hang two tabs, each decorated with a cross. Since the IVc. it was worn by Eastern bishops, and borrowed by Western.

"Teach the faithful, don't amuse them," Pope Celestinus wrote the Bishops of Narbonne and Vienne in 428 A.D., concerning a distinctive costume, *pallium* and *cincture*, concocted by the Gallic bishops. By the late Vc., however, the *pallium* was considered an ornament peculiar to the Pope, and sent by him, at first, to honor distinguished prelates of various ranks.

By the IXc. as a symbol of his delegated authority, the Pope granted it to archbishops. The Anglo-Saxon Chronicle records Robert of Jumièges' return from Rome in 1051 with the pall; his deposition in 1052; the refusal of 2 subsequent Popes to recognize Stigand (see Bayeux Tapestry) as archbishop, until he finally receives the pall in 1058 from Benedict X. After the XIIIc. an archbishop could not exercise his authority before receiving the pall, for which payment had to be made.

Pileolus: non-liturgical skull-cap worn by Catholic prelates under mitre and tiara.

Pastoral Staff (Bishops' Crozier, Archbishops' Cross-Staff): insignia of cardinals, bishops and abbots of the Catholic church. It is a five-foot staff of wood or metal, carried in the right hand, held in the left during benediction.

Heads were originally of four types: *shepherds' crook* (which continued to the XIIc. in Ireland); *knobbed; T* (typical of abbots, cont. to the XIIIc.) and in the IXc. *bent crook*, often snake-headed, from which present crozier developed. This became the predominant type in the XIc. and by the XIIIc. supplanted other types. The snake was elaborated into tendrils, with knob below, from which, by the XIV c. a scarf was suspended (now, abbots only).

The *Cross-Staff* of an archbishop does not

necessarily supplant the pastoral staff, both of which are frequently carried together, preceding the archbishop (not carried by him).

Pontifical Ring (*Annulus*) of bishop of Catholic church, derived from signet, and used since at least the VIIc. It is worn on the middle finger of the right hand (or forefinger, or in the case of the XV-XVIIc. Papal ring given to cardinals, thumb) and being massively set with a large stone, is worn over the glove, or shows through a slit in the glove.

Pectoral Cross of a bishop of the Catholic church has been worn over his vestments only since the XVIc.

Rochet (*G. Rock*): vestment, not strictly liturgical, of Catholic prelates and also of Anglican bishops. It is a modified alb of fine linen or lawn. In the Catholic church it is now knee-length, having been long in the XIIc.; and has narrow sleeves with a border of lace, embroidery or lining color.

The Anglican rochet, resembling the Catholic of the Middle Ages in its length, differs from it in the size of its sleeves, which increased in size, from the Reformation to the XVIIIc., at which time the huge ruffle-edged sleeves, tied at wrist with black ribbons, were transferred to the *chimere*.

Stole (*Orarium*): liturgical vestment of Catholic church for Mass, never processional use. It is a long narrow strip of material, usually silk, now decorated by three crosses, at ends and middle, and fringed at hem, and worn over the shoulder in different ways, characteristic of deacon, priest or bishop. It may have descended from the fringed *orarion* given by the IIIc. Emperor Aurelian to be waved in applause at the games.

In the IVc. it was established in the Eastern church, and specified as wear for the deacon who, dressed in white and with the folded stole over his left shoulder as badge of office, would welcome visitors at the guest house. It seems to have been introduced in the VIc. from the East into Gaul and Spain, and from there have gone to conservative Rome by the VIIIc. In 755 A.D. a Western bishop, arriving at the basilica on horseback, changed into fresh garments, with amice and stole. He would have worn a stole even in travelling, as a symbol of his priesthood (as did St. Hugh of Lincoln, as late as the XIIc., but now only the Pope does). It assumed by the IXc. approximately its modern shape: long, narrow, end tabbed, fringed, even finished with bells or tassels. Subsequent changes were straight strips in the XIII-XIVc., and in the XVI-XVIIIc. ends widening to shovel shape, decorated with crosses.

Rationale: Episcopal vestment of Catholic Church =*pallium,* worn over chasuble; now, by a specific few bishops. Rabano Mauro believed all church vestments to be derived from those of the Jewish priesthood. This is probably true only of the *rationale* which first appeared toward the end of the Xc. in a breastplate form almost identical with the *ephod* of the High Priest, and was favored by the German bishops of the Middle Ages. It has had *T* and *Y* forms, and is now a humeral collar composed of front and back sections.

Surplice: *Superpelliceum*: *Cotta*: Liturgical, but not blessed. Originally, as the Latin name shows, worn over fur-lined garments. White linen like the alb, (which, since the XIVc., has been reserved for mass); trimmed with lace or embroidery; great variation in sleeves. Originally long, it began to be shortened in the XIIIc. and by the XVIIc. was very short.

Tunicle (*Dalmatica Minor*): peculiar to subdeacons at Mass; bishops wear it beneath the dalmatic, but always under chasuble, never under the cope. It is a plainer, narrower-sleeved dalmatic, without clavi, often fringed, originally white, the alterations of which parallel those of the dalmatic. It was the sub-deaconal costume in the VIc. in Rome, and in Spain (where deacons wore alb, not dalmatic).

In the IXc. tunicle not dalmatic, was the liturgical dress of Roman cardinal-priests. From this time through the Middle Ages the tunicle was worn by acolytes. By the XIIc. bishops, hitherto garbed in tunicle or dalmatic, wore both together.

Monastic Background

399 A.D.: Monasticism introduced into Rome from East; worked West.

IVc.: Cassian and St. Jerome mention cowl as part of monk's dress.

529 A.D.: St. Benedict founded Monte Cassino, which by VIIc. had vast influence. The Benedictines were the only great order in the West, between the decline of the Columbans and the XIc.

590 A.D.: "Monasticism ascended the papal throne in the person of Gregory the Great" (Milman), who sent St. Austin to England where he became Archbishop of Canterbury.

614 A.D.: St. Gall, disciple of the Irish monk Columban, founded the Swiss monastery of St. Gall. The influence of the Columban hermits was immense but short-lived.

English missionaries to the continent:

680-755 A.D.: St. Boniface to Germany.

827 A.D.: Denmark, Sweden.

Xc.: Christianization of Norway begun; missionaries to Slavs.

XIIc.: Christianization of Sweden completed.

IX-Xc.: Degradation of papacy.

910 A.D.: Cluniac reform under Abbot Odo.

XIc.: Decline of Cluny.

XIc.: Religious revival:

1039 A.D.: Vallombrosa, and its lay brothers.

1084 A.D.: Carthusians.

1095 A.D.: Fontevrault, double order, men, women.

1098 A.D.: Cistercians, with lay brothers.

All these, like the Benedictines were contemplative, concerned with saving their own souls.

Canons Regular, Augustinian. Contemplative, plus holy orders.

Crusades, Military orders:

1023 A.D.: Knights Hospitallers: Militarized later.

1118 A.D.: Knights Templars.

1190 A.D.: Teutonic Knights.

XIIc.: Regular and secular clergy under absolute jurisdiction of bishop; some monks free of bishop's jurisdiction. Growing criticism of Church wealth.

XIIIc.: Rise of mendicant* preachers, teachers, universities; decline in XIVc. Like the military orders, active; saving souls and bodies of others. Friars: free of bishops' jurisdiction; no authority but Pope.

1210: Franciscans (Grey Friars) (Poor Clares, female).

1216: Dominicans (Black Friars).

1245: Carmelites (after 1287, White Friars).

1256: Augustinians (Eremites).

1535: Jesuits.

Monastic Orders and Dress

Just as the costume of nuns today is essentially that of married women or widows of the Middle Ages in their *barbe,* so all the elements of Monastic costume, habit, cowl, scapular, etc., had been or were still being worn by the laity. Even after these had become specifically monastic garments, the honor of meeting death or being buried in monks' costume might be accorded to lay persons. It must be remembered that a monk was not necessarily a priest; although he might be one, a large proportion of monks were not priests.

Cowl (Cucullus); hooded outer garment, common to both sexes during the Middle Ages, but accepted, from IVc., as essential part of monks' costume. Cowls of both summer and winter weights were prescribed for his followers by St. Benedict. In the ninth century it was forbidden priests as distinctive of monks. The monastic cowl

and habit are of the same color. The cowl of the Augustinians is still a separate hood; that of the Franciscans small, but attached to the habit; the cowl of the Cistercians, Benedictines, etc., is a great hooded mantle worn as choir dress. It exists, vestigally, on the cope, as the *scutum.*

Scapular: narrow, poncho-like garment now forming an essential part of monastic garb, and worn over the habit. It was a farm-laborers' apron when St. Benedict prescribed it as the work-garment of his monks. A hood, and later, shoulder flaps were often added. The front and back were sometimes connected by straps at the sides, to prevent flapping. By XIIIc. had to be worn by monks even at night.

Benedictines (Black Monks); from first half VIc., monks living in common, and in study, lives of discipline and obedience. They amassed great libraries like Monte Cassino; were early missionaries (today, teachers); did manual work, practicing all the arts and industries; and attended 7 or more services a day. All dressed alike according to the prescription of their founder St. Benedict at Monte Cassino, in "undyed" black wool garments, which came in summer and winter weights:—a sleeved habit; hooded sleeveless cowl (*cuculla,* a slave's garment by law in 382 A.D.), not more than 2 cubits long (cubit-length of arm below elbow, 18" 22"), as a sign of humility; scapular as work-apron; shoes and stockings. Funnel-shaped sleeve of the XIVc. retained in modern habit.

Cluniac: reformed Benedictine, and therefore black-garbed monks, under the customs of Cluny from 910. All the Cluniac Congregations of Europe were under the rule of the Abbot of Cluny, who thus became one of Europe's most powerful figures. The Romanesque Church of Cluny was, until St. Peters' in XVIc., the largest church in Europe, and the richest and most magnificent in its ceremonial.

Carthusians: ascetic monks, living in isolated cells, each with its own garden, and workshop, as established by St. Bruno, 1084, at the Grande Chartreuse. They illuminated manuscripts, carpentered, gardened, ate alone, meeting only at Mass and Sunday dinner. They wore "rude garments" and a hair shirt; now a habit of white serge.

Fontevrault (and other double monasteries from VIIc.): associations of monks and of nuns, under Benedictine rule, living parallel lives in neighboring but separate establishments, both under the rule of the Abbess of the aristocratic nuns, herself a great lady, like St. Etheldreda at Ely; or, at Fontevrault, a member of the French royal family.

Cistercians (White or Grey Monks): association

---

* Francis of Assisi and the earlier mendicants had literally obeyed the command "Sell all that thou hast and give to the poor." The friars, however, soon accumulated the wealth they had condemned in the Bishops, but declared that it belonged not to themselves but the Pope. They obeyed the recommendation to evangelical poverty literally: "Money, the accursed thing, they would only touch with gloves on their hands." G. M. Trevelyan, Eng. in the Age of Wycliffe, Longmans, Green, London, 1904 ed., p. 150, note 3.

of monks, each house under the rule of its own Abbot, crystallized c. 1112 at Clarevaux by St. Bernard and a group of noblemen. Dedicated to the Virgin, it was an offshoot of the Benedictines, and rose in importance during the XI-XIIc. decline of Cluny, from which it radically differed in its ideals of functional, unostentatious simplicity. Manual and field labor given a great place; a great number of illiterate lay brothers were admitted as farmers, shepherds and work men; the Cistercians became the greatest of the monastic architects, developed the vaulted style which led to Cathedral Gothic; organized and improved farm, land and mine management; led the English wool trade, and accumulated vast properties; the active life was beginning to gain in importance.

William of Malmesbury (1125-35), writing of the foundation, and regulations of the Cistercians says:

"They wear nothing made with furs or linen, not even that finely spun linen garment which we call staminium (shirt); neither breeches, unless when sent on a journey, which at their return, they wash and restore. They have two tunics with cowls, but no additional garments in winter, though if they see fit, in summer they may lighten their garb. They sleep clad and girded. . . ."

To distinguish themselves from Cluny, they first wore a brown habit; then a gray or white habit, with a brown, or, later, black scapular. The Trappists are an offshoot of the Cistercians.

Augustinians: There are many sorts.

The *Augustine Eremite Friars* started with XIc. hermits, gathered together in mid-XIIIc. into the 4th mendicant preaching order. Luther had been an Augustinian. They dressed in black, and became "barefoot friars" in 1570.

The *Augustinian Canons Regular* are associations of priests, headed by a Prior, not an Abbot. They take vows similar to those of cloistered monks, but live lives of service to a parish. The English Austin "Black Canons" wore a long black cassock, under a white rochet, with a hooded black cloak.

The *Praemonsterian* Order of *Canons Regular,* founded 1120 by St. Norbert, were preachers dressed in white.

The *Gilbertines,* founded in England in mid-XIIc., were a double order; the Canons under the rule of St. Augustine, dressed in black with a white cloak; the women were under Cistercian rule.

The *Trinitarians* were Canons Regular, established in 1198 to recapture prisoners from the infidels; they still do rescue work in Africa. They wore white with a red and blue cross.

Canons Secular: lived similar lives in the same association, without taking vows, and while retaining their own incomes, in addition to receiving their share of that of the association. By the late XIc. established with enormous success in England. In the XVIc. time of Leo X, English Canons Regular "dressed in violet, like other clergy," said a contemporary account. Now generally dressed in white, sometimes with a scapular, but essentially and characteristically differing from other ecclesiastical dress in the wearing of the *Rochet.*

Franciscans (*Friars Minor, Gray Friars*): originally a confraternity of mendicants, founded by St. Francis of Assisi, 1209-10, and dressed like the poor and sick among whom they worked with idealism and spiritual fervor. Duns Scotus, Roger Bacon, Bonaventura were Franciscans. They wore a coarse gray habit (now brown), with a small attached hood, and a characteristic cord belt. They might not ride a horse or wear shoes.

Poor Clares: order of Franciscan nuns, founded 1214 by St. Clara. From the earliest times there were nuns, as well, of all the great monastic orders, the Abbesses frequently being the sisters of the founders, as in the case of St. Benedict.

Friars Minor Capuchins: reformed Franciscans (1525), attempting to return to the ideals of the founder. Bearded, bare-foot, and with a conical pointed hood on habit.

Dominicans (*Black Friars, Jacobins*): originally (1216) mendicant preachers and teachers; (Thomas Aquinas); painters (Fra Angelico); conservatives, in charge of the Inquisition; many houses of nuns. Dominicans dressed only in wool; white tunic, black cloak and hood. By 1220 rochet replaced by scapular.

Carmelites (*White Friars* after 1287): originally mendicant friars, in whose costume there have been many changes. They now wear a white cloak over a brown habit. Their first costume of girdled tunic, scapular and hood, was of black, brown or gray. The cloak worn over it was composed of vertical stripes, 3 black, 4 white. At this period they were called *fratres barrati* or *de pica* (magpie). By 1287 the white wool cloak was adopted (White Friars).

Jesuits: members of the Society of Jesus, religious order founded by the Spanish St. Ignatius Loyola in 1535. Rigorously chosen, trained and disciplined; teachers and missionaries, under the motto "Ad majoram Dei gloriam." No specific garb was prescribed by the founder: Jesuits are usually dressed like Spanish priests of Loyola's time.

MONASTIC MILITARY ORDERS AND THEIR DRESS

Military religious organizations arose during the Crusades. For whatever purpose they were originally founded, they all degenerated into aristocratic military clubs as they accumulated wealth, from the bequest of the pious at home, or by conquest, plunder, exploitation and trade.

Knights Templars: earliest, and prototype of the military religious orders of the Catholic Church. In 1118 a band of 9, "Poor Knights of the Temple" from Northern France, banded together to protect pilgrims to the Holy Land. At that time they were without rule or habit, except that they were short-haired, rough bearded, and never wore parti-colored garments. They enjoyed immunity from excommunication and received many "rogues and impious men, robbers and committers of sacrilege, murderers, perjurers, and adulterers," who had gone to the Holy Land to plunder, or to save their souls. In 1128 they adopted the rule of St. Benedict, and with it the Cistercian (reformed Benedictine) white wool habit, with a red cross, granted the order mid-XIIc. by Pope Eugenius III. This cross appeared also on their half-white, half-black banner called *Beauséant*, which floated from the great round tent of the Grand Master, who with 7 dignitaries ruled the order. These personages, and those unmarried knights who were under permanent vows, wore the white habit, as, in a closed version, did the chaplains: the brown or black capes of the sergeants and menials were likewise charged with the red cross of the order, the motto of which was *Non Nobis Domine*. The Knights quickly rose in numbers and power. With their fortified Temples all over Europe, leading to Asia, they became the founders of international banking, and the financial districts of London and Paris grew up around their headquarters and bear their name. At the height of their power, jealousy and scandal led to their trial and suppression (1312).

Knights of St. John of Jerusalem (*Hospitallers, Rhodes, Malta*), were started during the First Crusade to defend pilgrims and nurse the sick. They were established under Augustinian rule, and at first wore any clothing, so long as it was poor.

The first reference to the military side of the Order is in 1200. In 1248, the knights wore a long, wide black tunic with a white cross on the breast; it had supplanted a black *cappa clausa* which proved inconvenient in battle. In 1259, Alexander III gave the infirmarians a black mantle with a white cross, and to the knights a red surcoat with a white cross.

Like the Templars, they were ruled by a Grand Master and 7 dignitaries, including a Marshal for the European knights, and another, the Turcopilier, in charge of the native troops. Unlike the Templars, the knights, whether under vows or lay "subscribers," had to be aristocrats and legitimate. This was not the case with the sergeants and infirmarians. The order was cosmopolitan, predominantly French.

The order, dissolved by Pope Clement in 1314, was reorganized as the Knights of Rhodes, which they took over. They were now a federation of national "langues," not French-controlled. The order turned into the leading sea-power of the Mediterranean while opposing the Turks. In 1523, they removed to Malta. Their membership, disturbed by the Reformation, was effectively ended by the French revolution, although the order is still in existence.

Teutonic Knights: Their order was modelled on the Knights Hospitallers. Like the Hospitallers, it was aristocratic, requiring 16 quarterings; but unlike them, it was intensely German, not cosmopolitan. Its beginnings were made during the 3rd Crusade at the siege of Acre, when a tent, made of their sails, was used as a hospital ministering to German wounded. In 1192, they were regularly established under Augustinian rule, with privileges like those of the Hospitallers and Templars, as a combined hospital and military order, supported by the rich traders of Bremen and Lübeck; ruled by a Grand Master and 5 dignitaries, it had lay members as well, dressed in white with a black cross.

As "missionaries to the Baltic pagans," they conquered and exploited E. Prussia, in XIIIc. They were magnificent, aristocratic and cultured landowners and traders, whose great glory began to fade after their defeat by the Lithuanians at Tannenberg in 1410; in XVIc., they finally withdrew from East Prussia.

The Papal *Knights of the Holy Sepulcher* were supposed to have been founded by Godfrey of Bouillon; in 1496, Pope Alexander VI granted them a red Jerusalem cross with Latin crosses at the angles.

The aristocratic Spanish military orders grew out of an earlier Portuguese one.

St. James of Compostella (*of the Sword*) was believed to have been instituted by Ramiro II, king of Leon, but it probably dates from Pope Alexander III in 1175. The badge is the red lily-hilted sword of St. James (Santiago).

The *Knights of Alcántara* (1156) and *Calatrava* (1158), organized to fight the Moors in Spain, carry the cross fleury, respectively red and green.

After the fervent crusading days were done, knightly orders continued to develop, but their character was honorary, bestowed by a ruler, rather then ecclesiastical. As we come upon illustrations of their insignia, we will take up the *Garter*, founded in England in mid-XIVc.; the *Annunziata*, established in 1360 by Amadeus VI of Savoy; the *Golden Fleece* of the Burgundian dukes and the later Empire, which was started in 1429-30; and the French orders of *Saint-Michel* (1469, and *Saint-Esprit* (1578.) (See also Heraldry.)

1. Apparel of neck
2. Orphrey of
   Chasuble
3. Chasuble
4. Sleeves of Alb
5. Apparels
6. Maniple
7. Ends of stole
8. Alb
9. Apparel of Alb
   The stole is worn
by priests crossed
in front and fas-
tened by girdle.

327

1. Apparel of neck
2. Dalmatic or
   tunicle
3. Orphreys of
   Dalmatic
4. Sleeves of Alb
5. Apparels
6. Maniple
7. Apparel of
   Dalmatic
8. Alb
9. Apparel of Alb
   The stole is worn
by deacons over the
left shoulder.

328

329

330

1. Miter of which
   there are three
   sorts:
   1·pretiosa
   2·auriphrygiata
   3·simplex
2. Crozier
3. Apparel of neck
4. Chasuble
5. Pallium
6. Orphrey of
   Chasuble
7. Maniple
8. Dalmatic
9. Tunic
10. Apparels of
    Alb
11. Gloves
12. Ends of stole
    worn without
    crossing
13. Alb
14. Sandals
15. Buskins

1. Cope   5. Apparel
2. Morse   6. Hood
3. Orphrey   7. Girdle of
4. Alb   Alb

327. Priest Vested for Mass.

328. Deacon Vested.

329. Archbishop Vested for Mass.

330. Priest in Cope.

The Dark Ages: Feudal Power

VII-XI Century Background

THE unification of costume during the first six centuries was followed, between Justinian and the Crusades, by a period of establishment of regional differentiations which the Crusades in turn helped to amalgamate into European costume. It is helpful to recapitulate the forces, the influence of which will appear in costume.

The Lombard invasion divided Italy into three elements: Byzantine, (Ravenna), Lombard, and the Papacy. Justinian (527-65) failed to unite Western Europe, but did reconquer Italy from the Ostrogoths and gain a foothold on the Spanish pininsula against the Visigoths (cf. VIc. sarcophagus, Xc. and later Visigothic material). The empire he left was a stable one; it declined after his death, but Constantinople, in the VII-VIIIc. withstood Persian and Mohammedan sieges, and was ravaged for the first time in 1204 by Crusaders. The dispersal of its looted treasures spread its civilization over all Western Europe. Greek Byzantium accepted image-worship in the VIIc VIIIc., stood at its height in the IX-XIc., and its elements remain clearly in the art and costume of Russia, which accepted Greek Orthodox Christianity after the baptism (Xc.) of its ruler, Vladimir.

The Western church, which was in its infancy in the IVc., expanded with the spread of monasticism in the IV-VIc., from Italy to France, and to the British Isles and Ireland, during the Papacy of Gregory 1, (590-604). Back to the continent and over the world there spread from the two islands the horde of missionaries, Christians since Caesar's time, who formed one of the most notable civilizing forces of history, such as St. Boniface, to Germany, and the Irish monks with their distinctive manuscript style, to the French monasteries already established at Tours and Poitiers, and to St. Gall in Switzerland, founded 614 by the most famous follower of the Irish monk Columban.

The great infiltration of the Goths was over. The Visigoths had come to Spain in 378, and had been its Kings 415-711; Alaric and his Huns at Rome, 410; the Vandals in Africa; the Burgundians and Franks; the Angles, Saxons and Jutes to England from the IVc.; the Ostrogoths in Italy.

In 711 the Saracens had crossed the Mediterranean into Spain and founded the Moorish kingdom of Granada, which endured to 1492.

The Gauls helped to spread the Roman culture with which they had begun to be familiar in Caesar's time. Christianity grew; civilization and rising power seemed its concomitants: Clovis and his Franks were converted on a battlefield in 496; the Burgundians in 517; the Visigoth King by his Frankish wife in 550; the Lombards by the end of the VIIc. The Xc. Norsemen were converted and civilized by the XIc. into the superb Normans, who held England; and wrested from the Mohammedans the two Sicilies, where their contact with Mediterranean culture helps to make understandable their spectacular rise.

The VIII-XIc saw the gulf between Latin and Greek cultures widening, and Western Christianity on the defensive, leading to the Crusades. New strength was given the degraded Papacy of the late IXc. to the early Xc., through the Cluniac reforms of Odo, and its connection with the rising power of the new German Empire under Henry III-IV, and the increasing power and dignity of the College of Cardinals.

Within half a century, under the Conqueror's third son, Henry I, London had begun its rise to pre-eminence. Norman merchants from Rouen on the Seine had traded with England in wine and fish for a century, under special privileges; now they flocked to their new capital on the Thames bringing craftsmen of all sorts. They did not attempt to exploit the English, and Norman taste, elegance and dress quickly spread.

Dress of Britons, Gauls and Franks

Our information about the dress of the Gauls and Britons is based on some eye-witness accounts; bas-reliefs on Roman arches, probably somewhat compromised with Roman costume; Gallo-Roman statues showing hooded cloak variants; actual costumes found in Danish peat-bogs; and metal objects fished out of the rivers or dug up.

The Britons, their skin dyed or tattooed blue with woad, loaded their arms with gold bracelets, sometimes weighing as much as 16 oz. each. Fur was available and warm. Cold and the shapes in which fur came led to closer-fitting garments and to tailoring, as against the loose, cool, primarily rectangular Mediterranean costume. The leather work of their sandal-moccasin shoes was admirably sophisticated. Hemp and good woolen materials were woven, even in twilled and diapered designs; they wove patterned, multi-colored braids and tapes, fringes and nets. The colors they loved and the bright woven stripes and checks of their materials impressed Roman observers. There was a woolen trade with the British Isles which by the VIIIc. was sending an especially good cloth to the Continent. Silk was familiar to them, through the Romans, before they knew cotton, a cape of which created a sensation on the streets of Tours in 580.

Their original garments, when made of woven materials, seem to have been less tailored than those of skins; their smocks short and sleeveless. With Roman citizenship or familiarity, this smock grew wider, longer, girded, long-sleeved: became a tunic. Their cloaks were of the many practical varieties, saggum, paenula and poncho-like garments which the Romans had incorporated into their own dress.

The Gallic *breeches* (Lat. *braccae*, Fr. *braie*) had a drawstring at the top, which, by the XII-XIIIc. was threaded through the waist-band to give some points of attachment for longer hose.

Under the Merovingians and the Carolingians a sock-like boot to the calf, or a fabric hose (*chausse*) was drawn up over the breeches. Other forms of breeches were tied at the ankle, or strapped under the foot. Looser varieties of breeches, and longer hose were bound around the leg with puttee-like or cross-gartered bands. Later we see the hose tied below the knee so that the wide top hung down in a cuff: or a knot tied at the top of short hose, made them serve as a sort of fitted boot; worn, by the XIIIc., over longer hose, pulled up in front to fasten at waist-band of breeches.

The Gauls seem to have been extremely shoe-conscious. It is from *gallicae*, the word for their shoes, that the French *galoche* and our word *galoshes* derive. The VI-VIIIc. boot-hose, *pedule*, was considered almost a Frankish uniform. For six hundred years, until the advent of long gowns for men, it is the legs, their decoration, wrappings and footgear, which form the most interesting and varied part of male costume.

Charlemagne (who donned Roman costume on only two occasions in his life) wore a linen shirt under a knee-length tunic, together with bands for his legs, and a small cap. But the shirt, though no longer uncommon, is not yet obligatory male wear, and the head is commonly uncovered (except in travelling or working in the fields) until the end of the Middle Ages, when the lengthening point of the travelling hood, wound around the head to get it out of the way, led to the hat.

There are not many remains of armor between the VIIc. and the Crusades.

Frankish leaders of the Merovingian period are known to have worn helmets and cuirasses. Soldiers had their heads partly shaved, and the rest of the hair dyed red, braided and wound protectively around the head, and held by a leather band. They carried small, round, convex shields; 32″ swords, narrow an ddouble-edged; or the single-edged *francisque*, a sword which could also be thrown; 20″ single-edged dagger; barbed javelin;

long-headed iron-tipped lance; and a battle-axe.

A monk at Saint-Gall, who saw Charlemagne at the end of the IXc., says that he and his men were "literally encased in iron; the emperor wore an iron helmet, his arms were protected by plates of iron, his thighs by scales of the same; the lower part of his legs was protected by greaves, and his horse was clad in armor from head to foot." Charlemagne's soldiers, by his laws, wore armlets, helmets, leg-pieces, and carried shields. The finely tempered long swords of the Iron Age were given names, like Weyland's "Mimung," Charlemagne's "Joiuse," and King Arthur's "Calibran" (Excaliber). (Quoted from Demmin.)

Women's costume for many centuries was based on a tunic, wider than the under tunic (A. S. *cyrtel*, Eng. *kirtle*), which had close sleeves and fell short of the ground and served as house or work dress. This might and later did have a linen shirt beneath. Over the tunic a *Mantle* was worn; head was covered by a veil susceptible of arrangement.

By the XIc. gloves and handkerchiefs were in established use, the *fichu* decorated the tunics of both men and women, and men's hair, after Charlemagne, was worn short.

ARMS AND ARMOR

Charts of development of arms and armor of the VII-XVIIc. (illustrations 435-446) have been massed, for convenience, under the chapter: "Knighthood in Flower." Arms and armor of the VII-XIc. are discussed in the captions of illustrations 334, 339, 342, 344, 370-374. Illustrations 165-170, on helmets, may also be consulted.

DEVELOPMENT OF XI-XII CENTURY DRESS

In the XIc. the long garment of the gentry reappears. Called the *bliaud*, the upper tunic is not the Roman tunic, but a cut and fitted gown (by mid-XIc. laced tight at sides or back, and showing the undergarment through the lacings) gored at the sides for additional width in the skirts, and with shaped sleeves. It was worn long by women; and from below the knee to very long by men.

It reflected many oriental influences. The Eastern dalmatic had continued in use in the Carolingian, and in the deliberately Byzantine Ottonian courts, whose contacts with the growing Italian sea power facilitated the passage of Byzantine traders and goods to Germany. The Normans, after recapturing Sicily from the Mohammedans, 1061-91, had carried oriental trends back to the continent and to England, and with the Crusades, all Christendom was brought into contact and trade with the East, so that the *turban*, introduced into Persia only in the Xc., had spread to Europe by the XIc.

The *surcoat*, a sleeveless upper garment, worn both by knights over armor, and by ladies, appears mid-XIIc.

The sleeve of this tunic was typically tight in the upper arm. It either broadened out into a wide funnel, showing the tight sleeve of the under tunic, *chainse,* or continued tight and widened very suddenly and extremely, below elbow, perhaps just above wrist, trailing to the ground and so long that it had to be knotted up, or with a stone tied in the end, might serve as a weapon. By the end of the XIIc. a plain wide sleeve appeared, much longer than the arm, so that it had to be turned back, or hung over the concealed hand.

Decorative bands, orphreys,* heretofore at neck and wrists, moved to horizontal positions around the upper arm, and across the bottom of a shortened and narrowed upper skirt, showing the extremely full skirt (now frequently trailing, and of another, usually lighter color), of the under garment, *chainse,* or kirtle.

While the under tunic often served alone for house wear (in which case it was usually girdled and edged in the older style at wrists, hem and down the front) both garments were now commonly worn, not only by women of the nobility but by those of the class first styled "bourgeoisie" in 1134 by Louis the Fat, and the rapidity of whose rise may be gauged by the fact that in 1374 Charles V ennobled all the bourgeois of Paris. Beneath these two upper garments was worn a linen *chemise,* the tucked or embroidered edge of which showed as the neckline of the upper garments rapidly lowered.

Under the *bliaud* men wore a shirt, frequently long and wide, and breeches, onto the belt of which were laced the hose.

The *cape,* oblong or semi-circular, which had been, for a short time in the XIc., fastened uncomfortably on the left shoulder, is soon fastened in front by a cord running across the chest, where a lady would hold it with two fingers, in a gesture typical of the Middle Ages.

Toward the end of the twelfth century came the introduction of *pelissons,* fur-lined over-garments for men and women. A little later the short Angevin mantle which gave him his nickname was introduced into England by Henry Courtmantel. For travelling, the old paenula and pluviale with capuchon were worn as hoods through the Middle Ages, particularly after the last third of the XIIc., but until the end of the XIVc. men went ordinarily bareheaded.

Berets and *brimmed hats* like the Greek petasus (especially for travelling) were the headwear in the later XIIc.

The pre-invasion English gentleman wore his hair long, a churl's was cropped. The long hair of the English was accepted by the Normans, replaced their own high-clipped short hair, and was brought back by them to the continent. Like the beard, it became standard there, although subject to much criticism and attempted regulation. The Normans shaved; beards became fashionable after the conquest. Henry I allowed a bishop to cut off his hair and beard in 1104. By the XIIc., beards were censored; by the XIIIc. they were definitely less common.

Women wore their hair parted and flowing, or braided, or wound about with ribbon, from the early XIIc.; completely uncovered or bound by a fillet for young girls. The veil of married women was smaller, circular, held in place by a circlet or crown.

Girdles were important. By XIIc. two were worn; one wider, at natural waistline; another knotted below. They were woven like orphreys on narrow looms.

Chief articles of jewelry were large high brooches, set with massive stones, fastening the slit bodice at the throat; there were similar stones on crowns and circlets. There were also clasps for the cords of the cape.

As for shoes, pointed toes (invented, William of Malmesbury said, by Foulk of Anjou to hide his ill-formed feet) begin to appear; wooden patterns were devised for bad weather; high boots, often with turned down cuff were not uncommon through the XIIc.

Materials are dotted with small all-over designs. Embroidery is applied in geometric bands. As cut ceases to be purely utilitarian, decoration becomes fanciful, and the three most typical elements of the costume of the Middle Ages appear: *particolor,* or *mi-parti; dagging,* slitting of edges, from German; *fur.*

The small furs, suitable for lining over-garments, lend themselves also to decorative piecing, and are lavishly used. The Anglo-Saxon Chronicle records, 1074, the gifts of King Malcolm of Scotland and his sister Margaret to Edgar as "great presents and much treasure to him and his men, skins adorned with purple, sable-skin, gray-skin, and ermine-skin pelisses, mantles, gold and silver vessels." Henry I received from the Bishop of Lincoln a fur-lined cloak worth £100.

As the knights' armor became more completely concealing, the necessity of distinguishing one from another was met by the development of armorial bearings, which apparently commenced (early XIIc.) with fur-decorated shields, soon elaborated with the ubiquitous color. The beginnings of armorial bearings are clearly shown on the Bayeux Tapestry, but the first recognizable bearings are the golden "lioncels" on the shield of Geoffrey of Anjou, a wedding gift (1129) of his father-in-law, Henry I of England (see Ill. 396).

---

* Increasing use of decorative orphreys. They were woven on narrow looms by monks and ladies from VII-XVc., while patterned materials had to be imported from the East, before the XIIIc. rise of Italian factories.

331

332

333

334

331-333. VIIc. Gospels of Durrow. (Trinity College, Dublin.)

Symbols of Sts. Matthew and Mark. Irish priest, in patchwork mantle and multi-colored shoes; tonsured in the Celtic manner, the tonsure of St. John or, mockingly, of Simon Magnus, by which the front hair was shaved from ear to ear. In allusion to this period of tonsure were the first two words of the Druid prophecy about St. Patrick: "Adze-head will come with a crook-head staff, in his house head-holed (*chasuble*)."

332. IXc. 820 A.D. Gospels of MacRegol. (Bodleian Library, Oxford.)

St. John with his symbols: the saint is tonsured according to the method variously called British, Ro-

man or St. Peter's, used in France, Spain and Italy until the late Middle Ages, after which it was retained for monks and friars, but reduced in size for clergy. During this period of illumination the folds of what was probably a garment of solid color were indicated as multicolored stripes; a thousand years later, French painters begin to experiment with not dissimilar analyses and syntheses of color. These are typical examples of the crude, raw color and interlaced manuscript style disseminated by the Irish missionaires).

334. VIIIc. 700 A.D. Found at Vendel, Uppland, Sweden. (State Historical Museum, Stockholm.)

Helmet decoration: Warriors wearing coats of ring mail, helmets, swords, lances analogous to the equipment of the Danish and Norman invaders of England.

335

336

scs michael   scs gabriel

337

335. XIII-Xc. (Church of Santa Maria in Valle, Cividale del Friuli.)

Persian-Hellenistic stucco figures. Six female saints wearing under-tunics with tight sleeves, embroidered at the wrist, beneath super-tunics with wide sleeves, the sleeve edges and hems banded with jewelled embroidery. One figure still bears the clavi: her neighbor to the left wears an embroidered mantle. Four wear Byzantine collars and headdresses. The figure at the extreme right carries her hand beneath her mantle, holding it up in the Byzantine manner.

336. 741 A.D. (Rome, S. Maria Antiqua.)

Romanesque wall painting. St. Cyr, in tunic and dalmatic with clavi, and decorated pallium. As in the Gospels of MacRegol, the shadowed folds of a plain colored garment are rendered as multicolored stripes.

337. VIIIc. Celtic-Teutonic-Franco-Byzantine; Illuminated Manuscript. (Treves Capitular Library.)

Saints Michael and Gabriel: in dalmatics with clavi and pallium. Compare with Gospels of Rurrow and MacRegol for evidences of the manuscript style brought to the Continent by the Celtic monks.

338. IX-Xc. Carolingian (Valenciennes Ms. 99, 31x) Apocalipsis Figurata.

The illustrations on this page are from three of the many manuscript versions, between the IX-XIIIc. of the *Commentaria in Apocalypsem* of Beatus of Valcavado (730-798). The only female figure ever shown is the Scarlet Woman, riding upon the Beast. In this example, her tunic still carries the clavii; collar and headdress still very Byzantine.

339. IX-Xc. Carolingian. (Valenciennes Ms. 99, 34x) Apocalipsis Figurata.

Knight on horseback, with a saddle blanket, but without a saddle; first used in Europe in IVc. Before the VIIc. introduction of stirrups, the warrior used his lance as a vaulting pole. Stirrups are dependent from a harness, to which the saddle blanket is strapped. His cape is fastened by a circular brooch, paved with stones, of a type already current for several centuries. Dots probably a method of enlivening the delineation of folds, but the period of small all-over designs on nothing is approaching.

340. Xc. 975 A.D. Spain. (Gerona Cathedral 60) Beatus.

Peaked saddle of oriental type, typical of Middle Ages. Definite stripes now used, horizontally and vertically. Hooded for travelling; patterned leg bandages.

All photographs courtesy of Morgan Library, New York

341. Spanish Visigothic 976 A.D., from Monastery of San Millan de la Cogolla. (Madrid, Escorial Ms. D. I. I.) Codex Aemilianensis.

This manuscript, executed by Velasco and his pupil, Sisebuto, shows the Visigothic Sovereigns of Leon, under whose reign the book was written.

Clundeswith (641-652): who carries in his hand what well may be the *mappa* of a late Roman consul. *Receswith* (649-672): by whom the Visigothic laws were issued, 645 A.D. *Egica* (687-701). *Queen Urracha*: decorated veil. *Sancho I* (955-967). *Ramiro III* (967-982), son and grandson of the traditional founder of the crusading Order of the Knights of St. James of Compostella. *Velasco*: the scribe with his tablets. *Sisebuto*: the bishop, wearing the mitre which came into use during Xc.; pastoral staff. *Sisebuto*: the notary, with his tablets. (See page 145.)

342. XIc. Carolingian. From the Monastery of Fulda.
(Rome, Vat. Reg. Lat. 124.)

German work, showing Louis le Debonnaire, the
last Carolingian, looking no more forceful than he
was: his tunic is treated to give a debased approximation of Roman armor; the shirt set on the low line
of the abdomen-protecting moulded lorica; the second
belt across the breast. His cape, half a crescent in cut,
and tied at the shoulder, is typical of the period. He
is wearing Frankish sock-boots, *pedules*. The use of
the letters of the Greek alphabet as a decorative background had begun in earlier centuries; words and sen-
tences were used as decorative embroidered bands.

Fulda, founded 744 by a follower of St. Boniface,
and endowed by the Carolingians, was the greatest
Benedictine monastery in Germany, ranking with
Monte Cassino in Italy and St. Gall in Switzerland.

343. End IXc. Carolingian, from Ratisbon. (Munich,
Stadbib. Cod. Lat. 14345.)

A tonsured ecclesiastic, in a dalmatic of the original form, tunic, and fine shoes, is being stoned by
men in girded tunics (by now definitely shortened to
above the knee) and sock-boots over breeches.

344. IXc. (Trier. Stadtbib. s. 31). Apocalypse.

The soldiers' shield is becoming more convex; its
boss more prominent. The tunic is above the knee;

346

breeches are cross-gartered or bound, above shoes. The cape, in cut, is between a half-crescent and a semi-circle. Heads are typically bare. The costume of the male saint is now set by tradition: the female saint is dressed as a lady of the period.

345. End IX-mid Xc. (St. Gall Lib. Cod. 250). Pen drawing.

Andromeda, in a short-sleeved super-tunic with embroidered bands and shoes.

The Monastery of St. Gall was founded in 614 by the most famous disciples of Columban, the Irish monk who traveled the continent, France, the Vosges, founding the great Swiss Monastery.

346. Xc. Ottonian. German. (Conde Museum, Chantilly) Registerum Gregorii.

Otto II enthroned, surrounded by the provinces, Germania, Francia, Italia, Alemania, paying homage. Otto II (955-983) held splendid court at Rome and died there after being crowned Emperor of both Rome and Germany by Pope John XIII, having restored Benedict VII to the Papacy, and secured the election of Peter of Pavia as John XIV, during the decadence of the Papacy. The costumes are deliberately Byzantine, as befitting the heir to the Holy Roman Empire. The band of embroidery on the upper arm will be seen persisting halfway through the XIII c.

347. Xc. 980-990 A.D. Ottonian from Reichenau. (Heidelberg Univ. Lib. Cod. Sal. IXb.)

Enthroned Virgin: *Ecclesia*. In this ms., illuminated in the VIIIc. Benedictine Monastery of Reichenau, she is dressed like a late-Roman matron, with Byzantine superhumeral collar and headdress.

348. Xc. before 920 A.D. (St. Gall, Stiftsbibliothek, Cod. 22). Psalter Aureum.

King David, in a short tunic, with decorative banding at hem, neck and cuff of the tight sleeves. Had the sleeves been wide, their edges would not have been decorated. Breeches, sock-hose and decorated shoes. Fringed cape, tied and clasped on left shoulder.

349-350. End Xc. Ottonian from Reichenau. (Munich State Lib., Cod. Lat. 4453. Gospels of Bamberg Cath. Treasure, Cim. 54.)

349. Provinces of Slavonia, Germania, Gallia and Roma paying homage to Emperor. Byzantine-clad females. Slavonia: white tunic with black and pearl-edged scarlet superhumeral, violet cloak decorated,

like those of all the others, in gold bands set with scarlet circles and edged with pearls. Germania: pale green cloak over bright blue tunic, decorated gold superhumeral. Gallia: plain white tunic, rose overgarment slung like cape. Roma: bright blue undergarment, orange-yellow overgarment; gold-decorated scarlet napkin over hands, Byzantine-fashion, as she offers jewelled tribute.

350. Enthroned Emperor and his suite. Probably Otto III, "The Wonder of the World," who was crowned German King, 983, later King of the Lombards, made his cousin Bruno, Pope Gregory V, and was by him crowned Emperor in 996 at Rome. There the Emperor lived in a court modeled on that of Constantinople, and rather in the style of the preceding century.

The Emperor wears a white under-tunic, a violet tunic richly banded in pearl-edged, gold bands, encrusted with red and blue stones. Pale green mantle simply fastened on right shoulder. Dark green shoes,

ornamented in red and white, over scarlet hose. The white-bearded sword-bearer on the Emperor's left wears decorated scarlet hose, lavender sock-boots, under a white tunic and deep plum cape. The ecclesiastics on the right are both bishops, tonsured, but not yet wearing the mitre which makes its first appearance in this century. Their white palls, decorated with red crosses and red-fringed end, are worn over chasubles, still tent-like in form, one dark blue, the other violet; both gold-edged. The gold-edged yellow dalmatics carry, on the clavi, the tuft-like decorations (both being red), which had developed outside Italy in the IXc. The golden stole, hanging straight, as worn by a bishop, has the oblong tabbed end, which started in IXc. Violet stockings and sandals.

351-354. End Xc. Anglo-Saxon. (British Museum). Tenison Prudentius.

Prudentius (348-c. 410), the early Christian poet, was a nobleman and a lawyer who retired to a monastery at 57; of his many books the most influential, "Psychomania," is an allegory of vice and virtue, portraying the Church in its struggle with paganism.

This English Prudentius Ms. shows the circular Anglo-Saxon cloak, both whirling, and lying in folds over the arm. All classes dressed alike. Men wore a linen shirt (A. S. *syrec*); breeches (A. S. *bréc,* "breeks") which were usually of linen also; a girded tunic (A. S. *roc,* German, *roc*-coat) which was of wool, with circular-cut, knee-length skirt; a short mantle, frequently circular, fastened on the right shoulder or in front; and ankle-high shoes.

Women wore an ample outer tunic, with a more fitted garment (A. S. *cyrtel*-kirtle) beneath; a very large mantle, one end of which is shown fastened around the waist; and a veil, the length of which can be seen on the figures of the dancing female in the girded tunic (352). Practically the dress of a Roman matron.

355

356

355-356. XIc. 1078-81.

355. *Nicephore Botaniate and his wife, Marie,* protected by Jesus Christ.

356. *Nicephore Botaniate,* Emperor of the Orient, accepting, on the recommendation of the archangel Michael, the works of St. John Chrysostome, presented by that saint.

These engravings were made in 1844 by the Count Auguste de Bastard after a manuscript in the Bibliothèque Royale (now the Bib. Nat. in Paris) No. 79 in the Fonds de Coislin. They show Byzantine costume in its Eastern development from which Russian costume evolved.

The saint is dressed as a bishop of the Eastern church, in *omorphion* (pallium), caught on the left shoulder; *phenonion* (equivalent of chasuble, worn from IVc., usually shortened in front); *epitrachilion* (stole; in Eastern church, a strip with an opening for the head at one end, hanging down in front); *sticharion* (alb), with a *zone* (belt) which is indicated by the blousing, although not shown; and *epimanica* (separate cuffs, allied to the liturgical gloves of the Roman church). A form of dalmatic, caught together but not sewed at the sides, called *saccus*, was worn from the Vc., though not by the saint shown here; a bishop would wear it now. He is tonsured in the short clip which the Eastern church allowed, in place of the shaved Roman tonsure.

The archangel illustrates the change which took place in the Byzantine chlamys with tablion, soon after Justinian. Hitherto flowing, so soft that the left

hand beneath could be used, still covered by it, in the typical Byzantine gesture which we still see at Arles in the XIIc. the chlamys has now become so stiff, of embroidered and jewelled brocade, that it has become necessary to cut the lower edge sharply up to free the left arm, after which the hemline again drops. The shape of the tablion is no longer simply rectangular. His tunic has embroidered superhumeral and hem-band; he wears embroidered Byzantine shoes.

The long brocade tunic which the Emperor wears, standing between these two, is decorated at the knees and center front of the pearl-studded superhumeral, with the conventionalized flower and leaf forms into which the roundels and orbiculi of the IVc. have altered.

As shown with his wife, the Emperor wears, instead of the chlamys, the vestigial *toga palmata* of a late Roman consul; a wide strip of stiff embroidery wound around the body. At the left arm, where it would be hopeless to attempt to drape it, an entirely different piece of soft stuff emerges from its end, to be thrown over the left arm. He carries in one hand the Roman consul's *mappa.*

On the costume of the Empress, nothing remains of the *toga palmata* or *praetexta* but a strip dropping from beneath the Byzantine collar, and the crescent-shaped apron to match—a formalization of the drape of the *sinus* under the right arm and across the body. There is no attempt here to commemorate the draped end hanging over the left arm.

The Emperor and his wife are essentially dressed alike, as Western Europeans will be, after the Crusades, and in materials more luxuriously elaborated, and sleeves more sophisticatedly cut than we will see, even then, in the West. Their sceptres, head-dresses, shoes are typically Byzantine. The band of embroidery across the upper arm passed into Western costume and will be seen until well into the XIIIc.

357. Early XIc. Anglo-Saxon. (London, Victoria and Albert Museum.)

Ivory carving of Virgin, Child and three wise men. The Virgin wears the typical costume of an Anglo-Saxon lady. Over her head the couvre-chef of the married woman or nun, in this case held in place by a circlet. Her mantle, closed in front, might have fastened on the left shoulder in the previous century. Two very full tunics; the upper (A. S. *cyrtel*-kirtle) is the shorter, and its bell-sleeves and hem have a patterned edge. The girdle, which does not show, would, certainly in the previous century, have been a folded, wide strip. The three kings wear the longer tunic with bell sleeves of this century, and their full circular Anglo-Saxon capes fall in stylized folds. The tiny figure on the roof wears garments with the fitted top, neckline and widening sleeve of the new type.

358. XIc. French. St. Pierre. (Moissac.)

Gravestone of Abbot Durand. The amice which the Abbot wears around his neck is at this period just beginning to be decorated. The chasuble with orphreys, is still tent-like, the sides not yet trimmed away. The dalmatic was granted to abbot's use in XIc. Early use of tunicle with dalmatic. Alb has been embroidered since Xc. Long stole. Sandals of early fenestrated type. Pontifical ring on middle finger of right hand. Pastoral staff of an abbot, not in this case bent, but an elaboration of the shepherd's crook.

359. XIc. Spanish. (Burgos, Santo Domingo de Silos.)

Stone relief of *Journey to Emmaus*. Three male figures wearing the longer, more fitted outer garment of this century, over a long, wide under-garment. The sleeves, wider at the wrist, are not typically bell-shaped. Pouch, decorated with cockle shells of Pilgrim is the *gypcière* (from F. *gibier*, the game which the hunter put in the pouch) increasingly important throughout the next two centuries.

360

361

362

360. XIc. Spain. (Burgo de Osma. Cath. Arch., 2. Cod.)

Beatus manuscript. Not only the rider's garments but the background and the bodies of the horses are covered with the small all-over patterns typical of the period.

361-363. XIc. 1028-72 Spain-S. France. (Paris Bib. nat. lat. 8878.)

361. *Beatus of Liébana or St. Sever,* executed by Stephanus Garsia. The only female shown in Beatus manuscripts is the Scarlet Woman. Her undergarment has long, tight sleeves. Over it she wears a short-sleeved, girdled tunic with a fuller skirt than heretofore. The rectangular mantle over her head is caught at center-front by an enormous clasp, and is surmounted by a small circular veil; decorated shoes.

362. The Kings and merchants lament the

fall of Babylon: The small, all-over design of grouped dots is typical of the period. Full circular capes, fastened on either shoulder. Loose breeches and shoes like sock-boots. Hair will remain short until after the Norman conquest of the long-haired English. The crowns and head-coverings worn in Spain during this and the centuries immediately before and after, are full of interest and special character.

363. Soldiers: Their capes, like those of civilians, close either on the right, or on the inconvenient left shoulder. Their kite-shaped shields, derived from the Frankish, are shorter and wider than the Norman, and like them decorated, though not yet heraldic.

Photographs courtesy of Morgan Library

364-65. XIc. 1014. German. (Bamberg, Cathedral Treasure.)

Coronation tunic of Henry II.

Of the 4 coronation ceremonies of the Roman Emperors, the 2 most important were that in which he received the imperial crown from the Pope at Rome, and the German coronation ceremony at Aix-la-Chapelle. This tunic formed part of the German regalio.

The X-XIc. tunic is shorter, often above the knee; neck, cuff, and hem embroidered. The diagonal neck-closing ends in XIIIc.

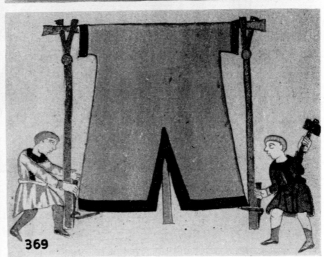

366-369. XIc. 1023. Italian. (Monte Cassino. Monastery Library.)

Mediaeval Encyclopaedia by Rabanus Maurus (766-856), abbot of Fulda.

366. De monacchis: Benedictine bishop, monk and abbot, dressed according to the directions of St. Benedict, founder of this monastery and order, in hooded sleeveless black wool cowl, over habit; and shoes and stockings. The monk wears a long working scapular; that of the abbot is fastened together at the sides. The bishop's crozier is of a very advanced type; that of the abbot of an earlier sort.

367. De coniugiis: Byzantine influence is still visible in the unbelted women's gowns, and in the placing of decoration on the simple home costumes of these noble Italians.

368-369. De tentoriis: Workmen in tunics, breeches, hose and shoes, dyeing bed-curtains and an unfinished long tunic.

370-374. XIc. Anglo-Norman. (Bayeux Cathedral.)

Bayeux Tapestry. The tapestry was probably commissioned by Odo, bishop of Bayeux (who had fought in the Battle of Hastings, and was William the Conqueror's brother) for the decoration of his cathedral; and was more nearly contemporary than was formerly believed. It is 20″ wide and 231′ long, contains 72 scenes worked in 8 colors. Packed full of information, it shows Halley's comet (which had glowed for 7 nights in 1066), and the earliest representation of a court dwarf in Europe, carefully marked as such above his head. (See Appendix.)

William of Malmesbury describes the English and Normans at the time of the Conquest, only 30 years before his birth:

English: short garments to mid-knee; hair cropped; beards shaven; arms laden with golden bracelets; skin adorned with punctured designs. "They were accustomed to eat until they became surfeited, and

370

370. Shield bearings. 371. Jazeran armor. 372 (left). Harold being offered the crown by 2 members of the Witan, one of whom carries the official axe. 372 (right). Harold as King, with Stigand the archbishop. 373-374. Warriors.

to drink until they were sick. These latter qualities they imparted to their conquerors. As to the rest, they adopted their manners."

Normans: "were and are even now proudly apparelled, delicate in their food but not excessive; a race inured to war, and can hardly live without it; fierce in rushing against the enemy, and where strength fails of success, ready to use stratagem, or to corrupt by bribery. They live in large edifices with economy; envy their equals; wish to excel their superiors; and plunder their subjects, though they defend them from others; they are faithful to their Lords, and though a slight offense renders them perfidious, they weigh treachery by its chance of success, and change their sentiments with money. They are, however, the kindest of nations, and they esteem strangers worthy of equal honor with themselves; they also intermarry with their vassals. They revived, by their arrival, the observances of religion which had everywhere grown lifeless in England. You might see churches rise in every village, and monasteries in the towns and cities built after a style unknown before." William allowed the enemy dead to be properly interred; returned Harold's body to his mother without taking the ransom she offered; and was crowned by Archbishop Aldred, being careful not to use Stigand, who was not canonically an archbishop.

The details of Stigand's unprincipled 50-year climb to power fill much space in the Anglo-Saxon Chronicle. He appeared in 1020 as Canute's chaplain; got his first bishopric in 1043, and was deposed in 1044 (the year of the great famine) because of his influence over the king's mother; succeeded to the Bishopric of Winchester in 1047 (the year when even the fishes froze). Stigand's rival, Robert of Jumièges, archbishop of Canterbury, came back from Rome with his pall* in 1051, was banished the next year, and Stigand was finally established as archbishop in his place. Then followed 6 years of failure to receive recognition from Rome: Stephen IX died; the new Pope, Benedict X, granted Stigand his pall, but was himself deposed; then papal legates arrived in 1070 to depose Stigand, who died in prison.

Stigand is tonsured, and without mitre, which did not appear until XIIc.; he wears a plain *amice;* his famous *pall;* a chausuble, long in back, cut short in front; *alb* with large sleeves (undecorated until XIIIc.); *stole* with fringed ends: and he holds in his left hand the *maniple* (which, after XIIIc., will be worn over the left arm).

* See Ecc. Cost. for its necessity.

371

Harold's courtiers are shown with high-clipped Norman haircuts, which the Normans abandoned in favor of the longer hair of the Anglo-Saxons, a style which they took back with them to the Continent, where it remained standard for several hundred years.

William's cavalry is shown attacking the *testudo* (tortoise) shield-wall of the English, who fight still as described by Fridegarius at Zülpich in 612 A.D. "In their weapons and their manner of fighting, the bands of Angles, Jutes, and Saxons who overran Britain were more nearly similar to the Franks than to the German tribes who wandered south." The Franks fought at Poictiers as 200 years before, in deep column or wedge.*

Both armies wear conical "Norman" helmets with nosepieces, and hooded *hawberks* (*birnies*) of the chain mail, which had come from Scandinavia. Rings are either sewn on a foundation, or are linked together. There are overlapping scales of jazeran armor (see Norwegian tap., Ill. 411). Other hawberks are of quilted material or leather (small recumbent figures). These hawberks have short wide sleeves; they are of knee-length (in late XI.; lowered to calf, mid-XIIc; shortened again to the knee, mid-XIIIc.); they are slit, front and back, for comfort in riding, and so could have been tied about the leg, trouser fashion, as they seem sometimes to be.

The forearm is protected by the long sleeve of the under-garment, probably quilted against chafing. The legs are covered, and further protected by spiral or cross-gartered leather strips, above a separate shoe.

Archers, on both sides, are unprotected by mail, as they will continue to be until XIIIc.; they shoot from the earlier, low position.

Both armies show 7-foot spears with distinctive pennons, indicating rallying points; javelins; maces (one, with a knobbed head, can be seen flying); and swords with broad blades, stout plain cross-guards, and knobbed pommels. The English use, in addition, the Danish battle-axe.

Shields are of two types: the very long, kite-shaped shield, used by both armies, is slung by shoulder-straps, *gigues,* and held by a loop on the back, *enarmes.* The circular Danish shield, of wood with a center boss and reinforcements of iron is used only by the English.

The shields are decorated in armorial spirit, but the devices cannot be identified as those of any of the known Norman families of the end XIIc.; the same characters reappear carrying differently blazoned shields. Malmesbury (1119) tells of William, Earl of Poitou, "a giddy, unsettled kind of man," who after his return from the Crusades, "wallowed in the sty of vice, and rendered absurdities pleasant by a kind of satirical wit." Among several wonderful anecdotes, he relates that Poitou abducted the wife of a viscount; he was madly in love with her, and placed her figure on his shield, wishing to "bear her in battle in the same manner as she bore him at another time. Being reproved and excommunicated for this by Girard, bishop of Angoulême, and ordered to renounce this illicit love: 'You shall curl with a comb,' said he, 'the hair that has forsaken your forehead, ere I repudiate the countess,' thus taunting a man whose scanty hair required no comb." This is still decorative fantasy, not imposed on future earls of Poitou.

* J. Horace Round: *The Commune of London and other studies,* Archibald Constable & Co., London, 1899.

375

376

377

378

375-378. 1080-1150. German. (Library of St. Peter's Monastery.) Salzburg Antiphonary.

The new costume of women, and the new long gown of gentlemen (as well as the familiar short one) is shown beside the standardized long religious costume of saints, and two liturgical costumes: bishop and deacon.

The mitre of the bishop shows the beginning of the horned effect which it started to assume in the XIIc. He wears an elaborate pall over a chasuble; it has the embroidered edge which did not appear until XIc.; dalmatic, notched, but still sewed together at the sides; stole with the tabbed ends of IX-XIIIc.; alb, with the embroidered cuff which had come in the previous century; and embroidered liturgical shoes.

The deacon is wearing the dalmatic, distinctive vestment of deacons; alb; stole; and maniple, which until the XIIc. was sometimes carried in the left hand, sometimes worn, as it now is, and as he does, on the left arm.

The saints wear the straight tunic, and pallium, instead of the fitted garment and chlamys of the gentlemen, whose sleeves, while cut tight as before, are so long as to wrinkle up the fore-arm.

Job's wife wears the fitted and shortened upper tunic, with a decorative band across the hem, and sleeves widening, funnel-shaped, from a tight upper-arm. The cuff of the tight sleeve of her undertunic is also edged with embroidery, and she, as well as one of the gentlemen, wears the little scarf which appears to be worn at this time only in Germany. Her headdress is the turban which spread so rapidly westward from its introduction into Persia, only a century or two before.

Knighthood in Flower: XII Century

XII-XIV Century Background

THE soaring mediaeval religious impetus built cathedrals; it undertook crusades, which mingled and broadened the peoples of Europe and gave them great events to be celebrated in the Latin which was the common language of all educated people. Under the Templars' protection traders and preaching friars made their way East.

But feudal power, at its height in the Xc., was waning. The placing of the higher clergy among the nobility and the lower among the common people had led to the critical spirit out of which arose the mendicant orders. The struggle between attainment and privilege increased with the growing Universities of Paris, England and Italy, whose Latin-speaking scholars came, even on foot, from many walks of life and countries and wandered from university to university.

By the XIIIc. the centralized monarchical government had won over the feudal. Towns grew and were enfranchised, and the bourgeoisie who inhabited them rose into increasingly consolidated power. Guilds of craftsmen and merchants were formed; trade with Asia increased through the Mediterranean, opened up by travellers like Marco Polo; and the Baltic and North Sea trade was controlled by the Hanseatic League.

In the XIIc. a bourgeoise, no matter how rich her husband might be, was fined for dressing like a noblewoman. By the XIVc. she no longer imitated, she surpassed the noblewoman. This determination to wear what you chose developed the personal in costume; and fantasy and frivolity in dress followed the terror and masochism engendered by the plague of 1348-50, which reduced the population by a half. The resulting scarcity of workmen, who had been oppressed by the feudal nobility, as it simultaneously lost power and required wealth to keep pace with the bourgeoisie, made possible the revolutions of the common people in France and England in the second half of the XIVc.

A woolen mill had been established in Norwich in 1331 by Queen Philippa of Hainault with Flemish weavers, but the raw wool which formed so great a part of England's export trade was woven almost entirely by Flemish mills, and it was to protect this trade that the Hundred Years War was undertaken, as well as because of Edward III's claim to the throne of France, or the danger to the French crown inherent in the feudal Norman coastal possessions.

The slight alterations in costume between the XI-XIIc. have been discussed in the chapter "The Dark Ages."

The costume of Europe in the XIIIc., like its civilization, is French, and increasingly so as the court of Burgundy makes fashion in the XVc. The decline of the feudal nobility is clear by the time of the death of Charles the Bold of Burgundy in 1477.

Heraldry: Its Development

Heraldry is the science of armorial bearings as blazoned on the shield. O. Fr. *blason* originally meant shield. As armor improved in XIIc., shields became smaller; the embroidered design of the surcoat (hence "coat-of-arms," coat-armor), was transferred to the shield, and to the pennon and the trappings of the horse. Blasoning came to mean the bearings on the shield and, eventually, the description of the bearings.

Many factors entered into the development of armorial bearings:

A *Closed Helm* concealed the knights' identity. William the Conqueror had to remove his headpiece after the Battle of Hastings, to convince his men he still lived.

Seals, originally used by kings and great personages, came into universal use by gentry, colleges, guilds, in an age when few could write. The first signature of an English King is that of Richard II (British Mus. Cat. of Seals). These seals often show unblazoned shields, together with badges which, a generation later, are used to blazon shields. By mid-XIIIc. seals became armorial in character, and in 1520 seals and signatures were used together. In 1677 the signature, without seal, became legal on documents.

The *Crusades,* especially the third, were major influences. English, French and German knights had to be identified and rallied under a leader's symbol. Organization, distinguished deeds to be commemorated, brought the use of inherited surnames.

Inherited surnames related to the place of residence, the personal peculiarities, or the prowess of the bearer, his neighbors and tenants, or his office or occupation. Chamberlayne* cites great offices of honor from which surnames came: "Edward Fitz-Theobald long ago made Butler of Ireland, the Duke of Ormond, and his Ancestors, descending from him, took the surname Butler." Chamberlayne's own surname dated from 400 years before his time when Count Tankerville of Normandy was made chamberlain to the king of England. Saxons, Chamberlayne explains, often added "son" to the name or nickname of their father or mother. Saxon names were based on office: Spencer—steward; Kemp—O.E. soldier; place of abode: as Underhill, Atwood or Atwell, often abbreviated later to Wood, Wells; or color or complexion: Fairfax—fairlocks,* Pigot—speckled. With this, much more armorial use of *Canting or Punning Names as*: *Salle*—2 *sal*amanders *sal*ient in *sal*tire. Armorial bearings often gave a more accurate indication of relationship than surnames. The classic example is shown in the arms of the Lullings, originally Lucys, who had retained the canting Lucy coat-of-arms: 3 luces (pikes), after altering their surnames to that of their Yorkshire property.

Tournaments, of the XIIc. onwards: the decorative and social gaining over the utilitarian; magnificent pageants heightened by pennons and banners; streamered crests of knights; crests and armorial trappings of horse, all stemming from the original bearings of the shield. Opponents at tourneys were identified by the spectator's knowledge of blazoning, as football players are now recognized by the numbers on their jerseys. Blazonings began to be collected, codified, and controlled by heralds, and books on heraldry were published. If a gentleman owned a book, it was probably on heraldry; if he owned 10 books, half of them might well be about blazonings, like the library of a XVc. Paston, containing the first English book on heraldry (see English XIVc.)

The armorial shield was in actual use from the XIIc. to 1500. The Bayeux Tapestry, XIc., shows the beginnings of armorial bearings, on 3-foot kite-shaped shields. But these are not yet identifiable as inherited. In the first quarter of the XIIc. Paris armorers provided the English with shields decorated with designs, animals, lions, dragons, etc., but not yet differentiated arms.

The earliest known recognizable bearings were on the shield of Geoffrey of Anjou, 1129 (see illus.), the same golden lioncel used by his grandson, William Longueépée. From this time (when one man might use different arms at different times) to the XIVc., the science of heraldry was in the process of establishment. The rise of the great German tournaments was a major factor. It is stated by a XIVc. authority that the tournaments were open only to those bearings arms since four generations. The XIIIc. English tournaments were also important stimuli. In XIIIc. armorial bearings were hereditary in Spain and Italy, and beginning to be so in Sweden. Shields smaller.

The golden age of heraldry was the period from the XIVc. to 1500.

Coats of arms were established, hereditary; arms differed for sons, bastards, cousins, neighbors. By unwritten law, no two people bore the same arms. Froissart records the rage of Sir John Chandos at finding his arms born by the Marshal of the French King, Lord John de Clermont; because of the truce they had to wait until the next day to settle the matter by arms. Mounted men began to discard shields.

In 1347 we see the first English brass without shield (Wantone) and, in 1360, the last English brass showing shield as part of equipment (Aldeborough). The shield was retained by foot soldiers who did not bear coats-of-arms. To 1500 a lady bore her father's arms on her mantle; her husband's on her kirtle. After that she bore arms impaled; husband's dexter side, father's sinister; if arms appeared on mantle only, or were the same on mantle and kirtle, father's arms were used.

Blazoning developed functionally, out of structural elements of the wooden shield, covered with leather, tanned or furred, braced and reenforced, horizontally, vertically, diagonally with metal strips, edged and supplemented with metal bosses and knobs, all of which lent themselves to decoration. The heraldically undifferentiated crosses on the Crusader's shields, and the first application of bold simple color, followed the shield's structural divisions.

Crests, Wreaths, and Lambrequins. The rise of the tournament on the continent, particularly in Germany in the XIIc., and in England, in the XIIIc., favored the increasing use of the crest, surmounting the helm of the knight and the head of the horse; fans, feathers, birds, beasts, implements and objects of the same character as those used on badges and banners.

The earliest known crest is that on the second seal of Richard II; the lion of England mounted on a fan-shaped crest. But it was in Germany that the crest was most fantastically elaborated, with the back of the moulded leather cap, on which the crest was mounted, ending in flowing, scalloped *lambrequins.* The crest is separated from the coat-of-arms, above which it is set, by a crown, coronet, or rope-like twist of two colors. A lambrequin may fall from the crest to the shield, and the shield may be hung by "supporters," usually animal or plant. Supporters are personal; there may be several, and a person may change them during his lifetime. From James I's time, the coat-of-arms of England has been supported by the

---

* Edward Chamberlayne: The Present State of England, 38th ed., London, MDCCLV.
* A notably dark fairfax, the Parliamentary general (cf. Eng. XVIIc), was nicknamed "Black Tom."

Scottish unicorn and the English "lion" (actually a leopard since no more than one lion may be blazoned on a shield).

Badges and Banners: The use of badges and was cries* preceded that of armorial bearings. The banner bearing the lord's badge was enormously important as a rallying point†. In the reign of Edward III banners were large, increasing in size, to the 9-yard banner of a king and the 4-yard banner of a knight by the time of Henry VIII. Badges on garments helped to identify followers, who, in the XIVc., were otherwise not dressed alike until the liveries of the XIVc. guilds led to retainer's liveries in the XVc. (when they often remained armorial in character, after the XII-XIVc. passion for applying armorial decoration on everything had passed.) Froissart says that the Flemish soldiers from Alost, Grammont, Courtrai, and Bruges wore liveries to distinguish them from one another: some blue and yellow jackets; a welt of black on a red jacket; white chevron on a blue coat; green and blue; lozenged black and white; quartered red and white; all blue. In 1399, at the entry of Queen Isabella into Paris, 1200 citizens, mounted on horseback, dressed in uniforms of green and crimson, lined both sides of the road.

Richard of Bordeaux, in his tournament at Windsor, had 40 knights and 40 squires, clothed in green with a device of a white falcon.

Great families were as well-known and often referred to by their badges as by their names:

Broom (planta genista), from which the family name: Plantagenet.
Black Bull: Thos. P., Duke of Clarence.
Dun Bull; Blue Boar: Nevill.
White Boar: Humphrey, Duke of Gloucester.
Swan: Lancaster; from de Bohun.
Black Plume: Black Prince (P. of W. feather).
Silver Ostrich Feather: Beaufort.
Golden lion queue fourche: Suffolk.
Rouge Dragon: Wales.
Bear and Ragged Staff: Beauchamp, Earl of Warwick.
White Rose: York.
Red Rose: Lancaster; from Beaufort, Somerset badge) in Shakespeare.
Rouge Croix, of St. George: England.
Knots (resembling initial): Bourchier, Stafford, etc.
Silver Crescent: Percys of Northumberland.
Gold Portcullis: Lancaster; from Beaufort (end XVc. Tudor badge).

---

* France: God and Saint Denis; Montjoye Saint Denis; Bertrand du Guesclin: Saint Yves Guesclin.
** Banners also helped to approximate numbers. Froissart approximated the English and French armies opposed at Vironfosse: English; 74 banners, 230 pennons in all, 27,000 men, and King of England, Lord of Kus, Lord of Breda, Duke of Gueldres (nephew of King of England) and Sir John Heinault. French: 220 banners, 5,000 knights, 40,000 common soldiers, 4 Kings, 6 Dukes, and 26 Earls.

Collars: Heavy chains about the neck were an important part of costume from XIIc., particularly during XIV-XVc. They were, logically, utilized as marks of respect, fealty, and alliance.

There were the collars of orders of knighthood, such as: mid-XIVc. Order of the Garter, with its forms: Garter; collar of knots and roses with an enamelled pendant of St. George mounted (dates from Henry XIII); and the Lesser George pendant, showing St. George within the oval of a purple garter. 1362. Order of the Annunziata, founded by Amadeus VI of Savoy: collar of love-knots and roses. 1429-30. Order of the Golden Fleece, established by Philip of Burgundy: collar of fire-stones and steels; pendant fleece. 1469. Order of Saint-Michel, of Louis XI: linked cockle shells. 1578. Order of the Saint-Esprit, of Henry III of France: collar of HL and fleurs-de-luce; gold and white Maltese cross pendant with an outstretched white dove; often hung on blue ribbon.

There were also personal collars, as: XIIIc. Broom-cod collar of Charles V, sent Richard II by Charles VI, and worn by Henry VI, combined with the SS collar, signifying his claims to both kingdoms. XIVc. SS collar of the House of Lancaster. The most famous English collar, from its inception, while Henry IV was still Bolingbroke, it carried the White Swan of Bohun as its pendant. The SS collar was also worn by women. End XVc. The SS collar of Henry VII; rose or portcullis pendant. XVIc. Legal dignitaries also wear the SS collar; the Lord Chief Justice wears it today. Since 1545. Lord Mayors of London wear the SS collar; not granted them, but bequeathed by former mayors. Various other collars are worn by the mayors, of other cities, as: the triple chain, worn since 1670 by the Lord Mayor of York. Kings-of-Arms and Heralds still wear the SS collar.

The collars of the House of York were: Falcon and Fetterlock. Third quarter of the XVc. Suns and Roses; as pendants, the White Lion of March, the Bull of Clare, the White Boar of Richard II. 1485. Red and White Roses, of Lancaster and York combined into Tudor Rose of Henry VII. XVc. Collar of the White Hart, of Richard II; hart enclosed in park palings.

HERALDIC OFFICERS: "ANCIENTS"

Heralds had existed, as messengers, before armorial bearings; another facet of their work grew out of the XIIc. minstrels, who sang the deeds of victors after combat. Heralds wore the badge of their masters, and while on errands of war and peace, the person of the herald, as his master's proxy, was considered sacred, although the herald himself was a person of no rank whatsoever. As armorial bearings came into use, heraldic officers were concerned with the direction of tournaments, the counting and recognition of those killed in battle,* the funerals of peers and prelates, and questions of precedence. They controlled the use and recording of coats-of-arms, and collected information, in England, on regularly scheduled "visitations" through the counties.

English heraldry surpassed that of any other country, even arms-loving Germany, in its perfection of detail. All the heraldic officers seem to have been established early in the XIIIc. The Norroy King-of-Arms dates from late in the XIIIc. But the first picture of a herald bearing his master's blazon is of Flemish herald Gelré, 1369. The French King-of-Arms, Montjoye, with 10 heralds and poursuivants, was established by Charles IV in 1406, before the incorporation of the English College of Heralds by Henry V. in 1420.

The position of heralds was well established in England by 1420. In 1500 came the institution of ambassadors who took over many functions from heraldic officers; the use of private heraldic officers died out by the middle of the XVIc. and by the end of XVIIc. heraldic "Visitations" ceased.

Space for a striking display of the master's badge was first found on a short, wide mantle (see Gelré, Flemish 1369), such as that of the Blue Mantle poursuivant, until the XVc. introduction of the *tabard*. The wide loose front and back sections of the tabard offered such a suitable background for display that the tabard has remained the distinc-

tive garment of heraldic officers (see Beauchamp, Warwick Pageant), together with the baton of office (a rod or sceptre) and, in England, the SS collar; worn by the King-of-Arms (gold), heralds (silver); not by poursuivants. At coronations only, the Garter King-of-Arms wears a crown.

Heraldic officers were of 3 sorts: Kings-of-Arms, heralds, and poursuivants. Dukes and marquises were served, theoretically, by a herald and a poursuivant; barons and bannerets, by a poursuivant only. Heralds served as assistants and deputies of the Kings-of-Arms, and were named from places as: Leicester, Windsor, or the Hereford Herald of Humphfrey de Bohun, earl of Hereford. It was as Constable of Acquitaine that Sir Chandos kept the Chandos Herald. The names of heralds also signified their master's foreign possessions, as: Agincourt or Guyenne; or their pretensions, as: Jerusalem King-of-Arms.

Poursuivants were apprentice heralds; named from the badges of the house they served, as Vert-Eagle, poursuivant of Richard Nevill, earl of Salisbury; and the Crescent and Esperance, poursuivants of the Percys of Northumberland, the latter named from a Percy war-cry. Private heralds disappeared by the time of Elizabeth.

* After the battle of Crecy, Sir Reginald Cobham and Lord Stafford, with 3 heralds to examine arms and 2 secretaries to write down names, enumerated as dead 11 princes, 1200 knights, and 30,000 common soldiers. (Froissart.)

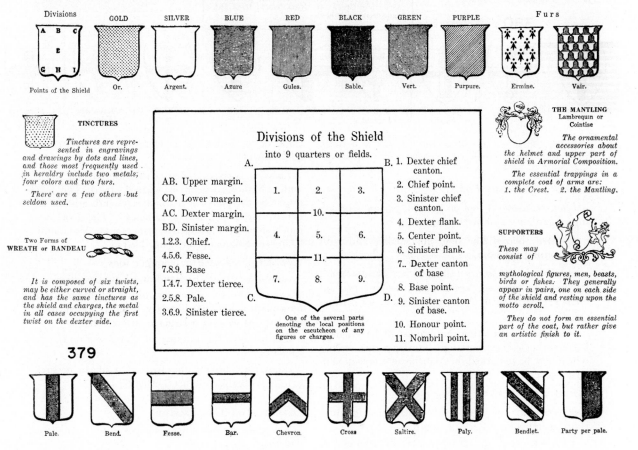

Divisions

| Points of the Shield | GOLD Or. | SILVER Argent. | BLUE Azure. | RED Gules. | BLACK Sable. | GREEN Vert. | PURPLE Purpure. | **Furs** Ermine. | Vair. |

TINCTURES

Tinctures are represented in engravings and drawings by dots and lines, and those most frequently used in heraldry include two metals; four colors and two furs.

There are a few others but seldom used.

Two Forms of
WREATH or BANDEAU

It is composed of six twists, may be either curved or straight, and has the same tinctures as the shield and charges, the metal in all cases occupying the first twist on the dexter side.

379

Divisions of the Shield
into 9 quarters or fields.

AB. Upper margin.
CD. Lower margin.
AC. Dexter margin.
BD. Sinister margin.
1.2.3. Chief.
4.5.6. Fesse.
7.8.9. Base
1.4.7. Dexter tierce.
2.5.8. Pale.
3.6.9. Sinister tierce.

One of the several parts denoting the local positions on the escutcheon of any figures or charges.

B. 1. Dexter chief canton.
2. Chief point.
3. Sinister chief canton.
4. Dexter flank.
5. Center point.
6. Sinister flank.
7.. Dexter canton of base.
8. Base point.
9. Sinister canton of base.
10. Honour point.
11. Nombril point.

THE MANTLING
Lambrequin or Cointise

The ornamental accessories about the helmet and upper part of shield in Armorial Composition.

The essential trappings in a complete coat of arms are: 1. the Crest. 2. the Mantling.

SUPPORTERS

These may consist of

mythological figures, men, beasts, birds or fishes. They generally appear in pairs, one on each side of the shield and resting upon the motto scroll.

They do not form an essential part of the coat, but rather give an artistic finish to it.

| Pale. | Bend. | Fesse. | Bar. | Chevron. | Cross | Saltire. | Paly. | Bendlet. | Party per pale. |

Color is never applied on color, nor metal on metal. The fur *vair* is *argent* and *azure* unless specifically blazoned. *Gules* (red) and *azure* (blue) come from the Persian *gúl* and *lâzurd* (lapis-lazuli), and show Arab influence from the Crusades.

The *Ordinaries,* conventional charges commonly found, are shown at bottom, Ill. 379. They are divided by border lines, *indented, engrailed,* etc., shown on Ill. 382.

The *Field* (background) may be semé (powdered or sown) with fleurs-de-lys, as in the old arms of France, crosslets, lozenges, etc. Crosses occur in great variety.

| A Cross Pierced | A Cross Voided | A Cross Surmounted | Couped and Surmounted Voided | Couped Fimbriated | Cross Quartered | Plain Cross Watered | Cross Interlaced | Quarterly Quartered |

 THE FILE OR LABEL, *Mark of the eldest son*

 THE CRESCENT, *The second son's mark*

 THE MULLET, *The third son's mark*

 THE MARTLET, *The fourth son's mark*

 THE ANNUET, *The fifth son's mark*

THE FLEUR-DE-LYS, *The sixth son's mark*

 THE ROSE, *The seventh son's mark*

 THE CROSS MOLINE, *The eighth son's mark*

THE OCTOFOIL, *The ninth son's mark*

380

Distinguishing marks applied to a Coat-of-Arms to indicate the various branches or cadets of a family

MARKS OF CADENCY

1, Cross of Calvery, a cross on three steps. 2, Latin Cross, a cross the transverse beam of which is placed at one-third the distance from the top of the perpendicular portion. supposed to be the form of cross on which Christ suffered. 3, Tau Cross, (so called from being formed like the Greek letter r, tau), or cross of St. Anthony, one of the most ancient forms of the cross. 4, Cross of Lorraine. 5, Patriarchal Cross. 6, St. Andrew's Cross, the form of cross on which St. Andrew, the national saint of Scotland, is said to have suffered. 7, Greek Cross, or cross of St. George. the national saint of England, the red cross which appears on British flags. 8, Papal Cross. 9, Cross nowy quadrat, that is, having a square expansion in the center. 10, Maltese Cross, formed of four arrow-heads meeting at the points; the badge of the Knights of Malta. 11, Cross fourchée or forked. 12, Cross pattée or formée. 13, Cross potent or Jerusalem Cross. 14, Cross fleury, from the fleur de lis at its ends.

LINES USED TO DIVIDE THE SHIELD

〰〰	Engrailed
〜〜	Invected
⌒	Ondé
2525252525	Nebulé
⋀⋀⋀	Indented
⋀⋀	Dancette (3 indentations)
⊓⊔⊓⊔	Embattled
525252525	Potent
⌐⌐⌐	Raguly
⊐⊏⊐⊏	Dovetailed
⋀⋀⋀⋀⋀⋀	Rayonne
⌒	Nowy
⊓	Escartelé
⌐_	Angled
⟋	Bevelled

| Cross Pometty | Cross Fleury | Quartered Fleury | Cross Crossed | Cross Nowey | Cross Degraded | Cross Fusilly | Couped and Fitched | Humetty |

Other charges: *Trees, Leaves and Flowers;* naturalistic, and conventionalized (as cinquefoils, fleurs-de-lys, etc.)

Beasts, Birds, and Fish:

Lion; rampant—1 foot on ground; passant—prowling; regardant—looking backward.

Leopard: blazed like lion, but smaller and with face fronting beholder.

Others, often *Canting* (allusive) as: Mauleverer—greyhound, "leverer"; Veel—calves; Griffin—griffon; Shelley—whelk shell; Arundel—martlets, for "hirondel."

Implements: also often canting, as: Malet—mallet; Ferrers—horseshoes; Forester—hunting horn—among which may be remarked the Manche, or conventionalized sleeve.

Roundels, Annulets, Lozenges, etc.

Differenced: to indicate descent, consanguinity, fealty, neighboring place of origin.

This was done in various ways: by changes in color, or in border-line, as engrailed for invected, by additions of:

Label, a horizontal strip across top part of shield, with 3-5 short dependent vertical strips. The label might be decorated in definite ways indicative of order of birth, (marks of cadency). The label was much used by Plantagenet princes (see Monmouth, Clarence; Salzman, Sur. Eng. Hist).

border, often used by younger sons

canton, especially England and Low Countries

escutcheons, of ordinaries, of small charges-seme-on a plain field. That is to say, usually a small quartered shield set over a larger quartered shield.

diminishing, the number of charges; France, not England

quartering, usually the arms of a queen or great heiress with those of her husband.

OFFICIALS AND ORGANIZATIONS

Religious organizations, colleges, guilds and cities had their coats-of-arms

Archbishops and bishops used their own arms impaled on those of their see (Eng.); sometimes combined, quarterly, or impaled (Continent, and Grand Masters of Hospitallers and Teutonic Knights)

Kings-of-Arms use official arms, as Garter King-of-Arms: argent, St. Georges cross on a chief azure an open crown within the garter, between a lion of England and a fleur-de-lys or.

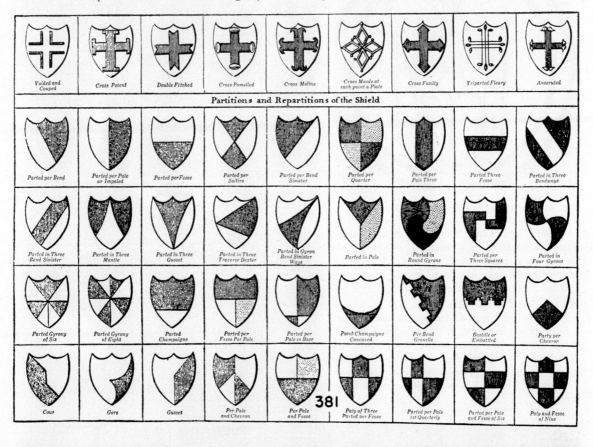

Voided and Couped	Cross Potent	Double Fitched	Cross Pomelled	Cross Moline	Cross Masde at each point a Plate	Cross Fusilly	Triparted Fleury	Anseruted

Partitions and Repartitions of the Shield

Parted per Bend	Parted per Pale or Impaled	Parted per Fesse	Parted per Saltire	Parted per Bend Sinister	Parted per Quarter	Parted per Pale Three	Parted Three Fesse	Parted in Three Bendways
Parted in Three Bend Sinister	Parted in Three Mantle	Parted in Three Gusset	Parted in Three Traverse Dexter	Parted in Gyron Bend Sinister Ways	Parted in Pale	Parted in Round Gyrons	Parted per Three Squares	Parted in Four Gyrons
Parted Gyrony of Six	Parted Gyrony of Eight	Parted Champaigne	Parted per Fesse Per Pale	Parted per Pale in Base	Point Champaigne Concaved	Per Bend Grenelle	Bastille or Embattled	Party per Chevron
Cour	Gore	Gusset	Per Pale and Chevron	Per Pale and Fesse	Paly of Three Parted per Fesse	Parted per Pale 1st Quarterly	Parted per Pale and Fesse of Six	Paly and Fesse of Nine

381

Chief	Chief Angled	Chief Chappé	Chief Bevelled	Chief Lowered	Chief Couped	Chief Supported	Chief Surmounted	Chief Corfu
Chief Rebated	Chief Embattled	Chief Potent	Chief Urdec	Chief Nebulé	Chief Engrailed	Chief One Indent	Chief One Label	Chief Arched
Chief Couvert	Chief Wavey	Chief Enmanche	Chief Double Arched	Chief Inverted	Chief Indented	Chief Charged with a Chapournet	Chief Quartered	Chief Point in Point
Chief Rayonne	Chief Vestu	Chief Vestu Sinister	Chasse	Chief Escartelé	Chief with One Embattlement	Chief Bevellways Couped	Chief Inclaved	Chief Nowed
Chief Dovetailed	Ajoure	Bar	Cloet	Barrulet	Cloetted	Bars Gemel	Barry of Ten	Brettled

382

383. XIIc. 1160-70. English. (Winchester Cath.)

Great Bible of Winchester: Queen. The "manche" of armorial blazoning is descended from the sleeve with a suddenly widened cuff. Queens are represented in very close-fitting gowns, girded very low, in a dipping line, by a knotted sash; mantle always worn.

384-385. 1160-70. (Morgan Library, 619.)

Scenes in the life of David and Samuel. From a folio Bible, executed at St. Swithin's Priory, Winchester, by the artist of the "Great Bible of Winchester," in gradations of cobalt blue; deep, strong vermilion; egg shell colors, from off-white to deep brown; with touches of a dulled light green.

Courtesy of Morgan Library (384-385).

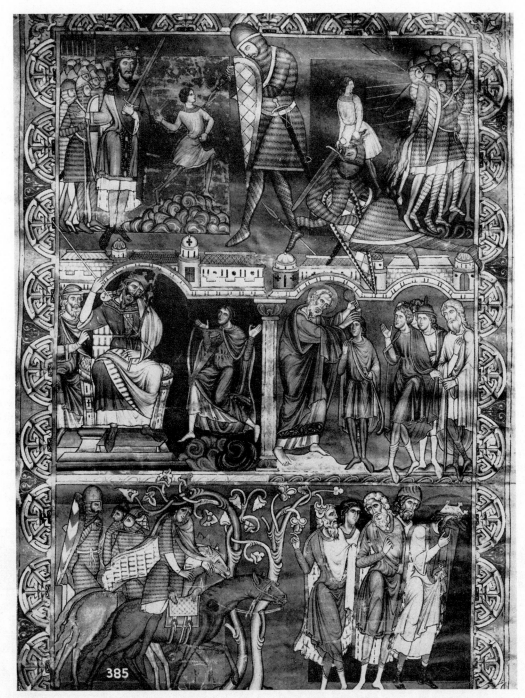

385

The women's costumes show the new sleeve, widening rapidly at the bottom, in a variety of cuts, one of which is so long that it must be turned back (lower l. corner).

The bishop's mitre shows budding horns; amice, as yet, undecorated; chasuble, bordered (since Xc.); pall; dalmatic; embroidered and fringed stole (IX-XIIc. shape); alb. The long garments worn by the saints are the standardized costume allotted to them since Roman times, and not to be confused with the long fitted garments of the gentry.

The King wears the rich dalmatic which came into regal English use in 1100 with Henry I. His ceremonial garments, like those worn by his gentlemen on state occasions, are longer; the hem of the long-sleeved under-tunic often hangs below that of the short upper tunic, or *hawberk*, in the general elaboration, accompanied by downward movement, which followed the Conquest. The principal hat worn by gentlemen is shaped like the XIc. soldier's *chapel-de-fer,* or the Greek *petasus.*

The most spectacular evidence of the new lavishness is in the use of pieced small furs, ermine and miniver, to line both rectangular and circular capes, which fastened on right shoulder or at center. The Scotch King Malcolm made presents in 1074 of pelisses and mantles of "purple" sable skins, gray skins, and ermine, as well as gold and silver vessels.

There is a parallel growth of interest in all-over patterns on garments (m. fig. in both lower right corners); both are allied with the rise of patterned armorial bearings.

Girdles are knotted at center front, with ends hanging, especially over hawberk and unbloused tunics which permit the effect to be seen.

William of Malmesbury records William II's anxiety, c. 1093, that his clothes should be extravagant, and describes his anger if any were bought at a low price. Men's hair flowed. There were repeated ordinances, forbidding or trying to control the length of the curved points of shoes (which Foulke of Anjou is supposed to have used to hide his deformed feet). "Then the model for young men was to rival women in delicacy of person, to mince their gait, to walk with loose gestures and half-naked, enervated and effeminate. A fierce flame of evil burst forth from what the King conceived to be liberty."

Henry I (1119) was harangued by Serlo, bishop of Sens, on his arrival in Normandy, upon the enormities of the time, one of which was "the bushiness of men's beards, which resembled Saracen's rather than Christian's, and which he supposed they would not clip lest the stumps should prick their mistress' faces; another was their long locks. Henry immediately, to show his submission and repentance, submitted his bushy honor to the bishop, who taking a pair of shears from his trunk, trims his majesty and several of the principal nobility with his own hands." The king returned from Normandy, still wearing his long locks, but his conscience bothered him, he dreamed of strangling by his hair, awoke, and chopped it off. All the knights copied this for a year or so; then went back to vying with women in length of locks, adding false hair if necessary.

Hose and shoes became more elaborate; the decorated shoes of the king are slit up the instep; the tops of loose wrinkled sock-boots are often turned down to show a lining of different color; the hose are now frequently decorated after the manner of the knight's spiral leg-wrappings, which now have feet, not separate shoes. Chain-mail is linked in sophisticated patterns. Chain hose (*chausses*) are used around 1150, as are also quilted or leather puttee-like wrappings, which they supersede in 1190.

The knight's hawberk, now almost invariably of mail, has a shorter, fuller skirt, eliminating the need for slits; the sleeves are typically long, ending in mittens, though occasionally still short, showing the sleeve of the *gambeson* beneath. The *coif-de-mailles* now surrounds the face closely, covering the chin, so that the helm is not always worn. The helm becomes increasingly less conical, and at the end of the century is supplanted by the rounded helm, still with nasal, which has appeared about 1150. The shield, still kite-shaped, is becoming shorter; it can no longer serve as a stretcher; its top is becoming flattened by 1180, and the boss disappears as armorial blazonings come to decorate the shield. The sword-guard has become lighter, and the knobbed ends curve away from the hand to ward the opponent's blade.

386

386. XIIc., before 1170. English. (Canterbury Cathedral.)

Canterbury Psalter. This psalter, written at Christ Church, Canterbury, by the scribe Eadwine, contains interlinear versions of the Psalms in French and Anglo-Saxon; it is the first psalter in French. The chasuble of the tonsured ecclesiastic has a forked cross, and is longer in back, over a checkered dalmatic. The warriors and shepherds are familiar; the vertical slit down the front of the tunic, stressed by bands, is very different from the superhumeral collar we have been seeing.

387. XIIc., 1180-90. English. (Canterbury Cathedral. St. Gabriel's Chapel.)

Wall painting: *Birth and christening of St. John the Baptist*. Ceremonial tunics, longer; longer capes, rectangular and circular, one hooded, all inclined toward center-front closing; decorated hose; studded shoes in sandal designs; sashes, knotted in front and decorated; hat like Greek petasus (see also on Winchester leafs, Ills. 384-85).

388-390. Early XIIc. French. (Vezelay.)

Vezelay, an abbey church in XIc., was added to in 1125-32, and in 1198-1206. St. Bernard preached the 2nd Crusade and Richard Coeur de Lion assumed the crown there.

These reliefs show many XIIc. developments: tightening upper body, combined with lengthening. The hanging sleeve of the seated figure, if pushed up, would give another typical effect of crinkling. Excessively prolonged sleeves were a fashion of 1100-60.

The tunic shows the characteristic crinkling; probably deliberately pleated; center-front and diagonal closing combined is typical of the century and ends abruptly with the XIIIc. Edges finished with narrow dotted or pierced borders of the early XIIc. Cape edges overlapped and were pinned together with a fibula in Byzantine days and long after; now barely meet and seem to roll away from each other.

Shoes have sandal-like fenestrations; sock-boots of 388 thrust into straps of wonderful, high wooden pattens for protection against mud.

391. XIIc. French. (Arles, St. Trophime, Exterior Portal.)

Procession of men: tunics to mid-calf, with dotted borders; decorated sock-boots; their hands covered in the old Byzantine fashion, which is responsible for the prolonged sleeve of the XIIc. tunic.

392-393. c. 1128. French. (Angouleme, Cathedral of St. Peter, Facade.)

Knights with long, floating veils from conical helmets; hooded shirts, apparently of scale-mail; heavier pike held at lower, horizontal position.

388

389

390

39[1]

394. First half XIIc. French, from St. Etienne Ch. (Toulouse Museum.)

Herodias and Salome: bearded king, center-parted long hair; 2 tunics, tight wrinkled length; one, like cape, decorated with orphreys. Virgin, with long, flowing hair and fillet; trailing clinging tunic; decorated shoes.

395. First half XIIc. French. (Clermont-Ferrand, Notre Dame du Port.)

Psychomania: knights in long tunics; mail hawberks of various patterns; one wears familiar conical helmet; other, the newer chapel-de-fer.

396. XIIc. 1129-51. French. (Mans Museum.)

Limoges enamel memorial plate: *Geoffrey of An-*

jou as lawgiver. "Martel," as Geoffrey was called before he became earl of Anjou at his marriage, having seized a castle and been warned of its owner's rage, said, "he would show the world at large how much an Angevin could excel a Norman in battle, at the same time, with unparallelled insolence, describing the color of his horse and the devices on the arms he meant to use."* These devices were still a matter of personal fancy, to be changed at will, but permanency began during his lifetime.

* William of Malmsbury in 1125.

The shield he uses here was given him by Henry I of England, on Geoffrey's marriage to his daughter Matilda, widow of the German emperor, in 1129. It bears the first known recognizable armorial bearings: the three golden lioncels carried by Geoffrey's bastard grandson, William of the Long Sword.

It was Geoffrey's habit of wearing a sprig of broom (*planta genista*) in his cap (see Scotch dress, XIXc.) which gave his descendants the surname of Plantagenet. The shield still protects the entire body; the central boss and functional cross still show. Helm: still

the modified phrygian-conical of the Conquest; but without the nasal, which was proved to have certain disadvantages, as when Stephen was captured and held by the nasal of his helmet at Lincoln in 1139. Sword; drawn, as lawgiver, is longer and more tapering. Mantle: lined with miniver. Two tunics, both long and both decorated with gold orphreys. Beard, long hair.

397. Mid-XIIc. French. (Chartres Cathedral, Royal Portal.)

The Twins: Without hawberk, showing the long tunic split up the front for convenience. In 1370, Sir John Chandos, tripping on his long tunic, was unable to avoid his death-wound. Shield: shorter; top flattened; has lost boss, but decoration is still based on construction, and is not yet armorial. Hair long, royal family till mid-XIIc.; then general.

398. Mid-XIIc. French, from N. D. de Corbeil. (Louvre.)

The Queen of Sheba. Dressed in the height of early mediaeval elegance. Hair: parted in the middle, hangs in four long tresses, bound in pairs and wound with colored and golden ribbons. False hair was worn by both men and women. Cape: long, semi-circular; orphrey along selvage edge. Upper tunic: bodice fitted, knitted or smocked. Queens wear two belts: one at normal waistline; another at hips, covering seam where full, trailing skirt is gathered onto the bodice; fastening at center-front by elaborately twisted and knotted cords, falling below the knees. Kirtle:

finely pleated and embroidered, shows above the upper tunic's neckline (considerably lowered, richly decorated, and massively clasped), and at the fitted wrist-length undersleeve. The kirtle sleeve is funnel-shaped, edged with fine pleating.

399. XIIc. French., from Bourges Cathedral. (Berri Mus.)
Queen. Tightly laced bodice, richly bordered, with great brooch; deep, pleated bag-sleeves; finely pleated skirt, widened by fan-shaped, coarsely pleated sections at the sides.

400. XIIc. French., from Bourges Cathedral. (Berri Mus.)
Bishop: unusual mitre, with one horn, worn in front; chasuble with Y-orphreys; decorated stole of modern shape; alb with large apparels above hem, and decorated cuff.

401. Mid-XIIc. French. (Chartres Cathedral.)
Queen of Juda. Hair hidden under small rectangular veil. Fibula on left breast, characteristic of Semitic dress since Hittite times, nearly one and a half millenia before. Upper tunic fitted at the shoulders with three small tucks, caught by buttons; under-tunic exquisitely pleated and caught by a smaller fibula. (See Ills. 25, 273.)

402. XIIc. Italian-Byzantine.

Ornaments; precious metals, and lead. Upper left, Saint George: wearing a practically Roman cuirasse with shoulder-lappets as a hawberk, over long tunic, ring-mail chausses with prick-spurs and knee-plates. Greek anchor cross on small kite-shaped shield.

Upper right, Noblewoman (seated, like Matilda on a sausage-shaped cushion, set on a chair similar to that of the King, St. Angelo in Formis). Her knees are draped with a rectangularly decorated table, possibly to protect her gown, since she wears a gauntlet, on which the claws of the hawk still show. Upper tunic, sleeveless, girdled, decorated with a scale design, is cut deep in the armhole and is split apart below the waist, to show the herring-bone design of the under tunic, which has shaped Byzantine sleeves and a band down the center-front.

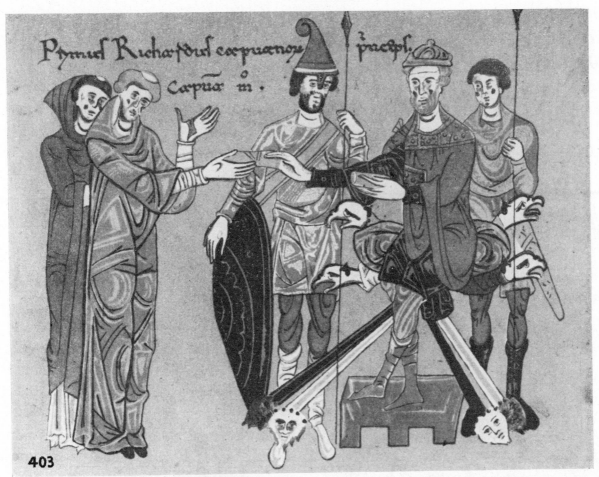

403

404

round nor kite-shaped, wears high, phrygian-conical helmet with nasal. Attendant with short wide sword, one monk wear thrown-back cowls.

404. XIIc. Italian. (Morgan Library, Mc. 493.)

Vita Mathildis, by Donizo, her chaplain. Matilda, Countess of Tuscany (1046-1115), was heiress to the greatest estate in Italy, which, deeded by her to the Papacy, formed the largest part of its temporal possessions. Courageous, steadfast and learned, she led her armies into battle on the side of the Guelphs (Papal) against the Ghibellines (Empire), and is known as "The Great Countess." Under her rule, the guilds, out of which the Republic grew, began to be established, and Florence started its rise.

Her wonderful conical hat is set over a veil, the arrangement of which indicates new tendencies; it surrounds the face, and is tucked under another garment at the neck. Her cape, in respect to its asymmetry, and the character of its embroidery, may be compared to those in Ill. 364, 365, 414. The embroidered sleeve of her upper tunic is widely funnel-shaped, but not notably tight in the upper arm. This is, in all its elements, the costume of a very rich and very great lady, less concerned with fashion than with a personal expression of suitable and dignified beauty and comfort.

Donizo, her chaplain, tonsured, wears his every-day tunic and sensible shoes. The body-guard's shoes show the new tendency to point.

403. XIIc. Italian. (St. Angelo in Formis.) Miniatures from the Register.

King's costume; impure and muddled Byzantine influences. Mantle has archaic shoulder fastening; tablion of the chlamys is gathered onto a sort of fitted superhumeral yoke. All legwear loose-fitting. The soldier whose shield is neither

405

406

407

408

405-408. XIIc. 1110-20. German. Stuttgart. (Landesbibliothek.) Stuttgart Passionale.

Three volumes illuminated at the Monastery of Hirsau. 405-406. Martyrdoms: St. Alban's executioner shows the new use of fur (see Ills. 384-85), in a pelisse, with the fabric of the garment serving as lining, and the fur mounted decoratively upon it. St. Alban's collar shows the new interest, both in the vertical line and in the center-front. His has a practical opening-slit; on wider collars the effect of the dependent center block is still often merely decorative. St. Alban's own costume, and those of the torturers

on the other plate, also show lengthening male garments; width introduced at hips by inverted V-shaped insertions; wider sleeves.

Two early Popes: represented in contemporary German dress, with archaic effects.

407. Pope Alexander I, "fifth in line from St. Peter"; outmoded form of mitre, with the daily dress of a dignified German gentleman. Tonsured ecclesiastics with him wear similar, shorter tunics.

408. St. Felix wears a long garment with diagonal neck closing of XIIc; combines features of dalmatic and Imperial regalia.

409

DNE DNE APERI NOBI

409. XIIc. German. School of Metz. (Berlin State Museum. Ms. 78A4.)

Foolish virgins: with flowing hair of unmarried women, some with fillets. Their gowns are as Byzantine as those shown in Ills. 1414-1417, but an interesting comparison may be made with the costume of Geoffrey (Ill. 396), in respect to the disposition and character of the small decorative motifs, and of the bar, not border, of embroidery across thigh of second figure from the left.

410. XIIc. Swiss. (Engelberg Monastery Library. Cod. 14.)

The lady who has something to confess wears her veil as a turban, with the end passed under the chin, barbette-fashion. Bodice, tight under the arms, widening immediately, to permit bloused effect and side fullness. Very long pleated XIIc cuffs, set below elbow of very tight sleeve. Her urgent friend wears a barbette under her chin (appeared mid-XIIc.), with a fillet. Tight bodice achieved by back lacing. Skirt, long, almost circular; gores added immediately below waist. Sleeves, very tight, with fantastically long pleated hanging bands laid across arm below elbow.

411. XIIc. Norwegian, from Baldishol Church. (Museum of Art and Industry, Oslo.)

Knight in ring-mail such as the Danes had brought to England in IXc., and the Scandinavians to Normandy in the Xc. Long hawberk, with coif-de-mailles which does not protect chin, and long sleeves which do not end in mittens. Conical helm with nasal. Prick spurs, lengthening pointed toes. Kite-shaped shield, decorated, possibly armorial.

410

411

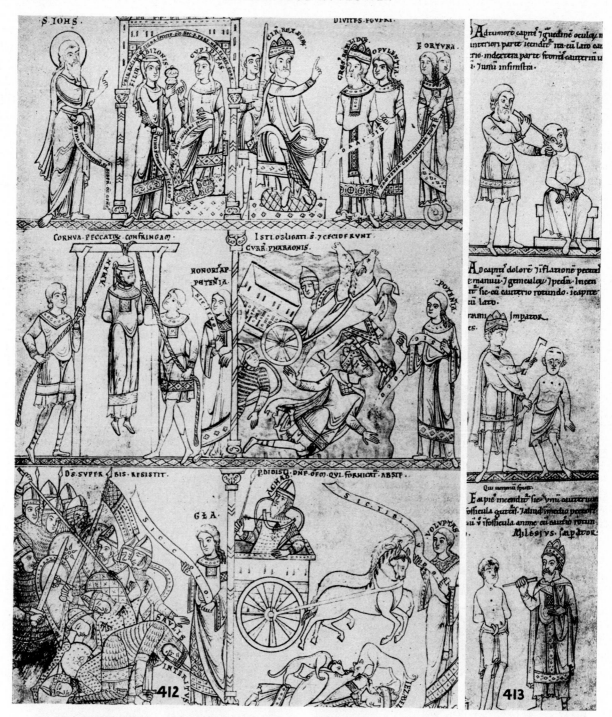

412, 413. XIIc. German. Regensburg (Ratisbon). Medical Examination Books.

412. Allegorical: Dress of both sexes shows increasing interest in center-front of top of bodice; as a vertical slit develops below base of neck, width of round collar will be seen to decrease. Decorated girdles close at center-front or side. Skirt of upper tunic is tucked into girdle on one side, giving a diagonal line to hem, showing garment beneath. For the rich, a third tunic appears; if three are worn, edge of uppermost is left plain; middle one of heavy, brocaded stuff, narrow in cut is bordered; lowest is full and plain, usually of linen. Unmarried women: bare, center-parted hair; wives: small draped and twisted veils.

Knights: hoods of mail, not enclosing chin, and frequently separate from short-sleeved hawberks. These, as well as chausses, made of linked mail, in many designs; of overlapping plates; and of studded cuir-bouilli. These are used, in combination, in the armor of one knight. Hawberks have heavy decoratively banded hems; are worn over full, slightly longer tunics. Shields: round, or knee-length and kite-shaped, with rounded or flattened tops. Helmets: conical, phrygian, or rounded. Swords: blade more pointed. Spears. Pennon.

413. Surgical operations: doctors and patients. Unnamed surgeons, dressed in short tunics. Hippocrates and Aesculapius: capes and embroidered hems. Those wearing crowns are referred to as Imperator, indicating founders of schools of medicine.

414-417. Alsatian. 1180. (Strassburg Library.)

Hortus Deliciarum, by the Abbess Herrade de Landsburg (fl. 1167-95), one of the very first encyclopaedias, almost entirely destroyed by fire in 1870.

414. King: standardized Xc. Byzantine costume, but with new fur lining in cape.

Bishop: mitre set in the new way, twisted so that the horns are at front and back, instead of at either side; pall; chasuble; dalmatic, with remnants of fringe decoration on clavi; fringed stole, of new straight shape; alb.

Two monks: one, with oblong mantle, given shape by being looped up at the shoulder; the other, cowled with interesting treatment of side-seam fastening. Men: servants wear shorter garments, closer fitting sleeves, than gentlemen; and do not wear mantles.

415. *Superba* and knights. The bodice of her full-skirted, trailing gown is laced tight at the sides; her sleeves have the new full cuff falling suddenly from a tight sleeve decorated with the persistent Byzantine

upper-arm band. Veil knotted into high turban with flowing ends; it was inevitable, in a century of such impetuous adventureousness in costume, that the susceptibility of the ends of the veil to arrangement should lead to such headdresses as those of the females of the Swiss plate (410). The toes of her decorated shoes show the effect of the new preoccupation with length.

The helms of the knights, all with nasal, show both the phrygian-conical form and the newer rounded top; and their shields, still long and kite-shaped, the new flattened top. Their knee-length hawberks of linked mail, slit in front, though showing increased width toward the hem, have the coif-de-mailles high about the chin, and completely developed fingers, not mittens. The front-knotted sash with its long ends hanging below the bloused tunic has led, especially on the new fitted garments where most effective, to an interest in belts which will increase during several centuries. Here the hanging-knot motif is used

Redder deus me... cedd laboni scort... suo... et deducer eo...in ... via mirabili

Sci ... iusti in d... gaudent cuoc ... elegit deus in here ... bitarem sibi

416

417

as the means of fastening a wide flat belt. The under-tunic with trailing, gored fullness is shown in its most extravagantly inconvenient form;* it will have to be slit, and is in Ill. 397.

416-417. Our Lord, in dalmatic and pallium, and 12 male figures in charming variations of standardized

Byzantine dress which had perhaps been revived by the Crusades (compare tunic, sleeve in Ill. 355).
* Two centuries later (1370), Sir John Chandos, trip-ping on ice, will entangle his legs in his "large robe which fell to his feet, blazoned with his arms on white sarcenet" (of his surcoat), stumble, and unable to avoid a lance thrust by a French squire, will meet his death. (Froissart)

418

419

418-419. Late XIIc. Swiss. (Morgan Library. M. 645.)

St. George and St. Oswald. Hem of tunic shows early use of "dagging," which started in Germany in the last third of XIIc., and spread rapidly. The use of dagging, particolor, and fur, gives to the costume of the Middle Ages its own particular character. A fur design is used to decorate St. Oswald's hose, and St. George's shoes have the sandal-patterned decoration brought by the revival of Byzantine fashions.

420-421. XIIIc. Norwegian. (British Mus.)

Chessmen of walrus ivory. King, queen, bishop, and foot soldier, as a castle: all rather backward. The bishop's chasuble has not been cut away; his mitre has the vertical band, but shows no impulse to spread into horns.

VISIGOTHIC SPANISH

Spanish civilization had developed out of the comparatively advanced culture of the Visigoths. From 415 until they were overthrown by the Musulman in 1711, the Visigothic sovereigns of Spain were under a disadvantage, particularly after the conversion of Clovis and 3,000 of his Frankish soldiers in a body on a battlefield in 496. The Visigothic kings adhered to the Aryan creed, while ruling a Catholic people. In VIc., King Ricared was converted, and the rulers gained the support of the clergy in their struggle to maintain their dynasty.

They were tolerant, considerably Romanized rulers. Their influence did not, like that of the Ostrogoths

420 421

422

423

upon her marriage to Alfonso VI.

This decorative period, which is that of a great national hero, the Cid, seems to me to be the most underservedly unexplained in all the history of costume.

422-423. XIIc. 1109 A.D. Visigothic Spanish. (British Museum. Beatus. Add. 11695.)

Four mounted knights and one foot soldier; enumerated, their garments and equipment are identical with those of Western Europe, but in detail there are considerable differences. All the hawberks and chausses are of overlapping metal scales or rings, not of linked chain-mail. The hawberk of the foot soldier, with its shaped sleeve, is extraordinarily long and narrow, and is not slit, as those of the mounted men simply had to be. The Roman lappets at his hem are probably a stylization of the folds of the tunic which shows at the cuff. The chausses have separate feet, with elaborate sandal designs, and prick spurs on the knights; their toes are lengthened and elaborated in the manner of the *solleret* which begins to appear in XIIc. The round shield with boss is very small, apparently a descendant of the two-foot Spanish *caetra* of IIc. B.C. Double-edged Germanic sword with a rounded point. The soldier (423), under his conical ribbed Germanic helmet with nasal, seems to have some misgivings, perhaps about his ferocious pike. The seven-foot Roman *pilum* came from the Iberian *gaesum*, which was originally a Celtic weapon.

Photographs courtesy of the Morgan Library

in Italy, die out with them but is still perceptible in Spanish art. Until the time of Charlemagne, Rome imposed little direction on the development of ritual costume in West Europe; the churches of Spain and Gaul were the last to conform to Roman use, which was brought to the continent principally through the agency of missionaries from the long-Christianized British Isles. Comparison with Bishops of XIIc. will show rate of development during IX-XIIc.

The cultures of the racial varied Mohammedan conquerors were too disparate for protracted, massive political effect, but with the Jews as intermediaries, the Mohammedans were princely patrons of learning and art. The Basques, holding off the Mohammedans, helped to seal Spain within its peninsula. Pilgrims to the shrine of St. James of Compostella brought practically her only contacts with Western Europe, until the XIIc. entry into the Spanish court of the cultured French ecclesiastics and knights who formed the entourage of the daughter of the Duke of Burgundy,

424

425

426

424-425. XIIc. Visigothic Spanish. (British Museum. Beatus. Add. 11695.)

424. Musicians. 425. The Scarlet Woman.

426. 1126-29 Spanish. (Oviedo Cathedral Archives.) Chartulary of Oviedo.

Ordoño I (850-866), King of Christian N.W. Spain, with his armor-bearer and two bishops, and Queen Mummadonna, between two maids of honor. The bishops, without miter, but with pastoral staffs, wear chasuble with Y orphreys, or pallium of a saint, under pall of bishop.

Nowhere else in this century will we find such sophisticated style as in the arrangement of the veils, and the placing of their plain mass, light or dark, against tunics the border decorations of which are subordinated to or eclipsed by the bold over-all patterns of the fabric out of which the tunics are cut, and in the case of the Visigothic queen, lined as well.

Courtesy of the Morgan Library
(424-26)

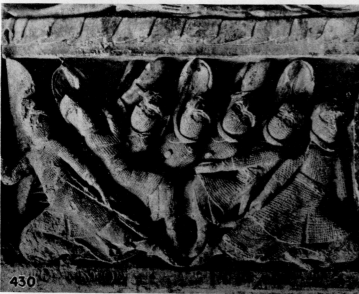

427-428. XI-XIIc. Spanish. (Barcelona. Crown Archives. Sp. 4546). Ms. de Fuedo.

Spanish costume shows much more use of elaborately patterned fabric than any other of the same period, although the era of fantasy and parti-colored garments is beginning, among people who long for colored patterns, which they cannot yet make, nor afford to import from the Orient.

Bishop: Mitre banded at the center, which will force top to spread into horns during XIIc. Patterned chasuble with orphreys; shortened in front from XIc.; pall; dalmatic, cut away at sides, is now colored; alb; maniple now fixed in wear over arm; pastoral staff with an early appearance of its scarf.

Gentlemen: parti-colored cloak and sleeveless tunic, slit to show short tunic which serves as sleeves for longer; lengthening hose; fenestrated shoes.

Lady: the way gown is cut away at sides and laced, on one side, over garment of another color, can be seen

clearly in XIIIc. Spanish *Book of Chess;* it foreshadows the universal sideless surcoat of XIVc. Turbaned head began to appear in Europe c. Xc.

429. Early XIIc. Spanish. [Burgos]. (Santo Domingo de Silos Cloisters.)

Male figure: cape draped, Byzantine-fashion, over hand, but new in lowering neck-line; and edges barely connected rather than overlapping.

430. Early XIIc. Spanish. [Burgos.] (Santo Domingo de Silos Cloisters.)

Entombment of Christ: knights wearing round-topped helms without nasals over mail hood affording maximum protection to face; scarf, draped about neck (see Ills. 392, 393); knee-length hawberk, short-sleeved, slit up front, over very long wide tunic. No mail chausses or spurs under these long tunics. Shield, almost body length with encircling curve.

431. Second quarter XIIc. Spanish. [Gerona.] (Baget.)

Wooden statue: simple tunic permits display of knotted fastening and long ends of richly studded belt.

432. Third quarter XIIc. Spanish. [Burgos]. (Solsona.)

St. Juliana and Devil: center-parted hair worn in 4 tresses; 2 tunics, fitted; upper tunic belted; shaped cuff laid on in pleats.

433. 1188 A.D. Spanish. [La Coruna]. (Santiago de Compostella Cathedral.)

Three Apostles: all-over fleurs-de-lys pattern; orphreys on tunic, pallium and scarf. Upper arm band persists through XIIIc.

434. 1163 A.D. Spanish. [Lerida]. (Solsona Cathedral.)

Virgin: bare head, long plaits, handsome orphreys, block of decoration at knee.

432

433

434

Feudal Lords and Kings: XIII Century

XIII CENTURY DEVELOPMENT OF DRESS

THE background of the XIII Century has been given under "Knighthood in Flower."

Nothing is more characteristic of XIIIc. costume, male and female, than the new sleeve, cut in one with the tunic itself. Starting often as low as the waist, it tapers to the wrist; the tunic has lost its fitted bodice and widens below a rather low bloused waistline. The whole effect is of one rather than two garments, even when, with the introduction of the knights' surcoat, similar sleeveless gowns (G. *sorket; sukeni*) are worn by women, and lead to the XIVc. *sideless surcoat,* which again exploits the use of two garments.

A variety of long, loose overcoats for men appears, often hooded, as are the shorter capes, worn with the shorter, fitted tunics (*pourpoints*) which develop for every-day wear, as hose, *chausses,* become longer and better fitting.

Coifs as well as hoods appear, for both men and women; and women's hair is gradually bundled up and braided into arrangements connected with the development of these enclosing head-coverings.

The emphasis on belts gradually moves to the pouches which now depend from them. Shoes are much plainer; the points lengthening with the century.

WOMEN'S DRESS

Tunic; cotte: sleeves tapering from waist to wrist. Garments skimpy around the chest, but no longer fitted; bloused at a low waistline. Whether belted or not, the belly is emphasized; then the garment spreads into skirts which are suddenly gored wide at the hips. Decoration is in horizontal bands; neckline lowered; *sleeveless surcoat* introduced. The use of orphreys, which, like the newer belts, could be woven by the ladies of the castle on a narrow loom, tends to lessen as Italian and Flemish textile factories are established and as Germany uses block-printing to decorate fabrics, antedating its use in book-printing.

Headdress: to the second quarter of the XIIc. ladies veiled, in public; through XIIc. long braids; end XIIc. *wimple* appears; early XIIIc. loose, with fillet (at home); first quarter of XIIIc., fillet widens into pill-box cap; mid-XIIIc. *barbette* appears; hair gathered into net (*crispine3*; headdress widens. Young girls wear loose flowing hair.

Cloak: semi-circular; front fastening; often fur-lined.

MEN'S DRESS

Tunics; cyclas or *cyclaton:* sleeves tapering to wrist: use of parti-color; dagged edges; fur-linings.

Overcoats: instead of capes; often hooded. Late XIIc. *pelissons;* fur-lined overgarment. End XIIc. *scapular;* poncho-like; caught but not sewed at the sides; often split up front. First quarter XIIIc. *garde-corps:* long, wide garment; sleeves voluminously gathered at top, and often so long that they were slit along the inseam to allow the arm to be used, while the sleeve of the garde-corps hung free. Second half XIIIc. *guarnache:* poncho-like; caught or sewed at sides; hanging, cape-like, down over shoulders.

Cowls and *Capes:* from third quarter of XIIc. hoods much used; lengthening point in back (*liripipe*); *chape; chapel; gugel; capuchon; aumusse.*

Headcoverings: since XIIc. berets, petasus, brimmed hats turned up in back; fillets. XIIIc. coifs, worn well into XIVc.; hats superimposed.

Accessories: girdles; pouches, *gypcière* (F. *gibier-*game) or *aumonière* (F. for alms). Mid-XIIIc., *fitchets,* vertical slits in outer garment to allow access to pouch, by both men and women. Gloves. Shoes (like women's), plain and increasingly pointed.

Underwear: Shirts. Mid-XIIIc. breeches (underdrawers) shortened; better hose-fastenings.

XIIIc. hose better shaped and longer; lead to shorter, tighter men's tunics, *pourpoints,* for everyday wear.

Improvement in fabrics was one of the factors leading to the wearing of the pourpoint and hose of the XIVc. Silk weaving was established in many Italian and some Flemish cities in the XIIIc. and more flexible materials were locally produced: good scarlet* wool in England; fustian (linen warp, wool weft) in Germany, which was also producing block-printed textiles.

The rise of tailoring was the other factor, starting in Germany, where the first guild of merchant tailors was chartered in 1153. By XIIIc. tailors were subdivided according to the categories of work performed, and women were supplanted by men-tailors. The tailors of Paris rose from 482 in 1292, to 702 in 1300, and were early divided into *tailleurs* (men's tailors) and *couturiers* (who did women's gowns).

DEVELOPMENT OF ARMS AND ARMOR: XII-XIVc.

The XIIIc. knight wore the chain-mail of the XIIc., with protective patches of plate or cuir-bouilli added at knees, over a padded and quilted pourpointed jack (*gambeson, hauketon*) and *cuishes* (covering thighs). With the rise of heraldry a new garment was worn over armor, the *surcoat*—sleeveless, silk or linen, suitable for the display of embroidered or painted armorial bearings.

Details of development of the various elements of armor were:

PLATE: The top of the *helm* was becoming rounded in mid-XIIc. and by the XIIIc. was flattened. The helm often enclosed the head and was supplied with vents for sight and breathing. By the end of this century it rested on the shoulders, chained to the belt and in the XIVc. to a plate on the breast. *Bascinets* were often worn under the helm. By the XIVc. these were visored and edged with mail to protect neck and shoulders. The *chapel-de-fer* was rather like our "tin-hats."

The *shield* was becoming smaller at this time. It was kite-shaped in mid-XIIc., triangular by the end of the century, then its top flattened; and by the middle of the XIIIc. it was heater (flat-iron) shaped. The *sword* becomes slenderer; quillons of the crossguard curved away from the hand. Up to mid-XIIc. it was worn under the hawberk,

drawn through the slit, then over the hawberk on a diagonal belt. By the end of the XIIIc. the sword (and dagger and helm) were chained to the belt; by early XIVc. chained to the plate on the breast. Sir Henry of Flanders was captured by his chained sword by an abbot. *Prick spurs; rowels* begin to appear in XIVc.

Both priests and women might go to war. Froissart tells of the archpriest, Arnault de Cervole, "an expert, hardy knight," who commanded 1600 men; and of the armed Countess of Montfort.

CHAIN: From the latter part of the XIIIc. to late in the XIVc. chain was linked in the manner called banded. A *coif-de-mailles* (*camail*) was worn over a padded arming cap or a steel skull cap. To the end of the XIIIc. this was in one with the hawberk, fastened by a flap (*ventaille*). Thereafter an iron mask was attached and by the XIVc. a mail edge, fastened to the bascinet, protecting neck and shoulders. The *hawberk* had long sleeves ending in gloves and became shorter, exposing the hem of the jack.

Chausses had knee-caps (*poleyns*) of plate or *cuir-bouilli;* laced up the back; prick-spurs (till mid-XIVc.). Metal *greaves* were worn over the chausses by the end of the XIIIc.

PADDED AND QUILTED: An *arming cap* was worn under the helm. The *jack* (*gambeson, hauketon*) was worn under the hawberk; this and the steel cap wree the only protection of common soldiers. *Cuishes* protected the thighs.

DECORATIVE: The *surcoat* was sleeveless, of silk or linen, decorated with a coat-of-arms. It was worn over the hawberk. It first appeared at the last quarter of XIIc., knee-length, slit front and back, open under the arm to the waist. It was quite common in the first third of the XIIIc. During that century it became gradually longer and then dangerously long, going down to the calf in early XIVc. It was cut off c. 1350.

Ailettes were tabs, standing on either shoulder, made of leather or parchment, decorated armorially. They appeared in the second half of the XIII century. The helmet had a *crest*.

---

* Scarlet was a material, not a color: a fine elastic wool, particularly suitable for making tights. It was dyed in many colors, of which a red was most successful and common; that red has now taken the name of the fabric.

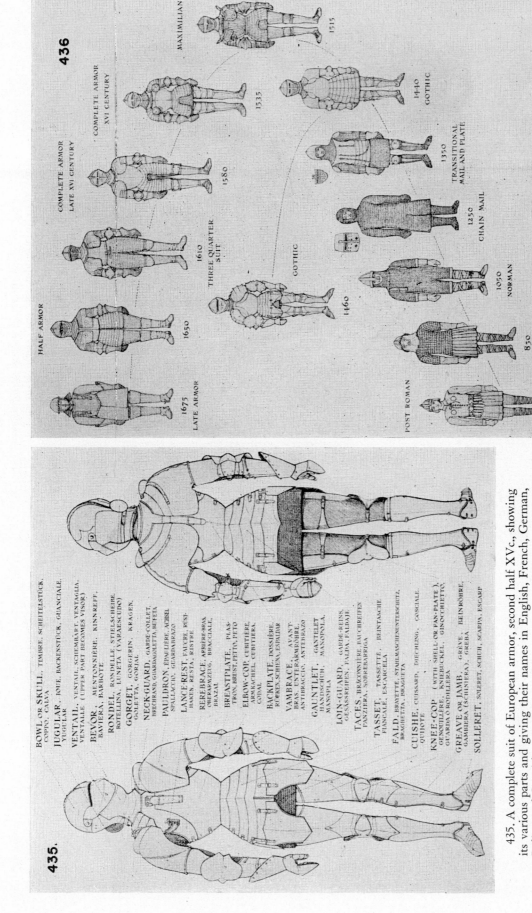

436

MAXIMILIAN   1515

COMPLETE ARMOR
XVI CENTURY   1535

COMPLETE ARMOR
LATE XVI CENTURY   1580

1610
THREE QUARTER
SUIT

1650

1675
LATE ARMOR

HALF ARMOR

1440
GOTHIC

1350
TRANSITIONAL
MAIL AND PLATE

1250
CHAIN MAIL

1050
NORMAN

850
FRANKISH

650

1460
GOTHIC

POST ROMAN

435.

BOWL OR SKULL. TIMBRE, SCHEITELSTÜCK,
    COPPO, CALVA.
JUGULAR. JOUE, BACKENSTÜCK, GUANCIALE,
    YUGULAR.
VENTAIL. VENTAIL, SCHEMBART, VENTAGLIA,
    VENTALLE (UPPER PART BECOMES VISOR)
BEVOR. MENTONNIÈRE, RINNREFF,
    BAVIERA, BARBOTE.
RONDEL. RONDELLE, STIELSCHEIBE,
    ROTELLINA, LUNETA (VARAESCUDO)
GORGET, GORGERIN, KRAGEN,
    GOLETTA, GORJAL.
NECK-GUARD. GARDE-COLLET,
    BRECHRAND, GUARDAGOLETTA, MIFETA
PAULDRON. ÉPAULIÈRE, ACHSEL
    SPALLACCIO, GUARDABRAZO
LANCE-REST. FAUCRE, REST-
    HAKEN, RESTA, RISTRE
RERE-BRACE. ARRIÈRE-BRAS,
    OBERARMZEUG, BRACCIALE,
    BRAZAL
BREASTPLATE. PLAS-
    TRON, BRUST, PETTO, PETO
ELBOW-COP. CUBITIERE,
    ARMKACHEL, CUBITIERA,
    CODAL
BACKPLATE. DOSSIÈRE,
    RÜCKEN, SCHENA, ESPALDAR
VAMBRACE. AVANT-
    BRAS, UNTERARMROHRE,
    ANTIBRACCIO, ANTEBRAZO
GAUNTLET. GANTELET,
    HANDSCHUH, MANOPOLA,
    MANOPLA
LOIN-GUARD. GARDE-REINS,
    GESASSREIFEN, FALDA, FALDAJE
TACES. BRACONNIÈRE, BAUCHREIFEN
    PANZIERA, SOBREBARRIGA
TASSET. TASSETTE, BEINTASCHE
    FIANCALE, ESCARCELA
FALD. BRAYETTE, STAHLMASCHENUNTERSCHUTZ,
    BRAGHETTA, BRAGUETA
CUISHE. CUISSARD, DIECHLING, COSCIALE,
    QUIJOTE
KNEE-COP. (WITH SHELL OR FAN-PLATE),
    GENOUILLÈRE, KNIEBUCKEL, GINOCCHIETTO,
    GUARDA O RODILLERA
GREAVE OR JAMB. GRÈVE, BEINROHRE,
    GAMBIERA (SCHINIERA), GREBA
SOLLERET. SOLERET, SCHUH, SCARPA, ESCARP

435. A complete suit of European armor, second half XVc., showing
its various parts and giving their names in English, French, German,
Italian and Spanish.
436. European Armor and its development during a thousand years
from A.D. 650-1650.

Courtesy of Metropolitan Museum of Art (435-463)

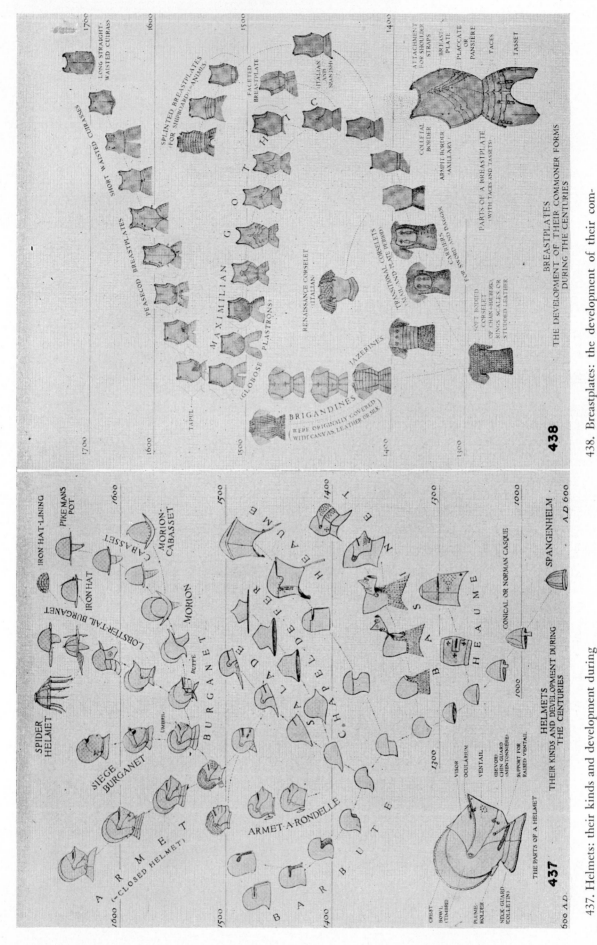

438. Breastplates: the development of their commoner forms during the centuries.

437. Helmets: their kinds and development during the centuries.

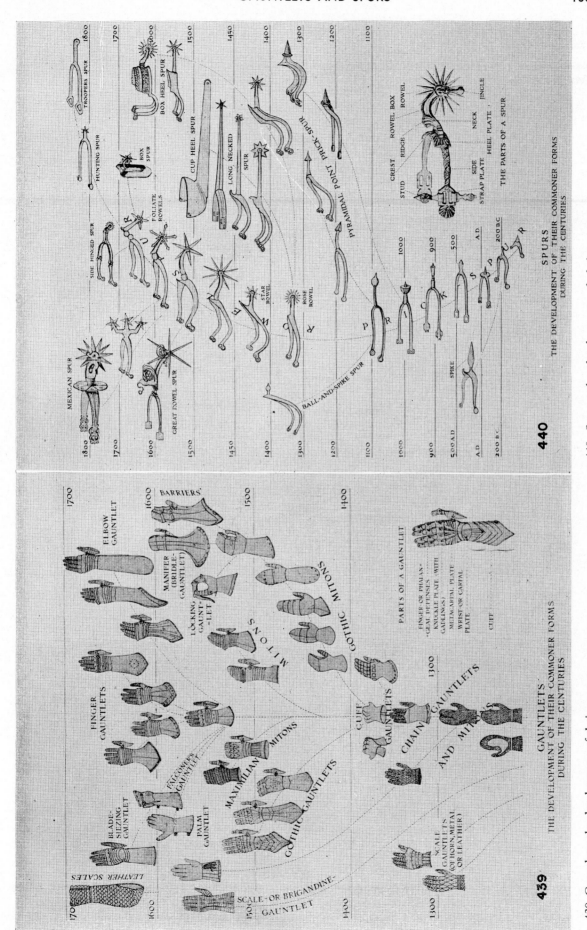

440. Spurs: the development of their commoner forms during the centuries.

439. Gauntlets: the development of their commoner forms during the centuries.

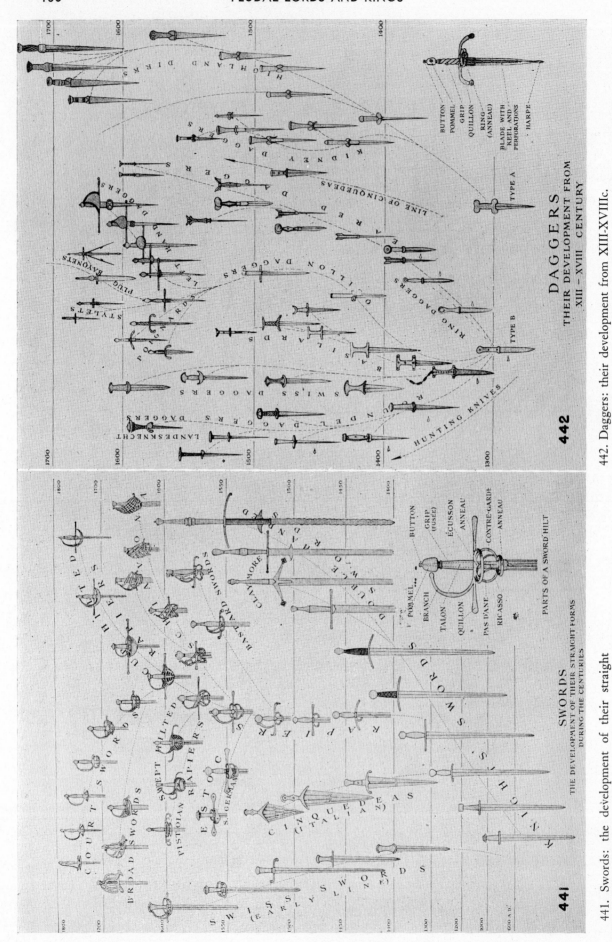

442. Daggers: their development from XIII-XVIIIc.

441. Swords: the development of their straight forms during the centuries.

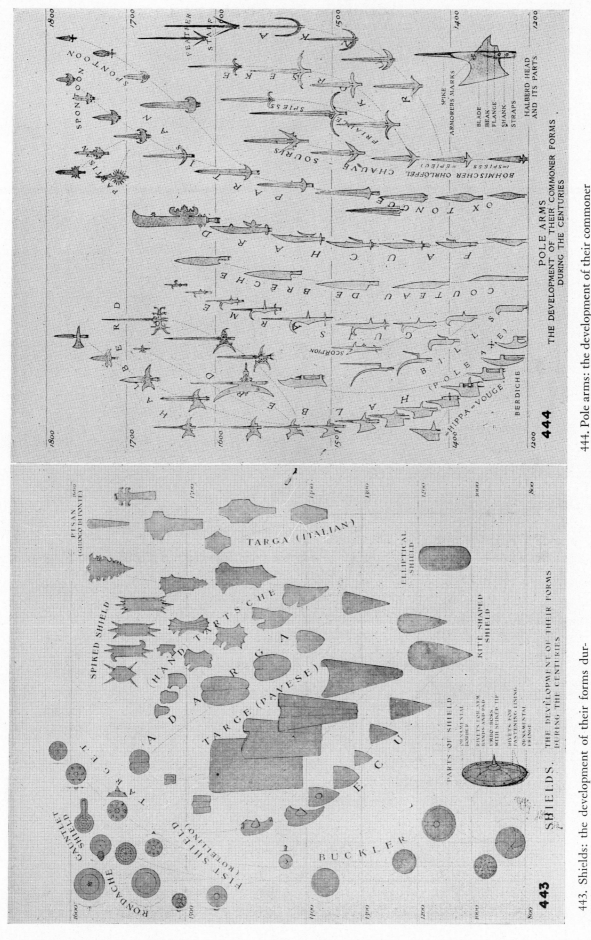

444. Pole arms: the development of their commoner forms during the centuries.

443. Shields: the development of their forms during the centuries.

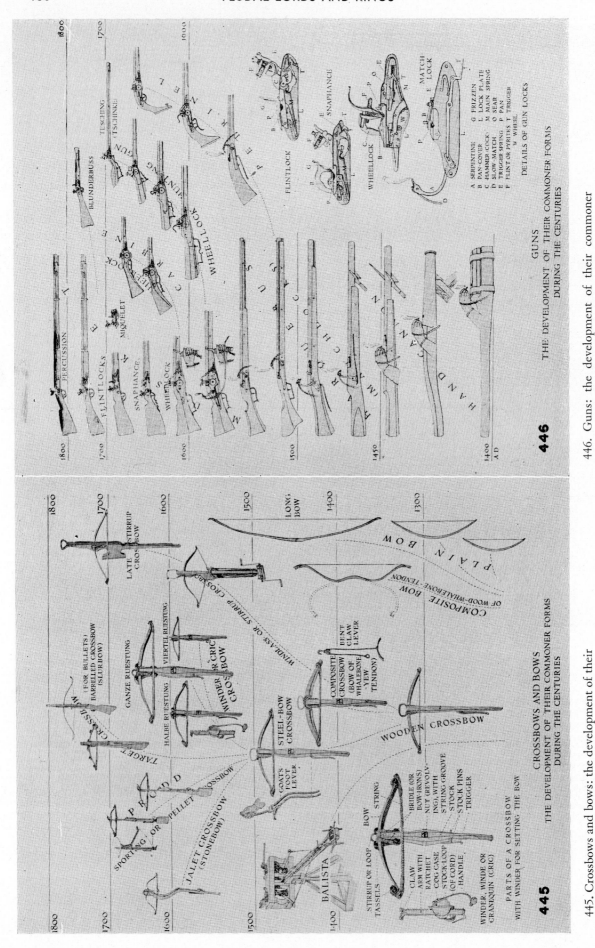

446. Guns: the development of their commoner forms during the centuries.

445. Crossbows and bows: the development of their commoner forms during the centuries.

447

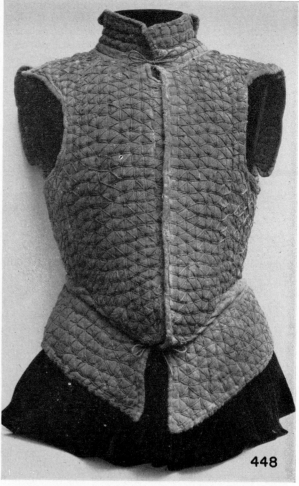

448

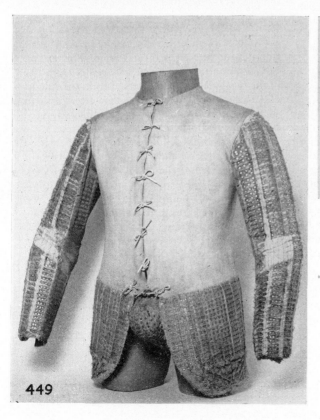

449

450

447. XVc. Spanish.
Brigandine covered with gold-brocaded velvet.

448. XVIc. English.
Jack: plates of iron laced between two folds of canvas.

449. XVIc. 1550. Italian.
Brigandine and brayette: leather, iron plates, brass studs, and silk.

450. XVIc. 1525. German. Maximilian.
Waffenrock; military skirt: quilted gold brocade (see Sir James Scudamore portrait, and Ill. 455).

In contrast to the jazeran, in which plates of leather,

horn, or metal were sewed on top of the fabric of the garment, the riveted brigandine and quilted jack were made of overlapping plates, scales, or bands of metal or horn, sewed between two layers of material, just as some forms of mail appear to have been covered with leather.

Brigandines were highly colored. Examples in the Metropolitan Museum are of red, blue, green, yellow, black, and white velvet, satin, brocade or leather.

In the dangerous days of Cellini, when everybody wished at least to appear protected, the doublet imitated the brigandine in appearance. Commines says that when the confederates marched to Paris in 1465, the troops of Charolois and the Duke of Calabria were in full armor and readiness, but those of Berri and Bretagne were "armed only with very light brigandines, or as some said, with gilt nails sewn upon satin, that they might weigh the lesse."

The brigandine often had protective skirts, or long, studded tassets down the thighs. The Metropolitan Museum Spanish brigandine has a separate gorget; and is covered in gold brocade, in imitation of the etched patterns used on XVIc. armor.

As the use of gunpowder increased, armor had to be made "proof" against it, and "proof marks" even entered into the design of its decoration. Proof armor was unbearably heavy, and armor was largely discarded in favor of leather by XVIIc.

At a time when a large proportion of the populace went armed, the civilian's padded doublets, stuffed trunk-hose, and thick pleated skirts, all developed out of the need to anchor armor firmly in place, prevent it from chafing, or replace its protection in a more comfortable way. A doublet was sometimes sent to the armorer as a pattern; our word "milliner" comes from the fine workmanship of the armorers of Milan.

Armor became ceremonial, rather than useful, during the XVIc. It aped costume in cut, and imitated the patterns of embroidery in its etched and colored decoration, as we see in Burgkmair's illustrations for the "Weisskönig," or in the work of Dürer, both of whom designed and engraved armor.

The tonnelet of Frederick of Saxony's harness is equivalent to a quilted "waffenrock" skirt. Grancsay shows a 1570 corselet with buttoned and tabbed decoration like that of a doublet; he compares Mytens' 1621 portrait of Charles I with the Barberini armor, to illustrate the way in which the breastplates became short-waisted, like the contemporary doublet, and in its decoration, followed the lines of embroidery or guarding of the doublet seams. He reproduces Ambrogio Figini's portrait of Lucio Foppa (Palazzo Brera, Milan), in which the etching of the armor and embroidery on the trunk-hose are identical. He also shows a military hat of metal, turned up on the side like a wide-brimmed beaver, with a socket to hold the plume.

* Grancsay: Mutual Influences of Costume and Armor, from which I have drawn the rest of this material.

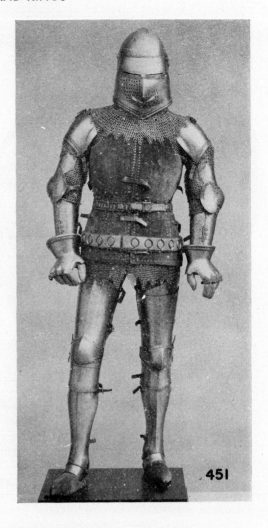

451. XVc. Italian. (Metropolitan Museum.)

Complete suit of Gothic armor (composed): transitional between mail and plate. This armor, unique in age and completeness, comes from one of the two great sources of early armor, the Citadel of Chalcis, near Thebes, taken by the Turks in 1470; the other was Rhodes, which they captured in 1523.

The brigandine, of large, shaped plates, with a fine globose breast and long skirts, was covered by fabric, as armor commonly was in XIV-XVc., to retard rusting, give color, and provide a place for heraldic blasoning; from XVc., color was chemically applied to the metal itself. This brigandine, originally covered with brocaded linen, has been re-covered in velvet with the original bronze rivets. Deep basinet, pointed visor; short-cuffed gauntlets; mail elements bordered with latten (brass).

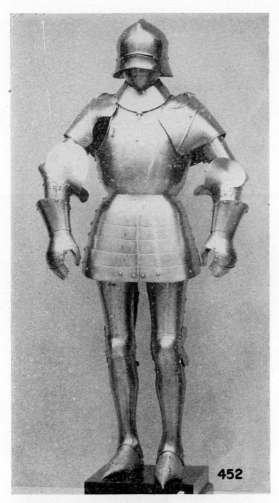

452

454

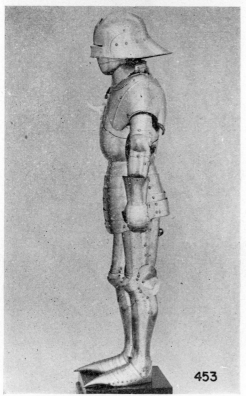

453

452-453. XVc. c. 1460. Italian. (Metropolitan Museum.)

Gothic armor: front and side views.

The simplest, most beautifully designed of all armor is the Gothic armor of XIV-XVc., which stresses a lean-waisted, athletic elegance of body.

The body, in a globose breastplate, is now well sheathed in plate, which is extended and flanged to deflect blows from the vulnerable shoulders and elbows. Deep skirt of many bands; wide-cuffed mitten gauntlets; salade; lengthening sollerets.

454. XVc. c. 1460. Italian Milanese. (Metropolitan Museum.)

Gothic suit, composed and with minor alterations; authentic elements bear the marks of the Missaglia.

Gothic armor, still beautiful and practical, is beginning to be ridged and fluted on the breast and around the armpits. The helmet, from Chalcis, bears the marks of the Missaglias of Milan, the greatest of all armorers.

The salade has given way to a beautiful fitted helm, prominently ridged and pointed into the "houndskull" form, with a hinged chin-piece which locks at its point. The neck is protected by a mail collar, with the additional protection of a tiny, round shield, set on a stalk, at the most vulnerable spot, in back. This form of casque, called *armet à rondelle,* was used in Italy from 1440 and in Spain, a half century in advance of the rest of Europe; and lasted into the early decades of the XVIc. Sabatons prolonged in 47 lames each, 2½ feet long; such footwear, which had sometimes to be chained up out of the way, is commemorated in the phrase, "to be on a great footing with the world."*

455. XVIc. 1510. German Augsburg. (Metropolitan Museum.)

Harness of Maximilian type, attributed to Frederick of Saxony, (1474-1510); part of a suite of armor (sometimes consisting of as many as 100 pieces) which could be interchanged for field, joust, or court use; preserved in the armory of the Teutonic Knights (of which he was Grand Master, 1498-1510), at Königsberg until the Napoleonic wars. An alternative breastplate in the Historical Museum, Dresden, is etched with the cross of the Order, a device, and Prussian eagles. Steel is forged, embossed, etched, and gilded in the puffed and slashed manner of contemporary dress which is also followed by the sollerets, now 6″ wide; visor, of face with mustache. Harness is from the workshop of Koloman Colmar, one of that great dynasty of Augsburg armorers called Helmschmied (see Germ. XVIc., Ch. Weiditz journey to Spain with Colmar's son to deliver armor to Charles V).

456. XVIc. 1527. French or Italian. (Metropolitan Museum.)

Harness of Galiot de Genouilhac, (1465-1546), who served Charles XIII, Louis XII and Francis I, as Master of Artillery. He accompanied Francis to the Field of the Cloth of Gold, and was captured with him and Anne de Montmorency at Pavia by Charles V.

"From the standpoint of practicality it is one of the best harnesses extant." Its helm retains the rondelle at the back of the neck. It is regally etched and gilded with the labors of Hercules, which were also used on his chateau at Assier. It was bought from the Uzès family, into which his daughter had married.

457. VIc. 1549. German Nuremberg. (Metropolitan Museum.)

Harness of Albrecht of Bavaria, nephew by marriage of Charles V. It bears the mark of the Nuremberg guild, and is possibly the work of Kurt Lochner. Albrecht became a member of the Order of the Golden Fleece at 17; the armor is etched with its insignia, the Virgin as its protector, and Peter and Paul, the Princes of the Apostles.

458. XVIc. 1550. French. (Metropolitan Museum.)

Parade armor of Henry II of France. The workmanship for this armor for state processions, made by Italian armorers in the Louvre workshop, had caused it to be attributed to Cellini. The best engravers of XVIc.: Dürer, Hopfer, Hans Burgkmair the Elder, all designed and engraved for

* Grancsay.

455

456

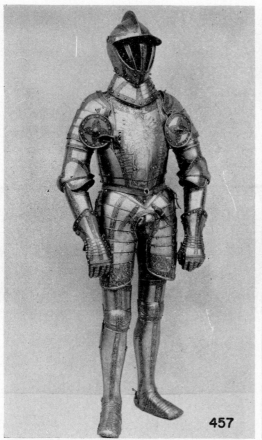

457

458

459

armorers, and many original designs like this have been preserved.

459. XVIc. 1550. German. Augsburg.

Armor of Charles V. This suit, for one of the greatest of all patrons of armorers, was made by Mathäus Frauenpreis (Frawenbrys) from the designs of Jörg Sorg of Augsburg, preserved in the Stuttgart Library. It is embossed, etched and gilded with a griffin, and the Columns of Hercules (in allusion to the efforts required by the Spanish conquest of America), and the fire-steels and flints of the Golden Fleece.

The support of puffs and slashed straps (equivalent to folds, in a more comfortable form), was required under the wide taces of the knight; the resulting trunk-hose also gave good leg protection to a foot soldier in a brigandine.

460. XVIc. 1555. Italian.

Harness of Anne of Montmorency, Constable of France. Anne of Brittany's godson and namesake (1493-1567), companion at arms of five kings of France, died of his wounds after the siege of St. Denis. His 50-pound fighting suit shows armor being reduced to its final form: a flexibly articulated breast-plate with long tassets. Its etched decoration includes the clasped hands of peace, which appear on his funeral monument (Louvre). The crest of the armet becomes more pronounced.

460

461

462

463

461. 1590. English. Greenwich. (Metropolitan Museum.)

Armor of George Clifford, third Earl of Cumberland (1558-1605). Clifford, who "was as merciful as valiant (the best metal bows best) and left an impression of both in all places to which he came,"* succeeded Sir Henry Lee as Queen's Champion in 1590. This beautifully colored black and gold armor is identical with that shown in his portrait by Oliver; every element bears Elizabeth's cypher, and the suit was probably made especially for the occasion at the royal armory at Greenwich. It is etched and gilded with Tudor emblems: fleurs-de-lys and open cinquefoil roses combined with true-lover's knots. The left gauntlet, which is similar but not identical, came from the suit of Prince Henry preserved at Windsor. (See Oliver miniature, 1590.)

462. XVIIc. 1633. Italian. (Metropolitan Museum of Art.)

Three-quarter suit, probably belonging to Taddeo Barberini, d. 1647. The blazon of bees of the Roman family of Barberini appears on the armor attributed to Pope Urban's nephew. The short waistline of contemporary dress, assumed by armor, and the wide-hipped taces which depend to the boot-tops, would make the upper part of the body look ineffectual, if it were not for the large shoulder-plates, which are stressed by the engraving and gilding, in braid-like embroidered patterns, and the sculpturing, tooling and silver studs of this suit. Burganet with umbril shading the eyes. The gauntlet is a leather glove, with a cuff and plate of metal covering the knuckles.

463. XVIIc. c. 1650. French. (Metropolitan Museum of Art.)

Half-suit of armor. Armor is progressively reduced in extent, and loses its fine workmanship, as the need for proof armor outweighs all other considerations; it becomes so heavy that it is abandoned in the XVIIc.

* Thomas Fuller, quoted by Grancsay.

464

465

466

464. XIIc. France. (Arles, S. Trophime.)

Gentlemen: hair approaching the rolled form at the nape of the neck, of XIIIc.; small fillets or crowns. Cape edges barely meet at shoulder closing. Width below the hips is obtained by pleated side gores.

465. XIIIc. French. (Paris Bib. Nat.)

Thomas de Roumeis, squire (d. 1264): from his tomb in the nave of the Abbaye de Toussaint, at Chalons in Champagne. As Roger de Gaignières traveled through France, turn of XVI-XVIIc., he was careful to have an enormous number of drawings made of tombs, many of which have since disappeared. The drawings which are particularly rich in examples of bourgeois dress have been reproduced in sets of loose plates by the Bibliothèque Nationale, and a number of them can be found in Piton. (See Appendix.)

Thomas is particularly interesting for the typical diagonal neck-closing of the XIIIc.

466. Second half XIIIc. French. (Florence, Bargello Nat. Museum.)

Bronze knight: floral fillet, over hair rolled at the nape: mail chausses and hawberk: coif about the neck; hanging mitten of the hawberk has become a pendant, decorative as separate mail gauntlets come into use: dagged surcoat.

467. First half XIIIc. French. (Montmorillon Notre Dame.)

The Mystic Marriage of St. Catherine: Saints at the right of the Virgin. Virgin, therefore with flowing hair, under a little pill-box cap. This wonderful dress combines most of the excesses of the late XIIc.-early XIIIc.; narrow upper body laced tight, blousing to stress the belly, jutting suddenly over the hips, and falling in crumpled heaps on the ground, and the most prolonged sleeve possible (see Ill. 389) with a dramatic cuff.

Dates varying from XII- IIIc. are given by various authorities for these lovely frescos, done in black, white, pearl gray, dark blue, green and brown. The costume would appear to be first half XIIIc.

468. After 1230. French. (Chartres Cathedral.)
Lady: fluted cap and barbette; cape with little rolled-back collar; cape-fastening has broken off statue; small brooch closes slit at front of neck, which is not stressed; exquisite belt.

469. XIIIc. French. Portrait head from tomb. (Walters Art Gallery, Baltimore.)
Noblewoman: stiffened linen cap, and barbette, with fine arrangement of veil.

470. XIIIc. French. (Bourges Cathedral.)

The Saved in the Last Judgment: middle figure at top: cap, barbette, sleeveless surcoat buttoned on right shoulder; low, bloused waistline below a tight bust, flows into a suddenly wide skirt.

471-472. XIIIc. French. (Chartres, South Portal.)

471. *St. Stephen, St. Martin and St. Laurent*: exquisite ecclesiastical embroideries of a fine period in church vestments. St. Stephen is dressed as a subdeacon in amice, dalmatic with apparels at hem and

cuffs, and with hem and slit sides fringed, alb, and maniple. St. Martin, as bishop of Tours, wears a conical mitre, amice, pall pinned in place over apparel of chasuble at center, dalmatic with 2 rows of fringe, stole, alb, maniple, and pastoral staff.

472. *St. Theodore*: as knight: mittened hawberk with coif dropped back, legs protected by mail *chausses* laced to sole; long surcoat; handsome sword on belt with low waistline; heater-shaped shield, hung over arm by *gigue;* lance with spirally furrowed hand-grip.

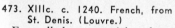

473. XIIIc. c. 1240. French, from St. Denis. (Louvre.)

Enamelled memorial plate: *Jean, son(?) of St. Denis*. Royal personage with fleur-de-lys sceptre; simple circular crown with mounting trefoils; cloak with narrow border dotted with jewels; narrow outer tunic with knotted belt (see Ills. 414, 415) and jewelled border; full under-tunic; slightly conservative, as royal dress is apt to be.

474. XII-XIIIc.* French. (Chartres Cathedral.)

Shepherds: summer, single tunic and covering; stiffening in top of hood, front to back. One bare-legged in boots; the other in loose, wrinkled *chausses*.

475. XIIIc. (Chartres Cathedral. North Portal.)

February warming himself: rectangular cloak fastened over short, hooded scapular; two tunics; drawers, hose without feet, shoes.

* Houvet, the director, says XIIc.; others say 1250.

476. XIIIc. before 1260. French. (Morgan Library.)

"Book of Old Testament Illustrations."

There is probably no more complete picture of the life and customs in the middle of the XIIIc. than is provided by these 46 illustrations. Plain people at work or rest; gentlefolk at home or abroad; knights and common soldiers in every sort of armor, and especially in garments worn beneath, or in place of armor, in camp or battle, are drawn in such variety and detail, that new information is revealed at each inspection. An explanatory Latin text was added by an Italian scribe in XIVc. The manuscript became the property of Shah Abbas, the Great King of Persia in 1608, and a description of each scene was added in Persian.

476. The Israelites are repulsed from Hai: The archaic helmets of the Conquest and the round Oriental shields carried by the defenders of Hai, are mediaeval conventions, to indicate warriors of alien race.

Knights: mail *coifs,* tied back from the temples, are worn alone, or under skull-caps, or flat-topped helms; mail *hawberks,* mittened; and *chausses* under plain surcoats. The fallen knight shows dagged sleeves of a quilted garment, worn between hawberk and surcoat. Heater-shaped shields; swords with various pommels and scabbards.

Men-at-arms: *pourpointed* or *gamboised* (quilted and studded) jacks; mittened, short-sleeved or sleeveless; one over another, the uppermost cut like a knight's surcoat, and sometimes dagged at the hem. Lacking the protection of the knight's mailed coif, the men wear a quilted standing collar; coif, covering the ears and tied under the chin, and arming-cap, surmounted by a studded *chapel-de-fer* or steel skull-cap.

Weapons shown, l. to r.: studded mace, staff with metal point, axe, glaive (long blade) falchion (square end, notched below, see No. 478), dagger, cross-bow. Standard: armorial.

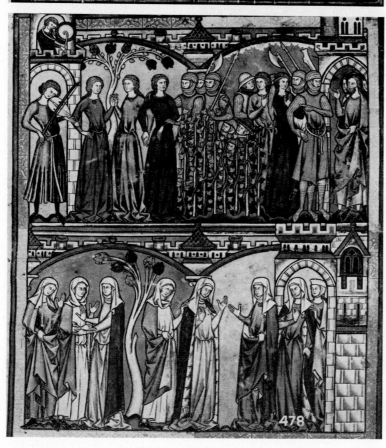

477-478. XIIIc. French. (Morgan Library.)

"Book of Old Testament Illustrations." 477. City of Hai captured and its king hanged (from an engine of war). Upper: Knights, armed as in 476, also with lance bearing a pennon, with 2-handed *glaive,* and with heater-shaped shields, one blazoned with 3 cinquefoils. Men-at-arms, as in 476; sappers and miners, with pick, actually using kite-shaped shields of Conquest type, which protect full length of body; crossbow with trigger, and hook for stringing bow hanging from archer's belt. Lower: Knights, the first with his *coif-de-mailles* thrown back, showing padded arming-cap under steel skull-cap; cords at waist of surcoats; sword-belts knotted in front; decorative scabbards, swords. Suppliant populace: 1st standing man in hooded scapular overgarment; *garde-corps* with short, slit sleeves on kneeling figure; *aumonières;* woman in sleeveless surcoat; man in short, hooded scapular on horse; boy in *capuchon.*

478. Bengamites win daughters of Sholoh as wives. Upper: Musician, parti-colored, dagged. Unmarried girls: flowing hair, fillets; effect of one garment, very long, wide and bloused; sleeves cut in one with gown which increases in length. Knights: coifs held back by cord; one with chapel over arming-coif, and collar, instead of coif-de-mailles; knight farthest right has slipped hand out of mail mitten. Weapons: axe, spear, bill, glaive. Lower: Travelling to Jerusalem, and now married; heads covered, some necks swathed; barbes, coifs, and cap; mantles, some fur-lined.

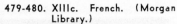

479-480. XIIIc. French. (Morgan Library.)

"Book of Old Testament Illustrations." 479. Boaz asks the foreman about Ruth.

Upper: gentleman on horseback, cloaked and gloved; on foot, wearing scapular with closed sides. Boaz, straw hat. Ruth, apron and gloves. Woman gleaner, netted hair and capuchon, thrown back. Other gleaners, cuffs unbuttoned, turned back; coifs or linen.

Lower: coifs, straw hats, hoods; hose; man's tunic slit in front, and tucked back out of the way into belt.

480. Ruth, Naomi, and Boaz. Upper: tendency of women's hair to be bundled up; woman's sleeveless surcoat; stockings striped horizontally. Lower: flailer in tunic, linen drawers, long hose. Flailer without tunic shows drawers rolled at waist around cord, to which ends of drawers are knotted.

481. XIIIc. French. (Morgan Library.)

"Book of Old Testament Illustrations." David and Goliath. Upper: Foot-soldier, pourpointed hawberk ending in gloves, not mittens, and with standing collar. Padded arming-caps, especially under engraved skull-cap of standard bearer, who wears a short jack caught together under arms. Same bearings on standard and on heater-shaped shield which is hanging on wagon, as do also chapels by their fastenings and pots (which undoubtedly suggested the chapel-de-fer) by their handles. Hair rolled at neck beneath coif. Lower: Goliath, wearing pourpointed *cuisses,* and *greaves* tied about lower leg; shield slung by *guige* and showing strap of *enarmes* on back. Very long lance with fixed cross-bar.

From "Book of Old Testament Illustrations," published in colored facsimiles by The Roxburghe Club, Oxford, 1927, with notes by C. O. Cockerell, M. R. James, and on armor by Charles ffoulkes, to which we are very much indebted.

482. Late XIIIc. French. Arras. (Morgan Library M. 730.)

Husband, wife and children: gowns of very simple cut, because of heavy, magnificent material. Arras, by XIVc. was the greatest centre of weaving in Europe; "Arras" another word for tapestries.

483

484

485

486

483-486. First half XIIIc. English. (British Museum.)
Drawings by Matthew Paris.

483. St. Christopher: holding his tunic up out of the water, discloses the manner of knotting linen drawers at knee (see No. 480.)

484. Archbishop, probably St. Edward of Canterbury, canonized 1247: Mitre pretiosa, horns set front and back (XIIIc.), low shape (until XIVc.); amuce with orphreys; pall narrow, decorated with tiny crosses; dalmatic, rich, diapered, bordered; tunicle, horizontally striped, fringed; alb with apparels; buskins of diapered material; episcopal ring, right hand; maniple over left arm; cross staff of archbishop. No stole or gloves.

485. King: a stalk of fleur-de-lys was supposed to have been used as a sceptre in the coronation ceremonies of the Frankish kings. With the establishment of heraldic devices in the XIIc. the fleur-de-lys was used on the arms of France: azure, semé de fleurs-de-lys or (Old France); changed, third quarter XIVc. to: azur, à trois fleurs-de-lys or (France Modern.) The king, under a green cloak lined with vair, wears a jewelled dalmatic with the horizontal-banded decoration typical of the XIIIc. The tapering sleeves are cut in one with the body and gathered onto a sort of superhumeral collar. Handsome buckled belt with long tongue. Shoes of diapered material, simple in cut.

486. Knight: in mail hawberk with mittens and coif. Palm of mitten shows slit which permitted use of bare hand. The flap of the coif and its method of fastening are clearly indicated. Drawers, chaussons, of mail; and chausses covered with metal bosses, laced down back of leg, ending in feet and prick-spurs, buckled on. His long slit surcoat, tied to hawberk under the armhole, bears the same crosses pateés used on his standard, and on the ailettes of either shoulder; with a larger cross superimposed in front. Sword and belt. His closed helm, with cords for fastening, is about to be placed over his coif by his lady.

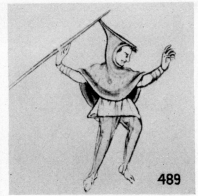

487. Mid-XIIIc. English. (British Museum.)

Matthew Paris: "Life of Offa."

Paris' "Offa" was one of the four old histories which John Stow persuaded Matthew Parker, Archbishop of Canterbury, to publish in 1571. All the servants in Archbishop Parker's house had to spend their unoccupied time with printing, engraving, and bookbinding; Parker had the first Anglo-Saxon typefaces cut. Offa was the VIIIc. king of Mercia to whom Charlemagne offered reciprocal protection for English and French traders, who in mediaeval times, travelled with their goods. English merchants already attended the French fairs, and an English trader was established in Marseilles in VIIIc.

Battle Scene: knights wearing the shorter hawberk, with narrowing mittened sleeves, like tunic of period; closed helms, or rounded helmet with nasal, or simply coif-de-mailles. Long armorial tabards to match heater-shaped or kite-shaped shields, with flattened tops. Quillons of sword, still straight, but deflect thrusts downward.

488-490. Mid-XIIIc. English. Salisbury. (Belvoir Castle. Duke of Rutland.)

"Rutland Psalter."

Short easy clothes of common men. Man at left has well-fitting hose, caught to his breeches, but they cannot come high enough to be covered by the skirt of his short tunic. The center figure wears hose without feet, very long but very loose, while the right-hand man is fighting in his breeches, without hose, but with shoes (compare breeches in Ills. 479-481.) These two wear hooded capes, *capuchons;* the top of the hood stiffened down the center; one also wears a linen coif tied under the chin.

From O. E. S. Saunders: *English Illumination*, Vol. II (487). From *Rutland Psalter*, Roxburghe Club, 1937 (488-90).

491. XIIIc. c. 1245. English. (Cambridge University Library.)

Matthew Paris: "La Estoire de Seint Aedward li Rei."

Edward the Confessor's marriage to Eadygth (or Edgitha), daughter of Earl Godwin. William of Malmesbury says that Edgitha was a woman "whose bosom was the school of every liberal art, though little skilled in earthly matters; on seeing her, if you were amazed by her erudition, you must absolutely languish for the purity of her mind, and the beauty of her person." The ascetic king never had carnal relations with her or any other woman.

Edgitha, in a horizontally striped gown, receives the fleur-de-lys sceptre. The fleur-de-lys entered regal costume with the XIIc. coronation of Philip Augustus. By the direction of his father, Louis VII, Philip wore a blue dalmatic and blue shoes, patterned in gold

"fleur-de-Loys," which referred both to the father's name and nickname, "Florus." Both Edgitha, under a flowing veil, and Edward wear open-topped crowns with foliated decoration above a low circlet, typical of XIIIc.

The blind earl, who gives his daughter in marriage, wears the new garment, the *garde-corps;* it is buttoned to the throat; its full sleeve is slit to permit free use of the arm in the tight sleeve of the tunic; it has a small cowl which can be drawn up over the beret. Bishop: gloves, maniple, mitre, amice, chasuble, dalmatic and alb, pastoral staff.

492. XIIIc. c. 1230. English. (Cambridge Univ. Lib.)

"Trinity College Apocalypse."

The Scarlet Woman: very Mae West, in comparison with the noble Edgitha above.

493. 1277 A.D. English. (Stoke D'Abernon, Surrey.)

Sir John Daubernoun: the earliest English brass; a knight completely armed in *mail*, with *surcoat;* clean-shaven. *Coif-de-mailles*: protecting chin, neck, shoulders; laced to metal *skull-cap*. *Surcoat*: long, slit up front, corners cut off diagonally, fringed; over mail *hawberk*: ending in mittens, strapped at wrist; over *haketon* (quilted) or *curie* (leather), protective against chafing; not seen. Mail *chausses*: with ornamented knee-caps, *poleyns,* probably of *cuir-bouilli;* and prick-spurs.

Shield: heater-shaped, charged with his arms in enamel: Azure a chevron or; slung by leather *gigue* ornamented by same crosses and roses as son's (see 1327 A.D.). *Sword*: ornamented pommel, slung in front in sheath fastened on wide *sword-belt*, which is supported in back by attachment to narrow braided *belt* of surcoat; *lance,* with pennon: bearing his arms.

494. XIIIc. Italian. (Bressanone.) Fresco.

Our Lady: In this extremely interesting illustration (which should be compared to Winchester Bible, 1170), the impossible silhouette of the previous centuries' ideal female figure is, as it were, drawn by the white outer garment upon the dark ground of the undertunic which covers a very matter-of-fact female torso. There is also the previous centuries' interest in the horizontal gathering of the material across the bodice. But in this case, the binding which finishes the sides, though furnished with eyelets, is so anchored at the waist and armpits that no lacing (see XI-XIIc. and XIIIc. Sp. "Book of Chess") is necessary, and none is indicated in the drawing: the eyelets are a flexible and decorative equivalent of an orphrey.

495. XIII-XIVc. North Italian. (Baltimore. Walters Art Gallery MS 153.)

Three knights in gloved hawberks, high coifs and chausses, under surcoats, the whole Romanized by the band about the chest and the low belt, simulating the bottom of the moulded lorica. Small, very convex shields protect the shoulder and very large chapels are worn over the coif.

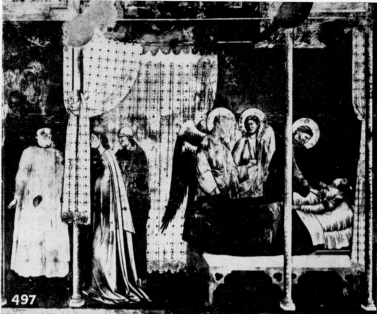

496. XIIIc. 1228. Italian-Byzantine School. (Subiaco S. Benedetto.)

Scenes in the life of St. Gregory: Portrait of St. Francis. Commemorates St. Francis' visit in 1218 to the first headquarters of the order he had founded a decade before. He wears the same clothing as the peasants with whom the Franciscans lived in joyous poverty. The Franciscans (who now wear a brown habit with a white knotted cord), are still, today, called "Gray Friars," from the original color of the habit.

497. XIIIc. Last decade. Italian. (Assisi.)

Master of the St. Cicely Altarpiece, or Giotto di Bondone. St. Francis curing an unbeliever.

Heads bound; or fur caps with drapery falling over the side from the crown, as though the headcloth of the 3rd figure from the left had been banded with fur, and its hanging ends lifted: or coifed, high felt hat.

The long, full tunics of elderly or important men are often fur-lined or hooded. The back-fullness is laid on in formalized pleats from the shoulders, with a hanging, pleated strip, which can be wound around the neck, if the garment has no hood; pocket-slit in the side seam under the pleats.

498. XIIIc. 1295-1300. Italian (Florence, St. Croce.)

Giotto di Bondone. Scenes in the life of St. Francis: The Saint renounces his father.

Looped-up overskirt of woman on left side is typical of the costume of simple Italian women (see XIVc. Giottos). The dignified men in the father's group wear an interesting variety of draped caps and fur hats, over coifs. Fur collars, muffs, with their long garments and overgarments. Group of ecclesiastics on right; children's dresses slit in front, the corner used as a pouch.

500. XIIIc. Spanish. Bur-
gos. (Fogg Museum.)
    Sepulchral Monument:
Don Diego Garcia:
    Spanish cap; notched
neck and deep armseye of
the Spanish sleeveless surcoat.

499. XIIIc. Spanish. Catalonia. (Solsona Museum.)
    Visitation: two women
in long patterned tunics
and mantillas.

XIIIc. Spanish Costume

Spain, relatively separated from the rest of Europe, had developed its own styles so strongly that much regional character and great richness were retained during the centuries between Spain's XIIc. introduction to the ways of the rest of Europe and her XVIc. position as Europe's first power. We then find all Europe dressed, no longer in the French, but in the Spanish style, which we call "Elizabethan." There are few books on costume in which these most de-veloped and integrated styles do not make a start-lingly sudden appearance; whereas they are, as it could only be, the rich result of a long-simmered stew of the most various elements: Iberian, Greek, Carthaginian, Roman Byzantine, Barbarian, Negro, Jewish, Syrian, Arab, Berber, and European. The permanent union of Léon and Castile had been completed by Alfonso the Wise's father.

Endless information can be extracted from the manuscripts of Alphonso the Wise, the many copies of *The Book of Chess,* and the *Cantigas.*

501-506. XIIIc. Spanish. (Escorial Lib. J. T. 6.)
"Book of Chess" of Alfonso X the Wise (1221-1284), King of Castile.

501. Alfonso, his secretary beside him, and two Moorish ladies.

502. Young prince (Don Sancho?), with his page, playing with a rich girl, attended by her maid.

503. Two court ladies.

504. Two noblemen.

505. Gentleman playing with a Moor.

506. A gentleman playing with a Jew.

Both men and women wear tunics with the tightest bodices found in this century. These are made possible by a set-in sleeve, so cut as to allow great freedom, which is additionally provided by a wide under-arm lacing, utilitarian elsewhere, but in Spain intensely decorative. Nowhere will the sleevelessness of the surcoat receive more emphasis through cut and use of contrasting bindings than here; and not, elsewhere, until XIVc.

The ladies of the rest of XIIIc. Europe, even though dressed in the sleeveless surcoat, are apt to have the look of wearing one, rather than two garments. These Spanish court ladies, however, have a distinct appearance of wearing three garments. The fitted tunic which the rich girl wears beneath her surcoat, has the set-in sleeve emphasized by embroidery into a yoke; below this, the laced portion of the bodice is made of contrasting, dark material, with the same light material as the sleeves showing through the lacing under the left arm, like a light chemise under a dark corset. As women's hair elsewhere is being braided or netted into widening headdresses, these Castilian ladies, with their stressed vertical lines, wear high, turned-up, patterned hats, with a patterned chin-strap as a barbette, over flowing hair.

On the men's tunics, the sleeve seams are emphasized by braid, as nowhere else in Europe (but not to the point of forming a yoke, as in the case of the court ladies), and are likewise laced over contrasting color. Their belts are rich, patterned rather than studded. Capes are edged with braid, and have flat braid fastenings, rather than the cord between jewelled clasps of the rest of Europe. The three-tined forked effect on the gentleman (right of 504)

is pure Byzantine; the main figure on the Disk of Theodosius, which was found in Spain, wears it. The cape (504, right fig.) has the one-sided collar (see Ill. 515) which is not caught together. But the companion of the young prince, for hunting with his falcon, has an analogous, but more fully developed actual armhole, cut into his cape on the right shoulder, and buttoned firmly into place. Chess and falconry were the chief occupations of the leisure of mediaeval nobles.

The dalmatic, cape, and headdress of the King are patterned with the lions and castles of his arms (Léon and Castile). His shoes are laced up the inside while those of others of the men have the fenestrated character of Roman sandals. The Moorish ladies with the King are barefoot, and wear one very wide, loose, transparent garment, and much jewelry at ears, neck, and headbands; this is the only jewelry worn by anyone in these illustrations.

The Jew wears a wide-sleeved, ungirdled tunic; the Mohammedan, a turban, and a vertically striped and buttoned gown, with the first tailored collar we have seen (outside of Persia), lining of plain material, and a fringed scarf twisted about the waist. His companion wears a surcoat of a Mohammedan brocade trimmed with fringe, and a coif surmounted by a sombrero.

Not only the sombrero, but practically all the decorative motifs used in these costumes, persist in use today in the costume of the Indians of Guatemala. The design of the hat of the court lady to the right is identically used in the weaving of one particular Guatemalan town; the wide-and-narrow braid edging is used in the costumes of Solola; the blocks of color (as on surcoat of rich girl's maid, and gentleman on left, 504) are used all over Guatemala, in fastening together strips from their narrow looms; only the lions and castles have been replaced in Guatemala by the double-headed eagle of Maximilian.

504

505

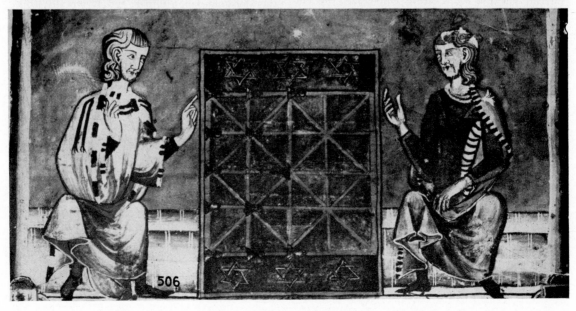

506

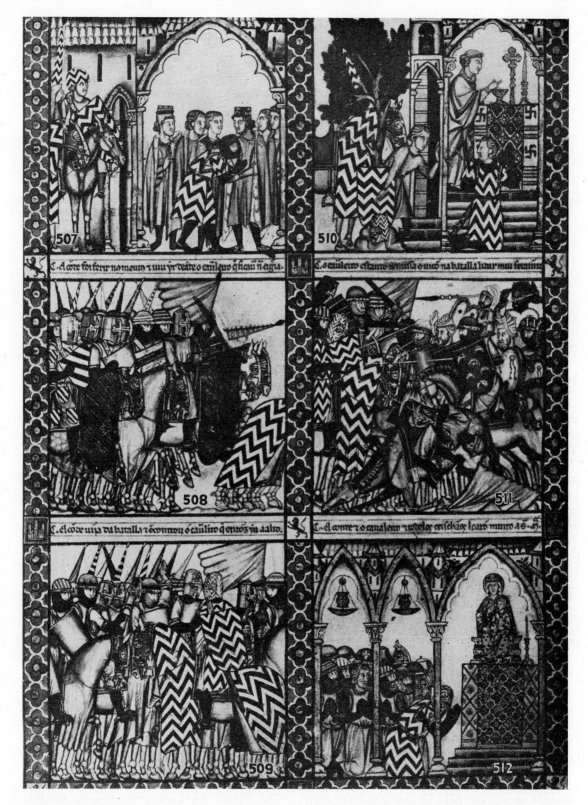

507-512. XIIIc. Spanish. (Escorial Lib., Roy. Mon., T. j. i.)

"Cantigas" of Alfonso the Wise: The story of Count Garcia and the devout knight.

Against Moorish architecture, all the belongings of the knight are covered with a blazoned design as simple and effective as the patterns of Queen Mummadonna and her maids. It is used on the cap of the squire who holds his shield, and the lance with its vertical pendant; on the knight's surcoat and on his horse's caparison. Beneath it, his horse is protected by chain-mail like the others, and like them, by plate on the head. His surcoat has cap sleeves like a XVc. tabard; like the other knights, he has a mittened hawberk, and coif high about the chin; over this the knights wear a variety of small round helmets and

closed helms, one of which is crested. The significance of glove as gage appears almost simultaneously
with the mitten of mail. The opposing army of infidels wears turbans and carries heart-shaped shields,
with tassels instead of the armorial bearings of the
Spanish knights.

The courtiers wear the pill-box hat of Spanish gentlemen, in one case brought under the chin like a
coif, and the surcoat, very much cut out and bordered in blocks of color which one sees in the *Book
of Chess*. The fur-lined capes have an asymmetically
raised and stiffened collar on the left shoulder, and
the Byzantine forked braid-fastening. Tonsured
priest: amice, chasuble, and alb.

**513-514. XII-XIIIc. German. (Cathedrals of Mainz and
Naumberg.) Reliefs.**

513. Men in hats; woman with cap and *barbette;*
in background, a hood (German: *gugel,* from *cucullus*); men's hair to shoulders, or parted behind
rolled bangs. 514. Men wearing petasus.

**515. XIIIc. Swiss. (Chapel, Hocheppen Castle, near
Bozen.) Wall painting.**

The Foolish Virgins: continuation of the costume
we have seen in late XIIc. German and Swiss illustrations; virgins, therefore they are bare-headed, or
with small embroidered cap, but long braided or
twisted tresses; fitted bodices; tight sleeve ending in
immensely prolonged, full band; trailing skirts with
gored fullness. Capes have become very important,
sometimes patterned, caught up on one shoulder in
a stiffened loop (see Ill. 404) which forms a sort of
collar, and is fastened from that to the smooth shoulder with clasp and cord.

**516. XIIIc. 1200-32. German. (Morgan Library, M. 710.)
"Abbot Berthold Missal."**

Salome: underarm lacing of tightly fitted bodice,
which draped down, outward, outlining the belly,
before the skirt begins to be gored into sudden width.
A scapular form of the sleeveless surcoat was often
seen in Germany: open down the sides, and projecting in wings over the shoulders.

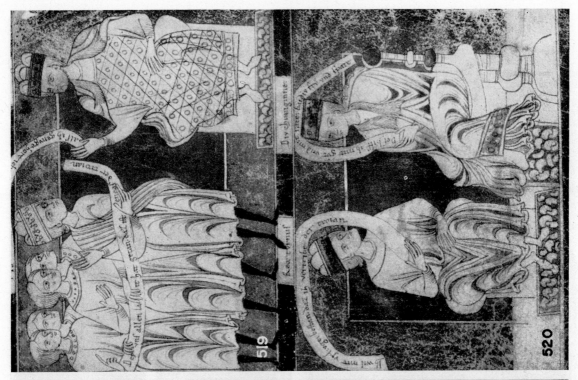

517-520. XIIIc. 1210-20. (Berlin State Library.)

Eneide by Heinrich von Veldeke (c. 1130-89). Askanius shoots Sylvane's brothers; storms and burns their father's city. These German costumes, like those of the rest of Europe, have narrowing sleeves in one with the tunic, even on the hawberks: archers unarmed, except for bows and quivers of arrows, and chapel; hair beginning to be rolled at the nape of the neck.

Sylvane's brothers, surprised in their everyday tunics, have snatched up swords, helms and shields, which like those of the fully armed knights show the heavily stressed decoration of Germany, the home of tournaments.

The court costumes are of the familiar longer, Byzantine type; crowns same German type as Regensburg illus.; the diapered dalmatic of the seated king is sleeveless like a surcoat; and the fur tippet is a typically German accessory, found nowhere else at this period. Armorial bearings probably originated in pieced patterns of fur, used to cover shields; compare knight (upper corner, l.) with executioner (1100-20, Stuttgart Passionale).

521. XIIIc. 1200-52. German. (Morgan Library, M. 710.)
"Abbot Berthold Missal."
Cowled over-garments with hanging sleeves; capes, caps and felt hats for travelling.

522-523. Early XIIIc. German. (Augsburg Cathedral.)
Stained glass: XIIIc. motifs: diapered, foliated, quatrefoils linked by squares (see necks, Eckhart, and Wilpert, this c.), horizontal stripes; eyelets; hats shaped like chapel-de-fer.

524. XIIIc. German. Wurzburg. (British Museum.)
"The Wurzburg Psalter."
Petasus for travelling; band around upper arm persists to mid-XIIIc.

525-26. XIIIc. 1210-35. German. (Strassburg Cathedral.)
Ecclesia, Synagogue: the narrow-sleeved XIIc. gown, with its very long wide skirt, is no longer laced tight in the bodice. It widens immediately below the armspit of the sleeve, which is cut in one with the tunic, although still tight under the arm. Center-front clasp typical of XIIIc.

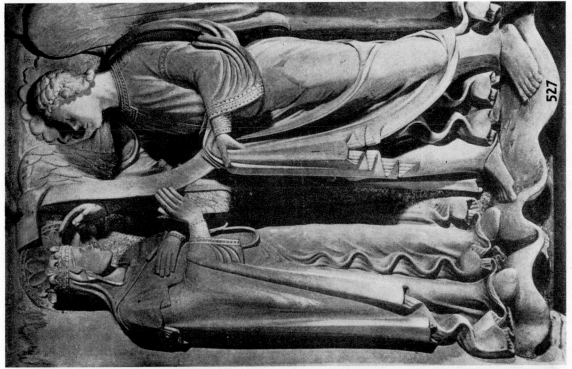

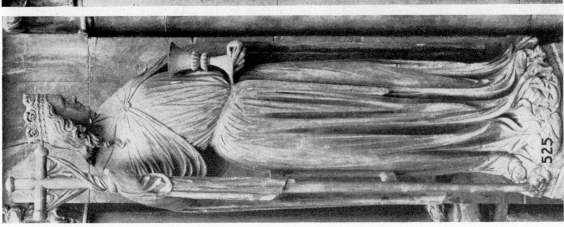

Foliated crown on flowing hair.

527. XIIIc. 1230. German. (Bamberg Cathedral.) Queen wears a low crown over a veil. There is just a suggestion in the sleeves of the undertunics, of the gauffered, pleated effects so evident in French costume second half XIIc. (Chartres, Corbeil). The angel, a fillet about his head, wears a long tunic of the Byzantine court type.

528

529

tally striped in orange-red, a gray-blue cape, and gilded jewelry.

Wiprecht's red cape, blue gown and shield are studded with great glass jewels. The fur tippet he wears is found only in Germany; cape fastens by an almost invisible cord running across breast from beneath jewelled roundlets on the shoulders. The rosette of decoration (see French XIIIc. Chartres; and Ill. 529) has been expanded into a decoration of the whole front of the gown; handsome belt; studded shield; flattened boss, not yet armorial.

528. XIIIc. 1230-40. German. (Pegau, near Leipzig, Klosterkirche.)

Painted monumental effigy: Graf Wiprecht von Groitzsch. The flamboyant character of German decoration becomes increasingly extravagant during XIIIc. It is frequently absurd, sometimes charmingly so, but often brutally heavy and tasteless. German sculpture of XIIIc. was often painted. One of the Prudent Virgins on the North Portal of Magdeburg Cathedral (1210-35) wears a yellow gown horizon-

529. XIIIc. 1249-80. German. (Naumberg Cathedral.)

Margrave Eckhart II, of Meissen and Uta, his wife: Eckhart wears a coif tied under his chin, over long but not yet controlled hair. The sleeves of his tunic are cut in one with the body and widen into it. Center-front clasp; fringed cape-fastening; wide belt, decorated with studding. Gloves, now very important, hang at sword-handle against shield, a placing characteristic of the period. Elaborately wound scabbard. Uta wears a coronet about her stiffened cap and *barbette* (German, *gebende*). Her cape, fastened from handsome shoulder-clasps, has the rolled collar which has reached Germany from France.

530. XIIIc. German.

Gravestone of Archbishop Siegfried III von Eppenstein.

Mitre aurifrigiata growing higher; pall (which was buried with its wearer); chasuble in a sort of diapered, all-over brocade; dalmatic brocaded in a design of small squares, plain lining; alb with band of the brocade of the dalmatic (a common XII-XIIIc. use) instead of orphreys, in the 4 blocks of decoration, used from XIIIc. on; embroidered liturgical gloves; ring; staff.

Two royal youths with crowns and sceptres. Capes with fringed fastenings; surcoats widely cut out around the armseye, to expose folds made by the excessively tight chest of the tunic, cut in one

with the sleeves of the garment. From the belt of the youth to the right hangs a jewelled pouch with tasselled ends, and a dagger, as well as a longer, broad sword with the wider, straight quillons and wrapped scabbard of XIIIc.

531. XIIIc. 1280. German. (Strassburg Cathedral.)

The King of the World: hair rolled smoothly at nape and above brow in French fashion, surmounted by coronet. His overcoat has short sleeves, slit for the passage of the arm, in the tight sleeve of the tunic; XIIIc. use of buttons to fasten up, or to decorate side-slits, as well as to close neck opening.

The smiling girl with flowing hair and fillet might very well not be wearing a girdle, although in this instance one may exist.

The Rising Bourgeoisie: XIV Century

XIVc. AND XVc. DEVELOPMENT OF DRESS

ARMOR and heraldry affected both male and female civil costume. The devices used on the knight's surcoat were also worn, "parted" (father's on right side, husband's on left) by ladies; and on the garments of retainers. This led to the general use of parti-colored (mi-parti, motley) garments (particularly as the non-armigerous bourgeoisie competed with the aristocracy in costume); and to the eventual rejection of parti-color by the upper classes, and its reduction to livery use alone.

Sumptuary laws multiplied each year during the XIV-XVc., as kings tried fruitlessly to control the manner of living of the steadily rising lower classes. In France, Charles V forbade the long pointed shoes, which the Church had always opposed since they made it difficult or impossible for the wearer to kneel at prayer. All the Edwards tried to control luxury in English food and dress. In 1363, Edward III forbade more than one meal of fish or meat a day to servants; in 1433, James I of Scotland forbade anyone less than a baron from eating pies or meats cooked by the new method of baking in an oven (instead of broiled over a fire). Sumptuary laws fell into disuse or were ignored, were repealed and reimposed. In 1463, Edward IV regulated the dress of all classes, since "the commons of the realm, as well men as women, wear excessive and inordinate apparel, to the great displeasure of God, the enriching of strange realms, and the destruction of this realm."

France led fashion; its influence was most strongly felt by England, with a time-lag of about a quarter century. Costume in Germany, Italy, and Spain, developed more regionally, in ways which later affected French styles. Italian costume exhibited fabrics of great sophistication and luxury. By second half XIVc. French garments became extravagantly short, tight, and padded, or long and dagged. These ways were common in England and Germany by end of XIVc.

As more elastic materials were produced, hose lengthened. The upper garments, to which the hose were laced, were shortened, tightened, and became padded. Belts, elaborate and across the hips in XIVc., tended to disappear in XVc., except over the carefully laid pleats of the long upper garments (new in second half XIVc.)

The lengthening *liripipe* end of the dagged (quainted) hood began to be wrapped around the head to form the turbanned *chaperon*.

Buttons were used in long rows by both male and female, until the advent of the *houppelande*. Gloves were generally worn in XIVc.; indispensable for the gentry by XVc.

DETAILS OF MALE DRESS

In the first quarter of XIVc., long gowns (except for elderly men and ceremonial occasions), and plain hoods had passed out of style.

Pourpoint, gipon, jupon, become the XVc. *doublet*: a padded, close-fitting, low-necked garment, worn under the *cote-hardi*. It had, typically, long tight sleeves. The garment became progressively shorter (eventually supporting the hose, laced to its eyeleted hem), more waisted and padded out at the breast (mid-XIVc.). With the extravagantly padded shoulders, *mahoîtres,* of XVc., padding invaded the upper sleeve as well. By third quarter XIVc., the sleeve often spread over the knuckles. When the sleeve of the *pourpoint* was short, wide, or pendant, the long close sleeve of another short body-garment appeared beneath them. Like the *cote-hardi,* the *pourpoint* assumed the high collar of the *houppelande* at end XIVc.

Gambeson, haketon, (G. *wammes*): body-garment of leather, or of padded and quilted stuff, not decorated; worn under armor, or as indoor garment of knight.

Cote-hardi: low-necked outer garment, laced or buttoned tight (center front opening, mid-XIVc.) with *liripipes* (later, lined *tippets*) hanging from elbow. This garment, too, became progressively shorter, from below knee (first half XIVc.,) to just above crotch (end XIVc.). Hem often dagged. By end XIVc., it too, appropriated the collar, sleeves, and pleats of the *houppelande,* which was supplanted by the *jacket, jerkin.*

The new, long outer garments of mid to third quarter XIVc. were the *houppelande* and Housse. The houppelande: (m. and f.), open down front; high, shaped collar; trailing "sleeves that slod upon the earth" (Richard II), usually funnel-shaped; bag-shaped in first third XVc: hanging, mid-XVc. Usually made of brocade; frequently fur-lined; edges elaborately dagged. The houppelande hung in formalized folds, tacked into place under the belt (the position of which was gradually lowered). Length varied from below knee, to dragging train for great occasions.

Housse: male use; tabard-like; buttoned slit at neck. If belted, only across the front.

Capes: short shoulder-capes of fur; or longer capes with dagged edges; fastened on one shoulder by buttons. Long only for travel, or as worn by peers, or members of knightly orders.

Hoods (G. *gugel*): dagged, with lengthening *liripipe*.

Hats: great variety, in beaver or felt. High conical; topper-shaped; pork-pie; and turned up in back. Arrangements of hood, bound around the head by the *liripipe,* with the dagged edge hanging, developed into the *chaperon* hat of end XVc. Plumes, end XVc. Pins, ornaments, and embroidery.

Hair: parted, exposing the forehead, rolled at the nape to mid-XIVc.; the rolled bottom became bushier. Late in XIVc., appeared the bowl-crop. The hair was combed in radiation from a spot on the crown, and cropped from bangs on the forehead in a continuous line which uncovered the ears. This line dipped in back toward the nape, but in most cases, the neck and head were shaved to a point well above the ears. The hair formed a sort of flat cap on the crown, no larger than a small Spanish beret of our own day.

Leg-wear: *Braies* shortened to drawers. *Hose*: becoming longer, better attached; often parti-colored; soles sewed on feet of hose, to end XVc.; codpiece attached to fork, as body garments shorten.

Shoes: ankle-height; front or inside lacing, or lappets. Simple cut; material often elaborate. Pointed toes, *poulaines* or *crackowes,* supposed to be of Polish origin, end XIVc.-end XVc. Wooden clogs to protect shoes from mud.

Boots: worn by travellers and huntsmen; not otherwise common until XVc.; elaborate, after 1450.

Belt: carrying *gypcière* pouch, writing materials and dagger, *anelace;* losing importance by mid-XVc.

DETAILS OF FEMALE DRESS

Women wore long, close-fitting, laced or buttoned garments.

Kirtle, Fr. *cotte*: close-fitting; tight buttoned sleeves; belted when worn under *cote-hardi,* which was buttoned down front; *liripipes* at elbow.

Sideless Surcoat: (Fr. *surcoat*); (G. *sorket*); very much cut-out armseye, edged with fur (England); with a plaquard or stomacher of fur (France); low neck; back cut wider than front; always prominently buttoned down center-front.

By mid-century women's gowns began to be divided into separately cut bodice and skirt; necks lower; sleeves longer. English robe: high neck; fitted laced back; arranged pleats at girdle.

Towards the end of the century came the *robe, houppelande*: new garment of women, as well as men. Very short-waisted bodice; wide, low, V-neck; wide belt, just under arm and breast; gored skirt, with wide border, often of fur: skirt so long that it had to be held or tucked up, or even carried by an attendant, thus revealing the material of the underskirt. For reasons of economy, luxurious material often appeared as a wide band on the lower part of the underskirt, matching the tight sleeve of the undergarment. Style is always capable of arising out of limitations, as in this case, just as well as out of profusion.

The cloak was now worn only on ceremonial occasions; the hood, by bourgeoisie.

During the first half of XIVc., hair was banded, by *wimples,* under the chin; was set in wide V-arrangements; caught in *crespine* nets. Hair in spirals at ears was replaced by vertical plaits, toward midXIVc. By the third quarter of the century, the wimple was passing and by the end of the century we see the horned headdress, *atours; hennin,* with veil; no hair showing; worn with houppelande. Long hair: brides, children, young girls, the Virgin, queens at their coronation.

A *girdle* was worn with *aumonière;* lady's dagger. Much jewelry and many buttons were used.

XIV CENTURY DEVELOPMENT OF ARMS AND ARMOR

Many of the examples we use to illustrate the main line of development of XIV-XVc. armor are English (in use if not in make) simply because these are the centuries of Crecy, Poitiers and the Black Prince, and of many of the plays of Shakespeare. It is most frequently English information that we require.

The finest armor in Europe, and much of the best worn in England, was of continental manufacture, Italian and German in particular.

Froissart records that Bolingbroke, accused of disloyalty in 1398, the year before he succeeded to the throne, asked Galeazzo Visconti, duke of Milan, to send him four armorers, together with magnificent armor from Lombardy, to wear in his life or death combat with the Earl Marshal, Mowbray, whose equally splendid armor was ordered from Germany.

The XIVc. was a period of superimposition of defenses, leading to the XVc. simplification of complete plate-armor (Eng. *alwite,* Fr. *harnois blanc*). Armor was expensive and good old-fashioned armor was not tossed away; it might even suit your action better. We find it in use, in combination and with additions, long after newer forms had become popular, so long as armor is used at all. The simple chain-mail defense of the XIIIc. lingered through the early XIVc., though defensive portions of leather and plate had already been added, and were constantly being supplemented by articulations at arm, hand and shoulder, at knee, leg and foot, until the sheathing of the entire body in plate was understood; and asymmetric sophistications were developed for special purposes. An articulated sheath of plate with mail gussets, over a leather garment to prevent chafing, was an infinitely more flexible and comfortable arrangement than half-a-dozen, or more, superimposed protections of leather, wadding and studding, and chain.

Mail was provided in a great variety of patterns, as the coif-de-mailles over arming-cap was superseded by the *camail* dependent from the *bascinet*. In battle or tournament, the helm was set over, and supported by the bascinet, until the XVc. when it rested on the plates of the shoulder and was used only in tournaments.

The loose surcoat, dangerously long at the end of the XIIIc.,* was shortened, tightened and dagged during the early XIVc. (and from 1321-46, into various forms of the peculiarly English military garment, the *cyclas*), into the fitted *jupon* of the late XIVc., out of which developed the XVc. *tabard*.

As the jupon (originally a civilian garment), tightened at the waist into the *justaucorps,* the belt at the waistline of the surcoat, as well as the diagonal sword-belt which it had supported, were replaced for both knightly and civil use by an elaborate and precious belt, worn horizontally and low on the hips, where it was held in place by hooks to the jupon; it supported the sword and slender *misericorde* of the knight and the heavier *anelace* of the civilian.

A series of carefully dated records of costume and armor exists, for a period of over 300 years, in the form of English and Continental brasses, commemorative plates of brass or latten, often enamelled, the finest of which were executed in Flanders and brought back to the East coast ports of England through which the Flemish wool-trade passed. Many of the best brasses and most luxurious costumes are those of rich bourgeois, wool-traders, mayors of towns, and their wives. These memorial plates suffered through Cromwell's destruction of the churches, and since then, through vandalism, carelessness, or simple greed for their value as old metal. But the recording of these monuments, through rubbings, became a

gentle but long-lived fad, from the end of the XVIIIc. These were accurately engraved and much published in the mid-XIXc. or the rubbings given to museums, often after the verger had cut up the actual plate to make a new foot-scraper for the church door, so that in many cases, these records are all that remain to us.

XIV and XV Centuries in England

The finest of guides to XIVc. England has just been published: Edith Rickert's *Chaucer's World,* Columbia University Press, N. Y., 1948. The great mediaeval scholar, author of the definitive critical text of the *Canterbury Tales,* died in 1938. She had amassed an immense amount of documentary material, uncovered for the first time by her research. This has been classified and combined with contemporary illustrations, to give a picture, painted by those who lived it, of London life, the home, training and education, careers, entertainment, travel, war, the rich and poor, religion, and death and burial, with a bibliography of manuscript and of printed sources. It is my dream of a good book come true.

The *Paston Letters* (ed. J. Gairdner, 3 vols., Archibald Constable & Co., Westminster, 1897) are among the great sources of information about English life in the XVc.

They show the rapid rise into the Norman society of Norfolk of the descendants of Clement, a Saxon bondsman and his bondswoman wife. His son, William, became a respected judge, under Henry VI; his grandson, John, married into county society, became the executor of the will of Sir John Fastolf (prototype of Shakespeare's Falstaff) and (whether by forgery or not), one of his heirs. His two great-grandsons were both knighted, and one became engaged to two ladies "right nigh to the Queen" by birth. Of his great-great grandsons, Sir William married the daughter of the Duke of Rutland, and was the ancestor of the first Earl of Yarmouth; and Clement became a celebrated naval commander, under Henry VIII.

In these letters, we meet most of the families of Norfolk and adjoining counties, whose effigies we use as illustrations: Northwood, Stapleton and Cobham, Felbrigge, Hastings, and Southwell, Say, Calthorpe and Arundel, Eresby, Rous and Warwick, as well as Edmond and Elizabeth Clere, the Pastons' cousins; and the family of the poet Chaucer, connections of the Pastons.

The "Bromholm Psalter" (illustration 534) comes from the nearby Cluniac Abbey to which the letters frequently refer.

There are letters from mothers and sons, about the management of country estates, and the pitched battles which were necessary to retain them; flirtatious Valentine letters; marriage arrangements; letters from wives, asking husbands to bring back dates and yeast, almonds, sugar and

---

* The persistence of old fashions is shown in the death of Sir John Chandos, who, at the end of XIVc. tripped over a long white surcoat, like that commonly worn 100 years before.

salad oil, articles of clothing and lengths of fabric, one of which tactfully concludes: "I would you were at home, liever than a gown, though it were of scarlet"; brothers writing each other to fetch forgotten garments, "iij longe gownys and ij.doblettes, and a jaket of plonket chamlett, and a morey bonet out of my cofyr . . . Sir James has the key," or telling how Sir James (mother's favorite priest) "is evyr choppyng at me, when my modyr is present, with syche wordys as he thynkys wrath me, and also cause my modyr to be displeased with me."

We have invaluable wills and inventories of Fastolf, as well as of many Pastons. These give minute instructions for funeral arrangements and tomb-stones; bequests to all the religious establishments, village inhabitants, poor, leperous, and the family; disposing of ten to twenty pages of plate, arras and tapestries, linen, room furniture, wardrobe, armor and books.

They also describe various processions and tournaments, and the costumes of the participants.

The *Paston Letters* show feudal English home life as ordered, mercenary and harsh. Marriages were arranged; property settlements of prime importance. As Scrope complains he was treated by his step-father, Fastolf, wards with property were "bought and sold like beasts." Places were found for children in the households of the great, and daughters were married and got out of the house, as soon as possible. English children were treated with a lack of tenderness which horrified the Venetian ambassador. In Renaissance Italy, children were not beaten after the age of seven; boys and girls were on the same footing, received the same educations; and the growth of personality was fostered. In feudal society, kings uncovered at the mention of other kings; the greatest lord was some king's "man," as his followers were his "men": all had and knew their places, and were scrupulous to give and receive all due honor, as we see in the headings of these letters of children to parents, and wives to husbands. The brutality of English family life was made bearable by the easiness of external social relationships in England. Erasmus noted the endless kissing which characterized the meetings of English ladies and gentlemen; and we find England in the XVc. notable for its external freedom, courtesy and fine manners.

The letters, which include those of servants, prove a widespread literacy; though the spelling is varied and phonetic, complicated by local pronunciations which still persist in English counties. Great lords and older knights like Fastolf are apt to sign letters written by their clerks; young men had been going to Eton and Cambridge since second quarter XVc. John Paston's library, in 1482, consisted of seventeen books: one, on chess, was produced by Caxton in 1474—the first book printed in England; four romances (one of which he "had off myn ostess at the george," and the other he "hadde neer X yer, and lent it to a dame"); six classics; four on blasoning; one on knighthood and the rules of tournaments and warfare; one of the new statutes of the kingdom.

532-533. XVc. 1477-85. English. (Formerly, Duke of Manchester.)

John Rous of Warwick: "Rows Roll."

Rous, the chaplain and historian of the Warwicks (see also Warwick Pageant, XVc.), in the "Rows Roll" lists the members of the family. These are Thomas, sixth Earl of "Warrewik" (1213-97) and his sister "Margeria," by his death Countess of Warwick; both in the costume of the XIVc. (See Appendix.)

534

535

534. XIVc. c. 1300. English. East Anglia. (Oxford Bodleian.)

"Bromholm Psalter": F o o l and wise man.

Fool wears a three-pointed pink cowl, ending in bells, over a loose gray tunic; and carries a fool's bauble with a bladder on the end, for noisy belaboring.

535. Early XIVc. English. Norfolk.

"Gorleston Psalter."

The Church had been criticizing and reforming itself throughout XIIIc. (see Monastic development). Friars had gone out from cloisters into active life. Whole categories of the clergy had become responsible to a far-off Pope, and were no longer under the jurisdiction of a near-by bishop. The people with whom they mingled knew and judged them as men. Rising lower classes had more money and could go on local pilgrimages. There was an immense amount of gusto and curiosity, and a good deal less automatic reverence.

All this was felt, even by cloistered monks; geese quack at foolish-looking animals dressed like important ecclesiastics, and illuminated missals begin to be very good fashion plates and embroidery pattern-books. They were the only ones available to their contemporaries, and are equally valuable to us.

536.

536. XIVc. c. 1310. English. Norwich, (Oxford Bodleian, Ms. Douce 366.)

"Ormesby Psalter."

Animal figures: left: fox; hair caught in crespine net, with barbette and circlet; hood thrown back. Right: conical beaver hat, worn over hood with short point. Knight and lady slaying unicorn: Lady: kirtle with XIIIc. sleeve worn under cote-hardi buttoned on right shoulder; crespine and couvre-chef. Knight: chapel over "banded" chain mail furnished with knee and elbow plates; ailettes bearing knight's device on shoulder of surcoat.

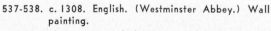

537-538. c. 1308. English. (Westminster Abbey.) Wall painting.

537. Siebert, King of the Saxons, founder of the Abbey, d.616.

538. Edward II (1284-1327) or Edward I.d.1307. Conservatism of the costume of majesty. In the early XIVc. representation of a VIIc. personage, Siebert is given gloves for dignity; an early XIIIc. hair dress;

archaic notes in low, simple crown; bloused tunic with wide orphreys at neck, hem and edges of cape, which is without shoulder clasp or fur lining.

Edward, almost contemporary, is shown against a background semé with lions passant gardant; gloved with great XIVc. elegance; late XIIIc. hair-dress; higher, more foliated crown and sceptre than those of Siebert; dressed in costume of majesty of

Sassetta: Journey of the Magi (*detail*).

XVc. c. 1430. Italian, Sienese.

preceding century; narrow orphreys, belt with long tongue hanging at center front over a slit tunic; cape fur lined, clasped on right shoulder.

539-552. 1303-14 A.D. English. (New York Public Library.)
"Tickhill Psalter."

539. Diagonal XIIIc. neck-closing; unused sleeve of overgarment; hat, with crown like point of hood, flopping forward. King's gloves, still an article of great elegance.

540. Saul: cape gathered onto embroidered collar, of Byzantine-regal sort. Abner: guarnache and hood worn over head.

541. Absalom: beret over coif; hood thrown back.

542. Jonathan: doffing tunic, showing shirt and braies tucked into hose.

543. Knights, surcoats below calf.

544. Musicians.

545. King: fine gloves.

546. Knight receiving from king helm with crest, and sword with magnificent belt and fastenings; separate mittens, apparently of flexible plates, hang on cords from sleeves. Slits in hawberk show mail chausses fastened like civilians hose, over braies; laced up back of calf; poleyns at knees.

547. King: familiar over-tunic with hanging sleeve. Knight: wearing accoutrements just given him by king, and shield.

548. King: doffing hawberk, worn over tunic. David: crook and embroidered pouch with tassels (gypcière), into which he gathers stones for sling-shot.

This manuscript, from the Lothian Collection, was written, illuminated, or perhaps merely gilded, by John Tickhill, prior of the Monastery of Worksop, which supplied manuscripts for Augustinian use.

553. 1310 A.D. English. (Trotton, Sussex.)

Margaret, Lady de Camoys: earliest English brass of a lady. Couvre-chef and wimple; enclosing face in manner analagous to coif-de-mailles of knight. Wimple, however, is often tucked into neck of gown.

Side arrangement of hair, with small curl at each temple, under fillet. Tunic (originally semé with enamelled shields); short loose sleeves, over kirtle; long tight buttoned sleeves.

554-555. 1325 A.D. English. (Westley Waterless Church, Cambridgeshire.)

554. Alyne, Lady de Creke, his wife: in carefully composed costume, all garments unified by identical embroidered edging; orphrey-like bands have b e e n superseded by asymmetric, often foliated running designs. *Couvre-chef* and *wimple;* looped plaits of hair. *Mantle:* fur-lined and with embroidered edge, fastened across breast by tasselled cord. *Surcoat:* sleeveless, very long, caught up; embroidered e d g e and hem. *Kirtle:* long tight buttonless sleeves; hem embroidered to match cape and cote.

555. Sir John de Creke: knight in mixed *mail* and *plate;* surcoat becoming *cyclas;* mustache. *Bascinet:* fluted, pointed, w i t h ornamental *prente,* worn over and laced to *coif-de-mailles,* which is not yet superseded by *camail.*

C y c l a s: shortened surcoat, cut off, *in front* only; slit at sides; tightened at body by lacings which s h o w under arms. Two *pourp o i n t s:* one studded with roses and fringed; one quainted leather. Mail *hawberk:* w i t h short, slit sleeves; hemline pointed down in front; *hauketon:* shows

beneath hawberk. *Chausses:* of banded mail, matching rest of mail equipment. *Poleyns:* cuir bouilli.

Plate defences: *rerebraces:* with lion's head *shoulder* and *elbow cops; vambraces:* beneath sleeve of hawberk; hinged around arm; *greaves:* strapped over chausses; *demi-sollerets:* laminated, protect feet;

spurs: rowell, now not uncommon.

Shield: heater-shaped; charged: Or on a fess gules three lozenges vair; *sword:* knob pommel; scabbard attached to *sword-belt* by metal catches.

Waist-belt of surcoat remains on transitional garment.

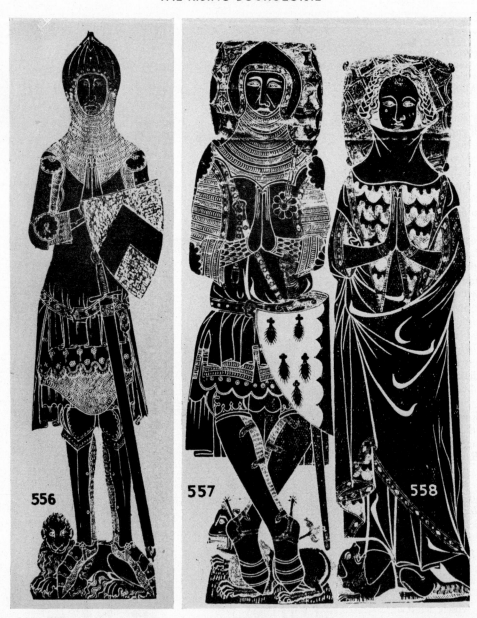

556. 1327 A.D. English. (Stoke D'Abrenon, Surrey.) Brass.

Sir John Daubernoun, son of Sir John, 1277: wearing mixed *mail* and *plate;* surcoat becoming *cyclas; camail;* moustache and beard. *Bascinet:* fluted, with dependant *camail,* of banded mail. *Cyclas:* very short front, slit sides, tightened under arms; without waist belt. *Pourpoint:* scalloped, fringed and studded. *Hawberk:* short slit sleeve; hemline curved downward in front. Hauketon, chausses.

Plate defences: *Rerebraces: roundels* protecting shoulder and elbow. *Vambraces:* under sleeve of hawberk; hinged. Poleyns (leather or plate). *Greaves:* strapped over chausses. *Demi-sollerets:* laminated; *prick-spurs. Shield: heater-shaped:* charged like fathers'. *Sword: sword-belt,* worn low; ornamented with crosses and roses of father's gigue.

557-558. 1330 A.D. English. (Minster, Sheppey.) Brass of French Manufacture.

557. Sir John de Northwood: wearing mixed mail and plate; surcoat into cyclas; camail. *Bascinet:* lower and rounder than 1327 Daubernoun, protect-ing ears; camail of banded mail with invected edge. *Cyclas:* short in front; sides and front slit; cut out under arms and bordered like sleeveless surcoat of lady. *Haubergeon:* slit front and sides, and at wrists. *Pourpoint:* quainted and grommeted. *Chausses:* incorrectly restored below knees.

Plate defences: *Rerebraces:* replaced by lengthened *roundel;* roundel on elbow of hawbergeon. *Vambraces:* scale-armor; under hawbergeon. *Mammelière:* on left breast; fastened to haubergeon, or to metal plate beneath (forerunner of breastplate); holding chain which secured helm. *Shield:* larger, very convex; hung on long studded gigue; charged: Ermine a cross engrailed gules. *Sword:* on low *belt;* worn farther to left.

558. Joan de Northwood, 1330: wearing a garment unique in England; occasional in France. *Gorget* "poked up with pins" to looped braids; without couvre-chef. *Surcoat:* sleeveless, lined with vair like hood which can be worn, buttoned over head, or as here, partially unbuttoned, as a cape; embroidered edges. *Kirtle:* embroidery of cuff and coat match.

559. c. 1325-35. English. E. Anglia. (Morgan Library, M. 700.)

"Du Bois Psalter."

Shepherd: hat, held by cord with movable slide, over hood; mittens; shoes with tongue. Small figure: in high flopping hat, over hood with liripipe; hood or collar on garment with funnel-shaped sleeves.

560. XIV-XVc. English. (San Marino, Huntington Library.)

"Ellesmere Chaucer."

The mediaeval excuse for taking a vacation was to go on a pilgrimage. Inns were usually dirty, and as dangerous as the roads, so pilgrims tried to travel in groups, for both fun and protection. The standard of living was at its highest in the monasteries; they served as the luxury hotels of the period. The monks welcomed the distraction of visitors; and educated people looked forward not only to exalted religious satisfactions, but to the cleanliness and good fare, to the intellectual cultivation of the monks, and to interesting and educational sights of beautiful manuscripts being illuminated, cheeses better made, fields and flocks more thriftily managed than anywhere else.

Wife of Bath: wide hat, held by cord like shepherd's; hood; netted hair; skirts and feet thrust into roughly hose-shaped bags; spurs over hose.

561. XIVc. 1326-27. English. (Oxford, Christ Church.)
Walter de Milemete: "de nob., sap., et prud. regum."
Crossbowman: aiming at a fire-box. Archers were for a long time unarmed. He now has plate protection at shoulder and elbow, as well as a chapel-de-fer and bavier. He is gloved; the hook for stringing his bow hangs from his belt.

562. c. 1350. English. (Gresford, Denbigh.)
Freestone memorial slab: a civilian. Guarnache with typical XIVc. lappets; standing collar; fastened over a close hood; shows sleeves of two tunics.

563. 1364 A.D. English. (Norfolk, Lynn Regis.)
Brass of Robert Braunch: compartment. Civilian. The new feathered hat over a hood which is buttoned under the standing collar of a short, loose tunic; this can be left open below the breast, because his long hose must be tied to a doublet.

564-574. 1340 A.D. English. (British Museum.)
"Luttrell Psalter."
Liturgical psalter written and illuminated in East Anglia for Sir Geoffrey Luttrell.
564. Man chasing a goose with his hood and staff; wide tunic tucked into studded belt; loose hose.
565. Lady playing with a squirrel, a common mediaeval pet, wearing a collar and bell. Lady in very long cote-hardi, tippet sleeves; hair in a crespine, under wimple and loose hood.

566-68. Milking ewes. Feed was scarce, and sheep could pick up a living on waste land. Tiny as these sheep were, their fleece made them the most profitable farm animal, as the English wool trade throve from XIIc. English agriculture was almost ruined during the XVc., as more land was enclosed for sheep, and fewer farmers were needed. Cheese-making from ewe's milk was abandoned when sheep became profitable. "They vse to wayne theyr lambes at 12 weekes olde, and to mylke their ewes fiue or syxe weekes," but this was "greate hurte to the ewes, and wyll cause them to . . goo barreyne."* The milker's hood can be fastened by its button. One of the women carrying milk wears a similar hood over couvre-chef; aumonière at belt. Her companion has a smocked apron. No perspective in these illustrations.
569. St. James as a pilgrim. Barefoot with staff, and cockle-shell (of a pilgrim to his own shrine at Compostella) fastened to the script which hangs from his shoulder, and on the turned-up, pointed hat worn particularly by pilgrims.
570. Men ploughing. It usually took 8 of these tiny oxen to draw a plough, but as many as 24 are known to have been yoked together, in working clay soil. Ploughman: hat like St. James', turned the other way, over a hood with a small tip; loose tunic, split up side seams; studded belt with hanging

* John ? Fitzherbert: *Book of Husbandry*, 1523.

564 565 566 567 568 569 570

sheath; work gloves; legs protected by bindings. Ox-driver: hood with tabs, which is seen at the neck, in various forms, throughout XIVc.; guarnache over tunic, slit up the front; also gloved.

571

572

potum dabis nobis in lacrimis in

573

t memores sunt mandatorum
ipsius : ipsius : ad faciendum ea :

574

571. St. Catherine; dressed as a queen of an earlier period.

572. Bishop: mitre and crozier more elaborate in form; amice, chasuble, dalmatic, alb with apparel, and episcopal ring over glove.

573. Archers: their leader wears a turned-back hat brim with a hood crown. Over the sleeve of his upper tunic, which is open at the side-seams of the skirt, he wears an arm guard; as do the other archers, into whose studded belts are tucked the wide skirts of their tunics, and their spare arrows.

574. Noble ladies travelling in a chariot. Carriages, originally made in Hungary, were a Flemish industry in XIIIc. This chariot, possibly the first in English use, was probably imported; similar ones are seen on the Continent.

Only very rich women or sick people rode in "whirlicotes," (whirl-moving, cote-house) or "folkwains." It was really much more comfortable to ride, but Elizabeth toured England in uncomfortable state in something not much more refined. When Richard II was married in 1383 to Anne of Bohemia, (who brought the side-saddle to England) whirli-

cotes and chariots were forsaken, Stow says, except at coronations.

This chariot has the usual 6-spoked wheel of the period, and no springs at all. Painted curtains, usually of leather, either rolled up or had window openings with curtains. A metal-sheathed box is fastened underneath, and there are rings for fastening luggage or dogs. There are a good many attendants, since the chariot had to be lifted around corners, until the XVIc., when a swivel was added to the front axle. This whirlicote is drawn by 5 horses in line. The first, between shafts, carries a driver with a very long whip; the front horses are between rope traces, caught to the shafts by pegs. The 4th horse is also driven; the lead horse is riderless.

The attendants on horseback all wear hoods with liripipes; over which 2 wear beaver hats. Rider (c.) has a scapular over hood and cote. The lady, who is passing her dog out to an attendant, wears a wimple. The sideless surcoats of the 3 young princesses are still very simple, bound at the edges with another color; veils from crowns set over braided, looped hair.

Comment alixand' fuit presente de un merueillous belle fonnes
encountre nature com honie + fuit nees in babilonie

575-584. 1338-44 A.D. England. (Oxford, Bodleian.)
"Romance of Alexander."
Gentlemen outdoors with king (575); and at *banquet* (576); showing a great variety of cotes-hardi and hoods. Without the hoods (in banquet scene), the cotes show wide bateau-neck and left under-arm fastening; they are parti-colored, motley, and (to left of king at banquet) armorial, as are the hooded capes

front of the skirt, through which to reach the belt (worn over the kirtle) from which hung aumonière, and even dagger. As sideless cotes are worn, and elaborated, the all-over embroidery tends to move to the kirtle (see Ill. 586). Hair is braided and massed over ears.

580. *Court ladies*: ceremonial sideless surcoats, which are of plain material, piped with another color, a line of fur, or braid, but never embroidered all-over; buttons down center-front and forearm of kirtle; hair elaborately braided and looped to a center part, over the forehead.

Windows, without glass, protected by oiled parchment, or shutters of wicker work or battens.

581. *Two ladies and four gentlemen*: all garments finely embroidered; gentlemen's pouches monogrammed; both hoods and cotes embroidered and dagged to match; ankle high, embroidered shoes. Arrangement of buttons and embroidery down front of ladies' cote; looped braids here pinned far back.

Minstrels and their music played an important role in the social life of a mediaeval court. Gaston de Foix gave 500 francs to the minstrels and heralds; and ermine-trimmed gold garments with 200 francs to the minstrels of the Duke of Touraine. (Froissart)

with dagged and slittered edges and long liripipes, which all wear in the outdoor scene above. Tippets and liripipes finish the sleeves of many of the cotes at the elbow, below which the sleeves, whether of cote or doublet, are buttoned to wrist. Buttons are also used down front of a diagonally striped garment. As the belt of the armed knight was lowered, so was that of males out of armor; all are furnished with gypcière and miséricorde, hung at center front.

577. *Musicians*: dressed, as are the servants at the banquet, very much like everyone else, but not invariably carrying a dagger with pouch.

578. *Ladies and gentlemen at games;* and (579) *with a falcon*: the round game presents the back view of the men's cotes and hoods. The cotes of the ladies have the same bateau neck as the men's; long skirts, frequently tucked up to expose the skirt of the kirtle which is frequently banded. Many of these cotes have buttons down the front; are embroidered all over; and have tippets and liripipes, lined with a plain color, at the elbow; and fitchets or latchets at the

PART OF THE CREST

582. *Women at games*: Cotes with tippets at elbow; some sideless, showing plain sleeve of kirtle, shorter skirt of which is exposed by trussed up skirt of cote, and is edged with a wide darker embroidered band, the color of the sleeves, on a lighter colored skirt. Couvre-chef and disordered hair, which had been arranged like that of the ladies.

583. *Masque*: mummers wearing capes, painted with animals, and with animal-head hoods. Women: parti-colored, plain, and all-over embroidered, with latchets.

584. *Fools*: in loose motley garments with extreme hoods (see Ill. 534), and sleeves cut with exaggerated point at elbow. The first figure from left has one of these sleeves; the other is so long as to conceal the hand.

585. 1347 A.D. English. (Brass of Flemish workmanship.) (Elsing, Norfolk.)

Sir Hugh Hastings, and contemporary personages: mixed mail and plate defenses; *cyclas* becoming *jupon; camail. Bascinet*: rounded top, movable vizor, with linked-mail *camail. Cyclas-jupon*: full-skirted like cyclas, but cut off all around to jupon length and fitted in body like jupon; charged with arms of shield. *Haubergeon*: hanging mail cuffs. *Hauketon*: wrist, below mail cuff. *Cuishes*: studded leather. *Chausses*: mail, without protective shin-plates; rowell-spurs.

Additional plate defenses were: *Gorget*: metal collar on which helm rested. *Rerebraces,* with roundels. *Vambraces*: over sleeve of hawbergeon. *Poleyns*: of cuir-boulli with metal spiked plates. *Shield*: very small, charged: Or a manche gules, with labels of three points argent. *Sword* (worn well to left); *sword-belt,* studded. *Helm* (shown on right above figure): flat-topped, perforated movable vizor.

Other personages (some lost) of Hastings brass: several without shields. The first English brass without shield is Wantone, 1347. Several hold lances with pennons; wear metal gorgets and shoulder-plates; spiked poleyns and coutes;

bascinets with pointed vizors. Dexter side: 1. Edward I, crowned, cyclas-jupon, charged France and England quarterly; 2. Thomas Beauchamp, Earl of Warwick; 3. Member of Despencer family (lost); 4. Roger, Lord Gray de Ruthin. Sinister side: 1. Henry Plantagenet, Earl of Lancaster; 2. Lawrence Hastings, Earl of Pembroke, whose shield, Hastings quartering Valence, is one of the earliest examples of quartering of arms of a lesser personage than king; 3. Ralph, Lord Stafford; 4. Almeric, Lord St. Amand, wearing the only *chapel-de-fer* over bascinet shown on any brass.

586. 1349 A.D. English. (Brass of Flemish workmanship.) (St. Margaret's Church, Lynn Regis, Norfolk.)

Margaret de Walsokne: Rich bourgeoise in costume of utmost luxury. Norfolk and Flanders are

587

closely related by the wool trade on which both
thrive. Their bourgeoisie rivals the aristocracy, which
competes in return. (See Appendix.)

Couvre chef and wimple; looped braids. Mantle:
embroidered edge, contrasting lining, cord thrown
back. Sideless surcoat: sleeveless, fur-lined; edge embroidered; wide neck, highest at center. Kirtle: tight,
buttoned sleeves; cuff detail; magnificent, all-over

embroidery.

**587. 1360 A.D. English. (Brass of Flemish workmanship.)
(Wensley Church, Yorkshire.)**

Simon de Wenslagh: Priests vestments. Matching
embroidery: amice; chasuble with orphreys; maniple
over left arm; stole, fringed; alb with apparels at
wrist and hem. The priest, like the ladies, wears the
simplest of pointed shoes.

588

589

588-589. 1350-60 English. From St. Stephen's Chapel, Westminster. (British Museum.) Wall paintings.

Sons and daughters of Edward III and Queen Philippa of Hainault. St. Stephen's, built in 1350, was glazed with stained glass designed by John Alemayne (whose name shows him an alien) but manufactured at Chiddingford. In tempera and metal leaf, overpainted in transparent oil; shows perspective.

Sons: camail attached to bascinet, heavily ridged all around; jupon with tightly fitted waist bearing England and France quarterly,* over hawbergeon. Extremities completely protected by laminated, hinged plate and mail gussets; belt, low; carrying sheathed miséricorde, right; sword, left.

Daughters: elaborately composed and unified costume. Foliated crowns over looped plaits of hair, decorated with same floral motifs which serve as buttons down front of cotehardi, which is completely sideless, and exposes body and sleeves of brocade kirtle; fur plastron extended over shoulders, from which hangs mantle, fur lined to waist, and bordered like skirt of cote, with an invected foliation.

* To ingratiate himself with the Irish, among whom St. Edward was a favorite, the English king used, in Ireland, banners bearing Edward's arms: A cross patence or, on a field gules, with four doves argent on the shield or banner as you please, rather than England and France. This was related to Froissart by Henry Castine, who had been sent in advance to try to make gentlemen of the Irish kings. They rode without breeches or stirrups, wrapped only in a cloak, and he had great difficulty in persuading them to wear silken robes, trimmed with squirrel and miniver.

590. 1350-60. English. From St. Stephen's Chapel, Westminster. (British Museum.) Wall painting.

Edward III: King: not robes of majesty; but insignia of kingship assumed over dress of contemporary gentleman. Cloak, fur lined, closing on right
shoulder. Shoulder cape of contemporary gentleman,
done in ermine; remains henceforth as part of insignia of kingship. Very high, foliated crown; gothic
sceptre. Justaucorp, the short fitted cote-hardi of the
XIVc., with bordered liripipe sleeves, same brocade as

tight under-sleeve. Important belt at lowered waistline. Pointed shoes, magnificently embroidered.

Courtiers: high felt and beaver hats, one with
plume (increasingly used). Parti-colored capuchon
with embroidered band and cartridge-pleated edge,
worn over justaucorps and under-tunic of matching
brocade; tiny buttons; diapered shoes. Parti-colored
hose and shoes; magnificently bound swords; tunic
with vertical stripes.

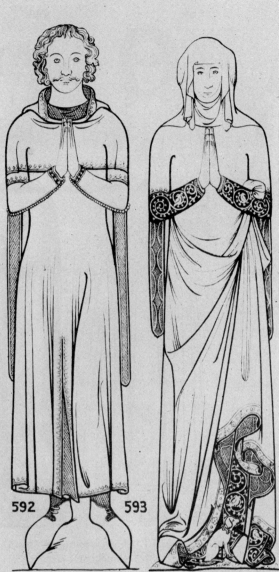

591. c. 1360. English. (Aldborough, Yorkshire.) Brass.

William de Aldeburgh: camail and jupon; mustache. *Bascinet*: high, convex (standard to end of century), covering ears, laced through vervelles to camail of linked mail. *Jupon*: cloth or leather; quainted edge painted or embroidered with arms born by shield; tightly fitted over body-armor. *Haubergeon*: linked mail. Sleeves and chausses of mail reduced to gussets as plate armor sheathes extremities more efficiently. *Cuishes*: pourpointed leather.

Additional plate protection: *Epaulieres; rerebraces; coutes; vambraces; poleyns; greaves;* articulated *sollerets. Gauntlets*: with articulated metal finger- plates. *Shield*: last brass in which shield is shown as part of equipment. Large, convex, charged: "Azure a fess per fess indented and . . ." between three crosses botony, or, the dexter cross charged with an annulet for difference. *Sword*: on *baldric,* embroidered with castles; *miséricorde* (from now on, indispensable part of knight's equipment).

These brasses (592-94) indicate the wealth which the bourgeoisie attained by XIVc. Sir John Fastolf's will (Paston Letters, 1459) refers to "Sir Philip Braunche, Knight, my brothyr-in-law, that deyde and was slayn in Fraunce," and the Paston's cousin Elizabeth Clere will be married to his grandson.

592-593. 1364. English. (Flemish workmanship.) (St. Margaret's Church, Lynn Regis, Norfolk.)

Robert and Margaret Braunch: his chaperon and cote-hardi, with liripipe sleeves and center-front slit, are unified by identical linings and a foliated embroidery edge into a typically composed costume; tight buttoned sleeves of under-tunic; shoes with pointed toes, ankle high, closed by parallel lacings. Lady: couvre-chef and wimple; cote-hardi fur lined throughout; over kirtle scrolled with rich embroidery.

594. 1376. English. (Flemish workmanship.) (St. Margaret's Church, Lynn Regis, Norfolk.)

Robert Attelath: fur-lined cloak closed on right shoulder by 4 buttons; hood, which could button tight at throat, here worn thrown back. Tunic with contrasting lining closed down entire front and at wrist by grouped buttons. Embroidered sleeve of under-tunic prolonged and spread over knuckles; like Ill. 601, allied to gloves with cuffs. Pointed shoes, notched at ankle and buckled.

595-596. 1364. English. (Ingham Church, Yorkshire.) Brass.

596. Sir Miles de Stapleton: camail and jupon; mustache, beard. *Bascinet*: laced to *camail* through *vervelles. Jupon*: cuir-bouilli; quainted edge; studded. *Haubergeon*: banded mail; gussets of mail at armpit and elbow; mail chausses have disappeared. *Cuishes, poleyns* and *jambes* of studded cuir-bouilli.

Plate defenses: *Epaulieres; rerebraces; coutes; vambraces; sollerets;* articulated. *Gauntlets*: steel *gadlings* on knuckles. *Baldric*: metal plates, linked; carries *sword* and *miséricorde*. No shields.

595. Joan (Ingham), wife of Miles de Stapleton: *Hair*: looped braids; jewelled *fillet*; small *veil. Cotehardi*: wide necked: *liripipe* at elbows; buttons at center-front; skirt short; beltless, so provided with *fitchets* to reach *aumônière* hung from belt or kirtle. *Kirtle*: tight buttoned sleeves, spreading over knuckle (compare with gauntlet in Ill. 600: knightly styles influence dress of ladies; wimple was equivalent to coif-de-mailles).

597. c. 1370. English. (Cobham Church, Kent.) Brass.

Maude, Lady Cobham: nebulé headdress, of superimposed gauffered layers, and veil. Sideless cotehardi, buttoned down center-front and with short skirt, bordered at hem and up slit sides. Sleeves of kirtle buttoned from shoulder to spread over knuckles.

598-599. 1384. English. (Southacre, Norfolk.) Brass.

599. *Sir John Harsick*:* camail and jupon; shield no longer part of equipment, but still an important method of identification, a little more personal than a calling card today. Froissart, meeting the March Herald, asks: "March, what are the arms of Henry Castide, for I have found him very agreeable . . ."

Helm: with crest, orle, lambrequin (above figures). *Bascinet*: laced to camail of band mail. *Hawbergeon*: jupon; bearing arms of shield: Or a chief indented sable. As epaulieres, rerebraces, coutes, vambraces; and cuishes, jambes and sollerets, curved, hinged, and articulated, enclose the extremities almost completely, the sleeves of the hawbergeon and the chausses exist only vestigially as gussets of mail at elbow and armpit, knee and foot. Rowell spurs; gauntlets with gadlings; belt, elaborate and low; sword worn at left.

598. *Katherine, Lady Harsick* (née Calthorpe): braids looped over fillet; mantle with cords through fermail: kirtle, with sleeves buttoned from shoulder to spreading cuff, and bearing the arms of Geslingthorpe, assumed by Calthorpe: Ermine a manche gules, impaling Harsick.

* Blennerhasset, Bleverhasset, abbreviated to Harsset, etc.

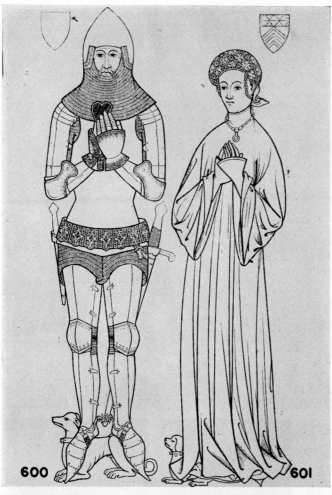

600   601

602

600-601. 1397. English. (Brandsburton Church, Yorkshire.) Brass.

600. *Sir John de Saint Quintin*: camail and jupon. Camail, hawbergeon and gussets of ring mail. Plates, hinged, articulated, buckled, finely chased, covering arms and legs. Gauntlets with cuffs of mail. Magnificent belt; sword borne far to left; miséricorde. Arms blazoned on small shields in corners.

601. *Lora de Saint Quintin*: crespine headdress, padded, covered with jewelled network concealing hair; small veil in back; and looped pearls at ears. Robe: high necked, wide sleeved, ungirdled, very wide skirt, fur lined. Kirtle: sleeves extending over hand.

602. XIVc. 1380-85. English. (London National Gallery.)

Wilton House Diptych.

The most beautiful embroidery in Christendom was done in England during XIII-e.XIVc., and vestments of "English work" were ordered from Italy. The magnificent Sion Cope c. 1300, in the South Kensington Museum, and its accompanying stole and maniple have the coats-of-arms of 124 donors of the vestments worked into the orphreys.

The effigies of Edward III's sons, especially William of Hatfield, at York Minster, show them in beautifully embroidered garments. The actual garments —the "atchievements" of Edward the Black Prince, in war and peace, hang at Canterbury: helmet, gauntlets, shield, and embroidered surcoat laced in back. There is a portrait of Richard II as king, in robes embroidered all-over with R's and roses. The English-made gilt-latten effigy of Richard II and his first wife, Anne of Bohemia, in Westminster Abbey, show both in magnificently embroidered garments. (See Appendix.)

The Wilton House Diptych, against a gold ground, represents (l. to r.) King Edmund: ermine-lined and collared green cloak, blue gown patterned in gold birds collared together by crowns, a blue under-tunic and red shoes. Edward the Confessor: white, with blue under-tunic sleeves prolonged over the hand. John the Baptist: gold lined with pink. Richard II in a red houppelande, covered with the badge of the White Hart in gold, and lined with brown fur. All kings with jewelled brooches.

603.

604.

605

606

603. XIVc. c. 1300. Italian. (Bologna, Museo Civico.)
Master of Manni. Pope Boniface VIII.

This huge statue in sheet bronze, of the Pope who died in 1303, shows the tiara, the non-liturgical headwear of the Pope, signifying temporal power. It is white and was originally without crown. One crown was added in XIc. In other statues, Boniface is shown with two crowns, which he was the first to wear. It was not until 1314, under Clement V that the Pope wore 3 crowns on the tiara. A large jewelled morse was originally set at the neck of what I take to be the mozetta. (See Appendix.)

604-606. XIVc. c. 1305. Italian Florentine. (Padua, Madonna dell' Arena.)

Giotto di Bondone. Scenes preceding the Birth of Christ: the Meeting at the Golden Gate (604); Joachim's Dream, detail (605); Betrayal of Christ, detail (606).

604. Females in specifically Italian dress already seen in XIIIc. Giottos: sleeves cut in one with short-waisted bodice; skirt gathered on, and looped under at the hem in front to show underskirt, orange or rose, with gold, pale or bright green.

Italian way of handling the ubiquitous braids, drawn up behind the ears, forming a coronet above forehead, differs from the English fashion of braids looped on either side, in front of the ears. Italian women's heads are relatively uncovered, in comparison with the veils and wimples of France and England. The extravagance of the horned and heart-shaped headdresses of the rest of Europe, will, in Italy, become an extravagance of hair arrangement; the headdress will be a wreath or fillet; this will increase to a stuffed roundlet, and finally to a turban. The veil will always be gauzy. In Italy it is the wo-

men of the lower classes, or the elderly, who cover their hair (black-shawled women, c.). Two of the ladies wear tiny pill-box hats; one of them holds her mantle in place by means of a narrow patterned ribbon which permits her to catch up its trailing side with the same hand. The man at extreme left wears the dress of the peasant of all Europe: coif; belted tunic; loose-fitting, bound sock-boots.

The shepherd in Joachim's Dream (605), and the attendant in the Betrayal of Christ (606), wear the same peasant costume, with the addition of capes with cowls, or a petasus with cord by which it could be worn slung back.

607. c. 1305. Italian. (Same provenance as 604-606.)

Giotto di Bondone. Last Judgment: Group of the Blessed.

A group of monks in cowled habits, coiffed elderly gentlemen, and ladies in robes of the current cut; rich braid trimming at seams, and orphrey-like patches give an effect which is more Byzantine and ecclesiastic than is commonly worn. Hair simple,

often flowing, with coronet braids, crowns, fillets and bands; woman in dark robe wears a gauzy veil pinned, wimple-fashion, to braided hair.

608. c. 1317. Italian, Sienese. (Naples, National Museum.)

Simone Martini. St. Louis of Toulouse Crowning Robert of Anjou.

The saint who had ceded his throne, probably un-

der duress, to his brother, wears the robe of a Franciscan beneath his bishop's garments, all of which
bear armorial designs. The new king's dalmatic,
likewise, carries his arms in its clavi and orphreys.

609. c. 1328. Italian, Sienese. (Siena, Pal. Pub.)

Simone Martini. Equestrian portraits of Guidoric-
cio da Fogliana.

The surcote of the proud, victorious general and
the caparison of his horse are yellow, with the black
diamonds and a running design of green sprigs,
"fogliana," of his coat-of-arms. He wears a high-collared, wide-sleeved shirt of mail; legs and knees
armed in plate combined with mail.

Beyond the stockade is a mediaeval fortress with
moat, ramparts, and towers with projecting galleries;
and a military machine of the mangonel type, for
hurling stones.

610. XIV.c. Italian, Sienese. (Pisa, Campo Santo.)

Triumph of Death; detail. (Attributed to *Francesco
Traini,* also to *A. Orcagna.*)

Rich woven pattern and embroidery characteristic

of Italian costume from XIVc. Brocade cote-hardi
with short wide sleeves lengthened into liripipes;
more richly lined and edged than in other parts of
Europe at this period. Close sleeves of the kirtle are
likewise of striped or patterned stuffs. Growing importance of the glove; the lady with the falcon wears
two, rather than the necessary one gauntlet (see Ills.

629-30). She alone wears a wimple and complete head-covering, made necessary by the sport. The others wear *roundlets,* stuffed turbans in the spirit of the increasingly seen coronets of braids, worn by the central figure. The third wears a simple pleated arrangement, connected with the elaborate male *chaperon* of continental Europe. Chaplet of flowers on rolled hair of man on right.

611. XIVc. Italian, Sienese. (Siena Academy.)
P. Lorenzetti. Carmelites.

The early black-and-white "magpie" dress of the Fratres baratti.

614

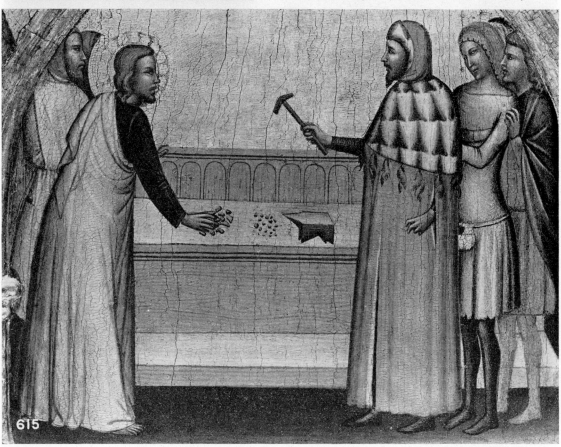

615

612. 1331. Italian, Sienese. (Siena, S. Francesco.)
Ambrogio Lorenzetti. Saint Louis of Toulouse before Pope Boniface VIII: detail of crowd.

Italian male headwear: hats worn over hood or integrated into hood; sheer coif; stiffened, turned-up brim with draped crown; and two wide-brimmed, flat-crowned hats. Wide-necked, sleeved tunics; fur lining seen through breast-slit. Patterned materials.

613. XIVc. Italian, Sienese. (Pisa, Campo Santo.)
Francisco Traini, also att. to *A. Orcagna,* or *P. Lorenzetti:** The triumph of Death: Last Judgment and Hell; Thebaid.

Hawking and hunting on horse and mule-back.

For journeys and hunting, women wear wimples and veils; and men, similar arrangements or hoods, gloves (not only for hawking), and high, conical hats with brims turned up in back. The head is always well protected. The king's crown is imposed on his hat, which is worn over a coif below which the hair is rolled. Jewelled brim of female rider, set over veil and wimple, which fill in low neck of brocade gown. Early prevalence in Italy of brocaded and striped materials. Embroidered borders of king's robe, with its cap sleeve. Sophisticatedly cut liripipe end of the short sleeve of the cote-hardi, worn over plain doublet. Follower, in brocade cote-hardi with funnel-shaped sleeve, wears hood of same brocade. Cripples at right: bearded, while gentry are clean-shaven. Tunics: one-piece, or with set-in sleeves. Old hag: head-covering of lower classes.

* In the case of varied attributions, I have tried to use that preferred by the Frick Art Reference Library.

616

614. 1330-40. Italian. (Wash., Nat. Gall. of Art.)
Bernardo Daddi. St. Catherine.

Crown over characteristically Italian braids, martyr's palm; brown cloak; gold-embroidered, green cotehardi; both lined with white fur, which shows at the fitchet (emphasized by gold embroidery), behind her right arm.

615. XIVc. Italian. (Wash., Nat. Gall. of Art.)
Allegretti Nuzi (act. 1346-73/74). St. John and the Philosopher Crato.

St. John in blue robe and red mantle, is accom-panied by a hooded monastic figure, whose arms are tucked in the front of his scapular; band below hips connects front and back sections of scapular. Crato wears a red cape, lined in white fur; it is slit for the passage of the arms, and is necessarily split up the center-front: hood-facing and shoulder cape of fur, fringed with tails. Accompanying gentlemen in fitted cotes-hardi, with low belts and aumonières.

616. 1337-40. Italian, Sienese. (Siena, Palazzo Pubblico.)
A. Lorenzetti. Results of Good Government: City Life.

Badly damaged, but full of detail of costume, architecture, and street life, which make it worth examining with a magnifying glass.

The gowns of the playful group with the tambourine are worn loose, girdled, or with the skirts gathered onto a low-waisted bodice. With back to us, is a gown brocaded with huge dragon-flies; sleeves are delicately laced across a wide rectangular opening from wrist to elbow in back; lattice-work sandals show clearly below slit which separates short front from longer back section of skirt. A similar skirt (horizontally striped), has corners of back section

pinned up on side seams for freer action. Between these two, a diagonally patterned gown has slittered sleeves, and a series of increasingly larger purses, hanging like tassels, from the belt. The stretched-out arm of the man (next to the tambourine player) is slit and laced along the entire seam of the sleeve, which is cut in one with the body. The sleeve of the youth (following the riders, to the left) is baggy at the elbows in the newest fashion.

617. XIVc. 1338-40. Italian. (Siena, Palazzo Pubblico.)

A. Lorenzetti. Good Government: Allegory of Justice.

621

Procession of dignified citizen in long gowns, coifs, and hats with draped crowns (see Traini: Ill. 613). Women in allegorical costume.

618-619. XIVc. Italian. (Siena, Acad. of Fine Arts.)

Bartolo di Fredi. Scenes from the life of the Virgin.

The saints are, by convention, very richly dressed, in brocade garments with fitchets, which are given an archaic Byzantine look by the use of patches and bands of embroidery.

620. XIVc. Italian. (Pisa, Campo Santo.)

Andrea da Firenze. Three Scenes in life of St. Ranieri.

Old gentleman: fur-lined cape; side slits for arms; short gown; contrasting hose and shoes. Child: caped cote-hardi; front closing, tiny ball buttons; separately cut, very flaring skirts. Group of 4 women, right of psaltery player: puffs pulled through slashes at sleeve-top; convex neckline; short, flaring overgarment. Beside her: interesting flapped cap (see XVc.). Girl with pigtails: sleeves buttoned from knuckles to elbow; braid definition of seams and edges.

621. Mid-XIVc. Italian. Florentine. (Assisi, San Martino Chapel.)

Puccio Capanna. Life of St. Francis, detail: Band of Musicians.

The elaborately imaginative dress of this band of street musicians corroborates Machiavelli's statement about Florence in 1350: "The people being conquerors, the nobility was deprived of all participation in government, and in order to regain a portion of it, it became necessary for them not only to seem like the people, but to be like them in mind and mode of living. Hence arose those changes in armorial bearings, and in the titles of families, which the nobility adopted in order that they might seem to be of the people." Under such conditions, there is always a concomitant rise in popular standards.

Parti-color in a very Italian and sophisticated form, enriched with patterned and pleated fabric, braid, and jewelry.

Saint, and singers, r.: characteristic short, clipped bang which accompanied bobbed hair of XIVc. men: this clipped tuft and the ends (carefully rolled by the more elegant) show even when a close coif is worn. For centuries, hair is more beautifully arranged in Italy than anywhere else in Europe.

The yoke of Italian women's dress is reflected in the flute-player's outer garment; a cape-like section, well down on the shoulders, appears to be attached to the cote-hardi. The standing collar, and flaring, stiffened cuff of the cittern-player's matching inner sleeve, are far advanced in sophistication. Fine details of neck-closings: double clasps of stones; turned-back tabs.

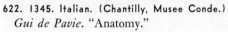

622. 1345. Italian. (Chantilly, Musee Conde.)
Gui de Pavie. "Anatomy."

Slit and hooded, fur-lined gowns with fitchets and liripipe sleeves; row of tiny buttons down outseam of undersleeve.

623-624. c. 1345. Italian. (Morgan Library, M. 735.)
Boniface de Calabria. "Thesauro di cavalli."

Bag sleeve, padded bosom, and high collar of the houppelande affecting the cote-hardi, even of a veterinarian, during first half XIVc.

625-626. 1356. Italian. (San Gemignano, Collegiate.)
Bartolo di Fredi. Old Testament Scenes.

625. Carpenters: aprons, or skirts of tunic tucked up to hold nails. Sock-boots, often without hose. 626. Shepherds: hooded overgarments of comfortable scapular type. Riding hat; plumed, brocade crown; brim turned up in back; cord knotted under chin.

627. XIVc. Italian. (Chantilly, Musee Conde.)

Bartolommeo da Bologna. Allegory.

Knight in surcoat with dagged edges; tight, low-waisted, with the peculiarly full-bellied and portly look of Italian costume of first half XIVc.

Lady mounted astride: veil, which in XIVc. Italy indicated an arduous outdoor trip, a saint or virgin, an elderly woman, or one of the lower classes. Legs protected by rather shapeless, spurred boots, clasped down the outside, and mounting above knee; worn in XIVc. by riders of both sexes. (See Ill. 560.) Embroidered, fur-lined, slit garments with lengthening liripipe sleeve-ends. Pleated, *gugel-like* headdress of woman, developed out of hood thrown across head (see Ill. 628), bound by liripipe end.

628. Late XIVc. Italian, Lombard. (Paris, Bib. Nat. Ms. Lat. 757.)

"Book of Hours for Franciscan use." St. Ursula and the Virgins.

Brocaded or embroidered *cottes,* two of which are high-necked. Turbans and bindings of coronets appear to be affected by the reticulated *kruseler* headdresses of adjacent Germany; looped German braids. Hood with enormously elongated liripipe, thrown over head; the wrapping of this liripipe about the hood, thus worn, led eventually to the extravagant forms of *chaperon.*

629-630. XIVc. Italian. (Florence, Sta. Maria Novella.)

Andrea da Firenze, and assistants. Allegories of doctrine and scenes from the life of Christ; called "Church Militant and Church Triumphant."

629. Worldly temptations: St. Dominic confessing a knight. In these frescos, celebrating the achievements of the Dominicans, the saint wears the hooded, black-and-white habit of his order, together with the scapular which became obligatory in 1220.

There is an infinity of details of the costume of both sexes: prevailing protuberant-bellied look of the long or calf-length garments; this is lost in the shorter, tight-waisted cote-hardi of the bearer, center. Yoked effects on viol player and small female figure (to left of center, bottom) also appear on garments of Italian male musicians. Patterned and embroidered materials, parti-color, dagged edges, fur linings. Hair of women, braided or flowing, relatively uncovered.

630. Lords spiritual and temporal. Throng of dignitaries, hooded and caped in fur. The gentleman in the short, light costume has been variously identified: from the French cut of his dress, and his pointed poulaines as the usurper, Walter de Brienne, Duke of Athens; and from the garter on his left leg, as an Englishman, perhaps an ambassador. (The records of the Order of the Garter, before 1416, have been lost.) Parti-color and diagonals on hooded cape (center, back to us). Gauzy cape of kneeling lady, whose headdress has the new, pushed-back look. By mid-XIVc., beards have begun to reappear; both forked and pointed.

631-632. XIVc. Italian. (Florence.)

A. Orcagna (?).

632. Tomb of Acciajulo Acciajuoli. The Acciajuoli were a family which, like the Medici, favored the lesser Florentine guilds in their struggle with the major guilds, who were aided by the Albizzi.

Costume of a rich, elderly Florentine, in its perfection. Braid-trimmed cote-hardi, as long and dignified as a gown; magnificently embroidered lining shows at slit front and tongue-shaped, liripipe sleeve. Fitchet behind sword handle. Handsome belt, fine buttons, gloves, and laced, embroidered shoes.

Linen coif; with hood, matching gown, folded and thrown over shoulder. It was often carried thrown across the head; the point, as it lengthened, was used to bind the whole in place, bringing about the draped turbans, *chaperons,* of e.XVc.

631. Tomb of Lorenzo Acciajuoli. Armorial surcoat vanishing. Vambraces and cuishes of leather, metal banded and studded. Hawberk with sleeves to just below the elbow; scalloped metal collar. Pauldrons and poleyns with lions' heads.

631

632

Jupon: dagged border in leaf design. Belt is high and narrow, so breast-chains still secure sword and dagger. Mail gussets between cuishes, jambes, and sabatons; rowelled spurs. Cuffed gauntlets. Fur-lined cape, with embroidered edge, fastened on right shoulder.

633. 1386. Italian. (Florence, Bigallo Coll.)

Niccolo di Pietro Gerini, and assistants. The return of lost children, by the captains of the Misericordia, to their mothers.

Wimples are not worn in Italy, probably because of the climate; more enveloping headwear is seen in N. Italy because of climate and propinquity to continental style (see Ill. 628). The headdress of the Italian woman is based, as it will be for centuries, on the hair itself; it is rolled and twisted with ribbons into coronets, or a roundlet is set over hanging, braided hair on richly dressed women; small caps and veiled heads are seen particularly on poorer women.

633

634. XII-XIVc. German. (Metropolitan Museum.)

Fragment of natural linen, block printed in green. Wood-block printed fabrics, in imitation of Italian brocades, often using silver and gold, began to appear in the Rhineland, end XIIc. They apparently antedated block printed initials on manuscripts, which led to the invention of type.

635. XIV-XVc. German. (Victoria & Albert Mus.)

Fragments of block-printed linen: Upper right, Rhenish: eagles, fruit and leaves in dark purple.

636. XIVc. Scandinavian. Herjolfnes, Greenland (Copenhagen, National Museum.)

Brown twill dress. Viking garment found in grave in the Norse colonies. Ungirded gown worn by men; others show slits, *fitchets*, in side seams of front, as in men's and women's gowns in continental Europe; tongue-shaped gore in front is characteristic of Viking gowns.

637. XIVc. German. (Heidelberg University Library, No. 848.)

"Manessa Codex."

The most important record of XIVc. German life and dress is the "Manessa Codex," a collection of the songs of 300 minnesingers, made by Rudiger Manesse (fl.1360-80/4), though dates of 1310 and 1330-40 are sometimes given to the ms.

637. *Dietmar von Ast,* (d.1171), a S. German-Austrian lyricist. This illustration was made by the artist referred to as Hand G.

The lady wears a white *barbette* banded under the chin, over long blonde hair; rose surcote with gold collar and blue lining; dark green kirtle with gold cuffs. The trader has a brown petasus with cords to hold it on; blue

cape lined with green; red tunic; brown hose. He exhibits belts and gypcières in black, blue and gold; hanging below is a shield and typical German helmet.

638-641. XIVc. German. (Heidelberg, University Library, No. 848.)

"Manessa Codex."

638. *Messenger from Limburg*: the peacock of the crest of the messenger's helm perches in the tree which serves as "supporter" for a shield, blazoned with 3 maces, (e. arms of the City of Limburg). The kneeling messenger wears a green surcote, patterned with white A's (equals amor ?), and lined with red; matching *ailettes* at shoulders; red spurs. The lady holding his helm wears a white *barbette;* blue surcote lined with white fur; gold-edged rose kirtle.

639. *Herr Gösli von Ehenheim*: Battle with swords from horseback. The knight (r.) in gold mail and helm; gold trappings and surcote, lined with pink. The crest of knight and horse is a green parrot with a red beak, sitting on a white nest; flowing pink *lambrequin*. His opponent: diagonal blue and red stripes with gold stars, lined with yellow; gold helm and crest, knobbed in red. Ladies watching from parapet: yellow, pink, and gray surcotes, patterned in white lines and dots; braided, flowing or veiled heads.

640. *Der von Wildonie*: a fast combat with fists, shields, and swords. Helm with knobbed horns and lambrequins. Small shields of hand-combat; other plates show the tiny wrist-shield, no larger than a saucer. Diapered shoes.

641. *Meister Heinrich Frauenlob*: music school. Canting arms; the "woman he loves" is blazoned in white and gold on a green field. Teacher: ermine collar and lining on purple and white robe, dotted in gold. Left to right: parti-colored green and purple cote-hardi; pink with yellow hose and black shoes; red; green and white horizontal stripes, red and white wreath; fiddler in red and purple, lined with white fur; red and green diagonal; parti-colored purple and blue, striped in red and white; pink and white.

Plates in the "Manessa Codex" show every detail of mediaeval life: sappers working underground; the defence of a castle by bowmen, aided by ladies with rocks; harvesters with sickles; Susskind the Jew from Trimberg, his traditionally yellow hat (flat, with an Oriental knobbed steeple-top), painted in gold.

642

643

644

645

646

647

642-647. XIVc. 1307. German. (Berlin State Library.)

"Codex Baldwinii": Emperor Henry VII's Journey to Rome.

642. Pope Clement makes Henry's brother, Baldwin, Archbishop of Trier: red hats had distinguished cardinals from 1252, but were not worn with liturgical vestments until red biretta was granted cardinals, third quarter XVc., by Paul II. These gloved cardinals wear fur capuchons fringed with tails over fur-lined tabards; the use of the dalmatic at solemn high mass had been granted to the cardinal priests of Trier in 975 by Benedict VII. The mitres of the Pope and the Archbishops all show a concave rake. Pope: amice, chasuble, alb, embroidered gloves and shoes. Archbishops: mitre aurifrigiata, amice, pall, chasuble, dalmatic, alb, maniple and gloves, crozier.

643. Travelling: Baldwin, in a red cap, is dressed like the others (who ride bare-headed) in a capuchon of fur or cloth with slittered edge, the hood generally worn down; over fur-lined tabard; gloves. Knights: in long full surcoats, ungirt and undecorated; over mail hawberk and chausses. They wear a variety of head protections, notably the pig-faced bascinet with pointed vizor, chapel, and rounded bascinets. Mail camail, hawberk and chausses. Small shields; note tiny wrist-shield slung at waist of kneeling messenger.

644-45. Men-at-arms: cross-bow men and other foot soldiers are now given mail protection.

646. Pennon and banners. 647. Messenger, and servants at banquet: all in similar parti-colored garments; within a century the idea of uniformity, designated by costume, will be well on the way to establishment.

Royal ladies at banquet: high gorgets pinned wide to hair (see Ill. 558).

648. XIVc. c.1341. German. (Soest, Staatsar-
chivs.)

"Das Soester Nequambuch."

Soest in Westphalia was a flourishing
Hanseatic town; its codified laws of the
XIIc. served as a model for the rest of
Germany. Our illustration from a manuscript history of the early days of Soest
shows homage to the archbishop; its costume, being historical, looks back toward
the XIIIc., while that of the "Younger
Titurel," below, looks forward to the XVc.

Bishop: mitra simplex, mantle with
large jewelled morse, cassock, pontifical
gloves. The long, hooded gown of the
chalice-bearer has the XIIIc. horizontal
stripes and hanging sleeve, from which
emerges the narrowing sleeve of the undertunic; it is fur-lined, slit up either side
of the front. The falcon-bearer, hawking
gauntlet on right hand, game pouch,
gypcière, in left hand, wears a fur-lined
tabard over his long tunic.

649. XIVc. Bohemian. Fernberger-Dietrich-
stein Ms.

"The Younger Titurel," by Albrecht, the
Poet.

The originally close-fitting cote-hardi
feels the influence of the houppelande, to-

ward the end of XIVc., and becomes full. It is still belted low in the knightly manner, but has become shorter. The sleeveless form (left) has also taken the standing collar from the houppelande. The cote-hardi of the central figure keeps the band at the upper arm, in fur, as do the high-belted cotes-hardi of the ladies, one of which has ermine liripipes; looped-up braids of last quarter XIVc.

650. 1357. German. Brass of Flemish workmanship. (Stralsund.)

Albert Hovener: luxurious dress of rich bourgeois, shown on one of the finest Flemish brasses. Tabard; fur-lined, hooded, with horizontally banded chaperon-like shoulder caps. Cote-hardi; also fur-lined, long, slit up front, sleeveless, and edged with same in-

vected foliated embroidery as tabard. Doublet; tight buttoned sleeves of brocade cut on diagonal. Shoes; buckled, shaped like sollerets of knight.

651. 1369. German. (Lubeck.) Brass.

Bruno de Warendorp: Chaperon with diapered band and slit edge. Cote-hardi; buttoned body, plain sleeves, to which is gathered, low under a fine belt, a rather long, full slit skirt. Beard.

652. 1394. German. (Paderborn.) Brass.

Bishop Rupert: Mitre, with elaborated edge, rising and becoming convex. Almuce-like tippet edged with fur tails; for choir wear, hung about neck. Wide-sleeved everyday cassock, worn over fur-lined garment with tight sleeves, and another with sleeves prolonged over knuckles and scalloped. Beard.

653

655

654

653. c. 1375. German. (Private coll., Assisi.) Statue (wood, gesso, painted?).

German noblewoman: crown; over gugel (capuchon, cucullus) the corded edge of which is equivalent to the pleating around the face in French examples; mantle, with band border and floral brocade collar showing at left shoulder; robe with full skirt gathered onto fitted bodice under wide, tongued belt (see Ill. 351).

654. 1377. German. (Neckersteinach Chapel.) Brass.

Ritter Hennel Landschaden and Lady: knight of camail-jupon period. Bascinet; camail and hawberk with drooping hem (see Ill. 600); under a jupon which has a quainted edge, and is probably of plate, from breast of which run chains to sword, miséricorde, and (over shoulder) to tilting helm (shown behind figure) with crest of king's head. Other plate defences are decorative in their cut-out shapes rather than in superimposed design, as in Ill. 600: epaulieres, rerebraces, vambraces, cuishes, genouillieres, jambes, sollerets; rowel spurs; gauntlets with articulated fingers.

Lady: zig-zag headdress, G. *kruseler* (kraus equals crinkled, plaited); mantle, with brooch at center front; kirtle.

655. XIVc. 1390. Bohemian. (Prague Cathedral.)

Peter Parler: St. Wenceslas.

The *barbute* worn by the Xc. ruler of Bohemia, who was murdered by his brother, has apparently been affected by the bandings of a bishop's mitre, in token of his canonization after death. Extremely rich belt with anelace, over a laced leather *jupon* with a deeply foliated dagged edge (see No. 631.)

to the hair, the arrangements of which will widen and elaborate with the century. The long, full, ungirded supertunics of the knights have a front slit which shows the lining, and a hood which is beginning to lengthen into a liripipe.

L. to r., on a vermilion bench: Man in light periwinkle blue; man in dark cobalt; woman in mulberry rose with medium blue sleeves: Woman in medium blue, white sleeves; woman in vermilion with light blue sleeves; man in dark cobalt, with vermilion sleeves.

657. XIVc. c. 1390. French. (Poitiers, Palais de Justice.)

Chimney piece: Jeanne de Bourbon, d.1377, wife of Charles V. Classic example of the sideless surcoat of France, with its wide and heavy plastron, made of fur in winter, which is able to support a strip of massive buttons down the center-front. The sleeves of the kirtle are now close-fitting, extended across the knuckles: the kirtle is girdled low, under the surcoat, with a narrow but rich belt. Hair is massed over the ears, in jewelled crespine nets, with crown or coronet.

658. 1362. French. (Paris Bibliotheque Nationale.)

Agnes Eliote, bourgeoise of Mans. (See Appendix.)

659. 1380-90. French. (Paris, Maurice de Rothschild.)

Les tres belles heures de Notre Dame of the duke of Berry.

Male bourgeois costume has altered little from that shown in the Old Testament Ills. 476-81, except in richness; the same close white coifs, show the little *dorenlot* bang in front, often curled up over the coif; or the hair is worn combed back, "bobbed" and rolled. Ankle-length, hooded over-garments are richly furred as the bourgeoisie prospers.

The hood has been relegated to bourgeois use; women now wear it, carefully fitted, and with a prominent row of buttons, but it is always worn unbuttoned. The same gowns shown so explicitly in XIVc. English use are worn by these French bourgeoises, on a slightly more bosomy and wide-hipped figure: low-necked, ungirded gowns, fitted or loose, with fitchets in the skirts and liripipes or tippets at the elbows of close sleeves. Rich bourgeoises wear richly furred capes; often appear in sideless surcoats with fur plastrons.

657

656. XIVc. French. N. Eastern. (Morgan Library, M. 805.)

Lancelot du Lac: the first embrace of Lancelot and Guinevere. Ladies in tunics, the under-sleeves of which are decreasing in width on the lower arm and will become entirely close-fitting with the sideless surcoat. The long, ungirded supertunics, by their deepening armholes and lowered necklines, presage the sideless surcoat which begins to appear, second quarter XIVc. The low neck is filled in by the wimple, which is pinned in a V

658

659

660-61. c. 1371. Belgian. (Brussels, Bib. Royale, 15652.)

660. Gelré: "Wapendichtenen Wapenbock."

Gelré's picture of himself is the earliest representation of a herald bearing his master's arms; in this case: azure a lion rampant or, queue fourché, armed and langued gules, of Renaud II and III, rulers of Guelderland, which included Nymwegen, Roermonde, Zutphen, Arnhem. Broken chain may signify Gelré's despair and retirement after his master's death.

661. The Emperor Charles IV receiving the hommage of different classes of society. Three bishops: mitre, staff, episcopal glove, pontifical ring, morse on cope, dalmatic, alb. Emperor: shortened, tightened surcoat of second half XIVc; knightly girdle, low on hips, carrying ring dagger (increasingly long); a few inches of mail skirt below belt; rerebraces, vambraces, elbow-cops with mail gussets; greaves; lengthening sollerets; gauntlets of mail and metacarpal plate. Forked beard; hair rolled outward.

King and gentleman behind him in a dagged hem wear long, formal gowns with new fuller sleeve; buttoned, standing collar precedes high fitted collar of houppelande; alternative manner of slinging the obligatory sword, when a belt is not worn.

Two men of lesser estate wear short garments, fullness laid in pleats, held in place by the new, massive, metal-mounted belts. Lesser men wear pointed soles, like poulaines, fastened on hose. Petasus turned up in back; high-crowned hats, round turned-up brims.

662

662. 1378-9. French. (Paris, Bib. Nat. Estampes.)

Charles V receiving the homage of Louis II, Duke of Bourbon, for the county of Clermont.

1. Charles V.	12. Mouton de Blainville.
2. Louis of Bourbon.	13. Hugues de Chatillon.
3. Charles, the Dauphin.	14. Jean de Vienne.
4. Louis of Orleans.	15. Edward de Beaujeu.
5. Louis of Anjou.	16. Chaumont.
6. Philip of Burgundy.	17. Gilles de Nedonchel.
7. John, Duke of Berry.	18. Renaud de Trie.
8. John of Artois.	19. John, the Bastard of
9. Pierre d'Orgemont.	Burgundy.
10. Bertrand du Guesclin.	20. Pierre d'Euxy.
11. Louis de Sancerre.	21. La Polpe?

The peers of France, originally 12 feudal lords, were considerably augmented in number during XIVc., as great nobles were honored by the crown. Peers' robes, developed in this century, are closely related to the civilian cloak of the period, buttoned on the right shoulder, as are the cloaks of late XIV-XVc. mayors and men of law. The robes of English peers, of red velvet, hooded and caped with ermine, 2-4 bars on shoulder indicating rank, were cut fuller than the narrow robe of the French peer, which offered a smooth display of armorial bearings.

#9 wears a chaplet of flowers, common in XVc. #1, 5, 7, 8, 19, as sons and brothers of the king, or descendants of St. Louis (the Bourbons), bear

663

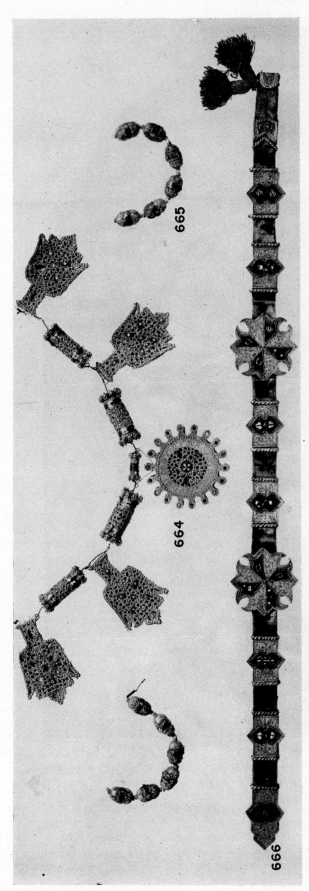

France quarterly, or differenced with a label. #3, 4, the little princes wear robes of the same tabard-like cut as those of the councillors in Ill. 663. That of the little Dauphin bears the canting dolphin and France quarterly. #1, Charles V wears a cape, the hood lined and tabbed with ermine; and gown semé with France ancient; as are also the undertunic and the short-sleeved, ermine-lined, long slit gown of Louis de Bourbon, #2, whose girdle carries a misericorde.

The onlooking commoners are being held back by a huissier in a quilted doublet with studded collar.

663. 1371. French. (Morgan Library, Ms. 717.)

Assembly of the King's Council, Toulouse: in parti-colored tabards, with bars on the shoulders, over parti-colored gowns, of orange, red and brown; and of orange and black. Compare with robes of the 2 little princes, above, and Chaucer's description of the serjeant of law, similarly dressed, with cape instead of tabard.

664-666. XIV-XVc. Spanish. Granada. (Metropolitan Museum.)

Jewelery; so-called "Hispano-Moresque." XIVc. Bracelets and necklace of gold, enamel, and pearls. XVc. Belt: copper-gilt and enamel.

667. XIV-XVc. Spanish. Granada. (Metropolitan Museum.)

Figured silk weaves; so-called "Hispano-Moresque," in red, blue, green, yellow, and white.

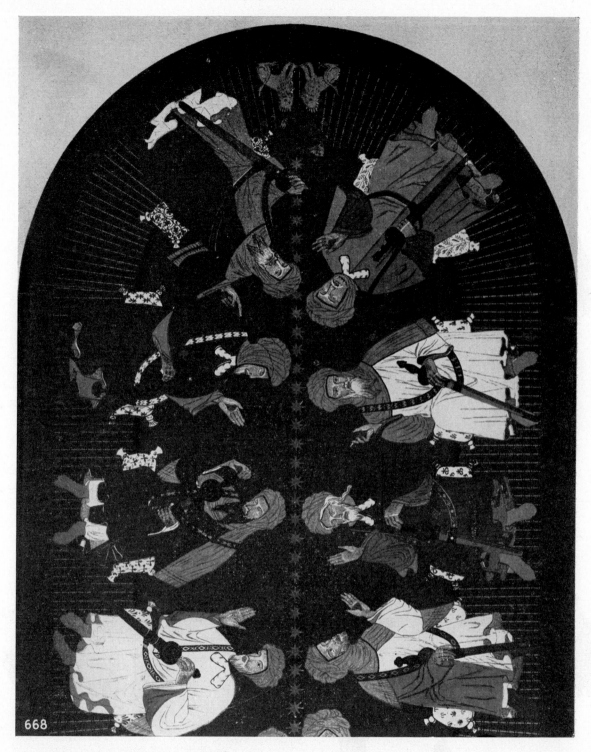

668

668-670. XIVc. Spanish. Granada. (The Alhambra.)
  Painted ceilings in the Hall of Justice.
    668. Heads of the Moorish tribes of Granada.
    669. Boar hunt: Christians and Moors.
    670. Battle between Moors and Christians.
  The painted ceilings of the Alhambra, ascribed to
Yousef I, d.1354, give infinite information about life
in Granada: architecture, costumes, and pastimes;
churches; palaces with courtyards, fountains, and
balconies; courtship, games of chess, hawking and
hunting with Moorish friends; battles between

mounted Moors, and Spanish knights and foot-sol-
diers.
  The Moors, defeated by the Cid in XIIc. had been
confined to Granada since XIIIc. Granada, which
they ruled until the conquest of the Moors at the
end XVc., was the richest and most civilized
city in Spain. The intermediaries between the Christians, who made up the other half of the population,
and the Moors, were the Jews. The Jews were poly-
glot and learned; during the three centuries in which
they had been protected in Spain, the highest aristo-

670

cracy and the princes of the Church had become of partly Jewish stock. I no longer remember which Spanish king was persuaded to sign a decree that all Jews should wear yellow caps; the next morning, his prime minister arrived with three yellow caps, for the king, the minister of finance, and for himself. It was the Jews' position as the hated tax-collectors which led to the first Spanish massacre of the Jews, preached by a priest in 1391.

By mid-XIVc., the Christian men, of high or low degree, will be found to have adopted the dress of men of their stations in France.

The cut of the cote-hardi worn by Spanish women, however, varies from that of the rest of Europe in several important details. (see lady struggling with wild man). Spanish costume was not homogenous, even among the predominantly Spanish aristocracy, in various parts of Spain. But Weiditz, in the XVIc., shows Castilian ladies dressed very much like the Alhambra paintings, and the same sleeveless surcoat still persistent in Barcelona, while Basque dress was as distinct as their tongue.

The surcoat is opened down the entire center-front from neck to hem, and is closed by rows of the ubiquitous buttons; in Spain, however, they are small and are frequently used in groups. There is no plastron on the front. Where a plastron is applied, elsewhere in Europe, it reinforces the front of the surcoat, and permits the use of much heavier and more important buttons, set close together in a row, which must stop when the plastron no longer exists to support their weight.

In the most specifically Spanish form of the sideless surcoat, the sides are cut away, in a different mode from the French-inspired concave sweep from shoulder to hip. From the horizontal line of the hem of the Spanish shoulder-cap, the side is cut away on a diagonal, rather than a curved line; it is edged with a piping or a relatively narrow braid. The Spanish skirt gains width below the hips by diagonal cutting of the side seams, rather than by gathering its material on, below the hips where the much more rigidly reinforced French surcoat will keep it from dragging.

The Renaissance Begins: XV Century

XVc.-Early XVIc. Background and Development of Dress

Protests of clergy, sumptuary laws of kings could not control the extravagance of XIV-XVc. costume, which exploited the superfluous, the fantastic, even the deforming.

The poulaines, forbidden to the French by Charles V, became so elongated that their points were chained to the knees. Edward IV. failed, as had the two preceding Edwards, when he attempted to regulate the dress of all classes in England.

To the already established German modes of dagged and slittered edges were added, by mid-XVc., the fantasy and luxury of the Burgundian court fashions. France, weak under the Valois, invaded with Burgundian aid by the English, had lost its position as the center of European civilization. Philip the Good of Burgundy, having fallen out with the English, concluded the Treaty of Arras with Charles VII, by which Philip was greatly enriched. During the second third XVc., while the French were still involved in the expulsion of the English, the superb court of Burgandy became the greatest in Europe, devoted to learning, the arts, and the fostering of Flemish industry and commerce. The Burgundian possessions were dismembered, after the death in battle of Philip's son, Charles the Bold; and France, under Louis XI, and Charles VIII, began its new rise. In a little more than a century, France, under Louis XIV. will again lead fashion.

But at the end of the XVc. the great new influence is that of Italy. The superb civilization attained by her city-states during the XIV-XVc. was spread over Europe, as a result of the Italian campaigns of Charles VIII and his successor. Italy's richly patterned silks and velvets, lavish with metal, were a revelation to her northern neighbors. Ladies in castles had woven decorative bandings on narrow looms; wood-block cutters in Germany had produced printed materials from XII-XIVc., after the demand for manuscripts had led the great German monasteries to mass-production methods of cutting blocks to print the capital letters. Packs of playing cards (showing costume) were produced by German and Italian engravers in second quarter XVc.

Saracen weavers had produced brocades in Granada from early times, and the Norman lords of Sicily had brought Greek weavers to Palermo in the XIIc. The mild Tuscan climate, ideal for silkworm culture, brought these weavers to Lucca in the XIIIc. From there they spread to Florence, Genoa and Venice (where, by the end XIVc magnificent brocades of silk, velvet and metal were produced) and to Bologna and Milan.

The vicissitudes of Italian life under the despots led Italian weavers to emigrate in XIV-XVc., particularly to France and Flanders. They set up, in Paris, Rouen, Lyons and other cities, what were to become the great silk-weaving centers of the XVII-XVIIIc. The revocation of the Edict of Nantes was, in turn, to force Protestant weavers to emigrate to England and Germany at the end of XVIc.

XV Century Italy

Italy, in the XVc., was merely a "geographical expression," made up of the republics of Florence and Venice; Naples, under an Aragon king; Milan, a duchy ruled by the Visconti, and their successors, the Sforza; and a number of lesser states ruled by families which had risen to power during the Age of the Despots in XIIIc.; Ferrara, under the Este; Mantua, under the Gonzaga; Urbino, under the Montfeltro; Rimini, under the Malatesta; Genoa which like Parma and Verona, had many masters, including the Doria; and the Papal States, accretions to the Church's inheritance from Matilda, Countess of Tuscany.

These self-made rulers were inevitably men of immense capacity. Unless their descendants had qualities of their own, they could not expect to maintain their dynasties, as many did for centuries, merely by money and ruthlessness.

In the generation following a *condottieri* com-

mander, risen from the peasantry and married into the aristocracy, it is not surprising to find children of wide interests, great culture, and taste.
This is particularly true of the Este, Montfeltro,
Gonzaga, and the Medici, whose power in Flor-

ence was gained a little later and by other means
than those of the early military despots.

Italy's political and geographical differentiations
fostered the development of a form of dress specific to each.

671-672. XVc. Italian. Tirol. (Cast. del Buon Consiglio.)

Fresco: 12 months of the year, represented by the
appropriate occupations of nobles and peasants.

671. *Taurus*: Ploughing with ox-team and horse,
together; harrowing; sowing fields and garden protected by wattle fence. Farm outbuildings; one with
wattle sides and thatched roof is probably a crib for
storing grain, which requires ventilation.

672. Left. *Gemini*: Walled town and its church.
Ladies and gentlemen eating and courting among
roses. Compare Gemini and Cancer with Ills. 807-10

for the classic houppelande and its Italian variations.
The exaggerated houppelande collar of northern
Europe is usually replaced in Italy, by a long-favored
standing collar. Stuffed and twisted roundlets, such as
the Italians like as headwear, often take the place of
precious chains, around the neck.

672. Right. *Cancer*: Peasants among tile-roofed log
out-buildings. Instead of diagonally strung baldrics,
the Italian male houppelande shows here the use of
two belts, at high waist and at hips, fastened together
by a vertical strap in back, (gentleman, lower right.)

672

673. 1410-20. N. Italian. (Wash., Nat. Gall. of Art.)

Pisanello. Portrait of a Lady. (*See also* Color Plate, No. 2.)

Italian version of Burgundian court costume. While the conventional collar is rarely found on Italian gowns, it is used here with great sophistication. The hair, clipped high on the neck, in service to the European idea of hairlessness, is otherwise shown and handled in a specifically Italian way. Instead of being enclosed in the conventional jewelled, reticulated net, it is drawn forward, and bound around in a coronet arrangement with the ends looped back, and ending in a little lock. Hair thus treated, but with the ends brought forward and bound together into a unicorn's horn will be seen in the Italian-influenced S. French frescos of a marketplace. The decorative use of simple pins will also be noted in XVc. Flemish costume. The stuffed roundlet which is set on the hair, is in the twisted Italian form; its decoration in a eyelet-studded, rather than a reticulated pattern. Over her blue and gold velvet gown, she wears filigree beads, and a flat collar of jewelled buttons, instead of the usual linked chain with pendant.

673

674-678. c. 1400. German-Italian. Tirol. (Castel Roncolo, near Bolzano.) Frescos.

Sleeves spreading over the knuckles, and extremely short male cotes-hardi are seen all over Europe, end XIVc. But the cape-like unbeltedness of the male cote, and the relatively uncovered heads, with roundlets and garments, are Italian, as are the striped patterns, and the sleeves of a different color from the body of the garment.

Courtesy of Frick Art Reference Library

.674

675

679-692. XVc. Italian. Lombardy. (Manta Castello.)

These frescos (allegorical) from the north of Italy, near the French border, show French styles relatively unaffected by Italian regionalism. Blazoned surcoats of knights; tilting helm, held by lady in sideless cote-hardi; leaved roundlets, frequently worn with armor, XVc.; and high clipped male hair.

Coryat mentions the rooms hung with painted coat-of-arms in Italy, and in Germany, where even the walls of inns were affected.

676 677

678

693. c. 1420-30. Italian. (Wash., Nat. Gall. of Art.)
Master of the Bambino Vispo. Adoration of the
Magi.

694. c. 1405. Italian. (Florence S. Maria Novella.)
Fresco.

Student of Spinello Aretino. Episode in the life of
St. Gregory.

Physician and friends: little change from the costume of learned, elderly men of XIVc.; in fact, von
Marle dates the picture "after 1387."

695. XVc. Italian. (Florence, S. Maria del Carmini.)
Fresco.

Masolino da Panicale (?). Raising of Tabitha: detail.

Young men in full, knee-length cotes-hardi of the
latter part of first quarter XVc.; with bag sleeves.
Brocade gown has sleeve with furlined slit at elbow
through which arm can be passed; here the arm

hangs concealed within the sleeve. Turban-like chaperon; Phrygian bonnet (Ills. 804-5); dependent scarf
of chaperon little used in Italy.

696-698. 1400-44. Italian. (Siena, Spedale.) Fresco.
Domenico di Bartolo. Hospital Scenes.

696. Nursing children: The heads of women of the
lower classes in Italy follow the general European
rule, and are covered by a veil or coif, but the coverings are close and exploit the hair; they do not deform or obliterate the natural head, as elsewhere.
Turban arrangement of bound hair, center. Italian
gowns have a short bodice, with natural round neck;
the skirts are often cut separately, and gathered onto
the high waist in careful, formal pleats. Shoe soles retained natural shape in Italy.

697. Tending patients: Doctors wear gowns, coifs
and caps, of the previous century; but hair is bowl-
cropped; no longer rolled at the nape. Hospital beds:

division between parallel bars forms head of one bed, foot of next; no springs; mattress tied like a hammock to end posts. Tasseled and corded velvet cushion on which man, wearing underdrawers, is bleeding. Walls fur-hung against chill.

698. Enlarging the hospital: Cut of doublet of man on ladder; division between body and skirts of garments, of men as well as women, in Italy. Short upper sleeve, with fur cuff, as worn also by children's nurses. Tights still short; worn with drawers. Architect, seen through arch; plain gown with sleeves of brocade. Perspective is now well understood.

699-702. XVc. 1440-50. Italian.
(Florence, Academy of Fine
Arts.)

Four cassone panels: The wedding of Boccacio Adimari and Lisa Ricasoli.

The same colors are used throughout this picture: black, brown, black or white and gold brocades, plain gold, dark green and a henna red, or vermilion. But three categories of costume are strongly differentiated. The wedding procession is magnificent, pale or somber, dressed entirely in black, white and gold, in combination. The dress of the spectators is intermediate between the muted color of the procession, and the bright clothes of the servants. Both spectators and servants wear parti-colored hose, (which combine 3 colors in one plain and one composed leg.) But the spectators use red in headgear and hose only; their body garments are black, brown, brocade, gold, or dark green, with narrow brown fur, or ermine. The servants' body garments use the brightest colors, sometimes parti-colored, and an additional orange-red appears in their clothing.

Tabard effects appear on the dress of ladies, gentlemen, and servants alike.

The high necklines of the gowns of Italian ladies are emphasized by necklaces worn high about the throat.

In the wedding procession (699) (l. to r.), the little page wears a green tabard, lined with white fur, its sleeves slit throughout their length; vermilion doublet and hose. Seated lady: white and gold robe with V-neck of Italian type (see Ill. 709); slit to show black and gold kirtle; white headdress with a small Italian rolled turban. Seated older lady: black gown; white and gold headdress of the current European type. Lady with monstrous black and gold turban: trailing overdress of black, unbelted and slit, tabard-wise, lined with gray; in Italy the long gown is shortened in front, not held up, as elsewhere. Lady leading procession: slit pendant oversleeve, now stiffened and stylized beyond usability; French headdress.

The spectators at the end of the panel (702) (l. to r.): ermine hat with vermilion crown; brownish-black tabard; black doublet; hose, vermilion, and black and white. Vermilion chaperon; brownish-black doublet, under a brown-furred black garment, belted in gold; black, and black and white hose. Tall black and gold turban; black doublet; vermilion gar-

699

700

ment, lined and edged with white fur; dark green, and black, white and green hose. Tall green hat; brown and gold brocade doublet; brown tabard and fur; black and white, and vermilion hose. Creamy-gold chaperon with a long knotted end; dark green tabard lined with greenish white; brown-black doublet; vermilion hose. Man leaving: vermilion chaperon, black tunic and hose.

In the panel of musicians and servants (700) (l. to r.): boy in red doublet, with brown and black hose drawn very imperfectly over white drawers. Servant with dish: black doublet; green and white hose, both parti-colored. With standing dish: vermilion and green tabard; black hose. 1st musician: vermilion hat; gold tunic with wheat (probably a

badge, see Ill. 706); black and white, and vermilion hose. 2nd musician: hat with orange brim
and green crown; dark tunic; green, and black and
white hose. 3rd.: orange hat; dark green tunic; vermilion, and black and white hose. 4th.: green cap;

vermilion garment; green and white, and black hose.

703. XVc. Italian, Florentine. (Metropolitan Museum.)
    Attributed to the *workshop of Filippo Lippi*. Man
and woman at a casement.

704. XVc. Italian, Umbrian. (Metropolitan Museum.)   Elizabeth Montfeltro, wife of Robert Malatesta, the
Domenico Veneziano. Portrait of a girl, perhaps   great *condottieri* leader.

707

708

705. XVc. Before 1450. Italian. (Berlin, Kaiser Friedrich Museum.)

Domenico Veneziano (?) Portrait of a young woman.

706. XVc. 1435-8. Italian Venetian. (The Louvre.)

Antonio Pisanello. Ginevra d'Este.

The bald appearance toward which the European woman of XVc. strived, is compromised in Italy, by interest in the hair itself. Small caps, turbans, and twisted rolls of mixed colors, are always subordinate to hair, flowing, coiled or braided.

The coiffure in Ill. 704, while affected by the head-dresses of N. Europe, allows bound hair to end in little loose tassels (see Ill. 673).

The Italian houppelande avoids a high collar, never stresses a V-neck, is always modest, relatively high-necked, mounting by mid-century to the base of the throat, but consistently sloping down in back.

Pleating, which becomes stylized all over Europe, is particularly fine in Italy, where cartridge pleats are set into plain material at an early date (see Ill. 703). Belt: never of great importance or worn unnaturally high.

Early use in Italy of slit oversleeves, which lend themselves to the Italian preference for differing sleeve and gown. The undersleeve is often of the male doublet form, upper half slightly padded and gathered onto a close undersleeve. There is a still further tendency to differentiate the sleeve from the gown by the use of embroidery, as in Ills. 703, 706.

Red-headed Ginevra (1419-40), of the ruling house of Ferrara, who was probably poisoned by her husband, Sigismondo Malatesta, wears on her gown a sprig of the juniper (purple berries) for which she was named. Cream-colored gown; lavender-brown belt; brown pearl-embellished embroidery on the hanging sleeve. Fur binding, always narrow in Italy, is replaced here by twisted ropes of red, brown, and cream; red inner sleeve; creamy hair ribbons. Her hanging sleeve is embroidered with the *impressa* seen on her brother Lionello's medals: a two-handled crystal vase, banded in pearls, chained from the handles to anchors; the vase is filled with leafless budding branches, which send out roots at the bottom of the vase.

The early interlaced Irish style loosened into scrolls, stylized flowers, and quaint animals in XIVc. Now, we see flowers represented quite literally in XVc. manuscripts, mixed with naturalistic insects as recognizable as the 3 varieties which flutter above Ginevra's head. The missal was also a pattern book; every tendril of a pea-vine, every leg of a caterpillar will be carefully worked in XVIc. embroidery.

707. c. 1460. N. Italian.

Engraved "Tarocchi" cards, so called: 50 cards representing all classes of men, arts, sciences, music and astrology; found pasted and written over in a manuscript of St. Gall, completed Nov. 28, 1468; in the style of Ferrara, Tura and Cossa, and are probably Venetian, and not by Montegna. From the front, the body of the jacket, fitted like a doublet, appears to carry doublet sleeves; jacket sleeves, probably not wearable, hang from shoulder in back. Flaring skirt, gored into high waistline, loosely belted at hips.

708. c. 1460. Italian, Florentine.

Att. to *Maso Finiguerra.*

709

710

Engraved series of the 7 planets: Mercury.

Florentine street scene: At left, a goldsmith's booth, exhibiting flagons, platters and precious belts; an engraver works on a plate; (engraving originated as an offshoot of jeweller's work and was extended to armor). Above, a painter decorates a wall in fresco; assistant grinds colors, which must be available while plaster is still wet. In center foreground a gentleman eats and drinks with a very coarse creature. At right, two learned gentlemen look over books together, while a boy winds a clock; above,

an old man blows a bellows for an organist.

709. c. 1460. Italian, Florentine. Att. to *Maso Finiguerra*. Engraving: the Fight for the Hose.

Specifically Italian wide skirts, gathered or laid in cartridge pleats onto short bodices with V necks; belt unimportant; emphasis on dependant brocade sleeve or sleeve of doublet type, with the upper fullness sometimes stressed by fur band above elbow. Heart-shaped headdresses, as well as Italian flowing hair and turbans. Clogs on feet of center figure. Cap and costume of a fool.

710. c. 1465-70. Italian, Florentine.

Engraving: an Allegory of Love and Death. French influence strongly shown in costume of center figures.

Woman: high, veiled hennin; flat collar spread in wide V over shoulders, and filled in with gauze; important necklace and belt; tubular cuffed sleeve. Men: high doublet collar; extremely short jacket with padded shoulders and tubular sleeves; horizontal neckline emphasized by chains from shoulder to shoulder. Decorative use of words, already seen in French costume; but the fabrics are Italian, particularly in the use of pattern on gentleman's sleeve.

Tights of gentleman and musician show the new use of pattern in late XVc. (see Ill. 906). Long tights and short jackets require use of codpiece (here tied into place at the top), instead of underdrawers (see Ills. 709, 714). The musician's jacket shows new trends: open front; lacings across shirt, which is also exposed by slashing doublet sleeve below elbow. While his jacket has shortened, its sleeves, ornamental rather than useful, are of the same brocade as the jacket; they retain their old length, but the supremacy of the Italian sleeve over the rest of the garment has begun to wane.

The effect of pointed French shoes is given by stem and sepal-like additions to the toe of the shoe.

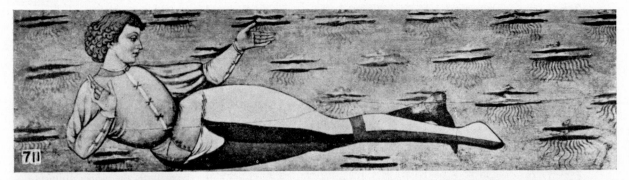

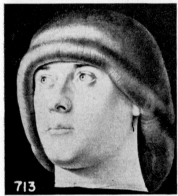

711. c. 1450. Italian, Florentine. (London, Earl of Crawford.)
Cassone panel.

712. Italian, Venetian. (Bergamo, Acad. Carrara.)
Pisanello. Lionello d'Este, (1407-50).

713. c. 1450-60. Italian, Venetian. (Metropolitan Museum, Bache Collection.)
Giovanni Bellini. Portrait of a young man.

714. c. 1445-50. Italian, Florentine. (Florence, Uffizi.)
Florentine youths playing the game of "civetta,"
a stylized, posturing outdoor game of well-born
Florentine youths.

Pisanello was first of all a medalist who has left
many records of wonderful hats, haircuts, and collars. He had been on intimate terms with Lionello by
1430, and worked for him again, 1441-8. This portrait is almost identical with Pisanello's medals, celebrating Lionello's 1444 marriage; it shows him in
dark red and gold, with pearls, a knot of gold in

back, and the same hair.

Bowl-cropped hair, like d'Este's, became full and
fluffy in Italy by the 50's, and developed into the
beautifully cared-for, extravagantly designed *zazzara*
of the Bellini young man.

The page on the Crawford cassone gives a classic
picture of mid-XVc. Florentine youth: bobbed,
banged hair; doublet with low standing collar, with
bosom, but not upper sleeve, padded and loosely
laced like the lower sleeve, to show shirt; red and
white parti-colored hose, not yet completely developed, are laced to the firmly buttoned skirt of the
doublet; being without cod-piece, they are worn over
drawers. (See Ills. 696-698.)

The same garments are worn by the "civetta" players; onlookers in very high turbans and bonnets.
Tabard (extreme right) is a Milanese fashion. Bag-
sleeves (center back) were particularly worn in
Venice. Little Italian boys wore shirts and doublets,

even socks and hose, but nothing resembling drawers.

URBINO AND THE MONTFELTRO FAMILY

The Court of Urbino was small, rich, peaceful, devout, beautifully organized and very learned. It contained one of the finest libraries of the age, and
housed many scholars, among them the mathema-
tician and painter, Piero della Francesca, but none
more learned than the Duke himself. At no court was
the education of the youthful nobility entrusted to
it more scrupulously supervised; the Duke, who
moved unarmed among his people, was equally devoted to their interests, and loved by them.

715, 715A. 1465-66. Italian, Umbrian. (Florence, Uffizi.)
Piero della Francesca. Portraits of Federigo I. di
Montfeltro, Duke of Urbino and Battista Sforza, his
wife.

Donors and their families had long been shown on
wings of altar-pieces, and events in the lives of
princely Italian families pictured in fresco, but this
small wood panel and its companion showing her husband are the first portraits in the modern sense.

Federigo, the great condottieri leader who had lost
the sight of his right eye, and broken his nose, in a
tournament in 1450, wears a red hat like that of
Lodovico Gonzaga, and jacket, its collar stitched in
darker red.

Battista, his second wife, is dressed in black, with
gold brocade sleeves; her blonde hair dressed with
white and gold.

716. XVc. 1445. Italian. (Metropolitan Museum.)
Giovanni di Paolo. Garden of Paradise.

Monks and nuns, prelates and gentlefolk. Left to
right. Upper row: 2 gray friars; a Carthusian talking to a dedicated lady in red; Cistercians in work

clothes; a fashionable young man conversing with an
angel; a hooded Trappist talking to a gentleman; a
youth hand in hand with a female angel.

Middle row: a nun, who looks like a Dominican,
but wears a blue-gray mantle, with an angel; Benedictine nun and Bishop of the same order; an angel
with a pope; a cardinal with a youth.

Lower row: 2 ladies in houppelandes, red and
blue, with monstrous turbans; 2 youths; 2 Dominicans; a Cistercian nun, with another nun, all in
white, and a Franciscan.

FERRARA AND THE ESTE FAMILY

The N. Italian city of Ferrara, despite the vio-
lently disordered personal life of some members of
the ruling family of Este, high taxes and a spy system, was, for two centuries, a very efficiently managed and prosperous city, the most modern in Italy,
with the best university of its time. Its citizens felt
secure from mishandling by its well-paid and disciplined army; and, spared from the wars which rent
the rest of Italy, Ferrara flourished under two excellent rulers: Lionel d'Este (1407-50) and his brother,
Borso (1413-71). Borso's court was both magnificent
and cultivated; its painters included Ercole Roberti,
and those "strange . . wild" painters, Turra and
Cossa, who used scenes of Borso's life in their frescos of his Schifanoia Palace. The third brother,
Ercole, was the patron of Ariosto, and the father of
two of the most notable and astute ladies of the Renaissance. The lovely, learned and short-lived Beatrice
d'Este (1475-97), wife of Ludovico (il Moro) Sforza
of Milan was the patron of Leonardo, Bramante and
Castiglione. Her sister, Isabella (1474-1539) established a brilliant court about her when she became

716

marchioness of Mantua; she was the patron of Mantegna, Raphael and Giulio Romano; and sister-in-
law of the third great lady of the Renaissance, Elisa-
betta Gonzaga, duchess of Urbino. The Este of the
XVIc. were the patrons of Tasso.

717-719. XVc. 1441-8. Italian.
  Antonio Pisanello.

717. Studies of costume of the Court of Ferrara. (*Milan,
Pinacoteca Ambrosiana.*)

718. Woman and two men in long flowered gowns.
(*Bayonne, Bonnat Museum.*)

719. St. Anthony and St. George. (*London, Nat. Gall.*)
These illustrations show the culmination of the Italian
preoccupation with hair and sleeves. The hair-mass of

717

718

Italian women, under the influence of the European ideal of hairlessness, was drawn up and back (see Ill. 706); where it was later bound into or surmounted by swelling turbans. Bowl-cut male hair, a manifestation of the same ideal, takes on height and bulk, in Italy.

On these Ferrara courtiers, the large beaver hats and dagged chaperons of Europe proper are exaggerated, and supplemented by specifically Italian forms of piled-up turbans. The winged, cape-like sleeves of the Ferrara court are emphasized by fantastically heavy fringes of fur, quite different from the flat furs used for linings and narrow bindings, and by multicolored fringes of dagged material. They make the superfluity of dagging in German costume (see Ills. 976-79) look almost utilitarian.

The Italian emphasis on sleeves almost obliterates the rest of the houppelande, however full and trailing it may be, on the lady and turbanned gentlemen.

St. George, wearing a plumed Tuscan straw hat, is in silver Gothic armor of second quarter XVc. The mail is almost completely sheathed in plate. The armor shown in the sketch has developed refinements of protection, which have been worked out for the different requirements of right and left sides of the body, in respect to the manipulation of lance and horse. Shoulder plates as large and badly fitted as St. George's appear in other contemporary pictures. His fur-bordered surcoat, embroidered with his cross, is thickly quilted and pleated, after the manner of contemporary dress, and of the *bases* or *waffenrock* skirts of knights. Long rowelled spurs on wide-toed sollerets. (See Appendix.)

719

720-723. XVc. Italian. Lombard School. (Milan, Casa Borromeo.)

Casa Borromeo frescos: details.
720. Society games.
721. Ball player.
722. Card player.

723. Card players.
Wonderful North Italian compromises between the European ideal of baldness under an exaggerated headdress, and the Italian love of turbans, braids, and the hair itself; the turban is made of monstrous braids, or is drawn up, hair-like, over pads.

724

725

726

724-725. XVc. Italian, Florentine. (Metropolitan Mus.)

Sano di Pietro di Menico. Cassone panel: Solomon and the Queen of Sheba.

Conventionally orientalized; especially soldier, Solomon, and conical hat crowns and flat collars of upper classes. Lower classes; contemporary Italian musicians in characteristic parti-color (see Ills. 699-702); camel-leader, in background, shows hose, doublet and haircut.

726. XVc. 1445-53. Italian Sienese. (National Gallery of Art, Washington.)

Giovanni di Paolo. Adoration of the Magi.

(*See also* Color Plate, No. 1: c. 1430. *Sassetta*: Journey of the Magi.)

Loose riding boots, with or without turned-down tops of another color, on figures to left, show seam on inside of calf to ankle where foot of boot is set on. Slit cape-like sleeves, of same length as garments (see Ills. 699-702, 714, 740).

727. 1430-40. Italian, Florentine. (Cortono, Baptistry.)

Fra Angelico. Altarpiece: Annunciation.

Richly decorated, bloused garments of allegorical or angelic figures.

728. c. 1450-60. Italian, Florentine. (National Gallery of Art, Washington.)

Fra Filippo Lippi. Head of the Madonna.

Veil wound and draped, in combination of fantasy with contemporary usage.

Fra Angelico (1387-1455) entered the Dominican monastery at Fiesole in 1407, was transferred to San Marco in Florence in 1436, and in 1445 went to Rome. Vasari says that he declined an archbishopric offered by the Pope, on the grounds of his own unworthiness, and suggested a more suitable candidate. The utterly sainted painter knelt in prayer before starting work on his fervently devout, unworldly, sexless paintings, with their exquisite gradations of pure color enriched with gold.

Fra Filippo Lippi (1406/12-69) was a very different sort of man and painter. He was warm, human, rich, and much more colloquial than *Fra Angelico.* He was the son of a butcher, orphaned early, and put by his aunt among the Carmelite friars at the age of fourteen. Although a devout man by nature, he was under vows by circumstance rather than vocation. He painted prolifically and profitably, but always under the pressure of having to provide for six marriageable nieces. Vasari says that he was abducted by Barbary pirates during a trip in 1431-37. In 1450 he himself abducted from a convent a beautiful girl inmate, pupil, or novice named Lucrecia Buti, who had been serving as his model for a religious picture. She was the mother of his son, *Filippino Lippi* (1460-1515), a painter at the age of ten, pupil of his father's pupil, Botticelli, and, like his father, one of the greatest painters of his time.

XVc. North Italian (see Ill. 673).   Pisanello: Profile Portrait of a Lady.

Courtesy of National Gallery of Art, Washington, D. C. (Mellon Collection)

729. 1449. Italian, Florentine. (Rome, Vatican.)

Fra Angelico. St. Lawrence Giving Alms.

The saint, a papal deacon, in a dalmatic with tassels in front and back (a usage which continued through the XVIc.), brocaded in the flames of his martyrdom. The poor: women's heads covered; men's hooded, in manner of earlier period; pouches and wallets; interesting details of shoe fastenings.

729

730-731. XVc. Italian, Florentine. (Metropolitan Mus.)

School of Pessellino. Two cassone panels: Scenes from the story of the Argonauts.

732. XVc. Italian, Florentine. (Metropolitan Museum.)

Cassone panel: Story of Esther.

On cassone panels illustrating biblical and mythological scenes, the costumes are frequently orientalized: this is particularly true of 730, less so of 731, and much less of 732, which, except for the conical hats, shows contemporary dress of second half XVc. (see Ills. 699, 702, 709, 710). These costumes, coming between those in Ills. 699-702, show massive, mounting male hats, in some interesting variations with turned-up brims.

733. XVc. c. 1450. Italian, Florentine. (National Gallery of Art, Washington.)

Master of the Jarves Cassone. Journey of the Queen of Sheba.

734. XVc. c. 1460. Italian, Florentine (National Gallery of Art, Washington.)

Paolo Ucello (?). Battle scene. As in previous cassone panels, we are given, in detail, fortified castles, interiors, and domestic architecture; processions with floats drawn by caparisoned horses; sailing ships, barges, and row-boats. The Jarves Cassone shows a fortified artificial harbor. Except for conical hats and pigtails, and some orientalized men (as usual, soldiers or worthies in long gowns) these are gentlefolk of N. Central Italy in mid-XVc.

Costume originating between the Arno and the Po (cf. Florentine and Ferrarese courts) is characterized by a distinctive use of pattern. The design is not the result of cutting from an all-over patterned brocade; it appears to be embroidered on portions of the costume, particularly on chest and sleeves. This effect could be achieved, in most cases, by the use of specially woven brocades; with borders and analogous, but not literally repeated motifs, which would permit the slight dissimilarities we see in r. and l. sleeves (see Ill. 710).

The Medici Family and Florence

The Medicis were an extraordinarily gifted family, under whom their city reached a point where a citizen thanked God "that he was a native of Florence, the greatest city in the world, and lived in the days of the magnificent Medicis." After 500 years we are still in their debt.

Exceptional though they were, they typify the rise that was everywhere taking place. Until mid-XVIc., their history is so mingled with that of Italy's other great families and cities, and of France, that they may well be used as a point of reference.

At the beginning of the XVc. Florence was a republic, of which only the members of its twenty-one guilds were citizens. The leader of its army was always a foreigner; the aristocracy, now ineligible for membership in its governing body, still manoeuvered elections.

Florence had ousted the usurper, Walter of Brienne; it was now the most flourishing commercial city of Europe, pre-eminent in the cloth trade and in banking; its *florin* was the standard gold coin of Europe.

In contests with the seven major guilds, controlled by the aristocratic Albizzi, the minor guilds were repeatedly aided by a family of bourgeois bankers, who added to their popularity by instituting tax-reforms, by their generosity to the plague-ridden populace, and by their commissioning of works of art for the adornment of their city; meanwhile increasing their fortunes by their loans to the King of England, to the princes of the Church, and to the Sforzas of Milan, all powerful allies in an age and country of precarious balance.

The Medicis, as a family, were characterized by the greatest financial and political astuteness; by the most varied intellectual, literary, and scientific interests; by marvellous taste in art and literature; and by a remarkable personal simplicity, kindliness, bonhomie, tact, and commonsense. Their faults were largely those of their age. They were a rather short-lived family, undistinguished for physical beauty, except for fine eyes and hands.

The Medici Palace was called "the hotel of all the Princes of the world"; but however luxuriously they lodged their guests, the life of the family was so simple that the Pope's son, who married Lorenzo's daughter, at first thought that a slight was being put upon him when he moved into the Medici Palace after the wedding, while his retinue continued to be entertained magnificently in another of the family palaces, which had been allotted to him before the wedding.

The high-minded gravity of the first three Medici generations changed, with rising Florentine fortunes, to the joyous lavishness of Lorenzo the Magnificent's time. Temporarily impaired by marriages with arrogant aristocrats, the essential Medici qualities would reappear in the following generation. Intellectual and artistic interests were made the fashion in Florence. This influence could still be felt in the XVIIIc., and was one of the reasons why so many cultivated English aristocrats lived or visited in Florence.

The accomplishments and changes in the Medicis and their city may be briefly summarized:

Under the founding *Giovanni di Bicci* (1360-1428), Florentine life was consciously austere; luxury controlled by sumptuary laws, administered by "foreigners," one of whom describes his difficulties: "When, obeying the orders ye gave me, I went out to seek for the forbidden ornaments of your women, they met me with arguments such as are not to be found in any book of laws. There cometh a woman with the peak of her hood fringed out and twined about her head. My notary sayeth, 'Tell me your name, for you have a peak with fringes.' Then the good woman taketh this peak, which is fastened round her hood with a pin, and, holding it in her hand, she declareth that it is a wreath. Then going further he findeth one wearing many buttons in front of her dress, and he saith unto her, 'Ye are not allowed to wear these buttons.' But she answers, 'These are not buttons but studs, and if ye do not believe me, look—they have no loops, and moreover there are no buttonholes.' Then my notary goeth to another who is wearing ermine, and saith, 'Now what can she say to this? Ye are wearing ermine,' And he prepares to write down her name. But the woman answers 'Do not write me down, for this is not ermine, it is the fur of a suckling.' Saith the notary, 'What is this suckling?' And the woman replies, 'It is an animal.'"

Works of art were commissioned, however, by the guilds, from Ghiberti and Donatello; Giovanni, who built for his city the Foundling Hospital designed by Brunelleschi, was the patron of Masaccio and other painters, and the first to have fresco used to decorate the walls of a private dwelling. He left his sons immensely wealthy, and we are told by Machiavelli: "He never sought the honours of government, yet enjoyed them all. When holding high office, he was courteous to all. Not a man of great eloquence, but of an extraordinary prudence."

Cosimo (*Pater Patriae*) (1389-1464). Built Medici Palace, 1440 (discarding Brunelleschi's plans as too pretentious), and many public and religious buildings. Art collector; patron of architects, sculptors, and painters, particularly Fra Angelico and Lippi. Scholar; founder of the world's first public library, 1444. Cosimo was influential in having the Council of Ferrara moved to Florence, where he became intimate with the great scholars of the Eastern Church; out of this came his founding of the Platonic Academy, and the financing of expeditions to the Orient to collect rare Greek and Roman manuscripts, many of which were the only copies to survive the fall of Constantinople. Since study of early Church manuscripts showed the supremacy of the bishop of Rome to have been founded on the forged Decretals and Donation of Constantine, Cosimo bears an inadvertent part in bringing on the Reformation. The fall of Constantinople, fatal to the trade of Florence's rival, Venice, consolidated in Florence the refugee scholars and mss. of the East. Florence, long a Guelph city, had been the refuge of Pope Eugenius IV, who took its culture back with him to devastated Rome; his successor, Nicholas V, who founded the Vatican Library, was the former librarian of the Medicis.

Cosimo's conduct of the affairs of the Republic led it to confer on him the title of "Pater Patriae." Machiavelli tells us that: "He was one of the most prudent of men; grave and courteous and of venerable appearance. His early years were full of trouble, exile and personal danger, but by the unwearied generosity of his disposition he triumphed over all his enemies and made himself most popular with the people. Though so rich, yet in his mode of living he was always very simple and without ostentation. None of his time had such an intimate knowledge of government and State affairs. Hence even in a city so given to change, he retained the government for thirty years." And Gibbon says: "Cosimo was the father of a line of princes whose name and age are almost synonymous with the restoration of Learning. His credit was ennobled into fame; his riches were dedicated to the service of mankind; he corresponded at once with Cairo and London; and a cargo of Indian spices and Greek books were often imported in the same vessel."

Piero il Gottoso (*the Gouty*) (1416-1469). Became head of the family, by the death of Giovanni, who had been trained to the succession because of the life-long ill-health of his older brother; when this permitted, the gentle and scholarly Piero had proved himself a most successful ambassador to the courts of France and Milan, and to Venice. One of the many alterations in the Medici coat-of-arms was that granted Piero by Louis XI: the use of the lily of France, on one of the Medici balls, colored blue.

There appears to be no connection between the three balls on a pawnbroker's sign and the Medici arms, as is so often stated. The red balls of the Medici, on a gold ground, varied in number with the generations: the earliest form was two red balls; nine balls, eight of them red (Giovanni di Bicci); six red, one blue (Piero); five red, one blue (Cosimo). (Details of Medici crests are given in Young's *Medici,* p. 135).

Piero, who commissioned the Gozzoli frescos in the Medici Palace, married Lucrezia Tornabuoni, a poet, and one of the first of the new generations of learned ladies, who later became the glory of the XVIc.

Lorenzo the Magnificent (1449-1492). Head of his family at twenty; and probably the most variously endowed man the world has seen. Machiavelli says, "He governed the Republic with great judgment, and was recognized as an equal by various crowned heads of other countries. Though notably without military ability he yet conducted several wars to a successful conclusion by his diplomacy. He was the greatest patron of Literature and Art that any prince has ever been, and he won the people by his liberality and other popular qualities. By his political talents he made Florence the leading state in Italy, and by his other qualities he made her the intellectual, artistic and fashionable center of Italy."

Commercially less astute than his forebears, Lorenzo was a scholar; loved the company of learned men; financed trips to collect manuscripts in the Orient, and maintained a staff of copyists for their dissemination; founded the Universities of Pisa for Latin, and Florence for Greek studies; contributing about $15,000,000 to learning. He was a poet, encouraging the use of his native Tuscan instead of Latin; the center of a gay and brilliant literary company, among whom were the fabulous Pico della Mirandola and Politian. He enlivened Florentine life with fire-works, pageants and tournaments; was a sportsman who loved the country and the hunt; was interested in agriculture and husbandry. He founded a free school of sculpture, where he discovered the fifteen-year-old Michelangelo; Botticelli was his court painter; he was the patron of the other great painters of his time, particularly Leonardo, Raphael and Perugino.

He was gay and courteous, charming, simple and helpful; he romped with children and threw snow-balls in the streets. By his marriage to an Orsini, he had three sons, the eldest of whom, Piero, married another arrogant Orsini, and was banished from Florence.

The period of the Medici exile (1494-1512) began with the victorious entry of Charles VIII into Florence at the head of 20,000 men; Italy viewed the potent new weapon, conceived by his father: the standing army. But to the French mass the meeting was even more revealing: here was a great civilization, an undreamed-of refinement of luxury; a standard to be equalled and surpassed. Even fine cookery, which we think of as French, was an Italian art, brought to France by Catherine de' Medici; here the French got their first notions of subtle food.

Without the Medici, Florence was torn by dissension and corruption; her prosperity declined, and in her uncertainty, profligacy increased. Longing for direction and ripe for an attack of bad conscience (for she had a long history of high standards), Florence passionately embraced the precepts of the reforming Dominican monk, Savonarola. She became a city of Puritans, plain of garments and way of life; her citizens, among them quantities of her painters, flocked into monasteries. At Savonarola's behest great bonfires were made in the public squares of her "vanities," indecent books and pictures, carnival gear, rouge and gauds, which a Venetian tradesman tried to buy for 20,000 gold florins.

Savonarola's attacks on the vile Borgia Pope led to his eventual torture and martyrdom in 1498. The amiable Cardinal Giovanni became head of the house of Medici; with the death of the unfortunate Pietro, whom they had driven out with his detested Orsini wife, and with some pressure from Pope Julius II, the Florentines recalled the Medici.

Cardinal Giovanni, later Pope Leo X, Lorenzo's second son, was an agreeable epicurean who, though he perhaps did not say, "Since God has given us the Papacy, let us enjoy it," horrified the papal household by wearing hunting costume and riding boots. His Medici entertainments and patronage made Rome gay and brought artists for the embellishment of the city, but he was without his father's real scholarship and taste.

Giuliano, Lorenzo's third son, whose exile had been passed in the cultivated court of Urbino, was a true Medici, talented, attractive and simple. Upon his return as ruler of Florence, he shaved his beard in conformity to the Florentine manner. Leo X, on his accession, transferred the rule of Florence to his nephew, Lorenzo, while offering to make Giuliano Duke of Urbino, at the expense of his former hosts, which he refused. Sent to France as a papal representative, he married there, was made Duke of Nemours, and died soon after.

Lorenzo, Pietro's dissolute son, had the insolence of his Orsini mother, by whom he had been brought up in exile, unaffected by Florentine standards. Bearded, like the foreigner he was, he ruled Florence; was made Duke of Urbino by the machinations of Leo X, who contrived with Francis I, to marry him, at Amboise, to Madeleine de la Tour d'Auvergne. He survived, only by days, her death after childbirth, leaving the baby Catherine, who was to become Queen of France, and a great Medici in her own right.

Giulio, nephew of Lorenzo the Magnificent, who became Pope Clement VII, was a brilliant, learned and adroit Medici, but crafty and cold; his deviousness helped to bring on the Reformation, and was personally disastrous.

As the elder branch of the Medici weakened, at the end of the XVc., the younger, descended from Cosimo's (Pater Patriae) younger brother, began its rise.

Giovanni "Populano" (1467-98), attractive and cultivated, became the third husband of Catherine Sforza, the great Countess of Forli. This brilliantly learned, accomplished, and immensely courageous woman, who led her troops in battle and at one time lived in armor, was the daughter and granddaughter of condottieri commanders, of peasant stock, who had risen to power and great marriages with the Visconti and the House of Savoy. Although her first husband was a Riario, nephew of Pope Sixtus IV, and so an enemy of the Medici, she had been in love with the family, since a visit to them in her childhood.

Giovanni delle Bande Nere (1498-1526), her Medici son, became in his short life the greatest soldier in Italy, the first to realize the importance of the infantry, and to exercise personal attention to the needs of his men. He wore nothing to distinguish him in battle from his black-armored troops (*Bande Nere,* Black Bands), who adored him; and who, from his death until their own, wore mourning for him. Giovanni married his distant cousin, Maria Salvati.

Cosimo I, their son (1519-74), the capable and pitiless Grand Duke of Tuscany, brought his duchy to its greatest prosperity and power. He built the Pitti Palace; his collection of Etruscan art was the world's greatest; he founded the first botanical gardens; established a tapestry manufacture which surpassed those of Flanders; rehabilitated the textile trade; concerned himself with all technological improvements in the utilization of the natural resources of his land, seacoast, and their defense.

Francis I, eldest son of Cosimo I, had a passionate love for art, literature and the sciences, particularly chemistry; he learned to fuse quartz, from which he fabricated vases which still exist; established porcelain manufacture; built the Uffizi; and began the improvements of the port of Leghorn.

Marie de' Medici ,Francis' daughter, brought the richest dowry of any Queen of France to her marriage with Henry IV, and died in abject poverty. She was a beautiful, amiable and unintelligent creature, immensely concerned with dress, on which it is probable that no woman ever spent more.

Ferdinand I, second son of Cosimo I, the reluctant cardinal who never took holy orders, was a courageous and generous ruler; he collected Greek and Roman art objects; was the real creator of the port of Leghorn, to which his decree of toleration brought prosperity, in the form of refugees of all races and religions.

The greatest days of Tuscany and the Medicis ended after the first-quarter of the XVIc. though the family continued to rule for another century.

735-738. XVc. 1468-9. Italian. (Florence, Medici-Riccardi Palace.)

Benozzo Gozzoli. Frescos: The Journey of the Magi.

735. Youngest of the three kings, on horseback. 736. Detail, with leopards. 737. Detail, children on horseback. 738. Detail, procession and landscape.

Life Magazine, Dec. 24, 1945, furnished complete color reproductions of these frescos. Commissioned by Piero de'Medici, they recalled a magnificent pageant which the 19 year old Gozzoli and 23 year old Piero had seen in 1439, during the meeting of John Paleologus, Emperor of Byzantium, and Pope Eugenius IV. in an attempt to reconcile the Roman and Orthodox churches. As a tactful reinforcement of Pius II.'s renewed efforts to the same end, the Patriarch of Constantinople and the Emperor are represented as two of the three kings, the third being the young Lorenzo de'Medici.

In the foreground of 738, l. to r., we see Piero il Gottoso, shown bareheaded, in reference to his invalidism; his second son, Giuliano, whose love of the hunt is symbolized by the bow which his Negro carried before him; Lorenzo the Elder, ancestor of the cadet line of the Medici, humbly mounted on a mule; and his older brother, Cosimo (Pater Patriae), the trappings of whose horse bear the seven balls of the current Medici arms, together with the peacock feathers which he had chosen as his personal emblem.

The riders are followed by a crowd containing many recognizable portraits of members of the Platonic Academy, bearded Eastern scholars, and clean-shaven Florentine notables; among whom we have Gozzoli's self-portrait, wearing a cap edged with the words, "Opus Benotti."

In Italy the doublet has not assumed the high collar of France; but the V-line in back, (into which the high collar fits) is used here in a specifically Italian way: in front, across the base of the throat, the neckline of the jerkin barely shows the tiny standing collar of the doublet; in back, instead of mounting, the line of the collar of the Italian doublet slides backward, while the neck of the jerkin, cut in the low V, exposes the brocade of the doublet. The Italian jerkin is often sleeveless, even skeletonized (Cosimo P.P.), and the sleeves, when they do exist, are usually split lengthwise to feature the sleeve of the doublet (page, preceding Lorenzo).

735

The commonplace sleeve of the rest of Europe is worn here only by Lorenzo, who is dressed like an elderly European gentleman, rather than an Italian; and by the Negro, whose cartridge-pleated jacket is of one stuff and does not have the backward-slipping Italian neckline.

Lorenzo the Magnificent's costume is that which he wore in his tournament of 1469, studded with rubies and diamonds; his cape-like sleeves, of the same length as the skirts of his jacket, in the Italian way, are split below the elbow only, to show only the fore-arm of his doublet sleeve, in the Medici red and gold. He rides the white charger, which was given him for the tournament by the King of Naples; its trappings bear the seven balls of his father's reign, which will be reduced to six when he rules. His attendants also wear their tournament costumes.

Parti-colored garments and hose are here worn only by servants (handsome jacket of attendant preceding Cosimo P.P.), the Negro, and the hooded walkers.

Mounted astride, on white horses with red and gold trappings, are Piero's three daughters, Nannina,

Bianca and Maria, wearing plumed and jewelled red and gold roundlets, golden jackets and sock-boots, scarlet doublets and hose. Not for three generations will the side-saddle be invented.

In 1605-7, Fynes Moryson found Italian women riders, married and virgin, apparelled like men, in close doublet; large breeches open at the knees, Spanish fashion, riding astride like men, but their hair like women, bare and knotted, or with gold net cauls, and feathered hats.

The Duke of Lucca, a ferocious soldier-enemy of the Medici is shown here, reduced to the status of a young sportsman, (carrying behind him the leopard which was his emblem), among the learned and civilized Florentines, one of whom symbolically halts his progress. The dismounting keeper of the other leopard, dressed in green, lets us see the contemporary saddle. In back, to l., a group of pages in wine-purple shows another Italian neckline, pointed both in front and back, disclosing a low-necked V of dark material; this bordered V-front neckline is often carried down into a c. front closing.

739

740

739. 1452-66. Italian, Umbrian. (Arezzo, S. Francisco.)
Piero della Francesco. Arrival of the Queen of Sheba. These austere and noble figures, clad in won-derful browns, greens and blues, with gold, white and black, show French influence in the slightly horned veiled headdresses.

741.

740. XVc. Italian. (Sienna, Palazzo Pubblico.)

Att. to *Neroccio di Bartolommeo de' Landi*. Preaching and Miracle of S. Bernardino.

Completely slit outer sleeve gives a tabard-like effect to outer garments, even when pleated and belted. Variation between fabrics of garment and sleeve, and narrowness of fur borders are typically Italian.

MANTUA AND THE GONZAGA FAMILY

Less only than the Medici court were the learned and enlightened courts of the Gonzaga of Mantua, the Este of Ferrara, and the Montfeltro of Urbino.

Coryat, at the end of the XVIc., describes Mantua, and says, "This is the Citie which of all other places in the world I would wish to make my habitation in, and spend the remainder of my dayes." Here it was that "a mountebanke, the first I ever saw, played his part upon a scaffold." Mantegna's relationship with Mantua began even before the 1460's, when he was housed there in the employ of the reigning family.

741. c. 1474. Italian, Venetian. (Mantua, Cast. di Corte.)

Andrea Mantegna. Marquis Lodovico II. Gonzaga, with his wife, Barbara of Brandenburg, and children.

The second marquis of Mantua, Lodovico Gonzaga (1444-78), was also known as Lodovico III, el Turco. The bald man to the left is probably his secretary, Marsilio Andreasi. Behind Lodovico's wife is her favorite son, Gian Francesco (born 1446).

The gray-haired man next to him is Bartolomeo Manfredi, the astrologer of the Gonzaga family. The identity of the man in rich secular costume, standing between Lodovico and the astrologer, is uncertain: some authorities consider him to be the future marquis Frederico I; others, Francesco, the cardinal, second son of Lodovico. The boy-pronotary next to the marquis is his youngest son, Lodovico, who, born in 1459, was already appointed bishop of Mantua in 1468. The girl, holding an apple, may be one of Barbara's younger daughters, Paola or Barbara. The slim youth, before the pillar, is Lodovico's fourth son, Rodolfo, b.1451, killed on the Taro in 1495.

The costume of these men, if compared to French examples from Foucquet onward, show French influences on Italian characteristics. Italian male garments exploit the natural body, where French fashions overwhelm and deform it. They are becoming shorter, though not so short as the French; fuller and squarer, with a padded doublet bosom; but with less padding at the shoulder and upper sleeve of the doublet than in France. The horizontal is played against the vertical at every opportunity; low doublet collar-line, unbroken in front; bateau neck of jacket; natural waistline; width of hem against the columns of neck and legs; simple tubular sleeves; carefully laid cartridge pleats. The tiny cap, and the hair carefully curled from it, are further refinements of the Italian use of these two impulses. Simpler materials are now used; brocades are less spectacular in pattern; subservient to the lines of body and garment. The shoulder line is not confused by humps of padding of the French mahoîtres, nor do the flat edging furs used in Italy flare out the jacket skirt; they follow, enhance, and yet oppose the repeated vertical lines of the fine pleats. Shoes: natural, as is usual in Italy. Gloves: new, not a hawking gauntlet. The costume of the bald secretary at left might be from a Foucquet, except for the bare back of his neck, where a French jacket would have shown a high doublet collar. The simplification and unification of sleeve with the body of the garment is seen in the women's costumes, also; the bodice is gradually taking on importance; the round collar and V plastron are now defined, even when all are of patterned brocade. Female dwarf beside Federigo's wife.

742. c. 1474. Italian, Venetian. (Mantua, Castello di Corte.)

Andrea Mantegna. The meeting of the Marquis Lodovico and Cardinal Francesco Gonzaga.

Lodovico's second son, Francesco, was the first cardinal of the house of Gonzaga. The youth in ecclesiastical costume who holds the cardinal by the hand is Lodovico, the youngest son of the marquis. The little boy who grasps the hand of the young Pronotary Lodovico is Sigismondo, son of Federico and grandson of the marquis. The other boy shown in profile is the oldest son of Federico, Gian Francesco III, afterwards fourth marquis of Mantua and husband of Isabella d'Este the discriminating, if grasping, art patron, and the greatest lady of the Renaissance. The man to the right in front is Fed-

erico, the next heir. The man next to him is supposed to be Mantegna himself. The youth in profile, just visible between Lodovico and the Cardinal is Gian Francesco Gonzaga, son of *el Turco.*

The city in the background is an imaginary picture of the antique Rome, which shows the fortifications and famous classical monuments of architecture.

Many new usages: circular capes thrown back over the shoulder; slashing; and points.

Lodovico and two others wear the high, flat-topped hat which is seen on the elders of the Gonzaga and Montfeltro, and is sometimes called the "ducal mortier." (See Appendix.)

Doublet sleeves of the children and most of the men show the decorative use of knotted points, placed just below shoulder padding. Lodovico's upper doub-

743

let sleeve is cut out in the pattern of its brocade, widely slashed and filled in with plain materials. His tabard-like upper garment is belted in front; tights without a foot are strapped over his shoe. Lodovico's sleeve is of the new detachable sort, laced across the shoulder padding. Federico wears the new Italian cape, circular and folded back over the shoulder, which will become very familiar. Parti-color on one leg of hose.

743. XVc. 1467. Italian. (Metropolitan Museum.)

Fra Carnevale. Birth of the Virgin. (*See also* Color Plate, No. 4.)

Italian costume, both male and female, is becoming fuller, made of simpler materials, with a larger number of colors used in one garment. Bodice, sleeves and skirt are here shown in different colors. The sleeve is set on a dropped shoulder-line, so that the color of the bodice of the kirtle is also visible. Beads, seen at extreme right, are a new style.

The dirtiest European country was Germany. The Burgundians complained of the filthiness and bad manners of the Count Palatine's retinue; and "German" was synonymous with "dirty" in Italy, the cleanest and most civilized country of Europe. It was in Italy, that the handkerchief (handcouvre-chef, also called "napkin") can be said to have originated in the XVc. (We see it in Ill. 743 hanging from the girdle by a cord, on the fifth figure from the left; similar usage will increase through Tudor and Elizabethan costume.) The first handkerchiefs were large, up to 18″ square, of linen, lawn, or cambric, embroidered in colored or metallic threads, fringed or edged with lace, the corners often finished with an acorn or tassel. Miniature handkerchiefs, worn in the hat-band, were given as favors to their suitors by English ladies. By XVIc. handkerchiefs were in general use in Venice, and appear by the dozen in inventories of the wardrobes of the great all over Europe.

VENICE AND THE DOGES

The city and patricians of Venice resembled no others. Built on piles, over a marsh, and served by over 100 miles of waterways instead of roads, Venice was impregnable but landless; with no natural resources except salt, she was forced to import food and timber. Her situation made her the most logical port of embarkation for the Crusades, the outfitting of which greatly enriched her. After struggling with Genoa for the supremacy of the Mediterranean, she became the world's greatest mercantile marine power. She received special privileges and rights of settlement in Syria and Asia Minor; rigorous government control specified even the dimensions of her ships, which permitted their refitting from stocks at outlying depots, and their conversion into men-of-war; and required them to bring back materials from the Orient for the embellishment of the city.

Her aristocracy were not feudal warriors, but the leading members of her merchant guilds. "Venice was a joint stock company for the exploitation of the East and the patricians were its directory." Her civilization was magnificent but material, without the interest in literature and art of the courts of Florence, Mantua and Urbino; her great painters are those of her decadence: Mantegna and the Bellinis, in the XVc., and the later Carpaccio, Giorgione, Titian, Tintoretto, Veronese and Tiepolo. Canvas, as a painting's surface, was first used in Venice by the Bellinis.

A large part of the population had gradually become disenfranchised, though some fiction of republican government was maintained in the words: "This is your Doge, an it please you," with which the new ruler was presented to the people. The Doges of the Republics of Venice and Genoa were elected for life, as the civil, military and religious heads of their cities. In Genoa, Commines relates, the Dorias, who were gentlemen, could not become Doges, as could the Campoforgosi, who belonged to the same party, "for no gentleman is capable of becoming Doge by their law. . . . The nobility makes Doges, but cannot be made so themselves." The Venetian Doges, though treated with the greatest honor and ceremony, were actually less important than the cabinet, council and senate, whose figure-head they were.

Venetian seizure of the adjoining mainland, at the beginning of the XVc., was the beginning of her downfall. No allies wished to help maintain her trade supremacy; and with the loss of her trade with the East, after the fall of Constantinople, mid-XVc., and the discovery of the route to the Indies around the Cape, Venice was ruined.

Venice became famous for her damask fabrics, particularly velvet brocades; Murano glass; silvered mirrors; mosaic and inlay. Oriental rugs passed into Europe through Venice; her ships, carrying sugar to England, brought away raw wool, which was exchanged in Flanders for finished cloth.

744. XVc. c. 1476. Italian Venetian. (Metropolitan Mus.)
Gentile Bellini. Doge Andrea Vendramin.

745. XVc. Italian Venetian. (Museum of Fine Arts, Boston.)
Att. to Gentile Bellini. Portrait of a Doge.

744

745

746

747

748

746. XVc. c. 1470. Italian. (Kaiser Friedrich Museum, Berlin.)

G. B. Morone or *Michele da Verona*. Cassone panel: Betrothal of Jason and Medea.

Just such heads, veiled over a little flat hat, with hanging locks in front of the ear, and short-waisted spreading bodices, with more elaborately cut and puffed sleeves, are shown in the Venetian dress drawn

by Durer in 1494-5. In Venetian use, at that time, two immense buttons closed the skirt in front, and high pattens were worn.

747. XVc. 1473. Italian. (Perugia, Palazzo del Municipio.)

B. Caporale or *Fiorenzo di Lorenzo* or *Master of 1473*. Miracle of S. Bernardino.

Very long, or very short garments, showing French

influence: extremely abbreviated jacket and cape; some high doublet collars; slightly pointing shoes. Italian: in hair and headwear, some collars, and particolor of one leg of hose. Pendant sleeves, here thrown over the wrist, are sometimes seen knotted in back.

Sleeves are becoming simple, close-fitting and unified with the costume. But the impulse which made them pre-eminent, earlier in the century, persists: sometimes in actual separation from the garment (laced on: see Ill. 742); partly freed, as is Jason's outer sleeve; caught (angels: see Ill. 749); or barely tacked on. By the next century, sleeves will become interchangeable.

The differentiation in color, seen in gowns in Ill. 743, continues in these Jason and Medea illustrations; in the sleeves and their slashings, lengthwise or across the elbow; the plastron; underskirt; lining of overskirt; color of cord belt, cap and veil.

The youth in the Miracle of St. Bernardino (ext. background, c.) wears boots cut into a point high above the knee and decorated with stitching.

748. XVc. Italian, Sienese. (Met. Mus. of Art.)

Francesco di Giorgio. Chess Players.

Wonderfully dressed clouds of blond hair, with approximately the costume shown on the Gonzaga family (741). Inset cartridge pleats.

749. c. 1470. Italian, Umbrian. (National Gallery of Art, Washington.)

Provincial follower of Piero della Francesco. Madonna enthroned with Angels. Slashing and separation of sleeve from garment.

750. 1477. Italian. (Rome, Vatican.)

Melozzo da Forli. Sixtus IV. Nominating Platina as Librarian of the Vaticans.

Implacable enemy of the Medici, Sixtus excommunicated all Tuscany in retaliation for Lorenzo's "only fault . . . that he had not been murdered" in the attempt by Sixtus' Riario nephew. Sixtus became "speechless with fury" and died when Lorenzo's diplomacy deprived him of the support of the Sforzas in his attacks on Florence and Ferrara. He was, however, an enlightened patron of artists and writers; his great program of public works included the Sistine Chapel; he founded the Sistine choir, and was one of the founders of the Vatican Library.

The Pope wears a red skull-cap and cape, erminelined; white rochet and cotta.

R. to l.: a man in dark green; Cardinal Giuliano della Rovere, later Julius II; Platina kneeling, in a blue gown with red sleeves; Girolamo Riario, the Pope's nephew, the Medici's enemy, husband of Cath-

751

erine Sforza, Countess of Forli (who later married
a Medici), and future governor of the Pontifical
States, his hands hidden in the sleeves of his blue
gown (also a female usage, late XVc. French); Giovanni della Rovere, Prefect of Rome, in a violet gown,
was the Pope's favorite nephew, and son-in-law of
the Duke of Urbino.

751. c. 1461. Italian, Florentine. (Metropolitan Mus.)

Benozzo Gozzoli. St. Zenobius Resuscitates a Dead
Child. Clerics, monks and acolytes; gentlemen, circular sleeve turned up on shoulder in the manner of
the new usage of capes.

752. XVc. Italian. (Florence, Uffizi Gallery.)

Pupil of Antonio Pollaiuolo. Study of model in
XVc. Florentine costume. Eyelet holes on doublet
hem and sleeves for lacing points.

**753. 1470. Italian, Venetian. (Ferrara, Palazzo Schifa-
noia.)**

Cosimo Tura and Francesco Cossa. Fresco: Triumph of Minerva.

754. 1468-85. Italian, Florentine. (Pisa, Campo Santo.)

Benozzo Gozzoli and assistants. Fresco: Old Testament Scenes.

Men's and women's work clothes: shirts and drawers; doublet and hose; tucked-up dresses and aprons.

752

754

753

755. 1468-85. Italian, Florentine. (Pisa, Campo Santo.)

Benozzo Gozzoli and assistants.
Old Testament Scenes: detail.

756. 1470. Italian. (Ferrara, Palazzo Schifanoia.)
Cosimo Tura and Francesco Cossa.
Triumph of Minerva: detail.

Lacings of front closing caught by decorative hooks. Fullness of sleeve below shoulder is all that remains of padded sleeve of the doublet type of the first half of the XVc.

757, 758. 1468-85. Italian, Florentine. (Pisa, Campo Santo.)
Benozzo Gozzoli and assistants. Old Testament Scenes.

757. Construction of the Ark; the Deluge; and Noah Giving Thanks.
758. Construction of the Tower of Babel.

The padded width of last half XVc. is shown here at its Italian limit, fullness provided by the favorite Italian method of inset cartridge pleats. The idea of hand-covering is increasingly strong; several gentlemen at lower right carry gloves; the youth (second from right, 1st row), thrusts his hands into the bottom of his pendant sleeve, as into a muff.

The separation of sleeve from garment, notably in Flanders and Italy in last half XVc., continues; the sleeve which is being used as a muff is so little a part of the jacket, that the fur lining of the jacket shows around the armseye; the jacket sleeve is merely tucked on in back, under the doublet sleeve. The sleeve of the youth at extreme right is cut in one with the jacket, at the shoulder, but is free of the jacket, under the armpit.

759. XVc. Italian. (Padua, Church of the Eremites.)
Niccolo Pizzolo. St. Christopher.

755

756

756

757

758

The effect of fullness is enhanced by circular capes, wound about, or thrown over the shoulder (see Ill. 751). Fur-lined boots, with turned-down fur cuff and side-buckled closing.

760. XVc. Italian. (Ferrara, Palazzo Schifanoia.)

Cosimo Tura. Triumph of Minerva.

Gloves are not merely carried, but are worn on both hands (gentleman, right). Belts reduced to a cord, knotted in back. Hose, parti-colored, with boot-like pattens on one leg.

761

761. c. 1478. Italian. (Florence, Uffizi.)
Sandro Botticelli. The Return of Spring: detail.
To illustrate Politian's allegorical poem, in celebration of the second and most splendid of the Medici tournaments (that of his younger brother, Giuliano, in 1475), Lorenzo commissioned Botticelli to execute three paintings: The Birth of Venus (Uffizi); Mars and Venus (Nat. Gall., Lond.); and the Return of Spring (from the motto, "Le temps reviendra," which

appeared on the Medici standard, painted by Verrocchio, who had also designed the helmets worn by the brothers in the tournament). For an analysis of the pictures, see Young's: *The Medici,* Chap. VIII.

762. 1480. Italian, Ferrarese. (National Gallery of Art, Washington.)
Ercole Roberti. Giovanni Bentivoglio.
The ruthless but cultivated tyrant of Bologna wears a red cap; red-gold brocade jacket. with white fur.

763. 1483-4. Italian, Florentine. (Nat. Gall. of Art, Wash.)
Sandro Botticelli. Portrait of a Youth.

The blond youth wears a red cap, brown jacket with separate sleeves.

764-67; 770-75. 1490-1500. Italian. (Metropolitan Mus.)
School of Bramantino.

Panels from the frieze in the Gonzaga Palace,
S. Martino di Guznaja, near Mantua.

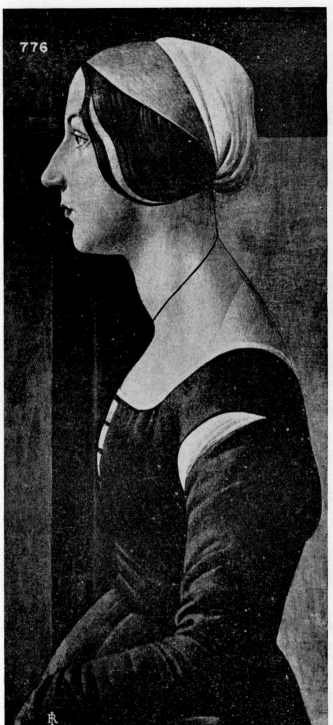

Doge, condottieri, and nobles with the long-flowing hair, the new bonnets and braid-trimmed outer garments with sailor collars, and the lady, the bound chin and tied-on sleeves, of the transition period.

768. XVc. 1487-9. Italian Florentine. (Metropolitan Museum, Bache Coll.)

Domenico Ghirlandaio.

Francesco Sassetti and son Teodoro.

Francesco, of the great Florentine bourgeois banking family, wears a purple cap, red gown, black cord belt and pouch. Teodoro: scarlet cap, gray brocade tunic edged with white fur, green doublet sleeves.

769. XVc. 1480. Italian. (Florence, Church of San Salvatore d'Ognissanti.)

Domenico Ghirlandaio.

St. Jerome.

Portable desk with lectern set on a table covered by the Oriental carpets which were first imported by Venice and spread through their agency throughout Europe in XVI-XVIIc. On its side hang the contemporary spectacles, which folded scissors-fashion to pinch the nose; inkwells, sand, scissors; cardinal's tasselled hat on shelf overhead.

779

780

776. XVc. 1489-90. Italian. (Florence, Pitti Gall.)
Sandro Botticelli.
Portrait of a Young Woman.
The Botticelli and Sassetti (Ill. 777) ladies show neckline, lowering and becoming squarer, laced bodices; and separate sleeves, showing shirt beneath. Succession of necklace styles: from the heavy jewelled collar, worn high on throat (see Ill. 715); ropes of pearls: cord caught at throat; coral beads, with Renaissance pearl pendant of Sassetti lady. Hair: loosening and flowing in locks; hair coverings, becoming simplified in arrangement of veils.

777. XVc. 1490. Italian Florentine. (Metropolitan Mus.)
Domenico Ghirlandaio.
Lady of the Sassetti family.
The lady wears a green moiré bodice, with sleeves of plain green silk; dark green lacings through gold catches; and a white fichu collar, in the new neckline of the XVIc. trend.

778. XVc. c. 1480. Italian Ferrarese. (National Gallery of Art, Washington.)
Ercole Roberti.
Ginevra Bentivoglio.
Ginevra wears a brown gown trimmed with gold, jewels and pearls; and a white veil, falling from a horned headdress, and carried under the arm (cf. exposed shirts of others).

779-780. XVc. 1486-90. Italian. (Florence, S. Maria Novella.)
Domenico Ghirlandaio.
779. The Birth of St. John the Baptist.
780. The Visitation (detail: Giovanni degli Albizzi Tornabuoni).

When Ghirlandaio was commissioned by the rich Florentine merchant family of Tornabuoni to redecorate the chapel, after the Orcagna frescos had been ruined by roof leaks, he used as models the painters, poets and leading citizens of Florence, and ladies of the Tornabuoni family. Until Lorenzo's day the Albizzi, leaders of the opposing party of the nobility, had been the most powerful family in Florence, and Giovanna, who had just been married, was the greatest beauty of the city.

The fashionable silhouette is definitely altering to one narrower and more severe. A stiff tabard-like outer garment, cut in a very low V-neck, falls loose over the short-bodiced, full-skirted gown we see on the attendants; the neckline of this under-gown is becoming lower and squarer, frequently exposing a line of the higher neck of the shirt. The greatest characteristic of all European costume, from the end of the XVc. through the first-half of the XVIc., is the increase, elaboration and combination of slashing and puffing, lacing and strapping.

We see lacing under arm (woman reaching for baby), down bodice fronts, and used (underbodice of visiting lady) in combination with strappings, such as catch the inner sleeve at the armseye, and cross the inner and outer elbow.

Many new usages are shown: the nightgown, worn by the invalid; the fan and handkerchief, carried by the great ladies; the use of embroidered edges on the hem of the elderly attendant's gown, and on the neck of the nightgown. Necklaces are now a narrow cord, caught at throat, falling between breasts; or bead necklaces with pearl and jewelled pendants. Lacings are often bead-strung, as across bodice of younger attendant. Hair arrangements have flowing side-locks, no head-covering at all, or a tiny cap or slight veil.

781.XVIc. 1597. Italian-German. (Met. Mus., Print Room.)

Att. to *Jost Amman.*

Venetian Gondola, from the illustrations of the great procession of the Doges, published in Frankfort, 1597.

781

782

Coryat describes the great height of Venice's 3-4 story buildings, made of brick and freestone, with pillars of white stone and Istrian marble; flat roofs, and open galleries hanging from upper stories; painted ceilings equal to those of the Louvre or Tuileries; and with windows of glass; and her checkered pavements, and mosaic walls.

There were no horses in Venice, but 10,000 gondolas—6,000 private and 4,000 for hire. The gondolas, with carved ends, had as many as 15-16 cloth-covered arches, and black leather seats with lace-trimmed white linen curtains below.

782. XVc. 1498. Italian. (Florence, Corsini Palace.)
Unknown artist. Execution of Savonarola in the Piazza della Signoria.

The fervid preacher, who denounced the powerful families of Italy and the corruption of the Papacy, was the virtual ruler of Florence after Cosimo de' Medici's death. He changed the pleasure-loving city to one of Puritan austerity in dress and manners. Carnival time in 1497 was celebrated by a bonfire of masks and "vanities" for which a Venetian merchant offered 20,000 gold florins. Alexander VI failed to buy off the dangerous man with a Cardinal's hat; then swore he should die "even were he a second John the Baptist." Florentine men began to resent their interrupted marriages; incited by Franciscans and Dominicans, Savonarola was arrested, tortured, and burned with two of his followers. The calamities which had been foretold by Savonarola for Florence under a Pope named Clement, came true in XVIc.

783. End XVc. Italian. (Milan, Brera Museum.)
Att. to *B. Conti.*
Madonna, SS. Jerome, Gregory and Ambrose, with Lodovico *il Moro* Sforza, Beatrice d'Este, and two sons.

These are the last generations of the 100-year old condottieri dynasty of the Sforza. Beatrice d'Este, the great patron of arts and letters, died before her husband. Lodovico, Leonardo da Vinci's patron, was driven from Milan in 1499, to die a prisoner of the French. One son, Massimiliano, died a pensioner of the French; Francesco Maria was reinstated, but on his death, the duchy went to Charles V.

Spanish styles influence the allied states of Naples, Milan and Florence. Naples is ruled by an Aragon king, and Lodovico had arranged the marriage of his nephew (Bianca Maria's brother), to the granddaughter of the King of Naples. Looped hair, often with a falling lock, as in Spain, is seen in Florence and Milan, and in the highest society, the bound Spanish pigtail appears as well. With this headdress, the forehead is bound by a narrow, flat, black braid with irregular edges; it does not have the thread-like character of the black cord worn around the neck in conjunction with short necklaces of enormous pearls.

784. XVc. c. 1493. Italian Milanese. (National Gallery of Art, Washington.)
Ambrogio de' Predis.
Bianca Maria Sforza.
The auburn-haired sitter, dressed in golden-brown brocade, formerly identified as Lodovico Sforza's

785

wife, Beatrice d'Este, is now generally believed to represent Gian Galeazzo's sister, Bianca Maria, during her engagement (signified by the carnation in her girdle) to the Emperor Maximilian whom she married in 1494.

The long queue, bound in pearls (which we will see in Spanish usage at the turn of the century, in combination with looped hair), is combined with a jewelled headdress and pendant. The pendant bears the Sforza emblems of branches carrying fruit; and the Sforza *spazzola* device, a brush with a ribbon tied to the handle (which was a great favorite of Lodovico, but had been in use by other members of the family at about the time of his birth); and the motto "Merito et Tempore," which each member of the family interpreted during his lifetime "according to his individual standards and ambitions." (See Appendix.)

785-787. XVc. 1490-95. Italian. (Venice, Academy of Fine Arts.)
Vittore Carpaccio.
The Legend of St. Ursula:

786

785. The English Ambassadors Before King Maurus; 786. The English Ambassadors Return to Their King; 787. The English Ambassadors Before King Maurus: detail.

Commines describes Venice, in 1495, to which he was Ambassador from the King of France: "The houses are very large and lofty, and built of stone; the old ones are all painted; those of about a hundred years standing are faced with white marble from Istria (which is about a hundred miles from Venice), and inlaid with porphyry and serpentine. Within they have, most of them, two chambers at least adorned with gilt ceilings; rich marble chimney pieces, bedsteads of gold color, their portals of the same, and most gloriously furnished. In short, it is the most triumphant city I have ever seen, the most respectful to all ambassadors and strangers, governed with the greatest wisdom, and serving God with the utmost solemnity."

Male costume of the Transition period was strongly affected by these Italian styles. The new diagonal line (shown particularly in the Return of the Ambassadors) is found, not only in the closings and wraparound of the cloaks of the young men, but in long gowns (m. near pillar in crowd before bridge), and in the braid trim of bias-cut cape sleeves (to left and in front of crowd), and in the revers of the cloaks.

The ambassadors' gowns have extremely long sleeves, widening below elbow; the plain high-necked gowns (in line, left of crowd) carry bead girdles. Doublets are excessively short, with sleeves much cut and laced; the lacings diagonal, or grouped horizontally.

Shirts are much exposed, with embroidery or braid holding gathered or smocked fullness. Hose are very long and well made; parti-color of one leg; and division of its decoration at knee. Boots are much worn; soft; slit at back seam; the tops turned down, showing another color, and pinked edges.

Gloves are not carried but worn, with embroidered edges and pointed cuff, weighted by a bead or acorn of precious metal. Doublet points begin to assume precious jewelled tags, aiglettes. Neck chains are heavy and handsome, often carry a pendant. Caps and hats of felt or beaver carry jewelled brooches and feathers; the larger hats, usually of beaver, carry clusters of plumes and a binding scarf.

The hair of the young men is particularly long and flowing; others have long and carefully rolled bobs; or are even clipped (rear: ambassador to Maurus). All are clean shaven.

788

788. End XVc. Italian, Florentine. (Met. Mus. of Art.)

Cassone panel: The War of Charles of Durazzo.
Left side: Charles enters Naples as Victor, 1381.
One episode in centuries of violent Neapolitan history and intrigue was Charles of Durazzo's capture of Naples and murder of its queen, Joanna I. She had named a distant cousin, Louis of Anjou, as her heir. René d'Anjou's claim on Naples, inherited by the French crown, together with the Orleans claim of Milan, were Charles VIII's excuse for the invasion of Italy in 1494, which revealed to the French masses a civilization beyond their dreams.

Durazzo's men are shown in the costume of the time of their invasion, more than a century before.

789-792. XIV-XVc. French Burgundian. (Dijon Museum.)

Claus Sluter. Four mourners.
To enrich the Carthusian monastery he had built at Champmol, Philip the Bold commissioned the Flemish sculptor, Sluter, to execute a magnificent altar tomb, with 40 alabaster figures representing mourners from all ranks of life.

Man: carrying large hat; wears small cowl over circular fur-lined cape, closed on right shoulder.

Bishop: the stole, which is worn, by a bishop, dependent from the shoulders, is here worn crossed, like that of a priest. There were many deviations of this sort during the Middle Ages; figure may be that of an honorary abbot, who is a simple priest permitted to wear pontificals; there are still honorary abbots in various parts of Europe. Mitre: rising and raking backward. Crozier; curve and tendrils becoming more elaborate.

Man: very new sleeve; full, gathered onto a long cuff of circular cut; buttoned tight at wrist; completely concealing hand of hanging arm; another expression of the idea manifested in prolonged sleeve of English bourgeois and ladies, and the shell-back gauntlet of English knights.

Carthusian monk: hooded scapular, held together by broad band, over fur-lined robe.

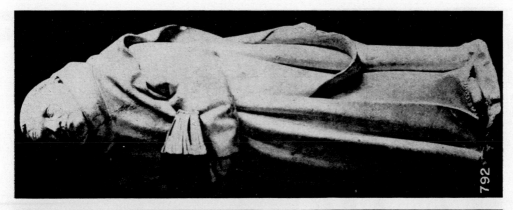

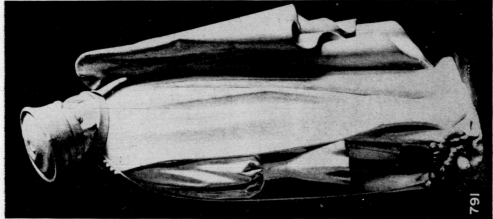

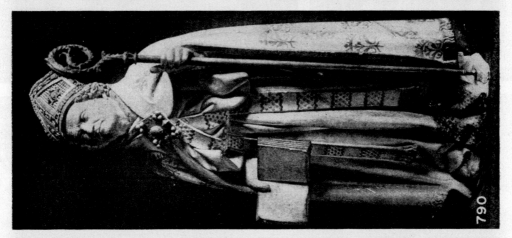

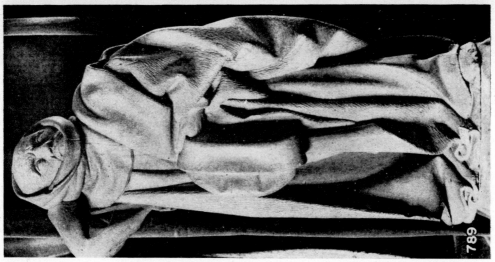

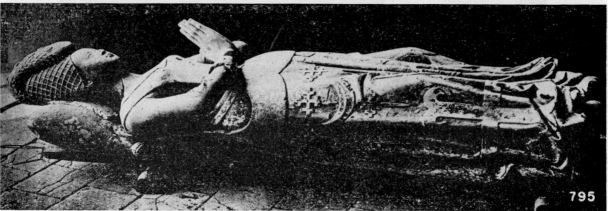

793. 1399-1401. French Burgundian. (Champmol Monastery.)

Claus Sluter. Isaiah: one of 6 prophets executed by Sluter for Philip the Bold, for the monastery where perpetual masses were to be said for the Duke's soul. Dressed in the costume of a rich gentleman of his period; tasseled pouches hang from handsome belt.

794. XVc. 1424-29. French.

Pierre de Theury. Tomb sculpture: Isabelle of Bavaria, wife of Charles VI.

The classic shape of the headdress of a great lady of the first-quarter of the XVc.; covered chin, of great lady or widow. Beneath the wimple and veil with fluted edge, the masses of netted hair, completely covering the ears, give the characteristic horizontal line to the top of the headdress, which, in full-face appears very wide; in profile narrow. The fact that Isabelle of Bavaria was completely bald and without eyebrows is supposed to have led, out of court snobbery, to the plucking of eyebrows and forehead, to give an exaggeratedly bald look to the unveiled head.

795. XVc. French. (Beuvil, Indre-et-Loire.)

Tomb sculpture. Jeanne de Montjean, d.1456.

796

797

798

By the third-quarter XVc. the netted headdress has become very high and narrow; ears, which have been covered for nearly half a century, are again beginning to be seen. The headdress is wired and padded to support the heavily jewelled netting and the horns formed by the stuffed roll. The skirt of her fur bordered cotte carries parted armorial bearings.

796-798. XVc. French. (Paris, Bibliotheque Nationale, ms. fr. 616.)

Livre de Chasse by Gaston-Phoébus.

One of the earliest books on hunting, the "Deduits de la chasse, des bestes sauvages et les oiseaux de proye," was translated into English in 1406-13 by Edward, Duke of York, under the title, "Master of Game." Of its author, Gaston III, Count of Foix (1331-91), called Gaston-Phoébus because of his beauty, Froissart, after his visit to the great court of Foix in 1389 says: "I never saw none like him of personage, nor of so fair form, nor so well made. . . . In everything he was so perfect, he cannot be praised too much."

It is probable that this copy belonged originally to Diane de Poitiers' father; he was reprieved as he stood on the scaffold, but his property was confiscated by Francis I. The book accompanied the king to the wars, and became part of the booty at Pavia. It was sold by a common soldier to the bishop of Trent. It was almost lost, and its binding badly charred in the 1848 fire in the Bibliothèque Nationale.

Start of the hunt (796): the Count's hooded robe, simple in cut, magnificent in its dragon-patterned brocade,* owes its dragging length to the influence of the houppelande. Its skirt, long in front, is necessarily slit partway above hem. The huntsmen wear high boots, laced up the outside of the leg, as well as the new bag sleeve. From the extraordinary collars of the houppelande, so much has been learned about cutting, that, by XVc., collars appear on garments worn by men of all classes. Horns slung by baldrics. Third man to right of count, and almost concealed, carries on his belt a wonderful pouch; a strap across its buckled flap holds a short hunting knife.

Tracking (797): huntsman in a broad brimmed straw hat, turned up in back.

Bear hunt (798): the mounted gentleman wears a short brocade gown of the houppelande type, collars on which are now becoming lower; bag sleeves, with a falling circular cuff, here thrown back. Precious collar of gold links is a new style. Hat, typical of the end of the XIVc., with Phrygian peak worn flopping forward. Strapped puttees. Dagging in leaf patterns has now invaded even the trappings of the horses.

---

* Gaston-Phoebus' personal emblem was a blazing sun; dragons, green with red and gold wings, were used as supporters by the Counts of Foix.

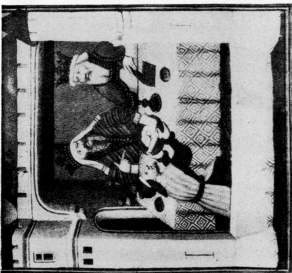 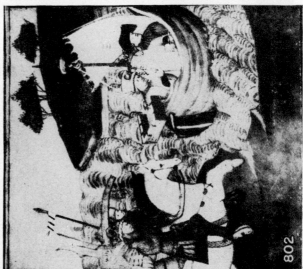

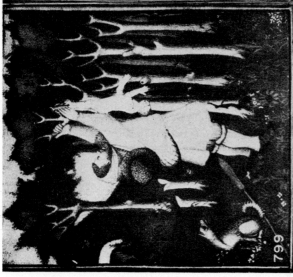 

799-803. XVc. 1409-19. French. (Paris, Bib. de l'Arse-
nale. No. 5193.)

Boccaccio of Jean Sans Peur.

This *Boccaccio,* one of the many fine manuscripts
which have come down to us in the libraries of the
Dukes of Burgundy, belonged to John, the son of
Philip the Bold.

799. Peasant: fur hat, worn over hood, but carried
slung back by a cord; net pouch, fastened to belt, and
slung above buttocks; socks with rolled top (cf.
huntsmen, Livre de Chasse), but without feet. (Right
panel) Banquet: oriental kings being served by man
in tabard-like garment; cloth of diapered mediaeval
pattern; flagon.

800. King: hood twisted and tied around brow;
from such usages developed the cockscomb turbans
worn with houppelandes, and later chaperons.

801. As the king hurdles the flames, his houppelande is presented almost in pattern form. It is of
brocade, ermine-lined; it has, typically, an extremely
high collar, flaring and trailing funnel sleeves, excessively dagged edges, and skirt slit high (in this
case, at side, rather than at center front as was more
common). His darker undertunic, also of brocade, has
bag sleeves. The onlooker (extreme right), shows
typical haircut of the first half of the XVc., cropped
high above ears; he wears an interesting very short
garment, in the nature of a jupon; it has, however a
rather full, baggy sleeve, and, under the influence of
the houppelande, a tiny slit in the front of its very
short skirts. His companion wears the forward-flopping hat already seen on horsemen of Livre de
Chasse illustrations; and pleated cote-hardi, the
sleeves of which are also set on in pleats. Both wear
parti-colored hose with sewn-on soles. Tapestry background and floor in typical diapered patterns.

802. On the little sailing ship, the king's two companions wear two typical forms of late XIV-e.XVc.
headgear: one, often seen in a taller form, in which
the crown resembles that of an opera hat, carries the
now fashionable medallion; the other is draped, made
from a hood, bound round by its liripipe into a turban, with the dagged hem of the hood falling in
pleats over the rolled edge.

803. King, in robes with parted armorial bearings,
being crowned by a bishop and two cardinals.

DOMESTIC ARCHITECTURE: MIDDLE AGES TO
XVIII CENTURY

Until the invention of the wrought-iron I-beam
in mid-XIXc., building height was limited to 5-6
floors. This was the first major advance over the
techniques practiced more than 2000 years before
by the Romans. Roman masonry was magnificent;
they manufactured brick, tile and glass in the re-
motest outposts of Britain. Their villas, built
around a court, which could be cooled by fountains and always provided a sunny or a shaded
area, had running water and hot-air ducts under
the floor which delivered heat in the "panel"
form which is heating's newest refinement in the
1940's.

With the fall of their empire, Roman culture re-
ceded toward its Italian sources. Its techniques
had only been imposed on Britain, and were largely forgotten there during the Dark Ages.

Concrete remained unused from Roman times
until the rebuilding of the Eddystone Lighthouse
in England in 1774.

Glass was used in English windows in VIIc.;
but in 758 A.D. Cuthbert, abbot of Jarrow, asked
the Bishop of Mainz to send workmen to supply
"windows and vessels of glass because the English
were so ignorant and helpless." The glass which
Bishop Wilfruth installed at Worcester in the first-
half of the VIIIc. was suspected of being of su-
pernatural origin. A knowledge of glass-making
was retained in Normandy, Lorraine and around
Barcelona; colored glass, appearing in churches
in late XIIc., was seen throughout Europe in XIII-
XVc. From XIII-XVIIIc., the finest glass was that
exported by Venice. Germany's ties with Italy
were close; and in 1453 Philip the Good established Italian glass workers in Flanders, which became another center, exporting to England. Glass
was in common domestic use in England by 1550;
in e. XVIIc., as we will see, the dramatic entrance
of coal as a fuel altered the entire industrial balance of Europe.

Knowledge of brick and tile making was retained in Germany and the Low Countries, which
exported brick to the east coast of England. Manufacture was recommenced in England in XIIIc.;
use increased through XV-XVIc., and after the
Fire of 1666 London was rebuilt largely in brick;
by XVIIIc., it was the most common building
material. Here, too, the Italians and Spanish were
pre-eminent and earliest, with magnificent decorative glazed terra cottas in XIV-XVc.; cool floors
of tile, and roof tiles which were not subject to
shattering cold. From XIII-XVIc., floors were
largely of tile: either the more durable red-brown
and cream-white encaustic tiles of England,
France, the Low Countries and Germany, or the
more colorful but tenderly glazed majolica of
Spain and Italy; or of marble. Where the floor did
not remain beaten earth, it was of stone, so long

as fires continued to be built upon it; then of tile or marble, lastly of wood.

In many places, stone is so good and plentiful that it has always remained cheaper than brick; as in N.E. England, up the Rhine, along the German seacoast and in parts of France. To Americans, brought up on weathered New England granite or New York gneiss, it is surprising to learn what a soft material newly quarried sand or limestone can be. In his specifications for St. Paul's Cathedral, Sir Christopher Wren required the stone to be seasoned for three years on a sea beach.

The most common building material in use through XVIc. was wood, which was becoming scarce in England and N.W. Europe. It was, in any case, so hard to fell, draw, adze and saw by primitive methods, and nails were so tedious to forge by hand, that timber was apt to be used only in the supporting frame. This was usually fitted together without nails, and the interstices filled in with interwoven wattles and mud (lathe and plaster), or later with brick. Diagonal bracing (as by projecting tree limbs) was often obtained by the actual use of trunks and limbs; with the increase of ship building the curved and seasoned timbers of old ships were worked into the framing. The patterns of the exposed dark wood frame and its light plastered stuffing were elaborated with infinite sophistication in the 4 to 5 story high, half-timbered houses of the Rhine Valley in XV-XVIc.; and with equal beauty in the lower, wider French and English forms of town or manor house or farm cottage. The upper stories were wider than the lower, to protect them from the elements, and to shelter passers-by and customers. A guild member's house was a combination of shop in front, opening out into the street, factory in back with a garden beyond, and living quarters above for the family and apprentices.

A wooden house in England before XVc. was about as weather-tight as grandfather's hayloft; its windows were glassless holes covered by batten shutters or wicker-work lattices which were hinged at the top and could be propped open in good weather. As in the castle, its fire was in the middle of the dirt or stone floor, and the smoke was supposed to go out of a hole in the roof. In Elizabeth's day a farmer's house is described as:

"Of one bay's* breadth, Got wot, a silly cote
Whose thatched spars are furred with sluttish soote
A whole inch thick, shining like a blackamoor's brows
Through smoke that down a headless barrel blows."

---

* Bay-16 feet, the module in multiplications of which a house was built, so many bays wide; during Tudor times, ranks of symmetrical bays were projected, stories high, from the face of the building, and were filled with windows in late XVIc.

Still, in 1628, "his habitation is some poore thatched roofe, distinguished from his Barne by the loopholes that let out Smoake, which the rain had long since washed thorow, but for the double seeling of Bacon on the inside." (John Earle: *Microcosmography*.)

Even in the bedrooms of mediaeval castles, smoke filtered out through slits high in the walls; the flue was a refinement, rare in Italy in XIIc., common in N. Italy by XVc. In cold N.W. Europe, the flue began to be common in XVc., and with the use of brick, late XVc., clusters of flues could be carried up in one chimney. The decorative value of tall chimneys was emphasized in French architecture in XV-XVIc. (See Ills. 807-810.)

The handsome house of Elizabeth's day was becoming well-lighted, comfortable and livable, and chimneys were making even unpretentious houses bearable. In 1577-89 Harrison says, "Old men yet dwelling in the village where I remain find things 'marvellously' altered within their sound remembrance . . . one is the multitude of chimneys lately erected in each village whereas in their young daies there were not above two or three but each made his fire against a reredos in the hall." (From: *Description of England in Shakespeare's Youth*.)

Roofs of cathedrals and palaces might be of lead or copper sheets; slate was used where found (see Ills. 807-810); tile, especially in milder southern Europe; wood shingles (East Anglia); and thatch.

In 1555, the Venetian Ambassador to England wrote, "In the North of England they find a certain sort of earth, well nigh mineral, which burns like charcoal and is extensively used, especially by blacksmiths, and but for a certain bad odour which it leaves would be yet more employed as it gives great heat and costs but little." Rising in veins to the surface, coal had been known in England since Roman days; by XIIIc. its use in the city of London had been forbidden, but as flues multiplied, it became practical, and early in XVIIc., the most important of all fuels. English patents for coal furnaces were granted in 1610; by 1616 no other fuel was permitted in English glass manufacture and the importation of glass was forbidden; by the third-quarter of the XVIIc. English glass was equal or superior to Venetian.

Now that the climate of N.W. Europe could be made comfortable all year round, Italy's Renaissance advantage of three good seasons to their one, was reduced to three against their present four; with a hot summer and inadequate fuel, Italy lost out in the new industrial age to England and the countries around the coal basins of Alsace and the Ruhr.

804-805. XVc. 1409. French. (Paris. Bibliotheque Nationale, ms. fr. 23279.)

Demandes faites par le Roi Charles VI, by Pierre le Fuitier, called Salmon.

804. Charles VI and Pierre Salmon. 805. Salmon presenting his work to Charles VI in the presence of Jean Sans Peur.

The basic plan of the great mediaeval dwelling provided a huge central hall, from which doors led at one end to the kitchens; from the other end, to the living quarters of the family. The size of the hall required the support of pillars and arches. Insufficient heat with much smoke was provided by a fire, often set on a raised hearth in the middle of the hall; in this case, there was no flue, and the smoke passed out through an insufficient hooded aperture in the high ceiling. By XIVc., tall screens blocked off draughts as doors were opened at the servants' end of the hall. Above these screens the musicians' gallery was placed.

At the master's end was a raised dining platform with long narrow tables, on one side of which diners sat in a row, and from the other side of which they were served. In great houses the attendants on the lord or lady were not servants, but young people of good family, sent there as they would now be sent to finishing school.* (See p. 298, footnote.)

The hall had a public and civic character. It was the law court, hotel, place of business and entertainment of the lord's domain, as the castle was the jail, source of supplies and place

of retreat for the lord's people and their cattle in time of danger. An overflow of guests was bedded down in the hall, and their servants in the stables.

The private rooms were usually on a higher level than the hall, set over the supply cellars; the "solar" was a combination bed-sitting room, much less draughty and smoky than the hall. Its fireplace was set against the wall, the smoke leaving by slits high in the masonry in the early days. It was the first fireplace in the building to be provided with a flue when these began to be built. The bedroom was therefore used as an audience chamber; Edward I and his queen were struck by lightning and almost killed in 1287, while sitting on their bed, surrounded by members of their court. A small low window with a wide sill served as a lectern (806).

The all-pervading chill of mediaeval court life is implicit in these illustrations: fur-lined gowns; tapestry-hung walls; curtained beds; double-hung windows; raised seats, draped with heavy fabrics and furnished with cushions under foot against the cold of the tile floors.

Pattern is now applied in a variety of ways. There are fewer borders and braids, except on conservative state robes (805). Floral and foliated asymmetric patterns, like those on the borders of illuminated manuscripts of the period, are variously used: diagonally (across bed-furnishings, 804, on certain portions [as sleeves alone] of houppelande). We see the familiar geometric designs in stained-glass windows, and diapered red and blue wall-hangings, but even the repeated patterns which we see on gowns and curtains begin to show increasing personal significance.

Typical of the XVc. is the increasing use of personal and identifying mottos, devices, badges and color. (See Ills. 807-810.)

In the course of the hereditary enmity between the houses of Orleans and Burgundy, Louis, Duke of Orleans, served notice of his intentions by adopting as his badge a knotty stick which he distributed as a gilded New Year's gift, in 1406, together with the motto, "Je t' envy" (I defy you), a dice-player's term. As a counter-device, Jean Sans Peur assumed carpenter's planes and levels, and, as motto, another dicing term, in Flemish, "Hic houd" (I hold it). After the assassination of Orleans, the Parisians said, "Le baton épineaux avait été raclé par le rabot!"† (The knotted stick was scraped by the plane.) These devices of Jean Sans Peur appear in the embroidery of his gown, and as pendants from his gold chain.

805. The canopies, fringed in red, black, and white (the colors of Charles VI), bear his motto: "Jamais." The hound with a crowned collar, which appears on his bed-hangings, and together with his motto, on the breast of his houppelande, was one of his emblems. The diagonal sprays shown on both are probably also significant.

---

* At the meeting of the Kings of France and England, Froissart tells us that "the Duke of Berry served the King of France with the comfit-box, and the Duke of Burgundy with the cup of wine; in like manner, the King of England was served by the Dukes of Lancaster and Gloucester. After the kings had been served, the knights of France and England took the wine and spices, and served the prelates, dukes, princes and counts; and after them, squires and other officers of the household did the same to all within the tent, until everyone had partaken."

The feudal period was extremely food-conscious: life was a feast or a famine, and when you had food, you gorged. A great lord assured himself of faithful followers by the profusion of his banquets; the sending of a dish from his own table was a mark of a king's favor; and it was a great compliment to send dinner ahead of you, and follow to help eat it.

† These symbols were used in place of actual names in political satires of the period, and were understood by everybody, just as "The Little Flower" meant Fiorello LaGuardia to the citizens of New York when he was Mayor. When an Englishman, in 1449, read a poem beginning: "The Root is dead, the Swan is gone, The fiery Cresset hath lost its light," he understood equally well that these were references to the Regent, Bedford: Humphrey, Duke of Gloucester; and the last Duke of Exeter.

Jean Sans Peur can also be recognized (extreme right) by his swan emblem, which is used all over his houppelande. The tapestries of the King's audience chamber are semé with the fleurs-de-lys of ancient France.

The houppelandes we see here are of various lengths, all fur-lined, with high funneling collars, elaborately dagged edges, and precious chains with pendants. The bag sleeve of the shorter garment shows under the long dragging sleeve of the houppelande; while the high houppelande collar has affected the collar of other male garments, designed to be worn without the houppelande. The headgears of the great gentlemen illustrate the late XIV-e.XVc. tendency to flop, either forward (turbans with Phrygian crown), or sidewise and back (those with hanging cockscomb, formed by dagged and pleated border of the hood, bound around the head).

806. XVc. 1409-15. French. (Paris, Bibliotheque Nationale, ms. fr. 2810.)

Merveilles du monde, by Jean Hayton, probably executed by *Jacques Coen* of Bruges.

Jean Hayton offering to Jean Sans Peur his story of travel, which was ordered by the Duke of Burgundy as a gift to his uncle.

807-810. XVc. 1409-16. French. (Chantilly, Conde Mus.)

Très riches heures du duc de Berri.‡ Executed by *Pol de Limbourg* and his brothers.

Jean de Berri, brother of the French king, and the greatest bibliophile of his time, maintained his own staff of artists and calligraphers. This book of hours was to have been the greatest treasure of his magnificent library; unfinished at his death in 1416, it was completed 65 years later by Jean Colombe. The occupations suitable to the 12 months of the year are shown against backgrounds of the chateaux he possessed or had built.

January: Banquet scene (807). The Duke sits at a banquet table, protected by a circular wicker screen from the excessive heat of the fire behind him. The decorations of the chimneypiece are all symbolic of his house or person: fleurs-de-luce of France; orange leaves; bears; wounded swans. The walls are hung with a tapestry of a battle scene, into which is woven an explanatory text. The floor is covered by a braided carpet. On the banquet table is set the great "salt cellar of the Pavillion," shaped like a ship,§ and surmounted by his bear and swan, which is recorded in the inventory of his estate. The sideboard bears a great deal of plate.

---

‡ Notes from M. le comte P. Durrieu's scholarly edition, with sumptuous color reproductions. LIFE magazine, Jan. 5, 1948, published all the plates in color.

§ Louis XIV's *nef* was a great gold salt-cellar in the shape of a ship, which all saluted in passing, as they did the king's bed; it held his salt, knives, and napkin between perfumed cushions and stood on the chimneypiece of the Cabinet of Medals when not in use.

808

807

Plate, in what seems to us like immense quantities, is meticulously described in XVc. inventories and wills. Sir John Fastolf's plate takes eight pages to enumerate, and that of Margaret Paston and Dame Elizabeth Browne is considerable. The most important pieces are named, like "his standing bowl called the Baron de St. Blankheare" (part of the loot of a naval engagement with the French), which Clement Paston bequeathed to his nephew. A lesser piece of Fastolf's is described as "a saltsaler like a bastell (bastile—small tower) alle gilt with roses weiying lxxvij unces."

From his bear (Fr. *ours*) badge, which surmounts this salt-cellar, Berri derived his pet-name for his wife, "Ursette."

Salt, indispensable and the symbol of hospitality, was a heavily taxed monopoly. The centrally placed salt-cellar was the most important piece of plate; the relative importance of the diners was indicated by their seating in relation to it.

Forks, though described in Miège's French-English dictionary of 1679, did not come into common use until the XVIIIc. Spoons were of wood or horn until XVc. A knife was the only common implement. Meat was at first laid in a slice (Fr. *tranche*) of bread, from which came the word "trencher," for the plates of wood (or for the rich, metal) which were the next refinement. Chinese porcelains had been seen in Europe in XIc., and fine ceramics had been produced in Moorish Spain since XIIc.; but the largely decorative ceramic wares of XV-XVIc. Europe were at least as costly as the finest plate, and were only for the very rich: armorial or portrait-decorated salvers, wine jugs, great vases, tankards, salt cellars, fruit bowls and floor tiles. Until the great English commercial china manufactures of the XVIIIc., wood, pewter, silver and gold utensils were usual.

The garments of Berri's chamberlain (behind him, with a staff, exhorting a reluctant man: "Approach, approach"), and those of the squires who serve, all bear his livery badge or colors, in some form; orange leaves; wreathed monograms; or the glowing crowns of the duke's own blue and gold robe appear on their gowns, hoods, or collars. Under the "ancien régime" it still took four people to serve a glass of water at court.

Parti-color and hoods are now used only on livery garments, such as these of green, red and white, or blue and white. Among the 15 robes in Fastolf's wardrobe is listed one, red, "of my Lord Cromwell his livery"; that is, Fastolf was the "man" of Ralph Cromwell, Lord Treasurer of England.

The scarlet-gowned cleric sitting beside the duke is the Bishop of Chartres, also a great bibliophile, and executor of the duke's will.

The houppelandes, typically fur-lined, slit, dagged, with wide sleeves, show a variety of collars: conveniently high (duke); high but turned back, as is the trend (chamberlain); low and standing; or with the V at the back completely unfilled by collar (squires with back to us, carrying scarves and napkins). The squire at the end of the table has sleeves pinned back over shoulders while serving. High-cropped hair; fur hats; precious collars; belts and diagonally slung baldrics, all hung with bells or badges. Puppies wandering over the table; greyhound with characteristic collar of XV-XVIc., being fed slices from a leg of lamb, instead of scavenging bones cast on the floor, as was usual.

April: Engagement (808). In the first warm days of spring, mediaeval society is always glad to escape into the open from the damp, dark cold of the castle (Ill. 672: Italian Tirol frescos). Large entertainments tend to be held out of doors for this reason.

In the background, the Chateau of Dourdain, in which the Duke's most precious belongings were held, and its little attendant village; pond with fishermen seining; walled garden with lattice for training grapes.

Fiancé: Blue houppelande has sleeves of same blazing gold crowns worn by Duke. His companion; white, edged with yellow fur; high black hat; red tights. Fiancée: White-bordered gown of light and dark gray-blue brocade; dragging cape sleeves; black feathered hat with red, yellow and white ostrich plumes (feathers new, in XVc.). Her companion: black and gold; her red and gold brocade undersleeve is edged with gold fringe, also a new usage. Kneeling ladies: In back: black gown, white trim; deep blue undergrown, and blue and gold stuffed roundlet. In foreground: pink, lined with gray.

May: Riding party (809). Beyond the woods, the town of Riom, capitol of the ancient Duchy of Auvergne, one of the Duke's possessions. The riders, celebrating May Day, wear the traditional garlands of leaves, and the "Livery of May," green garments given by the Duke to his entourage. The festive, bell-hung baldrics they wear here on May Day, have left us the phrase, "with bells on." But their wear was not confined to May Day and their size was often enormous. (See Hero: Ill. 906).

John Stow describes the May Day amusements of England in late XVIc.

The servants with horns wear parti-colored livery, with badges on their left shoulders. Second gentleman in procession seems young for the King, but wears the livery colors of Charles VI: red, black and white. The first three ladies wear the Livery of May in various shades of green; flowing undersleeves with edges of fringe. Men's garments belted high, as were the houppelandes of women. Collars and baldrics; bell-trimmed; caparisons of horses.

June (810): Harvest on the Ile du Palais, with Paris as the Duke saw it from the windows of his Hotel de Nesles, on the left bank of the Seine. The Pont Neuf now stands at the point where the postern gate is shown opening on the Seine. Beyond the walls and garden, slate-roofed except for two red tiled towers (back left), are the Palace, the Tower of the Conciergerie, and the Ste-Chapelle. Women gleaners: in blue and white; kirtles laced over shirt, and tucked up; heads wrapped. Reapers: in rose, white and blue tunics.

810

809

811. XVc. 1420-30. French. (Morgan Library, M. 453.)
Hours of the Virgin for Paris use.
Offices of the dead. Priests and acolytes; in center a robed member of a confraternity, with the symbol of the Virgin of the Ascension embroidered on the front.

812-815. XVc. Flemish. (Amsterdam Museum.)
Figures from a chimneypiece: Counts of Holland, Countesses of Holland.
The only sleeve which does not appear to have been worn by both sexes is
the bag-sleeve shown on the count with the top hat (814); a simpler form is
worn on an embroidered garment in John Foxton's *Cosmography*, 1408. An
unusual form of turned-up, jewelled brim appears on the other count (812).
The countess in the round turban is a typical figure of c. 1410; her companion,
in the butterfly headdress, more nearly approaches mid-XVc.

Photographs courtesy of the Victoria and Albert Museum

816. XVc. 1432. Flemish. (National Gallery, London.)
Jean van Eyck. Giovanni and Giovanna Arnolfini.
(*See also* Color Plate, No. 3.)

Italian merchant and his wife, lived in Bruges from 1420-1472. Arnolfini wears a tabard-like cloak, sable-edged, over tunic and hose; hat of finely braided straw. Lower l. corner: pattens worn in mud.

His wife wears a trailing gown edged with fur; lower part of her long bag-sleeves decorated with double thicknesses of the material of the gown, cut into petals and appliquéd, loosely, in banked rows. Kirtle, furred at the hem. Belt gold, embroidered in red. Hair confined, above ears, by netted cauls. The veil, which they support in the horned effect of the headdresses of first third XVc., is edged by layers of fluting (German: *kruseler* headdress), seen in the Low Countries, Germany and England. Wedding ring worn on second joint of finger.

817-819. XVc. Flemish.

Roger van der Weyden: Three portraits.

817. Portrait of a young woman, c. 1435. (Kaiser Friedrich Museum.)

818. Bracque family altarpiece: St. Mary Magdalene, c. 1452 (Louvre.)

819. Portrait of a lady, c. 1455. (National Gallery, Washington.)

Domestic pins are new in early XVc. Their use, decoratively, is typical of the Low Countries. They fasten interchangeable sleeves to kirtle (818), veils to coifs (819), and supplement or replace tapes in the typically Flemish headdress of the "beguine" type (817). Decorative pins are used on the falls of hoods, as elsewhere, but in Flemish portraits, these are apt to be in the form of naturalistic insects, bees or flies, such as might have alighted, rather than brooches or pendants.

Buckles, belts and tabs are extremely rich here, as all over Europe except in Italy; rings, everywhere, are worn on thumb or middle joint. Headdresses are set far back on tightly drawn hair, but the forehead is not plucked bald as in France.

The Franco-Burgundian court styles are worn by the upper classes, but women's clothing in Flanders is higher necked, much more bourgeois than in France.

At the end XVc., when male costume is affected by Italian fashions, women's clothing will be greatly influenced by these middle-class Flemish garments, with their variety of enclosing hoods, coifs and wimples: they lead directly to the Tudor fashions of Anne Boleyn and Henry VIII.

820-822. XVc. c. 1438-40. Franco-Flemish. (Metropolitan Museum.)

Tapestry: Arras or Tournai. Courtiers with roses,

Arras was the first great tapestry weaving center; there had been wool weavers there for ten centuries, because of the plentiful growth of madder, one of the oldest red dye-stuffs. In England, the imports from Arras finally led to the generic name of "Arras" being used for tapestry of any provenance. By second half XVc. many other towns, among them Tournai, supplanted Arras in importance.

We have already seen the collar of the high-belted lady's houppelande turning downward (see Ills. 808, 809). It has now been lowered into a flat collar, frequently (as in Rose Tapestry), of fur; the front opening has necessarily deepened, and exposes a triangle of the material of the kirtle beneath. The present gown has discarded the dragging, funnel sleeve of the houppelande; the new sleeve of the gown is long and close; below the elbow it widens slightly toward the wrist, where it is turned back into a cuff, matching the collar.

High, padded, heart-shaped headdresses, with streaming scarves, still occur well into last quarter XVc., as do the towering wired forms of gauze veil. Jewelled pin on veil. As these headdresses mount,

ears will gradually become uncovered again; ladies' eyebrows and an artificial hairline will be carefully plucked.

Both men and women strive to appear bald under their elaborate headgear. Men's necks and heads are shaved to a point well above the ears. The cropped head is often covered by a cap, over which the hat is set; until, and even beyond second half XVc., no hair will show beneath the stuffed roundlet of the chaperon, although the cap may appear.

The chaperon is a more convenient, ready-made descendant of the headdress worn with the houppelande, which each arranged for himself by winding the liripipe of his hood, turban-wise, over the pleated folds of its dagged hem, the unopened hood having been laid, like a shawl, across the head.

Like the ladies' gowns, the short garments of the gentlemen display a reduced form of the houppelande collar; the cote-hardi has become a jacket. The row of buttons in front has been replaced by hooks at neck and waist. The fabric of the *jupon* shows through this front gap. The jupon will acquire padding on bosom and upper arm; it will become progressively shorter and will turn into the *doublet,* to which the lengthening hose will be trussed by *points* through eyelets, and which will carry a standing collar. The pleats of the jacket are so carefully fastened that a belt is not required to hold them in place (822, smallest man, right). The bag sleeve of first third

XVc. has passed out of use, but its effect lingers in the cut of the wide sleeves. These are now slit from the shoulder again, showing the color of the jupon-doublet and permitting its close sleeve to be thrust through the fur-trimmed outer sleeve.

Parti-colored hose are declining in favor: where we do see them worn by gentlemen on Rose Tapestry, they differ only very subtly in color from each other: a light with a darker brown; green-gray with warm gray. They continue to be worn in Italy, and reappear in general European use, in very elaborate forms, during the Italianate period around the turn of the century. Shoes have begun to assume a long point.

823. XVc. 1440. French. (Rouen, Church of St. Ouen.)

Incised slab: The architects of the Church of St. Ouen.

These worthy men, moving in more modest circles, wear houppelandes of easy length, with bag sleeves, modified collars and handsome belts, over doublets with high collars. Comfortable chaperons are carried slung over their shoulders, by long scarves.

824-825. XVc. c. 1445. Flemish. (Mansfield, Hardwick Hall. Coll. Duke of Devonshire.)

Tapestry: Hawking.

These costumes, of the class of society and period of the Rose Tapestries, are much more Flemish and German in detail.

The sexual differentiations of the houppelande developed most acutely in France. Worn by both sexes,

the original difference was in the placing of the belt, always very high on women. In France, for the greater display of the belt, the bodice became close fitting, with a low V-opening which soon spread wide, uncovering the shoulders; it developed extremely narrow sleeves with a widening cuff, which might be turned down over the hand.

Here we see, instead, the old pleated fullness of the houppelande at the front of the bodice (see Ill. 817); the original funnel sleeve; or the bag sleeve which is worn by so many of the men on their short tunics; or the very wide sleeve, which we would expect to find on the robe of an elderly worthy. The front of the bodice fastens high, exposing none of the fabric of the kirtle beneath. The high collar has been turned back into the sailor collar, often so close around the throat that the necklace is displayed upon the fabric, rather than on the skin. The belt is handsome, but overpowered by the pattern and fabric around it.

Bag sleeves of both men and women have additional width gored in, halfway between shoulder and elbow (man, right of mill, 824; women lower r., 825).

The jackets of the men are bloused over the belt in a way which is much more German than French; as is also their dagging, which was a German origination. Dagging has gone far beyond mere snipped edges on hood and gown; it is now manifested in the appliquéing of petal-shaped pieces of material, as on Joan Arnolfini's dress (Ill. 816) and the Master of the Playing Cards, Ills. 976-79. (Cape at top left side of 825; sleeves of rider, lower left; brim of hat on rider preceding him; roundlet of headdress, woman, upper left.)

826. c. 1447. Franco-Flemish. (Brussels, Bib. Roy. ms. 9242-4.)

Chronicles of Hainault, by Jean Wauquelin. Executed between 1447-50 by various artists in the studio of *Guillaume Vrelant* of Bruges. Jean Wauquelin presenting his work to Philip the Good.

It is thought that this frontispiece may be the work of *Roger van der Weyden.* It shows the great duke, patron of letters and founder of the "Bibliothèque de Bourgogne," the collection of fine manuscripts still preserved at Brussels. Like his courtiers, the duke wears the costume of the gentlemen of the Rose Tapestries, but with the additional finish and elegance which made his Burgundian court the arbiter of elegance for all Europe.

Nothing could better oppose and conquer the brocades of his entourage than the plain fabric and superb cut of Philip's garments.

He wears the collar and pendant of the Golden Fleece, the Order which he established in 1429, in honor of his marriage to Isabel of Portugal.

Chamberlayne says, "Then, for Raiment, England produceth generally very fine Wool, which makes our Cloth more lasting than other Country Cloth, and better conditioned against Wind and Weather; and in such Abundance, that not only all Sorts, from the highest to the lowest, are cloathed wherewith; but so much hath heretofore transported beyond the Seas, that, in Honour to the English Wool, which then brought Such Plenty of Gold into the Territories of Philip the Good, Duke of Burgundy (where the Staple for English Wool was in those days kept) he instituted that famous military Order of the Golden

Fleece, after the English Garter, the noblest Order of Knighthood in Europe."

The Toison d'Or was worn by 24 gentlemen, of whom his young son (later Charles the Bold), and half a dozen others are shown, as well as by the Grand Master. In the duke's hand, what I had always supposed to be a walking stick, in the very latest fashion, proves actually to be a delicate hammer. In that day of emblems and badges, I suspect that it would be found to have some connection with the steels and flints of which the Collar is composed: it is possibly the baton of the Grand Master of the Order.

The shoulders of the duke's jacket show the padded *mahoîtres,* which become monstrously exaggerated during the next decade of doublet padding.

The front opening, no longer caught at the throat, spreads and is held at the neck by delicate lacings, exhibiting an embroidered shirt. To permit this, the doublet is also cut with a V-opening; only its standing collar shows above the fur which edges the neck of the jacket.

The roundlet of the duke's chaperon is padded into a spreading brim; its scarf is bound around it, under the chin.

All wear piked shoes. Stow writes to the "Cordwainers or Shoemakers Hall, which company were made a brotherhood or fraternity on the II of Henry IV. Of these cordwainers I read, that since the fifth of Richard II (1383) when he took to wife Anne, daughter to Vesalaus, King of Boheme [Wenceslaus was her brother; she was the eldest daughter of Charles IV, by his 4th wife, Elizabeth of Pomerania] by her example, the English people had used *peaked shoes,* tied to their knees with silken laces, or chains of silver or gilt, whereof in the 4th of Edward IV it was ordained and proclaimed that *beaks of shoon* and boots should not pass the length of 2 feet, upon pain of cursing by the clergy, and by parliament to pay 20 s. for every pair. And any cordwainer that shod any man or woman on the Sunday to pay 30 s."

To the duke's right is portrayed the Chancellor Rollin, in the outmoded gown of the conservative, now the characteristic dress of cleric or educator. It is slit for passage of the brocaded sleeve; hood thrown cape-wise over the shoulder. Rings on fore and middle fingers. Accompanying him, a learned worthy in a crimson gown, with a fine pouch at his girdle.

827-828. Same provenance as 826.

827. Carpenters and masons rebuilding town around a devastated castle.

Workmen in short doublets and jackets, slit at the side; skirts tucked up or protected by aprons. Man (second from left, hammering) and plasterer (extreme right) s h o w knots of the *"points"* by which tights are trussed to doublet.

Variety of sabre-like saws, adzes, hammers, trowels, and T-square. Woman (left, below ladder), shows back treatment of stuffed round turban; woman (extreme right) carries purse and knife on her low girdle.

828. Cardinal preaching in a courtyard.

To the familiar heart- and horn-shaped headdresses are added high hennins, gauzily veiled; high cylindrical hats, often, as here, with no veil; and also a great variety of the new hoods. These were often dark in color, and their draperies, of heavier materials, enclosed head and shoulders, falling in heavy folds behind. Meanwhile, we see the Burgundian fashions, worn by both sexes.

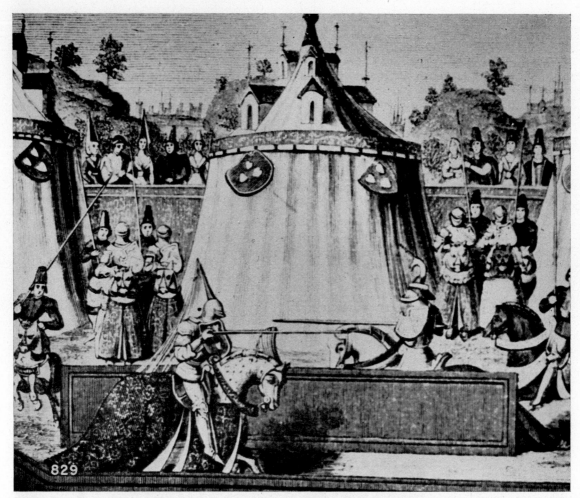

Ladies: bodices with very wide, low handsome buckles; narrowest possible sleeves, with turned-back cuffs of same color as collars.

Gentlemen: excessively short jackets, with padded shoulders and wide sleeves, too long for the arms; worn pushed up.

829. XVc. French. (British Museum, Harl. ms. 4379.)

Chronicles of England, France, and Spain, by Sir John Froissart.

A joust in the manner of one held at St. Inglevert in 1390, to fulfill a promise to the ladies of Montpelier. Each knight hung his shield before his tent. A shield blazoned with hearts hangs here on that pavilion; these are identical in form with the tents shown in Spanish manuscripts from XIIIc., and are brilliantly colored. In this picture they are white and blue, gold and green, and red and gold.* The helm of the French knight is topped by a hennin and veil, his lady's favors.

Stow describes the use of open spaces like bridges, or Smithfield (i.e. Smooth-field). In 1362, a joust was held during the first 5 days of May, before Edward III, his queen, and "the most part of the chivalry of England and of France, and of other nations, to which came Spaniards, Cyprians, and Armenians, knightly requesting the King of England against the pagans that invaded their confines." In 1374, Dame Alice Ferrers, Edward III's concubine, "as Lady of

the Sun, rode from the Tower of London, through Cheap, accompanied of many lords and ladies, every lady leading a lord by his horsebridle, till they came into West Smithfield, and then began a great joust, which endured 7 days after."

In a tourney at Saumur in 1446, organized by René d'Anjou, Robert d'Estoutville, provost of Paris, conquered his wife, Ambroise de Loré, in sword battle.

In 1467 (Edward IV), "the Bastard of Burgoine challenged the Lord Scales, brother to the queen, to fight with him both on horseback and on foot. The King therefore caused lists to be prepared at Smithfield, 120 tailors yards and 10 feet long, 80 yards and 10 feet wide" (Stow) with galleries. The first day's combat was with spears; the second on horseback, during which the Bastard's horse fell on him. The third day's combat was with pole-axes, and when one entered his helmet the Bastard relinquished his challenge.

A "Round Table" had a more theatrical and social character than a tournament. The participants sometimes masqueraded as Arthurian characters; by Edward I's time, their parts were rehearsed in advance.

Round Tables were not confined to the nobility. The burghers of Tournai gave one in 1331, and challenged other cities—Paris, Bruges and Amiens. There were processions with banners, jousts in the public squares; and the sport of chivalry lapses into an amusement for civilians. (See Appendix.)

* See It. End XVIc., *Assault on Empoli,* for origin of parti-color from these tents.

830-831. XVc. 1447. French. (Paris, Bibliotheque Nationale, ms. 2695.)

Traictié de la forme et devis comme on fait les Tournois, by René d'Anjou, executed by *Barthélemy de Clerk.*

René d'Anjou, king of Naples and Sicily, succeeded to the Duchy of Anjou, where he spent much time between 1443-70. His court wears the pointed toes and short tunics of France.

This manuscript, offered to Charles VIII by Louis de Bruges, Sieur de la Gruthyse, shows a tourney of the sort which Gruthyse had given, March 11, 1392, in which the colors of the Dukes of Brittany and Bourbon had been opposed.

It shows heralds and poursuivants in a variety of tabards, courtiers and attendants, with their masters' badges. Fringe-trimmed hat worn by René himself (see Ills. 985-86).

Commines (1475) tells how the King of France disguised one of his servants in a herald's coat and sent him with a message to the King of England, who gave him a favorable answer. "The king sent the Master of the Horse for the banner of a trumpeter to make his herald a coat of arms for the king was not so stately or vain as to have either herald or trumpeter in his train, as other princes have; therefore the master of the horse and one of my servants made up a coat of arms as well as they could; and having fetched a scutcheon from a little herald (called Plein Chemin, in the service of the Admiral of France), they fastened about him, sent for his boots and cloak privately, and his horse being got ready, he mounted, with a bag or budget at the bow of his saddle, in which his coat of arms was put."

830

831

832

832-835. XVc. 1448. Franco-Flemish. (Brussels, Bib. Roy., ms. 9967.)

Ystoire de Helayne, by Jean Wauquelin, for Philip the Good, executed by *Loyset Liedet* and *Guillaume Vrelant.*

832. Dining end of hall: opposite sideboard set with plate is a long canopied seat, in front of which a trestle table would be set for dining.

The long sleeve of Philip's gown is worn pushed up on left arm; close buttoned sleeve of doublet passed through slit of right sleeve, the more conveniently to handle his walking stick, a new fashion. Behind Philip, a shorter version of the same sleeve, seamed to balloon at the top, in order to enclose the padded upper sleeve of doublet (such as is shown on right arm of gentleman in cape, directly above Philip's right shoulder). Outer seam of doublet sleeve open below elbow, and caught together over a display of shirt sleeve.

Tall conical caps worn over new long bobbed hair. Flopping Phrygian bonnet, now conservative, worn with long gown. Medallions; collars with Golden Fleece pendant; or fine strands of chain emphasize horizontal line of shoulder; long pointed toes of "poulaines." Fool in motley, with bells on skirt of tunic, entering.

833. Henry, King of England, taking leave of his wife and confiding her to the care of his mother and the Duke of Gloucester.

Most of the costume elements are now familiar: longer hose fasten to shorter doublet, of which only the standing collar shows here, and permit extremely short jackets, closed in front and with a bateau neckline and extremely wide shoulders, supported by the padded doublet sleeve beneath. Carefully laid cartridge pleats, probably cut and seamed separately, on gentlemen's gowns. Body and flaring skirts of the jacket are separately cut and do not require a belt, which often hangs loose (Henry and gentleman behind wife's attendants).

The headdress of the Queen Dowager clearly shows the wire supports with hooked ends, which carry her veil. Short veils over eyes, sometimes set inside crown of headdress: high veiled hennins (attendant) have a small loop at the forehead by which they might be held steady. Cord necklace, falling between breasts will increase in popularity into XVIc. Gowns extremely long all around, must be held up to allow walking, in the typical female gesture of the century.

The preaching of the monk Thomas Conecte, against hennins, to a crowd of 20,000 women in 1428, led the women to burn their hennins in public. Conecte went on to Rome, attacked the dissolute ways of the Papal court, and was burned for heresy in 1434. After his disappearance, "the women that like snails in a fright had drawn in their horns, shot them out again as soon as the danger was over." (Spectator, ii, p. 98.)

834. Secret marriage of Ludie and Brisse, in the presence of the Archbishop of Tours and of Antoine.

In 1474, Philip de Commines tells us of the war-like bishops: "All the princes of Germany both spiritual and temporal, and all the bishops and free towns sent in their respective forces in great numbers. I was informed that the Bishop of Münster (who is none of the greatest), led into that army 6,000 foot and 1400 horse, all clothed in green uniforms, beside 1200 waggons; but his bishopric was hard by."

In England, until Henry I, bishops and abbots could make knights. William II was knighted by Archbishop Lanfranc. (Malmesbury.)

The first liveries seem to have been those of the chartered companies; guild members who had their own distinctive costumes, and were called "liveried companies," in the time of Edward III. The proliferating XVc. addiction to badges, mottos, scarves and liveries in the master's colors, led inevitably to the idea of uniforms.

But until the beginnings of a permanent army arose in the parish militia and cavalry established by Charles VII, the impulse toward uniformity could be shown only by small groups: followers of a feudal lord; members of a guild of craftsmen; or men of a certain town. Froissart describes Philip Von Arteveld's followers from Ghent, Alost, Grammont, Courtray and Bruges: "The greater part were armed with bludgeons, iron caps, jerkins, and gloves of *fer de baleine,* and each man carried a staff bound and pointed with iron. The different townsmen wore liveries and arms, to distinguish them from one another. Some had jackets of blue and yellow, others wore a welt of black on a red jacket, others chevroned with white on a blue coat, others green and blue, others lozenged with black and white, others quartered red and white, others all blue."

835. Capture of Helayne, who is led to the palace.

Townswomen in kirtles, such as the ladies wear under fur-collared robes. Its neckline is becoming lower, squarer, and often shows a line of the skirt beneath. Skirt protected by an apron, or looped up when long. Between the two skirts hangs a belt carrying pouch, keys or tassel, a usage which will continue in the XVIc. Modest horned headdresses, or hood-like coifs, such as plain women have long worn; toward the end of the century, the heads of ladies will become enclosed in bourgeois hoods.

Gentleman (lower right, back view), shows that the padded shoulders of the doublet, and its high, stiff collar require that the collar of the outer garment be reduced to a line of fur, horizontal in front, and dipping in back. Gentleman receiving Helayne: tall, conical hat ending in a fruit-like stem, such as appears on the modern beret; on this cap, the stem is elaborated into a tiny plume.

836. XVc. Before 1450. French. (Berlin, Kaiser Friedrich Museum.)

Jean Fouquet. Etienne Chevalier and St. Stephen.

Etienne Chevalier was Treasurer of France, under two kings, Ambassador to England, executor of the will of Agnes Sorel, and patron of Fouquet, (who became court painter to Louis XI). He wears a crimson jacket, of which we clearly see the cut, padded shoulders, bag sleeve, and high set-in collar, cut like that of a doublet.

St. Stephen: brocade-trimmed amice, dalmatic and tiny cap, set over tonsure. Both are most explicit representations of the bowl-cropped male head of first half XVc.

837. Before 1450. French. (Antwerp Royal Museum.)

Virgin and Child. Diptych panel by *Jean Fouquet.*

The work of Fouquet and other XVc. miniaturists gave promise of an indigenous school of French painting which did not develop, probably due to the competition of Italian painters for French patronage, at the conclusion of the Italian wars.

The Virgin, on a fringed and tasselled throne, and wearing a royal crown and ermine mantle, probably represents the first of the politically influential royal mistresses, Agnes Sorel, d.1450, mistress of Charles VII.

The front of her very long, laced blue-gray kirtle (see Ills. 810, 818), is cut in three gored pieces, one of which takes a diagonal curve from armseye to breast, where it curves downward to waist. Here the excessive length of the garment is roached up, and held by a marvellous belt. Jewelled crown, set on plucked forehead, over oblong veil with a border.

838. XVc. 1450-60. French. (Louvre.)

Jean Fouquet. Charles VII.

Charles wears a great beaver hat, embroidered on crown and brim. Collar of doublet shows above low fur collar of jacket. The method of squaring off the shoulders by darts, accommodates the padded mahoitres, and fosters the wide horizontal shoulder-line.

839-46. XVc. c. 1450. French. (Paris, Bibliotheque Nationale, ms. 6465.)

Grandes Chroniques de France executed by *Jean Fouquet.*

839. Arnoul, Archbishop of Rheims, and his brother Charles, imprisoned at Orleans, by order of Hugh Capet; King Robert chanting the office in the church. Primitive boots of King and groom, soft, wrinkled, wide; front seams, side opening. Moat and drawbridge; caparison of horse.

840. Arrival of Emperor Charles IV at St. Denis.

Charles V's uncle fell ill and had to be carried in a litter. (see note on "whirlecote," Eng.XIVc., Luttrell Psalter.) As Dauphin of the Viennois, Charles V had done homage to his uncle, the Emperor.

841. Edward, son of the King of England (Edward I), gives homage to Philip the Fair, for the Duchy of Aquitaine and other French possessions. Philip, seated in chair of state, his robes, carpets and walls semé France. Two sceptres; topped by fleur-de-lys, and by the open "main de justice" of benediction.

Edward's robes red; golden lioncels. Entourage of parliamentary dignitaries and courtiers: at r., puffs of shirt show through slashed lower sleeve of doublet; 2nd from r., belt of cord, knotted in front.

842. Marriage at Paris of Charles IV the Fair and Marie of Luxembourg.

Ermine-bordered robes of state; sideless surcoat, worn over kirtle with tight buttoned sleeves, and belt at hips, of previous century.

Bishop: stole worn crossed, instead of hanging.

843. Queen Jeanne d'Evereux before the assembly of barons and nobles, after the death of Charles IV, the Fair.

Nobleman facing Queen: cap barely set on cropped hair; hat carried slung over shoulder by its scarf; thumbs caught in low belt: the very pattern of the costume and posture of his class and time.

844. Entry of John II, the Good, and Queen Jeanne de Boulogne into Paris, after the sacre at Rheims.

Trumpeters' banners, sash of preceding horseman, caparison of King's horse, (head armed), all fleur-de-lys sown. Colored sashes were an early manifestation of the impulse toward uniformity.

Queen: less ceremonial costume; ermine-trimmed fashionable gown, cuff turned down over hand.

845

845. Entry of Charles V into Paris, preceded by the Constable Robert of Fiennes.

Another of the many gates in the walls of Paris. Fiennes wears the hat we associate particularly with Louis XI, scarf and drawn sword of office. He is preceded by identically dressed trumpeters, their hooded capes, almost vestigial, are decoratively slittered, a usage now confined to livery garments. Raised arms in doublet sleeve show jacket sleeve dependent from back of shoulder, and probably for decoration, rather than use. On unceremonious occasions, such sleeves were often knotted together in back, out of the way.

(*The order in which these pictures are placed does not indicate the correct chronology of the events described. Ill. 840 falls, historically, between Ills. 854 and 846.*)

846

846. Banquet offered Emperor Charles IV by King Charles V, in the Grand'Salle of the Palace, Paris.

Banquet table set on carpeted dais, up three steps, for greater ceremony. Walls specially hung; canopy for each personage.

Majordomo with staff and scarf; serving gentlemen with hanging jacket-sleeves; napkins over shoulders. Trumpeters: dagging persists on garments of servants.

From Fouquet: *Grandes Chroniques de France.* Paris, 1906. Berthaud freres.

847-48. XVc. French.
(Chantilly, Musee Conde, ms. 187.)

Book of Hours executed by *Jean Fouquet* for Etienne Chevalier.

847. Fouquet's patron (see Ill. 836) k n e e l s, partly armed, before the Virgin. He was not a gentleman by b i r t h*, and did not have a coat-of-arms; the plumed hat beside him bears the M and the fleurs-de-lys of the house of the king he serves, (see Ill. 8 0 7, squire in front of sideboard). The quasi-biblical soldiers combine contemporary armor w i t h fancifully cut and studded brigandines, a n d feathered helmets.

In the background, a castle fights off an attack by dropping fire.

* Under Charles XII and Louis XI the services of bourgeois like Chevalier and poor gentlemen like Commines, rather than of peers of the realm, were being utilized in confidential positions.

848. Carpenters with auger and adze. Trunks are now high and well-fitting; but for strenuous work, the points which truss them to the doublet are loosed (see carpenters, Ill. 827), and the back part will often be seen, hanging free, with no false modesty hindering.

849

850

849. XVc. 1456. French. (Paris, Bibliotheque Nationale, ms. fr. 9087.)

Avis directif pour faire le passage d'outre-mer by Frère Brochard, translated and executed by *Jean Miélot,* for Philip the Good.

The concave scallops of cape and mantle, reminiscent of dagging and therefore reserved for ceremonial or livery use, have a XVc. addition of tassels. Frère Brochard, with another tonsured ecclesiastic, and a learned gentleman (not a monk, but possibly a cleric), in a suitable long gown with belt and pouch. Gentleman (extreme r.) in a chaperon the crown of which is now a circular piece of material, gathered into the roundlet; it is no longer the hanging pleated coxcomb of the old hood. Short circular cape (back in use, last half XVc.), of ermine-lined brocade, in the new, unsymmetrical diagonal patterns, like those of King and gentleman to l. Beside him, one of the brimmed "hats," in the modern sense, which appear in increasing numbers (see Color Plate, No. 3).

850. XVc. 1469. French. (Paris, Bibliotheque Nationale, ms. fr. 19819.)

Louis XI presiding at a chapter of the Order of Saint-Michel.

Founded in 1469, the order at first consisted of 15 knights or noblemen. Under Charles IX the number was so increased that its decoration was called the "collier à toutes bêtes."

In this meeting in the Salle des Chevaliers, at the Monastery of Saint-Michel, we see, at l., Charles of France, duke of Guyenne, brother of Louis XI and other known personages; and behind the King, a bishop, 4 officers of the order, chancellor, clerk, treasurer, and the herald-at-arms, Montjoy.

The robes and collar show the scallop shells of pilgrims, alternating with knots, a much-favored new motif, which appears on sleeves, girdles, and hose attachments (see Ill. 852); and on the armor of the angels, which had been adopted in XVc. as supporters of the shield of the French kings.

851. XVIc. French. (Paris, Bibliotheque Nationale.)

851. *Jean du Tillet.* Louis XI.

This portrait of Louis XI is a XVIc. reconstruction of a contemporary picture; the work of an artist who was familiar with the Grand'Salle of the Palace, and its collections of portraits, before their destruction by fire in 1618. Collar of St. Michel. 2 sceptres.

852. XVc. 1458. French. (Munich, Codex Gallicus 6.)

The Munich Boccaccio executed by *Jean Fouquet.*

In Nov. 1458, the Duke of Alençon was tried and convicted of treason in the provincial court of Vendôme. When Fouquet, in the same year, began his illustrations for Boccaccio's "Le cas des nobles malheureux,"* he used as a frontispiece this freshly dramatic case of an unfortunate nobleman.

A parliament at which the King presided in person was called a "Lit de Justice" (originally, the long bench on which he sat). We have the most exact accounts of this "Lit de Justice de Vendôme," which have been exhaustively studied, in conjunction with Fouquet's illustration, by the Count Durrieu.** They agree to the last detail, and the portraits of scores of known individuals have been identified.

The courtroom is in the colors of Charles VII, red, green and white, decorated with the rose-stalks which were his emblem; and winged stags with crown collars, (the emblem of the two preceding Charles, and adopted by Charles VII) support the royal shield.

The King, dressed in blue, with 3 white ostrich plumes in his hat, has his young son, Charles, sitting just below him on the dais. In front of the King are the Chamberlain (Dunois, the Bastard of Orleans, companion-at-arms of Jeanne d'Arc) in scarlet robe and gold baton of office; and the Chancellor of the Realm, in gold-barred scarlet robe. Facing the chancellor and reading sentence is the court clerk; seated below him are four special notaries in ermine hoods.

To the r. of the King and young prince is a top row of lay peers, Charles of France, Charles d'Orléans, Gaston de Foix, etc. To the r. of Dunois, the Chancellor, Guillaume Jouvenal des Ursins, in his white magistrate's hood and scarlet robe with 3 bars, sits beside the 1st President of the Parliament

(two bars), and high government officials. Below them, legal functionaries in white hoods.

To the l. of the King, the upper row consists of the ecclesiastical peers of France: the Archbishop-Duke of Rheims, Bishop Dukes of Laon, Langres, etc. Below them, a row of lay gentlemen officials. Below them, the ecclesiastical councillors of Paris, in ermine hoods. Seated on the floor, the "Gens du Parquet," Procurer General, advocates, and councillors of the King.

By the end XIVc. white coifs had passed out of general use, and were considered characteristic of lawyers. A wardrobe roll of Richard II, 1391, lists: "21 linen coifs for counterfeiting men of the law at the King's play at Christmas." By the last quarter XVc., they were worn only by clerics and lawyers; the outmoded capes and hoods, with conventionalized tippets, worn over scarlet or violet robes, have become specifically court or academic costume.

Guarding the enclosure, and controlling the crowd, are mace-bearing attendants; and men of the King's guard, carrying glaives, and wearing uniforms in his colors. Two of these (in crowd to l.) have striped sleeves. Attendant in c. with mace: typical swelling torso of padded doublet; padded upper sleeve, under jacket, would give broad humped *mahoître* shape. Guards to r. of corner: brocade-filled V-opening of jacket is much wider-spread than heretofore; points, like those which connect doublet and hose, are here knotted, to hold in place the padding of the upper sleeve. Knotted cords will be seen on several spectators, taking the place of the elaborate belts of earlier days. Rear view of man in crowd, (ext.r.), jacket has an inverted V of cartridge pleats; large flapped bag. To his l.: high, spurred boots, top of a different color; knife slung in back. To his l.: circular cape with hooded collar; not a hood closed all around in the old style, as worn by the lawyers. On the r. edge of the picture, a man facing away from the proceedings is easily recognizable as Fouquet himself (if compared to his self-portraits: 1456, Vienna, Liechtenstein Gall.; and 1470, enamel plaque, Paris, Bib. Nat.).

---

* Boccaccio: *De casibus virorum illustrum*, translated into English by Lydgate (1370-1451) as *The Fall of Princes*.
** P. Durrieu: *Boccace de Munich;* and *Oeuvres de Fouquet*, in which material given here will be found in greatly amplified form.

XVc. Flemish (see Ill. 816).

Jan van Eyck: Giovanni and Giovanna Arnolfini.

Courtesy of National Gallery, London

853-55. XVc. 1450-60. Franco-Burgundian. (Paris, Bibliotheque Nationale, ms. fr. 24378.)

The Romance of Gerard de Nevers, and of the beautiful Euriant, his love, executed by *Giot Dangerans.*

This manuscript, ordered by Philip the Good as a gift for Count Charles de Nevers, illustrates the life and fashions of his Burgundian court, which so influenced all Europe.

853. Gift of a hawk: One wall of the room has been eliminated, as was the convention among missal painters, to permit the showing of life, indoors and out.

Since the period of the Rose Tapestries, the V-collar of ladies' robes has spread wider; the increasingly visible placard is now made of brocade or embroidery; it is not merely the fabric of the under-gown. The lady carries what definitely appears to be a rather short, circular-cut, fur-edged overgarment, with sleeves; so narrow that it can only be for female wear. At this period, when the character of the costume lies in its short bodice and clutched-up skirt, ladies are never represented wearing an outdoor garment, which would obscure the line of the costume, but which obviously must have existed. This is the first female outer garment, with sleeves, which we have seen; the close sleeves and uncluttered bodice, for the first time make such a garment practical. The pleats of the gentleman's jacket, reduced in number, are becoming formalized; they are probably cut, independent of the body, and inserted, like the cartridge pleats in the back of the jacket of the spectator in Ill. 852. The series of chains fastened across shoulders adds to apparent width. He wears a "hat," and soft high boots with turned-down tops. The chaperon is beginning to pass. Timber construction of outbuildings.

854. The viol player: Arrangement of sideboard, trestle table, and long seat, set with its back to the fire (Ill. 807, Très riches heures). Heavily studded window shutters. The man, dressed for riding, wears hip-length circular cape, closing in front, and high, loose socks.

855. Round dance at court: The excessively short garments of the gentlemen of the Burgundian court do not cover the buttocks; their unbelted width will also be seen in the "Sieur de Gavres" (Ills. 873-76). Feathered hat, at c. front.

The back view of a lady shows the fur collar, the loose tab-end of the high, wide belt, which is jewel-studded. The widening V of the neck is now being filled in by necklaces, or, as in the case of the Queen, by a line of gauze, in the manner of a higher-necked undergarment. The new Burgundian headdress, the *hennin*, is shown at its highest.

From Count A. Bastard d' Estang: *Costumes, moeurs et usages de la cour de Bourgogne, 1445-60.* Paris, 1881.

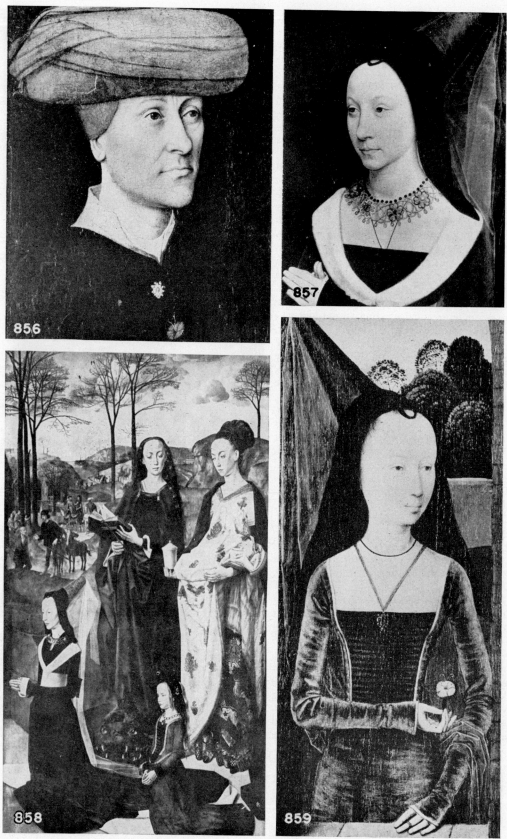

856. XVc. 1450-60. Flemish. (Metropolitan Museum, Bache Collection.)

Roger van der Weyden. Man with a turban.

Large, flattened red chaperon, without scarf, worn over skull-cap. Dark doublet with red collar; white shirt; jewelled rings. Pink held in hand indicated prospective marriage.

857. XVc. c. 1476. Flemish. (Metropolitan Museum.)

Hans Memling. Marie, wife of Thomas Portinari.

Compare with French costume, last half XVc.

Loops at forehead of steeple headdress were probably helpful in maintaining it in position.

858. XVc. 1473-5. Flemish-Italian. (Florence, Uffizi.)

Hugo van der Goes. The Portinari Altarpiece, right wing.

Tommaso Portinari, agent at Bruges for the Medici, was a lineal descendant of the father of Dante's Beatrice. The altarpiece was painted for the chapel of the hospital of S. Maria Novella in Florence, of which he was patron.

His family is dressed in the finest Franco-Flemish style. His wife has the M of her given name embroidered on her veiled hennin, and wears a jewelled collar painted by Memling. The daughter, whose laced bodice is seen on Memling's lady of quality, wears the band of a black hood, decorated with a brooch, over the flowing hair of a young girl.

859. XVc. Before 1480. Flemish. (Metropolitan Museum, Bache Collection.)

Hans Memling. Lady of quality.

Dark brown velvet hood; veiled gray hennin. Red velvet gown laced across a brown placard, and edged with white fur. The customary two necklaces, one thread-like, the other important, like that of Marie Portinari, or a flat braided gold chain with a fine pendant.

860-65. XVc. 1461. French. (Brussels, Bib. Roy., ms. 9392.)

Epitre d'Othea by Christine de Pisan (1364-1430), executed by *Jean Miélot.*

Christine de Pisan, of Italian extraction but reared at the court of Charles V, became a writer when left a widow with three children, at twenty-five. Her controversial feminist works brought her great fame, and tempting offers to live at foreign courts; adoring France, she remained there under the protection of Charles VI and the Dukes of Burgundy and Berri, by whom some of her books were commissioned. Her writings are filled with delightfully detailed pictures of the life of her times. The translation into English, by Stephen Scrope, was dedicated to Sir John Fastolf.

860. Diana with the young virgins: The high-waisted gown may be worn belted, or not; if it is, the belt is an important one. When worn low, the belt is a knotted cord, or slight chain.

861. Ceres sowing the earth: Shepherd with little house on wheels; farm horses with blinders and huge collars, hitched to a wheeled plough. Quasi-oriental touches are given to the headdresses of the mythological characters, who otherwise wear only their kirtles, which served as house and work clothes.

862. The rook advises the raven: The filling-in of the excessively wide V, which we have seen (see Ill. 855), is continued here, in the form of a bertha of gauze, reaching to the base of the throat. The V-line is reiterated by a cord, with heavy pendant, falling between the breasts, inside the tucker; as the neckline becomes squarer, at the end of the century, this cord will remain in use, in the XVIc.

Timber construction of thatched barn; wattle-fenced pastures.

863. Discord returning the golden apple to the table during the wedding feast of Peleus and Thetis: The now familiar dining pattern of sideboard, and fireplace warming the backs of diners, who sit beside, not opposite each other, at long narrow tables; dog underfoot, munching a bone cast from the table.

The squire serving at the l., wears the extremely short jacket, with his dagger slung in the new manner, over the buttocks. The sleeves of his doublet, almost entirely visible, as the jacket sleeve is slit through its length, are in their turn slashed along the entire length of the arm, and laced across the exposed shirt sleeve; the lacings are grouped. Thetis' crown follows the line of the roll of her high headdress. Cuffs spreading over knuckles; precious tab at free end of ladies' belt.

864. Atalanta's suitors vainly attempting to win the race from her: The neckline of her ermine-lined gown is now so low and wide that it cannot be held by fastening it to the exposed bit of the kirtle, alone. She wears an entire gauze bertha, with a standing collar, its transparency enhanced by the black cord necklace. Her buckled belt is as high, wide and stiff as possible, its tab finished with a stiff metal end, and decoratively large eyelets.

The suitor who is still on his feet shows to perfection the "points" which truss the long hose to the short doublet; which has the characteristic high collar, and the new open V, laced across the shirt bosom.

865. Ino sending cooked grain to be sowed: Dagged hoods, apron, pouch bag of workmen. The use of a high sock, on l. leg only, is undoubtedly connected with the specific job to be done.

From *Epitre d' Othea,* ed. by J. van den Gehyn. Bruxelles, Vromant, 1913.

866-67. XVc. c. 1477. Flemish. (Brussels, Bib. Roy., ms. 9231-32.)

La Fleur des Histoires by Jean Mansel, executed by *Simon Marmion.*

Useful rear views of costume are shown in this manuscript, executed for Jacques d'Armagnac, duke of Nemours (decapitated 1477).

866. Crowning of Charles V in chapel of castle. Towering veils of ladies of second quarter-second half XVc., supported by high horned headdresses or wire frames (see Ill. 883: Queen Mother). Jeanne de Bourbon, kneeling at prie-dieu, shows Queen's crown superimposed on folded veil of headdress; her sideless surcoat has the funnel sleeves of a houppelande; now so outmoded as to seem equally archaic, and equally suited for ceremonial wear. Ladies (3rd and 4th from l.), low V-neck, to girdle, finished with rolled edge. Charles V: coronation robes, and cape with conventionalized tippet.

867. Celebration of mass in church. Kneeling women at l. give rear views of the new hood, with its back folds enclosing head and shoulders. Longer and heavier head-draperies and cloaks are beginning to give to the costume of ladies an enclosed look which, for some time, we have seen in the costume of women of lower class. Rear view of horned headdress (women at front of group); and of vestments of ecclesiastics and acolytes. Hats of very shaggy beaver (on kneeling man, l. of ecclesiastics, and on standing gentleman with cane, at r.)

868-70. XVc. French. (Paris, Bib. Nat., ms. fr. 2644.)

Sir John Froissart's *Chronicles of England, France, and Spain.*

Four volumes executed for Louis de Bruges, Seigneur de la Gruthuyse. These three illustrations, from one of many Froissart manuscripts, give a full picture of mediaeval life, indoors and out, in city and castle.

868. The decapitation of Guillaume, lord of Pommiers, and his secretary, Jean Coulon, at Bordeaux in 1375 on suspicion of treason by the English who still held that territory.

Blindfolded men: shirts of period; doublet, top of hose, and attaching knots.

Executioner: trunks have codpiece, which came into use, third quarter XVc., as hose lengthened and short doublets no longer masked the division; doublet has bolero. Gentleman, c.: long garment, slit up sides like a tabard, is new. Shirts have assumed a standing collar, which shows through the break in the high collar of the doublet; but with the V-openings of male garments, toward the end of the century, the shirt will become collarless and low-necked.

Man to l. of him: back view shows method of cutting and fitting high collar which is properly the collar of the doublet; we see it used here on a jacket. The elements of male costume are becoming unstable and interchangeable: almost anything can be expected. The small male fig. (3rd from r.), shows the orthodox sleeve of a doublet, such as is worn by the executioner (in two colors and slashed) used on a long gown, which is slit up the front and full below the belt, but as tightly fitted in the body as a doublet. This is about as far as a robe can get from the old-fashioned loose gown of the elderly man on the left.

In c. background, a hat shop exhibits its wares, its shuttered sides raised to form a roof over the counter.

869. Louis II, Count of Flanders, receiving the deputies of the burghers of Ghent, after thei. revolt in 1353.

The prosperity of Flanders, whose cloth trade was dependent on the free flow of wool from England, (see Ill. 826; also Appendix), had been endangered since the end XVc. by the quantities of cloth produced in England* by immigrant Flemish weav-

869

ers, and distributed by the Hanseatic League. After three quarters of a century of conflict, the burghers, harassed by floods and the Plague, were finally subdued by the pro-French nobility, and the XVc. decline of Flanders became inevitable. The hemp rope, which the magistrates and burghers henceforth wore about their necks on a certain day of the year, in token of submission and penance, had been reduced to a blue ribbon by Evelyn's time (1641).

Louis stands on a dais, a rich brocade draped behind him, as protection against damp and draughts, and to heighten impressiveness. The sleeve of his jacket is slashed to show his doublet sleeve, slashed in its turn below its padded upper section, and strapped

over the shirtsleeves. His sword, like that of the cupbearer, is slung in front.

Gentleman with a hawk: tall cap with a stem like a beret; brimmed hat (to be worn over it) slung over shoulder by its scarf, which he holds in his hand, in a gesture characteristic of the period.

Squires and pages carrying flagons, wear tabard-like garments, cut well above the buttocks; very high and well-cut boots with piked toes and turned-down colored cuffs; rows of fine chains; long bobbed hair.

The suppliants wear the new plebeian hood† with slittered border, and the longer, fur-edged garments of respectable, well-to-do bourgeois; bags hanging from the belt, which is wide; while the gentry carry a sword or dagger on a narrow belt.

---

* In late Sept., 1465, John Paston writes Margaret to find out where William bought his fine worsted: "which is almost like silk . . . thou it be dearer than viijs. . . . I wold make my doblet all worsted for worship of Norfolk." She answers: "I have do spoke for your worstede" (which got its name from the East Norfolk village where it was first produced), "but ye may not have it tylle Halowmesse and thane I am promysyd ye challe have as fyne as may be made."

† Nevertheless, the 15-page wardrobe inventory of a bluff, out-door character like Sir John Fastolf (Paston Letters) enumerates more than 20 hoods, beside his blue hood of the Garter. Many of these are parti-colored, or if of one color, are half velvet and half damask; and the edges are often described as jagged. He had, in addition, four red or black riding hoods, a "great rolled cap," two other caps, one of which was knit, an impressive beaver hat, and one "strawen hattis."

870

870. Richard II and Wat Tyler's rebellion. Frois-sart, Chap. IX: "The populace were everywhere ris-ing against the nobility . . . On Corpus Christi day King Richard heard mass in the Tower of London, after which he entered his barge, attended by the Earls of Salisbury, Warwick, and Suffolk, and some other knights, and rowed down the Thames to Roth-erhite, a royal manor, where upwards of 10,000 of the insurgents had assembled. As soon as the mob perceived the royal barge approaching, they began shouting and crying as if all the spirits in the nether world had been in the company." The king spoke to the people, but "the Earl of Salisbury cried out, 'Gentlemen, you are not properly dressed, nor are you in a fit condition for a king to talk with.'" The king was prevailed upon to return to the Tower, and the infuriated rebels marched to London, destroying "all the houses of lawyers and courtiers and all the monasteries they met with."

Richard's barge is hung with his arms as would have been the walls of his chamber, or the caparison of his horse. A lacy crown is set above the brim of his beaver hat. His brocade jacket is as short and loose as possible. He is accompanied by dignified men in long gowns and draped hats, younger gentlemen in garments as short as his own; soldiers in studded brigandines; rower in a short sleeved doublet.

On the stern, a lord in a sugarloaf cap carries his beaver hat slung over his shoulder. The neck-chains of his companion are tacked in place at the shoul-ders; they fall lower in back than in front, following the line which permits the emergence of the high collar of the doublet from the back of the jacket.

The embattled populace wear visored sallets, chap-els, even old-fashioned closed helms; body armor, or studded gambesons over chain shirts; plate protec-tion of most legs, and some arms; and carry swords, spears, or pole arms, in variety: their own, their fa-thers' or their grandfathers' left-overs.

871

871. Third quarter XVc. French. (Paris, Bib. Nat., ms. fr. 2646.)

Froissart's *Chronicles*.

This illustration, taken from another Froissart manuscript, shows the events described in Chap. XXII. A party was given in the ball room of the Hotel de St. Pol, at the king's expense, in honor of the wedding of two members of the royal household. A Norman squire, cousin of the bride, had provided disguises of linen, covered with flax, the color of hair; in which six members of the party had gone to disguise themselves. The Duke of Orleans, entering late, and not knowing of the king's orders that the torches should withdraw to one side, upon the entrance of the wild men, snatched a torch from one of his own bearers, to try to identfy the dancers. The hemp, and the pitch with which it was affixed, caught fire and the dancers, of whom the king was one, being chained together, could not be separated. The king's young aunt, the Duchess of Berri, saved

his life by throwing her train over him. The Lord of Nantouillet broke loose and flung himself into a tub of dish-water in the pantry. Hugonin, the squire, and Sir Charles of Poitiers died on the spot; the Count de Joigny, and the Bastard of Foix, favorite son of Gaston-Phoébus, died at their own hôtels two days later. Queen: anachronistic robe and cape of royalty, belted low, but made of brocade; the cape carrying the contemporary wide, flat collar, and a standing sheer collar; gown with cuffs extended over the knuckles.

Ladies: widest necks and highest pointed hennins.

Orleans (under musician's gallery, with torch): wide opening of jacket shows doublet of brocade in a striped pattern, very different from the all-over patterns to which we are accustomed in France. (See striped Italian patterns of latter XVc.) Cuff spreading over knuckles, the effect of the fashions of one sex upon the clothing of the other.

Musicians in gallery: jacket sleeves slit lengthwise and slashed.

872. XVc. 1470. Franco-Flemish. (Louvre.)

Histoire de Charles Martel by Jan van de Gheyn, executed by *Loyset Liédet*.

Quarrel between Charles the Bald and Gerard de Rouissilon.

The photograph of this leaf, which shows wonderful exaggerations of the now familiar Burgundian costume was marked "Prayer Book, Louvre." Research shows it to be the missing leaf (in the Louvre) of Brussels ms.6-9.

873-76. XVc. (Franco-Burgundian. (Brussels, Bib. Roy., ms. 10238.)

Les Sires de Gavres.

In 1453, Philip the Good celebrated, at a great banquet, the battle of Gavres, in which the rebellious burghers of Ghent (see Froissart: Ill. 869) were finally defeated with huge losses. Laying his hand on a pheasant, brought in by heralds, he bound himself and his knights, by the "vow of the pheasant," to undertake a crusade. No attempt was made to carry out the project, but great sums were levied, and used for entertainments at court.

In contrast to the fine work of the Limbourgs and Fouquet, these are cheap, quick pen and wash illustrations, almost caricatures, but very spirited and informative.

When the Burgundian male costume had attained the limits of the idea of enormous width, squared and short, and the belts of the first half XVc. had been reduced to a cord, it was inevitable that it should occur to someone to loosen the tacking of the careful pleats, and let the jacket hang free, really square, really wide, as we see it in these illustrations.

873. Courtiers discussing the project with the Duke: back view of very short cape.

874. Disconsolate lady, bewailing her maidenhood and passing youth, by candlelight to her attendant; wears a hennin, veiled low over eyes; very wide belt and cuffs.

875. Marriage of the Duke's daughter: immensely wide fur borders of skirt which attendant holds up, over both concealed hands, in a characteristic female gesture of the period. Courtier: in fur-edged cape, open on r. shoulder.

876. The Sire de Gavres and his wife reunited: dagged hood indicates his journey. His companion holds one corner of his cape-like open jacket across his breast, after the manner of cloaks in Italy, toward the end of the century. Wife: hands characteristically concealed in fur cuffs.

877-78. XVc. c.1475. Flemish (Tournai). (Metropolitan Museum.)

Tapestry: presented by Pasquier Grenier, and wife, Marguerite de Lannoy, to Church of St. Quentin, Tours.

Priest: wedding; vested.

Woman receiving extreme unction: nightgowns not worn until end XVc.

Priest giving unction: every-day wear; long gown of any dignified gentleman.

Death-bed attendants, and kneeling donors: Flemish hoods, new (see Ill. 867).

Photographs courtesy of Morgan Library (873-76)
Metropolitan Museum (877-78)

879. XVc. Flemish. (Metropolitan Museum.)

Tapestry fragment: a noble company.

Details, extraordinarily fresh and bold, of the costume popularized by the Burgundian court, but with dramatically sloping shoulders, high-collared robes and jackets; doublets with still higher collars; and sophisticated combinations of solid color, pattern and texture, enhanced by the use of metal and jewels.

Lower row, l. to r. Truncated high cap, with tassel; jacket and doublet of different, equally bold brocades. Hennin and belt of brocade; wide neckline emphasized by flat, jewelled collar, two bias folds of sheer material, and elaborate wide necklace. Cape, closed on r. shoulder by four huge buttons; brocade collar and sleeves of doublet; towering, plain conical cap.

Upper row, l. to r. Brocade of the doublet and scarf, against plain masses of the gown; and of the soft, gathered shirt sleeves, unrestrained by lacings; necklace of twisted cord. Hat of brocade, with brocade scarf, and knot and plumes at sides; applied cartridge pleats on jacket. Brocade gown, with jewelled cuffs and mounting collar of plain material which serves to display necklace worn high upon it; scarved hat, softly pleated in at brow.

880. XVc. c. 1477. French. (Vienna, National Library.)

Book of Hours of Charles the Bold. Marie of Burgundy, at a shrine: depicting her marriage to Maximilian of Austria. Charles the Bold died in 1477, before the actual marriage of his daughter. Marie, seated in the shrine, before a picture of herself and her husband adoring the Virgin, is the quintessence of Burgundian elegance. Her hennin is embroidered with her monogram. (See Marie Portinari: Ill. 858). Her precious belt is as wide, and is worn as high as possible. The extremity of width and slipping shoulder has been reached in this bodice; partly to support it, and partly in the reaction of a woman of great fashion-sense, her entire bosom is veiled by a bertha of gauze, into the high neckline to come from 1485. This conceals the precious wide collar (see Portinari, also), which will be replaced by chokers with a pendant.

Marie protects the precious binding of the missal, and the pattern of its gilded edges, by the cloth over her hand. Two red dianthus, signifying their marriage, lie near the vase of naturalistically painted fleurs-de-lys.

Flanders, in close relationship with Venice, imported glass, and then set up factories of her own, from which window glass was imported into England in second half XVc. Small bull's-eyes, rather easily blown, and showing a center lump where cut off the rod, were an early form of domestic window glass.

881

881. XVc. 1479. Flemish. (Bruges, Hospital of St. John.) *Hans Memling*. Mystic Marriage of St. Catherine. Sideless surcoat with brocade skirt and train. An approximation of the bald-looking head in a mounting, netted headdress is given by braids under a projecting veil and coronet.

882. XVc. 1481. Flemish. (Brussels, Bib. Roy., ms. 13073-
    74.)
Chronicles of Flanders.
Engagement of Maximilian I and Marie of Burgundy.
By this marriage, the daughter of Charles the Bold
brought Burgundy and the Netherlands to the Hapsburgs. She wears the traditional ceremonious sideless surcoat and cloak, with the contemporary necklaces (see Ill. 857), and headdress over the flowing
hair of a virgin bride.
The Emperor's ceremonial robe, fur-lined and slit
up the sides, is collared in the new manner. He wears
the plumes of third quarter XVc. in a twisted fillet.

883-86. XVc. Flemish. (Metropolitan Museum.)
Life of St. Godelieve.
War-like bishops: (see Ill. 834).

887. XVc. c. 1480. French. (Morgan Library, M. 677.)
Hours of Anne de Beaujou (1460-1522).
Undershirt, laced kirtle and gown.

888. XVc. c. 1455. Flemish. (Penrhyn Castle.)
Dirk Bouts. St. Luke: self-portrait of the painter; glimpse of his studio.
Cut of fur-lined gown clearly shown.

889. XVc. 1487. Flemish. (Bruges, Hospital of St. John.)
Hans Memling. Diptych of Martin Nieuwenhove: hair in transition
from bowl crop to long bob; trimmed high up neck, but allowed to grow
long. Thumb ring.

890. XVc. 1487. Flemish. (Hermanstadt Gymnasium.)
Hans Memling. Diptych of wife of Martin Nieuwenhove: Flemish
hood; neckline rising and filled in with crimped gauze; important belt
with tab of fine goldsmith's work; wedding ring on middle joint.

891. XVc. 1491. Flemish. (Metropolitan Mus.)
Master H. H.

Portrait of a gentleman: Italian influence
on male costume, end XVc.; wide V opening of doublet and jerkin, laced across fine
shirt; squaring of neckline; small cap and
long bobbed hair.

892

892. XVc. c. 1495. Flemish. (National Gallery, London.)
Master of St. Giles.

St. Giles protecting a wounded hind. During transition, end XVc., differentiation of garments becomes difficult. Sleeves are transposed, and like plastron fronts, are often interchangeable. Jackets have separate pleated skirts, *bases* (see mounted fig.) Cloaks: collared, V-openings; or circular and thrown over shoulder in the Italian manner. Small caps, or the new bonnets with cut and turned-up brims, over bobbed hair. Boots (archer): turned-down tops of another color; soft and loose, clasped twice to fit below calf.

894. The Haywagon to Hell (detail)

895. The Table of the Seven Deadly Sins: detail, "Gula"

896. Seven Deadly Sins, "Invidia"

897. Seven Deadly Sins, "Superbia"

898. The Cutting of the Stone

H. van Acken (c.1460-1518), called Jerom or Hieronymus Bosch, from Hertogenbosch (Bois-le-duc), the strangely influential town of his birth (see Ills. 1102-02: Pilgrims), was Breughel's spiritual master although he died before Breughel's birth. Bosch greatly influenced Cranach, and worked for years at the Spanish court for Philip II; many of his teeming paintings are in Madrid.

No one ever painted everyday dress with more interest. Awls, needles, or arrows are stuck, usefully or decoratively, through hats as spoons and pipes are used in Breughel's day. He delights in skates and pattens, pouches and wooden shoes (like those of the patient in the operation), hand-me-downs and wonderful glimpses of dress from unusual angles. The way a lady, kneeling at prayer, has knotted her hanging pink sleeves together at the back of the skirt, is the cause of the "Temptation of St. Anthony" (Lisbon). The "Charlatan" (probably a

893-98. XVc. Flemish. (Prado, Madrid.)
Hieronymus Bosch.
893. The Garden of Earth's Pleasures (detail)

copy, at St. Germain-en-Laye), shows a mixed group of bystanders and gullible ecclesiastics (one wearing blue spectacles).

Bosch started painting very early, between 1470-75. "The Cutting of the Stone" and "The Garden of Earth's Pleasures" are early works; "Adoration of the Magi," c.1490; "Haywagon to Hell," 1510. The "Table of the Seven Deadly Sins," also late, shows Superbia (Vanity) wearing a brown skirt, under a pink gown caught up to show its white fur lining (see Ill. 906), primping from a large box which shows coral beads and fine girdles.

TRANSITION IN DRESS BETWEEN MIDDLE AGES AND RENAISSANCE: 1485-1510

About half way through the fourth quarter XVc., the costume of women begins to lose its fantasy and extravagance. Whether worn by Anne of Brittany, twice Queen of France, or by the middle and lower class women of the "Dance of Death," the costume (of Franco-Flemish derivation) is becoming severe, sensible and bourgeois. It is familiar to us as the costume worn by nuns, and that of the Queens on a deck of cards.

FEMALE: Necklines are higher; the front closing often laps (see Ills. 899-902) in just the curving line which the old spread collar would have made, had the lady been caught in a storm, and tried to clutch the revers together over her chest. But in the main, the neckline of the gown takes over that of the kirtle, becoming squarer. The horizontal line of the top of the plastron rises convexly (see Ill. 905). The old V-neckline is often laced back and forth over the kirtle, or over a plastron of brocade; back closings are also frequently laced. Wide sailor collars appear.

The sleeve of the robe is often of elbow length; frequently cuffed, showing the forearm in the sleeve of the kirtle. Though the wide, funnel sleeve is usual, close-fitting separate sleeves, pinned or knotted on at the shoulder, will appear, as Flemish and Italian influences affect all European costume, from 1485-1510; after this, German-Swiss trends will overtake them. Italian influence is more noticeable in men's costume.

The overskirt, which was formerly so long that it had to be held up, is now as short (and frequently shorter) than the underskirt, though both may show trains in back. It is less often caught up by the hands, but is now apt to be pinned, hooked, tied or tucked into fixed position (see Ill. 906). As skirts grow narrower, the overskirt is slashed to permit this permanent drape. The skirts of both garments are cut separate from the bodice and gathered onto it, in back only. The train, when looped up to the waistline in back, emphasizes the bustled look.

The belt is now a cord or light chain, often with a dependent end at c. front. The turned-up overskirt often reveals several decorative objects hanging from the belt of the kirtle: pouch bags, rosaries, prayer books, etc.

The heads of the poorer women are, as we expect, bundled up, but in a way related to the hoods which the bourgeoises, even the Queen, now wear. In comparison with the flowing veils of the Middle Ages, these lappeted Renaissance hoods are of relatively heavy stuffs, and often of dark colors or black. They enclose the head increasingly, as new methods of fitting them are evolved. Like nuns' headdresses today, the heavy line of the edge of these dark hoods is usually softened by a fold or ruching of light, usually white, stuff beneath. After nearly a hundred years of apparent baldness, or carefully concealed hair, these hoods reveal the hair, simply parted in the center, or drawn back.

Women's shoes, which seldom show, follow the same changes as men's.

MALE: As Burgundian supremacy in fashion wanes, and that of Renaissance Italy grows, men's costume relinquishes its padded shoulder width. The doublet loses its standing collar and assumes a normal waist line. Its close sleeves are often tied on, and are thus interchangeable. It is becoming vest-like: it often has a full skirt, but like the sleeve, this may be separate and interchangeable, as in the case of the cartridge-pleated *bases,* (Ill. 450: Waffenrock) which we find listed independently in contemporary inventories of costumes. The neck of the doublet becomes progressively lower; as on women's gowns it is frequently square, laced across a shirt or plastron, or lapped over.

The jacket or jerkin, worn over the doublet, is, as before, fuller than the doublet, particularly in the skirts; has wider sleeves, and is apt to have a collar of the sailor variety also seen on women's costume. The sleeve of the jerkin is frequently slit, not only longitudinally, as earlier, but crosswise.

Jerkin and doublet take on each other's attributes, and are not always identifiable.

Gowns are long, wide, closed down the front, sometimes girdled; and as before, fur-lined. Their sleeves and collar are those of the jerkin. The comfort and dignity of long gowns continue to make them appropriate for older men and ceremonial occasions. The shorter, ungirded gowns with wide collars are coats in the modern sense.

Cloaks are much worn. They vary in cut and length and frequently carry large collars; they are often thrown or lapped in the new diagonal line.

Hose now reach the natural waistline, where they are trussed to the doublet, as before. The codpiece is increasingly evident; it will presently be featured. There is a re-birth of the idea of parti-colored hose, but in a greatly elaborated Italian form; the legs may differ completely; stripes may be countercharged; there is a great deal of embroidery, which is now more frequently used at the top, to give the appearance of trunks (see Ill. 906), than in boot-like forms at the bottom of the hose, as it had been used earlier (see Ill. 807). The same effect is obtained by the use of interwoven braids, with puffs and slashes.

Slashing in patterns, through which the fabric of the doublet or shirt was exhibited, was used, particularly on doublet sleeves, from fourth quarter XVc. The practice was elaborated, and used all over costume, both male and female, through first half XVIc., and continued for a century thereafter.

Shirts increase greatly in importance as low-necked overgarments, lacings and slashings make them visible. The neckline of the shirt, gathered and embroidered in black, red or gold, lowers in unison with the neck of the overgarment.

Shoe form changes rapidly during this period. While retaining the point, the toes spread progressively, until end XVc., when they lose the point. While still wide, they become round-toed low shoes with straps. Backless slippers, into which the toe was inserted, as in women's "mules" today, appear at beginning XVc. Boots with turned-down tops are less used after first quarter XVIc. Loose sock-hose, which had long been used by all classes to protect tights in bad weather, begin for the first time to be knitted, in a form without heel or toe, worn strapped under the instep, like Uncle Sam's trousers.

The tall Burgundian caps are supplanted by beret-like hats, often pinched into the form we still see on the ecclesiastical biretta. These hats usually have a brim, or a section of brim, turned up; cuts in the brim, laced across, the lacings often knotted; ends hanging, or serving to secure the hat under the chin; these *bonnets* usually carry medallions. There are also wide-brimmed hats, frequently of beaver, immensely plumed (see Ill. 906). As in Italy, the head was frequently covered by a small embroidered cap, which was retained under the hat.

Hair is worn in a long bob, often with bangs; typically of shoulder length and natural, but varying from lank and unkempt to exquisitely trimmed and tended, especially in Italy.

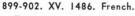

899-902. XV. 1486. French.

Danse macabre des femmes by *Pierre le Rouge;* pub. by Guy Marchant, Paris, 7 July, 1486.

899. The welcoming woman; the nurse.
900. The shepherdess; the woman with crutches.
901. The village woman; the old woman.
902. The second-hand clothes woman; the woman in love.

The allegory of the Dance of Death, in all its satiric bitterness, was repeated on thousands of wall paintings, woodcuts and engravings (one series by Holbein), and as a morality play, in France, Germany and England, from the days of the Black Death and the Hundred Years War.

903. End XVc. French. (Paris, Bib. Nat., ms. Lat. 1190.)

Anne of Brittany, wife of Charles VIII and of Louis XII.

904. XVc. c. 1494. French. (Paris, Beistegui Coll.)

Charles d'Orléans.

The little Dauphin, son of Charles VIII and Anne of Brittany, is shown in another portrait (Louvre) in brocade and the same sort of bib, with the brim of his cap turned down. Anne of Brittany's accounts have been preserved. She dressed the baby always in white and silver; we know how much she paid for silver cloth for his dresses, and that his caps were bought of Gorget of Tours for 50 *sols tournois*.

905. XVc. 1059-13. Franco-Flemish. (Paris, Cluny.)

Tapestry: *The Allegory of Smell*.

Allegories of the five senses, together with the Lady of the Unicorn, make up the famous set of six tapestries from the Cluny, among the 200 tapestries lent in 1948 by the French government to the Metropolitan and other museums in the United States. Against a rosy background, set with flowering plants, these predominantly red and blue tapestries show the lion of valor and the unicorn of purity holding the arms of the Le Viste family; red with two crescents set on a diagonal blue band.

906. c. 1490. Flemish. (British Museum, Harl. M.S. 4425.)

Roman de la Rose.
Carole (dance) of *déduit* (mirth) in a garden.

This volume, which belonged to Count Henry of Nassau, contains some of the great fashion illustrations of all time.

Illuminated manuscripts were the fashion plates of their day. As long as they were executed by monks, who had forsworn women but were perfectly aware of the difference between male and female, those differences were explicitly expressed. No matter how sack-like her garments, the Scarlet Woman in a XIIc. Beatus is very much a woman; all the new knowledge of bias cutting is used in XIIIc. to outline the belly or emphasize the provocative hip of the Foolish Virgins.

Then the troubadours began to sing of a romantic love, serving without reward, perhaps at a distance and for a lifetime. This was a civilizing notion, which required the relinquishment of brute manhood. Secular artists began to represent knights in long gowns, mooning around castles after the ladies they adored. With the advent of the houppelande, a beard is about all that differentiates Richard II from a woman in a similar garment.

The continuing process of refinement imposed an ideal of adolescent charm on both sexes. The Burgundian courtiers are exquisite page-boys, and Marie of Burgundy (Ill. 880) is a breastless girl whose hennin would fall off in a tussle.

But people and their dreams of themselves grow up. We see it happening in costume, at the turn of XV-XVIc. as it does physically: the adolescent girl matures more rapidly than the adolescent boy. In the Roman de la Rose, the girls are just beginning to turn, as they do almost overnight, into the women and housewives of the XVIc. Their dress is becoming simple and severe: a black velvet hood and a plain golden-brown gown with its train fastened up out of the way in back. The boys with them seem reluctant to grow up; their dress takes a last wild fling, as though trying to outdo an extravagance, the limits of which have already been reached; immense white hats are bound on with lavender scarves, and trimmed with spangled feathers more than half as long as their bodies.

The Flemish hausfrau look, reinforced by rigid Spanish coat-dresses and men's felt hats which are not removed in the house, give a characteristically masculine look to the costume of Elizabethan women. The male adolescence of the XVc. becomes diluted in Elizabethan men to a dandified elegance which gives an effeminate look to some of the most completely masculine men in history. By XVIIc., females are women, without having to be aggressive about it, and men are men, going about their empire-building and business.

The new sobriety of women is not complete in the Roman de la Rose illustrations, but it is already in sharp contrast with the dress of the men.

1. *female*: gold turban; pink gown, with light gray-blue undersleeves; green plastron laced with red; pale gold chain-girdle with pomander. 2. *male*: tiny red cap with jewelled brooch, over long flowing hair; black beaver hat, slung over shoulder of golden-brown doublet, gathered at neckline over padded, swelling bosom; bolero; doublet sleeves losing their upper padding; hose tops white, striped in pink, lavender-gray, and green; lower part black, embroidered with gold; cream-colored sock-boots; black, wide-toed shoes; belt threaded through a tasseled pouch. 3.*f.*: black velvet hood with golden-brown crown, pinned with a brooch; golden-brown gown with convex neckline, turned-down cuff of XVc.; shirt puffings pulled through outseam of lower sleeve; permanently draped overskirt; caught by a brooch; black underskirt. 4.*m.*: white beaver hat with immense, color-spangled white feathers, bound by lavender scarf, worn over green cap; red and green jacket with wide lapels and borders, over a black doublet; dark gray hose; black shoes with thick, broad toes, dramatized by the reduction to a minimum of the leather around the heel; sole also narrowed at the heel; another fine belt and pouch. 5.*m.*: tiny red cap with turned-up brim; lavender-gray coat with grass-green lapels and slit pendant sleeves; gray beaver with white plumes under arm; black hose and shoes.

6.*f.*:black hood with green crown; girdle with immense red, blue, and green cabochon stones; gold gown, its black-banded hem, pinned up to show black lining, gives the characteristic bustled look. 7.*f.*: red and gold cap over flowing hair; pink gown with gray skirt, turned up to show its ermine lining. 8.*angel*: white beaver with cut and turned-up brim, bound with pink and lavender scarves; dark gold wings; white garment embroidered with red roses and green leaves; wide gold and white belt. 9.*f.*: black and golden brown hood; pink gown trimmed in black and gold. 10.*m.* red hat; cobalt blue jacket with hem and sleeve ends slittered and cut; wonderful tasselled pouch carried in back; yellow-green doublet sleeves; yellow hose; black shoes.

Musicians: cloaks open on right shoulder; slittered edges; parti-colored hose (now livery).

11. *harp*: black cap; wide-sleeved vermilion coat, lined with red; 1 green, 1 red doublet sleeve.

12. *pipe*: red cap; coat with 1 pink and 1 lavender-brown lapel; hanging pink sleeve, fringed in gold; black doublet with 1 green and 1 black sleeve; parti-colored shoes and hose, alternately black, gold, and gray.

13. *drum*: black cap and doublet; red coat with 1 green and 1 lavender lapel; pink doublet sleeve slit over black; parti-colored hose, alternately gray, gold, and black.

15. *hero*: with staff and anachronistic dress; old-fashioned short gown with bag-sleeves and a fringed hem; red hose and hat with fringe (see Ills. 985-986: Housebook); girdle pendants, which are probably the large bells worn on belts and baldrics from e.XV-e.XVIc. In 1415, Marie of Burgundy had a collar with these hanging, pear-shaped bells. (See the livery of May and the servants in the Très-riches heures: Ills. 807-810.)

The gold border is painted naturalistically with many of the favorite motifs of XVIc. embroidery: pea-flowers, vines, and pods; butterflies, insects, and snails; strawberries and a peacock; fleur-de-lys, rose, dianthus, forget-me-not, and pimpernel.

13 12 11 10 9 8 7

906

Cefte gent vint
le Dune carole
Seftoient prz
a la carole

Et une dame leur chantoit
Q ui lieffe appellee eftoit
Bien fceut chanter et plaifaunont
Plus que nulle et mignotement
Son bel refrain nul bien lui fift
Car de chanter mernailles fift

Elle auoit la voir clere et fame
Laquelle neftoit pas villaine
Et tresbien se sauoit debriser
feur du pie et remoiser
Les gens la tenoient inte chiere
Pource quelle eftoit la premiere
De belle face et plainer
Courtoise eftoit et non vafhere
De loyaufete fut garnie
Et aufst de folas fournie

15 1 14 2 3 4 5 6

907-908. End XV-e.XVIc. c. 1502. French, Southern. (Issogne, Castello.)

Wall paintings. These Southern French wall paintings show costume of start of XVIc.; strongly influenced by Italian ways.

907. A mediaeval market place; draper's booth, with belts and caps hung on its open shutters. Traffic in strings of garlic and red onions, carrots, rutabagas; figs, plums and grapes; baskets of cabbage, melons and various squashes.

The simple roundlets and tiny caps favored by Italian women appear here, together with the new hoods. At l., the seated woman with spinning utensils at her belt, wears a horned roundlet; (braided hair was also brought together and bound into a similar point, second half XVc.). The new deep armseye of her sleeve is emphasized by the Italian differentiation in color.

The men wear the new bonnets with cut and laced-together brims. Padding is being removed from the tops of doublet sleeves; they remain full, but loose. This sleeve is also used on the jerkin. With the advent of pleated *bases,* separate and often interchangeable skirts to the jacket (Ill. 450) the doublet and jacket became less easy to differentiate. The gown of the man (c.), has the new broad, flat collar. Seams and edges are emphasized by lines of braid.

908. Tailor's shop: Parti-colored tights reappear, end XVc., in more elaborate forms than before (Ill. 906); in trunk-like patterns or multi-colored stripes, of Italian origin. Cut-out pieces of these tights, with codpieces, hang above the tailors. Their jerkins, in the new vertically striped materials, have the square neck of first quarter XVIc.

909

910

909. XIV-XVc. English. (Derby, Ashbourne Church.)

Tombs of John Cockayne (1404 A.D.) and civilian (1370 A.D.).

The knight: fringed surcoat bearing his canting arms of a cock. Aventail laced to bascinet through staples; cuff gauntlets; flowing moustache.

The prosperity of the XVIIc. cloth trade will be founded on the proposal of Sir William Cockayne, alderman and head of the Clothworkers' Company of London, that all cloth be dyed and finished in England before export.*

The civilian: cote-hardi, center-buttoned since mid-XIIIc.: precious belt, over the joining of the full skirt which gives sufficient solidity for attachment of hose; tasseled pouch; coif; hooded cloak caught on right shoulder.

910. XVc. 1400. English. (Nottinghamshire, Strelly Church.)

Sir Samson de Strelley, and wife Elizabeth.

The netted crespine has developed into jewelled boxes, surmounted by a coronet; from 1400 the boxes tend to descend and enclose the ears. Rising neckline filled in by a choker with pearl pendants, or by the SS collar, frequently seen on women.

---

* George Unwin: *Industrial Organization in the Sixteenth and Seventeenth Centuries,* Clarendon Press, Oxford, 1904.

911-12. XVc. 1400. English. (Gloucestershire, Deerhurst.)

Sir John and Lady Cassy.

The earliest remaining brass shows the Chief Baron of the Exchecquer, in the linen coif which, by end first quarter XVc., is worn only by judges, lawyers and churchmen (Ill. 928). The Baron of the Exchecquer, with judges and sergeants, made up the Order of the Coif. Fur-lined mantle with hood; under-tunic with sleeves extending over the knuckles, fastened by row of tiny buttons.

Lady Cassy, born Terri: reticulated headdress; long, loose gown, gored into a high buttoned neck; sleeves of kirtle extend over the knuckles.

913-14. XVc. c. 1410. English. (Lincolnshire, Spilsby Church.)

Knight and Lady (prob. 4th Baron, and 1st wife), of d'Eresby family.

Baron: armor of Transitional period, from mail to plate. Camail still worn under gorget and bascinet of plate. No jupon; breastplate, with mail gussets; and mail fringe below skirt of articulated plates, *fauld,* which supplants that of hawberk. Two belts; horizontal and diagonal. Orlé over bascinet; moustache.

Lady; houppelande (new gown, with high collar, flowing sleeves, belted high, fur-lined; largely replaces mantle). Inner sleeve, of length which heretofore covered knuckles, now falls back, as hand is passed through slit at wrist. Coronet over crespine headdress without veil; small net-covered bosses, above ears, until c. 1410.

915. XVc. 1401-1406. English. (Warwick, St. Margaret's Church.)

Thomas Beauchamp, Earl of Warwick, and Margaret, Countess of Warwick, born Ferrers.

One of the costliest monumental effigies ever ordered; made of latten.

Earl: armor of Camail period (see Ills. 591, 599) bearing Beauchamp arms. The ragged staff, which was a Beauchamp badge, is used on pommel and scabbard of sword, on roundlets at elbow, and on border of bascinet. The bear beneath his feet was another badge of his house. Moustache.

Countess: gown bears the arms of Ferrers; mantle Beauchamp. Nebulé headdress in late English form; sleeves extended over knuckles to end first quarter XVc.

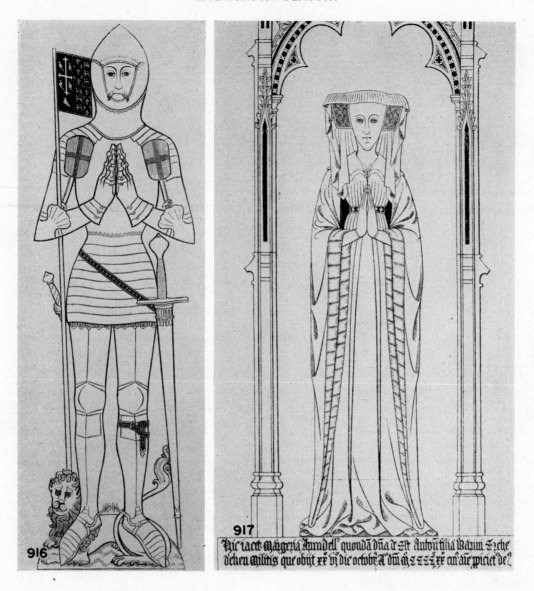

916. XVc. 1416. English. (Norfolk, Felbrigg Church.)

Sir Symon de Felbrigge, K. G.

Standard-bearer to Richard II, whose arms are shown on the banner he holds. Edward III was the first king to employ quartered arms (Azure, semé of fleurs-de-lys or, France, quartering gules, 3 lions passant gardant, England), which Richard II sometimes used (as here shown), impaled with the arms attributed to Edward the Confessor (azure a cross patée between 3 martlets or). He wears the Garter of the Order instituted in the middle of the XIVc.

Armor of Complete Plate period; bascinet, becoming more rounded; helm and gorget replace camail. Breastplate with oblong palettes (charged with a cross), protecting armpits. Skirt of taces, which increase in number; vestigial line of mail. Arms: articulated pauldrons, rerebraces, fan-shaped coutère, giving additional elbow protection, vembraces. Gauntlet: increasingly articulated but fingers not yet separated. Legs: cuishes, genoullières, jambes, sollerets, rowelled spurs. Belt: diagonal, holds sword, miséricorde at taces, right side; moustache; the Garter.

917. XVc. 1420. English. (Cornwall, East Anthony.)

Margery Arundell.

Houppelande: double collar, now worn flat (see Ill. 807). Headdress: netted cones of 2nd decade XVc. in England, wider, squarer, now covering ears; covered by shoulder-length square veil.

918-19. XVc. c. 1420. English. (Yorkshire, Harpham Church.)

Sir Thomas de Saint Quintin and wife Agnes.

Sir Thomas: Complete Mail period. Palettes of different shapes protect armpit; smaller, providing freedom of sword arm. Elaborate orlé on rounder bascinet. Belt: low, horizontal, and very elaborate, found till mid-XVc., though tendency is toward simpler, narrower, diagonal belts. Sword; handsome miséricorde. Below taces, elaborately scalloped mail edge. Moustache.

Agnes: collar of houppelande broader, flatter; belt lower, wider, more important; bag-sleeve of first quarter XVc. with gauntlet cuff. Bosses of reticulated headdress square, wide, cover ears; veil, shoulder-length, square.

920. XVc. 1492. English. (Sussex, Amberly Church.)

John Wantele.

Heraldic tabard, which appears c. 1425, in an early form; short sleeves cut in one with the garment; blazoned: vert 3 lions faces argent langued gules. Effigies are now frequently bare-headed and usually clean-shaven.

Stow, at the end XVIc., describes the tabard: "a jacket, or sleeveless coat, whole before, open on both sides, with a square collar, winged at the shoulders; a stately garment of old time, commonly worn of noblemen and others, both at home and abroad in the wars, but then, to wit, in the wars, their arms embroidered, or otherwise depict upon them, that every man by his coat-of-arms might be known from others. But now these tabards are worn only by the heralds, and be called their coats-of-arms in service."

921. XVc. c. 1420. English. (Kent, Herne Church.)

Peter Halle and wife.

Peter: Complete Mail period. Bascinet increasingly rounder; coutes fan-shaped. Sword-belt narrow, diagonal. No mail fringe below taces; no gauntlets; guarded rowel spurs. Clean-shaven.

Wife: classic sideless surcoat (persists nearly 150 years, from mid-XIVc.; its front placard being gradually reduced to a narrow strip); with accompanying cord-held cape. Pads of headdress beginning to assume heart shape, which will reach its culmination in third quarter XVc.

922-25. First quarter XVc. English. (London, Soc. of Antiquaries.)

Scenes from the life of St. Etheldreda.

St. Etheldreda, 660 A.D., was the daughter of the King of the East Angles. Twice married, but a perpetual virgin and an incorruptible corpse, she was the builder and abbess of the monastery of Ely. Bede tells us that "from the time of her entering into the monastery, she never wore any linen but only woolen garments and would rarely wash in a hot bath, unless just before any of the great festivals . . . and then she did it last of all . . . after having first washed the other servants of God there present. . . . She foretold the pestilence of which she was to die . . . (and) the number of those that should be then snatched away out of her monastery. . . . She was buried among them . . . in a wooden coffin."

Upper left to right: high horned headdress early form; headdresses, with round bosses, covering ears, surmounted by crowns (in other illus., by roundlets). Houppelandes; collars worn flat; variety of sleeves. Bishop, kings, ecclesiastics.

Lower left to right: masons wearing aprons; bowl crop of Englishmen's hair; Dead saint, with nuns, bishop, ecclesiastics, ladies and gentlemen.

926-27. XVc. c. 1427. French. (Paris, Bib. Nat., ms. lat. 1158.)

Book of Hours of Ralph Nevill, Earl of Westmorland (926), and Jeanne de Beaufort (927).

Ralph Nevill had 23 children; we are here shown 12 of his 14 children by Jeanne, his 2nd wife, together with 3 daughters-in-law. All wear houppelandes, or derivative garments, with flattened spreading collars

of end first quarter XVc. Sons wear bag sleeve (pokys—"pig in a poke"), which will soon be supplanted by the sleeve slit for the passage of the doublet-covered forearm. The women wear large heart-shaped French headdresses; the men show the English form of the bowl-cropped head; and wear the livery Collar of the White Hart. The blazoning of the coats of arms indicate the marriages, as: Nevill/Lancaster; England, York/Nevill; Mowbray, Plantagenet, Norfolk/Nevill.

928. XVc. 1430. English. (Essex, Gosfield Church.)

Thomas Rolf, Sergeant-at-law.

Not only the care of souls, but education, law, medicine, and charity had been administered solely by the Church. During XIVc., the separation of the professions began, at the time when long, loose, sober, hooded garments, currently worn by elderly men, were coming to be considered more suitable than others for clerical use. These garments, already antiquated, became fossilized in the dress of men (and women) of the Church, and of professional men, whose status remained semi-clerical although they might actually no longer be priests. The separation took place first in law, and last in education (within our grandparents' memory). The dress remains today in the robes of judges, monks, nuns, and hooded academic dress.

The coif and lappets of XIVc. are retained in legal dress in court or university in XVc. Sergeants are a privileged class, and wear a hooded cape of lamb's wool (budge) over a garment of the tabard-guarnache-scapular type, and a long gown.

A large colored plate (III) accompanying the informative explanatory text in the article on Robes in Enc. Britt., 11th ed., shows a law court, tempus Henry VI, and describes the difference between the different categories of legal dress shown there, and spectators and prisoners. Sergeants at law are more privileged than King's Counsel, and wear parti-colored robes (the "medlée cote" of Chaucer), in green and blue, diagonally or vertically striped in white. Judges, who belong to the same order, wear robes of the same form as sergeants but in scarlet, and their capes are furred with miniver; they wear XIVc. cloaks caught on the right shoulder, and coifs or furred hats. Variations in these colors, and the dress of King's Coroner, Attourney, Master of the Court, ushers, and tipstaff are discussed or shown. The whole set of 4 plates is reproduced from Archaeologica, Vol. XXXIX, 1863, p. 357-72.

929. XVc. English. (British Museum, Harl. ms. 4380.)

Mss. drawing: Treaty between the French and English.

930-31. XVc. 1458. English. (Leicestershire, Castle Donington Church.)

Sir Robert Staunton and lady.

Sir Robert wears a salade and Gothic armor showing increasing lamination for flexibility; and use of indenting, ridging and fluting of plates, calculatedly practical as well as decorative. Pointed, fluted tassets hang from the laminated fauld. Widely flanged guards at elbow; mitten gauntlets; English sollerets usually not piked, like ordinary footwear or armor of the continent.

Wife; heart-shaped headdress; less exaggerated than the French (see Jeanne de Beaufort, Ill. 927).

928

929

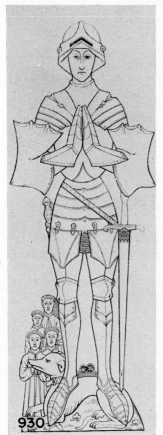

930

931

932

933

932-33. XVc. 1473. English. (Hertfordshire, Broxbourne Church.)

Sir John Say and lady.

Sir John's tabard, like his lady's mantle, was enamelled to show armorial bearings; Say: party per pale azure and gules, 3 chevrons or, each charged with another humette countercharged of the field;

and hers: Cheyny. Tassets increasingly fluted and indented; lengthening as fauld becomes shorter. He wears the Yorkist livery collar of Suns and Roses.

Wife: butterfly headdress of third quarter XVc. (see Ill. 833), short sideless surcoat, and heavy necklace characteristic of last half XVc. until superseded by fine knotted cords or bead chokers of XVIc.

934-38. XVc. c. 1485. English. (British Museum.)

Pageant of the Birth, Life and Death of Richard Beauchamp, Earl of Warwick (1382-1439), by *John Rows* of Warwick (1411-1491).

The illustrations for this life of the great warrior-Earl (son of Thomas B., 1400) furnish unique source material about military affairs of the period.

No. 934 shows the Earl in foot combat with Sir Pandolfo Malatesta at Verona. By casting down the baton which he holds, Sir Galaot of Mantua can end the combat, if he feels it necessary. The combat with battle-axes has been preceded by one with spears; the squires hold in readiness the swords for the encounter which will follow. Both were in complete armor, a rear view of which is given by Malatesta, whose crest is of plumes and jewels. The Earl's bascinet carries his bear and ragged staff, as crest. His sleeved tabard (see Ills. 830, 831), carries his bearings (see Ills. 532, 533).

935. The President of the "King's Court of France" receives three sealed letters from Warwick's herald, the letter he holds is sealed with a "maunche" (bag sleeve),* "the feyld sylver a maunche gowlys. The secund Pavys (shown above arch) hadde a lady sittyng at a covered borde worchyng perles/and on her sleeve was tached a glove of plate/and her knyght was called Chevaler vert/and his letter was sealed wt the Armes, the felde sylver &ij barres of gowles/ And he must just xv courses & that shulde be ij sadilles of choyes/the iij de pavys a lady sittyng in a gardeeyn makyng a Chapellet/and on her sleeve, a poleyn wt a rivet/and her knyght was called Chivaler attendant/And he & his felowe must renne x cours wt sharpe speres & wt out sheldys/his letter was sealed wt golde & gowles quarte a bordour of vere/ thies lettres were sent to the Kynges coort of Fraunce

/And a noon other ijj Frenche knyghtes received them & graunted their felows to mete at day and place assigned."

Herald, in sleeved armorial tabard, riding boots, and spurs (length of which is increasing). Swordbearer; long gown, handsome pouch. President and gentlemen; long gowns, jewelled collars and belts.

936. Richard, in armor and tabard, kneeling before Henry V, who wears parliamentary robes and crown, and is attended by sword-bearer and lords. To right, two Earls ride away, in full armor, wearing salades, one of which has a visor, the other a knob carrying a jewelled feather, both furnished with chin-pieces. They are preceded by Warwick's banner, borne by men-at-arms in studded brigandines, one over chain shirt, and with short sleeves of mail. All wear round salades, one over mail coif.

937. The Dauphin, and the Earls of Limoges and Vendôme defeated by the English. English archers, with bundles of arrows at their belts, in short brigandines over long mail shirts; protective cuff on left arm; barbutes on head. Behind them, spearmen, in visored salades. Warwick's banner borne by completely armed man in a closed helmet. Warwick in plumed helmet, mounted on plumed horse, which is given plate protection on head and neck. On right, crossbow men, with scimitar-like faulchions.

938. Richard kneeling before King on his return; followed by attendant wearing his ragged staff badge; on his doublet. Pennon with his bear and ragged staff. Horsemen with guisarmes and spears. King in trefoil crown, attended by hooded clerk and swordbearer.

The impulse toward uniformity is not new. The loyalty of feudal retainers had to be assured by food and clothing, which it was convenient to get in large batches, and so turned out alike.

Stow gives many lists of the expenses of Thomas of Lancaster for uniforms: in 1314, "1 cloth of russet for the bishop, 70 cloth of blue for the knights, 15 cloth of medley for the lord's clerks," and so on to a total of £460.15s, which dresses everybody down to the minstrels and carpenters. On other occasions, he got 65 cloths of saffron color for barons and knights in summer, or 100 pieces of green silk for the knights. This is uniformity, but of a sort, only.

Meanwhile, new loyalties besides the feudal arise. The solidarity of the city guilds sends 600 London citizens out to receive Edward I on his return from his wedding in 1300, dressed "in one livery of red and white, with cognizances of their mysteries embroidered upon their sleeves." The mayor, aldermen, and craftsmen of London met Henry V, on his return with French prisoners in 1415, in red, with red and white hoods; and Henry VII was met by the usual London worthies, "all clothed in violet, as in a mourning color," after Richard III's death at Bosworth (Stow).

The united loyalties (now to the Crown, instead

* As on the arms of Hastings.

935

936

937

938

or a feudal lord) of both factions are rewarded by Henry VII's Tudor collars of red and white roses combined. But it is still in feudal use that the first real uniforms appear. It is Stow again who tells us that Richard Nevill, in 1458, had "600 men, all in red jackets, embroidered with ragged staves before and after" who were "lodged in Warwick Lane; in whose house there was oftentimes 6 oxen eaten at a breakfast, and every tavern was full of his meat; for he that had any acquaintance in that house might have there as much of sodden and roast meat as he could prick and carry upon a long dagger."

939

939. XVc. English. (Eton College Chapel.)

Amoras sells his wife to the devil.

A great deal of English wall-painting was destroyed by the Parliamentary armies.

Anthony Wood of Oxford* said: "The pictures of prophets, apostles, saints, etc., that had been painted on the backside of the stalls in Merton college choir, in various and antique shapes, about the beginning of the reign of King Henry VII were daubed over with paint, by the command of the usurpers, about 1651, to the sorrow of various men that were admirers of ancient painting." Brass plates with inscriptions were torn away from gravestones; Wood failed to shame the despoilers, but as he says with satisfaction, "A. W. had before this time transcribed them, which were afterwards printed."

Standard Italianate male costume of Europe at the turn of the century.

* Life and Times of Anthony Wood, Antiquary of Oxford, ed. A. Clark, Oxf. Hist. Soc. 1891-1900, 5 vols.; vol. I, p. 309.

940

941

940. XVc. 1488. English. (London, Nat. Port. Gall.)

Lady Margaret Beaufort (Tudor), Countess of Richmond and Derby.

Henry VII's pious and well-educated mother (1445-1509), founder of Christ's and St. John's Colleges at Cambridge, and of the Lady Margaret professorships of divinity at Oxford and Cambridge, took a vow of celibacy in 1504, after being three times widowed.

Her cream-colored French hood, embroidered in light brown, and veiled in black, is worn over a white cap; black wimple edged in white; dark red gown with gray fur cuffs.*

941. XVc. 1491. English. (Durham, Hexham Priory.) Freestone.

Rowland Leschman, Prior.

A prior was the head of a house of Canons Regular; they were secular clergy, attached to cathedrals and their colleges, and receiving a share of the funds of the institution, while retaining their own property. They lived a modified monastic life, but became increasingly non-resident; and might, especially among the lower orders marry.† Leschman was a "Black Canon." A contemporary XVIc. account says that an English Canon Regular "dressed in violet like the rest of the clergy." He wears a hooded, sleeveless, semi-circular cape and white, pleated rochet, over a cassock, probably fur-lined.

942-43. XVc. 1488. English. (Norfolk, Stokesby Church.) Brass.

Edmund Clere, knight, and Elizabeth his wife.

While many of the finest monumental brasses were of Flemish make, imported sheet-brass was used in local manufacture at Ipswich, Lincoln, and as in this brass, at Norwich.

The Cleres, who appear throughout the Paston letters, married many Elizabeths. Sir John Fastolf's sister, who married Sir Philip Braunch had a daughter, Elizabeth. She, by her 1st husband, John Clere, had 2 sons: Robert, who married the Paston's beloved cousin Elizabeth, and had a son, Sir Robert; and Edmund, the name of whose wife does not appear in the Paston letters.

This may well be that couple, though he died in 1463; since his mother survived to 1492 his wife may have outlived him, and the brass thus be of a later date.

Edmund wears a large visored salade with beaver (chin protection); convexly ridged armor with unusual shoulder, elbow and thigh plates; and a collar of roses.

Elizabeth's gown retains its XVc. length in front, but is assuming a XVIc. severity of line, as its neck

942   943

becomes squarer and shows the material of the kirtle in front. Her headdress is becoming a hood, the front band rising in a gabled peak at the forehead.

As early as 1449, Margaret Paston asks her husband that he "wyld bye a zerd (yard) of brode clothe of blac for an hood fore me of xliiijd or iiijs a zerd, for there is nether gode cloth ner gode fryse (frieze?) in this twn." In 1454, she prays that he "woll vowchesawf to remembr to purvey a thing for my nekke, and to do make my gyrdill." No necklace appears in her long will of 1482, but she leaves to her daughter-in-law "a purpill girdill harneised with silver and gilt"; to her daughter Anne, "my best corse girdill blewe harneised with silver and gilt"; and to Agnes Swan, her "servaunt, my muster develys (gray wool) gown, furred with blak, and a girdell of blak harneised with silver gilt and enamelled." In the inventory of Agnes Paston's plate, the girdles are identified by the name of the goldsmith from whom they were ordered.

The gowns which the ladies describe or ask for, are of "a goodly blue, or else a bright sanguine," murrey, black, green, violet or gray. The men mention murrey, blue, French russet, tawny, black and puce (furred with white lamb); one sends for a new vestment of white damask, from which he will make an arming doublet "thow I sholde an other time gyff a longe gown of velvett ffor another vestment." The men repeatedly send for hose-cloth, black, or of "holiday colors."

---

* Mrs. Reginald Lane Poole: *Catalogue of Oxford Portraits*, 3 vols., Clarendon Press, Oxford, 1925.

† "The Saxon priests had known no rule of celibacy. About the time of the Conquest, Hildebrand's dreaded decree began to find its way into England, and by the XIVc. it had been a long-established rule that no priest should marry. But the old custom never died out completely among the parish clergy, though their partners were now in the eye of the law mere concubines. . . . Priests brought up their children without fear, if not without reproach."—G. M. Trevelyan: *Eng. in the Age of Wycliffe.*

From Cotman: *Sepulchral Brasses of Norfolk* (942-43).

944. XVc. Spanish. (Solsona, Museo Diocesano.)
Last Supper.

The usual mediaeval seating along one side of a long trestle table with one's back safe against a wall. Knives and serving spoons are the only implements. Wooden trenchers are used for cutting and eating portions of meat, but food and drink are served in superb Spanish pottery instead of the plate of the rest of well-to-do Europe. Plates are scraped onto a handsome tile floor for the dogs which lie waiting beneath.

945-46. Mid-XVc. Spanish, Catalonian. (Barcelona, Catalonian Art Museum.)
Father Garcia de Bernabarre (?) .
Banquet of Herodias (945); detail (946).

The costume of XVc. Spanish nobility was strongly influenced by French court fashions, and from second third XVc., by Italian styles. A comparison of these illustrations with the garments of Queen Isabella and Joanne the Mad, will show regional Spanish modes retained at the end XVc. in garments which exhibit the XVIc. conventual trend. We will see there these same extremely wide shirt sleeves, not laced or strapped into puffs, but falling free through the slit sleeve of the forearm; they will pass out of use in the XVc. But in the bell-shaped, stiffened underskirts (*farthingale, vertugale*) of these dresses, and in the great importance of the long V-openings of the bodice, with their display of the patterned undershirt, and (in the case of ungirded gowns) in the long, spreading V of the front openings, can be discovered the genesis of the peculiarly Spanish fashions which will affect all European dress in another century.

The padded edges of the bodice opening, to which the sleeves are laced at the shoulders, will become the characteristic roll, sewn into the armseye, between shoulder and sleeve, of the following century.

In all these Spanish women's costumes, we notice the complete absence of the extravagant outer-gown sleeve; sleeves are largely of the close doublet type. The extravagance of the Spanish sleeve is expressed in the spill of the (frequently) patterned shirt from some point in the lower arm.

The skirt, as in Italy, is rarely so long in front as to need holding up.

947-49. Mid-XVc. Spanish, Catalonian. (Barcelona, Catalonian Art Museum.)
Master of S. Quirse.
Retable of St. Clara and St. Marguerite; and detail.
Gentlemen and ladies, priests and pages, in these illustrations, wear costume of the French court type: padded shoulders; high doublet collars; and footwear. The wood-soled piked shoes of one page are identical with those shown in the Chronicles of Hainault; the other wears boots cut high at the knee and handsomely stitched.

The pages illustrate the difference in form between Spanish cropped hair and that of Italy and France.

The saint who kneels while she is being tonsured wears a short circular cape, which we see on other Spanish women of last half XVc. (see Ills. 951, 958).

950. XVc. Spanish, Catalonian. (Barcelona, Catalonian Art Museum.)
Master of St. George.
Retable of the Savior: detail.

951. XVc. Spanish, Catalonian. (Lerida Museum.)
Unknown Master.
Detail of retable.

952. Last quarter XVc. Spanish, Catalonian. (Madrid, Private Collection.)
Unknown master of the School of Lérida.
Detail of retable.

Spanish women's necklines though extremely varied in cut, remain comparatively high; but as necklines, all over Europe, become squarer, the top of the shirt becomes more important. Elsewhere the shirt is white and full, the rather horizontal neckline embroidered in color and metal. Only in Spain do we find these shirts made of stuffs in the bold striped patterns long characteristic of that country. The fullness of Spanish shirts is shown in the sleeves rather than in the body of the garment, and the shape of the shirt at the neck shows great variation, always in relation to that of the neckline of the gown with which it is specifically designed to be worn. The maid drawing water at the well wears the loose ends of her shirt-sleeves knotted.

Heads are covered more than in Italy, less extravagantly than in France. Close hood (central figure) is worn, also, by Mendoza's wife (954) under her huge crimped turban.

Cord and bead necklaces like these are seen in the last decades of XVc., particularly in Italy.

From Zervos: *Catalan Art* (947-49.)

953-54. XVc. 1455. Spanish. (Marquis of Santillana.)   955. XVc. Spanish. (Madrid, Nat. Gall.)
Jorge Inglés, or his School. Iñigo Lopez de Men-   *Letters of Ferdinand Bolea to the Kings of Aragon,*
doza and his wife.   *Castile, and Portugal.*

Don Carlos of Aragon, Prince of Viana (1421-61).
Viana was a charming and cultivated prince, who lived much in Italy because of the enmity of the stepmother by whom he was poisoned upon his return to Spain after the Catalan revolt.

956. XVc. 1455. Spanish. (Monastery, Sopetran.)
School of Jorge Inglés.
Panel: of Iñigo Lopez de Mendoza (Ills. 953-54).
His name implies that the painter of these pictures was an Englishman.

From the five children of Iñigo Lopez de Mendoza, Marquis of Santillana, d.1453, and his wife, daughter of the Grand Master of Santiago, were descended many of the greatest families in Spain: Velasco, Mendoza, Guzman, Medina Sidonia, and Olivares.

Mendoza and his attendant, like the prince of Viana, wear typically French garments of mid-XVc.: chaperon with streamer, or conical hat; padded shoulders; high doublet collar; precious chains with emblems; magnificent belts with pouches; and point-

957

958

959

960

ed poulaines. The doublet of the Sopetran panel is much more regional in its use of pattern, and of buttons on the sleeves and collar.

It is interesting to compare the way in which the skirt of the Mendoza lady is set onto a low waistline, with the ribbed effect obtained in quite different ways, on the skirts of the attendants in the Ill. 951. Her full sleeve tightens toward the wrist, where it widens suddenly into a little circular, falling cuff.

All these illustrations show floors of decorated Spanish tiles; braziers and tables of wrought iron; and beds set on a raised platform, over which is spread a specially woven thin carpet, the edges of which just reach the floor, such as are still used in Spain.

957. XVc. Spanish, Castilian. (Chicago, Deering Coll.) *Girard Master.*

St. Sebastian.

The saint might be almost any youth of the late XVc., except for the narrowing cuff of his short sleeve, the hanging end of shirt sleeve, and his footwear. The shoes of Spanish men of this period show delightful variations and combinations of cut and color; I regret that we have not space to show more.

958. XVc. Spanish, Catalonian. (Barcelona Cathedral.)
M. Nadal.

Retable of Saints Cosmas and Damian.

The lady wears the swelling turbans which we see in Italy and Germany, and upon the Lopez de Mendoza lady; skirt tucked, not held up, as in France, and with a square train; cape (see Ills. 947, 951); width of sleeve tucked into cuff.

959. XVc. 1460. Spanish. (Metropolitan Museum.)
Catalonian School.

Salome with the Head of St. John.

With a French horned headdress, Salome wears

earrings (see XIVc. Sp.); sleeves of her gown are of the male doublet type, with a line of fur where the padding would end; train square. The tabard-like overgarment with tippets in front, worn by the queen, is often seen in Catalonian paintings.

Meat was brought to table on platters, but was still eaten from trenchers of bread (Fr. *tranche*—slice), with a knife as the only implement, even in a great Spanish household, hung with brocade and floored with beautifully painted tiles. These were originally used in wall decoration, but have descended to the floor.

960. XVc. Spanish. (Barcelona, Catalonian Art Museum.)
Unknown Master.
Retable of the Virgin and Child.

961-68. Last quarter XVc. Spanish. (Burgos, Brotherhood
of the Knights of Santiago.)
Books of the Knights of Santiago.
Equestrian portraits of eight kings.

Three crusading military and religious orders of
St. James (Santiago) were established in Spain during the XIIc. The Knights of St. James of Compostella wore red cloaks, bearing the lily-hilted sword of
St. James; and those of Alcántara and Calatrava, the
cross-fleury, in red and green, respectively.

The eight kings, wearing mail shirts with short
sleeve characteristic of Spanish knights, may be compared with the knights in Ill. 984, in respect to the
late XVc. use of plumes, and of words, decoratively.

969. XVc. Spanish, Catalonian. (Lerida Museum.)
Espalargues.
Retable, from Viella.

970. XVc. Spanish. (Madrid, Lestieri Coll.)
Alfajarin Master.
St. Vincent and St. Lawrence.
Large, heavy brocades and decoration of Spanish
vestments (see Ills. 729, 751).

971

971. XVc. Spanish, (Madrid, Royal Palace.)
Att. to *Bermejo.*
Queen Isabella.
Isabella, "la Catolica," d.1504, the pious Queen
who undertook personally to underwrite Columbus'
explorations, and whose decisive intelligence was responsible for much of Spain's future greatness, wears
a gauze hood over a small cap, its ends caught together and finished by a heavy Renaissance pendant,

in a manner which we shall see in later Spanish use,
quite independent of headdress. The yoke which fills
in the square neck of her severe dress is embroidered
with the emblems of her personal inheritance of
Leon.

972. End XVc. Spanish. (Chantilly, Conde Mus., ms.
1339.)
Devocionario de la Reyna Da. Juana, by *Marcuello.*
Ferdinand and Isabella, with their daughter, Joanne
the Mad, mother of the Emperor Charles V, and
Queen of Castile in her own right.

Mother and daughter wear gowns with the severe
lines and square necks of the transition period, over
the stiffened Spanish bell-skirt; and with the immense
Spanish shirt sleeve pouring out of a close inner
sleeve.

972

973. XV-XVIc. Spanish. (Madrid, Prado.)
Juan Flamenco; also att. to *Franc. Gallegos.*
Beheading of St. John.
To accommodate the bell shape of the stiffened
underskirt, in Spain, the overskirt had either to be
draped or slashed. In this center front line, its edge reinforced with embroidery, and showing the decoration which overlaid the horizontal stiffening beneath,
we have the foundation of the Spanish skirt, and later
Elizabethan costume.

The great bound pig-tail, falling from a tiny cap,
appears in many Spanish pictures, and in Italian
portraits as well, such as Botticelli's Port. of a Young
Woman (K. F. Mus., Berlin), Piero della Francesca's
Port. of a Young Woman (Pitti, Florence), and
Sforza portraits (Ills. 783, 784).

Clogs, analogous to these very high, jewelled ones,
will be seen on Carpaccio's Venetian courtesans.

The enormous shirt sleeve receives varied treatment

here: it even assumes the puff of an upper doublet sleeve, and pours out of a superimposed lower doublet sleeve.

974. XVc. 1420. German. (Frankfort-on-Main, Historical Museum.)

Middle Rhenish School.

Garden of Paradise.

Women in domestic dress: bareheaded; kirtle, often belted low and bloused.

Knight: new bag-sleeve; gambeson, growing shorter-waisted; V-back, vertically quilted, over chain shirt with dagged fringe of mail.

Man at tree: short circular capes and hoods, less worn elsewhere than in Germany, where interest in dagging persists. Huge circular cuffs (see Ill. 791), capable of concealing hand.

Compare these and Ills. 976-79 with Ills. 824-25 and Color Plate, No. 3, for application of leaves and petals, derived from dagging; usage which persists into last quarter XVc.

975

975. XVc. 1425. German. (Passau, Niedernburg Convent.)
Lower Bavarian School.

Queen Gisela of Hungary, as Abbess of the Convent.

Garments of an important, elderly lady of first half XVc.: crown over wimple and veil with the crimped, *kruseler,* edge characteristic of German costume to end first half XVc.

BEGINNINGS OF ENGRAVING, XVc.

With packs of cards begins a new era in illustration: engraving.

Wood engravers had worked in Germany since XIVc. During XVc. they provided block-letters and illustrations to be inserted into hand-written books, as the demand outstripped the productive capacity of the monasteries. In addition to "block-books," they produced illustrations of fables, biblical history, dances of death, to be given away by the rich or sold by the church.

Next came packs of cards for various games. 1460 is the first definite date which can be given to any known pack but there is reason to believe that the Master of the Playing Cards was producing before 1466; and the importation of playing cards into Venice had been prohibited in 1441.*

Many artists of XV-XVIc. had been trained as goldsmiths, and were expert engravers; Daniel Hopfer, Hans Burgkmair the elder, and Jörg Sorg worked for the Augsburg armorers, as engravers and designers, and like Dürer, produced plates showing armor. The Cranachs, the Behams, George Pencz in Germany, Lucas van Leyden in the Netherlands, and Marcantonio Raimondi in Italy made plates which are especially valuable for costume information.

976-79. XVc. c. 1446. German-Swiss. (Dresden Library.)
The Master of the Playing Cards.

An Austrian writer of first half XVc. says: "Everyone dressed as he pleased. Some wore coats of two kinds of material. Some had left the sleeve much wider than the right, wider even than the length of the whole coat, while others wore sleeves of equal width. Some again embroidered the left sleeve in various ways, with ribbons of all colors or with silver bugles threaded on silk strings. Some wore on the breast a kerchief of various colors embroidered with letters in silver and silk. Still others wore pictures on the left breast. Some had their clothes made so long that they could not dress or undress without assistance, or without undoing a multitude of small buttons dispersed all over the sleeves, the breast and the abdomen. Some added to their clothes hems of a different color; others replaced hems by numerous points and scallops. Everyone wore hoods until the former headdress of men had disappeared. Cloaks were hardly long enough to reach the hips."

The large beaver hats, the largest of which carried clusters of plumes and a scarf for binding (see *Roman de la Rose,* Ill. 906, and Ills. 785-787) are new in Germany, and will travel over Europe during last half XVc.

* A. M. Hind: *A History of Engraving and Etching,* Houghton, Mifflin Co., Boston, 1923.

976

977

978

979

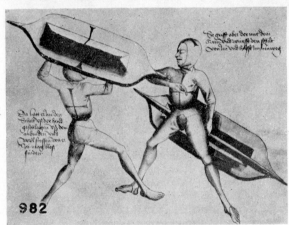

980. XVc. c. 1450. German-Swiss. (Metropolitan Museum, Print Room.)

Master E.S.

Sybil and the Emperor Augustus.

This plate is the early work of a German, probably from Strassburg, who seems to have been trained in the Upper Rhine or Switzerland under the influence of the Master of the Playing Cards.

Immense white turbans, striped across the weft in metal, neutral colors and black, are seen on German-Swiss tapestries of mid-XVc., worn with brocade gowns in bold color.

The sleeveless *sorket* is not much worn after mid-XVc.; this example shows the wide, over-long sleeve which becomes attached to the closed surcoat of last half XVc. German-Swiss necklines of mid-XVc. are inclined to square in some way, without actually being square. Front fullness begins high; it is gathered or loosely pleated into the neckline, and the gown is

immediately gored to great width. It may be belted high and bloused, full and loose, or it falls free in fantastic length and width. The front fullness tends to begin lower, as a panel of cartridge pleating, so that the upper bodice fits more closely. Meanwhile, the neck widens and rounds, exposing more shirt with its new embroidery; the skirt becomes more reasonable; but the sleeves grow longer and wider, and are often divorced from the material of the gown; they may be made of an entirely different material, or flow as a white shirt sleeve from a cap sleeve on the gown. (See Ills. 993, 994.)

Feet thrust into clogs, which are also worn by one of the men in the Master of the Playing Cards illustrations.

981. XVc. 1474. German. (Lubeck.)

Monumental brass:

John Luneborch, d.1474.

Lübeck, on the Baltic, one of the Free Cities and

head of the Hanseatic League, was governed by the aristocratic merchants who headed her great trading companies. Contact with Italy had spread over Europe such brocades as are used in this gown; typical of the fur-lined garments which developed out of the houppelande. Fine belt, with increasing numbers of handsome adjuncts.

982-83. XVc. 1467. Bohemian. (Duke of Saxe-Coburg-Gotha.)

Book of Fencing: *Code de Gotha* by *Hans Thalhofer*.

982. Fight with mace and special shield, in the combat called "The Judgment of God."

983. Fight with pole-hammer.

These illustrations, from a book of instruction in all methods of single combat by the master-at-arms, Thalhofer (fl.1443-67)), clearly shows the attachment by *points* of the shortening doublet to the lengthening hose, with their early form of cod-piece; "dressing left" or "right" was a late refinement of tailoring. In the battle with war-hammers we see sleeves set into a deep armseye, and carried almost to the collar-line, over the shoulder, after a German method of sleeve-cutting.

984-86. Last quarter XVc. German.

Housebook, by *The Master of the Housebook*.

No. 984 shows characteristically German form of women's dress of last quarter XVc.: very long and voluminous, fitting only around the shoulders; front fullness, loose or laid in cartridge pleats; sleeves tubular, but very wide and long, often gathered into armseye.

Increasing use of plumes: panache of horse, 984; male and female heads, 985-86.

Headdresses of wimple and coif are almost supplanted in Germany by last quarter XVc. by wound turban-like arrangements; often draped in spaghetti-like fringe (f. top, 985), which is also used on men's hats (bottom, 986); the ends of which are often individually knotted. A band under or around chin is often seen used by both men and women, particularly in German and Swiss examples: it is worn here (f. 986) and (984) by the man with cross-strapped pattens and short cape, the embroidered collar of which is set in (following the V-line which, in the jacket, used to permit the rise of the high doublet collar). Doublets are meanwhile becoming low-necked and laced across wide placards in the Italian manner. The horn player (bottom, right) shows trunks strapped under instep, to be worn with shoes.

985. Costume of mounted men shows the influence of neighboring Italy, but the Burgundian fashions also persist in the enormously long pointed shoes and pattens, and in the short, wide loose jackets (lapped over, as seen in Ills. 785-787, 873-876). New are the capes and hoods of women (see Ill. 867), here seen in a German form: buttoned hood and cape, showing new interest in centrally massed pleats. Knight being armed for the tilt shows decorative use of letters and mottos (see text, Ills. 976-79), on caparison of horse, shield, and guard worn on left leg to prevent its being crushed at the barrier; tilting lance and German tilting helm of end XV-early XVIc.; arm guarded by gauntlet. Persistence in Germany of slittering (trappings of horse, whose rider wears a short coat with embroidered revers or scarf). Garlands in male hair. (See Ill. 994.)

986. Top row: women riding astride (until well into XVIc.), with *gebende* turbans, or plumes in the hair arrangement. Fool with fife and drum.

Second row: male hat bound under the chin; jacket closed by knotted points. Knight tilting shows leg on right side, not requiring a guard; deflecting flanges of elbow-pieces; poulaine sollerets. Male hats: fringed; set-in crown on puffed turban; horsetail plume.

987. XVc. 1491. German. (Metropolitan Museum, Print Room.)

Der Schrein od' Schatzbehalten, Nuremberg, 1491, illustrated by *Michael Wohlgemut.*

Wohlgemut's woodcut is the first engraved representation of a coach (see Ill. 574); it is still much easier to turn the three horses than the rigid wheels.

The large turbaned and fur-brimmed hats worn indoors by women and men are exchanged, in travelling, for small hoods or hats over bound chins.

988. e. XVIc. German. (Brussels.)

Germanic Customs, in German.

989-90. 1494-5. German. (Frankfort-on-Main, Art Institute.)

Albrecht Dürer. Costumes of Nuremberg and Venice.

Dürer made his first Italian trip at 22; in other drawings of Venetian costume made on this trip (especially a front and back view, in the Albertina, Vienna) Dürer shows similar little flat hats set on the crown of a veiled head, with flowing locks in front of the ears; the same wide-necked, short-waisted bodice; longer and more elaborately cut out and puffed sleeves; the same two immense buttons closing the skirt front; and great feet in the bundled-up form of patten.

To his own observations during 6 years of travel in Europe in the last decade of the XVIc., the Englishman Fynes Moryson added in his "Itinerary"* a compendium of "the opinions of old writers": "In apparrell the Italian women are said to be neate and grave (only the Venetians shew their necks and breasts naked), the French light & variable, the Spaniards proud, the Germans foolish (perhaps be-

* Four vols., James MacLehose, for the Univ. of Glasgow, 1907.

cause they weare extremely straight sleeves on their armes, and guard one and the same gowne with many and divers coloured guards), the Flemmings fine (no doubt they, and especially the Brabanders, excell for white and fine linnen, and for generall comlines of their garments). The Spanish women are said to be painted, the Italians lesse painted, the French seldome painted, and sometimes the Germaine Virgins never that I observed (except those of Prussen have perhaps borrowed this vice from the Muscovites their neighbors)."

991. XVc. 1495-1500. German. (Vienna, Albertina.)

A. Dürer. Knight in armor on horseback.

Partially armed, with leather jerkin, hose, and sock-boots. Late XVc. salade, very much extended in back; monogrammed (reaching end of its use). Large pauldrons of late German Gothic armor, ribbed in the oncoming Maximilian style; plate protection of arms and of legs to knee only.

992. XVc. 1498. German. (Madrid, Prado.)

A. Dürer. Self-portrait at 26.

One of the handsomest of all pictures of the velvet-banded, German version of the Italian-inspired male dress of the turn of the century: gray, black, with gold-embroidered shirt.

More is shown, of a more beautifully pleated and embroidery-edged shirt, in Germany than anywhere else, whether its neckline rises into a standing collar of embroidery, or remains horizontal above a horizontal doublet neckline.

The extremely long hair which Dürer shows himself wearing for a decade or more is exceptional in Germany, and may be laid to the influence of his Italian trip.

993. Late XVc.-e. XVlc. German. (Dortmund, Propstei-Kirche.)

H. and V. Dunwege. Holy Kindred: altarpiece, wing.

Long, loose, full German gowns: variety of collars on rather high necklines; front fullness, from neck, or by inset cartridge pleats (in which case, belt hangs low, unrelated to the tacking which indicates natural waistline); long full sleeves. Headdresses of swathed turban type; or bound about, or falling over a swelling foundation.

994. End XVc. German. (Gotha Museum.)

Master of the Housebook, d.1505. Two Lovers.

Fine goldsmith's work fastens the rows of delicate chain, which maintain extremely wide neck-openings, and forms eyelets and tips for the cords at neck and sleeves lacings. These have replaced the important and precious belts of XIV-XVc.

Embroidery in red, black, gold or silver is used on the bateau necks of exquisitely pleated full skirts, and ladies' headdresses.

Italianate male costume, with flowing garlanded hair. Lady's sleeves, spreading wider to the wrist, would hang below the knees, and conceal the hands if not pushed up. The pink she holds is the sign of an engagement; if red, of a newly performed marriage, a favorite time for having portraits painted.

995.

995. End XVc. South German

Israhel van Meckenem, d.1503. The Feast of Herodias.

An immense mass of information about the transitional period in costume is given by this artist, who shows the influence of a stay in the Netherlands.

Arch, upper l.: Solider with pole-axe; doublet has appropriated the dependent sleeve of the jacket, in the form of completely unusable streamers, fastened beneath padded upper part of sleeve.

Gallery, l.: Men; buttoned hood; new slashed and laced bonnet.

Musicians, c.: All wear same livery badge; the new bonnets; new wide-toed shoes cut low around the heel; as well as old-fashioned poulaines. L.: interesting tight sleeve, of doublet-type, cut in one with dependent sleeve of jacket-type; slash exposing shirt at elbow. C.: horizontal slashes; long sleeve widening suddenly at cuff. R.: sleeve tight below elbow; full and slashed above, to show full puffed sleeve of shirt.

Balcony at r.: Man, new coat with lapels; long wrinkled tubular sleeves. M. (at r. edge) wears long coat, buttoned down back; separately cut skirt with clustered back-fullness; sleeve set in deep arms-eye.

Dancers, l. to r.: Ladies' gowns of 4 main types.

German: loose, with clustered cartridge pleats; long wide tubular sleeve on new coat with new lapelled fur collar; accompanied by turban.

Burgundian court: separate bodice and skirt; wide, low neck; important belt under breasts; accompanied by hennin.

German-Flemish: tight sleeves; long, wide opening laced across plastron; accompanied by a hennin, which is increasingly like a hood.

Flemish: separate bodice and skirt; relatively high necked; wide sleeves, showing undersleeves, and sometimes shirt-sleeves; belt not necessarily at waistline, and relatively less important than appended accessories.

Men, c. to r.: short Italianate jacket, sometimes with revers; laced or tied across plastron, which may be slashed. Shoes, pointed or with rounding toes.

996.

Codpiece, fastened with knotted points. Long gored coat, with deeply set in, wide sleeves.

996. XVc. S. German. (Metropolitan Museum, Print Room.)

Israhel van Meckenem. The Lovers.

Woman in much more bourgeois costume than any shown in previous illustrations. Enclosing headdress and gown with the new-lapped-over closing caught together with the new and exciting common pin. Her separate outer sleeve, set very low, is probably pinned on, too. Overskirt pinned up in front, probably permanently. (See *Roman de la Rose*: Ill 906.) Girdle hung with knife, pouch, and housewife's keys. Piked shoes and pattens, but her bedroom slippers, under the platform, have the newer round toe. Door latch closed by a knife, which everyone carries, and uses at table.

Culture Moves North: XVI Century

XVI Century Background

THE XVIc. was, like our own, a crucial century, during which the way of life of the next 350 years was established. It was a century of new freedoms, and of consolidation of power.

The discoveries of Africa, the New World, and ocean routes to the Far East coincided with the break-up of mediaeval restrictions. The religious and intellectual freedoms of the Reformation and increased literacy had been aided by the invention of printing.

The Black Death had doubled the wealth of the remaining population, and helped in the alteration of the old craft guilds into capitalist employers and traders belonging to the merchant livery companies, divided from the journeyman workers.

The increasing temporal power of the Papacy had a stabilizing effect. Rival city-states were welded into nations, with economies planned for commercial competition.

France, a howling wilderness at the end of the 100 Years War, recovered rapidly. An annual tax had been imposed by Jacques Coeur for the maintenance of Charles VII's standing army. The recalcitrant feudal nobility flocked to serve in the crown's cavalry, and were tied to the court for advancement. Henry IV used this regular income to improve internal communications, trade, industry and agriculture. The supremacy of the King was now well established, in a prosperous France.

The rulers of Spain, Portugal and the Empire made the mistake of deliberately hoarding, for their own aggrandizement, the riches brought by their explorations. While the condition of the lower classes was being improved elsewhere, their peoples were further repressed by inflation; the emigration of industry was not discouraged; and many valuable talents were lost, by persecution, to the Dutch. Repressive measures lost the Empire its possessions in the Low Countries, and its spectacular rise ended in failure.

The prosperity of Italy, South Germany and the Hanseatic cities was gone with the abandonment of the old Mediterranean trade routes from the Near East. Their bankers were weakened by their alliance, as money lenders, to the sterile financial policies of Spain and the Empire. The port of Antwerp took over the European distribution of goods brought from overseas by the Portuguese, until the calamities of 1585. By XVIIc. the Dutch, hospitable to refugees from Spanish persecution, controlled most of the profits of the Portuguese trade, and Amsterdam became a great industrial and commercial city.

The English, lacking the overseas riches of Spain, carefully developed their modest natural resources and their talents of seamanship, and encouraged the establishment of manufactures by refugee technicians, as the Dutch had done. Under the capitalism which Spain had rejected, her Protestant enemies throve and outdistanced her.

Development of Dress: German-Swiss Influence, 1510-1545

The Italian influences of end XVc. are superseded in e. XVIc. by German-Swiss fashions; these, in turn, give way to Spanish styles, toward mid-XVIc.

The slashed and puffed square width of German-Swiss costume influenced male garments, in particular, and invaded even gloves and shoes. English costume makes the least use of patterned materials, striped and slashed hose.

Men's Dress: The doublet and jerkin remain short-waisted, close-fitting, and difficult to differentiate. The low neck of the doublet rises and squares, finally assuming a collar. Sleeves are wide and slashed, but close at the wrist, and tend to separate into upper and lower divisions, analogous to those of the hose. *Picadils*: tabbed edge, below waist, or around armseye, last half XVIc. Jerkin, sleeved or not, assumes a square collar with notched lapels. *Bases* shorten and become less rigid. Gowns are of various lengths, with sleeves like those of jerkins; there are few cloaks.

The shirt's neckline rises, assumes a collar and delicate cord ties; the collar heightens, turns over, and takes on a gauffered edge, from which the Elizabethan ruff will develop.

Hose are divided into upper- and nether-stocks: i.e. breeches or *canions* (much slashed and puffed); and stockings (seldom so decorated, except among the Swiss soldiers); fastened together. Codpieces, *braguettes,* are increasingly evident. Garters appear; less practical than decorative.

Shoes: the short, wide, backless slippers become narrower, rounder and higher at the instep; slashed and jewelled.

The square-pinched, biretta-like bonnets, and caps, soon become relegated to the use of scholars and ecclesiastics and the elderly. They are supplanted by flat-brimmed, plumed bonnets; the plumes become reduced in number, and the nicked brim tends to droop, as it becomes narrower.

Bobbed hair commences to be cropped in the French manner, about 1520; and men, formerly clean-shaven, begin to wear moustaches and beards, which become square and wide; then lengthen.

With the increasing use of swords and daggers, diagonally slung, in the everyday dress of gentlemen, there is a decrease in the importance of chains, which tend to become cords or scarves, carrying a pendant. Increasing use of precious tags, *aiglettes; rings.*

Women's Dress: Women's gowns changed little until end first quarter XVc., and were less affected by German ways than men's clothing. Necklines arch and rise into yokes, and to high collars, c. 1540, when shoulder capes with collars appear, especially in Germany.

Outer sleeves widen into a great funnel, with a fur lining turned back into a cuff. Undersleeves are frequently interchangeable and have finished edges, instead of an outerseam, tied at intervals across puffs of shirtsleeves. The shirt collar rises, assuming a pleated edge; and shoes alter their form, parelleling male usages.

The skirt becomes of ground length, bell-shaped; and towards end first half XVIc. takes on an inverted-V front opening.

Hair retains its center front part, under regionally differentiated hoods, and the caps of Germany, Italy and Spain.

Goldsmiths' work appears in many, dependent forms: girdles, at hip line, with hanging pomanders; fur pieces with jewelled snouts and claws; aiglets.

DEVELOPMENT OF DRESS: SPANISH INFLUENCE, 1545-1610

The rigid and formal fashions of Spain begin to affect all European dress, after first third XVIc. The somber colors of the early part of the period become paler and brighter at the end. Lace is introduced into France from Italy in 1533 by Catherine de' Medici; its use increases enormously. Male costume seems effeminate, as women's clothing grows more masculine.

Male: Collars mount; waists lengthen, becoming corset-like with stiffenings. Padding, *bombast,* al-

ters the form of the torso into the *peascod* belly of the last quarter XVIc., accepted by both doublet and jerkin.

Sleeves, with *picadills* or a roll at the armseye, remain close, may have a dependant sleeve, and are supplemented by swelling leg-o'-mutton forms in last quarter XVIc.

Skirts of body garments diminish to picadills, as the upper hose shorten and are hugely padded at the hips, with their outer fabric vertically slit into *panes.* There are also loose, unpadded forms of upper hose, usually longer (*slops, galligaskins*). Close-fitting knee-breeches, *canions,* which extend below trunk-hose (trunk slops, round hose, French hose) appear; as do other forms of breeches, caught at the knee (*venetians*); or cut off like our shorts. Codpiece disappears during last quarter XVIc.

Slashing appears in small formal patterns, or long slits, *panes.* It is much used on leather: buff military jerkins; long, close, laced or buckled boots, and shoes are cut in tiny punctured (*pinked*) patterns.

Many capes are used; long and short; with and without sleeves. Gowns of all lengths. A tabard-like jacket called *mandilion* is often worn slung across the body.

Knit stockings come into use and are clocked, by last quarter XVIc. Garters become more elaborate.

Shoes, natural in form, cover the instep; frequently light in color. In last quarter XVIc. a tongue develops, under straps from ankle, laced across instep through eyelets; from the bow develops a ribbon rosette, later made of lace. Slippers are worn indoors, and mules, *pantoufles,* protect the shoe outdoors. Cork platforms rise in thickness under the heel; in last quarter XVIc., heels appear on shoes for the first time, and toes begin to square.

The gathered or fluted edge of the turned-down collar (*falling band*), is elaborated into many forms of pleated, starched and wired ruffs, which tend to fall again in first quarter XVIIc.; matching bands or ruffles at wrist.

Hats vary enormously in form and by country. The gathered crown of the flat hat rises, often to great height, as its brim diminishes. Broad-brimmed felt hats appear, as well as the tiny turbans of the French court. Emphasis on hat band.

Cropped hair lengthens, end XVIc. Beards commonly worn; variety of forms in last quarter XVIc. Guarded rapier is slung from a narrow flexible belt. Gauntlet gloves common, last quarter XVIc.

Masks worn. Men's ears pierced for one or two earrings. Much jewelry.

Female: Women's costume, like men's, is characterized by higher necklines, longer and more rigid bodies, padded hips, and the use of picadills and rolls.

The bodice is increasingly pointed at the bottom, and corset-like. Arched square of bosom filled with high-necked tucker; finished by a ruff, last half XVIc. Bare bosom, without tucker, last half XVIc.

The turned-back funnel sleeve is discarded, last half XVIc. All varieties of male sleeves are worn by women. The close sleeve of last quarter XVIc. may have a high, wide top. The hanging sleeve of end XVI-e.XVIIc. is elaborately shaped, slashed and trimmed; the under sleeve, in this case, matches the underskirt.

One-piece gowns, open, coat-like, and masculine, worn by upper classes. Similarly cut short jackets for outdoor wear.

Skirts, funnel-shaped, frequently with inverted V-opening; supported by Spanish farthingale, *vertugale,* last half XVIc., which aids display of pattern of underskirt. French roll support at hips, last quarter XVIc. alters silhouette from cone to wide cylinder. Ankle-length skirt worn around turn of century.

The French hood flattens across the top, then dips in the center. Its fall, when gauzy, is seen elaborately wired to frame the face. Bonnets and hats, identical with men's, much favored; small caps on the back of the head, last half XVIc., as hair tends to be dressed over rolls.

The hair at first mounts on either side of the part. Then the part is abandoned, as padding increases to an extent requiring the aid of artificial hair, in e.XVIIc. Pearls, jewels and feathers decorate the front expanse of hair; the back is reduced to a knot covered by a caul, to avoid interference with the high ruffs. With XVIIc. the hair at the sides tends to fall in loose locks.

The high-collared tucker opens and begins to spread in last half XVIc. As the tucker is reduced or abolished, the collar increases in width and height, and is starched or wired into a fan framing the face, or is drawn close about the neck in a cartwheel ruff, often seen above a bare bosom.

In Italy, necklines are generally lower, outside regions dominated by Spain, and the bodice is often padded into the male *peascod* belly of late XVIc.

Shoes, slippers and pantoufles like male varieties, but seldom seen.

Increased use of cosmetics and lace; pearls and earrings, hanging pomanders and mirrors; lace-edged handkerchiefs, masks; gloves, muffs; fur skins and scarves.

DEVELOPMENT OF GERMAN REGIONAL DRESS: XVIc.

The crown of Germany had never been entirely hereditary. The emperor king was also chosen by regional rulers: originally the Archbishops of Mainz, Trier, and Cologne, the King of Bohemia, the King of Bavaria who was also the Count Palatine of the Rhine, the Duke of Saxony, and the Margrave of Brandenburg. During the XIIIc. interregnum, the princely families tended to subdivide into endless small principalities, allotted at the will of the regional rulers. From the time of the Golden Bull of 1335, the power of the Electors increased, over both the Emperor, and the non-electoral cities and princes. Germany was thus prevented from being united, as France had been, with the waning of feudal power, by her kings from Louis XI to Louis XIV.

In the course of the XVIc., bourgeois costume, particularly that of women, becomes strongly differentiated by provinces, even by cities, forming the basis for later regional peasant costume. As everybody climbs the ladder socially, the bourgeoisie tend to become gentry, and their codified costume is taken over by the well-to-do peasantry. The regional styles of their people are worn by rulers, upon occasion or in partial form. (See Ill. 1003, and Spanish, end XVc.)

German regional dress is a very complicated subject, best covered by Hottenroth: *Handbuch der Deutchen Tracht,* Stuttgart, 1892-6. His material was taken principally from Jost Amman; D. Meisner's *Cosmographia,* 1606; Vecellio's *Hab. ant. & mod.,* 1590; and Winkler's *Stammbuch.*

Fynes Moryson's *Itinerary,* vol. IV, p. 204-18, describes the costume of Germany, Switzerland, the Low Countries, Bohemia, Poland and Denmark in 1591-5; and p. 217-38, the dress of Italy, France, Turkey, Scotland, Ireland and England.

The ways of regional costume are like the spot-patterns of insect species: they spread and alter gradually across plains and waterways, cross with new-met forms, and are stopped abruptly by natural barriers. A brief summary can only be rough and full of contradictions, as a century of time works its changes. But as a biologist's child, who was called upon to make a good many such charts during childhood, I have found it very interesting to spot each appearance of certain characteristics, in the illustrations of this century, on sheer tracings which could be set over a map, and to see how they filtered or stopped on the expected geographical basis.

Speaking, then, very roughly, we can say that fine pleating is seen in a great semi-circle running from Holland, through Lippe, Frankfort and Franconia, Bavaria (Nuremberg), and Saxony (Meissen), and into Silesia. In Nuremberg and Meissen it is used in the greatest quantities, on both capes and upper skirts of plain material, which at Nuremberg are often caught up in front. At the lower part of this swinging geographical line, pleating is often combined with headdresses bound around the chin.

Nuremberg shows wide, square necks, which tend to become filled in with gathered shirts and yokes; and, around first third XVIc., great cartwheel hats, the brims of which are often edged with ostrich plumes. These hats, with segmented color, or regularly caught decoration around the brim, are worn later, in a somewhat smaller form, in the middle Rhine Valley, around Frankfort, Heidelberg, and the Palatine.

The *heuke,* a cape flowing from the crown of the head and covering the body, is characteristic of the Low Countries, and is worn east to Bremen (where it is seen in the greatest variety, both of cape and top). In its pleated form, it is seen from Antwerp, up the Rhine and Main to Frankfort, and at Bremen. Its plain form appears from Holland to Bremen, and up to Cleves and Cologne. Something usually projects from the top of the *heuke.* On the plain cape, in Holland, Cleves, and Bremen, it was a long duck-bill in front; at Bremen, a long horn, curving upward, is set at the forehead of a pleated cape. A plate with a standing, tufted knob is set over both plain and pleated capes at Bremen; this plate follows the westward bend of the Wesser, and goes on to Cologne. There are also forms like inverted bowls with spikes. The edges of the *heuke* are wired out, in Belgium and Cologne, during the last half XVIc.

At Lippe, Westphalia, Frankfort, and east into Silesia, aprons are often finely pleated; but the aprons of the Rhine Valley are narrow strips, partly tucked in at the belt, in such a way that the corners stick out free below the waistline. At Heidelberg, the apron is folded lengthwise, and then in four sections across, the ironed creases utilized as decoration, as is sometimes done on white Flemish hoods. Both aprons and skirts are embroidered, or made of brocade or velvet to match the bodice, as well as made of linen.

Around Frankfort and in Westphalia the shoulder capes of Holland are much seen; in the Palatinate and the Alsatian side of the Rhine, short flaring jackets are worn with tiny plumed male bonnets and bell-shaped skirts without waist-fullness, often of brocade; like the Spanish coat-dress, these come into more general use, last quarter XVIc.

The yoked and often laced bodice runs from the Low Countries up the Rhine to Switzerland; through Frankfort, where its front decoration stresses a vertical or cross, rather than a horizontal, line; up into Westphalia and across to Saxony.

The furred and collared garments of Slavic costume affect clothing in the Baltic, Silesia, Bohemia, Austria and Bavaria, particularly at Salzburg and Augsburg: V-necks with wide-spreading revers running into high collars; fur-lined capes and jackets with great wide collars; wide headwear, often of fur; chins, ears and foreheads banded against the cold; full skirts; and, since this is the outer edge of the area in which pleating is much used, we find pleated skirts, capes, and aprons. Sheer pleating seems to replace fur, where warmth is no longer an absolute necessity, but where fashions are influenced by full, warm garments and the bulk and shagginess of fur.

The most common sleeve has a mounting cap at the shoulder, usually cut in one with the sleeve. This cap sleeve is sometimes pendant, especially at Augsburg; it is often cut off just below the shoulder, the lower sleeve being extremely close and of another material. The high cap is not often seen, however, with the square-necked bodices, and is less frequent with the V-necked, high-collared varieties. These bodices of the southeast usually have a dropped shoulder-line, finished to match the collar edge; and an under-sleeve of a different material, which if white, often emerges, full, from beneath the cap, and is gathered in again below the elbow into a tight forearm; this, if close fitting, is apt to be ornamented from the cuff-line. The bell-sleeve of XV-e.XVIc., beloved of Flanders, persisted longest in the costume of Cologne.

Moryson, late in the XVIc., found the Germans "of all . . . Nations least expencefull in apparrell, whether a man consider the small prices of their garments, or their long lasting. . . . Citizens and men of inferior ranke, weare coarse cloth of Germany, and only the richer sort use English cloth; and this cloth is commonly of a blacke or darke colour, and they think themselves very fine, if their cloakes have a narrow facing of silk or velvet. . . . The Gentlemen delight in light colours . . . and Italian silkes and velvets, but most commonly English cloth, for the most part of yellow or green colour." Swords (worn by gentlemen and doctors of civil law) "have plaine pommels to them, never gilded; and the scabbards (not excepting the Emperour) are alwaies of leather. . . . The Saxons instead of Swords carry Hatchets in their hands . . . and weare hanging daggers with massy sheathes of silver or iron." German men wore "shirt bands of coarse linnen, short and thicke, onely in Prussia I observed them to weare long ruffs, with rebatoes of wire to bear them up . . . but seldom made of fine . . . cambrick or lawne, but of their owne coarse linnen, such as I have often seene the Spaniards to weare. . . ." German "handkerchers are very large, and wrought with silke of divers light colours, with great letters signifying words . . . so as they seem more like wrought saddle clothes, than handkerchers."

The richest apparel in Germany Moryson found in Danzig, where men and women "without any decent distinction of degrees" wore silk and velvet; "and the women seem much prouder of apparrell than the men. . . . Daughters of Citizens and Merchants, as well married as unmarried . . . did weare chains of Pearle, worth 300-500 gulden" and "short cloakes . . . of silke or satten . . . and that of changeable or light colours with Petticoats and Aprons of like colours, but not so frequently of silke; and I have seene Virgines of ordinary ranke . . . daily weare Silke stockings."

Moryson found that German matrons in general wore high-necked gowns, very short ruffs set with "poking sticks as small as reedes," and little hats.

Virgins wore close linen sleeves, "for they esteem it the greatest grace to have the smallest armes, and their petticoates are guarded with some ten or more fringes or laces of silk or velvet, each fringe being of a different colour one from the other . . . as variable . . . as the Raine-bow."

"Citizens' wives put off their ruffes when they goe out of the house, covering their neckes and mouthes with a linen cloth for feare of cold, and they weare great heavy purses by their sides with great bunches of keyes hanging by chaines of brasse or silver; and all generally, as well married women as Virgines, goe with bare legges; and I have seene a Virgine in Saxony, refuse a paire of silke stockings offered her of gift; and the maide servants and married women of the inferior sort weare no shooes except they goe out of the house, and a great part goe also abroade bare footed.

"The married women hide their naked feete with long gownes, but the maide servants wear short gownes, and girding them up into a roule some handfull under the wast about their hippes (especially in the lower parts of Germany) many times offend chast eyes with shewing their nakednesse, especially when they stoope for anything . . . and in those parts of Germany, the Citizens' wives, like our little children, weare red and yellow shooes, and guilded at the toes.

"In generall, it is disgracefull to married women or Virgines (excepting at Augsburg, and some other few cities) to goe out of doores without a cloake, which commonly is of some light stuffe, as Grogram, or the like, faced with some furres, and at Heidelberg they never goe abroade without a little basket in their hands, as if they went to buy something, except they will be reputed dishonest."

Married women's heads are always covered, with a piece of velvet, hat or cap, "according to the use of the Countrey, and very many weare such crosse-clothes or forehead clothes as our women use when they are sicke.

"In many places the ordinary Citizens' wives have their gownes made with long traines, which are pinned up in the house, and borne up by maid servants when they goe abroad, which fashion of old onely great Noblemen used with us: And in many cities, aswel the married as unmarried Women, weare long fardingales, hanging about their feete like hoopes, which our Women used of olde, but have changed to short fardingales about their hippes."

Moryson remarks on the sober-colored or black garments of the Netherlands, and the extremely fine linen. "All women in generall, when they goe out of the house, put on a hoyke or vaile which covers their heads, and hangs down upon their backs to their legges. The vaile in Holland is of a light stuffe or Kersie, and hath a kind of horne rising over the forehead, not much unlike the old pommels of our Womens saddles, and they gather the Vaile with their hands to cover all their faces, but onely the eyes: but the women of Flanders and Brabant weare Vailes altogether of some light fine stuffe, and fasten them about the hinder part and sides of their cap, so as they hang loosely, not close to the body, and leave their faces open to view, and those Caps are round, large, and flat to the head, and are in forme like our potlids . . . used in the Kitchin; And these women, aswel for these Vailes, as their modest garments . . . and for their pure and fine linen, seemed to me more fair than any other Netherlanders, as indeed they are generally more beautiful."

Swiss citizens wear "large, round caps" like those of English 'prentices, together with cloaks, "whereas with us they are onely used with gownes, yea, and Swords also (which seemed strange to be worn with caps)." He describes their loose, vari-colored pluderhose. "The married Women cover their heads with a linnen coyfe, and upon it weare such caps as the men do (which are broader than we used in England) and commonly weare a linnen crossecloth upon the forehead. . . . The Virgins goe bareheaded with their haire woven up, and used short cloakes. . . . All . . . are apparrelled like the Germans, and affect nothing lesse then pride in their attire."

The Bohemians dress like the Germans, "and delight in greene, yellow, and light colours, but more frequently weare silkes and velvets than the Germans, and also false jewels of their owne." They also wear black cloth "with many laces and fringes of light colours, each fringe differing in colour." Prague draws so many foreign ambassadors and Italian merchants, that "the Bohemians are more infected with forraigne fashions, than the Germans. The married Gentlewomen attire their heads like our Virgines, and in like sort beare up their haire on the forehead with a wier." Like Germans, they wear short cloaks, long farthingales, and trains. "Citizens wives weare upon their heads large gray caps, rugged like gray Connie skinnes, and formed like the hives of Bees, or little caps of velvet close to the head, of a dunne colour, with the hinder skirt (or hinderpart) cut off and open. And upon their legges they weare white buskins, wrought with velvet at the toes; but upon their armes they wear large sleeves, and contrary to the Germans, thinke them to be most comely."

By late XVIc. few German men or women "weare gold rings, pearles, or Jewels: but Bohemia yields false stones like the oriental precious stones, yet of small or no value"; (garnets, and the glass which they had learned from Venice to manufacture in the XIIIc.; we get from them our stones for theatrical jewelry today). Moryson was shocked to find gentlemen wearing these false stones and rings of gold-washed brass. Women were seldom permitted chains, but "their Earles (vulgarly called Graves) and their Knights, sometimes weare gold chains, made of extraordinary great linkes, and not going more then once about the necke, nor hanging downe further then the middle button of the doublet."

997. XVIc. German-Bavarian.

Master M. Z.

Dancing party.

This S. German engraving shows both types of male costume of the Transition period: newer, squarer, fur-collared garments; and the slender Italianate forms, with capes, circular or with dependent points, and trunk-like patterns differentiating top and leg of hose.

Elaborate puffing and slashing have invaded both m. and f. garments; but as yet, only on the exaggeratedly long, narrow sleeves. Both sexes wear the slashed bonnet, over hair done up in caul caps or flowing.

In Germany and the Netherlands, ladies' gowns will presently lose their trains, as they have already lost their loose fullness; they will retain their high-belted, widely cut bodice, though this will tend to be filled in with yokes (notice strap across back of shoulders, f., l. center); and the swelling headdresses worn well back on the head.

Shoes: round-toed, still ankle-high, slashed and tied. Beards.

998-99. First quarter XVIc. Alsatian.
(Morgan Lib., M. 399.

Illuminated manuscript.
998. Gentry of Strassburg.
999. Peasants of Strassburg.

1000. XVIc. c. 1506. German.
(Brunswick, Ducal Mus.)

Lower Saxon School: altarpiece.
Mocking of Christ: detail of
center panel.

1001. XVIc. 1500-5. Dutch or Flemish. (Metropolitan
Museum.)

Unknown artist. Magdalena van Werdenberg, wife
of Jan, Count of Egmont.

Black and white costume of great distinction, in
velvet and the finest possible ermine. Simple Flemish
hood. The inner sleeve is rather loose and the shirt
sleeves are pushed up into transverse wrinkles; not
directed by the inner sleeve into becoming wrist
ruffles.

Balthazar Behem. The Behem Codex. XVIc. Polish.
(Cracow, Jagellonian Univ. Library.) Four plates from
the Behem Codex, the regulations of the guilds of Cracow,
were reproduced in color in "Vogue," for Dec. 1947;
therefore we merely indicate these easily available and
extremely valuable plates. They show the workrooms of
the artist's, shoemaker's, tailor's and cabinet maker's
guild members, with the tailors fitting customers, and the
shoemaker's wife taking the apprentice boys' mind off
their work.

1001

1002. First quarter XVIc. Flemish. (Metropolitan Museum, Bache Collection.)

Gerard David.

Nativity: side panel.

St. Vincent, in the robes of a deacon, stands behind the donatrice, whose coronet is set on her black Flemish hood. Orange-brown and silver brocade gown shows the convexly rising neckline, largely filled in, though not completely yoked in black velvet. The widening red inner sleeve, which funnels from the short sleeve-cap, originated from the white sleeve of the shirt.

1003. XVIc. 1502. German. (Meissen.) Monumental Brass.

Amelia, Duchess of Bavaria.

Costume of a widow of Meissen; bound head and chin; pleated cape with wide hanging bands.

1004. XVIc. 1517. German. (Meissen.) Monumental Brass.

Frederick, Duke of Saxony.

The breastplate of the bearded duke shows the fan-shaped flutings of the transitional period between Gothic and Maximilian armor; lengthening laminated tassets; broad toed sabatons; cross of Teutonic Knight on mantle.

1005-06. XVIc. 1504. German. (Frankfort-on-Main, Stadel Inst.)

J. Ratgeb. Claus and Margaret Stalburg.

1002

1003

1004

Claus' beaver is pinched into the angular shape seen in Flanders and W. Germany; it is worn at an angle, when set over a coif.

His rosary includes a pomander: *"pomme d'ambre"* (apple of ambergris)—a hinged, pierced ball, holding solidified perfume based on ambergris, civet or musk; used by both men and women, particularly in XV-XVIIc., to ward off infection or bad odors. In similar manner, Cardinal Wolsey held a clove-stuck orange during audiences.

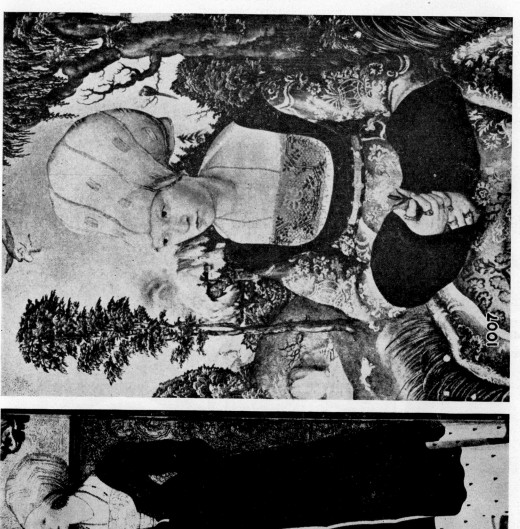

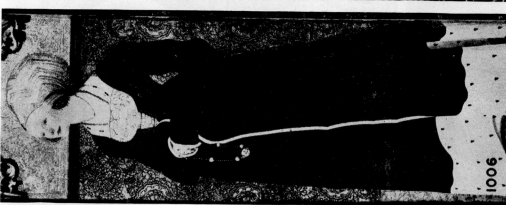

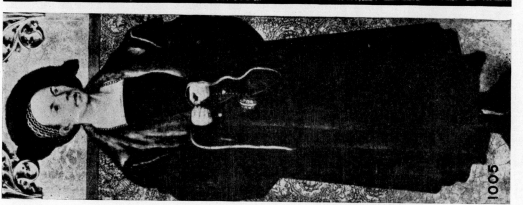

The gowns of the Cuspinian and Stalburg ladies are specifically German: extremely long, narrow sleeves; short-waisted, widely cut-out bodice, filled in by a plastron of magnificent and often jewelled embroidery, which is held in place by a scarf across the back of the neck; skirt of the new ground length. In the case of Margaret, this is extended into the bodice, the laced closing of which will be retained in the regional costume of German peasants to our day, though ousted by the Spanish styles of the gentry in third quarter XVIc.

The headdresses are also typical of Germany. Over jewelled cauls at the ears, embroidered gauze is drawn across the forehead and about the bulbous cap, set far back in the head.

1007. XVIc. 1502-3. German. (Winterthur, Coll. O. Reinhart.)

Lucas Cranach. Anna Cuspinian, née Putsch.

1008

Anna was the wife of Dr. Johannes Cuspinian, physician, scholar and rector of the University of Vienna, of whom there is a companion picture in the same collection.

In the background are a fire, a falcon, heron and parrot, symbols of her birth under the zodiacal sign of Sol.

Her rings (now worn on thumb as well) are more elaborate than those shown in English portraits. German belts, worn high, have fine buckles and are without pendants.

1008. XVIc. c. 1508. Flemish. (The Louvre.)
Gerard David.
Marriage at Cana.
Picture packed with details of Flemish costume and Italianate influences during the first decade XVIc.

A. Male donor in the usual long, richly bordered or fur-lined gown.

B. Jewelled fillet over flowing hair of a maiden. Gown seen in so many Spanish-Italian portraits of late XV-e.XVIc.: brocade, with tied-on brocade sleeves, cut out and laced across a great spill of white, embroidered shirt sleeve.

C., H., M. Dark Franco-Flemish hoods in various stages of development. The raked-back curves (M) of the later French hood are being evolved here by turning back the top of a narrow, straight-falling hood (C) to show the rich materials of its lining, under-cap, and the pleated or quilted gold gauze of still another cap beneath. As the hood tends to become more enclosing, its skirts are slashed at the shoulder (H) to form lappets (which will eventually come to be pinned up); brooch on falls.

D. Asymmetrical or lapped-over closings (see end XVc., Ill. 996: The Lovers) of jerkin; repeated lines of velvet trim, and shirt bosom smocked and embroidered into fine pleating (Ill. 992, Dürer: Self-portrait, 1498). Hair bound into a netted caul or turban.

E. Italianate garments; pleated shirt-front; hair cut in bangs across forehead.

F. Jerkin with carefully pleated skirts; shoe very much cut away, and strapped across instep.

G. Donor with rosary, in the white Flemish hood, which dips characteristically in the middle, and is folded and pinned or tied into shape at the nape, as the Franco-Flemish velvet hood will be. Wide-sleeved, fur-lined Flemish gown, with a convex neckline almost entirely filled in with black velvet.

I. Sheer gauze, treated like a white Flemish hood.

J. Lingering effects of the old horned and heart-shaped headdresses in veil drawn down to the forehead between knobs of hair (see Ill. 741: Barbara of Brandenburg; Gonzaga family). Alternative neckline, edged with embroidered bands, and filled with a fine white shirt (men D. and E.).

K. Bride with the ceremonious mediaeval cloak (see Ill. 529: Uta) caught by a cord between jewelled rosettes, over a contemporary Flemish fur-lined gown.

L. Turban, asymmetrically bound with narrow braid.

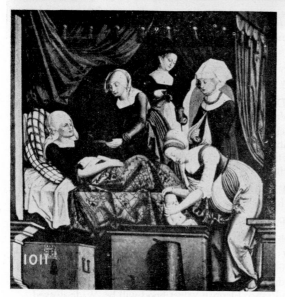

1009. XVIc. German. (Vienna, Coll. Baron van der Elst.)
Master of Frankfort, fl. 1490-15.

The Artist and his Wife.

The painter wears the beaver hat and flowing curls seen in Housebook illustrations (984-86), his wife a form of the béguine headdress. A rectangle of linen which has been folded is set so that the crease forms a dip over the forehead; the sides are crossed and pinned on either side; the back, which is often laid in careful folds, here falls free; and the hood is decorated with a pin in the form of an insect.

1010. XVIc. 1503. German. (Metropolitan Museum, Print Room.)

A. Dürer.

Coat of arms with skull.

The most wonderful of all flamboyant German

crests and shields, using the wild man's staff as supporter. Gown and crown seen in the illustrations of wedding parties and festivities at Nuremberg. (See Appendix.)

1011. First quarter XVIc. German. (Nuremberg, Germanic Mus.)

H. S. von Kulmbach. The Birth of the Virgin (lower half of panel).

1012. XVIc. 1504-5. German.

Albrecht Dürer. Espousal of the Virgin.

As in Ill. 1011, an attendant wears the great banded coif and pleated, low-necked mantle of the church-going dress of Dürer's native Nuremberg.

By the technique of their manufacture, straw hats are, of all head-coverings, the most hat-like in the

modern sense (see Color Plate, No. 3). Felt hats of analogous form will appear, last quarter XVIc.

1013. First quarter XVIc. Flemish. (Minneapolis, Inst. of Arts.) Tapestry.

Prodigal Son.

Bonnets, slashed, bound and plumed more extravagantly in Flanders and Germany than elsewhere, are worn by the gentlemen; set or tied over other bonnets, caps, flowing hair, or swelling turbans of the f. type.

The ladies wear bonnets of the m. type, set on hoods or twisted turban. Hoods have side flaps pinned up, and the back curtain brought over the crown of the head in a stiffened brim.

The men's doublets and wide-collared cloaks are of the below-knee length of first quarter XVIc. Dependent lower sleeve almost severed (m. at ext. l.) .

Use of knots, cords and tassels on pouches, girdles, necklaces and bonnets. Dagger.

Shoes: squarer toes, lower cut, held in place by ties across instep.

1014-1018. XVIc. 1507-12. German. (Berlin, Kaiser Friedrich Museum.)

Hans Baldung.

Adoration of the Magi.

Baldung worked in the Upper Rhine, at Strassburg and Freiburg.

At end XVc. armor tends to lose its fine Gothic form; it swells and widens, and takes on some attributes of contemporary male costume. Its surface is richly decorated by fluting, engraving, and combinations of metal colors. The breastplate of Maximilian armor becomes globular and short-waisted. The pauldrons enlarge and sweep across the breast and shoulderblades; a high collar of plate is added. The skirt of tassets becomes hippy and short-waisted, as it lengthens and encloses the thigh. The great helm is supplanted by visored armets. Sabatons take the form of the broad-toed shoe. The knight's sword and its hilt lengthen; its quillens widen.

Over his breastplate, used as a placard, the knight (l.) wears a pourpoint cut in one with its circular skirts. Beards, moustaches; separately or together.

The small caps of German ladies, like the bonnets of the men, are sharply tilted over left ear when worn with a netted caul; set level when the natural hair is exposed.

Braid is used on the sleeves and yokes of these gowns, in the diagonal patterns which we have seen, since the late XVc., on cloaks with dependent points, like that of the Negro king in finely striped tights.

G. van der Weyden.

Altarpiece; with donors: Arnold von Löwen and wife, Elizabeth von Breda.

The arms of the donors hang in the trees and appear on the sleeved surcoat of the knight (*Löwen*—lion), and on the mantle which his lady wears over her Flemish gown; identical, except for the lacings, with those of the XVc. R. van der Weyden portraits.

1020. XVIc. Before 1511. German.
        (Colmar Museum.)

Matthias Grünewald.

The Isenheim Altarpiece.

The garments shown on biblical characters in religious paintings are not always strictly contemporary. But the design which Grünewald, born in the Palatinate, gives to the mantle (which the f. ext. l. wears over her banded headdress) would seem to have been influenced, in its form, by the "heuke" of Holland and the Lower Rhine, and in its horizontal lines, by the banded fur cloaks of northern Germany.

1021-22. XVIc. Dutch. (Metropolitan Museum.)
Lucas van Leyden.

1021. The Milkmaid (1510).
1022. The Bagpiper (1520).

Barefoot women, with hose-like long drawers, beneath short, tucked-up kirtles. Loose hose of bagpiper, gartered, with sock-boots.

1023-26. XVIc. 1514. German. (Metropolitan Museum.)
Albrecht Dürer. Rustics.

Elastic as the hose of the standard-bearer appear, they are still cut from fabric. Knitting seems to have begun in late XVc., but the techniques of stocking knitting took about half a century to develop. Spanish or Italian stockings were occasionally seen in England before the mid-XVIc., but they remained a luxury until the invention of the stocking frame in 1589. Stubbes is indignant, in 1583, because "cloth (though neuer so fine) is thought too base," and people pay half a year's wages for a pair of stockings, "for how can they be lesse" (than a ryall, or 20 shillings) "when as the very knitting of them is worth a noble or a ryall."

The Swiss and German mercenary soldiers adopted and helped to spread the slashed and plumed style, of which we see the beginnings here.

Like the milkmaid and the bagpiper's wife (above), the dancing peasant woman wears a headdress of some pretensions; pleated apron, hung around the neck; pouch, knife, and keys at waist. Country men in hoods (which only they retain), pouches and knives, tattered hose and worn-soled boots.

1027. XVIc. c. 1515. German. Franconian. (Lichtenstein, Schloss Lichtenstein.)

Unknown artist.

Beheading of John the Baptist.

The soldier wears low-cut, square-toed black shoes and knotted garters; with yellow garments, diagonally slashed and puffed over black, and caught by black knots. White-plumed red hat slung over shoulders by knotted scarves. Short, square beard with moustache. Older man wears long rose gown, with brown fur collar and bonnet.

The lady holding the salver wears a brown skirt with a gold-embroidered, dark brown velvet bodice and sleeves, exposing much puffed shirt; slightly dependent belt, carrying a netted pouch and a case of toilet articles. White gauze drawn around white cap, embroidered in gold.

1028. XVIc. 1514. German. (Dresden, Picture Gallery.)

Lucas Cranach, elder.

Duke Henry the Pious.

Early in XVIc. Luther's friend, Cranach, became court painter to the Elector of Saxony. As perquisites, he was given a number of profitable monopolies. Painters were a variously gifted lot in those days; when an artist prepared his own colors, they were all chemists. Cranach was the proprietor of the only apothecary's shop allowed in Wittenburg; it remained in business until it burned in 1871. He was also given patents in printing, and sole rights to the sale of bibles.

The Lutheran duke, who succeeded his Catholic brother, and was the father of Maurice, the Elector of Saxony, wears a completely slashed costume: brocade-lined gown, doublet and upper hose, confined at the knee by embroidered, fringed garters, *krantz* wreath of dark and light carnations; heavy rope collar with pendant of clasped hands; continuously

linked collar of ribbon gold; huge jewelled pomegranate pendants finish the short sleeve of his gown; seal and other important rings; shell-decorated sword hilt and dog collar.

Moryson says everyone but "Virgines of inferiour sort, or Gentlewomen" who "weare a border of pearle," from the highest to the lowest, commonly "wear garlands of roses (which they call Crantzes)," worn only by women in winter; "but in Summertime men of the better sort weare them within doores, and men of the common sort weare them going abroade." He describes the method in which the rosebuds, damask for smell and others for color, are kept fresh all winter: laid in layers of rows on bay salt, sprinkled with Rhine wine, sealed with lead and kept in a cool, dark cellar; freshened with lukewarm water and Rhine wine for color, and rosewater for smell.

1029. XVIc. German. (Metropolitan Museum.)

Bartel Beham.

Leonardt von Eck.

The Bavarian Chancellor wears a scarlet judicial coif, pleated shirt with a ruffle-edged standing collar, and a full, low-necked beige gown, the cut of its sleeves providing fullness above the elbow, but on the outer part of the sleeve only.

1030. XVIc. German. (Munich, Alte Pinakothek.)

Hans Baldung.

Count Palatine Philip of Baden. Nowhere is body-linen now more beautifully embroidered than in Germany; Philip's shirt shows the standing collar which will be common in another decade. Over the long, bobbed hair of first quarter XVIc., he wears a fine flat hat, with slashed and laced brim and pendant; a jeweled roll, run through a ring, is set on the crown.

1031. XVIc. German. (Munich, Alte Pinakothek.)

Bernhard Strigel. Conrad Rehlinger, elder at 47.

The founder of the important family of traders with Venice was a man of such standing in his native Augsburg, that the Emperor Charles called on his services in a crucial new government, despite Rehlinger's Lutheran convictions and efforts to promote the Reformation.

Classic picture of a rich, middle-aged man of XVIc. Heads of elderly men and children, in cold climates, were protected by the mediaeval form of coif, or renaissance cap; hat was set over these for outdoor wear. In first half XVIc., combinations of hat and close-fitting cap, often decorated or netted, was fashionable, and not reserved for the old or bald.

The head must be uncovered before a sovereign, and the privilege of retaining a hat in his presence was an important reward. As new social classes rose and competed, the right to keep the head covered was jealously observed. Hats were generally worn indoors, by both men and women; men kept on their hats, for instance, in church and at table. Their removal was a real mark of respect.

1032. XVIc. German. (Sarasota, John and Mabel Ringling Museum.)

L. Cranach, e.

Cardinal Albrecht of Bavaria as St. Jerome.

After the manner of his times, the Elector-archbishop of Mainz (1490-1545), younger son of the Elector of Brandenburg, bought his cardinal's hat in 1518 with money borrowed from the Fuggers, and

repaid by Papal arrangement out of the sale of indulgences.

Erasmus' friend, and munificent patron of the arts, he sits under a chandelier made from the actual horns which served as pattern for the branched Flemish brass chandelier; lumps of crystal are hung from it in a primitive attempt to intensify the candle light. Table built on a platform to keep the feet warm. Chests, which have stood on the floor, are beginning to be hung as cupboards.

1033. XVIc. 1514. Flemish. (The Louvre.)

Quentin Matsys.

The Banker and his Wife.

Flemish garments have changed little since the XVc., but the shirt sleeve of the banker's wife now has an embroidered cuff, and a flat hat is set on her folded and pinned headdress.

Many fine objects: the illuminated missal with its clasp, backing and beautifully decorated edge; covered standing cup; box of nested weights for the scale;

repoussé bowl on the shelf; convex mirror in which we probably see the painter's self-portrait.

1034. XVIc. c. 1515. Flemish. (Metropolitan Museum.)
Bernhard Strigel.
Portrait of a German Lady.
Gold embroidered cap; gown of copper-brown brocade, edged with black velvet; shirt embroidered in gold, with colored motifs.

1035-36. XVI. 1516-18. German. (Metropolitan Museum, Print Room.)
Der Weisskönig, by Emperor Maximilian I.
1035. Illus. by *Hans Burgkmair.*
1036. Illus. by *Leonhard Beck.*
Der Weisskönig is Maximilian's autobiography, unfinished and finally printed in the XIXc.

The imperial regalia was kept at the favorite royal residence at Nuremberg. The city, not contained within walls like its rival, Augsburg, dominated a wide countryside, and was at the peak of its prosperity as the intermediary for the Oriental trade, between Italy and northern Europe. Watches were invented at Nuremberg; its artists were famous. A number of the Emperor's books were published there; he supervised their illustration by such Nuremberg artists as Dürer and Schäufelein; and the dress shown in them is that of Nuremberg. In the Burgkmair illustration, Mary of Burgundy, as a bride in

Burgundian court dress, is teaching French to Maximilian, with courtiers in turn-of-the-century costume behind them.

In the Beck illustration we see the costume of Nuremberg (see Ill. 1010, coat of arms with skull); the characteristic crowns set over banded or netted hair, looped up at the ears, with an untidy loose lock in front. Wide, round-necked gown, its skirt fullness bunched together at the waist in front, where it is very short; trailing into a square train; long, pushed-up sleeves, the transverse folds of which become repeatedly bound and slashed.

The man at the left gives a classic picture of the gentleman of Nuremberg in first third XVIc.: wide, plumed hat, slashed and overlapping brim; square, jutting beard and curly, full hair; short chain of immense links (of which Moryson still speaks at the end of the century); knee-length coat, immensely full, in carefully laid pleats, under a wide, slashed and tied "sailor" collar; and huge full sleeves, which are often seen gathered together at the bottom into a hanging ruffle. Immense peaked, slashed, and tied-on, wide-toed protective overshoe for travel.

1037. XVIc. 1531. German. (Metropolitan Museum, Print Room.)
Cicero: "Officia." M.T.C., Augsburg, 1531.

Illus. by *Hans Weiditz*. Clerks writing. Fullness inserted in cartridge pleats.

1038, 1039. c. 1520. German. (Denmark, Odensee.) *Claus Berg.*

Saints: painted wooden figures from altar.

Sculpture executed for a Danish church by a German artist from Lübeck shows what Moryson found later in the century. The Danes dressed like Germans, but particularly like Saxons; and the heads of gentlewomen, married or unmarried, were relatively uncovered, their hair "woven and adorned by rows of pearle . . . and borders of Gold." They also wore the standing Saxon collars.

The very low necks of e. XVIc. gowns tend to be-

come filled in by yokes, plastrons, and tuckers; but in Germany, where the décolletage was lowest, small capes, just covering the opening, began to be used at the end first quarter XVIc.; these came from the Low Countries, followed the Rhine and the North Sea and Baltic coasts, working their way inland.

1040. 1520. German. (Nuremberg, Germanic Museum.) *Master of the Mindelheim Kinship.*

St. Zosimus and St. Barbara.

The decline in taste and beauty of ecclesiastical garments has begun; mitres mount and decoration becomes heavy and ostentatious.

St. Barbara wears the new shoulder cape, with the

characteristic German sleeve of the late XV-e.XVIc.: overlong and widening at the wrist.

1041. 1524. German. (Munich, Alte Pinakothek.)
Matthias Grünewald.

St. Maurice and St. Erasmus.

St. Maurice in swelling, fluted Maximilian armor; large shoulder pieces with standing *passe-gardes, ränder;* broad-toed sollerets, and a pair of gentlemen's gloves. Jewelled wreath, allied to the *krantz* of fresh flowers, which were often combined with gilded nutmegs.

St. Erasmus: wheel of his martyrdom and coats-of-arms on the apparel of his alb.

Steel cross-bow man: slashings of hat brim progressively diminishing in width; imperfectly fitting hose, gartered for practicality; wide-toed shoes, almost entirely cut away and strapped over the instep, with the leather carried unusually high around the heel, for the same reason.

1042

1042. c. 1525. German. (Metropolitan Museum.)
L. Cranach, e.
Judith with the head of Holofernes.

1043-1045. 1525-30. German. (Vienna, Museum of Art.)
L. Cranach, e.

Three young women.

As the waistline becomes lower, the embroidered band of the plastron remains unchanged in width and position: the wide opening of the bodice is laced across the white shirt below. Belts, if worn, hang low over the pleated skirts, which like the laced bodices will persist in peasant costume. The massive and rigid Saxon collars are worn high on the neck, and here the largest chains appear. Rings of great beauty, in matched sets of 5, are worn on various joints.

The costumes favored by the wearers of these great plumed hats, set over pearl cauls, are a blaze of combinations of magenta, scarlet, orange, yellow with black and white. The plumed barett goes out of style, second third XVIc. and is supplanted by small flat hats, set level.

1043   1044   1045

1046-47. XVIc. c. 1522. Hungarian.

Unknown artist.

Louis II, Jagellon, King of Hungary, and his wife, Marie of Austria.

Marie, who holds a pink, symbolic of her marriage at 17 to the 15-year-old king, was early left a widow, and succeeded her remarkable aunt, Margaret of Austria, as regent of the Netherlands. She wears a jewelled collar and pendant of Hungarian workmanship. Beneath her crown, her hair is in one of the braided arrangements over the ears, which reappeared on young women, first quarter XVIc.

Louis is always shown in the anachronistic Italianate high doublet collar and filleted, flowing locks, persistent in Hungary.

1048. XVIc. 1525. German. (Vienna, Art History Museum.)

Bernhard Strigel.

Emperor Maximilian I and his Family.

The Hapsburg emperor, "the last of the knights," founder of the standing army of *landesknechte,* brave, cultivated but unstable, is shown in a picture painted after his death by his court artist. With him are his first wife; their son, Philip the Fair; two of Philip's children by Joanne the Mad, who grew up to be Charles V and Ferdinand I; and Philip's son-in-law, the King of Hungary.

Mary of Burgundy, who had died in 1484, is shown in the headdress and jewels of the period in which the portrait was produced. The long-jawed Hapsburg males have the bobbed hair of their period, and Louis the long, flowing hair of Hungary.

The wide, flat hat, c. 1525, is often furnished with ties by means of which the side lappets can be held in place, if turned up. The neck of the doublet is still low, in these portraits, as is that of the one shirt which appears.

1049. XVIc. c. 1525. German.
Hans Holbein, y.
The Standard-bearer of the Vallée d'Urseren.

In the Italian campaigns, the fashions of the Swiss mercenaries spread to the soldiers of the French and Imperial armies beside whom they served.

Holbein had lived in Basel from the age of 18, and maintained a house there for his family, although most of his work after 1527 was done in England. During a lean period at Basel, Holbein made this india ink and water color sketch for a stained-glass window.

As the use of slashing increases, there is a tendency to differentiate the legs by varying its direction, as was formerly done by the use of parti-color. Slashing was used on the front, rather than the back of garments, and is not often seen below the garter-line of the leg. This soldier wears gloves with a pendant at the cuff.

1050. XVIc. c. 1530. German.
Hans Sebald Beham.
Camp-followers.

One of Beham's many series of illustrations was of army life, soldiers of various ranks, provision and supply wagons. The commissary of a modern army did not exist; soldiers cooked and often had to forage for themselves; their women were permitted to tag along to do the K.P. and nursing, for which there was no other provision.

These Franconian costumes, with a fur collar from the district to the east, must have belonged to part of Nuremberg's large quota of 6,000 soldiers to the imperial army, seen by Beham before he moved to Frankfort. Fullness gored into the hem; wonderful pouches; knives from women's belts.

1051. XVIc. German-Swiss. (Basel Museum.)

Hans Holbein, y.

Lady of Basel.

The back view of this Swiss lady, one of a series of drawings of the costume of Basel, shows the method of drawing gauze around the embroidered cap. The bodice is filled in with a shirt, the high collar of which is edged by ruching; long banded and puffed German sleeve; skirt caught up in front to show a horizontally striped underskirt. In place of the high Flemish-German belt, we see a loose girdle with a massive pendant; so long that it must be knotted, it hangs down the back, instead of the front of the gown.

1052. XVIc. 1525-26. German. (Darmstadt Ducal Museum.)

Hans Holbein, y.

The Meyer Madonna.

Painted for Holbein's patron, the burgomaster of Basel, Jacob Meyer, it shows him with his first and second wives, his daughter Anne, and two sons, kneeling on an Oriental rug. Other portraits show these to have been in wide use, but still a luxury to be shown off.

The elder son wears a full-skirted jacket, trimmed with plain velvet bands; its upper sleeve cut in two sections, and caught by ball fastenings and tipped laces. Tasseled pouch.

Meyer's wives wear the banded chins and full, pleated capes of matrons of Basel in their Sunday dress. Dürer's colored drawings of Nuremberg cos-

tume (Vienna, Albertina) show how different were the house, church, and dance dresses of Nuremberg.

Anne's exquisitely pleated gown, and shirt with high collar, are banded with lovely embroidery. Her braided buns of hair are dressed over a band of embroidery, topped by a flower-crowned cap to match.

1053. XVIc. 1525. Austrian. (Metropolitan Museum.)

Hans Maler zu Schwarz.

Ulrich Fugger.

The German equivalent of the Medici was the great trading and banking house of Fugger. Always devoutly Catholic, it began its rise in the late XIVc., bore arms by XVc., and was ennobled a century later at the peak of its powers as bankers to the Hapsburg emperors.

Like the Medici, the Fuggers were people of taste, liberality, and interest in the arts; a number of them had literary talent and they collected a great library. The "Fuggerei" at Augsburg still standing after 400 years was an early example of a housing development for low-income groups.

The Fuggers maintained agents in the Orient and the New World and their commercial establishments covered Europe. From these houses, reports were regularly sent to the Golden Counting House at Augsburg, where they were translated and copied by scribes for issue in five languages to a list of subscribers. Out of these "Fugger News Letters" (some of which, 1564-1605, were published in 1924, John Lane, London), grew our newspapers.

1054. XVIc. 1530. German. (New York, Coll. Dr. F. H.
    Hirschland.)
L. Cranach, e.
Portrait of a Man.

1055. XVIc. 1535. German. (Metropolitan Museum.)
School of Cranach.
Portrait of a Man.

1056. Second third XVIc. Flemish. (Metropolitan Mus.)
Conrad Faber. (C. von Creutzenach).
Portrait of a Man. (George von Rhein?)

Moustaches and short beards at their greatest
square width; hair short; hats, caps and embroidered
cauls of rich, dignified men.

Loose shirt-fullness is associated with slashing, as
in Ills. 1054, 1056, where the short-waisted doublet
of first half XVIc. is slit up from the waist for additional display of the shirt, puffed out above the
breeches. All the shirts now have collars, three of
which are richly embroidered and finished with a
ruff. Collars begin to close with decoratively knotted
cords, black against the white shirt; as the neckline
rises, the ties will become white against a dark
ground.

In periods of extravagance and luxury, the garments of the very great are often distinguished by extreme severity, as are those of Fugger (see Ill. 826).

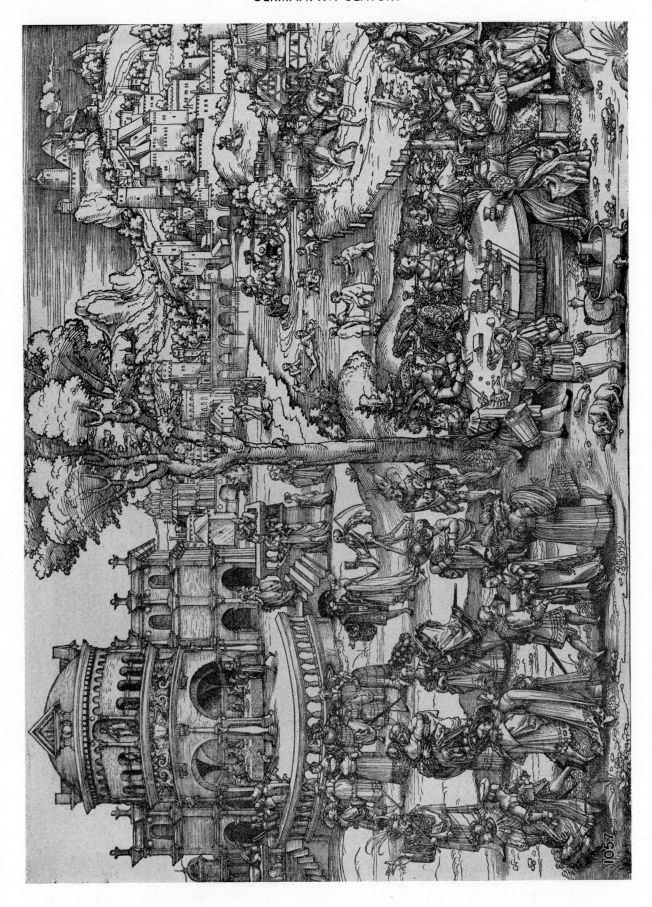

1057. End first third XVIc. German.

Hans Sebald Beham. Banquet of Herodias.

The free-thinking cronies and engravers, the brothers Beham and George Pencz, all born around 1500, and all important sources of costume information, were banished from their native Nuremberg in 1525. From 1531 until his death in 1550, H. S. Beham worked in Frankfort.

It would be impossible to crowd into one picture more information about the life of Nuremberg.

The men's costumes show inordinately large, slashed, laced and plumed hats, worn over hair, clipped or enclosed in a caul; many beards and moustaches. Skirts are becoming fuller and looser. Slashed doublets and hose, gartered; often striped on one leg.

Doublets with ballooning upper sleeves and full skirts. Wide, bulky, knee-length gowns. Musicians in motley.

Women's skirts are predominantly of ground length, finely pleated and horizontally striped. The skirt, when long, is bunched up in front to show a bordered underskirt. As bodies take on a normal waistline, precious belts are omitted; with the long skirt, a loose belt may be worn low (see Ill. 1051). Bodices are excessively low, though the entire décolletage may be filled in with a yoke, collared to the ears. The women wear hats of the male type; caps of two sorts: set on the back of the head and veiled with gauze, or small pill-boxes with arrangements of braids; or netted hair.

1058

1058. XVIc. c. 1535. Flemish. (Frankfort-on-Main, Stadel Inst.)

J. van Hermessen. Riotous party in a brothel.

The women of this low-class establishment wear the particular white hood and narrow, yoke-like black velvet tippet, which appear to have indicated their trade; over gowns (mostly red) with separate black or white sleeves.

As the garments of the male patrons show, the use

of slashing was not much extended to the rear of the body. Foreground, male figs.: yellow doublet with full green sleeves; scarlet hose; low-cut, almost heelless slippers like those worn by c. fig. in scarlet cap; late version of the slashed, low-necked doublet without skirt, and hose in yellow. Man in yellow doublet and old-fashioned waist-length hose of blue wears a rapier with a guarded hilt, which is just coming into use.

1059

1059. XVIc. 1535-40. Flemish. (Brussels, Count H. de Limburg-Stirum.)

Artist unknown.

Protestant Meeting in a Garden; also called Portrait of the Thiennes Family. Chateau de Rumbeke in the background.

The gown worn with the French hood in England, France and Flanders has a severe bodice, with a high, wide neckline; turned-back funnel sleeves, or one caught along the outer seam over puffs. Two older women wear white hoods of the earlier type.

Some of the men's jackets still carry pleated skirts, which, as they shorten, show the evolution of the slashed and gartered part of the hose into "paned" upper hose, slit into few divisions, and ending in a roll or slashed edge above knee. Collars with points, such as are shown on these jackets, will soon appear, heavily embroidered, on shirts. Slashed shoes of natural shape, covering the instep.

1060. XVIc. 1537. German. (Dresden, Picture Gallery.)

Lucas Cranach, elder. Duke Henry the Pious.

The Duke, whom we saw as a beautiful, clean-shaven and ringleted young man in 1514, is shown here with clipped hair and the widest, squarest and most elaborate of the beards now worn in Germany.

With his edged cape of mail he wears cuishes of moulded leather. The double-handed knight's sword has steadily increased in size; its quillons are wide, guarded only by a ring; it will go out of use altogether with the XVIIc. Swiss dagger in a magnificent sheath.

1060

1061. XVIc. After 1530. German.

Jörg Breu, elder. "Entry of Charles V into Augsburg." Marshal.

A series of woodcuts shows the entire procession, which celebrated the Emperor's arrival for the Diet of Augsburg. During his stay, the Emperor was lodged at the house of Anton Fugger, who celebrated the event by lighting a fire of cinnamon bark with one of his guest's bonds of indebtedness.

With his elaborate jerkin and boots with turned-down cuffs and the long spurs of the period, the Marshal wears arm-guards and gauntlets; and an armet with mentonnière and vizor, surmounted by a female figure and an immense panache of ostrich plumes, which are repeated on the chamfron (which with the crinet or mane-guard arm the horse's head and neck), and on the poitrel and croupe, which protect its body, fore and aft. He wears a two-handed sword in a handsome scabbard, and carries his marshal's baton.

Courtesy of the Metropolitan Museum of Art, Print Room

1062-65. XVIc. 1538. German.

Heinrich Aldegraver.

Wedding Festivities.

Aldegraver was a Westphalian goldsmith-engraver who worked at Soest and Paderborn.

The male flat hat was worn by women, in Germany as elsewhere, first half XVIc. It is shown here surmounted by a circlet. The characteristic posture of a woman in the low-necked, short-waisted German gown is determined largely by the dragging weight of the skirt (see Ill. 1051).

Wide collared jackets, braid trimmed and with cartridge-pleated skirts, or a similar unbelted cloak, are German fashions which were successful elsewhere. In their earlier form they show great upper-sleeve fullness; later a sleeve of normal cut, often worn pendant, is seen on the cape form, particularly. Elaborately slashed and gartered slops worn with nether hose which are often striped on one leg. Wide-toed shoes; extravagant German beard and moustaches. Musicians: badges on tasseled cloaks.

1066. XVIc. 1546. German. (Paris, Coll. I. Kleinberger.)

H. Mielich.

Pancratius von Freyberg zu Aschau.

The Bavarian nobleman wears one of the beautiful embroidered collars with long points, here ending in tassels, which appeared briefly in the forties.

It was in Germany that watches were first made, end XVc. They were at first globular, "Nuremberg eggs," and were necessarily carried or hung by a chain like a pomander. During XVIc. the mechanisms were refined until it was possible to make a watch small enough to be set on a bracelet or even a ring. The goldsmith's art was at its height; never had watch cases and faces been so beautiful. They were engraved, enamelled and jewelled in the form of crosses, octagons and hexagons, skulls, shells and animals. A typically Renaissance pendant, with a recumbent female figure hangs from his large-linked German chain.

The flat hat is losing its rigidity; as the crown is preparing for its rise, aiglettes are now set around the band of the hat.

1067. 1523-30. German. (Frankfort-on-Main, Stadel Inst.)

Bartholomaeus Bruyn, elder.
Portrait of a Patrician.

The Bruyns worked in the Lower Rhine valley, from Cologne to Amsterdam; the costume shows Flemish influences. Brocade hood over gauzy cap with pinned up lappets. Neckline filled in by a plastron of the "spangles" noticed by Moryson. Jewelled collar; shirt, the pleating of which is embroidered into a standing collar.

1068. XVIc. 1531. German. (Madrid, Prado.)

C. Amberger.
Frau Jörg Zörer.

Amberger worked around Augsburg. Bavarian costume south of the Danube has a special severity. Such headdresses and gowns as Frau Zörer's, with a yoke filled by a white shirt, still appear at the end XVIc. from Salzburg to Zurich, with the upper-sleeve fullness and tightening of the lower sleeve which we expect to find later in the century; around Salzburg the upper fullness is in a high cap, cut in one with the long, severe sleeve, while in Zurich this upper fullness is loose, like that of the son in Ill. 1052.

1069. XVIc. 1539. German. (Brunswick, Ducal Museum.)

B. Bruyn, elder.
Portrait of a Young Woman.

The Flemish-influenced costume of Cologne shows

the headdress specific to that city; its short-waisted gown of ground length, with the characteristically wide and magnificent belt and flowing bell sleeves of Cologne. Here the inner sleeve is of the male jacket type, especially beloved along the Rhine and into Switzerland.

1070. XVIc. German. (Munich Gallery.)

H. Mielich.

Frau Andreas Ligfalz.

Frau Ligfalz was the wife of an official in Munich where Mielich painted. Her logwood dyed blue-black gown, banded in velvet, with its tucker in the form of a *koller,* has the beautiful severity of south Bavarian costume. The bulbous cap, veiled over the forehead, the large amount of white at the top of the bodice, and the soft upper-sleeve fullness are seen particularly from the Nuremberg side of the Danube into Switzerland.

1071. XVIc. 1548. German. (Berlin, Kaiser Friedrich Museum.)

Unknown Saxon artist.

Portrait of a Woman.

The short, fitted shoulder capes which began to cover the low necks of German gowns c. 1525, were retained with later high-necked gowns, and into XVIIc. became part of the national dress of the Rhineland. Made of fur in the north, velvet-banded or embroidered, they are seldom as rich as that on this Saxon, whose headdress is typically based on a

1071

wide band, and exposes more hair than in other provinces. Eighteen rings, pearl bracelet, looped and knotted chains, precious girdle clasped at the side, and tasseled and embroidered handkerchief.

CLOCKS AND WATCHES

Herman Kirschner's oration in praise of travel in Germany, included by Coryat, says, "the art of making clocks that were in the time of Carolus Magnus brought into Germany by the munificence of the Persian Ambassador, which at that time were a great miracle to our people, the East and Persia her selfe that first gave them, having now received them againe from the hands and the wits of the Germans, doth greatly admire them, according as Augerius hath certified us."

Large clocks with bells, and often with elaborate mechanical figures of men, beasts and birds, which emerged to strike the hours, were set in cathedral and castle towers from Germany to England, during XIIIc. The first clock mentioned in England was set in a tower opposite the gate of Westminster Hall in 1288, and was paid for by a fine of 800 marks levied against a Chief Justice of the King's Bench.

The inaccuracy of the early mainspring was somewhat improved, second and third quarters XVIc., by the spirally wound fuzee; much greater refinements in the springs appeared, end XVIIc.

The first comparatively small clocks were made by Peter Henlein (1480-1542) of Nuremberg.

They had circular cases with hinged tops, and stood on a table, looking rather like a large inkwell. Louis XI (d. 1483) had one small enough to be pocketed by a courtier who was desperate from his losses at cards; however, it was apparently too large for the theft to pass undiscovered.

Henry VIII left seventeen standing clocks, with chimes and "Larums."

Watches were at first made of gilt bronze, probably because the early watchmakers were locksmiths. In Blois, in XVIIc., watchmakers had to buy their precious metals from guilds of goldsmiths and silversmiths. As in the weaving, dyeing, printing and engraving crafts, watchmaking families persisted for generations, and tended to marry within the guilds; there were women watchmakers, like Judith Lalement (whose name shows her German origin) owner of a factory in Autun in 1660. Many of the watchmakers were Protestants, who emigrated, bringing the trade to new countries, like England and Switzerland, which became pre-eminent in XVIII-XIXc. Rousseau came of a family of refugee watchmakers in Switzerland. Beaumarchais, author of "The Barber of Seville," son of the watchmaker Caron, first came to the notice of the French court when he published in the "Mercure" a protest against the piracy of his newly invented escapement; he made watches both for Mme. de Pompadour and the king, before purchasing a title.

Marvellously beautiful pendant watches began to be made in latter half XVIc., nowhere finer than in the French provincial towns; as at Autun by the Cusins (of whom Charles, who emigrated to Switzerland in 1585, was perhaps the greatest); at Lyons by the Combrets, from 1570; at Rouen, where in 1570, du Chemin made for Mary Queen of Scots two octagonal watches which were among the first to have rock crystal lids; as well as at Paris.

Elizabeth, who, like her sister Mary, loved watches, was served until 1590 by the refugee, Nicholas Urseau, and after 1580, by another, Bartholomew Nusam. Leicester's New Year's gift, 1571/2, to Elizabeth was a diamond-and-ruby-set watch, on a bracelet.

Great engravers like T. de Bry produced watch designs; the ring designs published in 1561 by Voerior of Lorraine show a ring set with a tiny watch, such as had already been worn in 1542 by Guidobaldo, Duke of Urbino.

Watches became the most luxurious of gifts, equalled only by snuff-boxes (from end XVII-XIXc.). They were worn in unnecessary multiplications; Marie de Medici unpinned a pair of watches from her gown and gave them to the Venetian Ambassador. In 1575, the Archbishop of Canterbury willed to the Bishop of Ely a watch set on a cane, as less reverend gentlemen had them set on daggers and rapiers. By 1622, watches small enough to serve as earrings were produced at Blois; and in late XVIIc., both Richelieu and Cagliostro wore a series of three-quarter inch watches as buttons.

This unnecessary display displeased the Puritans, who began to carry watches, for use only, concealed in pockets, as watches began commonly to be made small enough at the beginning of the XVIIc. As Puritan influence waned, watches continued to be carried in pockets; but by end XVIIIc., were commonly worn in pairs with two fobs, as was required in French court dress. Watches hung as part of ladies' chatelaines.

The beautiful rock crystal watches of XVIe.XVIIc., in octagonal and shell forms, or in crosses and skulls for the pious, were replaced in second half XVIIc. by charming enamelled forms. Multicolored golds began to be used in mid-XVIIIc.; and engine turnings, often covered by transparent enamel, in late XVIIIc.

The guild of English watchmakers was not founded until 1631. Many of its members were Quakers, like George Graham and Daniel Quare, inventor of the repeater watch. Alcock, Robert Smith, N. Vallin and the Jew, Isaac Symm, were among the great English watchmakers of the XVIIc. But it was the dead-beat escapement invented by Thomas Tompion (1639-1713) and improved by his pupil George Graham (1673-1751), which made possible the English watches of XVIIIc., the best in the world, until the magnificent plain, thin watches produced in Paris by A. Breguet (1780-1823). The firm of Breguet is still in existence; watches made by them soon after 1800 are perhaps superior to any produced since.

In late XVIIIc., Switzerland began to produce garish watches, especially for the Chinese trade, with engraved, jewelled and enamelled works visible through an inner cover of glass. France in XVIIIc. and Switzerland in early XIXc., provided charming ladies' enamelled watches in amusing shapes: banjos, lyres and flowers. The first good cheap watch was made in Switzerland, by Rosekopf, for 20 fr. in mid-XIXc.

1072   1073   1074

1075   1076   1077

1072. XVIc. 1560-90. French, Paris.

Watch by Nicolas Bernard: rock crystal case, bevelled in 8 panels; lid clear, lower part yellowish; metal hinge, finial, and snap.

1073. XVIc. 1580-1600. French, Autun.

Watch by Charles Cousin: case and cover of bevelled rock crystal, 1½" x 1⅛"; gold and silver face.

1074. XVI-XVIIc. French, Paris.

Watch by Melchior Adan (m)?: shell-shaped rock crystal, mounted in engraved metal; silver hour band.

1075. c. 1592. French, Rouen.

Watch by F. Hubert: oval case, enamelled with flowers and leaves in green, blue, and gold on white ground, spotted black; interior enamelled pale blue; crystal cover mounted in black and white enamel; hour hand only. F. Hubert's son, Etienne, made watches for Mary, Queen of Scots.

1076. XVI-XVIIc. 1590-1613. English, London.

Clock-watch by Michael Nouwer: engraved metal face; tangent wheel; screw adjustment.

1077. XVIc. 1610-30. French, Cartigny.

Watch by Denis Bordier: engraved silver dial, chain, and key. The Bordier dynasty of watchmakers had removed from Orleans to Cartigny, near Geneva.

1078

1079

1080

1081

1082

1083

1084

1078. XVIIc. 1620-39. English.
Watch by Nicholas Walter: silver, enamelled face.

1079. c. 1630. English, London.
Watch by Robert Smith in Popesnose Alley: engraved silver, plain and dotted bands; dial silver, engraved with tulips and marigolds; floral balance cock, tangent wheel, screw adjustment.

1080. XVIIc. c. 1638. English, London.
Calendar watch by Thomas Alcock: polished silver with outer case of black leather, studded with silver; face, engraved silver; revolving center disk black, semé silver stars, shows moon's phases; revolving outer disk gives days of month; tangent wheel, screw adjustment.

1081, 1084. Second half XVIIIc. German, Augsburg.
The "Great Ruby Watch" by Nicolas Rugendas, y. (c. 1670-1730); case enamelled with flowers in relief and natural colors, set with rubies.
Inside lid enamelled pale blue, black scrolls; face with black numerals, enamelled with tulips and roses in natural colors, Time, a sundial, and death's-head.

1082. XVIIIc. c. 1695. English, London.
Travelling clock-watch with striking alarm by Thomas Tompion; silver; movement signed by Tompion, one of the greatest innovators in watch-making.

1083. XVIIIc. c. 1710. French, La Rochelle
Watch by B. Hubert: gilt brass.

1085. XVIc. German.

Michael Ostendorfer. Landgraf Georg von Leuchtenberg (Upper Palatinate).

The pendant sleeve took new force from its use on these wide-shouldered cloaks (G. *Schaube*), and persisted after the simplification of the upper sleeve, becoming completely unusable and vestigial in late XVI-e.XVIIIc.

In Nuremberg c. 1530 the sleeve was often gathered, making the opening at the bottom unusable although the sleeve was slit elsewhere. The pendant sleeve was less used on women's garments; it appeared occasionally on the short, flaring jackets called *Schaubelein;* and an unused or unusable hanging sleeve was a feature of the severe coat-garments of Augsburg, fourth quarter XVIc.

XVI CENTURY ENGRAVING

The increased demand for engravings, midXV-midXVIc., was met by the great Flemish houses of commercial publisher-engravers: Hieronymus Cock, Brueghel's patron; Philippe Gall; and the family van der Passe (Crispin I, II, III, Simon, Madeleine and Willem) who spread from Flanders into England.

The XVIc. was the great era of exploration and interest in recording. Mercator and Hondius produced maps. Collections of costume plates of Europe, the New World and the Orient began to appear everywhere. (Queen Elizabeth will be painted standing on a colored map of Oxfordshire.) The trend began with the 2,000 plates of M. Wohlgemuth and G. Pleydenwurf: *Chroniques de Nuremberg,* 1493-1500. Weiditz' unique drawings of his travels, 1529-32, were not reproduced until our own time. But 17 editions of Sebastian Münster: *Cosmographie,* a sort of encyclopedia, were produced during XVIc., with translations into Bohemian, 1554, and French, 1562.

E. Vico of Parma (fl. 1541-67) produced about 100 plates of European costume which were the basis of the first great costume book, *Recueil de la diversité des habits,* published in France, 1562. This was followed by F. Bertelli: *Omnium feregentium nostrae aetatis habitus nunquam antehac aediti,* Venice, 1563; and the great works of Jost Amman from 1564-96.

Melchoir Lorch: *Turkische Tracht,* 1626, was a fascinating record of Turkish life by a man, who, like Weiditz, drew what he himself had seen in his travels during 1575 to 1581.

In the last quarter XVIc. there is a flood of such books; many artists producing several apiece, of which the most important is cited: J. J. Boissard: *Habitus variarum orbis gentium,* Malines, 1581;

the 500 plates of de Bruyn: *Omnis gentium habitus,* Antwerp, 1581, and his record of military costume; C. Vecellio's 600 plates, including Russia and Poland, in 1590, reproduced as "*Costumes anciens et modernes,*" Firmin Didot, Paris, 1859-60.

In 1590, the de Brys of Frankfort began their *Collectiones perigrinationem in Indiam Orientalem and Occidentalem,* with the purchase in England of drawings brought back from the first expeditions to Florida and Virginia; these were completed by Merian in 1634, and are reproduced in S. Lorant: *The New World,* Duell, Sloan & Pearce, N. Y., 1946.

At the end of the century came G. Franco: *Habiti delle donne Venetiane,* and his *Habiti d' Huomini et Donne venetiane, con la processione della serma. signoria et altri particulari Cioe Trionfi Feste et Ceremonie Publiche della noblissima città di Venezia,* 1610, reprinted by Ferdinando Organia, Venice, 1878; this shows meetings, councils, festivities, and home life of Venice. (At M.F.A. of Boston.) In 1601, J. de Gheyn: *Des habits,*

moeurs, ceremonies, façons de faire anciens et modernes. Meanwhile useful portraits were being produced by the Kilians of Augsburg (artists to the Fuggers); Goltzius; the brothers Wierix of Antwerp; and in England by Rogers, Peake, and Elstrack. They were followed by architectural and topographical plates, which include costumed figures, like John Speed: *Theatre of the Empire of Great Britain,* 1611, *Brittania Illustrata,* 1707-8, and Loggan's work.

In XVIIc. there are Crispin de Passe; Callot's Italian and gypsy plates; Bosse, Perelle, Aveline, Bérain, and the costume plates of Louis XIV's period, in France; R. de Hooge in Amsterdam; and the precious records of English and Central European costume made by the Bohemian, W. Hollar.

Reproductions of many of these will be found in the many volumes edited by G. Hirth: *Kulturgeschichtliches Bilderbuch aus vier Jahrhunderten,* Munich, 1923-5, and: *Les Grands Illustrateurs,* 1500-1800, Munich, 1888-91.

1086. XVIc. 1550. German. (Metropolitan Museum, Print Room.)

C. Amberger. Schlittenfahrt Königs Ferdinand.

Ferdinand, his grandparents' favorite, was brought up in Spain. But it was Charles V, despite all they could do, who inherited the Empire and his grandmother's Burgundian possessions. Ferdinand was made King of Austria, the Tyrol, the Hapsburg lands in S. Germany, and administered the Roman Empire ably for his older brother. Ferdinand married Anne of Hungary and Bohemia; when his childless brother-in-law, Louis Jagellon was killed, he laid claim to both kingdoms, and succeeded in becoming king of Bohemia. On Charles's abdication, Ferdinand became emperor. Riding in this wonderful sleigh, which the Augsburg publisher attests to be accurately shown, must have been one of the real pleasures

of his transplanted life.

1087. XVIc. 1551. Flemish. (Brussels, Musee Communale.)

Peter Pourbus, e. Adrienne de Buuck, wife of Jan Farragant.

The approach of lace can be seen in the working of sheer fabric, in the wrist ruffles of the Slossgen lady, and of Adrienne de Buuck, as well as in the cuff of her glove. Shoulder cape lined with stiff, diaper-patterned silver and white brocade.

1088. XVIc. 1557. German. (Metropolitan Museum.)

B. Bruyn, y. Lady of the Schlossgen Family of Cologne.

The ermine sleeves show the bell form, at the end of its use elsewhere but persistent at Cologne. Patrician girls of adjacent Hainault wear ermine aprons to match these sleeves. The yoke of the gown of Cologne is still open, the opening filled with pearled

1086

plastron, pendant and embroidery; pear-shaped pomander.

1089-90. XVIc. 1550. German.. (Philadelphia, Courtesy of the John J. Johnson Art Coll.)

Barthel Bruyn, e.

1089. Donor, Son and St. Peter.

1090. Donor's Wife, St. Anne, Virgin and Child.

The elaborate sleeves of the first half XVIc. are simplified in second half; show short Spanish caps or picadills in fourth quarter, when the hanging sleeve is largely unused and the short circular cloaks are worn as capes. The white cords which fasten the high shirt collars of the third quarter XVIc. often hang decoratively loose on the dark garments, the collar open.

The donor's wife wears the cap of Cologne with her Spanish coat-dress of velvet-edged brocade, furlined, over a satin underdress. This gown will be upper class wear during second half XVIc., particularly in Cologne, the Palatinate, Frankfort, Bavaria and Saxony, and will enter into the regional dress of Augsburg, as shown by J. Amman in 1586.

These gowns, moire-lined for summer wear, are often black. Black is much worn in XVIc. Germany in contrasting textures: velvet and cloth, moire, dull silk and brocade. Nothing could better set off the headdresses of sheer white or gold and pearled, the

is shown, with tactful touches of the costume of her province: the Saxon cap, its band set back of the ears, is worn with a garland (*krantz*); wide, precious Saxon color at base of the throat; rounded line of underbodice; finely pleated apron.

1092. XVIc. 1556. German. (Vienna Art History Museum.)
N. Mielich.
Anna, Duchess of Bavaria.

The duchess holds a jewelled fur piece, chained to a girdle which is finished with a tassel in place of the older pomander. Portraits are apt to exhibit new and precious objects, such as the clock in front of her little dog. Castles are still cold; hot-water bottles have not yet been invented; and small spaniels, in addition to being amusing, stay 4 degrees warmer than a human being, and are happy to lie cozy on a lap or even tucked against a toothache.

1093. XVIc. 1558. German. (Vienna Art History Museum.)
J. Seisenegger.
Ferdinand, Archduke of the Tyrol.

The Spanish-German costume of the Archduke shows a brown velvet hat, white ostrich; gown of copper silk, guarded by bands of matching metal galoon; white and gold doublet, laced with gold, match the hose; natural-colored nether-hose and shoes; brown gloves.

1094. XVIc. 1555-9. Italian. (Metropolitan Museum.)
G. B. Moroni.
The German Warrior.

The German warrior, like the son of the Emperor Ferdinand I, shows standard European upper-class dress of the 50's: doublet with longer waistline, shorter skirts, dropped shoulderline, simplified sleeve, braiding in vertical lines; paned hose, with a little bambast set low.

wonderful goldsmith work, or the color used in bodice and apron embroidery.

1091. XVIc. 1551. German. (Dresden Gallery.)
H. Krell.
Anne of Denmark, Electress of Saxony.
The coat-dress now worn by great ladies

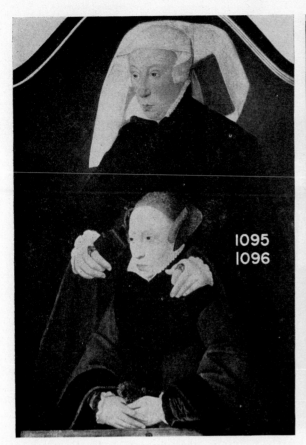

1095-96. c. 1560. German. (Berlin, formerly coll. R. von Kaufman.)

B. Bruyn, y.

Portrait of a Woman and her Daughter.

The mother wears the white béguine headdress of Flanders in its form specific to Cologne: excessively long falls looped and caught at the back of the head-dress. The extremely wide and magnificent belt characteristic of this costume can be seen in the portrait of a mother and four daughters (companion picture of father and four sons), by an unknown painter of Cologne at this same period, in the Dresden Gallery.

The daughter wears the wide cap with looped braids of a young woman of Cologne, together with the characteristically belled sleeve; its bodice is more completely closed since first half XVIc.

1097-98. XVIc. 1564. Swiss. (Basel Museum.)

Tobias Stimmer.

Jacob Schwitzer and his Wife Elizabeth.

Schwitzer was a leading citizen of Basel, head of the guild of wool carders. He wears black hat and shoes; red-brown brocade doublet; red upper-stocks with the cod-piece set in a diagonal, gored band; nether stocks and garters to match; black and gold dagger sheath with a silver cross.

Coryat found that the men of Basel and Zurich wore ruffs, never falling bands, and that the cod-piece remained in use, large and prominent; he and Moryson noticed the flat hats, like those worn by English 'prentices.

Elizabeth wears a wide coif, veiling the chin; brown, velvet-edged bodice, cream-colored apron, smocked and embroidered at the top, and tied on with knotted cord; ground-length skirt of natural colored satin (?), bordered in brown. Her fine belt, hanging by clasps over the pleated apron, carries the multitude of objects seen in Switzerland: a knife in its sheath, a "housewife" of sewing or toilet articles, as well as the usual fine pouch; gloves with an elaborate cuff.

1099

1100

1101

1102

1099-1100. XVIc. German. (Dresden.)

Att. to L. Cranach, e. (d.1553).

1099. Elector Augustus of Saxony, 1526-86 (1563).

1100. Anne of Denmark, Electress of Saxony (1564).

Tall embroidered hats with plumes, and short capes with high standing collars are a uniform of the Electors of Saxony in last third XVIc. The loose, *pluderhose* fullness between the panes of the upper hose is characteristic of Protestant German costume. Matching dagger and sword; embroidered gloves.

As in Ill. 1091, the Electress' Spanish gown is given regional touches: her underskirt has the Saxon cartridge pleating and an almost vestigial apron. Her sleeve, while much like that worn in Germany with this dress, has some regard for the Saxon regional dress in its third quarter XVIc. form. Its velvet bodice now has a puffed cap-sleeve like that of the Spanish gown, below which an extremely tight white sleeve has its forearm braceleted almost to the elbow with bands of embroidery; its hat is now a miniature flat hat, set horizontally over a pearled coif.

1101-02. XVIc. 1561. Flemish. (Budapest, Museum of Fine Arts.)

N. Neufchatel.

1101. Hans Heinrich, Pilgrim of Bois-le-Duc (Hertogenbosch).

1102. Mme. Hans Heinrich, Pilgrim of Bois-le-Duc.

It was not by chance that Bois-le-Duc produced Hieronymus Bosch, Brueghel's progenitor, this proud and somber man, and his pious Protestant-looking wife. Bois-le-Duc, a flourishing commercial town with the largest Gothic cathedral in Brabant, had begun to be attacked in XIVc. by the sort of conscience which led to the Reformation. The Confrèrie of Notre Dame, established there in 1318, in opposition to the corruption of the Church, admitted lay members, and came to be much concerned with charities. Its members believed that purity of soul and communion with God could be attained without the official intervention of the Church, and that theirs was the only true way.

Spanish influence is particularly strong in this immensely distinguished man's costume, simply guarded in velvet, with extremely high collar. The ruff, with hanging, decorative band-strings, is left open, as it is sometimes seen during third quarter XVIc. Poignard in superb sheath; rapier; fine pouch with a handkerchief; light gloves with a pinked cuff.

Women's hair in two braids was a Swiss usage which Coryat noticed in Basel, as in Zurich and Strassburg.

1103. XVIc. c. 1564. German. (Hamburg, Edouard F. Weber Coll.)

Ludger Tom Ring.

Lucia von Münchhausen.

The costume of Westphalia, where the Münchhausen family originated and Ring worked, is closely related to that of Cologne and of the triangle of Holland between Harlem, Leyden and the Rhine.

I have never seen the original of this picture, or been able to learn its colors. The headddess is worn with a garland (*krantz*). The high embroidered collar of the gown is clasped across the throat; the cape (*goller*) of velvet has a high collar and matches the deep cuffs. The top of the finely pleated apron is folded under and set beneath the woven belt. The front-laced bodice is of the same material as the finely pleated outer skirt. This, like the banded and pleated underskirt, is of ground length. Panelled room with surrounding bench.

1104-6. XVIc. c. 1575. German. (Metropolitan Museum.)

Ludger Tom Ring.

Christ Blessing the Donors.

These Westphalian costumes show the men in furred black.

The mother is in dark velvet with a close white hood. The daughter behind her, with looped braids under her simple cap, wears reddish brown. The elder daughter with the exquisitely pleated cap, clearly influenced by Holland, is in pinkish brown with the same deep cuffs and *goller,* woven braid belt and pleated skirt which we see on the others.

DRESS OF THE LOW COUNTRIES

The pictures of the elder Brueghel, of Antwerp, called "Peasant" Brueghel to distinguish him from his painter sons, "Hell" and "Velvet," show all the daily life of Flanders in third quarter XVIc.: carnival and Lent; illustrations of its proverbs, its children's games, the 7 Deadly Sins; soldiers, shepherds, peasants and beggars; weddings and dances, indoors and out. (See Color Plate, No. 7.)

It is hard to comment on the costumes in Brueghel. They are simple peasant clothes; the figures are too multitudinous to be indicated without a key drawing and numbers; new things can be found in them after years of familiarity.

Their peculiar richness comes out of the accidents and improvisations, even more than the intentions, of a thrift which borders on poverty. Worn garments are not thrown away; they are combined and supplemented: sock-boots over old hose; protective triangles tied above knees; a vest of one color over a shirt, over the tails of a still longer shirt; the color of an inner sleeve, rolled back or hanging below an upper.

These are hardworking, lusty people who like fun and color, must be comfortable and have no time or inclination for nonsense. The women's heads and chins are wrapped against the damp cold of their low land, which would take the starch out of anything they might be silly enough to pleat. They wear layers of skirts; the warm lining is one more color, when the skirt front is tucked up into the belt, and the darker underskirt bears the brunt of daily accidents. Skirts are short of the mud; aprons are never tokens of embroidered velvet here.

Except on soldiers, who have made the Swiss styles their own, there is no slashing, elaboration of upper hose, tailoring of cod-pieces: these latter necessities are reduced to tied-on triangles. Short breeches and sock-boots are added for warmth. Sleeves are comfortable; they neither constrict nor get in the way. The outermost of 3-4 body garments is apt to be practically sleeveless.

EUROPEAN DYESTUFFS

Dyestuffs are precious, local and hard come by, or imported and expensive. Garments are dipped, and lees of dyes combined, until the last bit of color is extracted; there is a serial richness of gradations of tones.

The Low Countries have always been the heart of the dye industry. Now the familiar mediaeval dyes are being supplemented by new dyestuffs, pouring in from the New World and the Orient, in XVIc.

The woad blues of Saxony are reinforced by the deeper blues of indigo. Until the invention of a fast green dye in 1811, green will be made by redyeing blue with yellow. (So be careful when you think of freshening your great-grandmother's patchwork. She would have washed it, since indigo is not water-soluble; but indigo is extracted by some dry-cleaning fluids, and the lovely greens may come back a nasty yellow, unless an expert is consulted. Even though the work dates from after 1811, the new dye did not immediately supplant old methods, and scraps from past generations were used.)

The madder of the Low Countries is the fast red of military and hunting coats until XIXc. The kermes of the cardinal's red gowns (used in Germany since XIIc.) is being replaced in XVIc. by cochineal imported by Antwerp from America.

Saffron yellow was the specialty of Basel; the safflower orange of Italy was part of the commerce of Frankfort.

There were the pale browns of German weld; Brazil wood red; the XVIc. purplish-blacks of the New World logwood; the orange-yellow series of fustic (combined with logwood for brownish-blacks); the lichen-purples of orchil and orseille, imported from Italy, but also locally present, to be scraped up patiently by sea-coast peasants, and still one of the beauties of the crofter-produced tweeds of the British Isles. There were other wood, bark and berry dyes, imported or collected, fast or fugitive; as well as all the rusty colors obtained from soaking iron scraps in acidified or chemically varied local waters.

With the great advances in chemistry of the XVIIIc. new dyes began to appear, but these XVIc. Flemings had at their command most of the dyes used until the invention of aniline dyes in second third XIXc. Everybody in Flanders knew something about dyeing, and their colors have a subtle, varied richness of which we have been deprived by standardization and fast colors, even though we have colors of which they could only dream.

1107. XVIc. 1566. Flemish. (Vienna, Art History Mus.)
Pieter Brueghel, e.
Murder of the Holy Innocents (left half).

The growing strength of the idea of uniformity is shown in the identical black-trimmed red jackets of the mounted Spanish soldiers. The manifest advantage of knowing your friends from your enemies was exploited in the garments of feudal retainers as it could not be with transient pressed soldiers or mercenaries. Colored scarves were a XVIc. attempt to consolidate these casuals, but lent themselves easily to trickery. There were few regular troops to be put into uniform before second half XVIIc.

The Print Room of the Metropolitan Museum treasures one of the invitations to the coronation of Matthias of Hungary. With it is included a woodcut of a black-clad rider, described as "a little pattern of a man," which the guests are asked to follow in outfitting their retainers, who will make the king's procession impressive. A lord now outfits his own men, at his own expense, not in his own colors, but for the aggrandizement of the growing central power of the king.

1108. XVIc. 1567. Flemish. (Munich Gallery.)
P. Brueghel, e.
Fool's Paradise.

An author, in a rose-colored doublet and hose with tied-on cod-piece, his writing implements hanging from his belt, sleeps on his fur-lined black gown; a peasant in dun hose lies on his flail; a soldier wears a dark gray doublet with red hose, seamed in black, in an elaboration of the Swiss style seen on Schwitzer.

1107

1109. XVIc. 1568. Flemish. (Louvre.)
P. Brueghel, e.
The Cripples.

Whether there is, or not, a punning relation in the fox-tails (emblem of the oppressive party of the Geuse) on the garments of the beggars (*gueux*), they help to make these some of the most loathesome creatures ever painted.

Europe was being ravaged by the new plague, syphilis, and fresh outbreaks of bubonic plague, the rat and louse-borne disease of poverty and filth. People turned scarlet or black and fell dead in the middle of a conversation on the street, and their better but infected clothing was snatched from their corpses by creatures like these.

1110. XVIc. 1569. Flemish. (Vienna, Art History Mus.)
P. Brueghel, e.
Peasant's Wedding.

There is evidence of Spanish oppression in many of Brueghel's paintings; the number of guests at such a Flemish wedding was limited to 20 by a decree of Charles V.

Bride with flowing hair in center, her wedding crown hung above. Women's simple béguine headdresses and velvet-yoked gowns with wide sleeves. Franciscan friar at the end of the table talking to an important townsman. Lappeted caps, retained in peasant use, could be tied under chin. Oblong wood trenchers instead of plates; no forks; everyone carries his or her own knife in a hanging sheath (even the

aproned baby on the floor, wearing a too-large hat with a peacock feather); wooden spoon stuck in the hat of the farm boy who is carrying in tarts on an unhinged barn door. Buttoned closing along shoulder seam, best seen on green-lined black coat of man pouring wine. Bagpiper's hats, feather or medals sewn on edge. Hose are, plainly, still of seamed cloth; garters, *points* by which hose could be trussed hang in pairs; the other server has a bunch of shoe-string-like points knotted to his hat.

1111. XVIc. 1569. Flemish. (Vienna, Art History Mus.)
P. Brueghel, e.
Dance of the Peasants.

Bagpiper's doublet, untrussed for comfort like the dancer's, shows pairs of grommeted eyelets, through which the points tie. Cap with a hanging medal over a white coif.

Flemish aprons come well around the body, on strings tied at the back, but like the narrow aprons of the Rhine valley, the top corners of the apron hang free.

Male dancer with knife, and spoon in his hat. His companion's best headdress is folded with some care; pattern of the back of the square yoke, seaming of sleeve and bodice clearly shown; pouch and key from girdle.

Beyond her: untrussed hose, with a tied-on cod-piece flap, are held up by a belt. In the group beyond the signboard of the inn, a fool in motley scarlet.

1108

1109

1112. XVIc. Flemish. (Vienna, Imperial Museum.)

Att. to *Pieter Brueghel, e.* The Shepherd.

This winning old wretch is delightfully dressed in a coat of many colors, stitched togethed with all his wife's left-over bits of wool.

His red cap is edged with blond fur. The jacket collar has the hooks and eyes, which we have suspected must be in use on the tight doublets of the gentry; it has a little bell as a top button. Great buttons covered with coiled cord fasten the jacket, which is of strips of natural, red, yellow, greenish putty, brown and blue, sewed with white, black, blue-black, red-brown and brown.

Diß ist ein Figur vnd eigentliche anzeygung eins gantzen Thurniers / wie der vor zeyten durch die Ritterschafft vnd vom Adel gehalten. Wie vnd was darinn / mit Seyl abhauwen durch die Grießwertel / Empfahung / Cleinoter abhauwung mit den Schwerdten / Straffung deß Schlagens / Schranckensetzens vnd außzihens / rc gehandelt worden.

1113. XVIc. 1566. German.

Thurnier Buch von Unsang Vrsachen Vrsprung, Frankfort-on-Main, 1566; illustrated by *Jost Amman.*

Fortunately for us, Jost Amman, a Swiss working in Nuremberg, was one of the most productive artists who ever lived. A pupil who worked with him for four years said that Amman produced enough during that period to fill a hay wagon. His woodcut books have been catalogued by C. Becker; *Jobst Amman,* Leipzig, 1851; and many have been reproduced, partly or entirely.

Among the most useful are the plates of this *Tournament Book,* 1566; *Trades and Workmen,* 1568 (all its 115 plates, as well as some from the *Tournament Book,* are reproduced by Hirth); military costume in the *Fronspergers Kriegsbuch,* 1577; *Costumes of the Catholic Church,* 1586 (of which the Print Room of the N. Y. Public Library has a copy, showing 102 plates of clerics, religious orders, lay members, and masked flagellants); the *Trachtenbuch,* published by Hans Weigel, Nuremberg, 1577; and the *Frauenzimmer Trachtenbuch,* published by S. Feuerabend, Frankfort, 1586 (reproduced in facsimile by the Holbein Society as *The Theatre of Women*), both of which show regional costume, particularly German. Amman illustrated books on everything from midwifery and cooking to tournaments; he also designed playing cards which are valuable for costume.

With the downfall of feudalism, the tournament had degenerated into an almost bloodless show. At the court of Henry VIII, it was intermixed with pageantry; under Elizabeth, it was reduced to a formula (see Ill. 1202: Queen's champion). The elements of pageantry were preeminent at the court of Catherine de' Medici's sons (see Medici Tap.). In France, and particularly in England the bourgeoise and yeomanry were advancing steadily into the gentry and nobility (see beginning of Eng. XIVc., Paston Family). Only in feudal Germany were generations of noble birth really important. The quarterings of 16 armigerous forebears were still necessary for entrance into German tournaments, where knights still solemnly sweated through the old knightly formulae. The inescapable element of pageantry was expressed, in Germany, in the panoply of the knight and his steed. Public squares, like bridges, were particularly suitable as tournament yards (see Appendix, Ill. 829: Stow).

Even in Germany, pageantry played an increasing part. In a celebration at the court of Dresden in 1591 (*Fugger News Letters*), for the christening of the child of the Elector of Saxony, the tilting ground was planted with 100 huge fir trees, decorated with oranges, pomegranates, pumpkins, live birds, and squirrels. The Elector led a procession of singing miners. Then 100 huntsmen brought in cages of bears, wild boars, wolves, lynxes, foxes, and small game. These were let loose and belonged to the person who caught them. Then larger animals were loosed to roam the tilting ground, guarded by dogs, who protected the populace when the wild boars charged. Four days of jousting, "run for money," then followed.

1114. XVIc. 1570. German. (Toronto Art Gallery.)
B. Bruyn, y.
Lady of the Vavasour Family.

Portrait by a German painter, of a Dutch lady, related by marriage to Sir William Vavasour.

With a white cap as fine and exquisitely embroidered as this one, the wide Dutch ruff is starkly plain. Spanish coat-dress with shoulder rolls patterned in the spirit of picadills. The separation of bodice from skirt is stressed by the picadill-edged point of the pinked satin doublet; the hips of the dark skirt are widened by the new bolster. The precious girdle tends to shorten. Gloves with a turned and slashed cuff.

1115. XVIc. 1577. Sweden. (Vastmanland, Ungso Church.)
Gravestone.
Elsa Trolle.

Flat hat set square on netted hair. Spanish coat with extremely high, wide collar. High-necked underdress with spreading collar and double ruff.

1116. XVIc. 1569. Dutch. (Metropolitan Museum.)
Dutch School.
Surgeon.

Quasi-ecclesiastical dress; surgeon's needle, other hand on a skull; hospitals and medicine are still administered by the Church.

1117-21. XVIc. 1581. Dutch. (Metropolitan Museum, Print Room.)
Omnium gentium habitus, or *Trachtenbuch,* Antwerp, 1581, engraved by *Abraham de Bruyn.*

Dutch, Belgian, and British sailors.

In first quarter XVIc., Weiditz shows Dutch seamen wearing these same clothes and the long wide breeches, which were commonly worn in Zeeland (where the sea was everyone's business), and which appear on Alsatian river boatmen. They were also a basic part of the dress of Basque men, who were the whale fishermen of mediaeval days, until Barents' discoveries led to Greenland whaling.

The Dutch sea-captain, holding an oar, and wearing around his neck the whistle which was his badge of office, shows braid trim and diagonal pockets; these will appear as a fashion at the turn of the next century, with loose breeches not unlike these, cut off above the knees like our "shorts." The similarity is so striking that the XVIIc. style, seen particularly in Spain and the Low Countries, must be an adaptation of this old-established seaman's style. In additional corroboration, the shorts show a useless but decorative buttoned side-slit, like those with which the long breeches of the Belgian and British sailors are provided for easy rolling.

Tall caps, bound close against the wind, are seen on all XVIc. seamen. The bare-backed galley slaves, chained together, which Evelyn observed at Marseilles in 1644, wore only these high bonnets, in red, and coarse canvas drawers.

1122. XVIc. 1577. German.
Trachtenbuch, Hans Weigel, Nuremberg, 1577; engraved by *Jost Amman.*
Burgher's daughter of Breslau, Silesia.

1123-24. XVIc. 1586. German.
Frauenzimmer Trachtenbuch, Frankfort, 1586; engraved by *Jost Amman.*

1123. Women's clothes are increasingly severe and masculine, and men's more blousy and effeminate, in Germany as elsewhere. With the apron, full, banded skirt, and rosary of the costume of Meissen, the high-born matron wears a circular cape and a hat with the heightening, pleated crown of the male variety. Moryson notes the short, jutting cloaks and hats in the form of an oyster-shell seen in Germany.

1124. The costume of a widow of Meissen, already seen on the Bavarian duchess, is one of the most striking of German mourning garments.

1125. XVIc. 1587. German.

Heindrik Goltzius.
The Standard Bearer.
No illustration shows better than this the artifically padded yet loosely effeminate male costume of the latter part of XVIc.: wreathed and plumed bonnet, worn with earrings (in male use, usually only one), and blowing curls; great loosely set ruff *à la confusion,* worn with the very pattern of the pinked peascod doublet at its most fantastic, its loose sleeves and galloon-guarded breeches laced and knotted along their open outer seams.

1126. XVI. c. 1585-1590. Dutch.

J. de Gheyn.
Mascarades.
Goltzius' pupil, who lived entirely in the Netherlands, did a series of 10 plates of carnival costumes in the spirit of the Italian comedy which was delighting Europe. (See XVIIc. Italian, Callot illustrations.)

With the high, puffed Italian bonnet, the musician wears loose Protestant *pluderhose,* with which the cod-piece survived longest; garters crossed behind and knotted above the knee.

The woman with her pouch, bunch of keys and aprons, show the pinned-on sleeve and shirt-puffs which have persisted in Flanders since early XVc.

Turkeys had been brought from the New World during this century. The wearer of the wattled turkey mask has the dashing new sombrero, embroidered as high felt hats often were, and with the very high crown of the last decade. Peascod doublet with overlapping skirts. Unpadded trunk-hose with cuffed canions and knotted garters. Shoes begin to show heels and mount over the instep into the tongue of the XVIIc.

1127. XVIc. 1594. German. (Metropolitan Museum, Print Room.)

P. Flindt. Woman.

Flindt was a native of Nuremberg. The border, brocade, embroidered apron, standing ruff, and pendant sleeve of Nuremberg's costume, at the end XVIc., are stylized here.

1128-29. XVIc. 1596. Flemish. (Metropolitan Museum, Print Room.)

Emblematica Secularis, 1st ed. 1596. Illustrated by *Theodore de Bry.*

With voyages of discovery and the new interest in strange and alien ways there comes a fanciful spirit of stylized exaggeration, which will be seen in Bérain's "inventions," in the potentates and American Indians of Louis XIV's pageants, and in Pillement's fantastic oriental flowers and chinoiseries in early XVIIIc.

The bell-like character of the skirts of the ladies of his city of Nuremberg at the end XVIc. occurs to a goldsmith like Flindt. De Gheyn's Dutch folk appear in grotesque carnival masks (see 1126).

A bizarre strain, seen in Flanders from Hieronymus Bosch in XVc. and in Brueghel, is combined with the stresses of years of existence under Spanish rule and religious differences, in the dichotomy of de Bry's symbolic Netherlands figures. The dress of a soldier at the turn of XV-XVIc. was indeed often divided down a center line, and striped and slashed into dissimilarity on either side. De Bry's soldier has an Italianate left side, after that manner; his right side has the newest collar, longer breeches, not packed with bombast, but with their padding and fabric quilted together. Adherents to Catholicism made these breeches their characteristic wear, as *pluderhose* were of Protestants. The ribbon tags at the elbow, fringed sash, garter-knots, and bows on the shoes are flowing. They differ from the former set rosettes as do the new sprays of hat feathers from the Elizabethan curled ostrich plume, both shown on the adjoining figure.

Outgoing and incoming fashions are set on opposing sides: the high-crowned Elizabethan hat, against the new, primarily military hat, the broad brim of which is cocked out of the way on one side; a small, formal multiple ruff against a wide loose one; a full sleeve with a wrist ruff, and a close, slashed sleeve with lace-edged cuff and braid-trimmed dependent sleeve; a doublet of normal waist length against its latest peascod form, prominently buttoned; loose *pluderhose,* crossed garters and rosettes, with higher trunk hose, canions, and a fringed knot; clocked hose with plain; pinked shoes with simpler ones which mount high on the instep. (See Appendix.)

1130. XVIc. 1597. Dutch. (New York, Cooper Union Museum.)

Hendrik Goltzius. The Dog of Goltzius.

Goltzius' dog is shown with the son of Thierry Frisius, the Flemish painter. Straw hat with wider brim and important hat band; ruff disintegrating into a collar, narrowly edged with lace and worked into open patterns, which are in themselves the origins of lace. Beautiful button and loop closing on jacket and on the bottom of the outseam of the new shorts, which have an embroidered edge. Pinking in small patterns. Rise of shoe into tongues.

1131-32. XVIc. 1524. French, Lorraine.

Gabriel Salmon (fl. 1504-42). Two Title Pages.

Salmon was court painter to Duke Anthony of Lorraine, whom Pierre Gringoire served as herald. Gringoire's *Blazon des Hérétiques* is a descriptive catalogue in verse of the heresies of Lutheranism.

The title page (1131) shows a figure, allied to the German-Swiss mercenary, dressed half as a peasant laborer, half as an armed nobleman. His costume is partly explained by a text in verse, which asserts that Lutheran heresy is discordant, contradictory, and makes itself ridiculous, like his dress. His body is tremendously elongated to signify the contempt and self-righteous pride which are the worst Lutheran vices. Their next worse sin is self-indulgence. They preach

"lubricité, erreur, et gourmandise," lure nuns from convents, urge priests to marry, and do not keep fast days; corrupt, venomous snakes writhe in his apron, and greedy rats gnaw the bag he carries.

Lance, spade, and book (nobles, commons, and clergy) signify the Lutheran destruction of authority, and of the existing social order; *"destruction de tous prelats, et diminution de la noblesse,"* while *"voullans commun* (i.e. the rabble) *vivre en auctorité."* The flames issuing from his body are another symbol of Lutheran destructiveness. The necklace may represent the vanity which Gringoire imputes to the Lutherans.

No. 1132 is the title page of de Seronville's *Victory over Lutherans.*

From George Clutton: *Two Early Representations of Lutheranism in France.* Journal of the Warburg Institute, I, 1937-38.

1133. Late XVI-e.XVIIc. Flemish. (Boston, Isabella Stewart Gardner Museum.)

Tapestries: Chateau and Garden Set.
Garden Scene.

Houses, affected by the architecture of Italy, have become lighter and airier, "fair houses so full of glass, thet one cannot tell where to become to be out of the sun or cold," Bacon described them. Their gardens, with statuary, fountains, arches, and far-set pavilions, are enclosed with walls of espaliered fruit; vegetables are as decoratively used as flowers. The exotic turkey, with a crane, takes the place of the falcon in every mediaeval tapestry, but the collar of the hunting dog has not changed since the time of Gaston de Foix.

The costume is that of the turn of the century. The lady standing in the center wears the bolstered, drum-shaped skirt, with a number of objects, including a looking glass, hanging from her girdle. The girdle now finishes in an important jewel, just below the point of the bodice. The hair is now uncovered, studded with flowers, with a jewel at the center of the forehead.

Her suitor wears a felt hat of the new "derby" shape, plumed and banded; a low, open band collar; cape; padded venetians; and high boots with turned-down tops.

The seated man wears a short, skirtless jacket, braided in the new diagonal way, over a pinked doublet.

The couple walking off to the right show the simplified, caped, male outline with an important hat carrying a spray of feathers; and the female silhouette, with hanging sleeves, of the Medici tapestries.

1134. XVIc. English. (Windsor, H.M. the King.)
Unknown artist. Arthur, Prince of Wales.
1135. XVIc. English. (London, Soc. of Antiquaries.)
Unknown artist. Edward IV.

In the second of these two XVIc. portraits of XVc. personages, Edward IV, d.1483, wears Italianate brocade garments, the jerkin caught by horizontal strings of pearls, each carrying a fine, identical pendant.

Arthur, who died in 1502, at 15, wears the Tudor collar of the Red Rose of Lancaster and the White Rose of York which his father, Henry VII, had assumed upon his marriage to Elizabeth of York, to symbolize the reconciliation of their factions; the roses are linked with tasseled cords, their loops filled with pearls. His bonnet carries the medallion of a saint, and its slashings are caught by precious studs. Jewels worth £15,000 had been imported from France for Arthur in 1501, when he married Catherine of Aragon. His shirt is edged with fine Spanish embroidery.

1136. XVIc. c. 1518. English. (Oxford, Corpus Christi College.)
Corvus, Hans Johannus.
Richard Fox, Bishop of Winchester.

The bishop, whom we see in surplice, scarf and episcopal ring, painted by a Flemish artist, came of yeoman stock. During his youth, he had become intimate in Paris with "the great rebel, Henry *ap* Tudor," as Richard III called him, in opposing Fox's appointment to a vicarage. Immediately upon Henry VII's accession, Fox was called into his service, be-

coming confessor, as he eventually was executor, of the king's mother, the Countess of Richmond. Fox received increasingly important bishoprics as sinecures, and as Lord Privy Seal devoted himself to statesmanship. The marriage of Henry VII's daughter, Margaret, to the king of Scotland led to the union of the two crowns in 1603, and to the union of the kingdoms in 1707. Fox negotiated the marriage of Catherine of Aragon to Prince Arthur. Fox upheld the legality of Henry VIII's marriage to his brother's widow, and continued in power, though Henry called him "a fox indeed," until ousted by Wolsey.

After his retirement from government, Fox devoted himself to the conduct of the richest English bishopric, and founded (1515-6) Corpus Christi College, where the New Learning flourished under Italian teachers of Latin and Greek.

1137. XVIc. 1511. English. (London, College of Arms.)
Westminster Tournament Rolls.
The Answerers and Trumpeters.

The Westminster Tournament was held by Henry VIII in 1511, to celebrate the birth of his short-lived and only son by his first wife, the widow of his brother Arthur.

The Roll shows: 1. the procession to the lists; 2. the combat; and 3. the return to court. This is the right side of 2: it shows Les Venants, the 8 Answerers, the caparisons of whose horses, in courtesy to the Queen, bear the roses of Aragon, the castles of Castile, the cockleshells of St. James, and the pomegranate flow-

ers of Granada. Behind them, the return signal, *"A l'hostel,"* is blown by the trumpeters.

With the rounded forms of the XVIc. Maximilian armor, the Answerers wear armets—round-topped, beaked tilting helmets; mitons; sollerets of the sabot-shape which has superseded poulaines, in armor as in civil dress; and gored *bases* of alternating plain and brocade strips.

ENGLISH PAINTING, XVIc.

Aside from Nicholas Hilliard and Isaac Oliver (both influenced by Holbein), the most characteristically English painters of the Tudor period are foreign born like the German Holbein; the Flemish Ewarth, and the Gheeraerts and de Critz families, who worked entirely in their adopted countries; the Italian Zuccaro; and the Flemish Sir Anthony Moro, and Sir Anthony Van Dyke in Stuart times. It is hard to know what to call them when they *were* English painting, but unless they worked only in England, we credit them to the countries of their birth. In the case of Holbein and others, who painted the dress of so many countries, captions combine their nationality with that of the sitter whose national dress is shown, as: German-English, etc.

1138. XVIc. 1527. German-English. (Basel Museum.)
Hans Holbein, the younger.
Sir Thomas More and family.

Made by Holbein on his first English visit, and given in 1528 to their mutual friend Erasmus, this study for the painting shows the costume of the English upper middle-class household described by Erasmus. "More has built near London, upon the Thames, a modest yet commodious mansion. There he lives surrounded by his numerous family, including his wife, his son, and his son's wife, his three daughters and their husbands, with eleven grandchildren. There is not any man living so affectionate to his children as he, and he loveth his old wife as if she were a girl of fifteen."

The caps of the older men are of the square, biretta-like forms which by this time have been pretty well relegated to scholastic, legal and clerical wear. More's long gown has slit, dependent sleeves. He wears the

SS color with a Tudor rose pendant, and carries a muff, as does Johannes More, dressed in a judge's cloak. Young Johannes wears a short gown with a standing collar and braid-trimmed sleeves, puffed to the elbow. The bulky fullness of Henry's gown is gathered onto a yoke.

The ladies wear the English gable hood, one or both lappets of which had begun to be pinned up, towards end first quarter XVIc. Crossed bands of striped material conceal the hair. Over these is worn a white cap, often fastened under the chin and edged by a jewelled frontlet. The whole is surmounted by the wired or stiffened hood; this is usually of black velvet with a band of decoration covering the front section; with the fashion of upturned lappets, their plain dark lining conceals much of this decorative outer strip.

The 15- and 20-year-old girls wear rounder linen headdresses, over caps which fasten under the chin and show the parted hair.

The gowns, of floor length, have low, sash-like girdles with tassels and rosaries. Square-necked bodices, on some of which the front opening lingers, are filled with sheer yokes, *partlets* or *tuckers,* or with bands and necklaces in characteristic variety; they are laced or looped across with ties and chains, and carry funnel sleeves with fur linings, turned far back. Quilting gives body to the undersleeves, which are tied together at intervals along an open outseam, over the loose sleeve of the shirt.

1139. XVIc. 1524. English. (Norwich, St. John's Maddermarket Church.) Sepulchral Brass.
John and Lettys Terri.

This is a provincial family, no member of which is dressed in the latest fashion. In Terri's case, the archaic garments are the ceremonial dress of a mayor. The scarf of office hangs over the tabard-like XIVc. cloak, buttoned on the right shoulder, and showing the wide sleeves of an equally old-style undergarment.

The sons wear the square-necked, full skirted jacket of the Transition period, which is that of the mother and daughters.

Lettys' gown is that seen in Franco-Flemish tapes-

tries—end XVc.: high, square neck; train pinned up over the bustle of the back gathers of the skirt; and is worn with the specifically English form of hood, the pedimental (or gable or kennel) headdress, edged with a jewelled band. Her girdle, with its Tudor roses, is of the new, lower, wider sort, which has something sash-like, asymmetric and dependent about it—an effect given here by the hanging rosary; these will be seen until the religious disturbances begin. It might well have been a "muskeball" (pomander).

1140-42. XVIc. 1527. German-English. (Windsor Castle, the King of England.)
Holbein, y.
1140. Mrs. John Clement (Margaret Gigs), inscribed Mother Iak (nurse of the royal children).
1141. Lady. 1142. Queen Anne Boleyn.
The attributed names are doubtful, but all wear delightful and unusual forms of the current domestic cap, with fur or felt hats. Pins are still a novelty, and are as proudly displayed as in Flanders.

1143. XVIc. 1527. English. (Metropolitan Museum.)
British School: formerly att. to *Holbein*.
Lady Guildford, aged 27.

This portrait shows the hood with the back curtain long, full, and still undivided, but with one of the front lappets pinned up. On her plain dark gown, the emphasis on the small, neat shoulder is provided by continuing the chains which are looped across the bodice. Below the familiar pendant with pearls is pinned a delicate jewelled spray. The stiffening of her undersleeve is provided by external seaming, spaced like the bodice chains.

1144. XVIc. 1534. German-English. (Metropolitan Mus.)
Holbein. Margaret Wyatt, Lady Lee, at 34.
Lady Lee wears a variation of the French hood, which had reached England c. 1515, and which can be seen in its classic form on Catherine Howard. Lady Lee's béguine-like black hood is set before the light-colored, raked-back, crescent front of the French hood. Her red-brown brocade gown shows many new attributes: the high, standing collar line of gown and shirt; leg o'mutton sleeves caught by beautiful paired aiglettes across puffs of orange material, with white shirt sleeve showing only in the frill at the wrist; inverted V-opening of skirt, scarlet underskirt; oval pendants, increasingly massive.

1145. XVIc. 1536. German-English. (Vienna, Kunsthis-
torisches Museum.)

Holbein. Queen Jane Seymour.

The hood is seen here in its final development,
with both red-and-gold lappets pinned up. Its back
curtain has been slit; the r. section twisted up in
back, and pinned into a "whelk-shell," and the l.
carried around to the r. shoulder. Her red velvet

gown, with pearl and ruby bands and magnificent
pendant, has an all-over pattern in gold bugles on the
turned-back sleeve. Over a shirt with black Spanish
embroidery frill, the undersleeves of silver brocade
are caught with ruby clasps. The V-opening of the
skirt from a natural waistline shows the same brocade, and a jewelled girdle with double pendants.

1146. XVIc. 1527. German-English. (Metropolitan Museum, Frick Coll.)

Holbein. Sir Thomas More.

The Chancellor wears the costume shown in the family group, including
the XVc. bonnet, its brim cut away in front, and laced across the crown,
which is characteristic of him.

The SS collar has been the official one of the house of Lancaster since
last quarter XVc.; it is shown with the Lancastrian portcullis of Beaufort,
which had become a Tudor badge in XVc., and a pendant Tudor rose.

1147. XVIc. 1532. German-English. (Berlin, Kaiser Friedrich Museum.)

Holbein. George Gisze.

This portrait is of a Danzig merchant, who lived in London as a member
of the Hanseatic League's privileged "Merchants of the Steelyard"; so-
called because, to the annoyance of the citizens, they were allowed to keep
their own scales on the premises, instead of using the official scales of the
City. They had been chartered by Henry III in 1259 to "bring hither as
well wheat, rye, and other grains, as cables, ropes, masts, pitch, tar, flax,
hemp, linen cloth, wainscots, wax, steel, and other profitable merchandise."
(Stow.)

Gisze wears a form of the practical "flat caps, knit of woolen yarn black,
but so light that they were obliged to tie them under their chins, for else
the wind would be master over them. The use of these flat round caps so
increased, being of less price than the French bonnet,
that in short time young aldermen took the wearing
of them" (Stow) and they were taken over by the
London apprentices as their very own. His black
gown is slit for the passage of the sleeves of the red
satin doublet, their upper fullness pleated in at the
elbow. Both jacket and doublet have the low, square
neckline which begins to disappear at about this
time. Shirt: gathered onto a cord at base of neck.

His table is covered by an Oriental carpet, such as
the Venetian rivals of the Hanse distributed over Europe; carpet manufacture was not begun in England
until later in XVIc. Accessories of trade: holder for
a ball of cord, seal, inkwell and quills, shaker for
blotting-sand, and scales.

1148. XVIc. 1526-28. German-English. (Washington, National Gallery of Art.)

Holbein. Sir Brian Tuke.

The first British postmaster wears a flat cap over
a black coif; chain with symbols of the Passion, over
a fur-collared black gown. Through its slit sleeves we
see gold and black checked sleeves of his doublet. A
tiny frill finishes the shirred, embroidered collar of
the shirt. He carries gloves.

1149. XVIc. 1536. German-English. (Florence, Uffizi.)

Holbein. Sir Richard Southwell.

Privy councillor and official of Henry VIII's court,
Southwell played an important part in the confisca-
tion of the monasteries, at the instigation of Thomas
Cromwell.

Standard costume of the period, with the collar
ties which will persist in use for another quarter century. In the 1560's, the high collar with ruff is often
worn open, with the cords hanging.

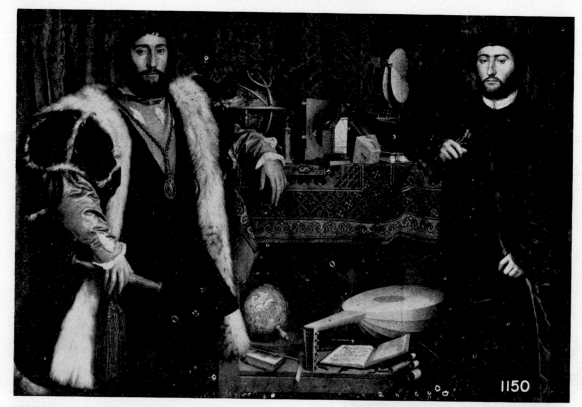

1150. XVIc. 1533. German-English. (London, National Gallery.)

Holbein. The French Ambassadors to London, Jean de Dinteville and Georges de Selve.

Dinteville is dressed in black and rose, with a chain carrying
a medallion of the Order of St. Michael, and a green and gold
tassel hanging from his girdle. His flat hat bears a silver skull
set in gold. Light, spotted lynx, with which his gown is collared
and lined, has become a favorite fur; lines of fur were much
used at the seams of the upper puffed sleeve, in both male and
female costume.

Selve, later Bishop of Lavour, wears the 4-cornered mozetta-
like scholar's cap, and a fur-lined gown of brown brocade.

1151. XVIc. c. 1537. German-English (Chatsworth, Duke of Devonshire.)

School of Holbein. Henry VIII.

This portrait of Henry VIII is a copy of one portion of the
Whitehall picture, later destroyed by fire, which the king order-
ed from Holbein in 1537; which showed him, his parents, Henry
VII and Elizabeth of York, and Jane Seymour.

There are few pictures of the young Henry, attractive, athletic,
learned and musical; but though puffy with disease, the sump-
tuously dressed 46-year old king is a figure of the most purpose-
ful power and intelligence. Not only his resolution and compe-
tence, but a great interest in wardrobe, and the personal means
to indulge it, were the king's legacy to his daughter, Elizabeth.

Henry's rivalry with the King of France was lifelong. He
grew his great golden beard when he heard that Francis was
bearded; he competed sartorially with Francis at the Field of
the Cloth of Gold; and his death-bed message to Francis to "remember that he, too, was mortal" scared Francis into his own
final illness.

Henry wears a high-collared doublet with white
puffs drawn through the interstices of its embroidery;
a vest, cut wide and low, and *bases* to match, of blue
trimmed with silver braid and ruby-set gold clasps
over white puffs. There are two white sashes, one of
which carries the dagger with its red and gold mounts
and tassels.

His gown is of red velvet, lined with sable and embroidered in gold. The upper part of its sleeve, which
is usable, is gored and banded with gold embroidery
done in cord; its unusable, hanging part is tubular,
separately made and set on at the back. What would
be the front (if worn) is vertically slit at the top, with

the tabs turned back to show an embroidered lining. Elaborate cod-piece mounted on nether garments. White hose with the Garter; slashed white shoes, rising high over the instep, have short, laterally spread, square toes. Black bonnet with a white plume laid

around the brim, the under side of which is sewed with gold tags.

Although the wall-hanging is probably of stamped leather, its pattern is a favorite for corded appliqué on costume.

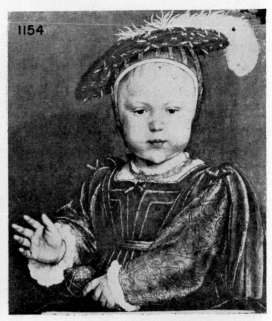

1152. XVIc. 1527-36. German-English. (British Museum.)

Holbein. English lady with rosary.

Back view shows the development of the pedimental hood. The back curtain has been supported, beneath, by a box-like extension of the gable-front. After the slitting of the curtain, the box had emerged, become independent, and the slit ends had been added to it. We see also the V-back of the square decolletage, and the pleats in the bodice, leading to the back fullness of the skirt.

1153. XVIc. 1527-36. German-English. (Oxford, Ashmolean Mus.)

Holbein. Woman walking.

She wears a gray dress with a black yoke; looped up by a catch slung over the shoulder, and by a tasseled yellow sash with rosary; beige underskirt; red petticoat; square-toed black shoes.

1154. XVIc. 1538. German-English. (National Gallery of Art, Washington.)

Holbein. Edward VI as Prince of Wales.

This portrait, presented to Henry VIII as a New Year's gift, 1539, shows the little son of Jane Seymour dressed in red and gold. Over a coif, he wears a flat hat with the single plume which had followed the profusion of feathers of the Transition period; its under-side is sewn with precious aiglettes, with which the gentry differentiated this enormously popular hat.

Lady Bryane, governess of the royal children, had great trouble getting clothes for them. This might be the very costume about which she wrote Lord Thomas Cromwell, just as Edward was getting his fourth tooth: "The best coat my lord prince's grace hath is

tinsel, and that he shall have on at the time; he hath never a good jewel for his cap." As king, the boy Edward was left entirely without pocket-money, and as Mary and Elizabeth were alternately declared illegitimate they were badly neglected in childhood. Anne Boleyn's accounts show that despite the disappointment of Elizabeth's sex, she did once go to some pains to order a milliner to measure the baby for caps of purple and of white satin with a gold caul.

1155. XVIc. 1543. German-English. (Metropolitan Museum, Bache Collection.)

Holbein. Edward VI.

Side view of the flat hat, worn tilted in the Italian manner after 1520, over cropped hair. Collar line mounting.

1156. XVIc. 1538. German-English. (London, Nat. Gall.)

Holbein. Christina of Denmark.

Granddaughter of Joanne the Mad and widow of the Duke of Milan, the beautiful Christina repulsed Henry VIII, saying that she "had only one head," and was remarried in 1540 to the Duke of Bar and Lorraine.

This is one of the few full length female portraits of the period; it shows her in a one-piece gown of black velvet mourning, sable-trimmed, and with delicate stitching at the frill of her shirt sleeve. She carries buff gloves.

1157. XVIc. 1539. German-Flemish. (Louvre.)

Holbein. Anne of Cleves.

Holbein was sent to Flanders in 1539 by Henry VIII to paint the portrait of his bride, who in the flesh Henry found "no better than a Flemish mare," and soon divorced. Ample settlement was made on her and she remained in England, a good-natured person who appeared at court in her endless lovely dresses, each "more wonderful than the last," decorated with the fine needlework which was her only accomplishment.

English male clothing of this period is much more influenced than female by German fashions. Anne's completely Flemish costume, compared with the gar-

ments of Henry, shows the parallel developments which so often occur in male and female garments, in respect to the cut-out front of the bodice (Henry: doublet) over its partlet (Henry: vest); and the puffed upper sleeve with its band above the elbow. The lower sleeve is funnel-shaped, like her skirt which was described as "without a trayne after the Dutche fassyon," at a period when English ladies' gowns, almost alone, retain them.

The tucker or partlet and the cuff-bands of the shirt are not of the Spanish embroidery seen so far, but of cut-work; this antedates lace, which in fact grew out of cut-work; lace has been made since XVc. and will be common by XVIIc.

Her headdress is typically Flemish. Over a tiny, pearl-edged cap is laid an oblong of lawn; on this is set a swelling cap, gold and pearl embroidered, with the motto "*A bon fine*," and a jewelled pendant pinned on the left side. Monograms and mottos continue to be used as they were in the XVc. Flemish hennins (see Marie Portinari, Ill. 858; Burgundy, Ill. 880): the wide belts of the hennin period have been much reduced, but Flemish belts continue to be precious and handsomely buckled, and in German and Flemish use, are worn high. Rings now appear in profusion; worn on the thumb as well as other fingers, they are small and simple in comparison with *carcanet* collars and pendants.

1158. First half XVIc. English. (Metropolitan Museum, Bache Collection.)

Master of Queen Mary Tudor. An English Princess.

The unnamed princess is dressed in brocade of a rosy red, much used at this time. Her shirt sleeves and yoke, which had gained a standing collar finished by a frill, are decorated in bands of Spanish embroidery. French hood over frizzed hair.

There are two portraits of Mary Tudor before 1533 by this painter.

1159. XVIc. 1540-41. German-English. (Toledo, Museum of Art.)

Holbein. Queen Catharine Howard.

Henry VIII's fifth wife wears a black satin gown; black velvet yoke with a standing collor; leg o'mutton sleeve (reputedly brought from Flanders by Anne of Cleves), its gold-embroidered black puffs caught by paired aiglettes; shirt ruffles of black Spanish embroidery.

She wears a brooch designed by Holbein, one of several for which his original drawings have been preserved. As was the case with the great salt-cellars and standing cups, important jewels were often given names. The stones from Mary, Queen of Scots' "Great Harry" were later set in James I's "Mirror of Great Britain."

On her slightly frizzed hair, she carries a classic example of the French hood; a white cap with a frill of gold tissue, under a raked-back crescent band, from which hangs a triangular tube of black velvet.

1160. XVIc. 1540-43. German-English. (Metropolitan Museum.)

Holbein. Lady Rich.

At about the end of its vogue, Lady Rich continues to wear the gable hood, but her high-collared bodice and standing shirt collar are both finished with the pleated ruffle, which foreshadows the Elizabethan ruff.

1161. XVIc. 1542. German-English. (London, St. Bartholomew's Hospital.)

Holbein. Henry VIII.

The aging king seems to have found this the costume most suitable to his infirmity and bulk. It appears in different colors, in various portraits, and was described in 1540 by Edward Hall: "His person was apparelled in a coate of purple velvet, somewhat made lyke a frocke, all over embrodered with flat gold of damaske with small lace mixed between of the same gold, and other laces of the same so goyng trauerse wyse, that the ground lytle appered: about whyche garment was a rych garde very curiously enbrodered, the sleves and brest were out lyned with cloth of golde, and tyed together with great buttons of Diamonds, Rubys, and Orient Perle, his swoorde and swoorde gyrdle adorned with stones and especiall Emerodes, his night cappe garnished with stone, but his bonet was so ryche of Iuels that few men could value them. Besyde all this he ware in baudricke wyse a collar of such Balystes (pink rubies) and Perle that few men ever saw the lyke."

In this case the coat is of dark gray, embroidered in gold, with ruby studs; the under-sleeve of snuff brown with emerald studs. It also appears in red and gold. Black hat with pearls, rubies and emeralds.

1162. XVIc. 1540. English. (Longford Castle, Earl of Radnor.)

Hans Eworth. Thomas Wyndham.

Eworth, whose name is variously spelled, was a Flemish painter who lived in England after 1543.

Wyndham, the navigator and explorer, who was drowned while returning from the Gold Coast, wears

a spruce-green leather military jerkin, paned in the current small, massed patterns. The combed morion of the second half of XVIc. infantryman, richly decorated, shown above; headpieces are now seldom worn in portraits. Red scarf of an infantry leader; touch-box (powder flask) hung from neck; date of picture on gun muzzle.

1163. XVIc. 1540. German-English. (Frankfort-on-Main, Stadel Inst.)

Holbein, y. Simon George of Quocote, Cornwall.

"Sir George of Cornwall," as he is also called in some titlings of this picture, wears the flattest possible hat of black beaver, plumed on the right and tilted sharply to the left, over cropped hair. The brim, decreasing in size and no longer slashed, is decorated with an enamelled spray of violas, an enamelled medallion of a saint, and small gold ornaments: crossed fish, vases, and lozenge shapes. Natural beard and moustache of midXVIc.

Shirt collar of black Spanish embroidery shows cords for fastening; embroidered ruffles at wrists are full and gathered but not yet formalized. Interlaced cord decoration of black sleeve; gown edged in white; inner garment red and gold.

1164-66. XVIc. 1548. English. (Lancashire, Sefton Church.)

William Molyneux and his two wives.

The Molyneux had lived at Sefton since the Conquest; William, his wives, and the local monument maker all appear to have been country-living conservatives who clung to the old fashions.

The ladies show the pedimental headdress in one

of its last appearances, and William wears an antiquated mail coif, under the XIVc. Lancastrian SS collar, which had been revived by Henry VII, late in XVc.

1167. XVIc. 1546. English. (Knole, Lord Sackville.) *School of Holbein.* Earl of Surrey.

Henry Howard, (1518?-1547), Earl of Surrey, eldest son of the third Duke of Norfolk, was brought up "at proud Windsor, where I in lust and joy, With a Kinge's son, my childish years did pass," as companion of Henry VIII's illegitimate son, the Duke of Richmond. Surrey nearly married Princess Mary, and Richmond eventually married Surrey's sister.

Surrey's haughty, rash, intriguing temper took him repeatedly from court favor to jail: for quarrels, for eating meat in Lent, for breaking London windows with Wyatt's son. He fought as one of the champions at the jousts in 1540, was knighted in 1541, received the Garter, and fought gallantly in many wars. But he was tried and beheaded, on the accusation of quartering his arms with those of Edward the Confessor (as his family continued to do after Mary's accession); he was actually feared to be plotting, with his father, against the king.

During four imprisonments, Surrey wrote his tender love poems to Geraldine, and made a translation of the Aeneid which is the first English blank verse. Of the transition between the Anglo-Saxon Chaucerian poetry and the Elizabethan Renaissance, Puttenham says: there "sprong up a new company of courtly makers, of whom Sir Thomas Wyatt the elder and Henry Earle of Surrey were the two chieftaines, who having travailed into Italy, and there tasted the sweete and stately measures and stile of the Italian Poesie, as novices newly crept out of the schooles of Dante, Arioste, and Petrarch, they greatly polished our rude and homely maner of vulgar Poesie, from that it had bene before, and for that cause may justly be sayd the first reformers of our English

meetre and stile." (From *The Arte of English Poesie,* 1589.)

Costume, with superb Renaissance appliqué and embroidery, shows trunk hose very slightly padded; slashed shoes still square-toed.

1168. XVIc. c. 1548. English. (Hampton Court, H.M. the King.)

Gwillim Stretes. Gentleman in Red, called "Thomas Howard, Earl of Surrey."

Stretes, a Hollander, was painter at the English court, c. 1546-1556, and completed some of Holbein's portraits. Entire costume is red, except for a white plume in the velvet hat and the Spanish black work of the white shirt; this has a high collar with a ruffle at the top, and at the wrists. The short, wide velvet gown has no dependent sleeve from the upper puff; it is satin lined, and like the jacket beneath, which is open to the waist, is trimmed with narrow lines of gold; wide trunk-hose, without padding or panes. A massive gold tassel hangs from the slung dagger, and the cuts on the shoes are emphasized by gold buttons.

1169. XVIc. c. 1548. English. (Windsor Castle, H.M. the King.)

Att. to G. Stretes or *School of Holbein.* Edward VI.

The eleven-year-old king was painted several times in this costume. In his hat, and that of the Gentleman in Red (1168) the pleated crown is just beginning its rise, which is indicated in the new diversion of interest from the underside of the brim toward what will become the hat band.

His ermine-lined gown of bright red velvet is guarded by gold bands; its collar is higher and narrower, the top of its sleeves less full than formerly worn. His jerkin of silver brocade has the new high collar, low waistline, slightly protruding belly, and overlapping skirts. Horizontal cords, spaced like the clasps on his father's 1544 coat, cross the corded bands of decoration, and button. His trunk hose are padded;

puffs are drawn through the cut-out pattern of their brocade and that of the jacket sleeves.

Black hat, shoes, dagger sheath and tassel; white hose. The first knitted silk stockings worn in England were given Edward by Sir Thomas Gresham, the merchant, whose trade with the Low Countries brought him into contact with such Spanish goods.

1170. XVIc. Before 1554. English. (Metropolitan Mus.)

British School. Lady Jane Grey.

Frances Brandon's accomplished and delightful daughter, who was for nine days Queen of England, and who was executed at seventeen, together with her father, Suffolk, and her husband, Dudley, wears her hair dressed over pads, under a ruche-lined cap, developed from the French hood; in other portraits, her cap shows a slight center dip.

The extremely high collar of her gown has a carefully goffered ruff, matching her wristbands; they are edged, though not yet with lace. Her gown shows the fur-slashed upper sleeve and fur collar of the coat-like, one-piece Spanish gown of mid-XVIc., which often has a high inner, as well as a low outer collar. Ropes of pearls will increase in use to the end of the century.

1171. XVIc. 1554 English. (Boston, Isabella Stewart Gardner Museum.)

Antonio Moro (Sir Anthony More). Queen Mary.

This portrait, by the Flemish artist who became an English knight, was sent to her prospective husband, Philip of Spain, and shows the daughter of King Henry VIII and Catharine of Aragon to have been "a little faded woman with a white face, no eyebrows, and russet hair. At thirty-seven, an old maid, disillusioned and wearied by years of cruel injustice." After his divorce from her mother, and Elizabeth's birth, Henry VIII had, for a long time, removed Mary from the succession. The diary of her extremely intelligent 11-year-old brother, Edward VI, relates that "The Lady Mary my sister . . . was called with my Council into a Chamber; where was declared how long I had suffered her Mass in hope of her reconciliation. . . . She answered That her Soul was God's and her Faith she would not change nor dissemble her Opinion with contrary doings. It was said I constrained not her Faith but willed her not as a King to Rule but as a subject to obey; and that her example might breed too much inconvenience." (See Appendix: Ponsonby.)

The restoration of the old religion, which cancelled the imputations of her illegitimacy, led to government persecutions for which she was not responsible, and her nickname of "Bloody Mary." She was actually a good and intelligent person, learned and a fine musician, who suffered from life-long ill health and extreme nearsightedness.

Mary, who wears a wide, flattened French hood over waved hair, and carries gloves with jewelled cuffs, is dressed in blue-gray velvet, with a characteristically plain bodice, and undersleeves and skirt of blue-gray brocade. Her standing collar has a frilled inner collar of Spanish embroidery, in addition to her shirt; the ruff is well on its way.

The queen loved jewels, as did her father and sister. By a ribbon from her short precious girdle, hangs the same reliquary which is also seen in a full-length portrait belonging to the Society of Antiquaries.

From her collar hangs one of Philip's many gifts, a diamond, with an historic pendant pearl "worth 25,000 ducats," called, from its travels "La Pelegrina." Found in 1517 by a slave to whom Balboa, in exchange, gave freedom, it became a prized jewel of the Spanish crown. After Mary's death it returned to Spain, was carried off by Joseph Bonaparte, and sold by Napoleon III to the Marquess of Abercorn. Because of its weight it was often lost; the pearl had been recovered from the upholstery of a settee in the English court, and from the folds of Queen Victoria's train, before Abercorn finally had a fastening bored into the end of the pearl. (See Appendix: Norris).

1172. XVIc. 1559. English. (Bettws-y-Coed, J. C. Wynne-Finch.)

Hans Eworth. Frances Brandon and Adrian Stoke.

Frances Brandon, mother of Lady Jane Grey, widowed by the execution of the Duke of Suffolk, was married the following year at 36 to the 21-year-old master of her horse, Adrian Stoke.

1173

We see her in the year of her death, dressed in a high-necked black gown with jewels and gold aiglettes. The neck ruffs and wrist bands, new at the time of her daughter's portrait, are now elaborately edged in gold. Black and gold French hood; slashed and jewelled gloves; fine rings.

Her young husband wears a lynx-lined black jacket with the standing collar of the 1560's and short sleeve, its slashings caught by gold tags; and an embroidered and slashed doublet, its ruffs edged with pink. The high male collar of the 1550-60's may be open or closed, and is often furnished with ties. It mounts straight up, and encompasses the ruff, which still appears to have some connection with the shirt; by the fourth quarter, the collar will be closely fitted and the formal band of the ruff will be fastened to its top.

1173. XVIc. 1567-8. English. (Metropolitan Museum.)

British School. Mary, Queen of Scots: the Duff-Ogilvy portrait.

The padded (*atifet*) arrangements of hair on either side of a c.part tended to be supplanted by unparted hair, drawn up over a pad, its height increasing into XVIIc. The feeling of a center part shows in the rolled edge of her tiny cap.

As the ruff (*band*) increased in size and became edged with lace, the fluted finish at the wrist of a close, or of a padded leg o'mutton sleeve, was usually replaced by a turned-back cuff, with lace. The closed circular ruff was commonly worn by married women.

Brantôme said that Mary looked like a goddess in everything, "even the barbarous costume of the savages of her country," that is, in Scot's dress.

Mary, who loved jewelry, especially pearls, wears only earrings and chains with this extremely simple costume. Through Mary's French marriage, some of Catherine de' Medici's best pearls passed into the English crown jewels.

Male infants, like this baby who became James I, wore women's gowns, in miniature, throughout the diaper period; then miniature male costume. Embroidered caps protected the heads of babies and elderly men; babies also wore every form of grown-up hat, in miniature.

1174. XVIc. 1566. Welsh. (Glamorganshire, Llanturt Major.)

Monumental effigy of a woman.

Nothing is known about the middle-class Welsh woman, whose memorial slab was found lying in a churchyard.

Women, as well as men, wore the plumed hat with a high pleated crown. The dress, with its wide ruff, shows the increase in padded rigidity of last half XVIc. The rectangular pattern, into which the covering of the leg o'mutton sleeve of a great lady would be puffed and jewelled, is achieved in this modest costume by a latticework of fabric bands. The outer garment, tight in the waist, full in the skirt and sleeveless, except for the picadills around the armseye, is open in a V to the waist, with its flat collar spreading wide over the shoulders.

1174

1175. XVIc. 1568-9. English. (Hatfield House, Marquess of Salisbury.)

Joris Hoefnagel. A Horselydown Wedding.

There are few more precious costume documents than this picture of a country wedding, where the gentry, bourgeoisie and country folk appear together. Women of all classes are seen to wear hats over hoods. The picture will repay much study.

1175

1176

1176. XVIc. 1573. English. (Nottingham, Wollaston Hall.
Coll. Lord Middleton.)

Unknown artist. Lady Willoughby.

During the reign of Elizabeth, the character of
jewelry alters: jewelled collars are replaced by draped
strands of pearls; and oval medallions by more elaborate pendants, showing better cut stones, increasingly
naturalistic enamel work in paler colors; miniatures;
cameos; mirrors; and watches of all shapes, octagonal,
fat and pomander-like, or flattened. (See Appendix.)

Both the form of the pendant and the spot at which
it is placed are now less often symmetrical. Lady Willoughby wears her enamelled mermaid pendant at
one side of her bodice, which is looped with strings
of pearls combined with beads.

Interest in the hat now centers on its band. This
carries the jewels formerly pinned to the under side
of the brim; and from it, clusters of plumes emphasize the heightening crown. The male hat, much
seen on women, is worn here, as was usual, with
loose uncovered hair and a tiny reticulated cap, set
on the back of the head. The hat, as well as the cap,
is often worn indoors by women at this period, just
as it is by men.

Lady Willoughby wears the one-piece open Spanish gown. Though it forms one garment with the
gown beneath, its separate, coat-like look is emphasized by the flat, turned-down collar and cuffs, worn
in conjunction with the 2 set ruffs at the neck, and
those at the sleeves of the gown beneath.

Both forms of collars and cuffs are finished with
a narrow purled edging of needlepoint lace. Brought
from Italy in 1533 by Catherine de Medici, lace-
making received government encouragement in Flanders. Refugees from the religious persecutions by

Spain in the Low Countries brought lace manufacture to England in the last third of XVIc., and lace
rapidly became the characteristic feature of late Elizabethan and XVIIc. costume.

The first laces were needlepoint, in the looped-
cord patterns worn by Lady Willoughby, or in rectangular patterns based on the warp and weft of fabric; cut work; and the drawn, darned and whipped
reticella laces.

Pattern books for lace and embroidery were widely
published in second half XVIc. all over Europe.
(Many are in the fine lace collection of Cooper
Union Museum.) With the appearance of pillow lace,
running patterns, analogous to those of the foliated
appliqués of e.XVIc. become possible. These patterns, followed by embroidery in the freedom of its
techniques, become the "crewel" embroideries of the
turn of the century and XVIIc., asymmetrically patterned with birds, fantastic flowers, and scrolled
leaves, under the added influence of printed India
fabrics.

In costume, as we see by these sleeves, interest in
cords and knots is being transformed into an interest
in ribbons and bows.

1177. XVIc. c. 1560-70. English. (London, Nat. Port.
Gall.)

Unknown Flemish artist; formerly att. to *Zuccaro.*
Robert Dudley, Earl of Leicester.

Elizabeth's favorite, Amy Robsart's husband,
brother-in-law of Lady Jane Grey, leader of the Protestant faction, and uncle of Sir Philip Sidney, who
died under his command with the troops sent to the
relief of the Low Countries, the Earl is the personi-
fication of the handsome, assured courtier. But his
enemies unfairly said, "he was the son of a duke,

1177

the brother of a king, the grandson of an esquire, and the great-grandson of a carpenter, and the carpenter was the only honest man in the family, and the only one who had died in his bed."

The Earl's court costume is advanced in style. The collar has reached the ultimate height, which "rose up so high and sharp as if it would have cut his throat by daylight." (Thomas Middleton: *The Ant and the Nightingale,* quoted in Morse: *Elizabethan Pageantry.*) The fluted edge of the shirt collar has become a developed ruff by the 60's, matching those at the wrists. Picadills at the top of the collar support the ruff; they also appear at armseye, cuff and bottom of the skirtless doublet. The doublet is now assuming the "peascod" belly form, is fastened by buttons in a close row (previously grouped), and is pinked in the new small punctures, combined with cuts. Sleeves, narrow in the 50's, widen during the 60's, when they begin to show padding. Incidentally, the word picadill is the diminutive of the Spanish *pica,* (spear); it was these cut edges, according to legend, which gave the name of Picadilly to the street leading to the house of the tailor who introduced the style in England.

Paned trunk-hose, whale-boned and padded, reach to mid-thigh and are squared off at the bottom; codpiece disappearing.

The Spanish-Italian bonnet, with higher, full crown, introduced in the 60's, surmounts a typically English head. The hair, not yet artificially waved, is brushed back, and down, in front of the ear in the beginning of the later love-lock. Although Stubbes

complained of the variety of the cuts of beard and moustache: "When you come to be trimmed they will ask you whether you will be cut to look terrible to your enemy or amiable to your friend," these long, sweeping moustaches and natural beard, with the jaw shaved above the line of the moustache, are specifically English.

From a precious chain hangs a medallion of the Garter, shown also above his right shoulder. The narrow belt follows, exactly, the waistline of the doublet: the belt is sometimes shaped, and is made flexible by metal swivel connections. Front and back attachments of the sword, with elaborately guarded grip, very wide quillons and anneau.

1178. XVIc. 1578. English. (Bisham Abbey. Lady Vansittart-Neale.)

Unknown artist. Sir Edward Hoby.

Hoby, whose uncle, Lord Burleigh, was the most important man in England, wears the high, stiffened hat of last third of XVIc., "standying a quarter of a yarde aboue the crowne of their heades," Stubbes complains.

It is often worn at a much more acute angle than Hoby, over his fluffed-out hair, wears this maroon-plumed black hat, with its band of gold ornaments and cluster of gold acorns toward the top.

Ruff embroidered in maroon, on high collar of slashed, cream-colored doublet, with buttons and embroidered edges of self-colored silk, and shoulder-line extended by a cap, instead of picadills or a roll. Maroon scarf.

1179. XVIc. 1574. Flemish. (London, Nat. Port. Gall.)

Unknown Flemish artist. James I, aged 8.

Mary Stuart's suffering during her pregnancy produced a rachitic child, who could not stand till he was seven, and who always slobbered, with a tongue which seemed too big for his mouth. As Charles I also had weak legs and an impeded speech, these failures were more probably genetic.

Costume of various "natural" colors with olive-green velvet slops. Full, loose, breeches (venetians) never have cod-pieces and usually fasten below the knee, and are finished here by a picadill slashing.

High-necked, padded doublet of stitched chamois-colored leather, fastened at top only, by 3 gold buttons; has pointing front and short, overlapping skirts; sleeves quilted over some padding.

Belt, sword-belt, dagger and sword cases all of red velvet. Gauntlet and falcon. Flesh-colored hose, shoes of pale natural-colored leather.

1180. XVIc. 1577 English (Oxford Univ., Bodleian Lib.)

Christopher Ketel. Sir Martin Frobisher.

Discoverer of the Northwest Passage, and with Drake and Hawkins, under Howard of Effingham, vanquisher of the Armada, the admiral wears a sleeveless leather jerkin, with picadill finish at arms-eye, waist and breeches. The high collar is cut in one with the body of the jerkin; the gores of the neck, like the front opening, are fastened by points which are left open below the throat, over padded, almost skirtless doublet, with rows of tiny buttons, and padded leg o'mutton sleeves of 1575-90, with pushed up length on lower arm.

These superimposed padded garments were terribly hot, and both men and women got relief by wearing them open to the waist. In the presence of the French ambassador, De Maisse, Elizabeth opened her gown to the navel.

Rapier on narrow sword-belt at waist of doublet; wheellock pistol of late XVIc. Light colored shoes, rising over the instep in what will become a tongue, when the strap closing of late XVIc. develops.

1181. XVIc. 1580. English. (Oxford, Ashmolean.)

Unknown artist. John Bull.

The English musician, organist to Elizabeth and James I, and probable composer of the national anthem, "God Save the King," was given permission to lecture at the university in English, instead of Latin, in which he was not proficient.

He wears an open cappa (which is now pretty well restricted to choral, ecclesiastic, legal and academic wear), with a fur-lined hood of brocade, and a superb "black work" collar.

Evelyn mentions the damask robes of the doctors of music in the procession into chapel of the companions of the Garter on St. George's day (23 April, 1667).

1182. XVIc. c. 1585. English. (London, Nat. Port. Gall.)
Unknown Flemish artist. Sir Philip Sidney in a mandilion.

The mandilion is a loose, tabard-like jacket, usually slit up the sides, and with sleeves pendant. It has the character of a cape, and is often rotated a quarter turn, and allowed to hang, as we see it worn here, "Collie-Weston-ward," as the Dean of Windsor described it. (Wm. Harrison: *Description of England,* 1577-8.)

The breeches, trimmed with braid to match the mandilion, have the diagonal pocket slits, often found on the variety of breeches which are cut off at the knee, like shorts.

1183. XVIc. 1588. English. (London, Nat. Port. Gall.)
Unknown artist: formerly att. to *Zuccaro.*
Sir Walter Raleigh.

The poet and historian, colonizer and explorer, who was for a decade a favorite of Elizabeth, and who after many misfortunes died on the scaffold by order of James I, introduced into European cultivation the tobacco and potato brought back by his captains.

He wears a costume of white, with black and silver. Soft, loose hair, continued into the beard; one earring only, as was worn by men. When Stubbes, in scolding women about fashions, comes to pierced ears he says: "Because this is not so much frequented amongst women as men, I will say no more. . . ."

Doublet of pinked white silk. Over the turned-down collar of the doublet is a sheer collar, matching the cuffs, shoulder cap, and band which extends beyond the edge of the doublet. The swordbelt below is trimmed in silver to match his paned velvet slops. His fur-collared black velvet cape is rayed with silver beads.

A full-length portrait by Gheeraerts, belonging to

Sir Stephen Lennart, shows Raleigh in 1602, dressed in brown, white, silver and beige, with his young son in dark blue and silver.

1184. XVIIc. c. 1610. Dutch.
Unknown engraver. Fleshly Disguises.

Although the funnel-shaped farthingale remained in use, another skirt was worn from c.1570-c.1615, which widened straight out from the waist, over a sausage-shaped bolster tied high about the hips.

In England, this French fashion was intensified into a drum-shaped silhouette, by a pleated ruffle going horizontally from the waist to, or beyond, the circumference of the skirt.

Since chairs could contain neither of these skirts, it became customary to sit on piled cushions on the floor, or on stools rather like a sawbuck with a stretcher top.

Restraining, fitted underbodices of heavy material (*vasquine, basquine,* from which our word *basque* comes) had been used in late XVc. The corsets of the first third XVIc. were rigid, hinged iron cages; these were replaced by flexible steel in Catherine de' Medici's time. In the latter part of XVIc., corsets were boned in patterns like those shown on these bodices, and were elongated and held firm by a center busk of metal, bone or wood. Below the waist, these corsets were finished with a roll and picadill, to support the skirt between the waist and bolster. The triangular front placard was often a superb example of embroidery.

This is perhaps a good place to explain the origin of the word "band-box." Neck ruffs (bands) were constructed by pleating immensely long strips of material onto a neckband. As ruffs grew wider and more elaborate, doubled and tripled, their laundering became the work of an expert. They were starched, often in color, set on a form, and gauffered

1184

with a sort of curling iron called a "setting" or "poking stick." The finished band was then set, for protection, into a low, wide "band-box." Ruffs eventually reached proportions which starch alone could not support; wire frames and stays, "underproppers" or "supportasses" had to be added. When these are withdrawn, in XVIIc., we see the wide bands falling limp.

Philip Stubbes has given us the most minute descriptions of ruffs, their starching and underpropping, as indeed he does of every other extravagant detail of Elizabethan dress; it is a temptation not to quote him by the page. The development of ruffs, Stow tells us dates from 1564 when "Mistris Dingen Van den Passe, born at Taenen in Flaunders, daughter to a worshipful knight of that province, with her husband came to London for their better safeties, and there professed herself a *starcher,* wherein she excelled, unto whom her own nation presently repaired, and payed her very liberally for her worke. Some very few of the best and most curious wives of that time, observing the *neatnesse and delicacy of the Dutch for whitenesse and fine wearing of linen,* made them *cambricke ruffs,* and sent them to Mistris Dinghen *to starch,* and after a while, they made them *ruffes of lawn,* which was at that time a stuff most strange, and wonderful, and thereupon

rose a *general scoffe* or *byword,* that shortly they would make ruffes of a *spider's web;* and then they began to send their daughters and nearest kinswomen to Mistris Dingen to *learne how to starche;* her usuall price was at that time, foure or five pounds, to teach them how *to starch,* and twenty shillings how to seeth starch. . . . Divers noble personages made them *ruffes, a full quarter of a yeard deepe,* and two lengthe in one ruffe. This fashion in London was called the *French fashion;* but when Englishmen came to *Paris,* the *French* knew it not, and in derision called it *the English monster."* (See sources on Tudor costume in appendix.)

Masks for outdoor wear came into use for both sexes during Elizabeth's time. Long masks were kept in place by a button, fixed on the back and held in the teeth. Masks of animals and grotesques were worn at carnival time, and by figures of Italian comedy.

Feather fans with a long stick remained in use in the second half of XVIc., even after the introduction of folding fans, on the Chinese model, by way of Italy in late XVIc.

The details of these gowns will be discussed, in their most exaggerated form, in the later gowns of Elizabeth.

QUEEN ELIZABETH

During her wretched childhood, Elizabeth was actually destitute of clothing. The royal governess wrote Lord Thomas Cromwell "beseeching .. that she may have some raiment, for she hath neither gown, nor kirtall, nor petticoat, nor no manner of linnen, nor foresmocks (pinafores), nor kerchief,

nor rails (nightgowns), nor mofelers (mobcaps), nor biggens (nightcaps). All these her grace must have. I have driven off as long as I can, that, to my troth I cannot drive it any longer." (E. Green: *Letters of Royal and Illustrious Ladies.*)

Elizabeth, in portraits of her as a princess, wears the classic Holbein costume; the gowns of the first years of her reign are rich but rather conventional. The tiny, slender queen, who never looked her age, was 50 before her vanity evolved the immensely personal style associated with her name.

Below a thickly painted face, great ruffs conceal an aging throat, though her bosom is often completely bare. Elizabeth, who seems to have had an over-active thyroid, complained of the heat while others felt chilly. Over her greying hair, curled auburn wigs mount, framed in wired-out gauze and dressed with the incredible jewels she loved, as all her family had loved jewels. Her fine hands are always on display, occupied with handsome accessories.

Elizabeth maintained a wardrobe of some 500 costumes: gowns prepared for the celebration of events which could be foreseen but were not certain; gowns to impress, startle, tell a story, or give warning.

Elizabeth's wardrobe was inherited by Anne, who had a parsimonious husband, and, we are told, had Elizabeth's gowns remade for her own use. This seems perfectly plausible (see Ill. 1362), until one looks at actual garments which belonged to Elizabeth (see Ills. 1187-89). They are so tiny that a good many 10-year-old American girls could not possibly get into them. Anne must also have been very small.

1185. XVIc. English. (Yale Univ., Elizabethan Club.)

Federigo Zuccaro. Queen Elizabeth.

Curled hair arranged within a jewelled wire frame, from which embroidered gauze falls, free and unwired. Ruff of reticella lace. French gown; moderate waistline; skirt with closed front; yoke and sleeves of jewel-studded embroidery; roll at armseye. Scarf and looped pearls lead to pendant with three nude figures. Ostrich fan with jewelled handle.

1186. XVIc. c. 1590. English. (Colonial Williamsburg, Va.)

Marcus Gheeraerts, e. Queen Elizabeth.

Gray tubular ruff and veil wired wide and caught to the sleeve of black gown, embroidered and jew-

elled in red, gold, black and pearl. Shoulders extended by roll and scalloped picadill. Gray undersleeve brocaded in Tudor roses and fleurs-de-luce in gold, rose and green.

Elizabeth appears to have liked a long line from neck to feet. We often find the centrally massed decorative bands of the Spanish gown used on the underskirt of her French dresses, where we would expect a pendant girdle; and this line is given unusual emphasis on some of her drum-shaped skirts with pleated cartwheel tops. When worn over hip bolsters, the inverted V-line of outer skirt of French gown must be cut in inverted U shape. Gloves with jewelled cuffs; feather fan caught on skirt.

Courtesy of the Elizabethan Club, Yale University (1185);
Frick Art Reference Library (1186)

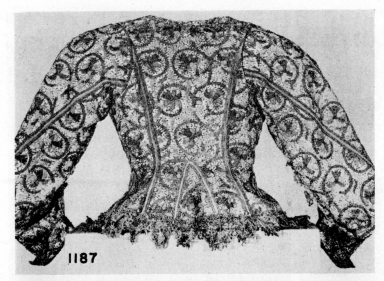

1187

1187-89. XVIc. 1578. English. (Boston, Museum of Fine Arts.)
1187. Jacket.

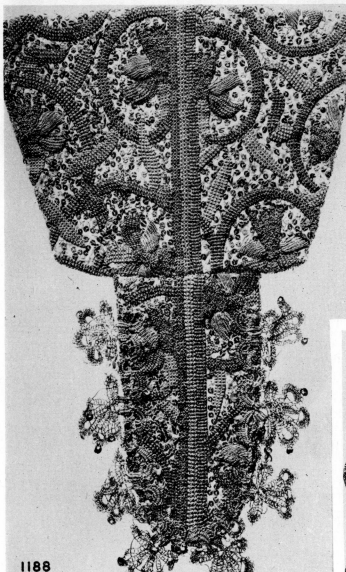

1188

1188. Stomacher.

1189. Embroidered coif in two parts.
These garments were left by Elizabeth as souvenirs after an overnight visit to Sir Roger Wodehouse, of Kimberly, Norfolk, August 21, 1578. They are done in gold, two shades of silver and gold sequins on natural colored linen, and show Elizabeth to have been a tiny creature.

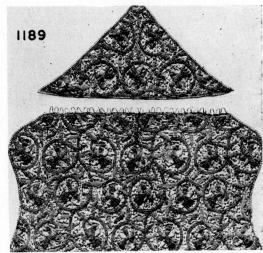

1189

1190. XVIc. English.

Crispin van de Passe, after *Isaac Oliver*. Elizabeth of England. (Costume of 1588, engraved 1603.)

The earliest portrait of Elizabeth in the drum-shaped farthingale, open standing ruff and wired veil, which she made her own, is Isaac Oliver's little ink and water color drawing at Windsor; from it, Rogers and Passe drew the material for their later engravings.

This white and gold costume is supposed to be that worn by Elizabeth when giving solemn thanks at St. Paul's for the defeat of the Armada. Its bodice, oversleeve linings and overskirt are of white satin brocaded in gold. The undersleeves, stomacher and underskirt have puffs of white silk caught to cloth of gold by pearls and rubies, with emeralds used in addition on the borders.

She wears the ropes of pearls which will be standard at the turn of the century (see Ills. 1290-95), and her curled wig, surmounted by the crown, is pinned with pendant pearls. She carries the orb and sceptre.

1191. English XVIc. Sept. 20, 1592. (London, Nat. Port. Gall. Bequest of Viscount Dillon of Ditchley.)

Artist unknown. Queen Elizabeth: the Ditchley Portrait.

This portrait of Elizabeth, standing on a colored map of Oxfordshire, commemorates her visit to Sir Henry Lee, Viscount Dillon's ancestor, at Ditchley.

Her creamy white satin costume is accented with coral. Crown, necklace and pendant of pearls, rubies and coral. Wired veil of gold gauze, edged with pearl-sewn gold lace and jewels.

Her short skirt is much fuller than in the van de Passe engraving; the overskirt has been given up. The hexagonal pattern of the skirt puffs, and the edges of her trailing sleeves are sewn with gold studs of varying forms, set with rubies, pearls and sapphires, and fastened in opposing directions.

A rose is pinned to her white ruff; a folding fan is fastened to her girdle by a knotted, coral-colored ribbon; she carries brown gloves with slashed gold cuffs.

Color reproduction of Ill. 1191 may be found in Morse: *Elizabethan Pageantry*.

1192. XVIc. 1594. English. (Hatfield House, Marquess of Salisbury.)

Marcus Gheeraerts, e. Queen Elizabeth: the Rainbow Portrait.

In this portrait, full of symbolism, the words "Non sine sole iris" (No rainbow without the sun) appear above the hand which holds the rainbow; the sleeves of her orange, fawn and olive costume are embroidered with jewelled snakes; the lining of her outer garment, with eyes and ears; a mailed glove is fastened to her ruff: it warns that she is powerful and fortunate, wily and wise, that she sees and hears all.

Her crown is set over a brim shaped like the headdress of the previous century but many items of her costume are prophetic of the century to come.

The coat-like outer garment is becoming separated from the gown beneath, and is worn off one shoulder. In the manner of the XVIIc., the bodice is of linen, embroidered in colored sprigs, and the lace edging of its low, spreading bodice is assuming the scallops of XVIIc. lace, though it is still of reticella. She wears a tiny neck ruff, and a wider ruff on the bodice; behind this, the wired gold veil has been cut off, horizontally, in the manner of the next century, and is separated from the flowing ends which now start from the neck. We see the beginnings of another XVIIc. fashion in the way her hair is dressed, with trailing locks at the side. In addition to the familiar knotted ropes of pearls, she wears pearl strands as bracelets.

1193. XVIc. 1592-4. English. (Hardwick Hall, Duke of Devonshire.)

Unknown artist. Queen Elizabeth: the Hardwick Portrait.

English ecclesiastical embroidery, last third XIII to first third of XIVc. was the finest in Europe. With the introduction of Spanish work in first third XVIc. there was a revival, which lasted through the XVIIc. The Reformation ended ecclesiastical embroidery, dispersed fine church pieces into secular use as wall-hangings, and left great knowledge and energy to be channeled into the decoration of caps, gloves, shoes and bags, gowns and jackets, shirts, collars, scarves and handkerchiefs, pillows, chairs and hangings.

The first Spanish-inspired "black work," often relieved in gold, was followed by multicolored embroidery with gold and silver, of scrolls and naturalistic flowers and animals; and petit point. Turkey work, in imitation of Oriental carpets, began to appear in third quarter XVIc.; raised "stump work" decorated mirror frames and boxes in XVIIc.; samplers, mentioned in Shakespeare, are seen from XVIIc.; bed, window and wall hangings, embroidered in silk or wool, appear second half XVIIc., and yellow silk embroidery on white at the end XVIIc. (See Appendix.)

Elizabeth herself did fine work, but among the greatest embroiderers of their time were Mary, Queen of Scots and the Countess of Shrewsbury, with whom Mary spent fourteen years of her detention in England. This fabulous lady, known as "Bess of Hardwick," was by four marriages the richest woman in England; she thought that she would never die as long as she was building the great mansions she loved, like Hardwick and Chatsworth; and she did die during a hard frost which stopped construction when she was ninety.

Bess of Hardwick is supposed to have given the white satin stomacher and kirtle of this gown, which she had embroidered in all manner and color of exotic birds, beasts and flowers, as a Christmas present to Elizabeth, who sent in return this portrait of herself in the finished gown, with an overdress of gold-embroidered green velvet.

The wired veil is now fastened to the edge of the bodice, under the ruff. The gown is very short, its underskirt finished with a pearl fringe. Gloves, indispensable, and now a favorite gift; round feather fan; pendant fastened to side of skirt by ribbons attached to point of stomacher; slashed and embroidered white shoes.

EUROPEAN TEXTILE DESIGN

The inspiration of the design of European textiles had always been Oriental: Byzantine, Saracenic, Persian, and to some degree, Chinese. The XVIIc. trade with India and China brought fresh Oriental motifs, which became the rage of the XVIIIc.

Meanwhile, during XVIc., a European interest in realistically drawn natural flowers is shown in missal painting, in tapestries, in embroidery, and in costume. Of all Philip Stubbes' castigations of Elizabethan ways, none now seems so extreme as his hatred of sweet smelling flowers and of women who wear "nosegays and posies . . . sticked in their breastes before." Naturalistic sprigs of flowers replace the stylized Ottoman pomegranate, cone and leaf designs. Patterns mount and spread in the *candelabre* designs of Louis XIV brocade and lace. Formal interlaced patterns turn into loose, searching tendrils. Stylized and fabulous armorial birds and beasts, facing left and right, give way to animals in the pursuit of the chase (see Ills. 905, 1704), to exotic animals like the whale and camel, to butterflies in flight, beetles and worms.

Trained decorative artists appear in the XVIIIc., as did Watteau from the atelier of Charles Audran, keeper of the Luxembourg collection; and Pillement and Philippe de la Salle, who studied design at the Académie des Beaux Arts, founded by Mazarin in 1648. Their fanciful improvisations on Chinese and Indian motifs were immensely influential. Chippendale was inspired by Chinese furniture; little pagodas and peaked bridges appear in European gardens.

The old interest in naturalistic flower forms persists, meanwhile, and is reinforced by the romantic rocks, ruins and graves, cottages and farm animals, which came with J. J. Rousseau's influence in second half XVIIIc.

The amusements and games, the allegorical figures, favored at the turn of the XVIII-XIX centuries, and such literal scenes as that of the Jouy factory (Ill. 1894) tend to become imprisoned, during the Classic Revival, in repeated medallion patterns, often showing notable buildings. Historical scenes are popular, both in hangings and in printed handkerchiefs, as Steele had foreseen, when he asked in the Tatler, #3,1709: "Suppose an ingenious gentleman should write a poem of advice to a callico-printer; do you suppose there is a girl in England, that would wear anything but the taking of Lille, or the battle of Oudenarde?"

As the Jouy factory (see Ills. 1955-60) ran down between 1810-20, the Alsatian and English manufacturers came into their glory. But their great period of delightful sprigged dress fabrics, and bold chintzes with flowers, fruits and birds, declines with the general debasement of taste in second half of XIXc., as red, brown and black Paisley shawl motifs are combined with magenta and purple cabbage roses (see Ills. 2562-70, 2425-28). For bibliography, see Appendix.

1194. XVIc. English.
    Elizabethan "black work."

1195. XVIc. English.
    Embroidery: petit point on satin, appliquéd pansies and thistles.

1196. XVIIc. English.
    Embroidery: polychrome silk and purl on white satin.

1197. XVIIc. 1672. English.
    Mirror frame of stump work; story of Jael and Sisera, signed A.P.,1672. "Stump work," raised, padded, and often gathered, free of the background was used to decorate boxes, purses and mirrors in XVIIc. England.
    "When my sister Jenny was in her sampler, I made her get the whole story without book, and tell it to me in needlework," Steele (as Sir Isaac Bickerstaff) says in the *Tatler,* # 84, Oct. 22, 1709.

1198. XVIIIc. 1715. English.
    Embroidered apron: white linen thread on white muslin.

1199. Late XVIc. Italian.
    Panel: Red cut velvet, brocaded in gold; compare with embroidery patterns.

1200

1200. XVIc. English. (Windsor Castle, H.M. the King.)
Isaac Oliver. Sir Philip Sidney.

The miniaturist, Isaac Oliver (1566-1617), son of a Huguenot refugee, was the pupil of Nicholas Hilliard and teacher of a son Peter, who became court miniaturist to James I. Evelyn took some relatives to court in 1660 to show them the king's collection of Oliver's work. Another fine Oliver miniature shows the Three Brothers Brown and their Servant, in 1597, their hat-crown wreathed in twists of "cyprus" mourning crêpe.

Sidney's dearest friend, Fynes Moryson, said of the grave, radiant, and chivalrous Protestant poet, diplomat, and soldier: "Though I lived with him and knew him from a child, I never knew him other than a man." While serving in the army of his uncle, Robert Dudley, Earl of Leicester, he doffed his greaves because his companion had none, was wounded in the leg, and died at 32, at Reimagen, in 1586. All London, as well as the court, wore sober clothes in mourning for him. His funeral procession is shown in Laut: *Sequitur Celebritas Pompa Funeris,* 1587.

High, hard hat, over curled, lengthening locks. Lace band, low at throat; and cuffs. Jacket with shoulders widened by a roll; decoration in vertical lines, (analogous to *panes*); skirts, cut and overlapping in manner of XVIIc. Very short trunks, puffed but not stuffed, over canions finished with lace cuffs.

Soft, high boots with spurs, of which the Spanish ambassador told James I: "I shall amaze my countrymen by letting them know at my return that all London's booted and apparently ready to walk out of town." Gloves; long rapier.

Young Englishmen of fashion are now making the Grand Tour of Europe, as they will continue to do into the XIXc. Many, like Moryson and Coryat are publishing accounts of their travels; Sidney was much influenced by having been in Paris on St. Bartholomew's Eve.

1201. XVIc. 1589. English. (London, Victoria and Albert Museum.)
Nicholas Hilliard. Sir Christopher Hatton.

Nicholas Hilliard (1537-1619), was a goldsmith of good English family. Inspired by Holbein's miniatures, he became the first of the long line of English miniature painters. As court "painter in little" to Elizabeth, he executed her 1585 Ermine Portrait, at Hatfield House. In 1588 he painted Robert Dudley, Earl of Leicester (belonging to the Duke of Buccleugh and Queensbury), and a drawing, 1580 (belonging to Archibald G. Russel), showing the widest possible farthingale. His son and pupil, Lawrence, was an equally accomplished miniaturist.

The dancing of the attractive Hatton brought him into favor with Elizabeth, whose pet name for him was "mouton" (lamb). His solid ability carried him to the Lord Chancellorship in 1588.

Photograph by gracious permission of H. M. The King of England

At this time he was made a Knight of the Garter, the emblem of which he wears over one high, soft leather boot, pinked for flexibility. His feet are thrust into pantoufles, slippers with high cork platforms, covering only the instep, worn out of doors over the shod foot. His turned-down band is of cut work, lace edged. Tudor collar (see Ill. 1134).

Stubbes says: "They haue corked shoes, pisnets, and fine pantoffles, whiche beare them vppe a finger or two from the ground, whereof some be of white leather, some of blacke, and some of red; some of black veluet, some of white, some of red, some of greene, razed, caruet, cut, and stitched all over with silke, and layd on with gold, siluer, and such like: yet . . . to what good vses serue these pantoffles, except it be to weare in a priuate house, or in a man's chamber to keep him warme? . . . but to goe abroade in them as they are now vsed altogether, is rather a lett or hinderaunce to a man than otherwise, for shall hee not be fane to knock and spurne at euery wal, stone, or poste, to keepe them on his feete?" They are so hard to manage that some men's legs swell up with the effort, and Stubbes describes with his usual gusto the ways in which they kick up dust or accumulate filth.

1202. XVIc. c. 1590. English. (London, Duke of Buccleugh.)

Nicholas Hilliard. George Clifford, third Earl of Cumberland as the Queen's Champion.

The dissolute, freebooting earl who commanded the "Bonaventure" against the Armada, does not wear the Garter with which he was invested in 1592. This portrait probably represents him in the tournament of Nov. 17, 1590, when he jousted in place of Sir Henry Lee.

The very suit of colored Greenwich armor in which Hilliard painted Clifford, will be seen among the photographs of the Metropolitan Museum Armor Collection (see Ill. 461).

He wears the queen's jewelled glove pinned to his gold-trimmed, plumed white hat; blue steel armor with eight-pointed gold stars; pale blue tunic, lined in white, embroidered in gold and green roses and leaves, and bordered in jewelled gold.

1203. XVIc. c. 1590. English. (Earl of Chesterfield.)

Sir James Scudamore.

Some elements of this suit are also in the M.M.A. Armor Collection. The old sectional goring of the *waffenrock* skirt is commemorated in the way in which braid is laid on here.

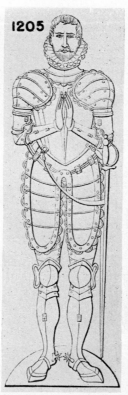

1204. XVIc. 1591. English. (Cornwall, Fowey.)
Monumental effigy.

Alice, wife of John Rashleigh, and daughter of William Lanyon.

England in XIVc. had no fleet. The foundations of the naval power of the Devon privateers of Drake's day were laid by "The Gallants of Fowey," following the French sack of the little port, which became the most important in Cornwall until midXVIc. The largest of the prehistoric stone cromlechs of Cornwall stands at Lanyon.

This country gentlewoman wears a modest roll under her short gown. The V opening of her bodice is filled by a pleated shirt with high collar and plain ruff. Her shoes show the beginning of a real heel, and the extension of the top of the heel enclosure into straps over the instep.

1205. XVIc. 1593. English. (Suffolk, Wrentham.)
Monumental effigy. Humphrey Brewster.

Complete armor of late XVIc. Ruff on high collared breastplate of peascod form; pauldrons spreading across chest; tassets, lengthening, like lobster tails, are buckled to skirt of breastplate. Scalloped finish used on costume also appears on armor. Gentlemen are now more often represented bareheaded, without hat or helm.

1206. XVIc. c. 1596. English. (Cleveland Mus. of Art.)
Isaac Oliver. Sir Anthony Mildmay.

Mildmay was Elizabeth's ambassador to the court of Henry IV of France, who "later complained of his coldness and ungenial manners."

The following description, signed W.M.M., is taken from the Bulletin of the Cleveland Museum of Art, Feb., 1927, no. 2.:

"This miniature must have been painted in or after the year 1596, for in it Sir Anthony is represented after knighthood had been conferred upon him. It is

in all likelihood an official portrait, painted as a memorial of the signal honor of ambassadorship. Sir Anthony stands before his tent, which forms an elaborate baldaquin at the back of the picture. He wears parts of a parade suit of armor, beautifully decorated with engraved bands of gilded arabesques. Across one shoulder, knotted beneath the gauntleted hand which grasps his court sword, is a blue sash edged with gold. His leg pieces have been removed and are shown on the floor near a cushion of crimson velvet. The right gauntlet lies on the table . . . covered with a blue cloth fringed with gold. There is also a pistol inlaid with ivory, and his finely-shaped helmet, gorgeously bedecked with a blue plume of curling ostrich feathers. Beyond is a chair, late Renaissance in style, and to one side an iron-bound chest, upon which is carelessly thrown a garment, perhaps a brigandine, perhaps only a velvet doublet, gold and purple, lined with blue."

His Greenwich armor lacks tasses. The concave scalloping of the skirt of the peascod breastplate can be compared to that of Sir Philip Sidney's jacket. The very short trunk-hose of a man of fashion of the last quarter XVIc. (and Stubbes, of course, has a great deal to say about that subject), have a horizontal strap woven through the panes. The sword is occasionally thrust through the panes in just this way. Ivory hose and shoes with tongue, under straps tied with blue bows. Compare decorative seaming of blue and white tent with that used on Sir Edward Hoby's costume (Ill. 1178). Long hair, and tiny beard and moustache, in one of the extravagant variations of end XVIc.

1207. XVIc. 1596. English. (Penshurst, Lord de L'Isle and Dudley.)
Marcus Gheeraerts,e. Barbara Gamage, Lady Sidney, and her children.

1207

The first wife of Sir Philip Sidney's brother Robert, who became Earl of Leicester in 1618, stands touching her sons: the year-old baby, who succeeded to the title, and his elder brother, who died young.

The use of light colors in both men's and women's dress increased during last quarter XVIc., and the whole family is shown dressed in white.

Lady Sidney's short gown shows many characteristics of English XVIIc. style. Its closed ruff, graded in width, frillier and less rigid, is worn lower and looser on the throat. The bodice has a shorter waist which has almost lost its point, and is differentiated from the skirt by its embroidery. The ruffle at the top of the skirt is smaller, less rigidly pleated, and a smaller bolster is used. The head is relatively uncovered; curled hair, loosely dressed, covers the ears.

Her older daughters wear miniature versions of the standard "Elizabethan" costume. Their petticoats show below their short skirts, as Elizabeth's often did. Twisted scarves outline the pointed waistlines, and a bow is tied around the arm of one.

The elder son, still in skirts, wears a diminutive peascod doublet, with a low-necked lace collar, sash and sword-belt, and carries a plumed hat with a high crown.

The youngest children all wear aprons. Black cords replace the knotted pearls of the older sisters. The baby's bells and rattle hang from his belt, and are slung, baldric-wise, over the shoulder.

1208. XVIc. After 1596. English. (London Nat. Port. Gall.)

Unknown artist. Sir Henry Unton, with scenes in his career.

Unton (c.1557-96) whose mother was a daughter

1208

of the protector Somerset, was a member of parliament and a personal friend and companion at arms of Henry of Navarre.

In this picture, his portrait, flanked by Fame and a skeleton, stands above the pageant of his life, pictured from left to right, with the sun and moon in the upper corners indicating the beginning and end. His birth takes place at "Wadlie," his family home, with scenes from Oxford life above; his marriage feast with dancing, as an orchestra plays in the next room; travels to "Venis, Paddua, across ye Alpes to the Low Countries and Niminggan"; his meeting at Cushia (Coucy?) with Henry IV, to whom Unton became ambassador in 1591; and his death while on a second embassy to France; the return of his hearse by land and sea; his funeral procession and sermon at Bolton Church; and his effigy. (Cust notes in National Portrait Gallery catalog.)

The earliest English representation of an umbrella is supposed to be the white one which Unton holds over his head, as he rides from the Alps to Padua, in the upper right hand corner of the picture. Like the Horseleydown Wedding, this picture is too complicated for comment, but will repay minute study with a magnifying glass.

1209. Late XVI-e.XVIIc. English. (London, Victoria and Albert Museum.)

Nicholas Hilliard. Miniature portrait of a gentleman.

Negligent curls. Ruff less studied, worn lower. Pale color; patterns of interwoven braid-like bands. The cape, apparently of the plush which came into use, together with beaver hats, during second half XVIc., is the short, full, circular one which commonly accompanies this costume, of extravagant leg o'mutton sleeves, peascod doublet, and the shortest possible upper hose (with or without canions).

Stubbes says: "Their dublets are no less monstrous the (*sic*) the rest; for now the fashion is to haue them hang downe to the middle of their theighes . . being so hardquilted, stuffed, bombasted, and sewed, as they can neither worke, nor yet well playe in them, through the excessive heate thereof; and therefore are forced to weare the (*sic*) lose about them for the most part, otherwise they could very hardly eyther stoupe or decline to the ground, so stiffe and sturdy they stand about them . . ."

1210. XVIc. English. (London, Nat. Port. Gall.)

Marcus Gheeraerts,e. William Cecil, Baron Burghley.

The Lord Treasurer of England, who had served Edward VI, Mary and Elizabeth, wears under his hat the coif, and carries the staff, of his office. The collar of the Garter is worn over the red velvet robes of the order, made bulky by the padding of the trunk-hose beneath, which reappeared larger than ever, c. 1590-1615.

XVI Century Spanish Costume

The immense contributions of the Moriscos to Spanish art and costume were carried to the Spanish colonies of the New World, and can clearly be seen in present-day Guatemala and Mexico.

The characteristic parti-color of the mediaeval Morris (= Morisco) dancers is still in use at the time of the final expulsion of the Moriscos in e.XVIIc. Fringe is much used, in blocks of color as skirt sections are now joined in Guatemala (where striped and figured Moorish patterns [seen in Ills. 668-70] and the reds and purples which they loved to combine were incorporated into the already expert indigenous weaving.)

The Moors wore many short loose jackets, as well as the sleeveless surcoats of the XIVc. Alhambra paintings; these persisted in everyone's use in XVIc., especially around Barcelona. In their XVIc. form, they were often cut straight across the front below the knee, with the entire back section dragging in a square train.

The row of buttons down the front of this garment becomes one of the features of XVIc. Spanish woman's dress, instead of the swinging girdle chains and pomanders of the rest of Europe. This row of buttons is enriched with braid, the ends of which are often fringed. There is an element of fringe in the Spanish way of using aiglettes; and indeed the over-all stripings produced by rows of braid on all the doublets of Europe was a Spanish way of using the Morisco's striped patterns. The constantly covered head of the peasant woman of Guatemala is that of a Catholic whose head must not be bare in church, where she may go several times a day—a Catholic concept strengthened by Islamic tradition: a woman's face is theoretically not to be seen by men (see Appendix: R. M. Anderson article). The mediaeval mourning cloak, in black, with a hood or liripipe, is constantly seen in both male and female use in church-ridden, death-loving Spain. A hooded red or black cape is ladies' outer wear; a short form, usually with an extravagant liripipe, covers the face of a self-flagellating *penitente;* and the whole idea persists to this day in the black lace mantilla.

The traditionally veiled head of Moorish women had already been considerably altered in Moriscan use, and no longer covers everything but the eyes. It is now a very long piece of material, gathered as tightly as possible into a band which surrounds the head and is fastened under the chin; this very full mantle, which was usually but not necessarily white, might be short for riding on a donkey, or long and fringed for street wear. Its great width could be caught up over an arm which wished to make the effective gesture of covering the face, or it could be looped up at the sides and allowed to flow free in back, which was both practical and decorative. Variations of this gathering around the face crept into use in Christian mourning cloaks.

There were also arrangements of diagonally folded kerchiefs over the head and shoulders; these stemmed from the Basque provinces and Navarre down into Castile. They were closed at the throat and down the front, with the points often tucked into the waistband, front and back. Over this, various headdresses were set; in Castile, this was often a small square. In the Basque country the top headdress was a fantastically tall horn, wound about with white, its point bent from the weight of a tufted end of binding or a mediaeval liripipe; there were constant strictures against the phallic indecency of these headdresses. In near-by Pampeluna (Navarre), the tall headdress was squared and often widened at the top; its white covering was drawn up over instead of twisted about it, and flowed down in back instead of being knotted at the top. The XXc. paintings of Miguel Viladrich Vilá (Hisp. Soc. of Amer.) show a forward-flopping Phrygian cap still a feature of Catalonian male costume.

A German scholar, in 1526, wrote: "In these mountains lies the land of the Basques, which has an impolite people and a peculiar language, which has nothing in common with the languages Italian, Latin, French, German and Spanish, and where the maidens are all completely shorn." The doctor was almost right. The nape of the Basque girl's neck was shaved like the bowl-crop of XVc. and the crown tonsured; from the remaining fringe all around the head two long, dank locks hung in front of each ear. These locks were also worn by young Basque men, and are seen on Moorish men and women, and ladies of Castile and Valencia in Weiditz' drawings (Ills. 1213-15). The looped hair of Isabella la Catolica (Ill. 971) shows this lock, beginning to break loose.

Basque skirts are short, full, and usually three in number, the outermost being turned up at the hips so that its hem makes a frill above the waistband of the apron; the bold horizontal or crossed patterns, characteristic of these aprons, are also used on the long, loose trousers of Basque men.

The old, old sleeve, prolonged and spreading over the knuckles, is worn all over Spain by both sexes, but it is now turned back to make a drooping cuff and show an additional color in its lining. The dropped shoulder-cap of Navarre is often elaborated with a frill, and shows an undersleeve which is full, if white, and of a different color than the bodice if close-fitting. In the Basque provinces and Navarre, bodices, undersleeves and layers of skirts are all of different colors: red, blue, green, yellow and purple; this varied use in color continued into XXc. as Viladrich's paintings show.

The dress of a Spanish lady developed a train, which had to be carried by an attendant as she walked to daily mass through mud or dust, on her high pattens. There were, classically, three skirts, definitely related by their hem decorations. The innermost was of ground length, fitting smoothly over a boned farthingale; this was sometimes worn alone, in house use, and is clearly shown in XVc. Catalonian wall-paintings. The second was only slightly shorter, its identical banding just clearing that of the underskirt. The outermost was short in front, dipping to meet the banding of the middle skirt in back, and was apt to show some fullness. The train, as it developed length and fullness, tended to become a square-ended extension of the back half of the upper skirt. The number of skirts was actually reduced to one, in grand wear, later in the century, but the appearance of superimposed skirts is always retained, in the way in which braid and puntas are applied; in a late effigy at the Hispanic Society museum, this impulse is reduced to a tuck above the trim of the hem.

Ladies of Catalonia, Valencia and Castile wear low-crowned, wide-brimmed hats, like a cardinal's or bullfighter's, trimmed with tufts or tassels on top of the crown, perhaps, and at each side certainly; under these, the brim is slit for the passage of a long cord, looped on the breast, which could be knotted tight under the chin. Great straw hats have long been worn by smocked Spanish peasants. Descerpz' "Recueil" (Fr., 1562) shows forms entirely different from the classic sombrero, worn by the Moor in the "Book of Chess" (Ill. 505). The long, bound tails of hair (Ill. 973), typical of Catalonia and Castile, also affected male costume (Ill. 1214).

We still see in Central America many other Hispano-Moresque details shown by Weiditz: poncho-like garments, sandals of many narrow leather thongs, and bound circlets to hold a shawl in place on the head. (See Ills. 1213-15.)

Weiditz travelled in a costume of a bloused smock and loose sailor trousers of yellow, diagonally striped in red, mittens, and a hood covering head and shoulders, under a feathered hat.

Weiditz shows a great deal of violet and olive green, or violet and red, used together in Spain; or a scarlet cape with a rosy-gray dress and dark red underskirt. Sleeveless surcoats were of brown, dark gray, or black striped with gold, and were worn over lighter or brighter gowns.

Lavender stockings are frequently seen with the red or yellow pattens, decorated in gold or silver. Leather shoes, usually black, often have the pointed, curled-up Moorish toe which we associate with a jester's costume, cut into points in back and at the instep (where bells would hang, in a fool's costume). Peasant men wear sandals which are handsome and imaginative, as footwear has long

been in Spain, and still is in Latin America.

The marriage of uncloistered priests had become so common, even in Spain, that the costume of their wives was governed by decree; one of the "Recueil" illustrations is of a Spanish priest's wife, and very gay and unfettered she is.

SPANISH PORTRAIT PAINTERS: XVI CENTURY

Few of the great painters of XVIc. Spanish portraits were themselves Spanish. But the Empire, rich, widely connected and pious, was a great patron.

Titian (1477-1576), the Venetian who painted the greatest of all records of Spanish costume, was never in Spain; he was twice called to Augsburg, in 1547 and 1550, to paint the emperor and his family.

Antonio Moro (1512-76) was a Fleming who worked in Madrid from 1552, followed Philip (II) to England at his marriage to Queen Mary, and returned with him to Spain after her death in 1558.

A. Sanchez-Coello (1515-90) was of Portuguese extraction, Spanish-born, Italian trained. He returned to Spain in 1541, became court painter to Philip II, and had a daughter, Isabella Sanchez, also a portrait painter.

El Greco (c.1545-1614) was a native of Crete who studied in Venice, and by 1577 was working in Toledo, where he lived like a rich man and died in debt among his beautiful possessions.

Juan Pantoja de la Cruz (1551-1608), Coello's pupil, was Spanish and painted at the courts of Philip II and III.

Liano and Bartolome Gonzales were also Spaniards.

Rubens (1577-1640), a Fleming and Catholic, was closely allied with Spain, through his connection with the Archduchess-Infanta Isabella Clara Eugenia. He worked in Spain for Philip III in 1603; entered the archducal household as painter in ordinary and familiar in 1609. Accustomed to the greatest society, literate and polylingual, he was not only a painter but a diplomat, who served as ambassador in negotiations between England and Spain.

Velasquez (1599-1660), of noble Portuguese descent, became in 1624 court painter to Philip IV, of whom he painted forty portraits besides innumerable pictures of his family, dwarfs and courtiers. He was official host and guide to Rubens, and with financial aid from the king, spent 1629-31 in Italy as Rubens had advised. He was recalled from a second trip to Italy, 1650-1 by the king who too badly missed his daily companion.

1211. XVIc. First Quarter. Italian. (Morgan Library, M. 52.)

Breviary of Queen Eleanor of Portugal.
St. Barbara.

A border of the large, naturalistic flowers, often on a metal-colored ground, typical of XVIc. manuscripts, is seen on this breviary produced in Rome for a queen who died in 1525. St. Barbara wears the age-old ceremonial sideless surcoat of royal ladies, the skirt of which tends to be made in lighter colors.

1212. XVIc. 1526. Italian. (Madrid, Prado.)

Titian. Isabella of Portugal, wife of Emperor Charles V.

The least-covered hair of first third XVIc. is seen in Spain, Italy and parts of Germany. With these looped arrangements of braids, there are usually loose locks, or as in this and other Spanish examples, soft puffs of hair at the ears.

The focal point of interest of all Spanish female sleeves into the XVIIc. is the line of the seam below the shoulder; this will be at least partly open, and emphasized by braid. Where the bell sleeve is cut close to the upper arm in England, and its hem deeply turned back, the Spanish sleeve begins to widen from the armseye, and is not apt to be turned up; it is shortened on Isabella by being caught up at intervals to the upper part of the undersleeve.

From end XVc., the low square neck is, in Spain, filled by a shirt or partlet embroidered in a vertically striped design, which tends to become spoke-like from the base of the throat. As Spanish embroideries spread through Europe, the shirt tends to disappear in Spain, except as an important frill at the top of high collars on closed bodices. With embroidered shirts like Isabella's, puffed undersleeves appear; but the characteristic undersleeve of XVI-e.XVIIc. is a perfectly simple, close-fitting one of the male doublet type, horizontally ringed throughout its length in narrow braid.

Isabella wears pearl earrings and necklace with a fine pendant, and an ornament at the part in her hair.

1213-15. XVIc. 1529. German. (Heidelberg, Germ. Nat. Mus. Library.)

Trachtenbuch von seinen Reisen nach Spanien, 1529, und der Niederlanden, 1531-2, by Christoph Weiditz.

This collection of 154 drawings, never published until our time, was sketched by a young goldsmith and medallist who accompanied his townsman, D. Colman, (of the family surnamed "Helmschmied" from their profession), on his trip to Spain to deliver to Charles V the suit of armor "with the wild animals," (now in the Madrid Museum), from the famous Helmschmied shop in Augsburg.

Wieditz' drawings, from which he had probably intended to make one of the very new wood-cut costume books, gives irreplaceable information about the dress of different Spanish cities and provinces, the Indians brought back by Cortez, sailor's dress, methods of husbandry and transport, and regional dress of France and the Low Countries.

1213. Dress of a Spanish noblewoman: Characteristically Spanish pigtail, covered in white, bound in red; triangular earrings of three spraying drops in a form which was old at the time of the Alhambra paintings; fan of spider-web pattern. Her rose gown, trimmed in green, shows full shirt sleeves, multiple skirts of various lengths, square train projected from the back half of the skirt, high pattens decorated with the usual zig-zag designs; all equally Spanish.

1214. Castilian peasant going to market: As in Central America today, going to market, which is held once or twice a week, was the greatest of social events; people come from all directions, and a Guatemalan peasant woman may walk as much as three days to get to one of the great markets, sell as few as five eggs, then walk home, perhaps to pick up what eggs can be found and start back, if she still feels gregarious. Her man may carry nets of crockery or drag five pigs, but he wears his best clothes, and recognizes the inhabitants of the surrounding villages by their special costume, just as they can tell where he comes from by his dress.

This peasant's costume shows strong Morisco influence, if he is not one himself, as seems likely; except in predominantly Moorish Granada, Christian, Jewish, and Moorish blood was inextricably intermixed. His intricately wound turban is of Moorish inspiration; it ends in a tab of their red, blue and white fringe. His yellowish cloak is edged with their toothed appliqué in red, blue and white. Hoods of one color, often lavishly decorated, set into "sailor" collars of another are favorite wear of XVIc. Spanish shepherds. From this peasant's hood falls a tail, in Morisco sections of color, blue, red and white, wound with red and gold, and fringed in green at each division of color. His green undersleeves show the favorite Spanish finish: the old funnel-shaped prolongation over the knuckles, turned back to form a drooping cuff. With full trousers he shows an Hispano-Moresque form of footwear of interlaced thongs which tie above the ankle like modern *alpargatas*.

1215. House dress of a Morisco woman and child: The woman has a red and white striped headdress, held in place by a bound circlet of green, white and blue, like that of a modern Arab. With a parti-colored red and brown vest she wears a loose white jacket, full trousers, and footless stockings characteristic of Moorish women (see Ill. 505). She may go barefoot, wear platform sandals with a wide strap over the instep, or slippers with curled-up toes, like those the child wears with violet stockings, a parti-colored red dress, buttoned in gold, and a mantle of green, white and gold stripes.

1216. XVIc. 1532-3. Italian.
(Madrid, Prado.)

Titian. Charles V and his Dog.

Few men have needed to be, more than Charles V was, able, p a t i e n t and adaptable. T h e w i d e l y spread Hapsburg empire, Spain and its Italian possessions, Burgundy and the Netherlands had to be kept in equilibrium, America conquered, France, Lutheranism and the Sultan combatted.

Charles was a great general, a capable rather than creative administrator, pious, but not bigoted, scrupulous, conventional a n d stubborn. He was ugly, but a fine figure of a man, with great dignity and taste, of personally decent and simple life except for gluttony; this led to agonizing gout, and in 1557 he retired from all his cares to a small house near a monastery, where he could enjoy country life, animals, children, reading and music.

Portraits by Titian, his favorite painter, show that Charles dressed wonderfully as a young man. He was accused of h a v i n g brought Burgundian luxury to Spain; but he was no more able than his mother had been to control by edict the lavish metallic decoration or silk brocades used at court; and in his own later days he dressed with simple sobriety.

With his black velvet bonnet, Charles wears a superb gold and white costume. His canions are of gold-striped white s a t i n, vertically paned and horizontally caught, to match the doublet which shows only at the lower sleeve, and through the slits of his cloth-of-gold doublet, corded in gold. As in the jerkins of Henry VIII and Francis I, the slits are part of its pattern; however, their small puffed cuts will pass out of use, while the slits seen here, low on the jerkin, will be extended to the breast, and will become an important fashion of the mid-century. Over these, Charles wears a cloak of white brocade, collared in sable, patterned with gold cord run through clusters of gold rings; white netherstocks and shoes; belt with sword, and dagger tasseled in white silk topped in gold; pendant of the Golden Fleece.

1216

1217. XVIc. Spanish. (London, Louis Raphael Coll.)
A. Sanchez-Coello. Queen Isabella, d.1539.

Hair is no longer looped about the ears; free locks persist at the sides but rise as the centrally parted hair begins to be brushed up from the temples.

In addition to the vertical cut, Spanish sleeves are subject to transverse cuts across the elbow-line; these may be in a horizontally set V from the inside of the elbow, in—and + forms, or in the inverted T form shown on these sleeves, one worn and one pendant.

The slashes of the bosom of the male jacket (1216) are lengthened on this very masculine jacket with its high collar and ruff, and close doublet; the horizontally banded doublet sleeve on women's garments shows a frequent subsidiary spiral effect, which will be influential into third quarter XVIc. Picadills at armseye and, in a scalloped form, at cuff.

Sheer scarf with pendant now separated from veil.

1218. Second quarter XVIc. Spanish. (Brussels Royal Gallery.
Copy of *A. Sanchez-Coello.* Margaret of Parma.

Charles V's able natural daughter, who followed her aunts as Regent of the Netherlands, holds a symbolic bridle in her hand.

Her clothing shows the startling and contagious masculinity of Spanish female dress of the XVIc.: male bonnet with rising crown, over hair dressed high, but retaining bunched loose hair, ornamented; jacket with picadill finish at high collar and waist as well as armseye; flowing sleeve slit and caught along inner seam; close masculine doublet with high collar and elaborate shirt ruffle.

1219. XVIc. c. 1554. Flemish. (Madrid, Prado.)
Antonio Moro.

Catherine of Austria, Queen of Portugal.

Charles V's fanatically bigoted sister, under whom, as regent for her grandson, the Jesuits dominated Portugal, shows the veiled forehead of her grandmother with hair bunched over the ears as it so often is in the '50s, pendant earrings of the triangular, tasseled Spanish form, and fine jewelled collar. Severe coat-dress, embroidered fall at high collar; buttoned bosom-slits matching braiding of upper sleeve; brocade undergarment; wide belt, coat-of-arms buckle; Italian fan; lace inset handkerchief.

1220. XVIc. c. 1550. Flemish. (Prado, Madrid.)
Antonio Moro. Emperor Maximilian II.

The eldest son of the little boy in the Strigel portrait lived mostly in Spain until 1550. His portrait is by a Fleming, court painter to the Hapsburgs from 1549 to his death in 1575, often classed among the Spanish and English painters whom he influenced.

Maximilian's jerkin of pinked and slit white leather has the lowered waistline of second third XVIc. and the highest possible Spanish collar, finished with a scalloped picadill edge bound in gold to match its cap sleeves and double skirts. It is worn over a beautiful close doublet of white braided in gold.

Paned trunk-hose, in their early form shown here, have bombast (stuffing) used only below the line of the crotch, and match the doublet sleeves.

Beautiful classic pouch of the period; superb rapier with well developed knuckle-guard, and *pas d'ane* below straight quillons. Black bonnet with tiny plume; cord emphasizes the parting of crown from brim. Collar of the Golden Fleece. Gloves. Slit shoes of natural form.

On the fringed velvet cover of the table stands his closed armet, which has a considerably developed neck-guard and plumes set in its comb.

1221. XVIc. 1553. Italian. (Naples Museum.)
Titian. Philip II.

Isabella of Portugal was loved in Spain as her husband could never be, by a people who resented his necessary attentions to other parts of his wide-spread

possessions. Charles ingratiated himself with his Spanish subjects, at the time of the birth of his only son, by killing a bull in the public square of Valladolid in honor of the event.

Philip was a pleasant blond young man, rather defectively educated by a tutor during his father's absence; he was hardworking, over-meticulous and proud; attractive in his family life, as was his father, and like him, of relatively simple personal tastes. His marriage to Mary Tudor in 1554, however, required a magnificent wardrobe, of which his valet, Andreas Muñoz, left a descriptive inventory, and which introduced Spanish fashions to the English court. (It is given in detail in Norris: *Costume and Fashion*: *The Tudors*.) These costumes were largely in black, white, gold and silver combinations.

Here his padded doublet, jerkin, hose (still padded low), and shoes are of pale yellow, embroidered in silver: the gown, of brown satin and sable with paired aiglettes, has lost its pendant sleeve; below its top fullness it has assumed a lower sleeve, which used to be that of the garment beneath, and which is short enough to show the actual jerkin sleeve.

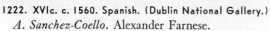

1222. XVIc. c. 1560. Spanish. (Dublin National Gallery.)
A. Sanchez-Coello. Alexander Farnese.

Farnese, who was Charles V's grandson by Margaret of Parma, followed Don Juan of Austria as governor of the Netherlands. As a successful general and diplomat, he consolidated the southern provinces into Catholic Belgium, loyal to Spain. During the struggle, however, Amsterdam acquired the trade of the port of Antwerp, as the more enter-prising Protestant part of the population took refuge in the Dutch Republic or England, enriching those countries and impoverishing Belgium.

Farnese wears the cloak with hanging sleeves slung like a cape across one shoulder, as it is usually carried; (see Sidney: Ill. 1182); it has a high collar and is notched into the beginning of our lapels. Increasing height of collar, and elaboration of collar edge into set ruff.

1223. XVIc. c.1565. Spanish. (Vienna Art History Mus.)

A. Sanchez-Coello. The Infante Don Carlos.

The wilful and disorderly lunatic son of Philip II died incarcerated about three years after this portrait was painted. The *Fugger News Letters* relate that he walked barefoot in the water with which he had caused his room to be deluged and had eaten nothing but ice-water and fruit for a week.

Like his cousin above, the Infante wears his sleeved and lapelled cloak as a cape. The panes of his shorter and wider hose show an effect of interlacing; this horizontal or diagonal interweaving was often actual, and the dagger is sometimes seen run through the panes like a darning needle. The shoe is becoming elaborated over the instep, where a tongue will develop at end XVIc.

1224. XVIc. 1569. Flemish. (Washington, Nat. Gall. of Art.)

Antonio Moro. Portrait of a Gentleman.

The gentleman, no longer considered to be the artist's self-portrait, wears a costume of black velvet and violet satin, with the highest of Spanish collars, open in front in the manner of the 60's and after.

1225. XVIc. 1564. Spanish. (Vienna Imperial Museum.)

A. Sanchez-Coello. Portrait of a Woman.

The Hapsburgs tried to keep their great empire in equilibrium by a network of politically expedient engagements and marriages. In 1559, Philip II took as his third wife Catherine de' Medici's eldest daughter, Elizabeth of Valois; and in 1572, Elizabeth of Austria, daughter of Maximilian II, was married to Catherine's son, Charles IX.

It is therefore not surprising to find, in a Spanish portrait which must show one of the ladies of the new queen, French dress almost identical with that worn by Philip's niece as Queen of France. In the Coello portrait, the gown has the Spanish collar, so high that it must be worn open, elaborately edged; and in the Clouet, seven years later, a completely developed ruff. Glove with slashed finger; handkerchief.

1226. XVIc. c.1575. Spanish. (Madrid, Prado.)

J. Pantoja de la Cruz. Infanta Empress Maria.

The Emperor Maximilian II's cousin-wife wears

the scarf we have seen on Isabella la Catolica and others of her descendants: Christina of Denmark and Isabella of Portugal; here it is finely crimped and falls from the head.

Wrist ruffles remained inconspicuous in Spain until the complete development of the lace ruff which they now match.

The great *puntas* of Spain hang from ribbon or braid tabs, where the smaller paired *aiglettes* of the rest of Europe branch out from the fabric to which they are sewed.

The shape of the typical slit, pendant sleeve of Spain will show more clearly on examples at the end of the century.

1227. XVIc. 1577. Spanish. (London, Earl of Northbrook.)
A. Sanchez-Coello. Don Diego, son of Philip II.
For little boy's costume, see Ill. 1173.

1228. XVIc. 1575. Spanish. (Metropolitan Museum.)
El Greco. Cardinal Don Fernando Niño de Guevara.

With his red biretta, mozetta and cassock and lace-edged white surplice, the cardinal wears spectacles fastened around the ears by loops.

Spectacles were perhaps the invention of Roger Bacon; they are first mentioned in XIIIc., and their use was developed in Italy. In their earliest form, they are like two reading glasses pinned together through the handles so that they could be spread in a V and set or held on the bridge of the nose; glasses of this sort hang at the side of the desk of Ghirlandaio's St. Jerome, and are worn with Caligari-like effect in the Florentine engraving of the same period, purporting to show the ritual murder of St. Simon of Trent. (See Appendix.)

Dark rimmed spectacles, fashionable in Spain in XVIIc., were used on the mask of Zerbino, one of the Spanish characters of Italian comedy.

1229. XVIc. 1578. Spanish. (Toledo, Church of Santo Thome.)
El Greco. Burial of Count of Orgaz, detail.

The Count of Orgaz was a devout gentleman of the XIVc. who, according to legend, was about to be buried when St. Augustine and St. Stephen, to whom he had been very devoted, descended from heaven and laid him in his coffin.

1228

1229

1230

The priest of Santo Thomé and members of the Covarrubias family have been identified among the portraits of notables of Toledo, in their mourning cloaks with the cross of St. James, great ruffs and pointed Spanish beards.

The dalmatic of St. Stephen and the copes of St. Augustine and the priest show magnificent orphreys of Spanish embroidery.

1230. XVIc. 1579. Spanish. (Madrid, Prado.)

A. Sanchez-Coello. Infanta Isabella Clara Eugenia.

The Infanta, adored by her father, and the greatest matrimonial prize since Elizabeth, was thirty when Philip II realized that he was going to die. The Cardinal Archduke Albert of Austria, who succeeded his brother as ruler of the Netherlands, was freed of his vows by the Pope and married to his cousin, the Infanta. Their joint rule as "the Archdukes" was devoted and competent; they concluded a truce which renounced any authority over the United Provinces and tried to repair the economy of the Netherlands. But they died childless, and their country reverted to an impoverished Spain, which relied on her treasure ships, now being successfully raided by the Zeeland-

ers and British. Meanwhile Spain expelled the Moriscos, her only good farmers and since centuries, her finest craftsmen, weavers and embroiderers, metal workers and pottery makers; these (since they alone prospered) must be the "sponges that soaked up all the Spanish wealth." Spain de-industrialized herself, as she had the Netherlands, and her glory decayed as the Dutch East India Company was being formed in 1600. (See Appendix: Trade.)

The girdle pendant is now becoming shorter, all over Europe; it has never been much used in Spain, where skirts have been massively decorated down the center-front for centuries; chains and pomanders would only tangle with studs and tags, braid and ribbon. The girdle is immensely rich in Spain, finished at the center by a pointing shield- or heart-shaped motif, matching the precious collar, and outlining the waistline as it lengthens and points.

The armseye roll is reinforced by tabbed picadills above and below; the sleeve of the gown is only an open strip behind the braided doublet sleeve.

She wears a high tilted bonnet, plumed on one side, over jewelled hair which is dressed in the unparted Spanish fashion, in a high padded pompadour.

1231. XVIc. c. 1571. Spanish. (Vienna Art History Mus.)

A. Sanchez-Coello. Queen Anne of Spain.

Philip married in 1570 his fourth wife, daughter of Maximilian 11, and mother of Philip III; she died before him in 1580, ill as he was.

She wears her parted hair rolled in the French way; chains of pearls; a tabbed picadill skirt on bodice, matching her shoulder-caps; dispensing with massive Spanish collar and girdle.

Ribbon loops (which will become extremely important in XVIIc.) have come into use on the jewelled puntas which catch her skirt and great sleeves.

She carries a handkerchief with lace insertion and edging in one gloved hand; gloves are beginning to be taken for granted; she wears only one, and its forefinger is slit to show a fine ring.

1232. XVIc. 1590? Spanish. (Metropolitan Museum.)

A. Sanchez-Coello. Infanta Isabella of Spain.

Hair and headdresses, in their most specifically Spanish forms,

mount to a point. Hats tend to disappear, in favor of jewels and rosettes set rather asymmetrically in the hair. Pearl earrings are worn in pairs; more elaborate earrings, often singly. Pearl ropes replace heavy jewelled collars. Folding fans are used. (See Ills. 1237-38 and 1290-95.)

Ruffs grow more enormous, and end in jagged points of lace. They tend to split and flatten, as on the Infanta (whose wire support with pendant fringe is clearly seen under the ruff-collar). Ruffs are frequently replaced by flat collars, wired high (1238). Reticella begins to be replaced by bone lace; and set ruffs at the wrists, by lace cuffs (which increase in width and importance); or, as in the case of the Spanish princess, by embroidered cuffs with lace-like notches.

Bodices also split and expose the bosom, though less so in Spain than elsewhere. Their points lengthen and the tabbed peplums deepen. Skirts become unified in cut and are gathered around the waist to accommodate hip bolsters; this forces the point of the bodice outward. The hip bolster has only the slightest effect on the cone-shaped Spanish farthingale at the end of the century; we never see the drum-shaped skirt with cart-wheel top used in Spain.

The sleeve we see here has been in long use in Spain. Tabbed wings now supplant the old roll at the shoulder; important jewels pinned on sleeve, just below shoulder.

The great era of braid has passed. Brocades in striped patterns are used in place of braid in tabs and on doublet sleeves, which are now braided only along their inner seam. Openwork galoon bands are now used, upon less austere brocades, lighter in color and delicately sprigged in smaller patterns. The somber stiffness of Spain is passing.

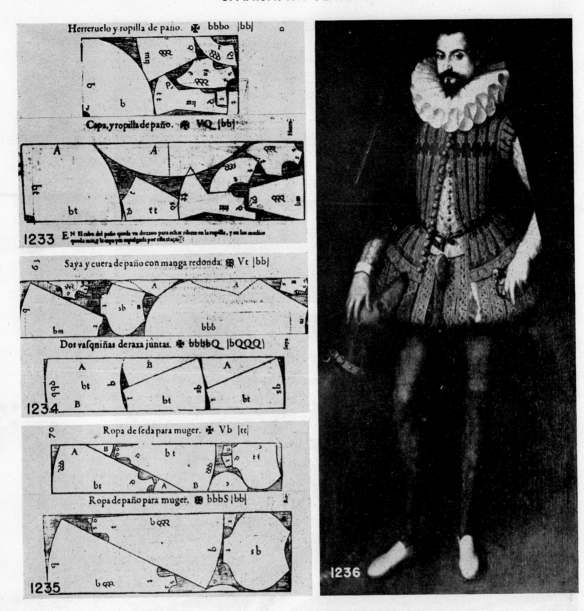

Herreruelo y ropilla de paño. ✠ bbbo |bb|

Capa, y ropilla de paño. ✠ VQ |bb|

1233 EN El cabo del paño queda vn doraso para echar ribete en la ropilla, y en los medios queda mitad la capa y vn espadigote por esta traça.

Saya y cuera de paño con manga redonda. ✠ Vt |bb|

Dos vasqniñas de raxa juntas. ✠ bbbbQ |bQQQ|

1234

Ropa de seda para muger. ✠ Vb |tt|

Ropa de paño para muger. ✠ bbbS |bb|

1235

1236

1233-35. XVIc. 1587. Spanish. (Metropolitan Museum, Print Room.)

Libro de geometria practica y traca, by Juan de Alcega, pub. by Guillermo Druoy, Madrid, 1587.

In the XVIc. flood of books on costume, it was inevitable that pattern books should appear. Alcega' is the first of these. (See Appendix.)

1233. A "wagtail" (which is certainly a wonderful name for a long-skirted jacket) and doublet of plush velvet; and a velvet cape and doublet.

1234. A skirt and bodice of velvet with round sleeves.

1235. A silk gown, and one of velvet.

1236. XVIc. (last decade). Spanish. London, Christie sale, June 27, 1924.)

Att. to *A. Sanchez-Coello.* Portrait of a Nobleman.

This gentleman's brown costume with mauve hose shows many new characteristics. He has the wide, boldly set ruff of the last decade; its shorter-waisted jacket with sleeve-wings, breast slits simulated by embroidery, longer skirts, and the XVIIc. impulse to be unbuttoned below the breast; short cape; very short, wide trunk-hose still carrying a cod-piece; shoes with soles but no heels, as yet.

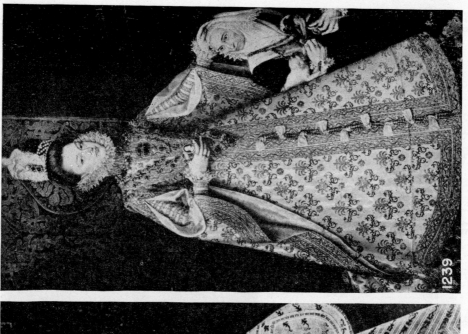

1237. Last decade XVIc. Spanish. (Paris, Coll. Lazzaro.) Att. to *A. Sanchez-Coello.* Portrait of a Lady.

1238. End XVIc. Spanish. (New York, George Mercer Coll.) Att. to *A. Sanchez-Coello.* Spanish Princess.

1239. XVIc. c. 1585. Spanish. (Madrid, Prado.) Att to *T. F. Liaño.* Infanta Isabella Clara Eugenia and the dwarf, Magdalena Ruiz.

Men's hats, whether worn by men or women, are growing higher and less gathered in the crown. The Infanta's plume, hair, and collar are higher, her ruff and skirt wider. The bell-sleeve, which never passed out of Spanish use, and is split along the inner seam in the Spanish way, trails to the long train of her gown; this is characteristically developed out of the back section, alone, of what is made to look like a short skirt over a longer one, by the use of braid.

Her attendant, a dwarf, kneeling with the monkey, has the headdress of Northern Spain.